Global Perspectives on Foreign Policy of Major Powers

Global Perspectives on Foreign Policy of Major Powers

Editor

Ajit M. Banerjee

ACADEMIC FOUNDATION
NEW DELHI

www.academicfoundation.org

First published in 2016
by

ACADEMIC FOUNDATION
4772-73 / 23 Bharat Ram Road, (23 Ansari Road),
Darya Ganj, New Delhi - 110 002 (India).
Phones : 23245001 / 02 / 03 / 04.
Fax : +91-11-23245005.
E-mail : books@academicfoundation.com
www.academicfoundation.org

Global Perspectives on Foreign Policy of Major Powers
Edited by Ajit M. Banerjee

ISBN 9789332703261

1. Financial crisis. 2. Globalization--Economic aspects. 3. Monetary policy. 4. International economic relations. I. Title.

DDC 338.542 23

Typeset by Italics India, New Delhi.

Printed and bound by The Book Mint, New Delhi.
www.thebookmint.in

For
Anila, Anjali, Arianna and Alexander

Contents

About the Editor/Contributors

Editor:

Ajit M. Banerjee is a consultant on foreign policy and governance. He was a faculty member of the National Institute of Public Administration, Consultant to Punjab government, and Government of India on management improvement. He was invited by the United Nations (UN) and assigned to the UN Economic Commission for Asia and Far East (ESCAP), as Regional Advisor, to assist Asian and Pacific governments on administrative reform, civil service restructuring, and capacity building for development. This was followed by appointment as Deputy Director of the UN Center for Development Administration. Dr Banerjee was the main architect of the concept of the Regional Center based in Malaysia. He was subsequently appointed Deputy Director of the Center. Later, he was assigned to UN Headquarters in New York as Special Advisor and Principal Coordinator for administrative reform, governance, and foreign policy programmes. He led over 50 UN missions to governments in Asia, Middle East, West Africa, and Caribbean countries dealing with these programmes, and advised on establishing foreign service training institutes. He was also part of a core group of specialists for political negotiations to several governments (Cambodia, Cyprus, Namibia, Haiti, Afghanistan), in peace maintenance and governance. His books include *Organization of Government of India,* published by Asia Publishing House; *Asian Civil Service,* published by EROPA; *Renewing Governance,* published by Tata McGraw-Hill; co-edited *Reinventing the United Nations,* published by Prentice-Hall; and *UN International Civil Service: Perceptions and Realities,* published by Academic Foundation. He has contributed numerous technical articles in professional journals. He obtained his MA from Maxwell School, and PhD in Public Policy as a Fellow in Social Sciences of the Rockefeller Foundation. Paul Appleby Award was bestowed on him 2013, for his outstanding service in Public Policy and Management.

Contributors:

James A. Baker, III, has served in senior government positions under three United States Presidents. He served as the nation's 61st Secretary of State from January 1989 through August 1992 under President George H.W. Bush. During his tenure at the State Department, Mr Baker travelled to 90 foreign countries as the US confronted the unprecedented challenges and opportunities of the post-Cold War era. He served as the 67th Secretary of the Treasury from 1985 to 1988 under President Ronald Reagan. As Treasury Secretary, he was also Chairman of the President's Economic Policy Council. From 1981 to 1985, he served as White House Chief of Staff to President Reagan. His record of public service began in 1975 as Under Secretary of Commerce to President Gerald Ford. It concluded with his service as White House Chief of Staff and Senior Counselor to President Bush from August 1992 to January 1993. He is presently a senior partner in the law firm of Baker Botts.

Tim Oliver is a Senior Lecturer in the Department of Defence and International Affairs at the Royal Military Academy Sandhurst, but writes here in a personal capacity. He is also a non-resident fellow of the Center for Transatlantic Relations of the Johns Hopkins University Paul H. Nitze School of Advanced International Studies, Washington D.C. Dr Oliver has worked in the House of Lords, the European Parliament, the German Institute for International and Security Affairs (SWP), RAND Corporation, and taught at University College London and London School of Economics

Jeffrey Mankoff is Deputy Director and Fellow with the CSIS Russia and Eurasia Program. He is the author of *Russian Foreign Policy: The Return of Great Power Politics* (Rowman & Littlefield, 2009) and a frequent commentator on international security, Russian foreign policy, regional security in the Caucasus and Central Asia, ethnic conflict, and energy security. Before coming to CSIS, he served as an adviser on US-Russia relations at the US Department of State as a Council on Foreign Relations International Affairs Fellow. From 2008 to 2010, he was associate director of International Security Studies at Yale University and an adjunct fellow at the Council on Foreign Relations. In addition to his policy research, he teaches courses on international security and Central Asia at Georgetown University's School of Foreign Service. Dr Mankoff has held academic fellowships at Harvard, Yale, and Moscow State Universities. He holds dual BAs in international studies and Russian from the University of Oklahoma and an MA, MPhil, and PhD in diplomatic history from Yale.

Quansheng Zhao is Professor of international relations and Chair of the Asian Studies Program Research Council at American University in Washington, D.C. A specialist in international relations and comparative politics focusing on East Asia, he is the author of *Interpreting Chinese Foreign Policy* (Oxford University Press, winner of the Best Academic Book Award by the Ministry of Culture of the Republic of Korea), and *Japanese Policymaking* (Oxford University Press/Praeger, selected as "Outstanding Academic Book" by Choice). His most recent edited book is *Managing the China Challenge: Perspectives from the Globe* (2009). His books have been translated into Chinese, Japanese, and Korean. In 2010, Dr Zhao received Sumiya Mikio Award as the first place winner for best essays in Japanese studies selected by the Chinese Academy of Social Sciences. From 1993-2009, he was a Research Associate at the Fairbank Center for East Asian Research of Harvard University; and from 1999-2008, he was Division Director of Comparative and Regional Studies at American University. He received his BA from Peking University, and MA and PhD from the University of California at Berkeley. He is a member of the National Committee on US-China Relations. He has also testified at the US Congress on China's high-speed railway system, and served as a consultant for the United Nations.

Steven Philip Kramer has been Professor of Grand Strategy at the Industrial College of the Armed Forces, National Defense University in Washington, D.C. since 1992. He was also Policy Advisor to the Assistant Secretary of State for European Affairs from 1996-2002, where he focused on long-term issues and on issues related to France. Dr Kramer has taught Contemporary European History and Government at the University of New Mexico and Georgetown University, served as a Council of Foreign Relations Fellow in the US Department of State, directed the Face to Face program of the Carnegie Endowment for International Peace, was the John J. McCloy Distinguished Fellow in Residence at the American Institute for Contemporary German Studies and was a Fellow at the Institute for the Study of Diplomacy at Georgetown. He has written widely on European politics and culture. His most recent books are: *Does France Still Count: The French Role in the New Europe* (Praeger/CSIS, 1994) and *Trouble in Paradise, Europe in the 21st Century* (NDU Press 1996), co-authored with Prof Irene Kyriakopoulos. He has also written *Socialism in Western Europe: The Experience of a Generation* and a biography of the cineaste Abel Gance. He received his BA in history from Brandeis University and his PhD from Princeton University.

Dieter M. Dettke is currently Adjunct Professor at Georgetown University teaching a course on "Europe and Russia: The New Security Dynamics and the Atlantic Alliance" and on "The Politics of European Security" at Georgetown University's Center for Peace and Security Studies as well as at the BMW Center for German and European Studies. He served as the US Representative and Executive Director of the Friedrich Ebert Foundation in Washington from 1985, until 2006 managing a comprehensive programme of Transatlantic cooperation.

In 2006, he joined the German Marshall Fund of the US as a Transatlantic Fellow and from September 2006 to June 2007 he was a Fellow at the Woodrow Wilson International Center for Scholars. He is author of *Germany Says 'No': The Iraq War and the Future of German Foreign and Security Policy*, and *Allianz im Wandel*, a book on European-American security relations and super power bilateralism. He also served as editor and author of *The Spirit of the Berlin Republic*, a book about Germany after unification. His most recent publication is *Hungary's Jobbik Party, the Challenge of European Ethno-Nationalism and the Future of the European Project* (published in 2014 by the Center for International Relations in Warsaw). Dr Dettke is a foreign and security policy specialist, author and editor of numerous publications on German, European and US foreign and security issues. He studied law and political science in Bonn and Berlin, Germany and Strasbourg, France and was a Fulbright Scholar at the University of Washington in Seattle in 1967-68.

Takashi Inoguchi, Professor Emeritus, University of Tokyo; President and the Chairman of the Board, University of Niigata Prefecture. Takashi Inoguchi became President and Chairman of the Governing Board, University of Niigata Prefecture in 2009. He is also Professor Emeritus, University of Tokyo and President, the Asian Consortium for Political Research. He served as Assistant Secretary General of the United Nations assigned to the UN University Headquarters (1995-1997) and as President, the Japanese Association of International Relations (2000-2002). Amongst the latest of which are *American Democracy Promotion* (Oxford University Press, 2000), *Reinventing the Alliance* (Palgrave Macmillan, 2004), *Political Cultures in Asia and Europe* (Routledge, 2006), *The Uses of Institutions* (Palgrave Macmillan, 2007), *Citizens and the State* (Routledge, 2009), *Globalization, the State and Public Opinion* (Routledge, 2009), *Japanese Politics Today* (Palgrave Macmillan, 2011), *The US-Japan Security Alliance* (Palgrave Macmillan, 2011). He is Director of the AsiaBarometer project since 2002 and the founding editors of two journals, *Japanese Journal of*

Political Science (Cambridge University Press) and *International Relations of the Asia Pacific* (Oxford University Press).

Rohan Mukherjee is a doctoral candidate in the Department of Politics at Princeton University. His writings on Indian foreign policy and security have appeared in journals such as *Survival, Global Governance, International Affairs*, and *International Journal*. In 2014-15, he is also a Visiting Fellow at the United Nations University (UNU) in Tokyo, working on an edited volume titled: *Deepening the Japan-India Partnership*.

Sartaj Aziz has served as Pakistan's Finance Minister from 1990 to 1993 and again from February 1997 to July 1998. He was Pakistan's Foreign Minister from August 1998 to October 1999. At present, he is Advisor to the Prime Minister of Pakistan on National Security and Foreign Affairs. He obtained a Bachelor's degree in commerce from the Punjab University in 1949. He proceeded to join the civil service of the state of Pakistan in 1951. Later, he travelled to the US and earned a Master's degree in development economics from Harvard University in 1963."

Aparna Pande is a Research Fellow and Director of Hudson Institute's Initiative on the Future of India and South Asia. After completing her MA from St. Stephen's College, Delhi University, and MPhil in international relations from Jawaharlal Nehru University, she received a Doctorate in political science from Boston University. She has authored the book titled *Explaining Pakistan's Foreign Policy: Escaping India* (Routledge, 2011). Her major field of interest is South Asia with a special focus on India, Pakistan, foreign policy, security studies, religion in politics, and political Islam. Pande testified before the US Congress (House Foreign Affairs Sub-committee on Oversight and Investigations). She has contributed articles to *The Melbourne Journal of Politics* and *Current Trends in Islamist Ideology*.

Natana J. DeLong-Bas is a leading expert on Wahhabism, Salafism, jihadism, terrorism and extremism, particularly Al-Qaida and ISIS, and women and gender issues in the Islamic world. She is a consultant to both the US and international governments, as well as international corporations and the media. She serves on the Academic Council of the Prince Alwaleed bin Talal Center for Muslim-Christian Understanding at Georgetown University, Washington DC, and the Board of Directors for the American Council for the Study of Islamic Societies. Dr DeLong-Bas is Visiting Assistant Professor of Comparative Theology and Islamic Civilizations and Societies at Boston College, Chestnut Hill, MA. She is the author of *Wahhabi Islam: From Revival and Reform to Global Jihad* (Oxford University Press, rev. ed. 2008; named 1 of the 5 best for understanding Islam by the Wall Street Journal), *Notable Muslims: Muslim Builders of World Civilization and Culture* (OneWorld, 2006), and *Women in Muslim Family Law* (with John L. Esposito, Syracuse University Press, second edition, 2001). She is Editor-in-Chief of *The Oxford Encyclopedia of Islam and Women* (Oxford University Press, 2013).

Yoav J. Tenembaum is a lecturer at the graduate Diplomacy Programme, Political Science department, Tel Aviv University, Israel. He has been teaching the core, mandatory course on The Shaping of Foreign Policy and Decision-Making. He has taught courses on Conflict Resolution, International Crises and on the Role of the National Security Advisor of the US President in Shaping Foreign Policy. He is Argentinean-born and has lived in various countries, including Argentina, Britain, the US (New York) and Israel. He holds a Doctorate degree in modern history from Oxford University and a Master's degree in international relations from Cambridge University. He read for his BA degree in history at Tel Aviv University, specialising in modern (diplomatic) history. Dr Tenembaum has been invited to deliver lectures on Israeli foreign policy in several countries on diverse academic and professional forums. Articles of his on diplomacy, international relations and foreign policy have been published in various journals, magazines and newspapers in the US, Britain, Argentina, Uruguay, Spain and Israel.

Leila Bijos has a PhD in Sociology, a Master's degree in international relations (technical cooperation), specialisation in political science, specialisation in foreign trade and third sector activities. She is a professor and researcher at the Master's degree in law at the Catholic University of Brasilia, Coordinator of the Internationalization of Higher Education at the Law School, Director of the Study Group Laboratory of International Politics, and member of Cathedra of UNESCO for Youth, Education and Society, where she has been teaching for 14 years and has been the advisor of more than 40 graduate level dissertations. She has been a visiting professor at the University of Hyderabad (India), University of Loja (Ecuador); a visiting researcher at the University of Tsukuba (Japan), University of Asia and the Pacific, Manila (Philippines); visiting scholar at the Center for Iberian and Latin American Studies, University of California, San Diego (USA); invited speaker at the Zentrum für Interdisziplinäre Forschung, University of Bielefeld (Germany), New York State University, Stony Brook (USA), Institute of Political and International Studies (IPIS), University of Tehran (Iran), University of Sevilla (Spain), University of Panama (Panama); and Research Fellow at the Annual Bank Conference on Development Economics (ABCDE). She has authored more than 50 publications, including *Mulheres Sul Americanas: O Presente Mais que Imperfeito* (2013), *Discriminação Étnica Racial: "Nikkeis" Brasileiros no Japão*, and *A Excelência da Democracia Brasileira e o Apoio da Sociedade Civil* (2013); besides co-authoring books on migration, regional integration, cultural diplomacy, and women in Latin America.

Tseliso Thipanyane was former Chief Executive Officer of the South African Human Rights Commission. An independent human rights consultant on human rights, democracy and good governance, an adjunct law lecturer on African human rights systems at Columbia University School of Law, an adjunct lecturer on African politics at Ramapo College of New Jersey, and a co-producer on human rights at AfrobeatRadio (WBAI 99.5FM New York). Advocate of the High Courts of South Africa and Lesotho.

Foreword

The significance and scope of foreign policy and diplomacy has increased over time. The key factors have been the rise in number of states, population growth, stress on national resources, increase in ethnic strife, and political and economic disagreement.

Much has been written about individual countries and their foreign policies. This book is unique as it attempts, in one volume, to enlighten graduate students of international studies how major powers formulate their foreign policy based on national, regional, and global interests.

After World War II, the British government promised to make preparations for their withdrawal from India. Lord Louis Mountbatten was appointed Viceroy, responsible for overseeing the transition of British India to independence no later than 1948. He was charged with finding a peaceful plan and securing Indian Independence as quickly and smoothly as possible. This was a strategic decision as part of the British foreign policy.

My own experience was when I accompanied my parents, Lord Louis Mountbatten, Earl Mountbatten of Burma, and Lady Edwina Mountbatten to India. I remained with them during my father's term as Viceroy of pre-Independence India and then Governor-General of post-Partition India through 1948, living with them in Government House, New Delhi, and during the summer at Vice Regal Lodge in Simla.

I congratulate the distinguished authors for providing their perspectives, and for the Editor, Ajit Banerjee, who put together in one volume, foreign policy of major powers.

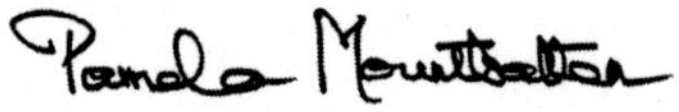

— Lady Pamela Mountbatten
India

Preface

This book is focused on the advancement of foreign policy as a major field of study through analytical presentation of evolving strategies covering 13 countries: the United States of America (USA), the United Kingdom (UK), Germany, France Russia, China, Japan, India, Pakistan, Israel, Saudi Arabia, Brazil and South Africa. The criteria for selection of countries is based on their stature regionally and globally. The US, UK, China, Russia, and France are recognised as major powers: they have a pre-eminent status because of their strength in military, economic, and security domain. These five countries are also permanent members of the United Nations Security Council (UNSC). Japan and Germany hold a strategic status because they are innovative economic centres. India is a nuclear country and has emerged as a regional economic and cultural hub, while Brazil and South Africa are now becoming economic entities in Latin America and Africa respectively. Saudi Arabia and Israel are key players in the Middle East for their economic and political reasons. Pakistan is located in an important geographical region of China, Central and West Asia and casts potential influence in trade and transport. It is also a nuclear state. Overall, in Africa, several analysts had expressed that two decades of elections and economic development will usher an era of democracy—but across the continent, militaries are resurging and dictatorial regimes are in control. There are only 19 states which have democracies (Drew Hinshaw and Patrick McGroarty, Review, WSJ, 7 December 2014).

The papers written by individual authors, and the views expressed therein are their own, and do not necessarily convey the opinion of the Editor and the Publisher.

The significance and scope of foreign policy has increased with the rise in the number of states and globalisation. Decolonisation provided impetus to several states. The end of the Cold War and the collapse of the Soviet Union unleashed yet another spurt of newly independent countries. The number of states increased threefold since 1945 and 193 of them are already members of the United Nations (UN). These countries—with different political systems, economic models and cultural orientations—cooperate and compete between themselves and in several international and regional organisations they have created for mutual benefit to advance their objectives and interests. All this has made international relations and foreign policymaking more complex.

We are living in a dangerous world. Terrorism is now global. Post 9/11 led to a war in Iraq and Afghanistan. Overall, the US is still the greatest military, industrial, and economic power. Europe's share in world economy is declining, the European Union (EU) is expanding in size, the growing inequality, and rising debt amongst its members is causing instability in its currency, the Euro. The UK continues to have political and strategic influence on world affairs, particularly through its financial and industrial power. While its economy is improving, the cost of two world wars and the loss of 'Empire' have impacted in its power base in foreign affairs. The rise of China as a economic and strategic force, has caused uncertainty with its neighbours in South China Sea. Japan is re-emerging as a potent economic force. India is another strategic and emerging economic force, although it suffers from massive poverty, illiteracy, and border conflicts with its neighbour, Pakistan. China, India, Pakistan, and North Korea are four nuclear powers in the region. A major question now is can Iran's nuclear capability be limited. The political situation in the Middle East continues to ravage the region. Egypt, Syria, Iraq, and Libya are volatile in the wake of Arab Spring. Israel is the only democratic country. In Eastern Europe, Russia which has the second largest weapons of mass destruction after the US is facing problems with its neighbours.

Literature in international relations and diplomacy is full of individual country's strengths and weaknesses. However, there is no single volume—a primmer of sorts—introductory treatise on foreign policy strategies of major powers globally, which would help put these policies in perspective. The Editor has attempted to address these issues with a view to fill the gap, based on his experience of over three decades with the UN on governance, public policy issues, and strengthening of foreign policy institutes in various regions through management development and structural refinement of these organisations.

Critical issues that could influence the foreign policy process include: political instability, and internal and external measures for maintaining peace and security. Additionally, high unemployment, inflation, corrupt practices in government, open borders without enforcement measures, and poor application of rule of law could be a hindrance in decision-making. Widening gap between the rich and poor is causing major imbalance, increase in poverty, as well as poor quality of education and social services. In planning foreign policy objectives, there could be instances where due to lack of trained personnel, the preparation of deeper analysis for realistic policymaking could suffer. Poorly organised ministry of foreign affairs, lack of technological devices for database, and established think tanks to prepare consistent alternatives with clear economic, security and military objectives are essential.

This volume will facilitate the readers to know the concrete issues that major powers are dealing with in their foreign policy for the 21st century.

Acknowledgements

This is the fifth book I have authored or edited. The Editor would like to thank all the outstanding authors and scholars for contributing substantive papers. They have enriched the strategic field of foreign policy of major powers covering selected countries in Asia, Africa, Europe, Latin America, Middle East, and the USA.

The Editor expresses his gratitude for the encouragement and support of H.E. President Martti Ahtisaari, Ambassador K.L. Dalal, Sir Richard Jolly, Mr S. Vardachari, Prof Yeshkel Dror, Prof Raymond Baker, Mr Myron Gordon, Mr Ethan Bronner, Dr Anirudho Basu, Ms Mary Ann Eliza Kimball and Ms Martina Paniagua, coordinator, UN Reference Team at Dag Hammarskjold library for assistance in preparing a table for economic and social indicators of countries included in the volume.

My highest appreciation is conveyed to Lady Pamela Mountbatten for the Foreword. Last but not the least, I am indebted to Mr Sanu Kapila, Publisher, Academic Foundation.

Finally, I respect the conventional wisdom of gratitude as an expression of love for my, wife Uma in my professional pursuit, besides my daughter Amita, Robin, my sons, Ajoy, Arun and Eva.

Introduction

President George Washington in his historic farewell address on 19 October 1796, declared that nation states "observe good faith and justice towards all nations, cultivate peace and harmony with all. Religion and morality enjoined this conduct, and can it be that good policy does not equally enjoins it."[1] This statement is so true in today's fast changing world as well.

Leopold Von Ranke emphasised the primacy of geography and external threats in shaping foreign policy, but later emphasised domestic factors.[2] The government seek to protect and promote their national interest through their foreign policy: such interest include maintaining sovereignty, territorial integrity, obtaining political stability as well as promoting trade investment, economic, social and cultural progress. In this context, these factors equally demand the presence of right military strength as an integral part of a modern country's foreign policy.

The significance of foreign policy is increasing. The major factors for this has been the increase in the number of states since 1945, mainly due to decolonisation, separation from existing states, increase in population growth and demand on natural resources, as well as ethnic strife, religious differences, and cultural and linguistic divide.

In recent history, the world went through two great wars, several major conflicts, and a range of disputes that perished millions of lives around the planet. The search for ideological conquest and weapons technology to back it up triggered the Cold War, and since

---

1. Yale Law School Avalon Project—Washington's Farewell Address, 1796.
2. Leopold_von_Ranke HYPERLINK: *http://www.britannica.com/topic/foreign-policy*

World War II (WWII), the development of deadly weapons shook the earth to the brink of extinction by use of nuclear weapons in Hiroshima and Nagasaki. In recent times, global terrorism since 9/11 has produced asymmetrical wars in several countries that have destabilised the daily lives of their citizens. Proliferation of small arms and light weapons have made conflicts more lethal. Wars, ethnic conflicts and natural disasters have forced 21 million people to seek shelter as refugees in other countries. Poverty, disease, and illiteracy have impacted on the majority of world citizens, most of whom live in emerging countries. Crimes have become sophisticated and so have the criminals in their techniques, methodologies, and reach. Environmental degradation and climate change now pose a security challenge to the existence of global order.[3]

Numerous new and some old challenges continue to anguish human life in the present century. As was the case with Vietnam, neither Iraq nor Afghanistan was a war of necessity; neither a justifiable choice.[4]

Editing a volume on foreign policy of major powers containing contribution of scholars and practitioners is indeed a stimulating experience. Each paper is focused on a particular country providing new information and analysis within the scope of broad outline provided to the authors. The writers were advised to follow the outline flexibly reflecting their experience and information base. The changing theoretical framework that is evolving in the context of major powers, the shifting perspectives and approaches on the subject do pose challenges. However, the essays presented in the volume written by acknowledged specialists provide rare insights for readers.

Foreign policy at the conceptual level, is in some ways at an incipient stage, struggling to develop a theoretical framework. Within the broad spectrum, foreign policy as a major field of study is essentially conceived as a strategic activity within the national context, discovering the latent potentialities in order to attain the goals based on national interest to protect and defend the country.

---

3. Banerjee, Ajit and Murari Sharma (2007). *Reinventing the United Nations.* Prentice-Hall. p.5.
4. Haas, Richard (2013). *Foreign Policy Begins at Home.* Basic Books. p.2.

The United States (US) is the oldest constitutional democracy. With the end of the Cold War, US became an economic power with influence over much of the world.[5] In this century, the influence remains strong but in relative terms, it is somewhat declining in economic output compared to China, India, Russia, Brazil, and the newly consolidated European Union (EU).[6] The US extended political influence beyond its borders and carried out missions to bring freedom and democracy to the greater part of the world. It has remained active in world politics. The US relied on military strength and balance of power. These policies were bold and imaginative.

James Baker's paper on foreign policy underscores the test of American policy during the coming years, which is based on three important propositions. First, the significant phenomena shaping world affairs today is the uniquely pre-eminent position of the US; second, how best to use that power in ways that advance our interest and values in the fundamental challenges confronting US policymakers; and third, even as we force a policy to promote these goals, we must also be aware of strategic overreach. These propositions could be reviewed one by one.

> By any standard, the US enjoys a unique pre-eminence in world affairs...our might is not limitless. But, compared to earlier great powers...we possess immense advantages over potential rivals. Our powers is perhaps most obvious in the military arena. The defeat of the Taliban clearly demonstrates our unparallel lead ability to project decisive forces across vast distances... No other country even begins to approach this capability, nor will they for decades to come. The US is also an economic powerhouse. Our output represents a quarter of world GDP.

British foreign relations since early days has focused on achieving a balance of power, with the objective of extending its predominant influence in the continent of Europe.[7] The British built up a very large worldwide Empire, which peaked in size around the 1920-1940

---

5. *http://en.wikipedia.org/wiki/Foreign_policy_of_the_United_States*
6. Ibid.
7. *http://en.wikipedia.org/wiki/Foreign_relations_of_the_United_Kingdom*

era, then began to shrink by the 1970s. Very little was left, but a "Commonwealth of Nations". After 1945, Britain reduced its overseas commitments. All the colonies became independent, and left an indelible mark in the emerging countries. Subsequently, it joined the EU.

Tim Oliver states that the United Kingdom (UK) has long been an active player in international relations. This is built in part on history, a requirement today to engage in a globalised world, and also a deep-seated desire within the UK that the country play a global role. To appreciate this role and what drives it, we need to examine how British foreign policy is made. We also need to appreciate the history of UK foreign policy and the long-standing debates about whether UK's foreign policy should prioritise ethical concerns, commercial links or the threats facing the state. We can then examine which international relationships the UK prioritises and why.

France is a major European country. It has played a prominent and historic role in the European and international history. It is a founding member of the United Nations (UN), and of the European Coal and Steel Community (the EU's predecessor). Its main allies are Germany, Italy, the US, and the EU. As a charter member of the UN, France is a permanent member of the Security Council.[8]

Steven Philip Kramer states that France got caught up with a series of crisis initially, and later on with the Franco-Prussian war in 1870. In 1940, France fell to Germany. These events indicate a lack of cohesion leading the country to humiliation in WWII. After the war in 1958, France introduced a model for planned economy and a welfare state. Thereafter, the leaders turned attention to the project of European integration and achieved regional leadership in partnership with West Germany. Despite France's central role in the creation of EU, the country's relationship with Europe has never been easy. Nevertheless, France made European integration the cornerstone of its foreign policy. Its leaders have been reluctant to yield national sovereignty to the supra-national institutions they helped to create.

8. *http://en.wikipedia.org/wiki/Foreign_relations_of_France*

Since 1951, Germany has been at the heart of European integration. The reunification in 1990, which saw East Germany merged into West Germany, promoted peaceful integration with its neighbours. Strong ties with the US remain central to German foreign policy.[9]

Deter Dettke indicates that a short historical review of the paper traces German foreign policy from the days of partition and beginning of the Cold War to the era of Détente and German unification as the crowning event at the end of the East-West conflict and the collapse of the Soviet empire. The partition of Germany initially became part of the structural foundation of the post-WWII international order, forcing West Germany to focus on economic recovery and reform. Assisted by the US Marshall Plan and committing West Germany firmly to European integration and Western institutions, the country was able to join the family of Western democracies in their efforts to contain the Soviet Union and to defend against the political and military threat it posed for the survival of the West. Under these circumstances, West Germany's national security strategy put European and Western political and military integration before unification as the only way to provide security for Germany and Europe, including nuclear deterrence.

Ostpolitik and Détente in the late 1960s and early 1970s led to a reduction of tensions between East and West, including between the two German states. Unification came as a serendipity for Germany and its Western allies when the Soviet Union realised that the costs of holding its empire together, if necessary with the use of military force, turned out to be too high. Economic and political reforms in the Soviet Union itself opened the way for German and European unification.

The new Europe that emerged after 1989 created by far the best geostrategic environment Germany ever experienced. After unification, Germany ended up again in a central position in Europe, but this time not as a military power imposing itself on Europe but as a civilian power. The culture of restraint will remain a crucial

9. *http://en.wikipedia.org/wiki/Foreign_relations_of_German*

component of German behaviour in the future. However, with the quest for normalcy and as a central power in Europe, Germany will also have to take on more responsibility in maintaining stability in Europe and of the international system. German leadership on the basis of geo-economic power will not be enough to secure the post-modern order that emerged after WWII. Multilateralism will always be at the centre of German foreign policy, but Germany will have to add military capabilities on the national level too in order to successfully act multilaterally.

With the breakup of the Soviet Union into separate nations, and the re-emergence of the nation of Russia, the world of pro-US and pro-Soviet alliances broke down. The big change during these years was a transition from a bipolar to a multipolar world. If they can avoid war, the coming decades can be peaceful and productive, provided there are no misunderstandings or dangerous rivalries.[10]

Jeffrey Mankoff states that foreign policy in Vladimir Putin's Russia centres on the tension between a desire to play the role of a traditional great power and the need to adapt to a world in which the very nature of power is evolving. Restoring Russia's international influence has also become a major component of Putin's strategy of domestic legitimating, especially as the Russian economy has slowed down in the aftermath of the global financial crisis and the onset of a major confrontation with the West, following Russia's 2014 annexation of the Crimean Peninsula and military intervention in eastern Ukraine. Increasingly central to this conception of Russia as a major power and independent global actor is an effort to differentiate Russia from the West, which Russian elites increasingly view as an antagonistic force. Russia continues to prioritise traditional measures of power, and while (as its actions in Ukraine, Syria, and elsewhere show) it can apply hard power effectively, it finds itself more and more isolated, the object of fear more than respect, and like its Tsarist and Soviet predecessors, the economic foundations of power in Putin's Russian Federation remain shaky. Shoring up those foundations will be in many ways Moscow's

10. "Foreign Policy After the Cold War", *www.boundless.com* "The History of American Foreign Policy".

greatest challenge, but one that ironically requires a greater degree of openness and international cooperation—especially with the West—than Putin's Kremlin seems inclined to accept.

Throughout the post–WWII period, Japan concentrated on economic growth. It accommodated itself flexibly to the regional and global policies of the US, while avoiding major initiatives of its own; adhered to pacifist principles embodied in the 1947 constitution. referred to as the "peace constitution"; and generally took a passive, low-profile role in world affairs. Relations with other countries were governed by what the leadership called "Omni-directional diplomacy," which was essentially a policy of maintaining political neutrality in foreign affairs while expanding economic relations wherever possible. This policy was highly successful and allowed Japan to prosper and grow as an economic power, but it was feasible only while the country enjoyed the security and economic stability provided by its ally, the US.[11]

Takashi Inoguchi presents a fairly detailed portrayal of Japan's foreign policy as it evolves in the 2010s. After a brief description of institutional actors shaping Japanese foreign policy, its three policy lines, big power aspiration, solid civilian power orientation and historical legacies, are examined in some detail. Then turning briefly to a longer term projection (1813-2033), the dynamics and dialectics of three major powers in East Asia, the US, China and Japan, are speculated, on the basis of their "red-line" preoccupations, i.e., primacy for the US, autonomy for China and peace for Japan. The current thrust of Japanese foreign policy under Shinzo Abe, 'Abenomics' and 'Abegeopolitics', are examined in some detail.

The new government in Pakistan, which was elected by its people, is poised to bring about major changes in the process of governance as well as economic reform. Going forward, it can play a major role in the region with its outstanding intellectual and professional capabilities in various fields.

Sartaj Aziz provides a strategic vision of foreign policy of Pakistan. He articulates that completion of the first year of the new

---

11. *www.boundless.com* "The History of American Foreign Policy".

government to review the foreign policy predicaments, as well as achievements, provides a list of goals and challenges that lie ahead for the country.

India's foreign policy has always regarded the concept of neighbourhood as one of the widening concentric circles, around a central axis of historical and cultural commonalities.[12] The end of the Cold War significantly affected India's foreign policy, as it did for much of the world. The country now seeks to strengthen its diplomatic and economic ties with the US, the People's Republic of China, the EU, Japan, Israel, Mexico, and Brazil. India has also forged close ties with the member states of the Association of Southeast Asian Nations, the African Union, the Arab League and Iran.

Rohan Mukherjee mentions that India has been described as an "improbable democracy." Indeed democracy is not the only improbable phenomenon to have taken root in Indian soil. The fact that India has risen from the ranks of the world's poor countries to become a frontrunner for great power status is the signal achievement of its astute leaders and energetic citizens over nearly seven decades. Starting with a foreign policy designed to avoid costly foreign entanglements, India has navigated the stormy waters of regional and international politics with reasonable success. India today has a large and growing economy, experienced military, nuclear weapons, and a young and dynamic population that continues to drive innovation and growth in knowledge intensive sectors.

There is of course much that threatens India's achievements and future trajectory. Deep social schisms along caste, religious, and linguistic lines; thriving armed insurgencies and separatist movements; enduring regional rivalries with Pakistan and China; and endemic poverty engulfing hundreds of millions of individuals are among the major challenges India faces today. In terms of institutional resources, India's able bureaucracy and political leadership have not always been able to translate their acumen into positive gains on the international stage. India's positions on democracy promotion and humanitarian intervention remain firmly

12. *India Foreign Policy and Government Guide*, Volume 1.

at odds with the global institutional consensus spearheaded by the West.

Nonetheless, India has done well on many counts—pursuing economic diplomacy, securing strategic autonomy, and carving out a greater share of benefits in international institutions. While much remains to be done, the fact that the Indian state remains not just a viable enterprise but a flourishing venture in its 67th year of independence, is in itself a remarkable feat of domestic and foreign policy, given the levels of poverty, institutional weakness, and domestic turmoil in which India began its journey in 1947.

Relations between India and Pakistan have been complex due to a number of historical and political events. Relations between the two states have been defined by the violent partition of British India in 1947, the Kashmir dispute and the numerous military conflicts fought between the two nations. Consequently, even though the two South Asian nations share linguistic, cultural, geographic, and economic links, their relationship has been plagued by hostility and suspicion.[13]

Aparna Pande attempts to explain why despite ties of history, culture, ethnicity and language, Pakistan and India still remain hostile neighbours more than six decades after partition of the British Empire in 1947. The chapter provides a historical context to the relations between India and Pakistan dating back to Partition, before discussing evolution of the foreign policies of these two countries. To understand India-Pakistan relations, there is a need to comprehend the underlying issues of their relationship. For each state, its national identity frames its foreign policy. The role of leaders and institutions in each country will be reviewed, as well as their conflicts and wars. A key part will be to examine the issue of military and economic parity which has defined and still defines how Pakistan views its ties with India. The influence of the Cold War on both countries' ties with other nations (including the US, China, Afghanistan and the rest of the Muslim world) and the changes that resulted with the end of the Cold War will be reviewed before assessing future prospects.

---

13. *http://en.wikipedia.org/wiki/India%E2%80%93Pakistan_relations*

Israeli foreign policy is chiefly influenced by Israel's strategic situation, the Arab-Israeli conflict, and the rejection of Israel by most of the Arab states. The goals of Israeli policy are therefore to overcome diplomatic isolation and to achieve recognition and friendly relations with as many nations as possible, both in the Middle East and beyond.[14]

Yoav J. Tenembaum dwells on Israel's foreign policy, both from a conceptual and historical perspective. It delineates the structural dimensions of Israel's foreign policy decision-making process, assessing the institutional and political aspects that have wielded their influence on it. The chapter deals with the major challenges facing Israeli foreign policy and the risks and opportunities entailed in them. Major historical landmarks in Israel's foreign policy are analysed, and pertinent conclusions are presented on their effect in the shaping of present and future policy.

China's foreign policy and strategic thinking is highly influential. China officially states it "unswervingly pursues an independent foreign policy of peace. The fundamental goals of this policy are to preserve China's independence, sovereignty and territorial integrity, create a favourable international environment for China's reform and opening up and modernisation construction, maintain world peace and propel common development." China's leaders have been regular travellers to all parts of the globe, and it has sought a higher profile in the UN through its permanent seat on the United Nations Security Council (UNSC) and other multilateral organisations. Closer to home, China has made efforts to reduce tensions in Asia; its relations with its Asian neighbours have become stable during last decades of the 20th century. "China's foreign policy today is summarised as the strategic ones with the neighbouring countries and with world's superpowers to strive for China's national interest (and most importantly the interest of the Chinese Communist Party) for creating a favourable environment for the country's domestic development for perpetual competition in the world in the long-run."[15]

---

14. *http://countrystudies.us/israel/106.htm*

15. *http://en.wikipedia.org/wiki/Foreign_relations_of_China*

Quansheng Zhao explains that Chinese foreign policy has experienced many different eras. We should therefore analyse the transitions between different eras, such as from the Mao Zedong era to the Deng Xiaoping era and later into the eras of Jiang Zemin and Hu Jintao. Currently, we have entered the new era of Xi Jinping and need to continue identifying the basic characteristics of China's "new" foreign policy.

This chapter examines in details the formation of Chinese foreign policy, focusing on the evolving role of think tanks. In recent years, public participation in the formation of Chinese foreign policy has noticeably increased, yet it still has considerable limitations. By providing a conceptual framework—interactions between the "inner circle" and the "outer circle"—this paper examines the limited impact of think tanks on policymaking processes of Chinese foreign policy. A key development under Jiang and Hu (and now under Xi) is the increasingly active and multi-layered channels between the inner circle (the top leaders in the Chinese government) and the outer circle (think tanks, intellectuals and scholars). There are seven channels between these two bodies, including consultations with policymakers, internal reports, conferences and public policy debates, policy NGOs (non-governmental organisations), outside-system discussions, overseas scholars, and epistemic community. This progress is due to three changes in Chinese society: the development of civil society, greater demand for policy input, and growing professionalism in the foreign policy apparatus. However, think tanks still face severe limitations, including a lack of ability to openly criticise official foreign policy due to the authoritarian nature of Chinese society and a lack of personnel exchange between think tanks and government agencies, owing to the continued peripheral status of think tanks.

Leila Bijos states that the end of the Cold War and the effects of globalisation induced the Government of Brazil to discuss Brazil's physical and functional identity, and how to leave its isolation and look forward to a more relevant role in the new international reality. The development of Brazil in the last two decades, combined with its broadening involvement in a complex and important international agenda including: human rights, inequality, programmes for eradicating hunger, Bolsa Escola (Family School Grant, cash transfers to poor families to enrol their children in the educational system), leadership roles in two United Nations Peacekeeping Operations, participation as a creditor in the International Monetary Fund (IMF), production and dissemination of biofuel, as well as other important international issues, were brought to the fore by a foreign policy that envisages the country's assuming a regional leadership role in Latin America. Analytical emphasis is placed on contemporary Brazilian foreign policy, its political context, contemporary aspirations and the patterns of its engagement in several economic blocs, political alliances, environmental protection of the Amazon, and questions relating to defence and security. Brazil is on the brink of becoming an important actor as a regional leader in South America, and an important partner to North American, European, Asian and African countries.

The African National Congress (ANC) believes that the charting of a new foreign policy for South Africa is a key element in the creation of a peaceful and prosperous country. Apartheid corroded the very essence of life in South Africa. This is why the country's emerging political leaders are challenged to build a nation in which all people—irrespective of race, color, creed, religion or sex—can assert fully their human worth; after Apartheid, our people deserve nothing less than the right to life, liberty and the pursuit of happiness.[16]

Tseliso Thipanyane writes that under the Apartheid era, South Africa's foreign policy informed by racist policies and practices was characterised by hostility and aggression towards its neighbouring states, and defiance of international norms and standards. The struggle against Apartheid, in contrast, was informed by a desire and determination to establish a democratic country that would live in peace with its neighbours and make a significant contribution towards a fair and just global order. This chapter reviews the role post-Apartheid South Africa has and continues to play in regional and international affairs in terms of its foreign policy. It focuses on the progress the country has made in translating human rights values

16. *http://www.foreignaffairs.com/articles/49408/nelson-mandela/south-africas-future- foreign-policy*

and principles which are reflected in the Constitution stating foreign policy positions. It also looks at challenges South Africa faces in the implementation of its foreign policy and how it balances its founding human rights values and principles with its economic and political interests in the African continent and an increasingly and changing and globalising world.

Saudi Arabia is a non-aligned state whose stated foreign policy objectives are to maintain its security and its paramount position on the Arabian Peninsula, and as the world's largest oil-exporter, and also to maintain cooperative relations with other oil-producing and major oil-consuming countries. Saudi Arabian stated policy is focused on co-operation with the oil-exporting Gulf states, the unity of the Arab world, Islamic strength and solidarity, and support for the UN.[17]

Natana J. DeLong-Bas analyses the complex interplays between components of Saudi foreign policymaking, historical and contemporary, focusing on the objectives of peace, prosperity, and stability that drive it. Saudi foreign policy reflects both multifaceted national needs and a multiplicity of identities, including national (Saudi), micro-regional (Arabian Gulf), macro-regional (Arab), and global (Muslim). Although Saudi foreign policy has proven sufficiently flexible to adapt to changing contexts, circumstances, and perceived strategic interests, it nevertheless has consistently maintained security at its centre. Following a brief historical overview of Saudi foreign policy, detailed attention is given to contemporary challenges and opportunities, including: domestic issues with an impact on foreign policy; strategic priorities that include keeping the Middle East free of nuclear and mass destruction weapons, promoting regional cooperation and security, and calling for global respect for religion; political priorities of creating and/or maintaining security in war-torn countries in the region, particularly Lebanon, Iraq and Egypt; economic and social priorities of using Saudi oil wealth for humanitarian and development purposes and expanding energy production and export beyond oil to renewable energy resources; and security priorities of addressing terrorism, including the rise

17. *http://en.wikipedia.org/wiki/Foreign_relations_of_Saudi_Arabia*

of Islamic State of Iraq and Syria (ISIS), the aftermath of the Arab Spring, the civil war in Syria, containing sectarian and religious rivalries, especially with Iran, calling for just solutions to long-standing conflicts, particularly in Palestine/Israel, and protecting its own borders, particularly with Yemen. In addition to these priorities, the paper calls for future attention to be given to Saudi government accountability to Saudi public opinion, the challenge of institutionalising Saudi foreign policy as succession issues loom, using Saudi financial power to promote regional, and thus domestic, security, and increasing Saudi independence, particularly from the US, in formulating its foreign policy for Saudi Arabia's own needs.

1

JAMES BAKER

The Case for Pragmatic Idealism

Foreign Policy and International Relations

My reflections on the global challenges that will test American foreign policy during the coming years are based on three simple but important propositions: first, one of the most significant phenomenon shaping world affairs today is the uniquely pre-eminent position of the United States (US) in world affairs; second, how best to use that power in ways that advance our interests and values is the fundamental challenge confronting US policymakers; and third, even as we forge a policy to promote these goals we must also beware of strategic overreach.

Let me take these propositions one by one.

First: By any standard, the US enjoys a unique pre-eminence in world affairs. As I will stress later, our might is not limitless. But, compared to earlier great powers—ancient Rome, Napoleonic France, and Britain at her peak just prior to World War I—we possess immense advantages over potential rivals.

Our power is perhaps most obvious in the military arena. The defeat of the Taliban and the overthrow of Saddam Hussein clearly demonstrate our unparalleled ability to project decisive force across vast distances.

Our services represent the best-armed, best-trained, and best-led military in the world. No other countries even begin to approach this capability, nor will they for decades to come.

The US is also an economic powerhouse. Our output represents almost a quarter of world GDP (gross domestic product). Moreover, our performance over the last two decades has significantly outpaced that of our traditional competitors such as Japan and the countries of Western Europe. And despite the scandals that rocked corporate

America earlier in this decade we remain at the forefront of economic efficiency, innovation, and entrepreneurship.

In addition, we wield immense diplomatic influence in the global arena. The US enjoys strong and durable bilateral relationships with a host of friendly countries. And we also play a leadership role in international organisations such as the United Nations (UN), the International Monetary Fund (IMF), North Atlantic Treaty Organization (NATO) and the World Trade Organization (WTO).

And last but not least, we represent an ideology—free market democracy—without a serious global rival. That model is clearly not triumphant everywhere. But the trend over recent decades has unmistakably been in the direction of democracy and free markets.

Our old international adversary—communism—has been swept into the dustbin of history. And no other ideology has risen to take its place. True, Islamic fundamentalism is a potent force. But, by definition, its appeal is limited to countries with significant Muslim populations.

In short, there is today no country or group of countries that can challenge our international pre-eminence. This may change as countries like China and India loom larger on the world stage. But for now and the foreseeable future, the US is the only true global power.

Now my second proposition: how can we best use our unparalleled power? I realise that this is a question easier to ask than to answer. But how well we answer it will surely determine if our current preeminence continues for years, decades, or even longer. So, I would like to offer a few ideas—10 maxims, if you will—that will help us find our way in the international arena—and the answer to that question.

First, we must be comfortable with using our power. In a real sense, we have no alternative. If the US does not exercise power, others will. We simply have too much at stake in the world to walk away from it, even if we could. This was true before 11 September 2001. But it is even truer today as we combat the scourges of international terrorism and proliferation of weapons of mass destruction.

We should also remember that the US has proven itself to be, (on balance), a powerful force for good in world affairs. Does this mean that we are perfect? Of course not. But in the major global conflicts of the last century—World War I, World War II, and the Cold War—the US played a historic role in defeating imperialism and totalitarianism. Other countries depend on our leadership. This is most obviously true of our allies in Western Europe, East Asia, and elsewhere. But even countries that are sometimes anything but friendly often seek our engagement.

Second, we need to recognise that even US power is limited. We cannot be, even if we wanted to be, the policeman for the world. And we should not be expected to be by those countries that would like that in today's unipolar world. Powerful as we are, we cannot solve every problem in the world. Iraq, for instance, has shown a limit of our military strength. In saying this, I yield to no one in my admiration for the magnificent performance of our men and women in uniform. But it is plain that our military services, which crushed the conventional Iraqi army within weeks in 2003, face altogether more intractable foes in insurgent groups and sectarian militias. Their task, I might add, is complicated by divisions within the Iraqi government and growing frustration among many Iraqis at the lack of basic security and services.

Our power is limited in other areas as well. As strong as our economy may be, we still need the cooperation of others in such areas as expanding trade and investment, and coordinating macroeconomic policy. The same is true in the diplomatic arena, where our influence can be constrained when we are unable to persuade others. Securing the support of China and Russia, for instance, will be critical in crafting a tough response to Iran's nuclear programmes. Not least, the exercise of American power is limited by the ability of our leaders to generate and sustain 'domestic political support'—a subject to which I will return at greater length later.

Third, we should be prepared to act unilaterally when the situation requires it. Unilateral action remains the first and surest test of a great power. But we should not undertake such action lightly.

For reasons that I will discuss, it is almost always preferable to act in concert with others. But when our vital interests are at stake, we must be prepared, (if necessary), to go at it alone.

Fourth. But we also need to appreciate the importance of allies. It is no coincidence that the three great global conflicts of the 20th century—World War I, World War II, and the Cold War—were won by coalitions. By securing allies, our policymakers can achieve important goals. Most obviously, partners allow us to spread the human and financial costs of any action. We can create what could be called an "efficient division of international labor."

In the Gulf War of 1990-91, for instance, a military coalition —the US, Britain, France, even many Arab nations, and others— was bolstered by financial support from Gulf Arabs, the Japanese, German and a number of other Western Europeans. Many forget that the Gulf War of 1990-91 cost the US hardly a nickel because at our request our allies provided this critical financial support. In addition, allies can help secure "legitimacy" for our actions. In the case of the Gulf War of 1990-1991, the UN Security Council's authorisation of force promoted support for action against Saddam Hussein in both the international community and (just as importantly), here at home.

Fifth, we need to use all the means at our disposal. These tools include moral persuasion, bilateral talks, and multilateral action. Such action can occur through formal institutions such as the UN, NATO, and the IMF. But it can also be pursued through "informal groups" like the coalition against Iraq during the 1990-91 Gulf War. "Effective foreign policy" embodies a continuum of action from private demarches to military intervention. In short, one size does not fit all when it comes to foreign policy. This is especially true today, as we confront the threats posed by international terrorism and the proliferation of weapons of mass destruction.

We require a comprehensive approach. Military action—such as the battle against the Taliban—must be part of it. But it is evident that this cannot be the sole solution. A successful approach must include the coordination of intelligence-gathering and law enforcement and international cooperation in areas such as money laundering, tighter border controls, and international pressure on rogue regimes.

Sixth, we should be prepared to "change course" if necessary. (We are doing just that now in our Iraq policy.) Consistency, of course, is an important element of foreign policy. It permits us to move beyond crisis management and facilitates the development of long-term strategies. Consistency can also foster stability by reassuring allies and setting down clear markers for potential adversaries. But when events change, we must be prepared to change with them. The rise of Mikhail Gorbachev in the Soviet Union, for instance, marked a dramatic shift in the worldview of the Soviet leadership. And it was therefore only right that Washington reach out to Moscow in ways unimaginable just years before.

Seventh, we need to recognise and accept that the US will sometimes have to deal with authoritarian regimes. In a "perfect world," we could perhaps work only with other democracies. Unfortunately, this is not a perfect world. And there is no sign that it will become one anytime soon. To be blunt, sometimes we have no choice but to work with governments that fall short, in terms of democratic practices and protection of human rights.

Easily the most striking example of this is our World War II alliance with Stalin's Soviet Union, one of the most murderous regimes in history. (Given the immediate and deadly threat posed by Nazi Germany, we had no alternative.) And during the Cold War, we made common cause with authoritarian regimes in Latin America, Asia, and elsewhere.

Today, our allies in the war on terror include countries in the Middle East and Central Asia that bear scant resemblance to Jeffersonian democracies. I cannot pretend that this is a satisfying state of affairs. But there is simply no alternative to it. This brings me to yet another maxim.

Eighth, we must be prepared to talk with our enemies. I don't say this because talking, *per se*, is a good thing, although there is something to be said for maintaining a bilateral dialogue if only to avoid misunderstanding and missteps. No: the fundamental reason for us to be prepared to speak to our enemies is that it is in our interest to do so. This is why we maintained an embassy in Moscow throughout the Cold War. And this is why even so staunch an anti-Communist as President Reagan was prepared to negotiate with the Soviets. Talking to hostile states—whether it was the Moscow during the Cold War or Damascus today—is not 'appeasement'. It was and is good foreign policy.

Ninth, we should be mindful that 'values' are important—but that they aren't the only thing. It is hash to say it, but sadly, we cannot formulate or implement American foreign policy according to the principals of Mother Teresa because when the body bags start coming home, you can't get support of a political policy when there is not an overriding national interest.

Promoting democracy and free markets is rightly central to US foreign policy. A freer, more prosperous world is a better world for our own citizens and people everywhere. But we must remember that that progress towards democracy and free markets is either inevitable or without its own strains. The example of World War I is sobering. It followed immediately on the heels of a period of unparalleled economic integration that some have called the "first golden age of globalisation." One of the most influential books of the pre-war period—Norman Angell's *The Great Illusion*—argued that general war had become impossible because of the economic advantages to peace. Yet we know what followed: one of the bloodiest periods in human history. The lesson: we should be very wary when talk turns to 'inevitability'. What man creates, man can destroy.

Moreover, both democracy and free-markets can be decidedly mixed blessings in the short run. Economic reforms can lead to strains that prompt populist backlashes. Nor can elections be counted upon to produce stable, responsible regimes. The popular success of Hamas among Palestinians and Hezbollah in Lebanon are cases in point. So, should we support free markets and democracy? Of course we should. But we should be especially careful of underestimating the difficulties that countries can face as they embark on the path to democracy. And we should remember that 'stability'' is not a dirty word!

Tenth and last, we must always remember that domestic support is vital to any successful foreign policy! The will of the American people is the final arbiter of foreign policy in our democracy. Generating (and sustaining) domestic support for foreign policy is in every way as important as the policy itself. Without that support, specific policies risk repudiation at the polls or public disenchantment with foreign engagement in general.

This brings me to one final proposition: We must be careful to 'avoid strategic overextension'. But the history of empires and great powers from Rome onwards does provide an important lesson. Power must be husbanded carefully. It is precious and finite. Spreading it too thinly can lead to disaster. Choices still matter. And so do priorities.

Let me make clear: I am anything but a 'declinist' when it comes to the US. I am absolutely convinced that our country's future is a bright one. But while the US may be the most powerful state in history, we are not omnipotent. Our society may be good. But it is not perfect.

As the theologian, Reinhold Niebuhr, wrote: "Great nations are too strong to be destroyed by their foes. But they can easily be overcome by their own pride."

The approach I suggest does not fall easily into traditional categories of foreign policy—'realism' or 'idealism'. It contains the 'best elements of both'. And it embodies one of our most distinctive national characteristics: we are a practical people less interested in ideological purity than in solving problems.

What I suggest could be called 'pragmatic idealism'. While firmly grounded in values, it appreciates the complexity of the real world—a world of hard choices and painful trade-offs. This is the real world in which we must live, decide, and act.

It is a world that Ronald Reagan understood. He was, famously, a man of deeply-held conviction. But he was also pragmatic. When I was his chief of staff, he often told me, "Jim—I'd rather get 80 per cent of what I want than to go over the cliff with my flag flying." The Gipper, of course, was right.

Such a balanced approach, I believe, can help us avoid both the cynicism of 'realism' and the impracticality of 'idealism'. It is based on an optimistic view of man but is tempered by our knowledge of human imperfection. It promises no easy answers or quick fixes.

But such an approach does, I am convinced, offer our surest guide and best hope for navigating our great country safely through this precarious period of unparalleled opportunity and risk in world affairs.

2

TIM OLIVER

Foreign Policy of Britain

Britain's Place in the World

Britain's place and power in the world is difficult to pin down. Britain is neither a superpower nor a small power. It can be considered a regional power but it retains interests in large areas of the world beyond Europe and the North Atlantic. Economically, the United Kingdom (UK) is no longer the industrial workshop of the world (as it was during the Victorian era) but it remains one of the largest and richest global economies. Britain's cultural and soft power is substantial, in part thanks to the global role of the English language, but also because of sport, media, achievements in education, science and innovation and political developments such as parliamentary democracy and Magna Carta. Britain has actively sought to be open to the global economy with the City of London and international finance a key part of the UK economy. Substantial immigration and emigration (the British diaspora is one of the world's largest [see Sriskandarajah and Drew, 2006]) links the UK to peoples all over the world. Britain's military capability allows it the capacity to project military power around the world, an ability that, while limited, is held by few others. The UK stands at the juncture of a wide range of international relations, for example, as a permanent member of the UN Security Council, North Atlantic Treaty Organisation (NATO), the G8/G20, a leading member of the European Union (EU) (especially on EU foreign and defence matters) and as a leading player in the Commonwealth. Closeness to the United States (US) has been a central aim of successive governments and, at times, has resulted in influence over US policy. In consequence, as former UK Foreign Secretary Douglas Hurd noted, Britain "punches above its weight" in international affairs.

However, we cannot be overly optimistic about the UK's position in the world. Britain's population, natural resources and geographical space are small and limited compared to some of the countries that span large areas of continents such as the US or Brazil. Britain, for example, imports large amounts of its food, energy, minerals and manufactured goods. Economically, the British people may be prosperous and, collectively, one of the richest in the world, but the UK economy has been in relative decline for a long period with Britain at one point labelled the 'sick man of Europe'. Long-standing problems with technological and industrial innovation, not to mention productivity, today face stiff competition from emerging markets. Britain's cultural power may be said to rest in a large part on the use of English in North America. Indeed, relations with the US or EU can leave it looking like British foreign policy and power rest on foundations that are not its own. Membership of institutions such as the UN Security Council are in part a legacy of World War II. In a number of places around the world, Britain faces a degree of resentment and hatred for imperial occupation and, more recently, because of complicity with human rights abuses, torture and regimes that have shown little sympathy for their population or international law.

One only need look to history to see that post-World War II, British foreign policy has mainly been one of the increasingly restricted ambitions, something termed 'declinism' (see Tomlinson, 2009). Britain's emergence in 1945 as a victor created something of an illusion. She had at one point stood alone in Europe against the Nazis, played a key part in the defeat of Germany and Japan, and commanded a place at the top table of international relations thanks to the British Empire. It was assumed by many in Britain that Britain would and should continue to play a global role. The reality was that the strain of war had seen Britain lose 25 per cent of its national wealth and the accumulation of massive debts; exports had collapsed and much-needed investment postponed (Dedman, 2010: 94). The independence and partition of India in 1947 meant the loss of the manpower of the British Indian Army. Post-war defence spending commitments for the Korean War (1950-1953) and the development of the British atomic bomb had to be balanced against the costs of rebuilding and of constructing a welfare state, something the British people had voted for in large numbers when they elected, by a landslide, a Labour government in 1945.

The squeeze on British power of these mounting costs was felt most painfully in the 1956 Suez Crisis. Egypt's nationalising of the Suez Canal led to a British, French and Israeli operation to occupy the Canal Zone, seen by Britain and France as crucial to their continued imperial positions in Africa, the Middle East and Asia. Military success on the ground was undermined by economic weakness at home. US anger at what it saw as a destabilising act of imperial aggression led to pressure on the Pound Sterling that Britain could not sustain. Britain's eventual withdrawal from Suez delivered a clear message: that Britain's ambitions to be an independent global power had been humbled by American economic power and political calculations (Reynolds, 2000: 203-06). It was a classic example of a state overstretched in its global commitments. In turn, Britain could not resist the further break-up of the Empire with a final withdrawal of garrisons from East of Suez by the early 1970s (Hyam, 2007: 327). The retreat itself saw British power humbled on numerous occasions such as when it was powerless to deal with the Unilateral Declaration of Independence by the whites-only government of Rhodesia (now Zimbabwe). Membership of the European Common Market in the 1973, although supported by the US, seemed an abdication of a global role—something we turn to later. Victory in the Falklands War of 1982 led to a revival of feelings of pride in British power, and of capabilities many thought Britain had long lost. But victory would not have been secured without a degree of largely hidden help from the US and France (Freedman, 2005: 379-89). Indeed, even under the Iron Lady—Mrs Thatcher—the military faced reductions in commitments, the Falklands War itself a result of the mixed signals given by the withdrawal of British military commitments to the islands (Freedman, 2005: 143). By the time of the fall of the Berlin Wall in 1989, the UK's main foreign, security and defence concerns were focused on Europe and the North Atlantic.

The post-Cold War world was to show further constraints. The newly found unity of Europe was shattered by division and weakness over the former Yugoslavia, a situation Britain was just as incompetent at handling as everybody else. Economic weaknesses came to the fore again in 1992 when the pound sterling was humiliatingly forced to withdraw from the European Exchange Rate Mechanism (ERM). British involvement in the 1990 Gulf War was substantial but defence cuts to cash in on the 'peace dividend' from the end of the Cold War saw Britain's forces significantly reduced. The domestic weaknesses of Prime Minister John Major's 1990-1997 Conservative Government saw infighting over Europe that tore the party apart. The newly elected New Labour Government led by Tony Blair had said little on the issue of foreign policy, concentrating instead on the need for domestic renewal. But Blair's premiership showed how, despite a long list of constraints, the UK continued to attempt and at times succeed in playing a global role. This ambition continues to this day, with the 2010 government—formed through a coalition of the Conservative Party and the Liberal Democrats —pursuing an ambitious foreign policy agenda, despite facing significant economic challenges.

Restricted ambitions and decline then seemed to be the narrative of British foreign policy, but let us not forget that ambitions there certainly were. The legacy of Empire meant Britain was destined to be involved in global issues as it withdrew from imperial territories. The UK's position as a victor in World War II meant the public and especially the political elite held expectations of a role in the world, as did allies who looked to Britain to fulfil such roles. As an advanced industrial economy requiring access to global resources and markets, Britain could not avoid the various associated political and security dilemmas. Added to this was how Britain's military capabilities, experience and proud martial history meant that military power was considered more of an option than for other similarly sized countries.

Who Makes UK Foreign Policy?

British foreign policy is directed by the UK's 'core executive', this being the Prime Minister, Cabinet, the Cabinet Office, certain departments such as HM Treasury and the Foreign and Commonwealth Office (FCO) and a complex series of units, networks and committees that try to coordinate the whole of British government (see Smith, 1999). Prime Ministers can appear to be the most important person in government, sometimes resembling a president such as in the US (Foley, 2000; Allen, 2001). They are not. Unlike a president they lack a national mandate. They depend on many sources of support such as a majority of MPs (Members of Parliament) in the House of Commons, Cabinet colleagues, support in their political party, and cooperation with other parties such as through a coalition or some other agreement. They also depend on their staff in 10 Downing Street and the Cabinet Office, a small department that serves the Cabinet and which coordinates the rest of government (and which in the event of a national or international emergency is home to COBRA—Cabinet Office Briefing Room A—that, chaired by the PM, operates as the central decision-making body handling the country's response to an emergency).

Prime Ministers then exercise predominance: "Predominance enables the Prime Minister to lead, but not command, the executive, to direct, not control, its policy development, and to manage, but not wholly dominate the legislature" (Heffernan, 2003: 350). Prime Ministers then have considerable influence, including over foreign policy, but they should not be seen as being the only influence. Prime Ministers also need to be weary, as *The Economist* (2002) noted in January, of being lured towards two traps: "One is to over-estimate Britain's part in world affairs. The other is to exaggerate the place of world affairs in their own job". Many Prime Ministers have sought solace from the drudgery of daily domestic government in international affairs. International summits and meetings to build close relations with other world leaders are important and can bring change, but they can also bring accusations of a Prime Minister becoming too interested in the glamour of international affairs (Russell, 2003).

The other three large departments traditionally associated with foreign affairs are the FCO, which is Britain's foreign ministry (see Dickie, 2004). Like other foreign ministries, it has traditionally played a role of a 'gatekeeper' between the UK and the outside world. Today, because of globalisation and UK membership of the EU, some foreign and domestic affairs are very similar. For the FCO, this means working with other parts of government to ensure Britain's foreign policy is unified and coherent. In recent years, it has prioritised its efforts in areas of the world where the rest of government lacks strong contacts and where Britain wishes to develop links.

The role of the Ministry of Defence (MoD) is, as a British General once noted, "to translate the Government's political objectives into military capabilities and military operations; it's therefore both a Department of State and the supreme headquarters of the Armed Forces" (Jackson, 2006). Britain remains one of the biggest defence spenders in the world, yet defence spending has faced significant cuts with an expectation that the military will do more with less. A desire to keep up and work closely with the US has had to be balanced with the urge to retain an independent capability and to avoid dependence on the same. Poor management of the MoD, especially over the period since 2001 when the British military was constantly deployed on operations, meant that by 2010, the MoD was in a state of crisis. Significant cuts and restructuring were brought in by the 2010-2015 government, with further changes likely beyond 2015.

Britain's aid ministry, the Department for International Development (DfID) has a mission, as set down in law by the International Development Act 2002, to support the international development agenda (House of Commons, 2008: 74). Assisting UK foreign or security policies, therefore, goes against some of DfID's ethos of providing aid strictly for poverty reduction and humanitarian relief. Spending on DfID has also sometimes been controversial. Despite cuts across the rest of government, the 2010-2015 coalition government protected DfID's spending and increased it to meet an international commitment by the UK to spend 0.7 per cent of GDP (gross domestic product) on international aid.

UK governments have long struggled to manage relations between these three departments and the many other parts of UK government that touch—increasingly—on foreign affairs. The March 2008 UK National Security Strategy was 'the first time the

Government has published a single, overarching strategy bringing together the objectives and plans of all departments, agencies and forces involved in protecting our national security' (Cabinet Office, 2008). It was intended as an attempt to grapple with the need for all of UK government to act coherently in response to the challenges posed by the wide-ranging threats the strategy mapped out. The document succeeded in cataloguing the risks in a more contemporary context, going beyond concerns about terrorism or invasion to encompass transnational organised crime, influenza pandemics, civil emergencies and climate change. In short, it stressed the interconnectedness of the domestic and the foreign. Yet it lacked focus and prioritisation and so struggled as a strategy.

In 2010, the incoming Conservative-Liberal Democrat coalition government updated the National Security Strategy as part of a long-awaited review of Britain's defences (Cabinet Office, 2010). Drafting was overseen by a new National Security Council, with its weekly meetings chaired by the Prime Minister. The Council also oversees implementation of the strategy. Published the day before the defence review, the strategy sets the context and ends of British security policy both at home and abroad. The context describes the threats, how they may develop and the UK's position in the world. The ends are the priorities that the UK will attempt to tackle. Unlike the previous strategy that lacked prioritisation, the 2010 strategy identifies 15 priority risks to UK security and breaks them into three tiers. The top tier lists terrorism, cyber security, international military crisis into which the UK is drawn, and national disasters such as floods and pandemics. The role of the following Strategic Security and Defence Review (SDSR) was to structure the UK's defence and security capabilities so as to be the ways and means of achieving these objectives. To ensure that they remain up to date, the SDSR will be reviewed every 5 years, with the National Security Strategy reviewed even more often.

Despite its central place in British democracy, the Parliament is rarely central to deciding UK foreign policy. Powers called the Royal Prerogatives, exercised by the Prime Minister and Cabinet, mean Parliament can be ignored and bypassed on a range of matters.

Parliamentary scrutiny is hampered by government secrecy and obstinacy, especially notable in foreign, defence and security matters. MPs also concentrate on domestic and local matters that are more likely to secure them re-election. This is not to say, however, that Parliament is completely irrelevant. Debates, parliamentary questions and parliamentary committees provide regular insights into government activity and thinking. All governments rest on a majority in the House of Commons and so the backbenchers of a governing party or coalition can cause trouble if they are ignored. A good example of this was the 2014 vote on whether the UK would support US led military action against Syria. The government was under no legal obligation to seek Parliament's approval, the power to go to war being a Royal Prerogative. However, a convention has developed of seeking Parliament's approval (except in emergency situations) on the deployment of UK forces and the controversial nature of the action over Syria meant the government would have faced significant political problems had it ignored Parliament. The government lost the vote in part not only because of bad management of its backbenchers, but also because of weariness in Parliament at British involvement in such military interventions.

Parliament's unease at the proposed action in Syria reflected the British public's own unease. The public can show mixed interest in foreign affairs. On the one hand they can, at times, seem keen. One only has to look at membership in and support for organisations such as Oxfam (founded as the Oxford Committee for Famine Relief) or Amnesty International (founded in London in the 1960s) to see that they are larger than those for political parties. Widespread support for campaigns such as 'Make Poverty History' or 'Live 8' and large demonstrations, most notably over the Iraq War, also signal a degree of interest. Concerns about terrorism can create lively debate, especially fears that some British Muslims have been radicalised as a result of UK foreign policy and so pose a homegrown terrorist threat. But large demonstrations and concerns about terrorism can be the exception. Even the issue of Europe has rarely played a large role in electoral results for the House of Commons. This is not to say that the public or all of British society is indifferent. London hosts a large number of internationally recognised think tanks such as Chatham House, Royal United Services Institute (RUSI) and the International Institute of Statistic Studies (IISS). London and the UK are also home to a network of international media organisations. British business, especially in finance, energy and—most controversially—defence, has had strong links with foreign policy.

Ideas in UK Foreign Policy

British foreign policy has long been driven by a series of ideas about Britain's place in the world and how Britain should behave. It has often been a question of balancing ethics and humanitarian intervention with trade and national security.

Ethics

Ethical concerns in foreign policy or debates about intervening in another state on humanitarian grounds are hardly new ideas in British foreign policy. But in 1997, the newly elected Labour government committed the UK more clearly than ever before to pursuing a foreign policy with an 'ethical dimension' (see The Guardian, 1997). Known more commonly, but inaccurately, as an 'ethical foreign policy', it committed the UK to supporting 'the demands of other peoples for the democratic rights on which we insist for ourselves'. For the Labour government, the national interest could no longer be defined by a narrow realpolitik. Instead, the UK would put values first making it a 'force for good' in the world.

The extent to which this represented a qualitative shift in foreign policy has been hotly disputed (see Wheeler and Dunne, 2004; Little and Wickham-Jones, 2000). On the positive side, the UK has made commitments to institutions such as the International Criminal Court (ICC), banned landmines, tightened the criteria on arms sales, prioritised debt relief, made the UK (through DfID) a world leader in international development, has made real progress towards spending 0.7 per cent of GDP on aid, promoted good governance around the world, and warned of the security and social justice implications of environmental degradation. However, the energy, food and economic (especially defence industry) needs of Britain have seen continued involvement with governments and business practices that are less than sustainable or scrupulous.

It was the use of military force for ethical purposes that the 1997-2010 Labour Government is vividly remembered for. British history is littered with military campaigns justified as being for the benefit of others. Under the Labour government, and in particular thanks to Tony Blair, the urge to intervene on humanitarian grounds reached a new apogee. The Kosovo War of 1999 was the largest and clearest example. Kosovo, a province of Serbia, had long been considered a potential flashpoint in the unstable and bloody Balkans. Tensions between the majority of Kosovar Albanian population and the Serb government finally led to an insurgency to which the Serbs responded with brutal force that mirrored previous tactics. Fearing an escalation of ethnic cleansing and a repeat of the humanitarian disasters of Bosnia and elsewhere in the former Yugoslavia, the UK, along with the rest of NATO, took military action to force a Serb withdrawal. No authorisation was given by the United Nations Security Council casting doubt on the legality of the operation that intervened directly in the internal affairs of another UN member state. For Blair, the conflict was a defining example of the type of problems faced in international relations. In April 1999, at the height of the war he outlined his ideas in his *Doctrine of the International Community*:

> The most pressing foreign policy problem we face is to identify the circumstances in which we should get actively involved in other people's conflicts. Non-interference has long been considered an important principle of international order. And it is not one we would want to jettison too readily. One state should not feel it has the right to change the political system of another or foment subversion or seize pieces of territory to which it feels it should have some claim. But the principle of non-interference must be qualified in important respects. Acts of genocide can never be a purely internal matter. When oppression produces massive flows of refugees which unsettle neighbouring countries then they can properly be described as "threats to international peace and security".

The experience of Kosovo gave Blair the experience and rationale to commit British forces to a series of other conflicts in Sierra Leone,

East Timor, the D.R. Congo and, on a much larger scale, to Iraq and Afghanistan.

While the Iraq War was not primarily fought for humanitarian reasons, the experience cast doubts over the idea of humanitarian intervention. The questionable legal basis and the large scale opposition raised questions about its legitimacy and legality; the human and financial cost in blood and treasure (to both the Iraqis, British and others) has shown the cost of such actions, especially when combined with a lack of adequate post-war planning; the failures in intelligence to support the case for action have brought home a realisation of how imperfect an instrument military intervention can be. Finally, the UK's apparent attachment to working with the US raises questions as to how committed the former is to the idea of 'the international community' (see Dunne, 2004).

So have we seen the end of the humanitarian or ethical drive in British foreign policy? No. Examples such as the 2011 intervention in Libya and the desire to intervene in Syria, show that the idea, whether termed as 'humanitarian intervention' or the more nuanced 'Responsibility to Protect' remains very much alive. It is important to recall that Robin Cook called for 'an ethical dimension' as opposed to 'an ethical foreign policy'. He accepted that a state such as the UK could not expect to undertake a purely ethical foreign policy and questions exist as to whether such a policy could ever exist. As Robert Self (2010: 252) argues of New Labour's record, "even at its most charitable, the record can only be described as mixed at best—and at worst it is inconsistent, hypocritical and characterised by precisely the same realpolitik pragmatism as its predecessors." As we see below, this remains very much a problem for the 2010-2015 coalition government.

Commerce

Critics of interventions such as Libya or Syria argue that the underlying reason for this and other interventions are commercial and as such about the realpolitik of energy security and power. Trade and commercial concerns have always played a central role in British foreign policy. The large amount of foreign investment in the UK and the equally large investments overseas held by UK banks, pension funds and investment firms mean the UK economy is uniquely vulnerable to global economic—and especially financial—problems and to the decisions of foreign business interests. The economic turmoil of the global recession of 2008-09 saw the UK hit hard. British diplomats have therefore been under pressure to help build international links for British business. Diplomats have long been under pressure to promote British business. Putting trade first presents problems of inconsistency and hypocrisy, in much the same way as when ethics is put first. There have been numerous examples. The 2010-2015 coalition government has been accused of encouraging export of weapons to states with questionable democratic credentials (Martin and Shipman, 2011). The previous Labour government has been accused of intervening to stop criminal investigations into possible £1 billion of bribery surrounding the £43 billion Al-Yamamah defence contract. Warnings by the Saudi government that they would cancel future orders, along with a BAE campaign to highlight the potential economic cost to the UK, led Tony Blair to instruct the Attorney General to terminate the SFO investigation on grounds of 'national security' (Self, 2010: 231-34). The term 'national security' is vague. Its use in this particular case led to accusations that Britain was being hypocritical and selective in its application of standards and ethics.

Key Relationships in UK Foreign Policy

In 1962, retired US Secretary of State Dean Acheson said

> Great Britain has lost an empire and has not yet found a role. The attempt to play a separate power role apart from Europe, a role based on a 'special relationship' with the US and on being the head of a 'commonwealth' which has no political structure, unity, or strength—this role is about played out.

Acheson's speech is still debated to this day. Like most countries, Britain has relations with numerous countries and organisations around the world. Which of these should or can be the most important is an important debate of UK politics as they can indicate what role Britain sees itself playing in the world.

US-UK Relations

Powerful demographic, cultural, political, economic and security (especially during the Second World War) links have bound the UK and US together since the 13 colonies that formed the US secured their independence from Britain in 1775. During his 'Iron Curtain' speech in 1946 in Fulton, Missouri, Winston Churchill argued that:

> Neither the sure prevention of war, nor the continuous rise of world organization will be gained without what I have called the fraternal association of the English-speaking peoples. This means a special relationship between the British Commonwealth and Empire and the United States.

His idea of a 'special relationship' has survived despite numerous pronouncements that it is dead or passé. Its Lazarus quality of regeneration is in part due to the fact that it is not just a single relationship but rather a series of interconnected ones in different policy areas that reflect hard-headed realpolitik as much as it does any emotional and cultural links (Marsh and Baylis, 2006).

If there is such a thing as a 'special relationship', then it can certainly be found in military and intelligence cooperation. British national security has since (and to a large extent during) the Second World War been based on cooperation with the US, either bilaterally or through NATO. As a result, the UK has often made the largest, most effective, non-American contributions to many extra-European US-led military operations, such as in the 1991 and 2003 Gulf Wars (Wallace and Phillips, 2009: 267). In Europe, the UK has worked to ensure that the US remains committed to NATO and the defence of Europe either when faced with the threat of the Soviet Union, in anti-terrorist operations or, following developments in Ukraine, to defending it against Russian behaviour. Cooperation extends into sharing the burden of nuclear and military technology [for example the Trident missile system that carries Britain's nuclear warheads, was sold to Britain on very preferential terms, while the US has gained access to sought after UK nuclear and military technology (see Self, 2010)], intelligence gathering [although this is, to an extent, also shared with Canada, Australia and New Zealand (Dumbrell, 2001: 124)], training and military planning. This intense level of cooperation and trust has provoked accusations that Britain has allowed itself to be used as 'Airstrip One' or, more recently, that the UK has configured its military to operate more as a contribution to US efforts than for Britain's own needs (House of Commons, 2010: 23-34). While this arrangement has not always been harmonious, for successive British governments the cost of such accusations has been worth bearing because from their perspective, the UK's needs often match those of the US.

While not quite so apparent, the economic side of the relationship was, for a long time, as important as the military one. US loans enabled Britain to fight the Second World War, then afterwards develop a welfare state and maintain global military commitments. For this, the US exacted a high price. British imperial trade preferences were dismantled, control of Middle Eastern oil given up and British power visibly undermined, all to the benefit of the US. Again, a realpolitik assessment by both sides drove the relationship. Even in the 1980s, Mrs Thatcher did not let emotion or a shared affinity with Ronald Reagan for neo-liberal economics get in the way of trade disputes, differences on energy policy and competition in financial services (Self, 2010: 87-93). Today, the UK and the US are part of a transatlantic economic area that is deeply integrated, with the UK as the biggest investor in the US and vice versa (Pollack, 2005). Despite this and the UK's 'Anglo-Saxon' economic model, the UK is often located in the European side of the relationship.

We should not, however, rule out the emotional appeal of cultural links and shared ideas shaping the relationship. Links are to be found in language and literature, the law and constitutional arrangements, demographics, religion, media and ethnicity. That said, we need to be cautious about taking them too far. Churchill was talking about a much larger relationship of 'English Speaking Peoples', and specifically the British Commonwealth, Empire and US. This then was a relationship much larger and equal in size than that of just the UK and the US. We should also be careful not to forget that, although the US is more familiar to Britons than a great many countries in the world, it nevertheless remains a foreign place.

Personal relations between Prime Ministers and Presidents often appear to symbolise the relationship. A good example was how Margaret Thatcher's relationship with Ronald Reagan verged on, to use the words of the British Ambassador Sir Anthony Parsons, a 'political love affair' (see Self, 2010: 88). But her close support for the US, like with many other Prime Ministers, was not built on a personal relationship but on a belief that the Atlantic alliance was the cornerstone to the security of the UK and the West.

At first glance, a shared political outlook was not something one would have assumed Tony Blair, a social democrat, and George Bush, a Texan conservative, would develop. Their closeness grew out of Blair's interpretation that Britain's national security depended on working with the US, analysis that required Britain to seek to exercise influence over decision-making in Washington D.C. Like so many Prime Ministers before him, he viewed the relationship as one based not narrowly on his personal rapport with Bush, but as being in the UK's national interest (Dunne, 2004).

Blair's support of the Iraq War saw him labelled as a poodle to American power and, in particular, to President Bush. This is a crude analysis obscuring a more complex relationship in which Blair can arguably be criticised for other more nuanced failings. Blair had been concerned about Iraq's WMD (weapons of mass destruction) from early on in his premiership. As he joked in the lead up to the Iraq War, "It's worse than you think, I actually believe in doing this" (The Economist, 2007). His more articulate defence of the war reflected his long-standing personal commitment to the issue. So he was very much his own man in reaching the conclusion that Iraq was a threat and that Britain's involvement was in its national interest. What he can be criticised for more easily was the way he approached President Bush and US decision-making. He favoured private discussion and criticism "behind closed doors" which gave the appearance of slavishness, something even Mrs Thatcher had managed to avoid in her close relationship with Ronald Reagan. Worse was that Blair appears to have offered largely unconditional support for Bush's invasion of Iraq. Any concessions that were given, for example, over the Middle East peace process, largely failed to materialise (see The

Guardian, 2004). These failings raised questions about the claim that Blair and Britain's privileged access equalled influence over US power.

Britain has often tried to position itself as a bridge between the US and Europe. For the UK, the aim is clear: to try and harness American power for British ends. For some, this is a means of cushioning the angst of imperial decline, for others a hard-headed realisation that Britain's security is only guaranteed through a strong Atlantic alliance. This has not always worked particularly effectively. Other European states also have close relations with the US. A Prime Minister also has a limited capacity to shape the agenda of a US President. The structure of US government also means the President does not determine all US foreign policy. It is important therefore to take a balanced approach to the relationship. On the one hand, we should not underestimate Britain's financial, military and diplomatic contributions to US efforts; at the same time, it is in Britain's national interest to ask what reciprocal gains it receives.

UK-EU Relations

Once described as 'an awkward partner' (George, 1998), Britain has rarely appeared either comfortable or united about its membership of the European project. As Prof Andrew Gamble (2003: 114) explains:

> The reason why the issue of Europe has been so persistent and so divisive is that there is a lot at stake. For the future of British politics there is no more important issue, involving as it does a reassessment of British identity, security and political economy, and a judgement about the relative priority to be given to Europe as opposed to other relationships, particularly those with America. Such choices occur rather rarely but when they do they often trigger political realignments which can constitute major turning points in the life of parties and states.

In the early post-war phases of European integration, Britain was supportive, but Britain imagined itself as a global power and so remained detached. This left a legacy that exists to this day of playing catch-up. Britain's eventual membership applications reflected a growing, albeit unwilling, recognition that not only were Britain's economic links increasingly determined by events within the rest of Europe, but that Britain needed to secure a place in the European organisation that was increasingly determining Europe's, and therefore Britain's, place in the world. When membership was finally secured in 1973, it seemed to some like an abdication of a global role.

This does not mean that Britain has never been a good European. It is important to distinguish between governmental and political relations. Britain not only holds a strong record of enforcing EU law, but the British government can also be an effective operator in Brussels in achieving British objectives (Bulmer and Burch, 2005). Britain, like other member states, works to upload its ideas so as to shape the wider EU, in turn enhancing both the EU and UK's power in the world. Britain has been quite successful in some areas, for example, pushing for EU enlargement or on financial regulations. In 2005, when French and Dutch voters rejected a proposed EU Constitution, one of the reasons given for the French rejection was that the constitution was too 'Anglo-Saxon'—even 'Thatcherite'—and would devastate Europe's social fabric (Reynolds, 2005). While such fears reflected more the debate in France about economic and social policy, they did highlight the extent to which successive British governments have been busy working to shape the EU.

It is the political relationship that is often the most fraught. Europe is rarely a vote-winner, with many Prime Ministers and governments preferring to avoid discussion of the topic. The issue of Europe has played a part in changing UK party politics, the UK Independence Party (UKIP)—which campaigns for Britain to withdraw from the EU—emerging in recent years as a fourth party of UK politics. Metaphors of war, particularly the Second World War, are a regular feature in the UK's print media when discussing Europe. While in other parts of Europe the impact of globalisation has been a major issue of public debate, in Britain it has been Europe. Yet the two are often two sides of the same coin. Unease about competition from overseas, immigration (from the EU or elsewhere) and dependence on others have been sensitive political subjects. A good example is the British political debate about sovereignty, which in relation to Europe is presented as a zero-sum game, rarely a positive one where Britain gains sovereignty from 'pooling' it with other EU member states so as to provide the EU and UK with more control over the forces that shape the two. The consequence is that British governments have been unwilling to acknowledge or highlight the consequences of Britain's deepening involvement in the EU project.

The EU's Common Foreign and Security Policy (CFSP) along with a defence capability are two areas which the British people might be surprised to learn their government has actively, albeit sometimes ambivalently, supported. Cooperation on foreign and security matters in European integration dates back to the 1970s. That this was also the beginning of British membership of the EU made it one policy area where Britain did not have to play catch-up. The end of the Cold War, the failure of the EU to deal with the disintegration of the former Yugoslavia, America's disengagement from European security matters and a desire by some member states, particularly France, to see a stronger role for the EU in the world, increased efforts to co-operate more in the foreign and security arenas. The UK's leadership in foreign and defence matters, along with that of France, meant there could be no viable CFSP or defence capability without UK involvement. It is one area where the UK clearly has led in terms of both capability and experience. France on its own could not achieve this. An agreement with France at St Malo to create a European Security and Defence Policy (ESDP) reflected a British desire to see improvements and efficiencies in European defence capabilities. At the same time, Britain (unlike the French) stressed the importance of NATO and relations with the US. The UK has also stressed that the areas of foreign and defence cooperation should remain strictly intergovernmental, meaning that member states have to reach unanimous agreement on decisions. No decisions or powers to enforce them would rest with supranational institutions such as the European Commission. Here lay the crux of the problem. As a leader in foreign, security and defence matters, the UK has been eager to see improvements that would make the EU a more effective operator in the world. This would, in turn, act as a means to allow British governments to exercise continued power in the world. However, Britain has been unwilling to allow changes to make decision-making easier with St Malo itself not living up to the expectations many had of it. One alternative has been for the UK, France and Germany, the big three, to work together as a trilateral as has been the case with the EU's Iran policy. But the extent to which they can be said to speak for the rest of the EU is disputed.

Britain's approach to the EU then can be described as Janus-faced, after the two-faced Roman God. One face shows awkwardness, ambivalence, suspicion, sometimes downright hostility and a desire to stand apart from European integration. This unease has reached such a point that the idea of Britain holding an in-out referendum has become something of a norm in UK politics (Oliver, 2015). At the same time, the other face is constructive, engaging effectively in the construction of EU policies intended to benefit and enhance both the UK and the EU. Of course, the UK is not the only member state who is awkward in the EU; this was highlighted by the rejections of the European Constitution by the Dutch and the French, both founding members of the EU. For Britain, however, there is something of a deeper problem. The EU is too often seen as a means to an end of upholding British power in the world or of ensuring that the Atlantic alliance with the US is maintained. Europe itself does not seem to be something Britain wishes to commit to as an end in and of itself. The concern for Britain is that the EU may be developing in such a way that London may find itself on the margins, unable to shape EU decisions for its benefit. The decision not to join the Euro, for example, means that Britain is not a member of an inner-group of member states who, on reaching agreements about the Euro, are making key decisions about the future of the EU without the UK's direct involvement (The Economist, 2011). A British exit from the EU —also known as a 'Brexit'—is regularly debated, with all of the main parties committed in some way to holding an in-out referendum. A Brexit would have significant implications for both the UK and the EU, potentially changing the wider geopolitics of European (Oliver, 2013). For pro-Europeans, this behaviour risks repeating previous mistakes, particularly Britain's approach after the Second World War when Britain remained aloof while key decisions were made that Britain later had to live with. For those more sceptical of Britain's EU membership it provides an opportunity to look beyond the EU to the wider world.

The UK and the World Beyond the North Atlantic

The UK's relations with Europe and the US are not just ends in themselves; they also serve as a means of furthering British interests in the rest of the world. We can look at three areas in particular that capture Britain's global role: the Commonwealth, relations with emerging powers and the UK's role in international institutions such as the United Nations (UN) and the World Trade Organisation (WTO).

The Commonwealth

The Commonwealth (and before it the British Empire) was, for a long time, the cornerstone of British power. In the post Second World War era, it appeared to be of equal importance to that of relations with the US and Europe. But decline had set in long before the War when the UK's imperial markets were shrinking rapidly. Defeats in war, especially the loss of Singapore in 1942, shattered pretentions of imperial power. The ensuing decolonisation was driven by a mix of strong independence movements, American pressure, the drain of military overstretch with expensive garrisons scattered around the world, Britain's declining economic power and a growing political unwillingness at home to support the idea of empire. The emerging Commonwealth did not live up to the expectations of it as a replacement for the Empire. Failures to deal with Rhodesia/Zimbabwe, and later splits over how to deal with apartheid South Africa, showed the weakness of the UK and of the Commonwealth.

In the post-Cold War world, the Commonwealth has undergone something of a renaissance. Membership has increased, and while there have been problems over Zimbabwe, Nigeria and Pakistan, the Commonwealth has not appeared quite as split as it would once have been. New Labour utilised Britain's international links to place the issue of African development at the top of the agenda of various organisations, including the EU and the G8/G20. A common language has also helped to increase long-standing demographic links making the Commonwealth the home of 2.7 million of the 5.5 million British citizens who live permanently abroad. That said, we should note that approximately 2.1 million of these Britons reside in just Australia, Canada, and New Zealand (see Sriskandarajah and Drew, 2006). The Commonwealth is also home to countries and regions that are emerging as new centres of global power. To these powers, the Commonwealth is not the most immediate or attractive means of furthering their growing interests. Therefore the renaissance has limits, as it remains debatable to what extent the Commonwealth can be said to act as a coherent political unit.

Emerging Powers

Speaking a few months after formation of the Conservative-Liberal Democrat coalition government, the new foreign secretary William Hague (2010) criticised the previous Labour government for failing to take up the opportunities presented by a changing international landscape. Relations had instead, he argued, been "ad hoc and patchy, giving rise to the frequent complaint from such governments that British ministers only get in touch when a crisis arises or a crucial vote is needed." For Hague, foreign policy had for too long been concentrated on Europe, the US and the Middle East. Such an approach would not serve Britain well given the shifts in the distribution of power that are leading to a more fragmented multi-polar world. In his view, the passing of the certainties of the Cold War and the diminishing unipolar moment compelled Britain to be prepared for a world in a constant state of flux. Managing therefore the myriad of problems this would present increased tensions over resources, or responding to failing states would require new alliances and an approach that was more nimble than before.

Hague's approach reflected a need to assuage international and domestic pressure as much as a need for a genuine 'fresh start'. Appearing distant from the US and the EU helped sooth some political concerns about both. Emphasising trade reflected the financial constraints faced by the new government. The extent to which this would actually be a new start, however, is debatable. Many previous governments had placed an emphasis on trade and building closer relations with powers such as India and/or the importance of addressing the needs of regions such as Africa. Many of them also found that they were limited by the realities and complications of day-to-day diplomacy such as balancing ethics and trade. Attempts to build closer relations with emerging powers were also taken forward by New Labour. Blair and Brown used Britain's position in the chair of the G8 to begin formalising the idea of the G8+5 which would bring more closely together the leading Western economies with those of Brazil, China, India, Mexico and South Africa. But this is not to deny that there is a need to change a situation where areas of the world have often fallen off the mental map of British foreign policy, for example Latin America. Brazil, for example, was for a long time a largely absent concern in UK thinking, but is now one of the world's top 10 economies, one of the BRIC nations and an emerging Atlantic power. Mexico, and even an advanced industrial economy such as South Korea, can struggle to appear in UK trade figures or be at the centre of foreign policy thinking. This raises questions of how to decide which countries should be prioritised and which relegated to the side-lines. Should this, for example, be based on economic measurements such as imports, exports and GDP, possible future growth, population, strategic importance, history or something else?

The UK faces several challenges relating to emerging powers. On the one hand, Britain seeks productive, stable economic ties that will benefit the UK economy. Another key challenge (and one that Britain by itself is arguably less well equipped to do) is managing their rise. Despite talk of globalisation binding the world together, the future may not turn out to be as harmonious as some hope. UK relations with Russia have deteriorated in recent years due to political assassinations, disputes over dissidents, Cold War levels of espionage and Russia's behaviour in Ukraine (Blitz, 2010). Moves by Russia, China, India and by smaller but potent powers such as Iran, Turkey and North Korea to bolster their military capabilities are already shaping the debate about Britain's future defence needs. The willingness of emerging powers to assert their positions internationally, flex their growing economic muscle and support regimes that are hostile to British interests point to a diplomatic world where UK foreign policy will be under intense pressure. In these circumstances, can Britain abandon old and trusted alliances such as the US and the EU? Will emerging powers pay more attention to the UK if it is not a close partner of the US and a leader in the EU? For Britain, these two relationships look set to the mainstays of British power. The uncertainties presented by emerging powers have not, so far, made Britain opt for a radical revision of its foreign policy priorities.

International Organisations

The UK's membership of international organisations is substantial. It belongs to more international organisations than any country except France. The growth in multilateral relations and the overlapping institutions involved in global or regional governance mean bilateral relations between the UK and other states are only one part of British foreign policy. Britain's permanent seat on the UN Security Council (UNSC), like the composition of the rest of the Council, reflects the politics of 1945. The UK has long supported reform of the Council to include permanent seats for Japan, India, Brazil and one African state. It does not, however, contemplate the loss of the British seat or its merger with the permanent seat of France to create a permanent EU position. At the same time, the UK and France have been busy cooperating closely with other EU members in UN votes (Smith, 2006). Permanent membership of the primary body for the settlement of international disputes means the UK is obligated and empowered to take an interest in the full range of global issues. The questionable legality of the Iraq War cast a shadow over the UK's commitment to the central place of the Security Council. Nevertheless, for the UK, the UN remains the appropriate level for efforts to protect the environment (the Kyoto Treaty was negotiated under the auspices of the UN), promote human rights and manage a wide range of issue areas from food (the UN's World Food Programme) through to the proliferation of nuclear energy (the International Atomic Energy Agency [IAEA], although independent, reports to the UN). The UK has pushed reform of other UN-related organisations such as the World Bank, which Britain lobbied to take a stronger approach to poverty alleviation and environmental problems during the Labour government. The credit crisis of 2008 saw Britain push for a stronger role for the International Monetary Fund (IMF), although Britain has been uncomfortable at giving up its allocation of voting powers in these organisations to reflect the changing balance of economic power in the world. Britain's international economic policy is shaped by its membership of the EU, WTO, UN, G8, Organisation for Economic Co-operation and Development (OECD), IMF, World Bank, the Paris Group and a host of other organisations listed below. This relationship is complicated by the fact that trade is an area over which the EU has sole competence to act on behalf of its member states. This makes the EU a trading superpower—an area in which its foreign policy is perhaps most coherent. This means that Britain is part of a much larger force that engages in trade wars with the US (or in the case of the Transatlantic Trade and Investment Partnerships, the largest ever trade deal) or disputes with China over copyright infringements. It also helps to highlight the fact that membership of international organisations has an impact on Britain's sovereignty. Membership imposes constraints; however this need not be negative. Sharing sovereignty over trade, just as in defence or foreign policy, can lead to a stronger position for the UK in disputes with much bigger powers such as the US.

Conclusion

Despite its limited size and relative decline, Britain has continued to actively engage in global affairs. This is a result of its history, of the strong economic and social links to the rest of the world, policies—ranging from economic openness through to humanitarian intervention—that successive governments have actively sought to implement and, finally, a strong desire amongst its decision-makers to shape the world around them. That decision-makers have been able to pursue such policies is in part owing to foreign policy remaining an area dominated by the executive with few checks from Parliament. While the Prime Minister is particularly important, other parts of the core executive also play crucial roles.

Britain's role in the world has been shaped by a number of ideas and relationships. Ethical concerns about human rights or good governance have had to be balanced with the need to preserve and bolster Britain's defence industry and respond to the risks facing UK national security.

Britain's key foreign policy relationships have remained with the US and the EU. While Britain is uneasy at appearing to be too close to the US, a desire to be close has been based an assessment by successive governments that it is in Britain's national interest to have close access to decision-making in the dominant global power. However, the extent to which this approach is delusional or even desirable remains a matter of debate. At the same time, the UK has become progressively embedded into a EU that is more than just the economic trading zone—some in the UK might think it is. Britain has been reluctant to fully embrace the idea of Europe.

Despite tensions in relations with the US and the EU, it is unlikely that they will be replaced as the most important relationships, even if we witness the emergence of a multi-polar world. In an era of uncertainty, Britain may fall back on its most trusted, albeit at times somewhat difficult and controversial, relationships.

References

Allen, G. (2001). "The Last Prime Minister: Being Honest about the UK Presidency", *Societas*.

Blitz, J. (2010). "Russian Spying at Cold War Levels, say Experts", *The Financial Times*, 2 July.

Bulmer, S. and M. Burch (2005). "The Europeanization of UK Government: From Quiet Revolution to Explicit Step-Change?", *Public Administration* 83(4).

Cabinet Office (2008). *The National Security Strategy of the United Kingdom: Security in an Interdependent World*. London: HMSO.

———. (2010). *A Strong Britain in an Age of Uncertainty: The National Security Strategy*. London: HMSO.

Dedman, M (2010). *The Origins and Development of the European Union: A History of European Integration*. Routledge.

Dickie, J. (2004). *The New Mandarins: How British Foreign Policy Works*. London: I. B. Tauris.

Dumbrell, J. (2001). *A Special Relationship: Anglo-American Relations in the Cold War and After*. London: Macmillan.

Dunne, T. (2004). "When the Shooting Start: Atlanticism in British Security Strategy", *International Affairs* 80(5).

The Economist (2002). "The Dashing Mr Blair. Britain has Lost an Empire but has at Last Found Tony Blair", *The Economist*, 10 January.

———. (2011). "The Euro and the European Union: Can Angela Merkel Hold Europe Together?", *The Economist*, 10 March.

———. (2007). "Pity, Fear and the F-Word", *The Economist*, 12 July.

Foley, M. (2000). *The British Presidency*. Manchester: Manchester University Press.

Freedman, L. (2005). *The Official History of the Falklands Campaign*. Routledge.

Gamble, A. (2003). *Between Europe and America: the Future of British Politics*. Basingstoke: Macmillan.

George, S. (1998). *An Awkward Partner: Britain in the European Community*. Oxford: Oxford University Press.

Hague, William (2010). *Britain's Foreign Policy in a Networked World*. Foreign and Commonwealth Office. 1 July.

Heffernan, R. (2003). "Prime Ministerial Predominance? Core Executive Politics in the UK", *British Journal of Politics and International Relations* 5(3).

House of Commons (2008). "British Foreign Policy Since 1997", *Research Paper* 08/56, 23 June.

———. (2010). *Foreign Affairs Committee, Global Security: UK-US Relations*. Sixth Report of Session 2009-10, HC114. 18 March.

Hyam, R. (2007). *Britain's Declining Empire. The Road to Decolonisation 1918-1968*. Cambridge: Cambridge University Press.

Jackson, M. (2006). "Defence of the Realm in the 21st Century", *BBC Annual Richard Dimbleby Lecture*. London. 7 December.

Little, R. and M. Wickham-Jones (2000). *New Labours Foreign Policy: A New Moral Crusade?* Manchester: Manchester University Press.

Marsh, S. and J. Baylis (2006). "The Anglo-American "Special Relationship": The Lazarus of International Relations", *Diplomacy and Statecraft* 17(1).

Martin, D. and T. Shipman (2011). "Hypocrisy Goes On: Cameron Takes Arms Dealers with him on Egypt Visit to Promote Democracy", *Daily Mail*, 22 February.

Oliver, T. (2013). "Europe without Britain: Assessing the Impact on the EU of a British Withdrawal", *SWP Research Paper*. Berlin.

———. (2015). "To Be or Not to Be in Europe: Is That the Question? Britain's European Question and an in/out Referendum", *International Affairs* 91(1): 77-91, January.

Pollack, M. (2005). "The New Transatlantic Agenda at Ten: Reflections on an Experiment in International Governance", in *The Journal of Common Market Studies* 43(5): 899-919, December.

Reynolds, D. (2000). *Britannia Overruled: British Policy and World Power in the Twentieth Century.* Harlow: Longman.

Reynolds, P. (2005). "An Anglo-Saxon Takeover of the EU?", *BBC News Online,* 11 May.

Russell, B. (2003). "Blair Jets Out While Cabinet Colleagues Take Time Off at Home", *The Independent,* 26 July.

Self, R. (2010). *British Foreign and Defence Policy since 1945.* Basingstoke: Palgrave.

Smith, K. (2006). "Speaking with One Voice? European Union co-ordination on Human Rights Issues at the United Nations", *Journal of Common Market Studies* 44(1): 113-37.

Smith, M. (1999). *The Core Executive in Britain.* Basingstoke: St. Martin's Press Macmillan.

Sriskandarajah, D. and C. Drew (2006). *Brits Abroad: Mapping the Scale and Nature of British Emigration.* London: IPPR.

The Guardian (1997). "Robin Cook's Speech on the Government's Ethical Foreign Policy", *The Guardian,* 12 May.

———. (2004). "Doomed to Failure in the Middle East: A Letter from 52 Former Senior British Diplomats to Tony Blair", *The Guardian,* 27 April.

Tomlinson, J. (2009). "Thrice Denied: 'Declinism' as a Recurrent Theme in British History in the Long Twentieth Century", *Twentieth Century British History* 20(2).

Wallace, W. and C. Phillips (2009). "Reassessing the Special Relationship", *International Affairs* 85(2): 263-84.

Wheeler, N. and Tim Dunne (2004). *Moral Britannia? Evaluating the Ethical Dimension in New Labour's Foreign Policy.* London: The Foreign Policy Centre.

3

JEFFREY MANKOFF

The Foreign Policy of the Great Powers: Russia

Foreign policy in Vladimir Putin's Russia centres on the tension between a desire to play the role of a traditional great power and the need to adapt to a world in which the very nature of power is evolving. The emphasis on Russia's standing as a great power owes much to history, that of the Tsarist Empire as well as the Soviet Union, when Russia was defined by a strong centralised state, a powerful military, and a fearsome reputation among its neighbours. Reinforcing it is the presence of security service veterans or *siloviki* (including the ex-KGB lieutenant colonel Putin himself) in key positions. Restoring Russia's international influence has also become a major component of Putin's strategy of domestic legitimation, especially as the Russian economy has slowed in the aftermath of the global financial crisis and the onset of a major confrontation with the West, following Russia's 2014 annexation of the Crimean Peninsula and military intervention in eastern Ukraine. Increasingly central to this conception of Russia as a major power and independent global actor is an effort to differentiate Russia from the West, which Russian elites increasingly view as an antagonistic force.

Russia's ability to give substance to its great power ambitions depends on its ability to adapt to a world that is increasingly interconnected, with non-state actors (from terrorist groups to NGOs [non-governmental organisations] to MNCs [multinational corporations]) playing a larger role in global politics and security. Since becoming president for the first time in 2000, Putin based his domestic appeal to the Russian public on reversing the economic and social collapse post-Soviet Russia experienced in the 1990s. Expansion of the Russian economy and stabilisation of the state created the preconditions for Russia to pursue its geopolitical ambitions. Yet this economic expansion was in many ways the product of fortunate timing. Russia's 1998 default precipitated a massive currency devaluation, pricing imports out of the market and allowing a gradual revival of industry; the period from 2000-2008 then saw a sustained rise in oil prices, which reached $147 per barrel before the onset of the global financial crisis. As Russia depends on energy sales for more than half of its budget revenue, higher oil prices allowed the Kremlin to pay off the debts accumulated during the 1990s, improve social services, and channel vast sums into reviving the military.

They also diminished the urgency of reform, and Russia's competitiveness continued to lag. The collapse of oil prices in 2008-09 exposed vulnerability of the Russian development model, but despite a brief period of liberalisation under Dmitry Medvedev (2008-2012), it was not sustained enough to force a change of course, and Russia's economy faced the prospect of stagnation, notwithstanding a return to high oil prices. With Putin's return to the Kremlin in 2012 in the face of a growing urban protest movement, geopolitical assertion replaced economic stabilisation as a strategy for legitimation. In the course of just a few years, Medvedev's push for modernisation and rapprochement with the West gave way to Putin's neo-imperial expansion in Ukraine and the greatest crisis in relations with the West since the Cold War.

Russia continues to prioritise traditional measures of power, and while (as its actions in Ukraine, Syria, and elsewhere show) it can apply hard power effectively, it finds itself increasingly isolated, the object of fear more than respect. And like its Tsarist and Soviet predecessors, the economic foundations of power in Putin's Russian Federation remain shaky. Shoring up those foundations will be in many ways Moscow's greatest challenge, but one that ironically requires a greater degree of openness and international cooperation—especially with the West—than Putin's Kremlin seems inclined to accept.

Russia in the World

While Russians remain divided on much of the substance of foreign policy, their divisions operate within the context of a broad consensus about Russia's role in the world. That is, the bulk of the Russian elite and, it seems, a substantial percentage of the public, continue to see Russia as a major global power, acting on the world stage according to its own national interests and playing a dominant role within the post-Soviet region. Its roots stretch much further back, but in the post-Soviet context, this consensus emerged gradually over the first decade of Russia's post-Soviet independence. Much of the elite, including Foreign Minister Andrey Kozyrev and acting Prime Minister Yegor Gaidar, pursued a strategy of integration with the West (Kozyrev, 1992). This strategy faced significant opposition, and when Kozyrev was replaced in early 1996, his successor, the old intelligence hand Yevgeny Primakov sought to restore Russia's standing in the world largely through a policy of differentiation from and confrontation with the United States (US)-led West (Tsygankov, 2011: 30; Mankoff, 2011: 6; Primakov, 2004). Primakov's strategy of frustrating the US in pursuit of Russian power failed in part because Russia in the late 1990s (especially following its 1998 default) was isolated and not in a position to make good on these ambitions (Sestanovich, 2010).

Putin, who outmaneuvered Primakov to emerge as Boris Yeltsin's successor in 1999-2000, took on at least some of the outlines of Primakov's approach to foreign policy though, at least initially, without the overt anti-Westernism (Tracy, 2000). Putin and his team maintained the emphasis on Russia's status as a great power, by virtue of its historical legacy, nuclear arsenal, and UN Security Council seat, but—in contrast to Primakov—argued that a great power Russia could nevertheless maintain close relations with the West in pursuit of common interests (Light *et al.*, 2003: 63-4; Trenin, 2002: 206-08; Lo, 2003: 3-4; Tsygankov, 2006: 26). This approach was reinforced by the 11 September 2001 terrorist attacks in the US, which Putin condemned and sought to use as a mechanism for positioning Russia as an indispensible partner for the US in the emerging global war on terror (Kuchins, 2006).

Russian Foreign Policy's Official Mind

The consensus uniting much of the Russian foreign policy elite is reflected in the series of conceptual documents on foreign and security policy produced by the Russian government, which provide at least a sense of the intellectual framework within which foreign policy is made. These include the Foreign Policy Concept (drafted by the Ministry of Foreign Affairs), National Security Concept (Security Council/Presidential Administration), and Military and Naval Doctrines. Updated roughly every decade, these documents reflect the assumptions of the ruling elite at the moment of their adoption. Not all of these documents focus explicitly on foreign policy, but they all touch in some capacity on Russia's role in the world, including a Long-Term Socioeconomic Concept to 2020 and an Energy Strategy to 2030, which discusses Moscow's ambitions to boost its energy production and rebalance its energy sales to Asia (Russian Ministry of Energy, 2010). A presidential decree adopted in May 2009 set out for the first time guidelines for developing short, medium, and long term strategies for Russia and to establish clear roles for the various institutions involved in the planning process, with the Presidential Administration's Security Council taking the lead. These conceptual documents consequently provide more direct guidance for strategic planning than in the past (Monaghan, 2013; Kremlin, 2014). The making of foreign policy, at the levels of both strategic planning and day-to-day decision-making is highly centralised, with the Security Council (currently headed by close Putin-ally, Sergey Naryshkin) taking on increasing responsibility, while the Foreign Ministry is responsible primarily for implementation (Monaghan, 2013; Giles, 2010a: 3-4; Tsygankov, 2006: 83).

Russia's 2000 foreign policy concept, released to coincide with Putin's installation in the Kremlin, captures the fundamentals of the prevailing strategic consensus well. It calls for turning Russia into "a great power and one of the most influential centres of the modern world," while creating a "democratic world order" (i.e., one not dominated by the US) (Russian Ministry of Foreign Affairs, 2000a). Under Medvedev, the language of these documents shifted somewhat, with iterations dating from his time in office eschewing the term "great power" while focusing more on foreign policy as a tool for promoting Russia's domestic development and modernisation as a strategic task (Mankoff, 2011: 16-7). With Putin's 2012 return to the presidency, most of these conceptual documents received an overhaul, reflecting an effort to leave behind the quixotic emphasis on modernisation that characterised the Medvedev years.

The most relevant overview of official Russian thinking on foreign policy can be found in the Foreign Policy Concept, adopted in its current form in February 2013. The concept lists nine priorities for Russian foreign policy, the first of which is "ensuring the security of the country, protecting and strengthening its sovereignty and territorial integrity, and securing its high standing in the international community as one of the influential and competitive poles of the modern world," (Russian Ministry of Foreign Affairs, 2013). This emphasis on sovereignty and territorial integrity has a particular meaning in the Russian context. Much of the ruling elite fears a repetition of the Soviet Union's collapse, an event that Putin once termed the "greatest geopolitical catastrophe of the [20th] century," and which many fear continues to stalk the Russian Federation thanks to hostile outside forces arrayed against it. The focus on Russia's standing in the international community, meanwhile, reflects the importance that Russia's elite places on remaining a global power (Putin, 2005).

Other priorities discussed in the Foreign Policy Concept also reflect an approach to diplomacy at odds with those of most Western powers. These include "establishing a just and democratic system of international relations based on collective decision-making in addressing global issues, on the primacy of international law, including, first of all, the UN Charter, as well as on equal, partnership relations among nations with the central coordinating role of the UN as the principal organisation regulating international relations;" in other words, securing Russia's right to be consulted on all major decisions affecting issues of global significance, preferably through the UN Security Council where Russian maintains a veto (Russian Ministry of Foreign Affairs, 2013).

Particularly relevant in the context of the Ukraine crisis is the Concept's emphasis on "ensuring comprehensive protection of rights and legitimate interests of Russian citizens and compatriots residing abroad," that is, giving Moscow a kind of protectorate over not only Russian citizens, but also "compatriots [*sootechestvenniki*]," or former citizens of the USSR who identify in some way with the Russian state. The concept of compatriots is further enshrined in Russian law, giving Moscow enormous scope to intervene in the affairs of its post-Soviet neighbours (though Moscow also maintains links with compatriot organisations further afield) (Russian Ministry of Foreign Affairs, 2013; Zhurovsky and Vykhovanets, 2013; Byford, 2012).

Similarly, the Foreign Policy Concept highlights the central role that the post-Soviet region continues to play in Russian strategic thinking. Notable is an emphasis on seeking to accelerate 'integration processes' within the former Soviet Union. Specific mention is made of the Commonwealth of Independent States (CIS), the largely moribund structure originally designed to facilitate a "civilised divorce" among the USSR's 15 republics, as well as the Collective Security Treaty Organisation (CSTO) and the Eurasian Economic Union, which Moscow plans to establish at the start of 2015. Ukraine is a country of particular focus, as a state with which Russia seeks to "build up relations...as a priority partner within the CIS, [and] contribute to its participation in extended integration processes," even though Ukraine itself has expressed little interest in these integration projects (Russian Ministry of Foreign Affairs, 2013).

Russia's National Security Concept and Military Doctrine lay out more precisely official thinking on the principal security challenges facing the Russian Federation, including Moscow's approach to issues of arms control, disarmament, terrorism, and information security. As with the Foreign Policy Concept, they reflect a worldview that prioritises traditional geopolitical threats over the kind of transnational challenges, such as terrorism, that security strategy in many Western countries now emphasise. The National Security Concept, released in 2000 and modified in 2009 with the publication of the so-called *Security Strategy to 2020*, contrasts the emergence of multipolar world in the aftermath of the Cold War with "attempts to create an international relations structure based on domination by developed Western countries in the international community, under US leadership and designed for unilateral solutions (primarily by the use of military force) to key issues in world politics in circumvention of the fundamental rules of international law" (Russian Ministry of Foreign Affairs, 2000b).

The 2009 Strategy, released during Medvedev's presidency, represents something of a departure in that it emphasises foreign policy as a tool for promoting economic and social development, and identifies raising the country's economic potential as a key component of national security. It argues that Russia's strategic priorities lie in:

> Social, political and economic transformations intended to create secure conditions for the realisation of Russian citizens' constitutional rights and freedoms, the stable development of the country, and the preservation of the territorial integrity and sovereignty of the state. (Russian Ministry of Foreign Affairs, 2009).

Nevertheless, it too criticises the post-Cold War global order, suggesting that,

> The inadequacy of the current global and regional architecture, oriented (particularly in the Euro-Atlantic region) towards NATO, and likewise the imperfect nature of legal instruments and mechanisms, create an ever-increasing threat to international security (Russian Ministry of Foreign Affairs, 2009).

While expressing an openness to deeper cooperation with North Atlantic Treaty Organisation (NATO), it argues that the success or failure of NATO-Russia cooperation will depend on:

> The preparedness of the alliance to recognise Russia's legal interests when engaging in military-political planning, and to respect norms of international law; and likewise NATO's readiness to consider the further transformation of these relations and the search for new tasks and functions with a [humane] orientation (Russian Ministry of Foreign Affairs, 2009).

The Security Strategy to 2020 portrays the major threats facing Russia as including "the policies of a number of leading foreign countries, directed at achieving predominant superiority in the military sphere, primarily in terms of strategic nuclear forces, but also by developing high-precision, informational and other high-technology means of conducting armed warfare, strategic non-nuclear arms, by unilaterally creating a global missile defense system and militarising space," along with the proliferation of weapons of mass destruction. Terrorism, meanwhile, is discussed largely in the context of threats to public safety requiring a law enforcement response (Russian Ministry of Foreign Affairs, 2009). That said, Putin and others have in the past cited terrorism as a tool that hostile states use to weaken Russia, as well as an outgrowth of extremist ideologies (Yasmann, 2004).

The *Military Doctrine* (2010) goes farther, in that it identifies the expansion of NATO and efforts to endow the Atlantic Alliance with global responsibilities as a "danger," indeed the top danger, to Russia (though in official terminology, a danger [*opasnost*] ranks as less severe than a threat [*ugroza*]—and the decision to term NATO expansion a danger rather than a threat is therefore significant) (Russian Ministry of Foreign Affairs, 2010; Giles, 2010b: 1). As the *Military Doctrine* was published at the high-point of the Medvedev era, Western analysts have been puzzled by the emphasis on external threats and the seemingly discordant note in what was otherwise a period of significant rapprochement between Moscow and the West. If anything, the *Military Doctrine* rolls back some of the more progressive elements contained in the *National Security Strategy to 2020*, released the previous year, which prioritised foreign policy as a tool for development more than a response to physical threats (Giles, 2010b).

One area in which the 2010 *Military Doctrine* is more dovish, however, is in its elaboration of Russia's approach to nuclear weapons. In response to the near-collapse of Russia's conventional forces, then-Defense Minister Pavel Grachev announced in November 1993 that Moscow was abandoning its Soviet-era pledge to not use nuclear weapons first in a conflict, without specifying what contingencies would incur a nuclear first strike (Schmemann, 1993). The 2000 version of the *Military Doctrine*, meanwhile, established that Moscow would employ nuclear weapons in response to a conventional attack "in situations critical for the national security of Russia and its allies" (Nezavisimaya Gazeta, 2000). The 2000 National Security Concept meanwhile specifies that these contingencies include armed aggression and threats to the territorial integrity of the Russian Federation (Russian Ministry of Foreign Affairs, 2000b). The updated 2010 *Military Doctrine*, in contrast, restricts the circumstances under which Russia is prepared to use nuclear weapons to contingencies threatening the very existence of the Russian state, without mentioning defense of allies (Russian Ministry of Foreign Affairs, 2010). These more restrictive provisions however, did not invalidate the previously existing commitments. In response to a question about the possibility of Ukraine seeking to restore its sovereignty over Crimea by force, in a July 2014 press conference, Foreign Minister Sergey Lavrov referred to the provisions of the 2000 National Security Concept in warning Kyiv against making the attempt, implying the possibility that Moscow could respond with a nuclear strike (Lavrov, 2014; Keck, 2014).

Power, Sovereignty and Identity

An important subtext to official thinking about Moscow's global role is an emphasis on Russia as a sovereign state existing in a world that is still defined by a struggle for mastery among several powerful states. Sovereign in this context means not only exerting control over all of its territory and freely choosing its international engagements, but also that Russia can decide whether or not to be bound by any ideological or normative restraints, and with the ability to structure its own politics as it sees fit. The international order, meanwhile, is defined in Russian thinking less by the existence of international norms and institutions, which merely reflect the interests of the primarily Western states that created them, and more by the continuing struggle among states to protect their interests. As Putin (2014a) remarked to the Russian Public Chamber (a kind of state-sanctioned umbrella for NGOs) at the height of the Ukraine crisis:

> It is not some kind of peculiarity of the present day. No one anywhere ever wants powerful rivals; international life is a competitive struggle. It has always been like this.

This emphasis on sovereignty has in recent years even extended to making a virtue of Russia's strategic isolation. Putin (2014b) noted to the Security Council in late July 2014 that "Russia, thank God, does not belong to any alliance. To a great extent this guarantees our sovereignty." Unlike the US, Russia does not have any true allies, though it does theoretically maintain mutual security guarantees with some of its neighbours through the CSTO. On the one hand, Moscow is critical of US alliances, which, it argues, allow Washington to project its power far from US borders, incusing along Russia's own periphery. On the other, it argues that alliances by their nature entail a partial loss of sovereignty. This loss of sovereignty is especially evident with Germany and Japan, states that were before the Second World War major powers, but which after 1945 found themselves hosting US military forces and enmeshed in treaty relationships with the US that, in Moscow's view, deprived them of their ability to act autonomously on the international stage.

For a time in the mid-2000s, the concept of "sovereign democracy" was in vogue. Championed by Kremlin ideologist Vladislav Surkov, "sovereign democracy" was an effort to legitimate Russia's increasingly authoritarian form of government by arguing that it reflected Russia's own needs, and that, as a fully sovereign power, Russia itself had the right to determine what its own version of democracy looked like (Lipman, 2006). Sovereignty is also an important component of Russia's approach to information security. In contrast to Western powers, Russia views information and the means of its dissemination mainly through the lens of domestic stability. That means prioritising the state's ability to control the domestic information space, recognising that control of information is often a tool for conflicts (Heickerö, 2010: 17-21).

While the rhetoric of sovereign democracy has since fallen by the wayside, the Kremlin has increasingly invoked a narrative of nationalism—both ethnic and historical-statist, emphasising Russia's isolation among hostile forces that would seek to weaken and even dismember it. This nationalism appears partially aimed at mobilising public support in the aftermath of the protests that broke out in the wake of Russia's falsified December 2011 parliamentary elections, and also contained a geopolitical element, in that it includes encouraging belief in external threats and invoking patriotism to bolster the political status quo.

This ethnically tinged patriotism was particularly visible in Putin's speech to the Russian parliament in February 2014 announcing the annexation of Ukraine's Crimean Peninsula. In seeking to justify the first act of forcible annexation in Europe since the Second World War, Putin spoke of Russia's commitment to protecting "Russians and Russian speakers," essentially creating a precedent for extraterritoriality that has been a source of concern in the Baltic states, Kazakhstan, and elsewhere with ethnic Russian minorities (Putin, 2014c). Similarly, the run-up to Russia's invasion and annexation of Crimea saw widespread public discussion of the "compatriot" issue in the Russian media and by Russian officials, including Putin. In early March 2014, Putin secured parliamentary backing for deploying Russian forces to Ukraine on the basis of protecting "citizens of the Russian Federation [and] our compatriots," (Putin, 2014d).

As several foreign officials and commentators pointed out, this invocation of an ethno-cultural protectorship recalls the justification provided by Nazi Germany for the Anschluss with Austria and the occupation of Czechoslovakia's Sudetenland in the 1930s (Kralova, 2014; Åslund, 2014). It also reflects a long-standing reluctance among Russian elites to see the other post-Soviet states as fully sovereign, legitimate members of the international community, a pathology that goes beyond the post-colonial *droite de régard* expressed, for instance, by France towards its former colonies in Africa.

Russia's solicitousness for the fate of compatriots abroad also reflects a broader turn towards ethnic nationalism under Putin. During the Soviet period, Russian nationalism was actively suppressed, since Lenin and other Bolshevik leaders equated it with "great power chauvinism" that threatened the balance between centre and periphery in the multinational USSR. Yeltsin sought to replace public usage of the ethnic term *russkii* with the neologism *rossiyan*, denoting a citizen of the Russian Federation regardless of ethnicity. Nationalist ideas, often nurtured abroad by the White émigrés and their descendants, nevertheless resonated at least in parts of the Soviet-era intelligentsia, and found more opportunities to flourish in the soil of post-Soviet Russia. From early in his tenure, Putin has promoted and patronised nationalist thinkers, both those from the past as well as their contemporary successors. One figure whom Putin has frequently invoked is the White Russian philosopher, Ivan Ilin who called for creating a renewed elite and re-forging Russian identity on the basis of traditional Christian values (Hill and Gaddy, 2013: 105-07).

In giving succor to ethnic nationalists, Putin has however had to walk a fine line, since Russia remains a multiethnic country, with a large and increasingly restive Muslim minority concentrated in the North Caucasus and in major cities. Tension between ethnic Russian nationalists and mostly Muslim minorities represents one of the starkest dangers to Russia's stability, not to mention to Russia's image in the Muslim world. One response has been to position Russia as an active player in the Muslim world, for instance seeking observer status in the Islamic Cooperation Organisation and rhetorically supporting the Palestinian cause—although this position became less and less tenable with the onset of the Arab Spring and Russia's full-throated backing for secular dictatorships like that of Bashar al-Assad in Syria.

Putin's tenure in the Kremlin has also coincided with the emergence of the concept of a "Russian World [*Russkii Mir*]," or a sphere of Russian cultural influence that, in turn, gives Moscow leeway to exert political influence (notably, this concept uses the term for ethnic Russians—*russkii*). The pillars of this "world" are the Russian language and the Russian Orthodox Church, and while its geographic scope is potentially quite large, the focal point remains the three East Slavic states of Russia, Belarus, and Ukraine (Maliukevicius, 2013; Saari, 2014). The identification of Belarus and Ukraine, which have been independent states since the Soviet collapse, as "Russian" reflects a reluctance to accept the legitimacy of Belarusian and Ukrainian nationalism, which Russian elites have downplayed since the Tsarist era, or the complete sovereignty of Belarus and Ukraine as states. Speaking of the crisis in Ukraine, Putin has reiterated on several occasions that Russians and Ukrainians (as well as presumably Belarusians) are "one people" whose tripartite division is an accident of history (Putin, 2013). This brand of nationalism is dangerous precisely because its fulfillment requires the redrawing of frontiers and rejection of the post-Cold War order.

Energy

One of Russia's most important sources of influence in the post-Cold War world is its massive reserves of oil and natural gas, which it sells to customers in Europe, the post-Soviet region, and, increasingly, to Asia. Much of Europe and Eurasia are heavily dependent on Russian gas (unlike oil, gas is not for the most part a globally arbitraged commodity, meaning that supplies cannot be quickly substituted). Increasingly over the past decade, customers have become conscious of Russia's proclivity to manipulate gas supplies to generate political leverage.

Yet effectiveness of this energy "weapon" remains questionable. First, Russia's energy reserves are a wasting commodity; existing fields are in decline and state gas monopoly Gazprom will struggle to develop new production sites in absence of significant foreign investment and technology. Global markets are changing as well, especially with increased global production of LNG (liquefied natural gas), the development of hydraulic fracturing ('fracking'), and the possibility that the US will soon become a major LNG exporter, including to markets that Russia currently dominates (Deutch, 2011). The perception that Russia manipulates energy for political ends will if anything accelerate this shift to alternate suppliers (and alternate energy sources).

But for the time being, Russia has substantial leverage over its customers in Europe and the former Soviet Union, although it too is reliant on its ability to sell energy in these markets—especially Europe, which accounted for more than 77 per cent of Russian gas exports in 2013 (while the revenues from energy accounted for more than half of Russia's state budget) (BP, 2014). Until recently, a major complicating factor in this relationship was the fact that the pipelines bringing Russian gas to Europe all crossed either Ukraine or Belarus, giving these transit states the ability to interfere with sales across their territory in order to put pressure on both Russia and its customers in the European Union (EU). In both 2006 and 2009, disputes between Moscow and Kyiv over prices and unpaid debts (against the backdrop of the Orange Revolution that installed a strongly pro-Western government in Kyiv) led Gazprom to cut sales through these pipelines, with Ukraine responding by siphoning off gas destined for Europe. In 2009, Gazprom then halted all sales through the Ukrainian pipeline, leaving users in southeastern Europe without gas for more than two weeks in the middle of winter (Pirani *et al.*, 2009).

Yet in 2011, a new pipeline opened beneath the Baltic Sea, bringing Russian gas directly to Germany while cutting out the transit states. This Nord Stream pipeline, with a current annual capacity of 55 billion cubic meters (bcm)—roughly a third of Russia's sales to the EU—significantly increased Russian leverage over Ukraine, which it could now bypass without affecting supplies to the EU. Indeed, when the next Russia-Ukraine crisis broke out in early 2014, Russia responded by halting gas supplies to Ukraine, while continuing uninterrupted sales to the Europeans who, meanwhile, remained reluctant to impose sanctions on Russia over its intervention in Ukraine largely because of their (uneven) dependence on Russian gas. Notably, the three rounds of European sanctions announced between the annexation of Crimea in February 2014 and Russia's refusal to halt its support of separatist rebels in Ukraine's Donbas region in late July deliberately did not include Gazprom (Baker *et al.*, 2014).

Another offshore bypass pipeline, South Stream, is slated to run beneath the Black Sea to Bulgaria and on to Italy, though the Ukraine crisis has called into question the EU's willingness to allow purchases of Russian gas to further increase. Nord Stream and South Stream (if built), are designed in large part to buttress Russian leverage over the transit states, by giving Gazprom the ability to cut them off without affecting its profitable European markets, regardless of whether these pipelines prove profitable. In that regard, they are not commercial ventures so much as tools of Russian foreign policy, overseen by

Gazprom, a state-controlled behemoth whose goals have always been more political than economic (Goldman, 2010: 2-7).

Control of pipelines also contributes to Russia's ability to keep the other post-Soviet energy producers in its political orbit, although mismanagement and the emergence of new customers has eroded Russian dominance in both the Caucasus and Central Asia. Since at independence all of the South Caucasus and Central Asian energy producers relied on pipelines across Russia to reach foreign markets, Moscow was able to block competitors' access to its pipelines, undercut producers from neighbouring states by selling its own resources on their domestic market at a subsidised price, and prioritise the sale of its own oil and gas in the profitable European market (Stulberg, 2007: 94-99).

Yet the resulting vulnerability led many of the energy-producing post-Soviet states to seek alternatives. Kazakhstan and Azerbaijan opened up their oil sectors to foreign investors in the early 1990s, while Azerbaijan worked with Georgia and Turkey to build a pipeline (Baku-Tbilisi-Ceyhan, or BTC) that facilitated direct oil exports to Europe (LeVine, 2007: 137-200). Along with a parallel gas pipeline that opened in 2006, BTC dramatically reduced Azerbaijan and Georgia's economic dependence on Russia, allowing them much more foreign policy flexibility. Similarly, new pipelines between Central Asian energy producers (especially Turkmenistan) and China have reduced Russian economic, and hence political, leverage in recent years.

Russia has tried to maintain and in places reassert its control over the energy distribution system in the former Soviet Union, particularly in countries that depend on it for oil and gas. Moscow has taken control of the pipeline networks in Belarus and Kyrgyzstan in recent years in exchange for economic assistance and debt relief (Kramer, 2011). It made similar offers to Ukraine on numerous occasions, and the question of who would control Ukraine's pipeline network was long among the most fraught issues in Ukrainian politics (EurActiv, 2013).

Since many of these states buy most of their oil and gas from Russia, price subsidies are another tool of Russian influence.

Gazprom typically charges its post-Soviet customers lower prices than those paid by European consumers, though even within the former Soviet Union, prices for Russian gas have tended to vary with state of relations between the consuming state and Russia. A reduction in these subsidies can create economic chaos. The 2006, 2009, and 2014 Russia-Ukraine gas crises were all precipitated by Gazprom's efforts to raise the price Kyiv pays for its gas. Higher gas prices, in turn, have played a major role in Ukraine's accumulation of debt to Russia, and thence to Russian efforts to take control of the Ukrainian distribution system so as to settle these debts. Moving to commercial prices for gas and reducing domestic subsidies is consequently one of the central demands made by the International Monetary Fund (IMF) and other members of the international community seeking to place post-revolutionary Ukraine on a stable foundation. Similarly, the decision to reject subsidies from Gazprom, despite the resulting higher prices, was a key element in Georgia's efforts to escape Russian influence.

Regional Contexts

The Foreign Policy Concept and other conceptual documents are, at best, a rough guide, but they do reflect the basic assumptions underlying Russian foreign policy. These include the importance of international law as embodied in the United Nations Charter and the central role of the UN Security Council, as well as the centrality of interstate relations. The concept of an "international community" based on a set of shared values is largely alien to the Russian understanding of global politics. In this understanding, it is the interactions of states, especially the major powers, which provide the substance of international relations. For that reason, Moscow directs most of its efforts to managing relations with major states, including the US and China, as well as the main European powers (especially Germany). Then again, the focal point and locus of most major confrontations between Russia and the West is the post-Soviet region, which Russian officials and scholars increasingly refer to as Eurasia (Vinokurov and Libman, 2012: 44-65, 201-12; Trenin, 2011: 83-7).

Eurasia

Having endured a long history of invasions from the east, south, and (especially in the 20th century) west, Russia is acutely sensitive to the need to insulate itself from external dangers. Russian elites have viewed the maintenance of a belt of states under Russian suzerainty or, at the very least, too weak and isolated to pose a threat to Russian security, as a core security interest since the Tsarist era. At the same time, the Soviet legacy and the persistence of Soviet-era institutions, mindsets, and relationships keep these states organically tied to Russia, although those bonds continue to weaken over time (Marsh and Gvosdev, 2009). Independent of its security concerns, Russia's great power ambitions centre on maintaining the post-Soviet region as an area of "privileged interests" (as Medvedev [2008] described it in the aftermath of the 2008 Georgia conflict). This Russia-centric Eurasia is envisioned as both a bridge between Europe and Asia, and a geopolitical pole in its own right.

The states of the former Soviet Union, which much of the Russian elite continue to regard as part of a less than fully sovereign "near abroad," are where Russian power and influence remains most visible. Tools of Russian influence include the presence of Russian minorities and their associate compatriot organisations in several of these states, military deployments, the "soft power" of a common culture (including the dominance of Russian media outlets), migration (millions of migrants from these states have moved to Russia in search of work, fueling ethnic tensions in Moscow and other cities), and in some states, the existence of "frozen conflicts" sustained by Russian involvement (Mankoff, 2014).

The continued importance of the post-Soviet space is one of the keys for understanding Russia's foreign policy behaviour, and is in many ways the most salient issue in Moscow's relations with other major powers. The major quarrels between the US and Russia have centred on Washington and Moscow's respective relationships with states like Ukraine and Georgia, which Russia fears as potential outposts of a West that it still views as hostile. Especially since the first of the so-called "colored revolutions" in 2003-04 in Georgia and Ukraine, Moscow has also become extremely wary of uncontrolled political change in the region, which is frequently depicted as part of a US strategy to weaken Russian influence by installing pro-Western governments that, in turn, will seek to move closer to NATO, if not as a prelude for regime change in Russia itself (Carothers, 2006). On several occasions, Moscow has sought to prevent, and reverse, political transformations in these countries, as it did throughout the crisis that led to Viktor Yanukovch's ouster in May 2014. Checking the spread of Chinese influence, especially in Central Asia, has also emerged in recent years as a Russian goal, though so far at least, Moscow seems less worried about Chinese actions in Central Asia than it does about Western actions in Eastern Europe.

While limiting external influence in the post-Soviet region has long been a central aim of Russian foreign policy, reintegrating the post-Soviet states under Russian leadership has become a more prominent goal of Russian foreign policy since Putin's 2012 return to the presidency.

After years of fighting a rearguard action against the expansion of Western influence, entities like the Eurasian Economic Union are part of an effort to go on the offensive by creating an alternative set of institutions dominated by Russia. The centrepiece of these plans is the Eurasian Economic Union, comprising Russia, Belarus, Kazakhstan, and likely in the near future Armenia and Kyrgyzstan as well. Critics, including former US Secretary of State Hillary Clinton have portrayed Russia's push for integration as an effort to "re-Sovietise" the region (RFE/RL, 2012). The tactics may have changed, but Eurasian integration is in keeping with Russia's efforts to simultaneously re-assert itself as a major global power (with a Russian-led Eurasia acting as a pole of a multipolar world, alongside the US-led West and a Chinese-led Asia-Pacific) and limit the penetration of outside influences into the post-Soviet region (Putin, 2011).

Integration limits the ability of other post-Soviet states to reorient their economies away from Russia—whether preventing Ukraine from signing a free trade agreement with the EU or stemming the flow of Chinese goods into Kyrgyzstan. It also supports Russia's larger ambition of asserting itself as one of the pillars of a multipolar global order since, in the official narrative, the ability to muster a coalition of like-minded states behind it (by whatever means) is one symbol of Russia's global influence, alongside its nuclear weapons and seat on the UN Security Council. Integration projects such as the CSTO, the customs union, and the Eurasian Economic Union are thus less clubs of equals like NATO or the EU, and more an outgrowth of Russia's interests into which smaller neighbouring powers are coerced into participating. The economic and geopolitical benefits, unsurprisingly, are heavily tilted in Moscow's favour, and Moscow uses a mix of carrots and sticks to encourage its neighbours to join (Inozemtsev, 2013).

The push for Eurasian integration is also linked to the ideological turn underway in Putin's Russia in recent years. The intellectual and spiritual underpinning for post-Soviet integration lies in the so-called Eurasianist movement, whose antecedents stretch back to the early years after the Bolshevik Revolution, but which has taken on a more imperialist, anti-Western tinge in recent years under the leadership of the ideologue and Moscow State University Professor Aleksandr Dugin (Laruelle, 2008; Barbashin and Thoburn, 2014). Underlying much of Eurasianism is the British geographer, Sir Halford Mackinder's assertion that Eurasia, the "world island," acts as the "geographic pivot of history," and that control of the Eurasian landmass is therefore the key to a state's ability to amass global power (Mackinder, 1919; 1904). In addition to this geopolitical element (Dugin's magnum opus is called Foundation of Geopolitics), many Eurasianist thinkers posit that the Eurasian people share a common cultural-biological destiny which predisposes them to act in opposition to the peoples of Euro-Atlantic littoral (Barbashin and Thoburn, 2014). Although Putin discusses projects like the Eurasian Economic Union in terms of economic advantage, Dugin, along with other political figures and publicists with ties to the Kremlin, make the connection between Eurasian integration and the broader project of establishing Russia as the core of an anti-Western geopolitical bloc (Pushkov, 2012).

Their ideas also underpin Putin's renewed emphasis on the cultural void between Eurasia and the West. They call attention to the West's embrace of issues such as gay rights in order to assert that the West has moved away from its Judeo-Christian roots and become decadent, while Russia is in the throes of a spiritual renewal that casts it as the defender of "traditional" values common to all of the peoples of Eurasia (Putin, 2013). This assertion of "traditional" values also reflects the rising profile of the Russian Orthodox Church as a pillar of the state, the existing political order, and Russia's geopolitical interests (Druzenko, 2011). Similarly, Moscow supports various social organisations, churches, political parties, and other traditionalist-minded groups throughout the former Soviet Union. Russia's own quixotic campaign against homosexuality in the years since Putin's return has much to do with this effort to emphasise the ideological and moral distance between Russia and the West, in part as a means of bolstering Russian influence abroad (while the former Soviet Union is the main target of these efforts, appeals to such traditional values also resonate in places such as the Middle East and Africa, not to mention certain parts of Europe) (Snyder, 2014).

The West

Russian institutions, as well as the elites manning them, remain highly focused on the West, especially the US, since it is Washington that still provides the mirror against which Moscow compares its own global standing. Early in his tenure, Putin sought to bandwagon with the US in order to not only position Russia as a key partner in the global war on terror, but also because the past decade has witnessed significant volatility in US-Russian relations. This volatility results in part from the fact that both countries have interests across the globe, but comparatively little interdependence or integration between them. Events in locales as disparate as Afghanistan, Syria, Ukraine, and Vietnam have ramifications for US-Russian relations. Yet the level of trade and investment ties between the two countries is comparatively low; consequently, neither country has a major economic stake in maintaining good relations. Moreover, the ideological and institutional legacy of the Cold War remains strong, especially in Russia, where officials lament that Washington no longer pays as much attention to Russian interests as it did in the Soviet era. Russia's reduced importance to decision-makers in Washington contributes to the unilateralism that many Russian observers decry.

Moscow's relations with Washington have mostly turned around three issues: the state of Russian domestic politics, competition for influence in the post-Soviet region, and issues related to global order and perceptions of US hegemony. Central to the Russian emphasis on sovereignty is a belief that outsiders should not tell Russia how to structure its own politics. The US, conversely, has a kind of genetic predisposition to favour democratic, or at least liberal, governments, in part out of a belief (often false) that such governments will be more supportive of US foreign policy aims. This preference for democratic regimes is especially pronounced in post-Communist Europe, where the end of the Cold War was seen as heralding a democratic breakthrough [what Samuel Huntington (1993) called the "third wave" of democratisation]. The US-Russian relations have been best when Russia appeared to be moving towards greater openness: under Boris Yeltsin in the early 1990s, during the early liberal phase of Putin's rule in 2000-2003, and during the presidency of Dmitry Medvedev in 2008-2012. Similarly, US-Russian confrontation has been greatest during periods of political retrenchment in Moscow.

The goals of domestic liberalisation and closer ties with Washington are mutually reinforcing, since a more liberal Russia is one more likely to enjoy Washington's favour, while the benefits of close ties with the US strengthen the hand of liberal reformers within Russia (Solov'ev, 2004). Owing to the association between the US and liberal democratic ideology, relations with the US also serve as a kind of proxy within Russian political debates. Figures seeking to pull Russia in a more illiberal, nationalistic direction therefore have an incentive to demonise the US and to inveigh against US global hegemony. It is hardly surprising then that Putin's efforts to shore up his domestic support, following the demonstrations of December 2011 and May 2012, have coincided with a turn against the US and US global influence and growing public antagonism towards the US. As in Latin America, the Middle East, and elsewhere, Russia's anti-Americanism is an effective tool for nationalist mobilisation and a distraction from domestic failings (Satter, 2013).

Developments in Russia's post-Soviet periphery are another driver of US-Russian relations. Putin's post-9/11 efforts at cooperation with the US largely ceased with the coloured revolutions in Georgia and Ukraine. Russia interpreted these revolutions in the context of the Bush Administration's democracy promotion agenda, which, Moscow charged, was motivated less by a desire to spread the benefits of democratic governance than by a desire to make the world safer for American hegemony by installing friendly regimes in strategically important regions. At the same time, suspicions of American complicity led Russian elites to fear that the US nursed similar ambitions towards Russia itself (Kara-Murza, 2005; Trenin, 2006).

In both the 2008 war in Georgia and the 2014 interventions in Ukraine, Russian perceptions that the US-led West, especially NATO, was encroaching on its sphere of influence precipitated drastic actions—the occupations of South Ossetia and Abkhazia in 2008 and Crimea, followed by support for separatist rebels in Ukraine's Donbas region in 2014. Underlying these crises are two dramatically different narratives about the political changes taking place in Georgia and Ukraine. The US viewed the coloured revolutions, as well as the Ukrainian protests that ousted Yanukovych as spontaneous demonstrations of popular sentiment against corruption and misrule. In Russia, these revolutionary outbursts appear less spontaneous and more part of a deliberate campaign of US "soft power," carried out by Western-funded NGOs and abetted by a Western media that remains innately anti-Russian. Indeed, Moscow's own support for quasi-NGOs, including compatriot organisations, was in many ways a direct response to the perception that Western governments were using similar tactics to oust pro-Russian regimes (Babich, 2005). Putin (2014b) remarked in July 2014 about the fall of Yanukovych:

> Today...countries conducting independent policies, or those that simply stand in the way of someone else's interests, are becoming destabilised. They do this by means of so-called color revolutions, or to call a spade a spade: coups instigated and financed by outside forces.

The struggle for influence in the post-Soviet region is also connected to a more global perception that the US has failed to take Russian interests into consideration, even when Moscow was intent on cooperating with Washington. Many Russians view the period since the end of the Cold War as one in which the West, led by the US, has repeatedly taken advantage of Russian weakness in order to advance its strategic frontiers closer to Russia's borders. Russia continues to view NATO as a tool for containment, even as it regards the post-9/11 globalisation of NATO's mission as a threat to the multipolar, UN Security Council-based global order that Moscow prefers. Russian efforts to subsume NATO into a broader mechanism for European security have met with little interest in the West. Ironically, growing perceptions of a Russian threat on the part of many Eastern European members have led to a renewed focus on NATO's original mission of territorial defense (Vershbow, 2014). The most sensitive issue in this regard is NATO expansion, beginning with the admission of the Czech Republic, Hungary, and Poland to the Atlantic Alliance in 1999. The prospect of Georgia, Ukraine, or other post-Soviet states joining NATO has always been something of a red-line for Moscow, and a major factor in the decision to use force against Georgia in 2008 and Ukraine in 2014.

Notwithstanding Putin's push for counterterrorism cooperation after 9/11, Russia reacted strongly to NATO's subsequent expansion in 2004 (when the Baltic states joined along with Bulgaria, Romania, Slovakia and Slovenia), as well as the invasion of Iraq, the US withdrawal from the 1972 Anti-Ballistic Missile (ABM) Treaty, and the coloured revolutions. The US-led bombing of Serbia in 1999 sparked a crisis in bilateral relations, as to a lesser degree did the invasion of Iraq in 2003; both of which Russia had sought to block at the United Nations. While Russia had long-standing ties to both Serbia and Iraq, more fundamental was Moscow's inability to influence US actions.

Following the Cold War, an era when Washington could do very little without gauging Moscow's reaction, the realisation that the US no longer cared was a major blow to Russian amour-propre. In his inimitable way, Putin identified the problem in a 2007 speech to the Munich Security Conference, charging that:

> One state and, of course, first and foremost the US, has overstepped its national borders in every way...in the economic, political, cultural and educational policies it imposes on other nations (Putin, 2007).

Moscow's support for a 'democratic' and 'multipolar' world order centres precisely on its interest in constraining the ability of the US to project power in the face of Russian objections.

Asia

To a significant degree, it shares this agenda with China, feeding concerns in the US about the possible emergence of a Sino-Russian axis capable of challenging the US-led global order. The reality is more complicated. While Russia's elite and institutions have long been focused on the West, recent years have seen a concerted effort on the part of the Kremlin to deepen engagement with Asia. In part, these efforts are instrumental, as Moscow turns to Asia (especially China) in order to reduce its dependence on the West. Yet with Russia's eastern reaches lagging badly behind its European core, and with more and more of the global economy concentrated around the Pacific Rim, Moscow has a clear interest in harnessing Asia's dynamism to support its own development. Russia nevertheless faces significant challenges as it carries out its own "pivot" to Asia, including fears of excessive dependence on China and a widespread perception in the region that Russia is, at best, an interloper with little to contribute to Asia as a whole.

The most important reason for Russia's growing interest in Asia is the need for economic development in Siberia and the Russian Far East, which lag badly behind Russia's European core in terms of manufacturing output, education, employment, etc. As early as 2006, Putin acknowledged that the underdevelopment of these eastern regions represented a threat to Russia's security (Putin, 2006). Russia fears that Siberia and the Far East will become colonial appendages to the dynamic East Asian economies (especially China), supplying raw materials, receiving little in return, and over time drifting out of Moscow's political orbit too.

At the same time, the onset of the global economic crisis in 2007-08 has fed into a perception among many Russians that the centre of global economic dynamism is in the process of shifting from the Atlantic to the Pacific, and that Russia stands to gain from reorienting its own economy increasingly to Asia (Kostin, 2012). As the 2013 Foreign Policy Concept notes, increased attention to the region is now necessary because Asia has become the world's "fastest-developing geopolitical zone, toward which the centre of world economy and politics is gradually shifting" (Russian Federation Ministry of Foreign Affairs, 2013). In the context of this global shift, Russia's principal aims in Asia include becoming a major transit route for trade and exchange between Europe and Asia, as well as developing Siberia and the Far East and shaping the development of regional architecture (Russian Federation Ministry of Foreign Affairs, 2013). Underlying all of these ambitions is the larger goal of securing Russia's role as a major global power at a time when the centre of global geopolitics is increasingly growing in Asia.

Far and away the most Russia's most important partner in the Asia-Pacific region is China, a country with which the Soviet Union nearly went to war in the late 1960s and which remained a strategic rival of Moscow's until the last days of the Cold War. Then again, since the late 1980s the relationship has undergone a profound improvement, and Putin has made further strengthening the bond between Moscow and Beijing a priority, especially as relations between Russia and the West have cooled in recent years. Many nationalist-leaning Russians appreciate China as a model for Russia's own development in the way that it has achieved economic and military power without political liberalisation. They also maintain a view of the world that aligns with that of Beijing, emphasising states' sovereignty and equality (at least among major powers) and rejection of the values-based foreign policy championed by many Western powers, principles that also underpin groups like the Shanghai Cooperation Organisation (SCO) and the BRICS (Brazil, Russia, India, China and South Africa), forum where Beijing and Moscow share a leading role (Lavrov, 2013).

The growing polarisation between China and the US at the global level seemingly lets Russia hold the balance of power between Washington and Beijing (Migranyan, 2014). Yet despite Moscow's global aspirations, Russia lags far behind both the US and China in terms of economic and military power. Moreover, China and the US are heavily interdependent (including massive Chinese holdings of US debt). Under the circumstances, neither Washington nor Beijing seems inclined to risk its relationship with the other for the uncertain prospect of a partnership with Russia. Especially as US-Russia ties have deteriorated since Putin's return to the Kremlin, that reality leaves Moscow's partnership with Beijing increasingly unbalanced. Indeed, China's position is now stronger on energy sales, at the UN (where its involvement in Ukraine has left Russia increasingly isolated) and in bilateral economic relations.

An example of this changing dynamic is the agreement, signed in May 2014, to build the so-called Power of Siberia (*Sila Sibiri*) gas pipeline from untapped deposits in Eastern Siberia to markets in China. Negotiations to construct the pipeline had been underway for a decade, with the major sticking point for much of that time being the price that China National Petroleum Corporation (CNPC) would pay for the gas. As Moscow confronted the possibility that the EU would eventually impose sanctions on its energy, it agreed to finalise the deal largely on Chinese terms. These included an advantageous price (of about $360 per thousand cubic meters that could be even lower because of pre-payments needed to finance construction), as well as granting CNPC an equity stake in both Russian state oil company Rosneft and an LNG project on the Yamal Peninsula (Mazneva and Kravchenko, 2014).

The growth of Chinese power has always been a two-edged sword for Russia. On the one hand, a stronger, more globally influential China contributes to the erosion of the unipolar world long derided by Russian foreign policy thinkers. Like Russia, China supports a global order based on the principle of absolute state sovereignty, rejecting the universalism of Western norms related to democracy and human rights. China never criticised Russia for using excessive force against rebels in the North Caucasus, or for rigging elections, cracking down on the press, or arresting dissidents. Indeed, at times Moscow and Beijing have banded together to call for a world less beholden to Western norms, leading some in the West to fear the emergence of a new authoritarian International, aiming to make the world safe for dictatorship and state capitalism (Halper, 2010; Ramo, 2004; Rachman, 2008; Kennedy, 2010: 461-77).

On the other hand, a stronger China poses a series of challenges for Russia as well, especially since, unlike the US, Russia shares a long border with China. Despite increasingly frequent diplomatic engagement and ringing declarations of partnership, the two states are at odds over issues ranging from bilateral security cooperation to regional security along the sensitive peripheries of Central Asia and Southeast Asia. China's military modernisation has depended heavily on Russian weapons, but many within the Russian security establishment have long been wary of transferring high-end technology to China. Reflecting a pervasive mistrust of Chinese motives, they fear the possibility that China could use such weaponry against Russia itself (indeed, Russia's military has carried out a series of exercises in its Far Eastern Military District in recent years designed to test the army's ability to repel a Chinese invasion) (Saradzhyan, 2010). They also recall Beijing's propensity for reverse-engineering Russian weapons, such as the Su-27 fighter jet, and selling Chinese knock-offs on the global arms market (Lague, 2013).

Yet Russia's estrangement from the West, which was building even before the start of the Ukraine crisis, has led Moscow to swallow many of these concerns. Military-technical cooperation between Russia and China was picking up again by the time protestors first took to the Maidan in Kyiv in the fall of 2013, although it was only in the midst of the crisis, in the spring of 2014, that agreements to resume the sale of Russian air defense systems, submarines, and combat aircraft were announced (Schwartz, 2014). Similarly, after the start of the crisis, Russia dropped its long-standing opposition to holding bilateral naval exercises with China in the vicinity of disputed islands off China's coast in the Sea of Japan.

Russia's reluctance to hold such exercises near territories claimed by Japan reflected Moscow's recognition of its risks becoming too closely tied to China in Asia, jeopardising its ability to develop Siberia and the Far East without seeing them drift into Beijing's orbit, and to be accepted as a full-fledged player in the emerging Asian regional security architecture. Even as Moscow has tightened its links with Beijing over the past decade-plus, it has sought to develop ties with a wider range of Asian players, including those like Japan (as well as Vietnam and India), that have difficult relations with China. Putin has made no secret of his desire to finally sign a peace treaty with Japan that would allow for a final settlement of the disputed Southern Kurile Islands/Northern Territories that Soviet forces seized in 1945 at the very end of the Second World War, but which are still claimed by Tokyo (Asahi Shimbun, 2012). Russia has also rejected Chinese pressure to abandon its joint energy exploration projects in the South China Sea with Vietnam, or to stop its sales of advanced attack submarines to Hanoi. Although China and Russia describe their relationship as a "comprehensive strategic partnership," they remain very much traditional great powers whose bond is cemented primarily by common interests in the context of their relationship to the US-led international order. Within their shared region, which also includes post-Soviet Central Asia, Beijing and Moscow continue to maneuver for advantage within an essentially zero-sum framework, one that the SCO and similar organisations does little to often.

Conclusion

The price for the sovereignty and independence on the international stage that Russia prizes is loneliness. The smaller post-Soviet states that remain in Russia's orbit (especially Belarus, Kazakhstan and Armenia) do so mostly because they lack good alternatives, not because they necessarily share Moscow's worldview or out of any kind of post-imperial nostalgia. All would like more extensive ties with the outside world, including with the West, but recognise that their economic and political dependence on Russia acts as a constraint. Russia's customs union and Eurasian Economic Union are for that reason a variety of what the Russian scholar Vladislav Inozemtsev terms "imperial integration," designed by and for the benefit of Moscow with little regard for the interests of other members (Inozemtsev, 2013).

Russia's relationship with the West, meanwhile, remains unstable, subject to unpredictable gyrations. Since the end of the Cold War,

Moscow has decisively rejected the model pursued by Germany and Japan after 1945, of accepting a US security guarantee in exchange for giving up their great power ambitions. Nevertheless, many in both Russia and the West have continued to hope for an eventual convergence, since, after all, Russia is culturally and historically very much a European country, and driving the Soviet collapse were the same humanistic values that scuttled Communism in Eastern Europe.

If there is a unifying narrative to Putin's time in power, it is the progressive rejection of a Western destiny for Russia. The Eurasian ideology peddled by Dugin and his ilk provides a pseudo-intellectual underpinning for this exercise, but more than any belief in a shared Eurasian past, it is an interest in establishing Russia as an independent global player that drives the political elite's embrace of this ideology. The effort to differentiate Russia from the West leads at times to an embrace of China, the most likely 21st century challenger to the Western-led international order, but this embrace remains heavily instrumental. In its current incarnation Russia, like China, is a lonely power rarely capable of cooperation on the basis of anything more lasting or durable than self-interest.

The crisis that began with Russia's infiltration into and annexation of Crimea in February 2014 represents the convergence of several strands in Russian foreign policy. The historically and geographically conditioned fear of invasion, coupled with the continued identification of Russians and Ukrainians as common people, makes the possibility of Ukraine's swerve into the West particularly sensitive in Moscow. Imperial nostalgia, reinforced by a belief that the West is in eclipse (and that Russia is ascending) has made it easier for Moscow to deploy military force against a neighbouring state, especially in the aftermath of NATO's unconstrained use of force in places like Serbia, Iraq and Libya over the past two decades.

Then again, the irony of the crisis is that Russia's actions are accelerating some of the very changes that Moscow is striving to prevent: the consolidation of a Ukrainian national identity on anti-Russian grounds, the reinvigoration of NATO (including the possible deployment of NATO forces ever closer to Russian borders), and Europe's efforts to lessen its dependence on Russia for energy. Even the post-Soviet states slotted for inclusion in the Eurasian Economic Union are having second thoughts, especially given the uncertain effects that Western sanctions will have on their own economies. It would be ironic indeed, if the lasting result of Russia's intervention in Ukraine, begun to keep alive the possibility of drawing Ukraine into this Eurasian bloc, ended by discrediting the whole concept of Eurasian integration *à la russe*.

Although Russia's estrangement from the West provides the backdrop for the crisis in Ukraine, the fundamental problem of Russia's place in the world in fact remains unresolved. Russia has always existed on the periphery of the West, and the question of whether or not it "belongs" to the West has exercised politicians, diplomats, artists and authors for close to a millennium. The Cold War ended in a burst of optimism that this centuries-old problem had at last been solved. But to the consternation of liberal Westernisers like Andrey Kozyrev, as well as leaders in the US and Europe, Russia was never ready to jettison the other, non-Western pieces of its history. Putin, who was initially seen as a liberal moderniser, has over time done more and more to reclaim Russia's imperial legacy, and to reconcile it with pieces of the Soviet past as well. His continued popularity is evidence that the push for a strong, independent Russia has touched a nerve, both among the political elite and within the public at large. Russia's Ukrainian adventure will likely end in tears, but the motives underpinning it will not go away, and the world will continue to face a Russia that is prickly, jealous of its sovereignty, and uncomfortable in a world shaped primarily by the West.

References

Asahi Shimbun (2012). "Putin Proposes Starting Over in Negotiations Over Northern Territories", 2 March.

Åslund, Anders (2014). "Anders Aslund: 12 Ways in which Putin's Rhetoric Resembles Germany in the 1930s", *Kyiv Post*, 21 March. *http://www.kyivpost.com/opinion/op-ed/anders-aslund-12-ways-in-which-putins-rhetoric-resembles-germany-in-the-1930s-340335.html*

Babich, Dmitry (2005). "Walk Softly...New Appointment Looks Set to Shift CIS Tactics", *Russia Profile*, 16 May. *http://russiaprofile.org/international/a1690.html*

Baker, Peter; Alan Cowell and James Kanter (2014). "Coordinated Sanctions Aim at Russia's Ability to Tap its Oil Reserves", *New York Times*, 30 July.

Barbashin, Anton and Hannah Thoburn (2014). "Putin's Brain: Alexander Dugin and the Philosophy Behind Putin's Invasion of Crimea", *Foreign Affairs*, 31 March. *http://www.foreignaffairs.com/articles/141080/anton-barbashin-and-hannah-thoburn/putins-brain*

BP (2014). "Statistical Review of World Energy", *http://www.bp.com/content/dam/bp/pdf/Energy-economics/statistical-review-2014/BP-statistical-review-of-world-energy-2014-full-report.pdf*

Byford, Andy (2012). "The Russian Diaspora in International Relations: 'Compatriots' in Britain", *Europe-Asia Studies* 64(4), June.

Carothers, Thomas (2002). "The End of the Transition Paradigm", *Journal of Democracy* 13(1): 5-22, January.

———. (2006)., "The Backlash Against Democracy Promotion", *Foreign Affairs* 85(2), March/April.

Deutch, John (2011). "The Good News about Gas: The Natural Gas Revolution and its Consequences", *Foreign Affairs* 90(1), January/February.

Druzenko, Gennadii (2011). "Geopolitics from the Patriarch: The Heavenly Kingdom *versus* the 'Russian World,'" *Russian Politics and Law* 49(1), January/February.

Dunlop, John B. (2004). "Aleksandr Dugin's Foundations of Geopolitics", *Demokratizatsiya* 12(4), Winter.

EurActiv (2013). "Push to Privatise Ukraine's Naftogaz Gains Speed", 10 May. *http://www.euractiv.com/europes-east/push-privatize-ukraine-naftohaz-analysis-519653.*

Giles, Keir (2010a). *Russia's National Security Strategy to 2020*. Rome: NATO Defense College.

———. (2010b). *The Military Doctrine of the Russian Federation 2010*. Rome: NATO Defense College.

Goldman, Marshall I. (2010). *Petrostate: Putin, Power and the New Russia*. New York: Oxford UP.

Halper, Stefan (2010). *The Beijing Consensus: How China's Authoritarian Model Will Dominate the Twenty First Century*. New York: Basic Books.

Heickerö, Roland (2010). *Emerging Cyber Threats and Russian Views on Information Warfare and Information Operations*. Stockholm: Swedish Defense Research Agency.

Hill, Fiona and Clifford Gaddy (2013). *Mr. Putin: Operative in the Kremlin*. Washington, DC: Brookings Institution.

Huntington, Samuel P. (1993). *The Third Wave: Democratisation in the Late Twentieth Century*. Norman, OK: Oklahoma UP.

Inozemtsev, Vladislav (2013). "The Folly of 'Imperial Integration'", *CSIS Russia & Eurasia Blog*, 6 Dec. *http://csis.org/blog/folly-imperial-integration*

Kara-Murza, Sergey G. (2005). *Eksport revolyutsii: Yushchenko, Saakashvili...* Moscow: Algoritm.

Keck, Zachary (2014). "Russia Threatens Nuclear Strikes Over Crimea", *The Diplomat*, 11 July. *http://thediplomat.com/2014/07/russia-threatens-nuclear-strikes-over-crimea/*

Kennedy, Scott (2010). "The Myth of the Beijing Consensus", *Journal of Contemporary China* 9(65): 461-77, June.

Kostin, Andrey (2012). "Russia Should Focus on Asia as Europe Fights the Crisis", Interview with RT, 3 September. *http://rt.com/business/russia-asia-crisis-kostin-241/*

Kozyrev, Andrei (1993). "Russia: A Chance for Survival", *Foreign Affairs* 71(2), Spring.

Kralova, Simona (2014). "Crimea seen as 'Hitler-style' land grab", *BBC*, 7 March. *http://www.bbc.com/news/world-europe-26488652*

Kramer, Andrew E. (2011). "Gas Deal with Belarus Gives Control of Pipeline to Russia", *New York Times*, 25 November.

Kremlin (2014). "*Podpisan zakon, ustanavlivayushchii pravovye osnovy strategicheskogo planirovaniya*", 1 July. *http://www.kremlin.ru/acts/46126*

Kuchins, Andrew (2006). "A Turning Point in US-Russian Relations?", *Carnegie Endowment for International Peace*, 20 November. *http://carnegieendowment.org/2006/11/20/turning-point-in-US-russian-relations.*

Lague, David (2013). "China Eyes $3.5 Billion Russian Arms Deal Despite Ire Over Sukhoi Copy", *Reuters*, 27 March. *http://www.reuters.com/article/2013/03/27/us-china-russia-arms-idUSBRE92Q0PE20130327*

Laruelle, Marlène (2008). *Russian Eurasianism: An Ideology of Empire*. Baltimore, MD: Johns Hopkins UP.

Lavrov, Sergey V. (2013). "*Vstupitel'noe slovo i otvety Ministra inostrannykh del Rossii S.V. Lavrova na voprosy SMI v khode press-konferentsii po itogam peregovorov s Ministrom inostrannykh del KNR Yang Jiechi*", *Russian Ministry of Foreign Affairs*, 22 February. *http://www.mid.ru/bdomp/ns-rasia.nsf/1083b7937ae580ae432569e7004199c2/c32577ca0017458644257b1a0042813b!OpenDocument*

————. (2014). "*Vystuplenie i otvety na voprosy SMI Ministra inostrannykh del Rossii S.V. Lavrova v khode sovmestnoi press-konferentsii po itogam peregovorov s Ministrom inostrannykh del Italii F. Mogherini*", *Russian Ministry of Foreign Affairs*, 9 July. *http://www.mid.ru/brp_4.nsf/newsline/ACCAC19C442BDFDC44257D10004542C7*

LeVine, Steve (2007). *The Oil and the Glory: The Pursuit of Empire and Fortune on the Caspian Sea*. New York: Random House.

Light, Margot, John Lowenhardt and Stephen White (2003). "Russia and the Dual Expansion of Europe", in Gabriel Gorodetsky (ed.), *Russia between East and West: Russian Foreign Policy on the Threshold of the Twenty-First Century*. London: Frank Cass.

Lipman, Masha (2006). "Putin's Sovereign Democracy", *Washington Post*, 15 July.

Lo, Bobo (2003). *Vladimir Putin and the Evolution of Russian Foreign Policy*. London: Royal Institute of International Affairs.

Mackinder, H.J. (1904). "The Geographical Pivot of History", *Geographical Journal* 23(4), April.

————. (1919). *Democratic Ideals and Reality*. London: Constable.

Maliukevicius, Nerijus (2013). "(Re)Constructing Russian Soft Power in Post-Soviet Region [sic]", *Baltic Security & Defense Review* 15(2): 70-97.

Mankoff, Jeffrey (2011). *Russian Foreign Policy: The Return of Great Power Politics*. 2nd ed. Lanham, MD: Rowman & Littlefield.

————. (2014). "Russia's Latest land Grab: How Putin Won Crimea and Lost Ukraine", *Foreign Affairs* 93(3), May/June.

Marsh, Christopher and Nikoals K. Gvosdev (2009). "The Persistence of Eurasia", Policy Innovations, 5 November. *http://www.policyinnovations.org/ideas/commentary/data/000152*

Mazneva, Elena and Stepan Kravchenko (2014). "Russia, China Sign $400 Billion Gas Deal After Decade of Talks", *Bloomberg*, 21 May. *http://www.bloomberg.com/news/2014-05-21/russia-signs-china-gas-deal-after-decade-of-talks.html*

Medvedev, Dmitry (2008). "*Interv'yu Dmitriya Medvedeva Rossiiskim Telekanalam*", *The Kremlin*, 31 August, *http://kremlin.ru/transcripts/1276*

Migranyan, Andranik (2014). "Washington's Creation: A Russia-China Alliance?" *The National Interest*, 10 July. *http://nationalinterest.org/feature/washingtons-creation-russia-china-alliance- 10843*

Monaghan, Andrew (2013). "Putin's Russia: Shaping a Grand Strategy", *International Affairs* 89(5): 1228-29.

Nezavisimaya Gazeta (2000). *Voennaya Doktrina Rossiiskoi Federatsii*. 22 April.

Pirani, Simon, Jonathan Stern and Katja Yafimava (2009). "The Russo-Ukrainian Gas Dispute of January 2009: A Comprehensive Assessment", *Oxford Institute for Energy Studies*, February. *http://www.oxfordenergy.org/pdfs/NG27.pdf*

Primakov, Yevgeny (2004). *Russian Crossroads: Towards the New Millennium*. New Haven, CT: Yale UP.

Pushkov, Aleksey (2012). "Interview with Mezhdunarodnaia Zhizn", 10 March, *http://interaffairs.ru/read.php?item=8335*

Putin, Vladimir (2005). "*Poslanie Federal'nomu Sobraniyu*", *The Kremlin*, 25 April. *http://archive.kremlin.ru/appears/2005/04/25/1223_type63372type63374type82634_87049.shtml*

———. (2006). "*Vstupitel'noe slovo na zasedanii Soveta Bezopasnosti*", *The Kremlin*, 20 December. *http://president.kremlin.ru/appears/2006/12/20/1548_type63374type63378type82634_115648.shtml*

———. (2007). "Putin's Prepared Remarks at 43rd Munich Conference on Security Policy", *Washington Post*, 12 February, *http://www.washingtonpost.com/wp-dyn/content/article/2007/02/12/AR2007021200555.html*

———. (2011). "*Novyi integratsionnyi proekt dlya Yevrazii–budushchee, kotoroe rozhdaetsya segodnya*", *Izvestiya*, October 3.

———. (2013). "Vladimir Putin Meets with Members the Valdai International Discussion Club. Transcript of the Speech and Beginning of the Meeting", *Valdai Discussion Club*, 29 September. *http://valdaiclub.com/politics/62880.html*

———. (2014a). "*Vstrecha s chlenami Obshchestvennoi palaty Rossiiskoi federatsii*", *The Kremlin*, 9 Jul, *http://www.kremlin.ru/news/46177*

———. (2014b). "Zasedanie Soveta Bezopasnosti", *The Kremlin*, 22 July. *http://www.kremlin.ru/news/46305*

———. (2014c). "Address by President of the Russian Federation", The *Kremlin*, 18 March. *http://eng.kremlin.ru/news/6889.*

———. (2014d). "*Vladimir Putin vnës obrashchenie v Sovet Federatsii*", *The Kremlin*. 1 March, *http://kremlin.ru/news/20353*

Rachman, Gideon (2008). "Illiberal Capitalism: Russia and China Chart Their Own Course", *Financial Times*, 8 January.

Ramo, Joshua Cooper (2004). *The Beijing Consensus*. London: Foreign Policy Centre.

RFE/RL (2012). "Clinton Calls Eurasian Integration an Effort to 'Re-Sovietize,'" 7 December. *http://www.rferl.org/content/clinton-calls-eurasian-integration-effort-to-resovietize/24791921.html*

———. (2014). "Gazprom Takes Over KyrgyzGas", 10 April. *http://www.rferl.org/content/kyrgyzstan-gazprom-buys-kyrgyzgaz/25327986.html*

Russian Ministry of Energy (2010). "Energy Strategy of Russia for the Period up to 2030", *http://www.energystrategy.ru/projects/docs/ES-2030_%28Eng%29.pdf*

Russian Ministry of Foreign Affairs (2000a). "*Kontseptsiya vneshnei politiki Rossiiskoi Federatsii*", *http://www.ln.mid.ru/ns-osndoc.nsf/0e9272befa34209743256c630042d1aa/fd86620b371b0cf7432569fb004872a7?OpenDocument.*

———. (2000b). "National Security Concept of the Russian Federation", *The Kremlin*, 10 January. *http://www.mid.ru/bdomp/ns-osndoc.nsf/1e5f0de28fe77fdcc32575d900298676/36aba64ac09f737fc32575d9002bbf31!OpenDocument*

———. (2009). "*Strategiya Natsional'noi Bezopasnosti Rossiiskoi Federatsii do 2020 Goda*", 12 May. *http://www.mid.ru/bdomp/ns-osndoc.nsf/e2f289bea62097f9c325787a0034c255/8abb3c17eb3d2626c32575b500320ae4!OpenDocument*

———. (2010). "*Voennaya Doktrina Rossiiskoi Federatsii*", 5 February. *http://www.mid.ru/bdomp/ns-osndoc.nsf/e2f289bea62097f9c325787a0034c255/2a959a74cd7ed01f432569fb004872a3!OpenDocument*

———. (2013). "Concept of Foreign Policy", 12 February. *http://www.mid.ru/brp_4.nsf/0/76389FEC168189ED44257B2E0039B16D*

Saari, Sinikukka (2014). "Russia's Post-Orange Revolution Strategies to Increase its Influence in Former Soviet Republics: Public Diplomacy po ruskii", *Europe-Asia Studies* 66(1): 50-66, January.

Saradzhyan, Simon (2010). "Russia's War Games: Preparing for Conflict with the East", *International Relations and Security Network*, 26 May. *http://oilprice.com/Geo-Politics/International/Russias-War-Games-Preparing-for-Conflict-with-the-East.html*

Satter, David (2013). "Russia's Anti-American Foreign Policy", *Wall Street Journal*, 22 September.

Schmemann, Serge (1993). "Russia Drops Pledge of No First Use of Atom Arms", *New York Times*, 4 November.

Schwartz, Paul N. (2014). "Russia Announces Sale of S-400 to China", *CSIS Russia & Eurasia Blog*, 30 June. *http://csis.org/blog/russia-announces-sale-s-400-china*

Sestanovich, Stephen (2010). "The Dinner Guest", *The American Interest*, 1 March. *http://www.the-american-interest.com/articles/2010/03/01/the-dinner-guest/*

Snyder, Timothy (2014). "Fascism, Russia, and Ukraine", *New York Review of Books*. 20 March.

Solov'ev, E.G. (2004). *Natsional'nye Interesy i Osnovnye Politicheskie Sily Sovremennoi Rossii*. Moscow: Nauka.

Stulberg, Adam N. (2007). *Well-Oiled Diplomacy: Strategic Manipulation and Russia's Energy Statecraft in Eurasia*. Albany: SUNY Press.

Tracy, Jen (2000). "Primakov Clears the Way for Putin", *Moscow Times*, 5 February.

Trenin, Dmitri (2002). *The End of Eurasia: Russia on the Border between Geopolitics and Globalisation*. Washington, DC: Carnegie Endowment.

———. (2006). "Russia Leaves the West", *Foreign Affairs* 85(4), July–August.

Tsygankov, Andrei P. (2006). *Russia's Foreign Policy: Change and Continuity in National Identity*, Lanham, MD: Rowman & Littlefield.

———. (2011). "Preserving Influence in a Changing World: Russia's Grand Strategy", *Problems of Post-Communism* 58(2), March/April.

Vershbow, Alexander (2014). "Looking Towrads the Wales Summit", NATO, 13 June. *http://www.nato.int/cps/en/natolive/opinions_111056.htm?selectedLocale=en*

Vinokurov, Evgeny and Alexander Libman (2012). *Eurasian Integration: Challenges of Transcontinental Regionalism*. Houndsmills, Palgrave Macmillan.

Yasmann, Victor (2004). "Analysis: The Kremlin After Beslan", RFE/RL, 8 September, *http://www.rferl.org/content/article/1054735.html*

Zhurovsky, Alexander and Olga Vykhovanets (2013). *Compatriots: Back to the Homeland*. Russian International Affairs Council, 31 May, *http://russiancouncil.ru/en/inner/?id_4=1908#top*

4

QUANSHENG ZHAO

Changes and Continuities in Chinese Foreign Policy and Policymaking

Chinese foreign policy has experienced many different eras. My early research on Chinese foreign policy, *Interpreting Chinese Foreign Policy* (1996), analysed the Mao-era policies to the Deng-era and continued into the eras of Jiang and Hu. Now, as of 2014, we have entered the new era of Xi Jinping and need to continue identifying the basic characteristics of China's 'new' foreign policy. As China's economy and international influence continues to grow, it is only natural that the Xi regime's foreign policy has increasingly drawn attention globally.

Overview

In order to better understand the era of Xi, it is imperative to recall the past experience since 1949, when the People's Republic of China (PRC) was founded. China has since experienced enormous internal and external change. After the communist government shifted its domestic focus from revolution to modernisation due to the change in leadership—from revolution-minded Mao Zedong to pragmatic Deng Xiaoping—the PRC's foreign policy adapted to the demise of Cold War bipolarity and the emergence of a more complex balance of power. Facing these dynamic changes, the PRC has been forced to adapt not only to maintain its strength and reputation in the international community, but also to assure its basic survival.

Let us begin with the widely-accepted fact that China has acquired the status of a great power in the international system, rather than an outsider that challenges existing norms. The country's population of more than 1.3 billion is the largest in the world, its economic output has become the second largest in the world, and its military capabilities are on the rise. The PRC's ability to affect peace and stability has been an important concern of China's neighbours and other nations in the global community. Long after the Soviet Union's collapse in 1991 altered the strategic landscape, this recognition of China's importance has grown stronger. This perception is especially valid given China's growing economic clout, but other vital issue areas—such as the global environment, weapons proliferation, and human rights—are directly affected by China.

An examination of Chinese conduct in foreign policy reveals a mixture of rigidity and flexibility. The government is rigid in terms of sticking to basic principles but is flexible in practical and technical matters. The non-negotiable principles (*yanze-xing*) are those that involve vital national interests such as regime legitimacy and internal power politics. The negotiable principles (*linghuo-xing*) are those regarded as lesser priorities. The status of an issue may change depending on timing, domestic conditions, and the international environment. Similarly, Chinese leaders make a distinction between 'essential' and 'rhetorical' principles. Essential principles express China's vital and enduring national interests, including its defence and assertion of sovereignty. Beijing's adherence to these principles will be consistently firm. Rhetorical principles, by contrast, often serve secondary goals that lie outside the immediate scope of policy objectives and are thus open to negotiation.

From Revolution to Modernisation

To understand Chinese foreign policy today, one must pay close attention to the historical legacies that the PRC faced when it was established in 1949. Those legacies stemmed first from the 'hundred-year humiliation' that China experienced prior to the PRC's creation, then from the internal chaos that attended the final years of civil war (1946-1949). After establishment of the PRC, Chinese foreign policy can be divided into three eras that correspond to the regimes of Mao Zedong (1949-1976), Deng Xiaoping (1978-1997), and post-Deng (1997-present) under three consecutive leaders Jiang Zemin, Hu Jintao, and Xi Jinping. One may notice that the central change during the PRC's first half-century involved the shift of national priorities from "revolution", a key concept for Mao, to "modernisation", the focus of his successors.

The Hundred-Year Humiliation

The period known as the hundred-year humiliation spanned roughly from the Opium War of 1839 to the rise of the Chinese communists in the final years of civil war (1946-1949). During this period, China experienced repeated invasions from Western imperial countries such as Great Britain, Germany, France, and Portugal; and from neighbouring powers such as Japan and Russia. Britain's victories over China led to enormous Chinese concessions and the loss of Hong Kong. China was effectively carved up during this period by several foreign powers. France occupied the southwest region, Britain the Yangtze River area, Germany the Shandong province, and Japan and Russia the Manchuria area and the far west.

Among the most important of these, latter encounters was Japan's vectoring in the Sino-Japanese war of 1894-95. China was forced to sign the Treaty of Shimonoseki in which it had to acknowledge the independence of Korea and cede Taiwan to Japan. Animosity toward Japan intensified in the late 1930s and early 1940s as Japan invaded and occupied most of China's territory. Millions of Chinese citizens were killed, injured, and tortured during this struggle—the most notorious incident of which was the Nanjing Massacre of 1937.

Another foreign intervention that left a troublesome legacy in China was the US government's support of Chiang Kai-shek's Nationalist regime during the final stages of China's civil war. American support of Chiang's corrupt and unpopular regime, which persisted despite several attempts at mediation, left traces of distrust toward Washington that remain evident even today. This tension is especially apparent in relation to the island of Taiwan, where Chiang's forces relocated after their defeat and created a government in exile that was long recognised by Washington and its allies as the official government representing the entirety of China.

Mao's Revolutionary Era

After the civil war, the victorious communist regime of Mao Zedong assumed control of a country that decimated by these conflicts. China's weakness was apparent in all dimensions—political, economic and military. After the communist victory in 1949, the PRC was left severely weakened and vulnerable. The combination of anti-imperialist struggles and internal fighting created a tremendous chaos and political uncertainty that left most of the Chinese people in poverty. Mao stuck to his belief that China must undertake 'continuous revolution'. He recognised that the establishment of a socialist society did not automatically lead to a genuine embrace of the new ideology by the masses. While seizure of political power and ownership from the exploiting classes could be completed within a relatively short period of time, it would take many generations to eradicate remnants of their old ideas and habits. From this, Mao concluded that the struggle and the revolution must continue.

In terms of the PRC's global environment, the Cold War balance of power was dominated by two opposite blocs—capitalist and communist. Virtually every country during that period was forced to make a choice between aligning with the US or Soviet blocs. China was no exception. This bipolar structure profoundly affected Chinese foreign policy under Mao, who signed a Friendship Treaty with Soviet leader, Joseph Stalin in 1950. China's alliance with the Soviet Union was consolidated further after the Korean War began in the summer of 1950. Together with the unsettled issue of Taiwan, the lasting effect of the Korean War was that China remained in a confrontational relationship with the US for the next two decades.

The new Chinese leadership was confronted with the immediate need to establish its legitimacy, and urgent task that was complicated by the rival regime in Taiwan. Domestically, the hostility between Taiwan and the mainland was regarded as a continuation of the civil war. Internationally, it involved the issues of representation in the United Nations (UN) and regime recognition in the international community. Both Beijing and Taipei (Taiwan's capital) claimed that they were the sole legitimate representative of China. The issue of

Taiwan, therefore, became critical to the PRC's initial foreign-policy calculations.

Central to Mao's new government was the importance assigned to communist ideology. Although during part of the mid-1940s Mao hoped to develop a cooperative relationship with the US, the PRC chose a policy of aligning with the Soviet Union. Beijing's decision to side with Moscow against Washington was a predictable result of the US-Soviet Cold War, which had divided the world into two hostile camps. Mao's idea that China must support a world revolution prevailed among the top leadership in Beijing. He pushed his revolutionary ideas to fight against 'imperialism' (such as shown by the US), 'revisionism' (a charge made in the 1950s and 1960s against the post-Stalinist Soviet Union), and 'reactionism' (a label for India's behaviour, as it had engaged with China in a border clash in 1962). All three were viewed as components of a conspiracy to encircle China. These politically strategic considerations during the era of Mao overshadowed other aspects of Chinese foreign policy. In East Asia, China supported North Korea and North Vietnam in their wars against the US. Those countries that stood with the US, such as Japan, South Korea, and South Vietnam, were labelled "running dogs of American imperialism."

As Sino-Soviet relations worsened, leading to a military clash along the border in 1969, Mao condemned Moscow's behaviour and started to improve the PRC's relations with the US. At the same time, President Richard Nixon significantly softened US policy toward Beijing, hoping that the PRC would help with a smooth US withdrawal from Vietnam and create a vital wedge in Washington's struggle against Moscow. Thus, starting in 1971, China and the US began the long process of rapprochement, leading to Nixon's historic visit to China in 1972 and the establishment of diplomatic relations in 1979. Even after the Sino-American relations improved, however, Mao continued to advocate struggle against the two Cold War superpowers.

Chinese foreign policy also was affected by domestic factors during this period, especially the Cultural Revolution of 1966-1976. Internally, the Cultural Revolution was launched to purge "capitalist roaders" from the leadership of the Chinese Communist Party (CCP). Externally, Mao continued to push his idea of 'world revolution'. During the peak of the Cultural Revolution, China isolated itself from the outside world as much as possible, making its population one of the least informed about events elsewhere in the world. The PRC paid a heavy price for this dogmatic and isolationist foreign policy, lagging far behind most other countries economically. Strategically, China was encircled by the two superpowers and hostile neighbours, creating a threatening environment. Although in the 1970s Mao made efforts to break the isolation by seeking rapprochement with the US, Japan, and most of the Western powers, his revolutionary rhetoric and dogmatic principles remained fundamentally unchanged.

Deng's Push For Modernisation

The death of Mao in 1976 brought the 10-year Cultural Revolution to an end. After a two-year transitional period under the leadership of Mao's hand-picked successor, Hua Guofeng, Deng Xiaoping achieved the status of China's permanent leader in 1978. This change of leadership marked the beginning of a new period in contemporary Chinese history. The Mao era was a radical revolutionary period highlighted by the Cultural Revolution. The Deng era, by contrast, was a period of pragmatism that led to "a new situation in all fields of socialist modernisation." In this respect, the Deng era was a postrevolutionary era, clearly different from the period under Mao's rule in its national priorities and behaviour toward the international system.

Under Mao, the regime emphasised revolutionary objectives: dramatic and sweeping social and political reform in the domestic arena and survival as a communist nation in the international environment. This period was characterised by an emphasis on revolutionary ideology, a general disregard for prevailing international norms, and extreme sensitivity to outside threats. In the era of modernisation, China moved beyond a single-minded preoccupation with world revolution. As nation states became increasingly interdependent, particularly in terms of economic integration, the PRC gradually recognised that the concept of regime survival had broader meanings. Deng warned that China faced the danger of losing its *qiuji* (global citizenship) if its economy failed to catch up with that of the other major powers.

In the beginning of 1980, Deng identified several tasks for China to pursue in the decade ahead: to preserve a stable international order, to work on the country's "reunification" with Taiwan, and, most importantly, to step up the drive for its economic modernisation. The country quickly underwent a series of domestic reforms, particularly in the economic realm, that pushed the PRC's foreign policy to become more open to the international community.

Four reasons explain Deng's dramatic change in policy. First, as domestic tensions were eased in the post-revolutionary era, Deng acquired greater self-confidence. This confidence was boosted by an emerging national consensus that China must concentrate on economic growth rather than the all-consuming ideological campaigns that prevailed during the Cultural Revolution. Importantly, economic modernisation hastened China's integration in the global economy because it required greater contacts with capitalist nations that were in a position to help China achieve its economic goals.

A second rationale underlying Deng's shift in foreign policy was that China's international profile had grown rapidly in the years preceding his rise to power. In 1971, the UN voted to admit Beijing as the sole representative of China. As a result, the PRC gained not only UN membership, but also the permanent seat on its Security Council that was previously held by the Taiwan regime. China's arrival as a legitimate actor on the world stage was further punctuated by the visit by President Nixon in 1972 and by the subsequent establishment of diplomatic relations with Japan and the Western European countries. All of this prompted Deng to pursue a less antagonistic foreign policy, particularly toward the Western industrialised countries. His approach was well received overseas as many countries switched their official state recognition from Taiwan to the PRC, a trend that further enhanced China's international stature.

During most of the Mao era, China's actions reflected a strong dissatisfaction with the existing international order. Beijing vigorously criticised existing international organisations, particularly the UN. Even after the PRC joined the UN and gained a permanent seat on the Security Council, its suspicion of the UN and other international organisations still persisted. This outsider position, however, was destined to become a thing of the past when China instituted its reforms under Deng. The PRC began to participate actively in international governmental organisations, including the World Bank, the International Monetary Fund (IMF), and the Asian Development Bank. Generally, China now plays a constructive rather than a disruptive role in these institutions.

Third, even before Deng took power, the influence of communist ideology was increasingly yielding to pragmatism. China's conflicts with the US in the 1950s and 1960s, and with the "revisionist" Soviet Union in the 1960s, stemmed from considerations not only of national interest but also of ideology. Beginning in the 1980s, ideological considerations gave way to economic concerns, which in turn compelled Beijing to engage the industrialised states that were formerly declared its enemies. No longer did China regard itself as the centre of world revolution. Instead, its leaders often called for world peace and avoidance of intervention in other countries' internal affairs.

In this respect, Deng adopted an 'independent' foreign policy that sought both a friendly relationship with the US and improved ties with the former Soviet Union. In practice, however, Deng moved closer to the West, which was better able to meet the demands of China's modernisation drive than was the Soviet bloc or today's Russia. In terms of national security, China's policy also became more flexible, as was seen in China's proposal to set aside territorial disputes in the South China Sea and other areas. Deng also moved Chinese foreign policy from one of "liberation of Taiwan by force" to a notion of one country-two systems. In 1978, he told a group of visiting US legislators that Beijing had adopted a policy of 'peaceful unification'.

Finally, Deng was keenly aware of the rapid economic development taking place elsewhere in East Asia, particularly in countries surrounding China. These included Japan and the newly industrialised economies (NIEs) of South Korea, Taiwan, Hong Kong, and Singapore. Of the "little dragons," all but South Korea were societies composed entirely or chiefly of ethnic Chinese citizens. Recognition of the intensifying economic competition in East Asia stimulated fundamental changes in Beijing's interpretation of national survival and reinforced the notion that economic competition was no less vital to China than political and military confrontation. Deng realised that China was not only far behind the industrialised countries, such as the US and Japan, but also lagged behind its small neighbours. This status was particularly clear in the high-technology industrial sectors in which the NIEs excelled.

In a revealing departure from previous practice, Beijing became willing to accept all kinds of foreign aid, from World Bank loans to disaster relief funds and Official Development Assistance (ODA) from Japan and other industrialised countries. Numerous forms of economic cooperation were established between China and the West, including massive volumes of foreign direct investment (FDI) and a growing number of joint ventures with foreign corporations. All of these measures, of course, reflected China's shift from the "command economics" of communism to a market-driven model that allowed for private enterprise and embraced closer ties with the capitalist powers.

The new orientation of Chinese foreign policy was proclaimed by Deng in the wake of the Tiananmen Square crackdown of June 1989, when a student-led Chinese pro-democracy movement was crushed by military forces, provoking severe economic sanctions from the West. This situation was further complicated by the collapse of communism in Eastern Europe in 1989 and the disintegration of the Soviet Union during the next two years. The central elements of this strategy were that China should avoid confrontations with the US (the only superpower), that it should not assume leadership of the post-Soviet socialist world, and that the former should not intervene in the internal affairs of other countries. In Deng's words, China should "go beyond ideological considerations," "detach (itself) from concrete events," and "try to avoid controversy." If such strategy were followed, he predicted, China would become a modernised country by the middle of the 21st century.

Xi Jinping's Proactive Foreign Policy

Deng's successors, Jiang Zemin, Hu Jintao, and most recently, Xi Jinping, have more or less followed Deng's policies both domestically and externally. Xi Jinping, however, unlike his predecessors, has been perceived as moving towards a more "assertive" posture of foreign policy and away from his guidance to "avoid controversy" (Bremmer, 2014). This proactive stance reflects several domestic realities for Xi. First, Xi has a strong support publicly and within the government because of his early experience of being an aide to the Defense Minister of PRC as a young man (Dittmer, 2014). Moreover his "China Dream," the vaguely defined goal of China as a global major power, including asserting maritime territorial sovereignty, is an acceptable rallying point for PLA leadership and their support of foreign policy (Ji, 2014; Dittmer, 2014). Xi also recognises that his personal and regime legitimacy rest upon continued economic growth, corruption control, and nationalism (Rudd, 2013). Although lower than recent years, China maintained a 7.3 per cent GDP (gross domestic product) growth rate in 2013, while Xi continues to rally the Chinese public around optimistic plans for poverty reduction, reducing the income gap, and raising the minimum wage (Heberer, 2014; Dittmer, 2014). Xi's anti-corruption movement, which began almost immediately after coming to office, not only strengthens public trust of the government, but also brings government officials and PLA leaders under control by disciplining dissenters (Heberer, 2014). Xi has moved on to strengthen Chinese nationalism in a number of ways. First, Xi has broken away from Mao and other predecessors in drawing on Chinese history, Confucianism, and other traditional ideology to strengthen pride in China (Tatlow, 2014). Second, Xi's proactive foreign policy strengthens domestic nationalism and, in turn, leads Chinese citizens to push for even more proactive foreign policy abroad (Zhang, 2014).

Within Xi's foreign policy, relations with the US remain the greatest concern (Heilmann and Schmidt, 2014). During his state visit to the US in 2012, Xi urged for a "New Type of Great Power Relations" including more cooperation and respect for each other's core national interests; however the Obama administration has not reacted much to those overtures (Rudd, 2013). At the same time, the US "Asia Pivot" or "Rebalancing to Asia" has left China feeling encircled—despite US assurance that the Pivot has nothing to do with Chinese containment. Due to economic inter-dependence, Xi wants to avoid a confrontation with the US above all, being forced to balance proactive diplomacy with compromise in his relations with the US (Heberer, 2014).

Japan is another of Xi's major foreign policy concerns. Since the 2012 nationalisation of three uninhabited islands in the Diaoyu Island (called "Senkaku" Islands in Japanese) change by the Japanese government, tensions between Japan and China have remained high, while neither has displayed any willingness to compromise over the disputed islands. As Chinese and Japanese leaders refused to meet about the issue, political relations are cold, yet as the stalemate drags on, economic relations grow cold as well (Heberer, 2014). For two countries so economically interconnected, this is worrisome to both, leading to efforts from both sides over the past several months to improve relations in ways that do not compromise their stance on the island dispute. At the time of writing, it is hoped that Xi and Abe will shake hands and hold a brief meeting on the sidelines of the APEC meeting in November 2014 (Fackleroct, 2014).

Russia continues to remain as a key partner in Chinese foreign policy. As a result of the major Western backlash against Russia after its annexation of Crimea in early 2014 and subsequent military incursions in eastern Ukraine, Chinese relations with Russia have seen some new momentum for further development. On one hand, Xi could not condone the unilateral annexation of Crimea for what it implies for disputed regions in China; but on the other hand, China's adherence to the principle of non-interference meant that Xi could not condemn Russia (Ding, 2014). The simple action of refraining to condemn drew thanks from Russia. China subsequently opposed and refused to join in on sanctions proposed by the G7 and the European Union (EU), calling sanctions unhelpful (Reuters, 2014; Irish Times, 2014). Amidst these warming relations, Xi and Russia's Vladimir Putin signed a 30-year $400 billion gas deal in May 2014 and are working towards a second deal of a similar scale (Johnson, 2014).

This serves China's growing need for international sources of natural gas as well as Russia's need for international buyers while European sanctions set in. Since the initial gas deal, Chinese-Russian relations have continued to warm, promising more cooperation between the countries, which is certainly welcome to Xi as he moves to hedge against the US Asia Pivot (Green, 2014). Yet, this growing friendship is unlikely to drastically transform international dynamics in Asia as Russia's primary region of concern remains Eastern Europe.

In addition to the foreign policy priority countries of the US, Japan, and Russia, the PRC also actively maintains relations with countries in the EU, Association of Southeast Asian Nations (ASEAN), and other regions of the world, although these relations remain largely economic at present. Largely due to the EU's frequent lack of unity and ability to take decisive action over foreign policy issues, China largely limits its relations with the EU to economics, a relationship necessary to both (Heilmann and Schmidt, 2014). In addition to foreign direct investment and trade to ASEAN and China's other Asian neighbours, China also invests actively in Africa and Latin America. Although Chinese FDI to Latin America is dwarfed by US FDI in the region, it makes up 13 per cent of total Chinese FDI (Mallén, 2014). Chinese FDI to Africa, while only 3 per cent of China's total, dwarfs all other sources of FDI to the continent (Nisen, 2014). In both Latin America and Africa, China has been willing to extend FDI and assistance to non-democratic leaders, often providing infrastructure projects needed for local economic development in return for natural resources (Sun, 2014a).

Xi has given particular attention to Africa since coming into office, visiting Africa on his first international trip as President during March 2013 (Sun, 2014b). He has also been much more active in African security concerns than any of his predecessors. Also in 2013, China dispatched 170 PLA troops to Mali with the UN Peacekeeping Operations, donated to the African Union for Mali's peacebuilding, and engaged in naval cooperation with Djibouti, among other efforts (Sun, 2014b). Xi's efforts in Africa may be an attempt to fulfil China's economic needs, as well as to display China's role as a responsible, global leader (Sun, 2014b). Indeed, under Xi Jinping, China appears to be moving beyond purely economic relationships with developing countries, leveraging more power.

Developments in the Post-Deng Era

Having examined Chinese foreign policy evolving from the era of Mao since 1949, to the era of Deng, all the way to the current era of Xi, this paper now turns towards the development of policymaking process in the post-Deng era. It is particularly important to pay attention to the continuities and changes since that time. Regarding major changes in the political process, what I have called the "scope and degree" of participation in the policymaking process, the scope has enlarged and the issues have become more diversified. There are more vehicles and channels of participation in the policymaking process. Having said that, we should also pay attention to the continuities in the policymaking process. Namely, that political power is still highly concentrated. The nature of the regime has not really changed; the regime is still authoritarianism in nature and the monopoly of the communist party in policymaking remains.

Instead of a general overview of the policymaking processes, this paper will analyse the evolution and role of think tanks in China, focusing on their impact on the policymaking process. I will employ the concept called "limited interactions between the inner circle and the outer circle" (*quan nei* 圈内 *and quan wai* 圈外) to characterise this relationship. Special attention will be paid to the channels between the policymakers and think tanks.

The policymaking process of Chinese foreign policy has primarily involved three governing actors: the party, the government, and the military. Instead of examining these institutional actors, this paper will focus on the role of policy communities and their impact on the making of Chinese foreign policy. Peter Haas and his associates published a group of articles in 1992 in *International Organization* on "knowledge, power, and international policy coordination." Haas specifically raised the concept of "epistemic community," referring to a "network of professionals with recognised expertise and competence in a particular domain and an authoritative claim to policy-relevant knowledge within that domain or issue-area" (Haas, 1992).

These professional networks, also known as policy communities, become influential because of the nature and complexity of the issues involved. Think tanks are an important part of these policy communities. As in western societies, policy communities and think tanks in China have exerted increasing influence on the direction of foreign policy, although there are noticeable limitations (Brookings Panel 2008).[1]

In July 2009, a three-day think tank summit was held in Beijing, primarily focusing on solutions to tackle the financial crisis. In attendance were Li Keqiang, then China's Vice Premier; Romano Prodi, former President of the European Commission and former Prime Minister of Italy; and Henry Kissinger, former Secretary of State of the US, among others. China's newly established "super think tank"—the China Center for International Economic Exchanges (CIEE), headed by retired Vice-Premier Zeng Peiyan, sponsored this summit (Renmin Ribao, 2009). Against this background, the following studies will examine the impact of policy communities and think tanks on Chinese foreign policy.

Institutions

It is only natural that in recent times attention has shifted to the link between Chinese foreign policy and China's domestic environment as the country continues to undertake profound reforms and the rise of China becomes a focus of world attention. A few studies have examined general influences of Chinese think tanks in the Chinese national policy process.[2] This paper, however, focuses primarily on foreign policy dimensions.

In China, the most well-known think tanks working on foreign policy issues are research institutes under various government

1. For some interesting discussions, see "Think Tanks in China: Growing Influence and Political Limitations," Panel Discussion at the Thornton China Center of the Brookings Institution, Washington, DC. 23 October. Transcript available at: *http://www.brookings.edu/~/media/Files/events/2008/1023_china_think_tanks/20091023_china.pdf*
2. See, for example, Xufeng (2009). For Zhu's early work on this subject see, Xufeng (2006).

agencies. In 2014, the Chinese government revealed the top 10 think tanks in China.[3] From a survey study conducted in the West in 2013, there are five China-based institutions among the top 100 think tanks in Asia (McGann, 2014).[4] With reference to these two lists, we

3. These think tanks are: Development Research Center of the State Council; Chinese Academy of Social Sciences (CASS); Peking University; Tsinghua University; China Center for International Economic Exchange; Party School of the Central Committee of CPC; Academy of Microeconomic Research, NDRC; Fudan University; Shanghai Academy of Social Sciences; China Institute for Reform and Development. For a discussion of the top think tanks in China, see Lin (2014).

4. Top Think Tanks Worldwide (Non-US) Ranked Globally: (Top Asian Think Tanks—China-based institutions are in bold):

9. Chinese Academy of Social Sciences (CASS), China

13. Japan Institute of International Affairs (JIIA), Japan.

14. Korea Development Institute (KDI), Republic of Korea.

18. Carnegie Moscow Center, Russia.

20. Carnegie Middle East Center, Lebanon.

21. Asian Developmenyt Bank Insitute (ADBI), Japan.

28. China Institute for Contemporary International Relations (CICIR), China.

30. China Institute for International Studies (CIIS), China.

40. Singapore Institute of International Affairs (SIIA), Singapore.

42. Turkish Economic and Social Studies Foundation (TESEV), Turkey.

46. Institute of World Economy and International Relations (IMEMO, RAS), Russia.

48. Institute of Southeast Asian Studies (ISEAS), Singapore.

49. Korea Institute for International Economic Policy (KIEP), Republic of Korea.

51. Centre for Civil Society (CCS), India.

52. Center for Strategic and International Studies (CSIS), Indonesia.

54. Institute for Defence Studies and Analyses (IDSA), India.

61. Institute of Defence and Strategic Studies (IDSS), Singapore.

63. Center for Economic and Social Development (CESD), Azerbaijan.

64. Shanghai Institutes of International Studies — China.

67. Association for Liberal Thinking (ALT), Turkey.

77. Center for Free Enterprise, Republic of Korea.

79. Development Research Center of the State Council, China.

81. The Energy and Resources Institute (TERI), India.

82. Council on Foreign and Defense Policy (SVOP), Russia.

84. East Asia Institute(EAI), Republic of Korea.

85. Moscow State Institute of International Relations (MGIMO), Russia.

99. Bangladesh Institute of Development Studies (BIDS), Bangladesh.

can list some of top think tanks in China that are most influential in foreign policy issues. Here are some most well-known examples:

Chinese Academy of Social Sciences (CASS).
China Institute of International Studies (CIIS).
China Institutes of Contemporary International Relations (CICIR).
China Institute for International Strategic Studies (CIISS).
Development Research Center of the State Council.
China Center for International Economic Exchange (CCIEE).
Shanghai Institute for International Studies (SIIS).
Chinese Academy of Military Sciences of the People's Liberation Army (CAMS).

CASS, directly under China's State Council, is the largest and most comprehensive government think tank in China. A number of research institutes under CASS are dealing specifically with international affairs and foreign policy issues, as is clearly indicated in their institutional names, such as "American Studies," "European Studies," "Japanese Studies," "Asia-Pacific Studies," "Russian, East European and Central Asian Studies," "West Asian and African Studies", "World Politics and Economic Studies," "Latin American Studies," "China's Borderland History and Geography Research," etc. CIIS falls under the Ministry of Foreign Affairs and contributes directly to policy analyses on current affairs. CICIR, a Ministry of National Security affiliated think tank, is known for its size in research staff, broad topics of research, as well as internal channels of policy recommendation. The Shanghai-based SIIS has served as an alternative and flexible window for Beijing's foreign policy establishment. In addition, two military think tanks, CAMS and CIISS, are under the People's Liberation Army (PLA), specialising in strategic and security issues. All these institutions have had relatively long history, playing important roles in various policy areas. There are also new think tanks, such as the earlier mentioned CIEE, but many of them tend to concentrate on economic policies.

Let us now conduct a brief review of previous studies in this regard. An early example is He Li's "The Role of Think Tanks in Chinese Foreign Policy" (2002), where detailed analyses were conducted on the historical development and structures of Chinese think tanks

(Li, 2002). Another early example comes from the September 2002 issue of *China Quarterly*, which was dedicated in large part to the study of China's think tanks with discussions including many foreign policy topics. In this issue, Tanner (2002) examines the evolving think tank system in China by using the case of China's growing commercialisation, and the new generation of think tanks that it has spawned. He continues to assert that generational change is evident in China's previously unstudied network of public security think tanks. These institutes, according to Tanner, have been in the forefront of importing and incorporating more sophisticated crime-fighting tactics and less class-based theories of social unrest.

Shambaugh (2002) argues that over the past two decades, China's foreign policy think tanks have come to play increasingly important roles in Chinese foreign policymaking and intelligence analysis. He provides a detailed analysis on the think tanks' structure and processes by offering historical perspectives on the evolution of this community. Shambaugh further argues that these think tanks often offer important indications of broader policy debates and competitions between institutions and their staff. Glaser and Saunders (2002) focus their research on civilian foreign policy research institutes and their increasing influence. They argue that a more pluralistic and competitive policy environment has given analysts at think tanks more influence, but has also created new competition from analysts and authors working out of traditional research institutions.

Gill and Mulvenon (2002) bring their research focus to the national research community in Beijing by arguing that this community is dominated by think tanks and other research organisations affiliated with specific governmental institutions. Furthermore, they point out that the PLA maintains its own set of internal and affiliated research bodies, performing a variety of intelligence, exchange, and research functions. Naughton (2002) examines economic think tanks in China. He states that although these think tanks are all government sponsored, they offer important alternatives to the policies and advice available within the formal governmental bureaucracy. He notes, however, the emergence of independent think tanks along with a significantly growing network of policy advisors to China's top leaders. Sometimes these policy advisors play a more important role than think tanks.

Johnston (2004) conducted a careful study on Chinese middle-class attitudes towards international affairs. Although not directly related to think tanks, the general argument of the article and the development of civil society in China are relevant to the subject matter of this paper. There are also an increasing numbers of PhD dissertations and Masters theses focusing on this subject—some of which have recently been turned into books or journal articles. For example, a dissertation-turned book entitled, *Chinese Foreign Policy Think Tanks and China's Policy toward Japan* (Liao, 2006), has provided a detailed study to update the evolution of China's think tanks and their relations with Chinese foreign policy. The author has also attempted to bring the study into a broader theoretical framework that will integrate recent developments in the conceptualisation of Chinese foreign policy (also see, Yahuda, 2006). Bondiguel and Kellner's (2009) article provides a detailed analysis of the role of think tanks in China's foreign policy.

The importance of think tanks in Chinese foreign policy and other decision-making processes has also drawn attention from scholars in China. The internet journal entitled *China's Strategy*, co-published by the Center for Strategic and International Studies (CSIS) and the Chinese Media Net, Inc. (CMN), is another example of the attention being given to Chinese think tanks. In the first issue published in January 2004, the journal contributed a special section entitled, "Decision-making mechanisms under the fourth generation of Chinese leadership." In this issue, all articles are written by Chinese scholars in China, making it a good complement to the above mentioned *China Quarterly* collection. Zhong Nanyuan published his analysis on the status of Chinese think tanks and their relations with the Hu Jintao-Wen Jiabao leadership. Ding Dajun examined the participation of intellectuals in the decision-making process. Zou Lan studied the influence of think tanks on finance, environment, and public crisis management. Zhang Wei focused his research on economic policies. Hong Xiaohu researched new mechanisms of defence policymaking. As for foreign policy decision-making systems, Sun Zhe analysed their evolutionary characteristics under the new leadership.[5]

Changes and Continuities

Major changes in Chinese politics and foreign policy occurred between the eras of Mao Zedong and Deng Xiaoping. Deng's policy of reform and openness fundamentally redirected China's development, both domestically and internationally. The era of Jiang Zemin and the leadership of Hu Jintao can be seen as a continuation of the Deng era in terms of general directions, yet these leaders had their own characteristics as well. It is therefore necessary for us to examine changes and continuities between these different eras.

Zhao (1992) characterised the changing process of foreign policy in China as that from Mao's era of vertical authoritarianism (i.e., one-person domination) to Deng's era of horizontal authoritarianism (i.e., collective decision-making). This article also pointed out that although intellectuals demonstrated increasing importance, they had not yet become an independent entity in China's political life. They had gained more freedom to discuss policy issues internally, but externally or publicly, they were obligated to support official party lines. Think tanks had a fairly high degree of freedom to conduct internal discussions on a variety of issues but it was difficult, if not impossible, for research institutes to voice dissenting points of view openly. A scholar who was allowed to discuss foreign policy issues in public was expected to explain and validate only the official party lines.

Over times, the scope and degree of participation by think tanks and policy communities have enlarged in the post-Deng era as leaders have vowed to continue Deng's policy of reform and openness. Jiang Zemin and Hu Jintao encouraged think tanks and policy communities to participate in the policymaking process in a variety of ways. The most salient participation was in economic policymaking. In analysing the development from the era of Deng to

---

5. All can be accessed at *http://www1.chinesenewsnet.com/gb/index.html.*

those under the leadership of Jiang and Hu, one will see increasing interactions between the leadership and policy communities.

Channels Between the Inner and Outer Circles

The following analysis will be focused on the relationship between the top leaders, known as the inner circle, and the think tanks, which form a part of the outer circle of the policy community. In Sun Zhe's paper on decision-making in Chinese foreign policy mentioned earlier, he divided the process into inner and outer circles.[6] In this article, I would like to define inner circle (*quan nei* 圈内), or the centre, as that which includes key policymaking individuals and organisations in the party and the government. The outer circles, which I will refer to as the outer circles (*quan wai* 圈外), include the news media, universities, think tanks, etc. The key development under Jiang and Hu is the increasingly active and multi-layered channels between the inner and outer circles. I have developed a notion of seven channels between these two bodies, as discussed below.

Channel 1: Consultations with policy-makers

In recent years, the Communist Party and government organisations have begun to make systematic consultations with think tanks and policy communities on specific policy issues, including foreign policy. The Foreign Ministry, for example, has its own mini-circles for consultation over policy issues, the most interesting and noticeable of these being a practice of invited lectures by think tanks and policy community scholars for the Chinese Communist Party (CCP) politburo. Recent examples are the lectures on international relations and foreign policy issues given by invited scholars Qin Yaqing (of the Foreign Affairs College) and Zhang Yuyan (from the Academy of Social Sciences) to the top leaders in the politburo.[7] These kinds of interactions provide opportunities for scholars to exercise direct influence on the opinions of top leaders.

6. Sun's article can be accessed at *http://www1.chinesenewsnet.com/gb/index.html.*
7. Interview with Prof Jin Canrong of Renmin University, Washington DC, 7 May 2004.

It is, nevertheless, a fairly rare occasion for intellectuals to do so and one cannot expect too much in terms of policy impact.

In addition to the above mentioned lectures, there are also issue-oriented debates and discussions among policy communities and between intellectuals and policymakers. In order to ensure this kind of policy debate, a proper political and intellectual atmosphere is necessary. It is impossible, for example, for such policy debate to occur during a totally closed period, such as the Cultural Revolution. Deng Xiaoping's reform and openness initiatives, beginning in 1978, opened the door to the possibility for such policy debate. At first, it appeared regarding internal economic policies, particularly in the debate over command *versus* market economies. It gradually expanded to the foreign policy field. Rozman (1987), for example, made a detailed record of such debates on the nature of the Union of Soviet Socialist Republics (USSR) and the relationship between China and the USSR during the period of 1978-1985. This kind of debate has flourished more and more since the 1990s.

One case in point is the debate on China's entrance into the World Trade Organization (WTO) and the issue of globalisation. In the late 1990s and early 2000s, prior to China's accession in December 2001 to the WTO, heated discussions and debates took place to deliberate upon the pros and cons of the issue (Misra, 2003). In his field research in Beijing, Garrett (2001) investigated these internal deliberations within Chinese think tanks and Chinese leaders' dialogues with them, which provided some useful input in China's policy toward the WTO.

Channel 2: Internal reports via government channels

As mentioned earlier, under some government agencies, there are a number of official think tanks which may also deal with foreign policy issues. Another type of official think tank is *zhengfu canshi-shi* (政府参事室) meaning 'governmental consulting division'. This kind of *canshi-shi* exists at both the national and provincial levels. At the national level, there is a State Council supervised *canshi-shi*, with 35 consultants. At the provincial or city levels, there are 41 governmental consulting divisions with more than 1,000 consultants (Wen, 2004).

A traditional way for think tanks to exert their influence has been through internal reports to top leaders. Leading foreign policy organisations and agencies such as the Ministry of Foreign Affairs, the Ministry of State Security, and military organisations have their own research institutes. There are long-established channels through which scholars may submit research papers, policy analyses, and recommendations to various levels of policymakers, including from time to time the top leaders. These policy recommendations are sometimes bold without ideological constraints. One of such examples is a suggestion in 2008 from researchers in the Party Central School that the CCP should speed up political reform in order to cope with the rapid development of Chinese society (Buckley, 2008; 2002).

Glaser and Saunders (2002: 608-14) describe four different types of influence exerted by think tank scholars. First, some scholars may have "positional influence," whereby they utilise their key positions in the government, such as within the China Institute of Contemporary International Relations (CICIR) and the China Institute of International Studies (CIIS). Secondly, those who possess expert knowledge in regional or technical matters are able to exert what is referred to as 'expertise influence.' The third type, "personal influence," is enjoyed by those individuals who are closely related to high-level government officials. For example, Yang Jiemian, Deputy Director of the Shanghai Institute of International Studies, has considerable access to policymakers through his elder brother, Yang Jiechi, former Chinese Ambassador to the US and current Minister of Foreign Affairs. The fourth source of influence is called "experiential influence," which is held by those people who have accumulated valuable knowledge through extensive experience living and studying abroad.

I would like to add a fifth source of influence; that is, retired veteran diplomats. These retired government officials have not only accumulated enormous firsthand knowledge abroad, but perhaps more importantly, also have extensive personal networks within the foreign policy apparatus. This is true because human networks have always been important in Chinese society, and China's foreign policy apparatus is relatively exclusive and segregated. In many cases, these retired officials still serve as advisors to the foreign ministry or work in some semi-official governmental institutions, such as the Chinese People's Association for Foreign Affairs. Qian Qichen, China's former Foreign Minister and Vice-Prime Minister, was believed to continue to have enormous influence on foreign policy issues several years after his total retirement from the government and the party. Therefore, the degree of influence of think tanks may depend on the sources of influence that individuals possess.

In addition to personal influence, one other factor to consider is the evaluation system that exists within the government. Senior-level officials, sometimes top leaders, often provide comments (known as *pishi* 批示) on think tank reports. They also rank the usefulness and importance of each report submitted by a think tank and these evaluations are then attached to the reports when they are circulated. Receiving a *pishi* from top leaders can help policy experts build both their careers and reputations as experts (Bondigues and Kellner, 2009).

Channel 3: Conferences and public policy debates

Another important channel for policy communities and scholars to convey their opinions is through conferences and public policy debates. Although these conferences and debates may not necessarily have a direct impact on policymakers, they do carry weight in influencing public opinion. The relatively recent practice of discussion and debate of current international affairs in the Chinese news media, including that on the Central Chinese Television (CCTV) network and in major newspapers (such as *People's Daily* and its affiliated *Global Times*), are good examples of such public dialogues. In general, the degree of freedom for this kind of debate depends on the degree of sensitivity. For example, there are few public discussions of the North Korean nuclear crisis (and even though some exist, the debaters may get into trouble—see below), but there are a number of lively debates regarding US military actions in Iraq—one can hear both pros and cons in a true crossfire of opinions.

Research institutes affiliated with universities and various governmental agencies are the likely host for policy-oriented conferences. The Chinese Academy of Social Sciences has a number of policy experts who frequently participate in internal conferences for policy deliberation. Researchers from the Institute of American Studies and the Institute of Asia Pacific Studies are also good examples in this regard. These activities present excellent opportunities for researchers to voice differing opinions. There are also news media arranged public policy debates.

Professors and research fellows from leading universities, such as Beijing, Qinghua, Renmin, and Fudan, are the main participants in these internationally oriented conferences and debates. Increasingly, these scholars are invited to present their analyses on foreign policy at international conferences, on television programs and radio discussions, and in newspapers and popular magazines. For example, Qinghua University's Yan Xuetong and Chu Shulong are frequent commentators on CCTV programs. Beijing University's Jia Qingguo and Renmin University's Jin Canrong are often quoted in various media. Although many of them are quite visible in the public eye, these academic scholars in general do not necessarily have direct access to policymakers and therefore have little influence on policymakers in Beijing. Individually, however, a few of them may have various influences, depending on their personal networks and connections, as discussed earlier.

In a recently published paper, Li (2010) predicts a likely enhancement of the "military's influence and power in the years to come." Along these lines, several generals in the PLA have called for tough positions toward the US and Japan. Major General Luo Yuan of the PLA, for example, has accused the US of employing what he calls "gunboat diplomacy." He describes it as a process of the US first 'flexing' its muscles as a warning and then teaching a lesson with its 'fists.' General Luo cites the US's Naval Operations Concept approved by President Obama in May 2010 as the best example of this type of diplomacy. He also calls the Chinese "peace-loving people" and criticises the US for using hard power, not smart power (Yuan, 2010). Another example is PLA Major General Zhu Chenghu, who people refer to as a 'hawkish' General. In 2005, Zhu threatened to use nuclear weapons if the US intruded on the issue regarding the conflict in Taiwan. "If the Americans are determined to interfere, then we will be determined to respond," he said. "We Chinese will prepare ourselves for the destruction of all the cities east of Xian. Of course the Americans will have to be prepared that hundreds of cities will be destroyed by the Chinese" (New York Times, 2005).

An influential policy-oriented journal entitled *Zhanlue yu Guangli* [*Strategy and Management*], established in 1993, is affiliated with the Strategy and Management Research Society, a think tank headed by former Vice Premier Gu Mu. This journal often makes bold policy suggestions as a testing balloon for new directions (Rutwich, 2004). For example, in 2002 and 2003, the journal published two articles regarding China's Japan policy—one by Ma Licheng of the *People's Daily* and the other by Shi Yinhong of Renmin University. Ma and Shi strongly advocated a "foreign policy revolution" which would reprioritise Chinese foreign policy directions in terms of China-Japan relations. Both articles emphasise the necessity of viewing strategic interests above considerations for historical legacies in Beijing's calculations concerning Japan. Although these articles received strong criticism from some circles of Chinese society and became quite controversial, they nevertheless did produce some "new thinking" in China's Japan policy, as the authors had advocated.

However, disaster struck the outspoken journal in September 2004, after it published an even more controversial article on North Korea. The article, written by the Chinese economist Wang Zhongwen, was entitled "A New Viewpoint to Examine the North Korea Issue and the Northeast Asian Situation" and appeared in the journal's July/August 2004 issue. Wang criticised North Korea's nuclear policy and the country's leader, Kim Jong Il, for "practicing ultra-leftist politics and political persecution in order to maintain dynastic rule." The author further suggested that Chinese foreign policy should be readjusted according to new developments in North Korea and in the Asia Pacific region. The issue was immediately recalled and banned, and the journal itself was ordered to close (Tkacik Jr., 2004). This episode highlights how sensitive foreign policy-related discussions in open forums can be in Beijing's political circle. It is nevertheless remarkable that such an article was even published, especially when viewed in light of China's censorship practices a or decade two ago, not to mention during the Cultural Revolution. Generally speaking, policy communities now have greater freedom in voicing differing opinions and analyses on foreign policy issues (albeit not without risk) and today's scholars appear much more active than those in previous decades.[8] Policy communities are gaining greater freedom to discuss sensitive foreign policy issues.

Channel 4: Policy NGOs

Although NGOs (non-governmental organisations) are still a new concept in China, they are quickly being utilised by the Chinese government to conduct foreign policy activities. At the same time, there have been some attempts to set up non-governmental think tanks. A few government organisations have managed to transform into a semi-official or NGO status (Zhu and Xue, 2007). To be sure, many NGOs are not truly independent of governmental control. However, they sometimes appear to have much greater freedom and flexibility to conduct policy research and foreign policy related activities.

A clear example is the common practice of so-called "Channel II Diplomacy" (also known as "Track II Diplomacy"). This refers to the activities of retired government officials, scholars, and think tank members who actively participate in all kinds of forums, meetings, and other activities with their foreign counterparts. These activities are designed to facilitate exchange on sensitive issues, such as arms control or the issue of Taiwan, that may not be easily conducted by official diplomats. Graham and Kelley (2009) explain that Channel II diplomacy focuses on dialogue as a means of reconciliation in tense situations. Participants utilising the Channel II approach work to facilitate communication between disagreeing parties. Channel II diplomacy is also utilised for public relations and may "supplement and enhance track one diplomatic contacts" (Graham and Kelley,

8. For the active atmosphere of discussions, see Leonard (2008).

2009). To encourage and coordinate these kinds of activities, the Chinese Foreign Ministry established a new public diplomacy division in the spring of 2004. Assistant Minister of Foreign Affairs Shen Guofang announced in March 2004 that the new Division of Public Diplomacy was established to coordinate the dissemination of information and to influence public opinion.[9]

Channel 5: Outside-system (tizhiwai 体制外) discussions

Most of the channels mentioned above can be regarded more or less as government-sponsored activities. One must, however, also play close attention to *tizhiwai* channels, meaning outside-system discussions that may from time to time be beyond government control. This has been particularly true during the most recent decade since the 1990s in the new information age. As the control over public information has loosened, a variety of ways have developed for scholars to voice their honest opinions, some of which are not always aligned with the opinions of the Party. Many of these opinions resonate with the popular mood reflecting a strong nationalistic tendency. One example is a best-selling book published in Beijing in 1996 entitled, *A China That Can Say No*, which reflected a strong anti-American sentiment (Qiang *et al.*, 1996). Thirteen years later in 2009, the same group of authors published another best-seller, *Unhappy China*, advocating China's leadership role in the post-financial crisis era with strong nationalistic sentiment (Xiaojun *et al.*, 2009). These ideas are in sharp contrast to *tao guang yang hui* (韬光养晦: to conceal your capabilities and keep a low profile) mainstream thinking of Chinese foreign policy, initially raised by Deng Xiaoping in the early 1990s.[10]

In the age of the Internet, it is difficult, if not impossible, for any government to control its citizens' access to information. In the era of Mao and even at the beginning of the Deng era, the Chinese government maintained tight control over the news media. The gatekeeper for this control was the Propaganda Department of the

9. *World Journal*, 10 May 2004, A4.

10. For Deng's guidelines for Chinese foreign policy, see Zhao (1996).

CCP. In the Internet age, however, this control has been greatly challenged and largely broken. During the spring of 2004, a Beijing University Associate Professor, Jiao Guobiao, posted an article on the internet entitled, "Taofa Zhongxuanbu (Denounce the Propaganda Department)" (讨伐中宣部). This article advocated the need for greater freedom from control by the Party and the government for the news media, and drew broad attention while provoking heated discussion on the Internet about information control in China. It is therefore a modern practice for scholars and policy community members to look at Internet discussion debates to ascertain the popular mood.

Internet discussion has drawn close attention from the central leadership. The Chinese Foreign Affairs Ministry, for example, has created a pop-up within its Chinese-language website asking for opinions of intellectuals and other ordinary citizens. Internet users can email their opinions to the ministry and can conduct discussions in the chat-room and can even chat regularly with senior foreign affairs officials (Gries, 2004).

It has become a pattern that whenever there is a dramatic and sometimes controversial international incident that involves China, there will be heated discussion about the event on the Internet. This happened in 1999 with the war in Kosovo and the subsequent embassy bombing incidents in which the NATO-lead bombers attacked the Chinese embassy in Belgrade. In a detailed survey study on the attitudes of Beijing students after the embassy bombing, Dingxin Zhao demonstrated that there is an apparent "rise of popular anti-US nationalism in China" (Zhao, 2002: 902).

Discussions can become more heated when the issue involves nationalism, as demonstrated by Internet discussions regarding the territory dispute between China and Japan over the *Diaoyu* Islands (or *Senkaku* in Japanese). In fact, China has begun to allow anti-Japanese demonstrations in several Chinese cities over territorial disputes. The 2010 protests began peacefully, but eventually became more rowdy, with some demonstrators holding racist signs calling for Japan to be "wiped off the face of the earth." A newspaper in Hong

Kong reported that the protests were organised by government-sponsored university groups (Assosiated Press, 2010).

Although the number of Chinese citizens with access to the Internet is still a small portion of the entire Chinese population, and it is difficult to fully represent popular mood, Internet discussion nevertheless plays an influential role in two ways. First, the government may be required to take publicly expressed opinions into consideration when making critical decisions, such as which country to work with on the high-speed railway project between Beijing and Shanghai. The issue of who to partner with (Japan or Europe) not only provoked heated debates among related government agencies and policy communities, but also became a controversial topic in public forums. The second role is a deterrent role as public awareness prevents scholars and policy community members from making conciliatory gestures on controversial issues in public appearances. Some scholars even feel deterred from making rational analyses when they are interviewed publicly, fearing a negative response afterwards on the Internet.

Channel 6: Overseas scholars

Another important source for policy communities' influence on Chinese foreign policy is from overseas scholars. Previously, this kind of influence was exercised by a few prominent individuals. Several Chinese-American Nobel Prize winners were invited to return to China to provide advice top leaders on a variety of issues, including foreign policy, but this kind of practice remains limited and lacks any systematic arrangement.

Since the 1980s, large numbers of Chinese scholars and students have studied abroad. Many of them have become professors and scholars in advanced industrialised countries, particularly in the US and Japan. A large portion of these scholars are focused on science and technology, but there are a small portion of them concentrating on the social sciences and humanities, including foreign policy and international relations. These scholars have organised themselves into academic exchanges and professional networking organisations.

A few have even begun to play a consultative role on foreign policy issues.

One such example is the Global Forum of Chinese Political Scientists,[11] established in 1999 by Chinese scholars in the US, China, Hong Kong, Taiwan and Japan. In addition to regular academic activities, such as sponsoring panels for the American Political Science Association annual meetings, it has a practice of conducting annual and semi-annual conferences, workshops, and mini-roundtables to discuss not only academic issues, but also policy-oriented dialogues and debates. This group has had activities in Washington DC, Hong Kong, Beijing, Shanghai and Tokyo. Through these kinds of activities, overseas scholars have gained the opportunity to conduct extensive discussions in both Beijing and Shanghai with their academic counterparts from such institutions as Beijing University, Qinghua University, Fudan University, Renmin University, the Chinese Academy of Social Sciences, the China Institute of Contemporary International Relations, the China Institute of International Studies, the Shanghai Academy of Social Sciences and National Defense University, among others.

Channel 7: Highly Specialised Professional Community

As think tanks and policy communities in the field of international relations and foreign policy studies have further developed, three types of policy-oriented epistemic communities have also emerged. The first type is the policy-oriented community which concentrates on issues in a specific policy area, such as arms control, missile defence, human rights, the WTO, etc. For example, Gill and Mulvenon (2002) argued in their study of Chinese military related think tanks and research institutions, that there have been considerable developments and an expansion of exchange programmes with foreign countries and research on military issues. Those think tanks and institutions include the National Defense University, China

11. For details of the activities of the Global Forum of Chinese Political Scientists, see the forum's homepage at: *http://globalforum.homestead.com/* The author was one of the participants that presented papers on a variety of aspects of Chinese foreign policy and policymaking processes, with a special reference to Beijing's Korea policy.

Institute for International Strategic Studies, the Center for Peace and Development, China Defense, Science, and Technology Information Center, the Foundation for International Strategic Studies, and the academy of military sciences. These issue oriented think tanks and organisations have developed extensive internal and external networking and have gradually become a policy community.

The second type of epistemic community is made up of regional or country oriented research institutes and/or scholars. In China, there are a large number of research institutes with scholars concentrating on a specific region or country, such as the US, Europe, Japan, the Middle East, Southeast Asia, Africa, and Latin America. Internal networking within each area of study is also well developed. The third type of epistemic community is connected to foreign research institutes and scholars. A few internationally oriented think tanks, both governmental and non-governmental, have well-developed connections with their counterparts abroad. The best examples in this regard are the China Institute of International Studies, China Institute of Contemporary International Relations, the China Reform Forum, and the Shanghai Institute of International Studies.

The Chinese foreign policy apparatus has varying degrees of contact with each of these epistemic communities and, through these channels, is able to obtain expert opinions from different angles, perspectives and backgrounds, which in turn improves policymaking deliberations. These widely established networks have also allowed policymakers to reach out for policy consultation and input, but at the same time, the development of these policy communities is irregular and therefore the function and impact also vary.

Reasons for Change

The above analysis has demonstrated enormous changes and development in terms of the greater role played by think tanks and policy communities in the foreign policymaking process in China. The greatest fundamental changes took place between the era of Mao and the era of Deng, as illuminated in my 1992 *Annals* article mentioned earlier. Chinese society in more recent eras—the eras of Jiang, Hu and Xi—has continuously undergone significant changes as it develops. The seven channels between the inner and outer circles in terms of policy input have reflected this change. There are three main reasons behind these social changes.

The first one is the development of civil society in China. Schwartz and Pharr (2003) in their edited volume, *The State of Civil Society in Japan*, conduct excellent analyses on the emergence of civil society. In Schwartz's (2003) definition of the term "civil society," he emphasised the following important elements: a nation state, cultural dispositions, a market economy, associations, and a public sphere (among others). In borrowing this analysis on Japan, we can see clearly how the recent developments in China have created a foundation for the growth of civil society. Ye (2003) argues that the "crucial measure of [the] presence [of a civil society] in any nation is the ability of NGOs to progress and develop." Using this measure, China is undergoing social changes that indicate the emergence of a civil society. It should be noted, however, that while Chinese society is becoming more pluralistic, China still has a long way to go before it can be said that a civil society in China exists. As mentioned earlier, Johnston (2004) has argued that the attitude of China's growing middle class toward international affairs has moved to "a greater level of nascent liberalism," which has in turn had an impact on Chinese foreign policy. The blossoming of a market economy and increasing room for private citizens in both economic and even political environments in the past two or three decades has created a new atmosphere.

Think tanks and policy communities can in turn utilise this public sphere (including such mechanisms as the news media and internet) to advocate their opinions. After a detailed study on the relationship between popular nationalism and Chinese foreign policy, Gries (2004a: Chapter 7) argues that "popular nationalists are not just influencing domestic politics; they are also beginning to influence the making of Chinese foreign policy." The difference therefore between the post—Jiang Hu era and Deng era is that policy communities now have greater freedom in voicing their dissenting opinions on foreign policy issues in terms of scope and degree (although noticeable limitations remain).

Another reason behind these changes is a greater demand for policy input. China's external relations have expanded rapidly as China has further integrated into the world community. Foreign policy issues are no longer limited to political, security and strategic issues, but also include other dimensions such as culture, economics, human rights, international organisations, and so on. These issues require broader participation, and the bureaucrats' capacity alone is not enough. In this spirit, the foreign affairs ministry and other government agencies have gradually established formal and informal consultation systems with think tanks and policy communities.

According to Haas (1992), there are four functions for epistemic communities to play. First, they will be able to elucidate the cause-and-effect relationships and provide advice about the likely results of various courses of action. Second, they can shed light on the nature of complex inter-linkages between issues. Third, they can help define the self-interest of a state or factions within it. And last, they can help formulate policies, and in some cases "decision makers will seek advice to gain information which will justify or legitimize a policy that they may wish to pursue for political ends." Similarly, epistemic communities in China, including think tanks, have performed these kinds of functions in the policy formulation process.

The third main reason for China's significant social change is the growing professionalism in the foreign policy apparatus. As a former Chinese diplomat told American researchers, "It used to be easy to be a Chinese diplomat. You just memorised the two phrases that defined the current policy and repeated them over and over. It's much harder now. You have to know about everything."[12] Diplomats and researchers alike have all increased their level of education. Many of them have experience studying abroad. Some of them even have MA and PhD degrees from the US, Japan, and Europe. Furthermore, through intensive interactions with counterparts in the West, Chinese diplomats have greatly shortened their learning curve and have increasingly become professionalised. Think tanks and policy communities are even more professionalised in their research

12. Quoted from Glaser and Saunders (2002).

activities and policy input. With this enhanced quality and quantity, it is natural that their voices are more frequently heard by top-level leaders of the foreign policy apparatus.

Future Directions

I will use the metaphor of a half-glass of water to describe the impact of think tanks and policy communities on foreign policy. The glass is half full in that there has been a noticeably increasing influence of think tanks in foreign policy communities, but at the same time we have to notice the half-empty part. There are still limitations in terms of policy inputs. This is particularly true when comparing China with Western countries or comparing China with other East Asian societies that have been deeply influenced by the West, such as Japan, South Korea, and Taiwan. One major difference is in terms of the degree to which official lines of foreign policy can be openly criticised or challenged. We understand that, for example, the George W. Bush administration faced enormous domestic criticism regarding the war in Iraq and Afghanistan. Japanese and South Korean leaders have also been openly challenged in their decisions to send troops to Iraq. These kinds of true policy debates over key foreign policy decision are still not imaginable in the current Chinese society, despite the significant progress that has been made.

One other limitation is in terms of personnel exchanges between think tanks and governmental agencies. It is common practice in the West and in Japan for scholars and policy community members to have opportunities to serve in the government and, when regimes change, for these government officials to be transferred to think tanks to do policy research. This kind of practice is still rare in Chinese society, if not completely absent.

When dealing with the increasing influence of think tanks and policy communities on Chinese foreign policy, Beijing clearly has to calculate the advantages and disadvantages. On the one hand, more policy input from think tanks and policy communities will increase the quality of decision-making and may also provide bargaining chips among the international community. On the other hand, as an authoritarian society, the Communist Party has been careful to protect its monopoly of power when making major decisions, including foreign policy decisions. With this kind of cost-benefit analysis, there will be inevitable ups and downs in terms of Beijing's control over intellectual life. The degree of policy communities' participation in foreign policy formation will correspond to the degree of party-state control over society.

In examining the impact of think tank policy communities on Chinese foreign policy (including its Korea policy), I analysed seven policy input channels. These types of policy mechanisms include consultations with policymakers, internal reports, conferences and public policy debates, policy NGOs, outside-system discussions, overseas scholars, and the epistemic community. One may develop even more models and channels to characterise policy input for China's think tanks and policy communities, but the above mentioned seven channels represent the main bodies for policy input. The recent developments in think tank and policy communities' participation in the foreign policymaking process in Beijing have achieved great progress; but at the same time there are also severe limitations. I call this phenomenon limited interactions between the inner and outer circles (*quan nei* 圈内 and *quan wai* 圈外). The limitation is largely from two sources. First, the nature of Chinese society is not completely open and remains authoritarian in nature, meaning it lacks a proper environment for true policy debate, particularly on sensitive issues. Second, think tanks and policy communities by and large have *quan wai* status and rarely have the chance to function in the *quan nei* circle due to the lack of personnel switches between policymaking organs and intellectual institutions. One may anticipate that as civil society continues to develop in China, there will be further demand for policy input and increasing professionalism in both governmental agencies and think tanks. It is likely that this will push scholars and policy communities to play even greater functions. In other words, the limits between the inner circle and the outer circle may become weaker in the years to come.

References

Associated Press (2010). "China Allows Rowdy Anti-Japanese Protests", *Associated Press*, 18 October. Access at: *http://www.google.com/hostednews/ap/article/ALeqM5iHLHN2ZfU4WqrEunnlFRJNWAlKpw?docId=2a615f1e487d4d0bb263fe64025b1020*

Bondigues, Thomas and Thierry Kellner (2009). "The Impact of China's Foreign Policy Think Tanks", Paper presented at the international conference *Global Think Tank Summit*. China Center for International Economic Exchanges. 2-4 July. Beijing.

Bremmer, Ian (2014). "Obama isn't the Only One with a Passive-aggressive Foreign Policy", *Reuters*, 19 June 19. Access at : *http://blogs.reuters.com/ian-bremmer/2014/06/19/obama-isnt-the-only-one-with-a-passive-aggressive-foreign-policy/*

Buckley, Chris (2008). "Elite China Think Tank Issues Political Reform Blueprint", *Reuters*, 18 February. Access at: *http://www.reuters.com/article/worldNews/*

Chung, Jae Ho (2009). "China's 'Soft Clash' with South Korea: The History War and Beyond", *Asian Survey* 49(3): 472, May/June. University of California Press.

Ding, Sheng (2014). "China's Dilemma in the Ukraine Crisis", *Asia Pacific Bulletin* 255, March 27.

Dittmer, Lowell (2014). "Asia in 2013: Peace and Prosperity amid Rising Tension", *Asian Survey* 54(1) *A Survey of Asia in 2013*): 1-11 (January/February).

Fackleroct, Martin (2014). "For Japan, Small Gesture Holds Great Importance", *New York Times*, 18 October. Access at: *http://www.nytimes.com/2014/10/19/world/asia/for-japan-and-china-small-gesture-holds-great-importance.html*

Garrett, Banning (2001). "China Faces, Debates, the Contradictions of Globalization", *Asian Survey* 41(3): 409-27 (May/June).

Gill, Bates and James Mulvenon (2002). "Chinese Military-Related Think Thanks and Research Institutions", *The China Quarterly* 171: 617-24, September.

Glaser, Bonnie S. and Phillip C. Saunders (2002). "Chinese Foreign Policy Research Institutes: Evolving Roles and Increasing Influence", *The China Quarterly* 171: 597-616 (September).

Graham, Sarah Ellen and John Robert Kelley (2009). "US Engagement in East Asia: A Case for 'Track Two' Diplomacy", *Foreign Policy Research Institute*: 84-86 (Winter).

Green, Michael J. (2014). "Should America Fear a New Sino-Russian Alliance?" *Foreign Policy*, 13 August. Access at: *http://shadow.foreignpolicy.com/posts/2014/08/13/should_america_fear_a_new_sino_ russian_alliance?wp_login_redirect=0*

Gries, Peter Hays (2004). *China's New Nationalism*. Berkeley, CA: University of California Press. p.134.

———. (2004a). "Popular Nationalism and the Fate of the Nation", in *China's New Nationalism*. Berkeley, CA: University of California Press. pp.116-34.

Haas, Peter M. (1992). "Introduction: Epistemic Communities and International Policy Coordination", *International Organization* 46(1) (Winter): 1-35.

Heberer, Thomas (2014). "China in 2013: The Chinese Dream's Domestic and Foreign Policy Shifts", *Asian Survey* 54(1) (*A Survey of Asia in 2013*): 113-28 (January/February).

Heilmann, Sebastian and Dirk H. Schmidt (2014). *China's Foreign Political and Economic Relations: An Unconventional Global Power*. Lanham, MD: Rowman & Littlefield.

Irish Times (2014). "China Opposes Sanctions on Russia Over Ukraine", *Irish Times*, 28 April. Access at:*http://www.irishtimes.com/news/world/europe/china-opposes-sanctions-on-russia-over-ukraine-1.1776366*

Ji, You (2014). "The PLA and Diplomacy: Unraveling Myths about the Military Role in Foreign Policy Making", *Journal of Contemporary China* 23(86): 236-54.

Johnston, Alastair Iain (2004). "Chinese Middle Class Attitudes towards International Affairs: Nascent Liberalization?" *The China Quarterly* 179: 603-28.

Johnson, Kieth (2014). "Hammered by the West, Putin Turns East", *Foreign Policy*, 18 September. Access at: *http://www.foreignpolicy.com/articles/2014/09/18/hammered_by_the_west_putin_turns_east_russia_china_gas_altai*

Leonard, Mark (2008). "China's New Intelligentsia", *Prospect:* 144, March. Access at: *http://www.prospect-magazine.co.uk/article_details.php?id=10078*

Li, He (2002). "The Role of Think Tanks in Chinese Foreign Policy", *Problems of Post-Communism* 49(2): 33-43, Mar/Apr.

Li, V. (2010). "China's Midterm Jockeying: Gearing Up for 2012 (Part 3: Military Leaders), *China Leadership Monitor* 33, June.

Liao, Xuanli (2006). *Chinese Foreign Policy Think Tanks and China's Policy Toward Japan.* Hong Kong: Chinese University Press.

Lin, Xu (2014). "Top 10 Most Influential Think Tanks in China", *China.org.cn*, 13 August 13. Access at *http://www.china.org.cn/top10/2014-02/03/content_31341799.htm*

Mallén, Patricia Rey (2014). "Is The Partnership Between China And Latin America Paying Off?" *International Business Times*, 8 May. Access at: *http://www.ibtimes.com/partnership-between-china-latin-america-paying-1581710*

McGann, James G. (2014) "2013 Global Go To Think Tank Index" *Foreign Policy*, January. Access at: *http://gotothinktank.com/dev1/wp-content/uploads/2014/01/GoToReport2013.pdf*

Misra, Kalpana (2003). "Neo-Left and Neo-Right in Post-Tiananmen China", *Asian Survey* XLIII(5): 717-44 (September/October).

Naughton, Barry (2002). "China's Economic Think Tanks: Their Changing Role in the 1990s", *The China Quarterly* 171: 625-35, September.

New York Times (2005). "Chinese Threaten to use A-Bomb if US Intrudes", *New York Times*, 15 July 15. *http:// www.nytimes.com/2005/07/15/international/asia/15china.html*

Nisen, Max (2014). "The US can't Best China's Ambitions in Africa", *Quartz*, 5 August. Access at : *http://qz.com/244912/the-us-cant-best-chinas-ambitions-in-africa/*

Qiang, Song, Zhang Zangzang, Qiao Bian *et al.* (1996). *Zhongguo keyi shio bu* [A China That Can Say No]. Beijing: Zhongua gongshang lianhe chubanshe.

Renmin Ribao (2009). "Global Think Tank Summit Wraps up in Beijing", *Renmin Ribao* (People's Daily), 5 July. Access at: *http://english.peopledaily.com.cn/90001/90783/91300/6693373.html*

Reuters (2014). "China Opposes Proposed EU Sanctions against Russia", *Reuters*, 01 September. Access at: *http://www.reuters.com/article/2014/09/01/us-china-russia-ukraine-idUSKBN0GW1TC20140901*

Rozman, Gilbert (1987). *The Chinese Debate about Soviet Socialism: 1978-1985*. Princeton, NJ: Princeton University Press.

Rutwich, John (2004). "China Orders Journal Closed Over North Korea Story", *Reuters*, 21 September.

Rudd, Kevin (2013) "Beyond the Pivot: A New Road Map for U.S.- Chinese Relations", *Foreign Affairs* 92(2): 9-17 (Mar/Apr).

Schwartz, Frank (2003). "What is Civil Society", in Frank J. Schwartz and Susan J. Pharr (eds.), *The State of Civil Society in Japan*. New York: Cambridge University Press. pp.23-41.

Schwartz, Frank and Susan Pharr (eds.) (2003). *The State of Civil Society in Japan*. New York: Cambridge University Press.

Shambaugh, David (2002). "China's International Relations Think Tanks: Evolving Structure and Process", *The China Quarterly* 171: 575-96, September.

Sun, Yun (2014a). "Africa in China's Foreign Policy", *Brookings*, April. Access at: *http://www.brookings.edu/research/papers/2014/04/10-africa-china-foreign-policy-sun*

———. (2014b) "Xi Jinping's Africa Policy: The First Year", *Brookings*, 14 April 14. Access at: *http://www.brookings.edu/blogs/africa-in-focus/posts/2014/04/10-jinping-africa-policy-sun*

Tanner, Murray Scot (2002). "Changing Windows on a Changing China: The Evolving "Think Tank" System and the Case of the Public Security Sector", *The China Quarterly* 171: 559-74, September.

Tatlow, Didi Kirsten (2014). "Xi Jinping on Exceptionalism With Chinese Characteristics", *New York Times*, 14 October. Access at: *http://sinosphere.blogs.nytimes.com/2014/10/14/xi-jinping-on-exceptionalism-with-chinese-characteristics/?_php=true&_type=blogs&_r=0*

Tkacik Jr., John J. (2004). "China's 'S & M' Journal Goes Too Far on Korea", *The Asia Times* 02 September. Access at: *http://www.asiatimes.com*

Wen, Ji (2004). "Remove the Secret Curtain from 'Governmental Think Tanks,'" *Renmin Ribao*, 10 April.

Xiaojun, Song, Wang Xiaodong, Song Qiang *et al.* (2009). *Zhongguo bu Gaoxing* [Unhappy China]. Nanjing: Jiangsu renmin chubanshe.

Xufeng, Zhu (2006). "China's Think Tanks: Roles and Characteristics", *EAI Background Brief* No. 306, 19 October.

———. (2009). "The Influence of Think Tanks in the Chinese Policy Process: Different Ways and Mechanisms", *Asian Survey* 49(2): 333-57 (March).

Yahuda, Michael (2006). "Chinese Foreign Policy Think Tanks and China's Policy Towards Japan", *Pacific Affairs* 79(3): 516 (Fall).

Ye, Zhang (2003). *China's Emerging Civil Society*. Paper presented at the Brookings Institution. June.

Yuan, Luo (2010). "PLA General: US Engaging in Gunboat Diplomacy", 13 August. *People's Daily Online*, Access at *http://english/peopledaily.com.cn/90001/90780/91343/7103900.html*

Zhang, Jian (2014). "The Domestic Sources of China's More Assertive Foreign Policy", *International Politics* 51(3): 390-97.

Zhao, Dingxin (2002). "An Angle on Nationalism in China Today: Attitudes among Beijing Students after Belgrade 1999", *The China Quarterly* 172: 885-905 (December).

Zhao, Quansheng (1992). "Domestic Factors of Chinese Foreign Policy: From Vertical to Horizontal Authoritarianism", *The Annals of the American Academy of Political and Social Science* 519: 159-76 (January).

———. (1996). *Interpreting Chinese Foreign Policy: the Micro-Macro Linkage Approach*. New York and Hong Kong: Oxford University Press. pp.50-54.

Zhu, Xufeng and Lan Xue (2007). "Think Tanks in Transitional China", *Public Administration and Development* 27(5): 452-64 (November).

5

STEVEN PHILIP KRAMER

The End of French Europe?

Things Fall Apart

On 29 May 2005, French voters rejected the draft of a new European Union (EU) constitution in a nationwide referendum. Although not unexpected, their vote plunged the EU into a long period of uncertainty. It also signalled that France itself is in crisis. In saying no to a draft worked out largely by their own leaders, French voters effectively disowned those leaders and, in the process, exported their country's crisis to the EU. European integration and the EU constitution had largely been French endeavours, and France had long been Europe's natural leader. A year after the vote, the key question that remains is whether the no vote, as well as the subsequent riots in the Parisian *banlieues* (suburbs) and the more recent mass protests against youth labour reform, has destroyed France's ability to lead the EU, an institution France did so much to create.

France has faced similar crises in the past. Following its 1870 defeat in the Franco-Prussian War and again after the disaster of 1940 (when France fell to Germany in a mere six weeks), France struggled to maintain its national security and its rank as a great power. It tried to recover from its failure in 1870 by establishing the Third Republic, rebuilding its military, and developing alliances against Germany. The French could not agree, however, on the underlying causes of the defeat, and this prevented the creation of a unified blueprint for rebuilding the country—a lack of cohesion that led to France's second great humiliation, in the early days of World War II.

The Author has given the permission to use his paper from the *Foreign Affairs* Magazine (July/August 2006 issue) which was published by Council of Foreign Relations.

After that war ended, France adopted a more creative approach to its reconstruction. Its leaders drew up a new model for a planned economy and a welfare state and in 1958, after another political crisis, established the Fifth Republic, adopting new political institutions that favoured the executive at the expense of the legislature. Starting in the late 1940s, France's leaders also turned to the project of European integration, using it to resolve the German problem and achieve regional leadership (generally in partnership with West Germany). France solved its own problems by solving Western Europe's. Its solution was an existential breakthrough for Europe; European integration served Europe's interests as well as France's.

France's grand ambitions now seem to have come undone. The defeat of the EU constitution in the referendum last year resulted from two factors: a general crisis in French society and the flaws inherent in the French concept of Europe. The first reflects the fact that the postwar French model—political, economic and social—no longer functions well. France lacks faith in itself; its elite is divided over fundamental questions and has lost confidence of the public. Its economy has suffered from slow growth for a decade, its social welfare model is under siege, and its system of ethnic integration has been challenged by the recent riots. Meanwhile, France's positions on the EU have become increasingly self-serving and defensive. An enlarged EU has chaffed under Paris' tutelage, and French citizens have grown alarmed about the implications of EU enlargement.

To be sure, despite France's central role in the creation of the EU, the country's relationship with Europe has never been easy. Although Paris made European integration the cornerstone of its foreign policy after World War II, French leaders have always been reluctant to yield national sovereignty to the supranational institutions they helped midwife; witness the defeat of the European Defense Community in 1954 (an attempt to establish an integrated European army within North Atlantic Treaty Organisation [NATO] to avoid the rearmament of West Germany on a national basis); and the near defeat of the Maastricht Treaty in a French referendum in 1992. Under the Fifth Republic, France has wanted contradictory things from European integration: a supranational bloc that could stand tall in the world, but also one that required minimal sacrifice of national sovereignty from its members. French officials believed that a European community based on inter-governmentalism (with decision-making resting primarily in the hands of the representatives of the member states) offered the best means of reconciling these two goals. But it was precisely this kind of inter-governmental EU that French voters shot down last May.

The vote should be taken as a warning: France needs to rethink its national strategy, just as it did after 1870 and 1945. Although French renewal is not a sufficient condition for the future development of the EU, it is a necessary one. Unfortunately, France has accomplished nothing on this front since May 2005. If anything, the situation has deteriorated.

Out of the Ashes

In his famous book *The Strange Defeat*, the great historian Marc Bloch describes his experience as a French reserve officer during the disastrous Battle of France, in 1940, and then uses his historian's training to explain the causes of the debacle. Bloch argues that France's rapid capitulation to the Nazis was not merely a military failure but the result of more fundamental problems in French society. Bloch's argument is relevant today: like France's military humiliation more than 60 years ago, the defeat of the referendum last year revealed a deep-seated crisis of legitimacy stemming from the government's failure to resolve long-term issues.

The aftermath of 1940 is also instructive. After the war, France's quick collapse produced a widespread belief that thorough-going change in the country's structure was necessary. But given the scale of the defeat and the fragmentation of French society, it took decades to establish a coherent response and to convince most of the French leadership and population to accept it.

The basic elements of the postwar French model (modified in 1958) included a strong executive and a weak parliament; an economic system with a large state sector and a significant role for state planning; an extensive welfare system that provided generous health care, retirement, and unemployment benefits and free higher education; support for European integration based on an intergovernmental model; the use of the Franco-German partnership as an instrument for maintaining peace in Europe and exercising French influence; the rebuilding of France's defense around a nuclear deterrent; and an ambivalent stance toward the United States (US), consisting of practical cooperation on concrete issues but doctrinal opposition to perceived US hegemony.

By the late 1980s, the new French model had jelled. For the first time in modern history, the French political class seemed to agree on basic issues of defense, foreign affairs, and economic and social policy. The alternation between left-wing and right-wing governments no longer resulted in significant policy shifts. Ironically, it was around this time that the model also began to fail.

The simplest explanation for France's current crisis is Jacques Chirac. Chirac has been better at defeating rivals and achieving power than he has been at using that power. Many of his difficulties derive from his failure to fulfill his 1995 campaign pledge to focus on "the forgotten man," he who has been excluded from the benefits of French society. In addition, Chirac has shown a tendency toward risk-taking and impulsiveness that has often backfired. For example, in 1997 he chose to dissolve the National Assembly early without first establishing a persuasive theme for the subsequent campaign. This led to a Socialist victory in the parliamentary elections, forcing Chirac to work with a Socialist Prime Minister, Lionel Jospin, for the next five years. Sticking with Jospin's Gaullist successor, the unpopular Jean-Pierre Raffarin (2002-2005) and holding an unnecessary referendum on the EU constitution were similar blunders. So, too, was Chirac's televised encounter with young people during the referendum campaign, when the elderly president seemed unable to respond to their concerns.

These missteps made it impossible for Chirac to consider running for reelection when his term expired in 2007, turning him into a lame duck. The president is the author of his own misfortunes and bears considerable responsibility for France's general problems. But

Chirac's failures also reflect underlying flaws in France's political and constitutional system.

The fundamental constitutional problem facing France today is the same one that has bedeviled it for 200 years: how to balance the powers of the executive and the legislature. France has lurched between governmental models that grant excessive authority to the executive and those that produce all-powerful parliaments. After the failure of the Fourth Republic helped Charles de Gaulle return to power in 1958, he created a new system (the Fifth Republic) that gave great leeway to the president and stripped the Parliament of most of its independence and power. De Gaulle also established a referendum mechanism that allowed him to renew his mandate with the people directly, further marginalising the legislature.

Ironically, this same referendum procedure has become one of the few ways for the French public to demonstrate its disapproval of the government and the president. Referendums can easily turn into plebiscites, and plebiscites into fiascos. Given this fact, submitting the EU constitution to the public for a popular vote was probably unwise.

Another grave problem in the French political system has been the replacement of a powerful anti-establishment party on the left with an equally powerful party on the extreme right. For over 30 years after World War II, France's Stalinist Communist Party (the Parti Communiste Français, or PCF) exercised a stranglehold over the country's political system. The PCF intimidated and weakened France's non-communist left, forcing it to choose between allying with the centre (and losing its base) or siding with the PCF (and losing its democratic credentials). This impossible choice helped ensure that France was ruled by a solid right-wing majority for many years after 1958.

Only François Mitterrand was able to tame the PCF—using its electoral support to win power in 1981, then keeping it hostage within his government, and finally nudging it into the dustbin of history.

Mitterrand's outmaneuvering of the PCF seemed at first to open the way to a less ideological political system based on a few large centrist parties. With the sidelining of the PCF, however, much of the populist and nationalist left simply switched sides, joining with the unreconstructed extreme right to create the powerful National Front. The National Front, which has been led by Jean-Marie Le Pen since 1972, promised to protect French workers from economic and social change, and to block immigration to their neighbourhoods. In the last 20 years, the party has become a durable, well-organised, and growing force of opposition, despite regular predictions of its imminent demise.

The National Front's rhetoric is fascist, racist, xenophobic, and often anti-Semitic, as well as staunchly anti-EU. Its vocal opposition to Arab and Muslim immigration has made bigotry an acceptable part of France's national dialogue, frightening minorities, tempting the conventional right to consider tactical alliances with it on the local level, and creating a bloc of no voters on any referendum concerning Europe. Le Pen's appeal, moreover, has made him the kingmaker of French politics. In 1997, the National Front threw the parliamentary elections to the Socialists. Then, in 2002, Le Pen came in second in the first round of voting for president, forcing Jospin out of the runoff and thus assuring Chirac's victory.

Since 2002, the Socialist Party has done little to rebuild its strength and unify a divided left. This means that in the next election, the National Front could once again make it to the runoff—beating out either the fragmented left or the fragmented mainstream right. Indeed, current infighting within the latter camp is playing into Le Pen's hands.

Seeds of Discontent

The root of the French public's political discontent is primarily economic, the result above all of chronic unemployment. After World War II, central economic planning and a large state sector helped France achieve 30 years of rapid economic growth. Starting in the 1990s, however, the government began liberalising the economy. State planning was reduced, nationalised industries were privatised, and French firms began to compete well globally. But unemployment has remained at around 10 per cent for two decades. The major cause of this problem has been France's highly restricted labour market, which makes employers reluctant to hire new workers in good times because they cannot be laid off during economic downturns.

To remedy this problem, French governments have tried to share employment by reducing the work-week to 35 hours, encouraging early retirement, and creating temporary public-sector jobs for the young. None of these measures has been effective at reducing long-term unemployment, and some, such as early retirement, have only increased the deficits incurred by the welfare state. Women, minorities and the young have remained particularly vulnerable.

Earlier this year, Prime Minister Dominique de Villepin attempted to address the problem of youth unemployment by creating temporary labour contracts for first-time employees under 25, which would have allowed them to be fired without cause in their first two years on the job. The measure was however unlikely to significantly reduce unemployment and it only enraged France's young people, who want the same kind of job security as their elders. The move was also unpopular with older working adults, who feared that it was the beginning of an effort to chip away at their job protections as well. The result was a month of strikes and protests, which ended when the government repealed the law.

Perhaps the hardest hit by France's unemployment problem are the country's ethnic minorities. Often called "immigrants," many of these people are in fact second-generation French citizens. In many ways, the riots they staged in the fall of 2005 were reminiscent of the inner-city race riots that rocked many major US cities in the 1960s. To be sure, the French riots were far less violent than their US counterparts. Yet in some respects, the situation for ethnic minorities in France today is worse than was the plight of African Americans in the 1960s. After all, American blacks had a mass civil rights movement to advocate on their behalf and gifted leaders such as Martin Luther King, Jr. American blacks were also represented in Congress, local government, and both major political parties. President Lyndon Johnson was sympathetic to their cause and pushed a variety of civil rights and social legislation through Congress that by the end of the century had produced significant results.

In France today, by contrast, the "outsiders" do not even share a collective identity, and they lack political organisation and representation in French politics. During the 1960s, white Americans at least viewed blacks as Americans, whereas in France, most inhabitants of the poor ethnic suburbs, whatever their actual nationality, are seen as foreigners by other French citizens. It does not help that many of France's ethnic poor are also Muslims at a time when Islam inspires fear throughout Europe.

American blacks, moreover, eventually came to benefit from affirmative action, which helped accelerate their transition to the middle class. France's republican creed makes such policies unacceptable to the mainstream. But as the riots showed, neglect (whether benign or not) of France's ethnic poor is no longer possible. Although only long-term policies will produce fundamental change, immediate action is necessary to show that the state is committed to helping them.

Such action, however, does not seem to be forthcoming. In the meantime, France's welfare state remains organised not along egalitarian lines, but in a guild-like fashion. Different professions retain different retirement systems and defend their privileges fiercely. Reform of the labour market and the welfare state is regularly blocked by groups with a stranglehold on the economy, such as railroad and metro unions. France's governments, remembering the near revolution of May 1968, back down from most confrontations with workers—as happened this spring. The result is deadlock.

The failure to reform is also justified by reference to bugbears such as globalisation and what Chirac, out of cynicism or actual belief, has called the ultraliberal current that could lead to an 'Anglo-Saxon and Atlanticist' Europe. No matter that France competes fairly well in a global world or that there is no single 'Anglo-Saxon social model' (the United Kingdom's [UK] is actually closer to the European welfare-state model than it is to the US'). No matter that some smaller European democracies, such as Sweden, are fairly successful in reconciling a vigorous, competitive economy and an open labour market with a higher degree of egalitarianism and social solidarity than exists in France.

Together, these factors have contributed to economic stagnation and festering social problems that are undermining France's influence in Europe. After all, how can Paris lead the EU—a largely economic organisation—when it cannot reduce chronic unemployment at home? France could not even manage to lower its budgetary deficit to three per cent of GDP (gross domestic product), as was required by the rules of the European Monetary Union; to avoid sanction, it had (together with Germany) to rewrite the rules.

Friends and Neighbours

As France's influence in the EU has waned in the last few years—and especially since the EU was enlarged in 2004—French leaders and the French public have begun to question whether the organisation still serves their interests. The French vision of Europe has rested on three principles: an intergovernmentalism that produced the least possible infringement on French sovereignty (especially the powers of its president), French leadership (or, at least, Franco-German leadership on French terms), and a "European Europe" independent of US dominance. Recently, however, all three of these basic principles have created problems.

The inter-governmental model, for example, carries a high cost. Protecting French sovereignty has meant opposing a strong European Parliament and the direct election of European leaders. But this has led to an EU that is technocratic and increasingly opaque to ordinary citizens, who have no voice in its policies. France's efforts, in other words, have helped create an EU that is hard to love, easy to fear, and can be voted down without much regret—as happened in last year's referendum.

Meanwhile, French influence over the EU has also started to slip. Until recently, Franco-German leadership of the EU went largely unchallenged, as had Franco-German leadership of its forerunners. When France and Germany worked together, they were usually able to create consensus; when they opposed an initiative, it failed. For years, there was no real alternative to their stewardship. The UK did not join the EU (then the European Community) until 1973, and it remained an outsider long after that because of its ambivalence toward European integration and unattractiveness of the British socio-economic model.

More recently, however, the situation has changed radically. Thanks to EU enlargement and the divisive war in Iraq, the Union now has several midsize members, such as Poland and Spain, that are unwilling to simply follow the Franco-German lead—especially since France and Germany appear more concerned these days with protecting their own interests than with protecting those of the EU as a whole. Meanwhile, London has become a more engaged EU player, and the UK now represents a more successful socioeconomic model than does either France or Germany. No wonder many in France feel they have lost their grip over the EU. Anxiety over that loss was reflected in the defeat of the constitutional referendum. Unfortunately, the vote only further weakened France's influence over the Union—something likely to worsen its anxiety in the future.

France's third principle—resisting US influence—has been a feature of French foreign policy for years. During the Cold War, France resented what it perceived as US hegemony in Europe; when the Cold War ended, Paris resented Washington's sole-superpower status even more. At the same time, France had usually stuck with the US (at least in its own fashion) when it mattered most—whether during the Cuban missile crisis or the Persian Gulf War.

This pattern changed in 2003; Iraq became a turning point in 50 years of French-US relations. In response to what was arguably the most unilateral act by a post-World War II US government (and one of its worst strategic judgment calls), Paris, while declaring the virtues of "multipolarity," followed Berlin's lead into confrontation with Washington. This made all the difference at the United Nations (UN); without French support in the Security Council, neither Russia nor China (to say nothing of the smaller states) would likely have taken on the US. With France at their side, they were emboldened, and together they dealt the US a stinging blow.

Tactically, France's UN diplomacy led to a brilliant victory: the humiliation of the US in the Security Council. Strategically, it was another of Chirac's blunders. France hardly managed to balance the US: Washington simply went to war without it. In the meantime,

France's action managed to disrupt both transatlantic relations: Washington rightly construed French advocacy of multipolarity as an attack on US power, and the EU, with little advantage for Paris or any of the other parties concerned.

Lost Leader?

Despite French voters' rejection of the EU constitution, France remains important to the Union. Paris has, however, lost its ability to lead the EU. This is bad not just for France, but for Europe as well, for the EU cannot hope to make any real progress in areas such as institutional reform and the forging of a common foreign and defense policy without France. Still, if France is ever to resume its leadership of the union, it needs to rethink its identity, its goals, and its strategies. Above all, it needs to overcome the paralysing fear of change—change that, if properly undertaken, would be salutary. Following World War II, France tried to solve Europe's problems by solving its own. The same needs to be done today.

This will require nothing less than a paradigm shift in the thinking of French elites and the French population at large. The French must accept the fact that the days of national and even regional economies are over. Globalisation presents opportunities, not just risks. To exploit them, France must make good use of its increasingly dynamic economy and strong scientific and educational base.

To improve its economic odds, France must restore the centrality of work as an instrument of empowerment and fulfillment. A freer labour market would help reduce unemployment and be more inclusive of minorities, women, and the poor. Promoting growth might mean accepting a little more insecurity, but French workers should remember that in a dynamic economy, they will be more likely to find new jobs if they lose the ones they have. Paris must place social benefits, such as pensions, retirement, and health care, within a national framework, one that is egalitarian and realistic. While other social democracies are raising the retirement age to above 65, France cannot continue to allow members of certain privileged groups (such as transport workers) to retire at 55 or 60. Rather than holding fast to a dysfunctional model and projecting its fears onto the outside world, Paris should encourage greater curiosity about the way other advanced societies (including France's neighbours) deal with labour and welfare-state reform.

By focusing more on economic growth and less on the defense of the French social model, the French government could help reduce its citizens' fear of immigrants, from both within the EU (the infamous "Polish plumbers," for example) and without. Historically, France has always benefitted from its immigrants, even if it has always resented them. To address matters today, France must start working harder to assimilate its non-European-born citizens. Last year's riots must be taken seriously. Paris should not merely improve services and opportunities in the *banlieues*; it must do away with de facto segregation. The best way to prevent French Muslims from developing a separate identity and turning to radical Islam would be to offer them decent employment and a shot at social mobility. Affirmative action in the US—even though it runs counter to US values—has resulted in social mobility for a vast portion of black Americans. Something similar should be considered in France, as should efforts aimed at facilitating real involvement of minorities in political life.

Such policies, along with a strong educational effort, might also reduce the appeal of the National Front. Eradicating it will not be easy—France has a long history of extreme right-wing parties—but doing so is crucial. The National Front only prospers when France's mainstream politics are defensive and limit genuine debate. The current balance between executive and legislative powers is tilted too far toward the former. When the public cannot effectively channel popular discontent and opposition through Parliament, it takes to the street. Contrary to conventional wisdom, moreover, French presidents are as much the victim of the current system as is the legislature, since they bear excessive responsibility for what does or does not get accomplished. At the very minimum, France should return to a system in which cabinet ministers are members of Parliament, and Parliament must be allowed to have stronger committees and greater budgetary powers. These changes can and should be made within the existing system; it is not necessary to invent a new one.

A less defensive France would be more effective as an EU leader. France will have to find ways to make the EU more transparent and more attractive to the citizens of Europe. This can no longer be done through inter-governmentalism, which means, in practice, technocracy and a democratic deficit. The current, incremental approach to EU reform—with successive inter-governmental conferences where member states tinker with the mechanisms of government—will not thrive now that the EU has 25 members. France must be prepared to abandon more of its sovereignty if the EU is to fulfill France's grander ambitions for Europe.

Finally, Paris must redefine the place of France and Europe in the world—and their relationship with the US. It should be apparent that the kind of intra-European split that occurred over the Iraq war cannot be repeated. France, Germany and the UK must make a genuine effort to bring their foreign policies closer into line. Perhaps Germany under Chancellor Angela Merkel will be more open to global engagement. Even so, it will remain for London and Paris to resolve the key issue that has long divided them: how to deal with Washington.

Relations with the US should be seen not as an end of strategy but as a means. Of course, this begs the question, a means to what? In order to answer it, French leaders must think long and hard about how they want the world to look in the future. Mobilising Europe around its own strategic vision, rather than obsessing over the US, should form the basis of a new European foreign policy that France might still be able to lead.

6

DIETER M. DETTKE

Germany: From the Ashes of War to the Centre of Power in Europe

Introduction

Germany arrived late as a nation in the concert of European powers and its path to nationhood was markedly different from its West European neighbours (Plessner, 1959). The Holy Roman Empire of the German Nation nominally lasted from 800 to 1806, a long time by any standard, but in the words of the French philosopher Voltaire was neither holy, nor Roman, nor an empire. It consisted of some 300 kingdoms, principalities, duchies and free cities. Even after its demise during the Napoleonic wars in 1806, there was no German state or nation to speak of replacing the old empire. What followed after the Holy Roman Empire was the German Confederation (Der Deutsche Bund) which emerged from the Congress of Vienna in 1815. Instead of the 300 entities of the Holy Roman Empire, the 'German Bund' consisted of some 40 kingdoms, principalities, duchies and free cities dominated by two great powers, Austria and Prussia. Whereas in Western Europe, in particular in Great Britain, the 17th and 18th centuries saw the beginning of a course of democratisation, Germany continued to struggle with the demise of the Holy Roman Empire. Defeated by Napoleon's armies, Germany began its *Sonderweg* (special path) as a nation without embarking on a course of democratic development. Bismarck achieved the unity of Germany and the establishment of the first German nation state not as the result of democratic developments, but by military victories over Austria and France. "For centuries"—Christopher Clark eloquently stated—"the German centre of Europe had been fragmented and weak; now it was united and strong" (Clark, 2012: 124).

Since 1871, the 'German question' was not unity or democratisation but the potential upheaval of the balance of power in Europe. "Too strong for Europe and too weak for the world"—in the words of Henry Kissinger—Germany's new role as the central power of Europe ultimately contributed to the breakdown of the balance of power system that Metternich and Castlereagh, the two great statesmen of the Congress of Vienna, had so carefully constructed. Although Bismarck was able to secure the role of an 'honest broker' for Germany within a delicate balance of power, his less able successors turned out to be incapable of keeping such a vulnerable system stable. In the summer of 1914, as a result of the murder of the Austrian heir to the throne in Sarajevo, Europe was at war again. In its aftermath, three empires collapsed—the Ottoman Empire, the Austrian-Hungarian Empire and the German Empire. The political and economic consequences were dramatic. Twenty million people, military and civilian, died and a decade later, Europe succumbed to the Great Depression with millions of people unemployed and prone to extremism. There is little doubt that harsh conditions of the Treaty of Versailles hugely contributed to the failure of Germany's first true democracy, the Weimar Republic. The loss of 13 per cent of its territory in Europe and one-tenth of its population in Germany, debilitating reparations as well as placing 'the sole responsibility' (*Alleinschuld*) for the war on the German Empire turned out to be a heavy burden for the new German democracy. True, the Weimar Republic also suffered from a number of internal weaknesses. For example, a constitution that allowed its own destruction from within and the persistence of past authoritarian thinking and too much tolerance for the enemies of democracy. In fact, the short lived Weimar Republic allowed a trajectory of German politics that not only tolerated but, because of the weakness of the democratic centre, encouraged extremism on the left and on the right side of the political spectrum. In fact, all European societies—not only Germany —after the World War I (WWI) became infected with left and right wing extremism leading to the "Age of the Extremes"[1] and the deadly confrontation between Fascism and Communism.

The rivalry between these two totalitarian ideologies dominated the first half of the 20th century only to end up in an even deadlier catastrophe than WWI. The Second World War (WWII) was indeed Germany's responsibility alone and as a result, 55 million people died, 25 million civilians among them. In the Holocaust Hitler's executioners murdered more than 6 million Jews. Among the victims of WWII were also 4 million German soldiers and 3.8 million civilians. The sheer destruction and the loss of life was particularly devastating for Eastern Europe and the Soviet Union. As the historian Timothy Snyder (2010) has shown, between 1933 and 1945, the mass killings of both the totalitarian Hitler and Stalin regimes together led to the death of an estimated 14 million non-combatants in a region that comprised what is now Russia, Poland, Ukraine, Belarus and the Baltic States. The Hitler regime alone was responsible for more than twice as many victims of mass killing than Stalin's Soviet Communism. The destruction of Europe as well as the genocide of Europe's Jews perpetrated in the name of Germany will always remain a heavy burden for the German people.

Strategic Priorities of the Divided Germany: Economic Reform and Recovery

Physically and morally defeated after WWII, Germany had to seek a new beginning as a nation and as a society and it had to find its way back into the family of nations as a divided country. Until 5 May 1955, Germany was legally an occupied country. The Four Powers that won WWII took over sovereignty, each one in its respective occupation zone on German territory as well as in Berlin. The three Western powers coordinated their policy in all matters 'German', early on focusing on the political, economic and social reconstruction of the country. In the East, instead of cooperating with the Western powers on the basis of the occupation regime, Stalin created facts on the ground that made the East-West division of Germany as well

1. The title of an important book on the history of the 20th century by Hobsbawm (1994).

as of Berlin inevitable. Given the geographically vulnerable position of Berlin as an island surrounded by East German territory under Soviet control, the Soviet Union by 1948 took serious steps trying to take over the entire Berlin area by blocking land access to Berlin. This violation of the terms of occupation regime amounted to a land grab and in order to preserve the Western rights over Berlin, the US began the most massive airlift in history in support of the people of Berlin. Ultimately, the US airlift faced down the Soviet Union and the territorial status quo in Berlin was restored. In the rest of the Soviet controlled areas of Eastern Europe, however, Soviet style communist regimes were installed. There was little the West could do because of the concession to Stalin at the Potsdam Conference that in the states bordering the Soviet Union 'friendly regimes' should be installed. The Baltic States were already annexed by the Soviet Union as a result of the Hitler-Stalin Pact. Poland, Czechoslovakia, Hungary, Bulgaria and Romania later became member states of the Warsaw Pact. With the exception of Yugoslavia's own model of communism, Stalin imposed his Soviet style system de facto as far as Soviet troops reached into the lands west of the original borders of the Soviet Union, including East Germany. Only Yugoslavia was able to preserve a high degree of independence and even played an important role in the movement of non-aligned countries.

Mindful of the catastrophic consequences of the Versailles Treaty after WWI, the Allied leaders in Yalta and Potsdam decided not to burden Germany with the exclusive responsibility for war reparations. They put the issue of reparations into the hands of each individual power in the four occupation zones. France, although defeated by Hitler's armies, was invited to join the three allied powers in the post-war governing of Germany. The Potsdam Conference addressed the immediate post-war needs in the defeated Germany, but it left the most important question unresolved: a peace treaty with Germany. Rather the decision was made that the Commanders-in-Chief of the Four Powers (the US, the UK, the USSR and the French Republic) would exercise supreme authority each in his own zone of occupation, and as a whole and jointly in their capacity as members of the Control Council. The purpose of occupation was the complete disarmament and demilitarisation of Germany as well as control of all German industry that could be used for military production, the destruction of the Nazi regime, re-education of Germans for the purpose of the development of democratic ideas, reorganisation of the judicial system and decentralisation of local self-government. But for the time being, no central German government was to be allowed. Finally and most importantly, the Potsdam Conference declared that the occupation of Germany should prepare for the eventual reconstruction of German political life on a democratic basis and for eventual peaceful cooperation in international life by Germany.

The Cold War began to cast its long shadow over Europe early on. Churchill eloquently described this development in his speech in Fulton, Missouri on 5 March 1946. Introduced by President Truman, Churchill declared "From Stettin in the Baltic to Trieste in the Adriatic, an iron curtain has descended across the Continent" and with regard to developments in Germany, he was well aware of the fact that the Soviet Union was about to build up a pro-Communist Germany in its area of responsibility. Thus with the onset of the Cold War, the partition of Germany became a fact of life and West Germany had to focus on the economic reconstruction of its part of the country and did so with fundamental reforms and establishing a true market economy. The US, Great Britain and France closely coordinated actions and policies in their occupation zones leading to the founding of the Federal Republic of Germany in 1949. In Eastern Germany, developments on the ground ushered in the founding of German Democratic Republic (GDR) as a state modelled after Stalin's Soviet communist system later in 1949.

Weakened in WWII and in view of the Soviet actions in Eastern Europe, Germany's West European neighbours felt that they needed the US for their protection against a possible new threat from Germany as well as against a Soviet Union seeking influence beyond the boundaries established at Yalta and Potsdam. Efforts to build new European alliances such as the Franco-British Treaty of Dunkirk in March 1947 turned out to be insufficient in view of the new post-WWII power constellation. The treaty saw the main threat in a resurgent Germany and tried to provide the instruments of containment should this occur. A year later, the Brussels Treaty included the Benelux countries in addition to France and Great Britain. But in the meantime, the Communist threat became more imminent for Europe and there was now not only a need to contain Germany but also the Soviet Union. In essence, Europe practiced a 'dual containment' strategy. Strong communist parties in Western Europe, in particular in France, Italy and Greece, opened new non-traditional ways of projecting Soviet power.

As early as the beginning of 1946, it became obvious that in the coming conflict constellation between the Soviet Union and the Western allies, West Germany needed to be part of the West. The Soviet threat appeared to be as dangerous—if not even more dangerous—than a resurgent Germany. In other words, Europe needed help and this could only come from the US. British and French pressure on the US prompted the latter to act. In view of critical domestic developments in particular in Greece and Soviet pressure on Turkey, President Truman decided to act. In a speech to a Joint Session of Congress on 12 March 1947, he declared that "it must be the policy of the United States to support free people who are resisting attempted subjugation by armed minorities or by outside pressures." Inspired by George Kennan, the Truman Doctrine became the official American strategy throughout the Cold War in Europe and worldwide. Together with the Marshall Plan, officially named 'European Recovery Programme', the Truman Doctrine defined the American post WWII foreign and defense policy.

West Germany benefitted from America's assistance economically as well as politically. The Marshall Plan paved the way for Germany to join its West European neighbours in the common effort of rebuilding the European economy and to begin a process of reconciliation. Only a year after the Truman Doctrine and as a result of much European pressure, the US Congress ratified the North Atlantic Treaty including its Article V that guarantees "that an armed attack against one or more of them in Europe or North America shall be considered an attack against them all." The parties to the treaty promised to assist each other, including the use of force in case of an attack.

By April 1950, the US had established its post-WWII strategy in full and spelled it out in National Security Council Report No. 68 (NSC 68) as a three-pronged approach of political, military and economic tools combating Soviet expansionism. NSC 68 became the central US Cold War document. West Germany, in spite of the division, benefitted from the Cold War insofar as it allowed a quick economic recovery. Fuelled by a currency reform and the principles of a social market economy, the country was able to overcome its wartime devastation and produce what became known as the German 'economic miracle'. The Cold War demand for steel, machinery, tools and manufactured goods, an area where the German economy was able to excel, grew rapidly, in particular after beginning of the Korean War. With help of the Marshall Plan, the country embarked on a massive modernisation programme that was also necessary because of the wartime destruction. New and state-of-the-art equipment and machinery contributed to Germany's regaining of economic strength.

Political Priorities in the Context of the Cold War: European Integration and Western Institutions

Most importantly, European integration paved the way for Germany to join the family of European nations on an equal footing. The Marshall Plan came with few strings attached. One important condition for US help was that under the European Recovery Programme, European countries were required to work together and develop a common European economic recovery programme. Thus the Marshall Plan indirectly helped to launch European integration, first in the Organization for European Economic Cooperation (OEEC) and later under Europe's own integration initiatives. The first of these initiatives was the European Coal and Steel Community (ECSC), with Germany as an equal partner. Launched with the Schuman Plan on 9 May 1950, the Treaty of Paris established the ECSC in July 1951. Germany was no longer isolated. The ECSC empowered Germany to take part in and share responsibility for key economic decisions. For a country that still suffered from its wartime wounds, the new equality that Germany was able to enjoy on the European level in spite of division and occupation, was a welcome gesture and an opportunity to engage in a new kind of decision-making. Multilateralism became a key foreign policy concept for West Germany. Its neighbours even promised to support Germany in its national goal of unification.

For a brief moment, however, the question of how to preserve the option of national unification, at least temporarily, interfered with the new promise of European integration. Just when the ECSC was in the process of being ratified in each member state, Stalin approached the US, Great Britain and France with his German unification initiative and Germany had to make a choice: Follow the siren song from Moscow or invest in Germany's European and Western future. In spite of considerable support for an exploration of the Stalin offer, the decision was loud and clear: In the interest of Germany's security, Western integration had to come first.

Membership in the ECSC was crucial for Germany because it was an important step forward in a process of reconciliation between Germany and its West European neighbours: France, Italy and the three Benelux countries (Belgium, the Netherlands and Luxembourg). Supranational cooperation in the European coal and steel industry, the classical war industries of the past, made war in Europe not only less likely, but made it rather impossible for these countries to go to war against each other. Thanks in particular to far-sighted French politicians like Robert Schuman and Jean Monnet, France and Germany, after centuries of rivalry and war, were now in a position to put conflict and enmity aside and begin to see their common future in a united Europe. The Schuman Plan of 9 May 1950 even opened prospects for a European Defense Community initiated by the French Prime Minister Rene Pleven in October of the same year. But this ambitious project officially launched in 1952 failed two years later in the French Parliament. Consumed in a bloody war over French colonies in Indochina, the French Parliament, as well as the French public in general, was not yet ready to share sovereignty with Germany in the delicate issue of defence.

As understandable as French reservations and concerns over a German rearmament were at the time—and rearmament would have been the inevitable consequence of the European Defense Community, the establishment of regimes in Eastern Europe modelled after the Soviet Union—if necessary by force—and de facto under Soviet control made it unavoidable to include the West German territory and the German economic potential in the efforts to contain Soviet expansion. The beginning of the war in Korea provided the ultimate push towards rebuilding German armed forces. The German government had undertaken first steps under the leadership of Konrad Adenauer in October 1950 by creating the so-called 'Amt Blank', an informal institution to look into future security needs of the Federal Republic of Germany. Adenauer indicated already on 3 December 1949, just months after the founding of the Federal Republic of Germany, that West Germany should seriously consider the creation of armed forces in the context of a European army and with a German contingent under European command in order to be able to contribute to the security and defense of the West.[2] When the Korean War began in June 1950, the question of a German rearmament was no longer 'whether' but 'when'. The assumption was that this would happen in the framework of a European Army, but that was impossible at the time. It still remains the most difficult aspect of European integration even today.

Instead, German re-armament took place within the framework of North Atlantic Treaty Organization (NATO) and a reformed Western European Union (WEU) and at the same time, the Federal Republic of Germany was recognised as a sovereign country, limited only with regard to allied powers over Berlin and the final status of Germany as well as a possible peace treaty including Germany's final borders. The West German evolution to a sovereign power became evident long before 1955. The 1952 General Treaty between the Western Powers and West Germany (Deutschland Vertrag in German) considered the Federal Republic of Germany already as a sovereign country. But being tied to the ratification of the European Defense Community, the General Treaty could not enter into force before 1955 because the French Parliament refused to ratify the Treaty on the establishment of a European Defense Community.

---

2. See the famous interview that Adenauer gave to the Cleveland Plain Dealer on 3 December 1949; Cleveland Plain Dealer, 14 December 1949.

But on an economic level, European integration turned out to be extremely successful. Once the Treaty of Rome launched the European Economic Community (EEC) in 1957 with common tariffs and institutionalised economic cooperation, integration quickly spilled over into politics transforming the European project into a larger political undertaking. Not only did the original six founding member states of the EEC (France, Germany, Italy, Belgium, Luxembourg and the Netherlands) move closer together and coordinate decision-making, their neighbours in the North and South of Europe, too, began to feel the magnetism of the new community in the centre of Europe. Enlargement was clearly in the German interest. Once Great Britain took the decisive step to join the EEC, enlargement became unstoppable. By the early 1970s, the EEC grew from 6 to 9 when, together with Great Britain, Ireland and Denmark became members. A decade later Southern enlargement was on the EEC agenda and Spain, Portugal and Greece joined the EEC. By 1990, the EEC had morphed into a full-fledged economic, social and political community. The European Community was born and, today, it is known as the European Union (EU) with 28 member states and still growing. The deepening and widening of the European project is arguably one of the most impressive peace building efforts ever, a civilisational experiment without precedent in human history. Together with the NATO, European integration created the safest and most productive political, economic and military environment for Germany in its entire history.

National Security Strategy during the Cold War: Western Integration Before Unification

No wonder then that Germany's belonging to the West had to put the goal of unification on the backburner. Security had to come first and that required Western unity against the perceived Soviet threat. West Germany's economic success story added to the assumption that the West German model of democracy and its economic achievements would not fail to become a magnetic force pulling East Germany—and perhaps even Eastern Europe—into the orbit of the West. Earlier strategic considerations included a 'roll-back' strategy of NATO and adding additional political pressure on the Soviet Union. Nuclear parity between the US and the Soviet Union made it impossible to implement such a strategy. The potential costs in case of war were simply too high. So Germany had to learn to live with partition and hoping that its political and economic model would prevail in the competition between East and West.

To be sure, more than 40 years of partition will always leave their mark on German life. The division of Germany was quite a painful experience. For the Federal Republic of Germany—also known as West Germany—partition meant first of all that there was another German state claiming to represent Germany, although, from West Germany's perspective, this second German state was an artificial creation of the Soviet Union and not a legitimate state. For West Germany, even on the basis of the results of the Potsdam Conference which left the final decision about the status and the borders of Germany open and to be resolved by a peace treaty, unity was the only legitimate constellation. On that basis, the preamble of the Basic Law, the constitution of the Federal Republic of Germany, adopted on 23 May 1949, declared that the West German states (Laender) as the authors of the Basic Law, "also acted on behalf of those Germans to whom participation was denied. The entire German people is called on to achieve by free self-determination the unity and freedom of Germany." The Federal Republic of Germany claimed to be the only legitimate German state (*Alleinvertretungsanspruch*) and tried to bolster this claim on the basis of the so-called Hallstein doctrine. Central tenet of the Hallstein doctrine was to prevent other countries, in particular West Germany's friends and allies, to officially recognise the GDR as a second German state in the international arena. Thus the most important foreign policy objective of West Germany after WWII was the restoration of German unity in a free and united Europe.

The Cold War confrontation between East and West made such a development impossible. At the time, the Soviet Union was first of all interested in keeping the territory of its East German zone of occupation within the borders of the Soviet Empire or, as an alternative, in preserving a good measure of influence over a neutral united Germany. Until 1989 and Gorbachev's peaceful revolution, only a Communist united Germany—or at a minimum a neutral united Germany—would have been acceptable for the Soviet Union. For Stalin and also for Soviet leaders after his death in March 1953, official recognition of the GDR as a state came first and unification only as a neutral Germany as a result of negotiations that would include the GDR. Even today, historians are still debating whether the 1952 Stalin notes should be considered as a serious Soviet offer to allow German unification. In particular writers and intellectuals who were willing to live with a neutral Germany and not as a member of the Western alliance and European integration, supported such a view. The more Soviet behaviour in Eastern Europe created the conditions for an exclusive zone of influence casting aside allied cooperation in the formation of a post-WWII order, the more it became obvious that the Western powers would need Germany on their side and ultimately also a German military contribution. The objective of the Soviet Union at the time was primarily to prevent the rearmament of Germany and its integration into European and Western institutions. The same is true for later proposals of a European Security Conference which put official recognition of the GDR as a state by the Federal Republic of Germany first. The Federal Republic of Germany, however, was not willing to allow negotiations on that basis; the partition of Germany continued throughout the Cold War and only mitigated in the 1960s and 1970s through the process of Détente between East and West.

Partition for the GDR firstly meant the deepening of Soviet control within the Soviet zone of occupation. To be sure, the Soviet Union following the example of the Western powers created its own 'German State'. But instead of allowing free elections on the basis of a multiple party system, political parties in East Germany were forced to operate in a pre-arranged block system with an in-built system of control of the official Communist Party, which took its orders ultimately from the military leadership in the Soviet zone of occupation, that is to say in reality from Moscow. Officially named the Socialist Unity Party (SED), the party was the result of a forced integration against the will of the larger Social Democratic Party

(SPD) of West Germany, which is the only legitimate successor of the oldest political party in Germany. As voters only had a chance to vote for a pre-arranged list in which the domination of the SED was predetermined, elections in East Germany in spite of the name 'German Democratic Republic' had nothing to do with democracy. The 99 per cent election results for the list dominated by the SED only confirmed the inherently undemocratic system of the GDR. On the basis of truly democratic elections, the GDR regime would not have had the slightest chance to survive in power. Large Soviet military forces were necessary in order to keep the GDR within the Soviet camp. More than 300,000 Soviet troops and over 200,000 dependents remained stationed in East Germany until 1989. Plus the GDR needed armed forces of its own to protect its borders not only against outside pressure, but also against the real danger of attempts of its own population to flee rather than to endure the lack of freedom inside the GDR.

During the entire Cold War, the two German states confronted each other on almost every level. The GDR was the weaker part of the two German states. A crucial factor was the economic success story of the Federal Republic of Germany after the War. Whereas West Germany was able to thrive not the least as a result of the Marshall Plan, East Germans suffered from a total lack of freedom under the Soviet occupation regime. Immediately after the war, the Soviet Union proceeded to implement its own reparation programme and dismantled almost the entire infrastructure of East Germany, including factories, industrial facilities as well as transportation systems. The entire railway system in East Germany was dismantled and rails taken up and transported back to the Soviet Union where they were used in the Soviet steel industry. East Germany was literally plundered and had to go through extremely difficult times getting back to a more normal life. The result of the disastrous Soviet occupation was mass emigration primarily to West Germany but also to other Western countries.

Between 1949 and 1989, 3.8 million people left the GDR. In June 1953, East German workers revolted against the dismal economic and social conditions in the GDR. Their uprising was brutally put down by

Soviet tanks and military personnel on 17 June 1953. West Germany tried to honour the victims of the brutal crushing of the uprising by making 17 June 1953 an official Memorial Day in West Germany. The Soviet response to the uprising led to a huge wave of emigration, and on 13 August 1961, the government of the GDR with the help and support of the Soviet Union erected the Berlin Wall in order to stop a development that—if unaddressed—would have led to a collapse of the GDR. The Wall divided the city of Berlin so that East Germans could no longer flee to the West through the open borders. But besides that, West Germans were also no longer allowed to visit friends and relatives in the Eastern part of Berlin and the GDR. Executed by East German security and border control forces against the rules of the occupation regime, the border control was total and ran along the entire border between East and West Germany, from the Baltic Sea in the north to Bavaria and Czechoslovakia in the South, altogether more than a thousand kilometres. Churchill's figurative iron curtain came down in the form of barbed wire and concrete.

In October of 1961, the Cuban Missile Crisis began. East-West relations reached their peak in the most dramatic confrontation so far. Nuclear war suddenly became a realistic scenario. Tensions were already high in 1953 during the uprising in East Berlin and the GDR. They reached new heights when the anti-Soviet uprising in Budapest in 1956 led to calls for Western help against the use of tanks and brutal Soviet military force against civilian Hungarian demonstrators asking for freedom and self-determination. During the Berlin Crisis in connection with the construction of the Wall, Soviet and American tanks drove up to the dividing line and took a threatening position. But since these events—as brutal as the Soviet military crushing of the uprising was—took place within Soviet controlled territory, Western intervention was difficult to contemplate and justify. President Kennedy preferred acceptance of the Wall over risking a war under the conditions of nuclear deterrence. The commitment to preserve the territorial status quo was again confirmed in 1968 when Soviet forces on the basis of the Breshnev Doctrine crushed the Prague Spring and used massive military force to keep Czechoslovakia in the Warsaw Pact. New literature now tries to show that at the time of the Berlin crisis, Western resistance and firmness against the construction of the Berlin Wall—the kind of firmness President Kennedy later demonstrated during the Cuban Missile Crisis—might have succeeded in preventing Soviet leader Khrushchev and GDR leader Walter Ulbricht from building the Berlin Wall and effectively closing the border with the West (Kempe, 2011). After all, the Soviet Union at the time was hardly in a position to withstand Western military capabilities, once they were fully deployed.

Cold War Foreign Policy Priorities: *Ostpolitik* and Détente

The Berlin Wall and the Cuban Missile Crisis brought political leaders in East and West to the realisation that deterrence could fail. War was a realistic possibility and that perception led to enhanced military and strategic planning as well as weapons modernisation programmes on the one hand, and the need to improve communication between the two hostile camps, on the other. Looking into the abyss of a nuclear catastrophe over the Cuban Missile Crisis prompted leaders to think harder about ways to overcome the East-West confrontation as such a situation could have brought about a nuclear war. Particularly in West Germany, a younger generation of political leaders developed ideas how to overcome the political and military standoff between East and West. The fact that West Germany was home of the world's largest concentration and troops, and weapon systems also contributed to launch arms control initiatives. Germans knew best that East-West cooperation was necessary in order to prevent a deepening of the existing partition. Millions of East and West Germans were directly affected by the hardening conditions of living in a divided country. It was only natural that German leaders would try to overcome the harshness of partition. Millions of families were separated with one part of the family living under dismal economic and political conditions east of the Wall and the other in the more prosperous West.

Critical thinking about ways to improve the situation between East and West first started in Berlin where the wall became the most powerful symbol of harshness of the division. It was the governing Mayor of the city of Berlin and future Chancellor of the Federal

Republic of Germany, Willy Brandt who initiated what later became known as the 'policy of little steps', meaning the initiation of family visits between citizens of West Berlin and their relatives in East Berlin. At the beginning, with an one dimensional process of allowing West Germans to visit East Berlin—not the other way around and on a mutual basis—the policy of little steps grew quickly into a much larger programme of family visits between West and East Germany, not the least because East Germany found lucrative ways to manage the visitor programme for West Germans. *Ostpolitik* started in Berlin with the realisation that in order to improve the situation of ordinary citizens in the GDR, communication and direct talks with the East German government were necessary.

'Change through rapprochement' became the German strategy of overcoming East-West tensions. Every official contact with the East, however, also meant a certain degree of recognition of East Germany and that West Germany wanted to avoid recognition in the interest of holding up the prospect of unification. Critics of *Ostpolitik* were quick to point out that official contacts with East Germany would lead to a deepening of the German partition. A year after the Berlin Wall was constructed, the Cuban Missile Crisis began and it was obvious from the beginning that the two pressure points—West Berlin surrounded by East Germany and vulnerable to Soviet military forces and Cuba, threatening the US even with sub-strategic Soviet nuclear missiles—were intrinsically related with the Soviet Union apparently in a dominating position. Without the firmness of President Kennedy in the Cuban Missile Crisis, the Soviet Union at the time might well have sought a victory against the West. But Soviet leader Krushchev overplayed his hand and had to backdown when faced with Kennedy's determination to stand his ground.

In the Berlin crisis, the crucial issue was the preservation of territorial status quo in Europe against Soviet pressure to change the post-WWII East-West arrangements. The more than three million people in West Berlin could have been Cold War victims. In the Cuban Missile Crisis, the nuclear status quo between the two super powers was at stake. Soviet missiles in Cuba could have exposed the US to blackmail. The result of the two parallel crises was Détente, in substance the recognition in the East as well as in the West that in the interest of peace, the territorial as well as the nuclear status quo needed to be respected. The key components of Détente were German *Ostpolitik* and Strategic Nuclear Arms Talks (SALT) between the Soviet Union and the US. On the German side, this included the acceptance of the GDR as a second German state in the international arena, most visibly expressed in the fact that the GDR was then onwards a member state of the United Nations (UN). The Federal Republic of Germany gave up the exclusive right to represent Germany and the GDR proceeded to establish diplomatic relations everywhere, including in West Germany's NATO and among European allies. Between the two German states, however, a special relationship prevailed insofar as the Federal Republic of Germany would not accept that the two German states would be foreign countries in their relations with each other. The distant goal of a united Germany in the future was thus preserved.

The process of Détente culminated in 1972 with comprehensive nuclear agreements between the US and the Soviet Union on the one hand, a Berlin Agreement, a Soviet-German Treaty on renunciation of the use of force and recognition of the territorial status quo in Europe on the other, including a German-Polish Treaty based on the existing territorial borders. Multilateral arrangements between East and West in Europe followed and in 1975, the Helsinki Final Act, for all practical purposes, amounted to an ersatz peace treaty in Europe. In principle, the Helsinki agreements were based on the territorial arrangements negotiated between US President Roosevelt, British Prime Minister Churchill and Soviet Leader Stalin at the Yalta Conference, mitigated only by new instruments of reducing military tensions between East and West and a careful lifting of the Iron Curtain so that people could benefit from greater openness between East and West in their daily lives. Economic cooperation greatly increased between East and West as a result of Détente. Old cultural ties in Europe could be renewed and military tensions were dramatically reduced through confidence-building measures and more transparency in general.

But Detente remained a fragile process way until the mid-1980s when Mikhail Gorbachev come to power in the Soviet Union and initiating a revolutionary process under the motto of *glasnost* and *perestroika*. Already shortly after the Helsinki Final Act and in spite of the strong symbolism of cooperation between East and West on the basis of the territorial status quo in Berlin and Germany as well as the SALT Agreements between the Soviet Union and the US, the Soviet Union invaded Afghanistan on Christmas Day 1979. Détente came to a standstill on the level of the two superpowers. After the 1980 presidential elections in the US, the new government under President Reagan increased pressure on the Soviet Union substantially. Calling the other superpower an 'empire of evil' and increasing military expenditures dramatically, the Reagan Administration even appeared to threaten the Soviet Union's military survival by creating a Strategic Defense Initiative (SDI) and replacing a military strategy of avoiding nuclear war with a more aggressive strategy anticipating military conflict with the Soviet Union, including a nuclear exchange.

Already during the Carter Administration, the US nuclear arms control took a backseat to necessary nuclear arms modernisation designed to counter Soviet nuclear forces specifically aimed at Europe. In particular, Soviet SS-20 nuclear equipped medium range nuclear missiles could reach every single European country and beyond, while at the same time sparing American territory with the exception of Alaska. Germany became the centre of the new Cold War tensions between the Soviet Union and the US as a potential host country for US intermediate range nuclear weapons countering Soviet SS-20 missiles. On the one hand, the 1979 dual track decision of NATO to counter the Soviet nuclear threat either through arms control or nuclear modernisation lifted Germany together with the two European nuclear powers, France and Great Britain, into the top echelon of NATO and Western political decision-making. German participation in any possible Western military strategy to counter the Soviet intimidation strategy of nuclear intimidation was crucial. Together with the US, Great Britain and France, Germany became a crucial partner in an informal NATO directorate, which was visibly demonstrated in the Guadeloupe Summit Meeting of 1979 between the leaders of the US, Great Britain, France and Germany. It was at the Guadeloupe Summit where the Western leaders formulated a response to the Soviet SS-20 threat.

In essence, the Guadeloupe decision of countering the Soviet SS-20 threat with US nuclear forces stationed on German territory, in particular a land-based Pershing II nuclear missile with the capability of reaching Soviet territory, caused profound concern for many Germans about their survival in case of a war in Europe; and this perception was shared in the GDR creating a new kind of German-German commonality of nuclear fear. The Soviet Union skillfully used this phenomenon for its propaganda against the Western nuclear response to the SS-20 threat. The German security dilemma gave birth to a powerful peace movement, visible in huge anti-nuclear and anti-war demonstrations. Faced with the fundamental security dilemma of keeping the option of unification open while at the same time resisting Soviet nuclear pressure, Germany correctly opted for security within the Western alliance. The choice was not easy. Those who put unification first had good reasons to believe that then on, unification would become a more distant goal than ever. It turned out that the opposite was true. The Soviet Union changed course and moved away from nuclear intimidation.

Unification: The Strategic Benefits of Patience

German unification came as a serendipity. It was totally unexpected and most likely would not have been possible without the profound changes that Soviet leader Mikhail Gorbachev introduced as *perestroika* and *glasnost*. The impact of his reforms not only changed the nature of the Soviet system in Eastern Europe by allowing free elections to take place. Ultimately, the reforms led to the collapse of the Soviet Empire on Christmas Day 1991, when Gorbachev ended the Soviet Union with the stroke of a pen and handed power to the democratically elected Russian leader Boris Yeltsin. Many Germans had given up any hope of ever living again in a unified country. In the years since 1945, the division of Germany had become a structural part of European security and many West Germans were more than willing to accept the new normal not least because of the economic success story of West Germany after WWII. As a result, West German pressure for unification was rather low. The fundamental departure of the Federal Republic of Germany from Germany's military past and its new identity as a civilian power helped enormously to make the revolutionary process of unification not only possible, but also acceptable for Germany's neighbours. There were concerns at the beginning, for example in France and Great Britain. But once the US put its full weight behind a united Germany that would remain a member of NATO while at the same time contributing to an acceleration of the process of European integration, the trajectory of a 'Europe whole and free' became the new consensus in Europe, both East and West. US support for German unification early on and the renewed American commitment to remain a European power made it easier for Germany's neighbours to accept the new reality in Europe. In the end, Gorbachev, too, preferred a united Germany as a member of NATO and the EU as the more stable solution for European security than a Germany unbound which, in his darkest fears, might even be tempted to rise again militarily, including to seek nuclear weapons as a matter of parity (on this delicate point see Adomeit, 2006). Insisting on a divided Germany was not necessarily in the Soviet Union's long-term interest. Any larger Soviet (and later Russian) design for Europe as a whole could not be built on the basis of a German partition. Germany would be needed as a partner for such a design and that required acceptance of unification. Similar considerations played a role in French and British thinking. Their influence in Europe as a whole would be difficult to establish on the basis of a divided Germany. In the end, as both Eastern and Western powers realised, a new Europe could only be built in partnership with a united Germany and not with a divided country in its middle. European public opinion on German unification at the beginning of the 1990s was surprisingly positive. Even in Poland, a country with its own history of partition, understanding for unification was substantial. Forty-eight per cent of Poles supported German unity and in most other European countries majorities were in favour of unification. Understandably, opposition in Israel was predominant. Only 25 per cent of Israelis supported unification (See the data in Dettke, 2009: 55).

Unification desire was much more prevalent in East Germany where East Germans had to suffer the consequences of WWII and live under Soviet rule without the many freedoms that West Germans were able to enjoy. Without a language barrier between the two German states and more access and communication between East and West as a result of Détente, East Germans appreciated Western achievements even more than many West Germans who took their individual freedom and higher living standards for granted. When Mikhail Gorbachev came to power in the Soviet Union in 1985 with the determination to modernise not only the Soviet Union but to apply the principles of *glasnost* and *perestroika* also in the Warsaw Pact, the GDR leadership was less than enthusiastic about the new course of Soviet foreign policy seeking closer cooperation with the West and in fact demilitarising the entire East-West relationship. After first refusing to join Gorbachev's reform efforts, the GDR leadership simply threw in the towel rather than fighting its own citizens who saw their future not in a reformed communist system, but in becoming part of West Germany. Not a single shot was fired in the entire unification process.

In East Germany primarily, the reforms from top in the Soviet Union opened the gates for unification. Promoting the idea of a 'Common European Home' Gorbachev, for all practical purposes, was willing to join the West rather than continue to fight for a communist system that already began to disintegrate before his own eyes. Wherever the Soviet leadership looked around in the world, there was a new political and economic dynamism in the making: China launched a profound economic reform programme based on market principles, the US recovered from a perceived decline and Europe began to embark on a comprehensive economic integration project implementing a single internal market for 300 million West Europeans. Only the Soviet empire and its East European members remained stuck in stagnation. When Gorbachev began implementing his programme of demilitarising East-West relations with revolutionary arms control agreements such as the INF Treaty, which removed a whole class of intermediate range nuclear weapons, or the CFE Treaty on conventional arms in Europe, which dramatically reduced the number of armed forces in Europe, East European communist leaders began to fear for their own future. Poland and Hungary began to join the reform process implementing their cautious democratic reforms. Others tried to withstand the reform pressure from within, including the GDR regime, at least initially. But all the communist regimes in Eastern Europe and the GDR quickly collapsed once Gorbachev ended the Breshnev Doctrine of keeping Soviet-type communist regimes in power, even at the cost of military intervention as in Prague in 1968. Instead he pronounced the Sinatra Doctrine, in essence refusing to prop up communist regimes using Soviet militarily forces if they had failed to survive on their own. By the end of 1989, the political landscape in Europe looked completely different. National independence came back with a vengeance. The Warsaw Pact turned out to be unable to survive and former members of the Pact such as Poland, Hungary and Czechoslovakia even began looking forward to become members of the EU and NATO.

The Way Forward: Civilian Power, Normalcy and Geo-Economic Politics

The new Europe that emerged after 1989 created the best geopolitical and geostrategic environment Germany ever experienced. For the first time in German history, the country, embedded in a deepening and widening process of European integration, was surrounded by partners and friends sharing membership in the EU and NATO. There were no longer territorial claims to be settled. In many ways, Germany after unification ended up again in a central position in Europe, but this time not as a power that imposed itself on Europe.

Germany's civilian power identity has deep roots in the complexity of German and European history and took on an even more profound commitment after unification. In a way it was written into the Treaty on the Final Settlement with Respect to Germany of 12 September 1990. In it the governments of the Federal Republic of Germany and the GDR reaffirmed their declarations "that only peace will emanate from German soil" (Article 2). The most visible sign of the continuity of its civilian power orientation was the structure of its armed forces. With armed forces of just about half a million plus reserves, the German Bundeswehr used to be one of the strongest and best equipped armies in NATO. That number changed to a much lower figure in the final settlement with respect to Germany. In place of a peace treaty with Germany, the so-called 'Two plus Four Treaty' between the Federal Republic of Germany (FRG), the GDR and France, Great Britain and the US, officially the 'Treaty on the Final Settlement with Respect to Germany' of 12 September 1990, stipulated the international conditions of German unification. For the German armed forces, the treaty required the FRG to reduce the strength of the armed forces of united Germany to 370,000 ground, air and naval forces. The treaty also stipulated that a united Germany will keep its commitment to the NPT Treaty, thus making sure that it would remain a non-nuclear power. Today, the reform of Germany's armed forces goes way beyond the criteria set in the Two Plus Four Treaty. Recent plans aim for German armed forces of no more than a approximately 175,000. This, for all practical purposes, excludes any future German military threat for its neighbours.

The 'culture of military restraint' will remain a crucial component of German behaviour. In fact, the civilian power paradigm helped pave the way for unification in spite of deep and serious concerns about the additional weight and power unification could put into German hands. In the long run, this could become a German question again, but short-term unification reduced Germany's economic power by way of lowering its per capita GDP. In France as well as in Great Britain, uneasiness about unification was considerable and openly displayed when French President Mitterrand was the first Western leader to visit Moscow after fall of the wall in early December 1989 and then made his first trip to the then GDR on 21 December 1989. In Great Britain, Prime Minister Margaret Thatcher not only openly clashed with German Chancellor Helmut Kohl in several European meetings over issues such as the final German borders, she also convened a special high level seminar with leading German experts and historians in the spring of 1990 to find out about the impact of German unification on Europe. One of the concerns emanating from this meeting was the fear that a unified Germany might seek control over all Europe.[3] Such a development appears to be much less likely than in the past. Europe has successfully shed its traditional military balance of power competition for a more benign and peaceful settlement of conflicts and differences. Unification already took place in that spirit and not as an attempt of maximising power.

The two Germany's—in the words of former Chancellor Willy Brandt—grew together as a result of a process that—peaking in cultural terms—rekindled older European cultural ties. Seen from Eastern and Central Europe, one can also speak of a "return to Europe" as Vaclav Havel put it so eloquently. For many neighbours of Germany in the East and West, however, a united Germany was not easily acceptable and German leaders were fully aware of the fact that to be accepted again as a normal power would take time and serious efforts of building trust. In order to prove that these and other concerns and assumptions were mistaken, Germany did everything to transform unification into a European project, taking up a concept first proposed by Thomas Mann, the concept of a *European Germany* and not a *German Europe*. Consequently, German unification also prompted a quantum leap forward in the process of European integration. The 1992 Maastricht Treaty not only launched the Economic and Monetary Union and ultimately a common European currency, the EURO, rather the political integration of Europe was greatly improved when foreign policy as well as justice and home affairs were added as new pillars in the institutional framework of European integration.

Germany's responsibility—not guilt; guilt will always be individual and not collective—for war, genocide and destruction will always stand in the way of normalcy. What Germany has achieved —it is safe to say—is reconciliation with its war victims. Every German government made serious efforts to seek reconciliation, in particular with Israel. Most of the efforts were gestures of material compensation and restitution. Given the magnitude of the Nazi crimes, full compensation will never be achievable. But between the

3. A detailed account of the meeting can be found in Winkler's (2000) seminal work on the history of Germany.

FRG—West Germany in the past—and Israel, a normalisation of diplomatic relations and even understanding and close cooperation in every field, including military cooperation, was possible. This is also true for Germany and France, which today is the indispensable partnership for European integration. The *Ostpolitik* relations between Germany and Poland as well as between Germany and the former Czechoslovakia—now the Czech Republic and Slovakia—have reached a high level of trust over the years.

The quest for normalcy and acceptance as a normal country has always been a very strong impulse for German foreign policy, and it is perhaps fair to say that these efforts have been remarkably successful given the heavy burden of the past as a result of German warfare. But from the perspective of victims, reconciliation is not the same as normalisation. It has to be more than reconciliation and forgiveness and amount to redemption. The key to redemption is remembrance and Germans can only find a way out of the shadow of its own past by not forgetting and—as the German philosopher Juergen Habermas put it—by embracing the "universalistic principles of human rights and a civilised mode of human interaction."[4] Normalisation for Germany would be the equivalent of redemption, and redemption is not in German hands (Dettke, 2009). What is in German hands is atonement, compensation and the willingness to reconcile, but redemption will always remain uncertain.

On the other hand, Germany cannot be on probation forever and should not allow itself to remain imprisoned in its own past. Accepting the uncertainty of redemption, Germany has to free itself and, on the basis of multilateralism, act as a normal power. But even on the basis of multilateralism, there is no easy way out of the German historical predicament. Germany can become guilty again by using force as well as by a failure to give help. The Balkan wars of dissolution taught Germans and Europeans the lesson that an early intervention can save lives and that reluctance or failure to act creates the moral burden of being responsible for the loss of human life as a result of reluctance.

---

4. Juergen Habermas as quoted by McAdams, (1997).

The example of too many cases of lack of support for victims of mass killings led the UN to develop the 'Responsibility to Protect' as a new norm of international law and behaviour. Precisely because of Germany's historical experience, the lesson can not only be "Never Again War". An equally important lesson from WWII and various post-WWII conflicts is 'Never again Genocide'.

It was the latter lesson that made Germany's military participation in the air war against Serbia possible and allowed the country to actively support the independence of Kosovo. The war in Kosovo was Germany's first military deployment beyond the boundaries of NATO. Part of Germany's civilian power paradigm was the commitment to use force only on the basis of a UN Resolution permitting and legitimising military action. In a 1994 Constitutional Court decision, the legal way for German troops to be part of military missions outside of NATO's boundaries was opened, provided the German Parliament would support such a mission and there is a UN mandate legitimising military action. It turned out, however, that in the case of Kosovo, Russia was determined to veto such resolution. NATO had to intervene without a legitimising UN resolution. Germany, faced with a clear and present danger of mass killings as a result of the use of Serbia's regular military forces against Kosovar civilians, supported the military intervention legitimized only on a NATO consensus to act. Germany accepted this procedure under the circumstances against the letter of its own civilian power commitment. Not acting would have created the bigger moral dilemma. The country could not simply remain on the sidelines in a conflict that might have ended up in genocide.

Kosovo demonstrated that the civilian power paradigm is no panacea. A civilian response alone would not have been able to prevent the threatening actions of the Serb military forces. Only two years later, the world was confronted with a powerful demonstration of the lethal destruction that terrorism can cause. The terrorist attacks on the World Trade Center (WTC) in New York and the Pentagon in Washington on 11 September 2001, where almost 3,000 people from more than 100 different countries lost their life, turned out to be a new challenge for global peace. The UN as well as NATO saw the attacks as the equivalent of military aggression. NATO invoked Article V for the first time in its history and the UN granted the US the right of self-defense, including a response with military means. The Global War on Terror as it is called in the US will be a long and difficult struggle. Germany fully supports international actions to combat terrorism and did not hesitate to support American air strikes against Afghanistan. The German government contributed militarily to the international effort to force the Taliban regime to comply with the legitimate demand of handing over the Al-Qaeda leadership as the perpetrators of the 11 September attacks and to allow justice to take its course. But this was impossible without a full military invasion of Afghanistan and Germany became part of the international coalition that helped defeat the Taliban regime. On behalf of combating international terrorism as recommended in UN Security Council Resolution 1368 (2001), Germany contributed some 5,000 troops, including special forces to the international mission in Afghanistan and renewed its mandate continuously for over a decade. In addition to International Security Assistance Force (ISAF) in Afghanistan, Germany also took on counter-terrorism missions around the horn of Africa and in the Mediterranean. Germany remains committed to support Afghanistan after the end of the UN mandate for the ISAF in 2014.

On the other hand, when the war in Iraq started, Germany refused to support the decision of the Bush Administration to invade Iraq, allegedly because of an illegal possession of weapons of mass destruction, including nuclear weapons. These weapons of mass destruction were never found even after several attempts of searching for their alleged presence in Iraq. In a way, the negative stance taken by the German and French towards the Iraq War supported by a majority in the Security Council, saved the UN from a possibly fatally damaging disaster, if the UN Security Council would have legitimised an intervention that turned out to be based on flawed evidence. The German refusal to support the US in the case of Iraq was not primarily a result of Germany's civilian power paradigm. It was a conflict of different world order concepts between the US on the one hand and France and Germany on the other, in particular the absolute insistence of the French and German on letting the UN inspection regime take its course before any military action could be initiated. Unable to obtain a majority for such action in the UN Security Council, the US interrupted the UN inspection process and invaded Iraq, thereby causing a deep split within the Western Alliance and Europe.

After Kosovo, Afghanistan and Iraq, the jury is still out whether or not Germany will continue to rely primarily on its civilian power paradigm. German behaviour in the Libyan crisis 2011 appears to point in that direction. In spite of UN Security Council Resolution 1973 (2011) supporting the establishment of a 'no-fly-zone' over Libya, Germany abstained from the critical UN Security Council decision to allow such a course of action. Whereas the abstention of Russia and China as veto powers de facto allowed the 'no-fly-zone' option to protect the civilian population of Benghazi to pass, the German abstention as a non-veto power was de facto a 'no' to the responsibility to protect the 800,000 civilians in the city of Benghazi from an imminent assault of Ghaddafi's regular armed forces on the city. In this case, the German government took the wrong decision in spite of the fact that Germany's civilian power paradigm would have allowed a participation in the military action that followed the UN mandate. On the basis of a UN Security Council decision, German participation in a coalition of powers using force would have been compatible with Germany's commitment to multilateralism too. In fact, its abstention was a deviation from the commitment to multilateralism as Germany sided with the four BRIC countries (Brazil, Russia, India and China) instead of helping to forge a EU consensus and a possible common action of the EU. Even more disturbing was the fact that Germany's position in the Libyan crisis undermined NATO efforts to implement a UN weapons embargo when the government, as a result of the abstention in the UN Security Council, decided to withdraw its military assets from the Mediterranean. Contrary to Germany's commitment to European integration, the country prevented the EU from acting in concert on an issue that clearly lies in the jurisdiction of the Mediterranean

Union and the EU commitment to the well-being of its Southern neighbourhood.

One possible conclusion one could draw from the rather idiosyncratic German foreign policy decision-making in major international crises is that the country has now achieved a degree of independence that can put in doubt the primacy of multilateralism in German foreign policy. There are also signs of a renewed emphasis on great power bilateralism. The highest growth rates for Germany's exports are now seen in the Chinese and Russian markets. German exports to China, for example, grew by more than 70 per cent between 2009 and 2010 (Kundnani, 2011). The new markets in China and Russia are increasingly important for an export nation like Germany. Almost half of its GDP (gross domestic product) is generated from its export industries. In the past, Europe appeared to be the answer to every single foreign policy problem. In fact, Germany helped create the impression that the country supports an eventual Europeanization of its foreign policy within a transatlantic framework. Such a development is no longer the only trajectory for German foreign policy. Great power bilateralism could well reduce—but not replace—the hard work of European consensus-building. Most likely, a country like Germany will not give up the ambition of increasing its power within the EU as well as within other multilateral institutions.

European and Western unity is crucial for effective German statecraft. One test case will be the role of Germany in the Ukrainian crisis. The Ukrainian crisis is a reminder that a post–modern order based on the rule of law is not a universally accepted self-fulfilling promise. Russia's Crimean land-grab is an example of an alternative non-Western authoritarian model of governance capable of violating accepted principles such as territorial integrity and a rules-based international order. In Asia, similar challenges might arise in connection with the rise of China and its future as a 'stakeholder' of the international system. Germany needs to act on the basis of Western commonalty in order to be effective. One obvious consequence of the debate will be the question of increased investments in military hardware and equipment for such a role.

In response to Russia's challenge of the post Cold War settlement which includes acceptance of the territorial status quo, European and Western unity will be essential.

Conclusion

Although the project of a European Constitution failed in national referendums held in France and the Netherlands, two founding members of the European project, deepening and widening of the EU is still a work in progress. European Treaty adjustments, most importantly through the 2009 Lisbon Treaty, paved the way forward into the 21st century. European integration not only survived the worst financial and economic crisis since the Great Depression, the reforms and institutional adjustments since the crisis began in 2008 made Europe stronger for future challenges. Germany—thanks to economic and fiscal reforms at the beginning of the 21st century—emerged from the economic and financial crisis that began in 2008 relatively unscathed. German leadership albeit cautious and hesitant at times contributed to navigate the Eurozone successfully through a deep recession, particularly in Southern Europe. In spite of an enormous debt and banking crisis, the Euro remained stable. There was no currency crisis and today, the Euro appears to be more acceptable than ever before, even in the countries hit most severely by the deep global recession. What is needed now is more creative European institution building to prevent future crises and this will have to be achieved under the condition of much national pressure so as to reduce the powers of European institutions. One example is the effort of Great Britain to renegotiate the European treaties. Other EU member states might follow with similar strategies under the influence of right wing anti-European parties.

The European debt and banking crisis catapulted Germany into a leadership position the country did not seek, but was unable to avoid given the sheer weight of its economy and the success of its economic model. In fact, based on its own historical experience which made the culture of military restraint part of the DNA of the new Germany, the country did not refrain from using its economic power. Germany developed its own alternative road to influence and even a high degree of independence as a geo-economic power, deliberately giving up the trappings of military might and focusing instead on the rule of law and economic governance. While these civilian principles and characteristics appear benign, geo-economic politics still follows the logic of conflict and competition.[5] As a geo-economic power, too, Germany can end up again in the position of being too strong for Europe, but too weak for hegemony (Kundnani, 2011: 43). But any German leadership as a geo-economic power—by definition—has to be based on consensus. A trading power can only achieve its goals in an environment that others voluntarily share. This will require extraordinary care and caution for a country that sees itself not only as a stakeholder of the liberal world order, but as a power to provide leadership in shaping the emerging post-modern rules-based world order that Europe wants to help create (*Gestaltungsmacht*).

The German question of the future might well be whether a post-modern geo-economic power can secure the post-modern environment it needs to survive. This issue is now at the centre of a German debate about the need of taking on more responsibility for peace and stability operations worldwide. Germany is still interested in becoming a permanent member of the UN Security Council. Its efforts to become a member failed in the first attempt to reform the UN system. Although compared with today's P-5 powers, Germany appears to be an 'incomplete power' (Serfaty, 2008: 40).[6] The issue might end up on the UN agenda again.

Historical experience tells us that behind every constitution stands an army to protect it and—as Robert Cooper (2003: 161) added—"behind the peaceful development of Europe in the second half of the twentieth century there has been NATO and American military power." It could well be that the constitution or the order that Germany needs for the survival of its own model—might be challenged by new neo-Westphalian powers such Russia and

5. On this important concept with regard to German foreign policy, see in particular the article by Kundnani (2011: 31-45). The aricle draws on earlier work by Edward Luttwak.

6. The term 'incomplete power' power is based on Simon Serfaty's term "complete powers" with reference to the US, Great Britain and France. Compared with these powers, Germany would be an incomplete power.

China. In the future, necessary protection of the European model will have to come more from Europe and less from the US. From a German perspective, multilateralism will always be at the centre of its course of action. But as one could observe during the economic and financial crisis beginning in 2008 and in the case of the Libyan crisis, Germany's new multilateralism will be less reflexive. It can no longer be taken for granted. However, a weakening of multilateral institutions is not in Germany's interest. It would make the country vulnerable again. For multilateral institutions to succeed, they need to have both the necessary physical strength and legitimacy in order to be effective. The problem is that the physical strength of multilateral institutions and the necessary means to act have to exist on a national level first, before they can be deployed multilaterally. The physical strength and the means to act cannot be compensated for and brought to bear multilaterally if they do not exist on a national level first. Germany will have to develop the necessary means to act multilaterally on the national level first.

References

Adomeit, Hannes (2006). "Gorbachev's Consent to Unified Germany's Membership in NATO", *Working Paper FG* 2006/11. Berlin: Stiftung Wissenschaft und Politik. p.4.

Clark, Christopher (2012). *The Sleepwalkers. How Europe Went to War in 1914.* New York. p.124.

Cooper, Robert (2003). *The Breaking of Nations. Order and Chaos in the Twenty-First Century.* New York: Atlantic Books. p.161,

Dettke, Dieter (2009). *Germany Says 'No': The Iraq War and the Future of German Foreign and Security Policy.* Washington DC and Baltimore. p.55.

Hobsbawm, Eric (1994). *The Age of the Extremes: The Short Twentieth Century.* London.

Kempe, Fred (2011). "Introduction" and "Epilogue", in Fred Kempe*Berlin 1961: Kennedy, Krushchev, and the Most Dangerous Place on Earth.* New York: Putnam Publishers.

Kundnani, Hans (2011). "Germany as a Geo-economic Power", *The Washington Quarterly* 34(3): 36 (Summer).

McAdams, A. James (1997). "Germany after Unification: Normal at Last?", *World Politics* 49(2): 299 (January).

Plessner, Helmuth (1959). *Die verspaetete Nation. Ueber die Verfuegbarkeit des buergerlichen Geistes* (The Belated Nation. About the Availability of the Bourgeois Spirit). Stuttgart. (originally written in 1935).

Serfaty, Simon (2008). *Architects of Delusion: Europe, America and the Iraq War.* Philadelphia: University of Philadelphia Press. p.40.

Snyder, Timothy (2010). *Bloodlands: Europe Between Hitler and Stalin.* New York: Basic Books.

Winkler, Heinrich August (2000). *Der Lange Weg nach Westen: Zweiter Band, Deutsche Geschichte vom "Dritten Reich" bis zur Wiedervereinigung.* Muenchenrlag: C.H. Beck. p.576.

7

TAKASHI INOGUCHI

The Foreign Policy of Japan as a Global Power

Japan is a global power. As such, this chapter looks back to see the historical roots of Japan's foreign policy and its development after the Cold War; looks to the present to examine Shinzo Abe's rise and his pro-active pacifist policy; and looks to the future of 2033 to speculate about the power dynamics of the three paramount East Asian powers, the United States (US), China, and Japan. In the first section, three pillars of self-recognition anchor the historical examination of Japan's foreign policy: self-recognition as a global power; self-recognition as a supporter of the US-led international system; and self-recognition of ontological insecurity. History is also significant in the third section. In looking toward 2033 and how internal and external issues of each of the three regional powers may unfold, we first look back to 1813 when Asia was at its last economic peak. Before I move on to sections I through III, I briefly describe the institutional arrangements and processes of Japan's foreign policy.

The Institutional Arrangements and Processes of Japan's Foreign Policy

Constitutionally, Japan's foreign policy is conducted by the Foreign Minister under Prime Minister's (PM's) ambit. Foreign Minister handles day-to-day matters of diplomacy and carry out designing and implementation of foreign policy in intermediate and longer term policy lines with broad instruction by PM. It is important to note that under the Constitution, the Foreign Ministry is in charge of security and diplomacy, whereas the Defence Ministry is in charge of equipments of weapons and personnel and operations for national defence as well as the designing and implementation of defence policy in intermediate and longer term policy lines again with broad instruction by PM.

The Defence Ministry was upgraded in the ranking of national bureaucracy from the Defence Agency in 2007 in tandem with the increasing emphasis on security cooperation with the US, the institutional manifestation of which is the two-plus-two meeting with the Foreign and Defence Ministries sitting together with their counterparts, say the State and Defence Department of the US government.

The past two decades since 1993-94, when the non-Liberal Democratic Party coalition formed the government for the first time since the Liberal Democratic Party was established in 1956, have seen the gradual increase in power with the non-bureaucratic component of the government as contrasted to its bureaucratic components. PM's Office has often been assertive *vis-à-vis* national bureaucracy, although it depends primarily on who is PM. Junichiro Koizumi and Shinzo Abe are two clear examples of semi-presidential PMs. One Democratic PM, Yukio Hatoyama, was an example of a PM who was not quite able to mobilise bureaucratic forces, although he was semi-presidential of a sort. Koizumi was semi-presidential with regard to pro-alliance and independence from China with his visits to Yasukuni and to Pyongyang not arousing noisy criticisms, whereas Abe was pro-alliance and anti-China with his visits to Yasukuni taken critically by the US, China and South Korea. Hatoyama was semi-presidential on alliance, whose position was taken as broadly anti-alliance by the US.

To push semi-presidentialism further, Abe has recently established the National Security Policy Agency under his direct arms. A glance from which ministries assigned personnel came enables one to see the dominance of the Foreign Ministry. It looks as if the National Security Policy Agency, the Foreign Ministry and the Defence Ministry were in broad harmony when Abe has vigorously been marching his Abegeopolitics by making trips to 49 countries in his first 20 months since December 2012.

The legislative branch has been quietly strong in exercising its influence on the executive branch by the power of brevity of parliamentary sessions (less than one half of 365 days except extraordinary sessions). Once government-sponsored bills end without votes in both houses, the government must start *de novo* in next sessions. When the number of government-sponsored bills rise, the legislative branch exercises its influence by prolonging committee and plenary sessions, thereby killing some bills. Not only pork-barrel bills but also controversial foreign policy related issues are such examples.

Japan's foreign policy is formed primarily by the Foreign Ministry. Yet when a PM who is strongly interested in diplomacy and defence appears, PM's semi-presidentialism often sways. The secret-preserving law passed in the 2014 sessions was such an example. The legislative branch's constitutionally accorded muscles in committees and plenary sessions sometimes manifest themselves, when committee chairs or both houses' presidents are politically strong men.

I

Japan's Foreign Policy as a Global Power

The end of the Cold War marked a shift from a bipolar international world order (Inoguchi, 1991; 1993; 1998; 2001; 2006; 2008a; 2008b; 2009; Gourevitch *et al.*, 1995), and Japan's foreign policy needed to respond and re-adjust to the changing outside environment. After the defeat of Japan in World War II, PM Shigeru Yoshida designed and implemented the country's post-war foreign policy framework. It is now called the Yoshida Doctrine (Kosaka, 1968). The Yoshida Doctrine prioritised the economic recovery and development of Japan and left its military defence to the US. Hence, the Tokyo government had the ability to respond to domestic disasters, but for its national security allowed US military to establish extensive military bases within Japan for regional operations. An example is the Korean War (1950-1953). Until 1960, the Japanese public had reservations about this policy and so contributed to the bumpy start in the Japan-US alliance.

By 1960, Japan's economic miracle had started, and with it Japanese public opinion about the alliance had become more positive. By 1960, Japan's Self-Defense Forces (JSDF) were well established and served to bolster the US position against the Soviet Union. Just as Japan's economy grew to be number two in terms of GNP (gross national product), so did the conceptualisation of Japan's foreign policy. At this point, Japan viewed itself as playing a systemic supporter of the US-led world order.

The bipolarity of world politics sharply ended with the collapse of communism in the Soviet Union and Eastern Europe. One of the founding structural cornerstones of the Japan-US alliance appeared to disappear along with the Soviet empire. Yet specifics of the alliance were somewhat vague, giving it the ability to adapt to the international environment (Inoguchi *et al.*, 2011). If the alliance looked adrift (Funabashi, 1999), then it was more appearance than reality. The 1990s saw Japan move forward in two directions. First, it focused on the United Nations (UN) Peacekeeping Operations and other activities (Inoguchi, 1995). The uncertainties that arose with the end of the Cold War allowed the role of the UN to be highlighted in Japan. Third world countries, trying to secure the support they once had in a bipolar world, acted out. Parts of the developing world struggled as civil war raged. Faced with such violence and desperation for local populations, the importance of the UN and its peacekeeping operations grew. Second, Japan actively sought to re-focus and re-boot the bilateral Japan-US alliance. The end of the Cold War was not the end of communism worldwide, that is, the ideology was and is still practiced by many regional states in Asia—China, North Korea, Vietnam, Laos, and Cambodia. Japan is acutely aware of these regional dynamics.

The 11 September terrorist attacks against the US shook the thinking of all state governments. In the ensuing decade, Japan sought a Defence posture that paralleled that of the US (Ikenberry and Inoguchi, 2003; 2007; Inoguchi *et al.*, 2011). The armed forces of both countries shifted their emphasis and orientation from land to maritime and air, and from the Soviet Union to China. Since the end of the Cold War, the Yoshida Doctrine has continued to be a main cornerstone of Japanese foreign policy, but with Shinzo Abe's second ascent to the office of PM in 2012 significant modifications have been introduced.

Three Pillars of Japanese Foreign Policy Post-Cold War

Three qualities distinguish Japan's foreign policy in the post Cold War period. First is recognition of itself as a global power. This assessment is more prominent among leaders than the general population of Japan (Tanaka, 2009; Kitaoka, 2009). It is also a moot point whether this assessment is shared among other state actors. Japan has pursued a low diplomatic stance since 1945. As a low-key actor, its influence is quietly acknowledged and moderately appreciated. Second is recognition of the supporting role Japan performs in the US-led international system (Inoguchi and Okimoto, 1989; Ikenberry and Inoguchi, 2003; 2007; Inoguchi *et al.*, 2011)—a system that is the product of the Japan-US security alliance, the Bretton Woods system, and the UN. Third is the persistent role that Japan's past actions, particularly those related to the war and its colonialism, have played in its ongoing ontological insecurity (Inoguchi, 2006; 2007; Zarakol, 2010; 2011).

If wider recognition is deficient for Japan's global power status, then recognition for its economic strength is more than ample. The economic strength of Japan is more than sufficient to qualify it as a global power. Key economic strengths include: ranked third after the US and China in GDP (gross domestic product); core economic fundamentals and indicators are robust; per capita national domestic product is high; elite-level technology; stable and coveted currency: ranked second largest creditor country after China; high and growing levels of Japanese FDI (foreign direct investment); history of high national savings rate; and large government deficits are counter-balanced by strong domestic sales of government bonds.

As all nations do, Japan seeks an honourable place in the world. The Japanese constitution stipulates this objective. The Tokyo government recognises Japan's position as a global power and actively seeks international recognition. An example is that in the early 2000s, Japan pursued a permanent seat on the UN Security

Council. Although the attempt failed, the desire remains. Coming from a position of strength in the arena of economics, technology, and finance, the Achilles heel for global power status persists in the arena of Japanese military and politics. Japan's constitution and its public pose a formidable roadblock to armed expansions outside self-defence goals. Lacking in combat experience, the JSDF are well armed and well trained in their high-tech weaponry. The ability and discipline of the JSDF are evident in the coordinated operations it undertakes with the US. The Japanese government is aware of the need for the JSDF to adapt to the changing international system, but it does not exceed a moderate defence budget in terms of GNP. Ringed by five military powers (the US, China, both Koreas, and Russia) and fully aware of China's long-range missiles aimed at US military installations on Japan and the Korean peninsula, Tokyo is keenly aware of its precarious position (Yan, 2006). China's nuclear capability serves as a counterweight to US power in the Asia-Pacific. Reports of declining US power combined with policy announcements of a US "return to Asia" heightens the sensitiveness of how Japan responds to China and North Korea as these events unfold (Hidaka, 2012).

A fragmented power centre is at the core of Japanese political weakness. It compromises professional competence, organisation, transparency and accountability of political parties and bureaucracy. Even in a crisis, politicians and bureaucrats face a fragmented power structure that is further slowed down by the cultural need for consensus building.

For 20 years Japan suffered a recession. Starting in 1991, the affected period is known by Japanese as the "lost two decades." During these difficult economic times, the government and business made important strides in two areas. First, Japanese companies ventured abroad in an effort to minimise risks and maximise benefits. Asia was the chief beneficiary of this new corporate strategy. The recession also forced Japanese companies to focus on research and development as part of an effort to reduce costs and improve quality. The impetus for efficiency is the second key achievement. During these years, Japanese business successfully reduced energy costs

Table 7.1

Japan-US Joint Public Opinion Poll

			Do not answer the question	Very bad	Bad	Neither good nor bad	Good	Very good
Question A	Do you think relations between Japan and the United States are good or bad?	Japanese respondents	5	4	37	20	34	1
		American respondents	6	2	6	34	41	11
			Do not answer the question	Do not trust a bit	Do not trust much		Trust more or less	Trust very much
Question B	Do you trust or do not trust the United States?	Japanese respondents	12	7	35		42	5
		American respondents	1	14	17		51	16
			Do not answer the question	Very bad	Bad	Neither good nor bad	Good	Very good
Question C	Do you think bilateral relations between Japan and China are good or bad?	Japanese respondents	5	8	53	18	16	--
		American respondents	2	5	17	48	25	4
			Do not answer the question	Do not trust a bit	Do not trust much		Trust more or less	Trust very much
Question D	Do you trust or do not trust China?	Japanese respondents	7	30	55		8	1
		American respondents	2	30	34		32	2

Source: Excerpts from the poll conducted in December 2011 jointly by The Yomiuri Shimbun and Gallup Organization, Yomiuri Online. 18 December 2011. (*http://www.yomiuri.co.jp/feature/fe6100/koumoku/20111218.htm*). Accessed on 10 January 2012.

Table 7.2

Japan-US Joint Public Opinion Poll

			United States	Japan	China	Both are important	Do not answer the question
Question E	Of the United States (Japan) and China, which country do you think becomes more important in politics?	Japanese respondents	55	--	32	5	8
		American respondents	--	42	52	1	5
			United States	Japan	China	Both are important	Do not answer the question
Question F	Of the United States (Japan) and China, which country do you think becomes more important in economics?	Japanese respondents	21	--	67	5	8
		American respondents	--	24	69	2	4

Source: Excerpts from the poll conducted in December 2011 jointly by The Yomiuri Shimbun and Gallup Organization, Yomiuri Online. 18 December 2011. (*http://www.yomiuri.co.jp/feature/fe6100/koumoku/20111218.htm*). Accessed on 10 January 2012.

through innovation. This positively impacted Japan's energy supply and energy efficiency. Hence, the "two lost decades" is somewhat incorrect.

Japan is a stellar supporter of the global system. The Japan-US security alliance is fluid in its scope and aims, thereby allowing it to change according to power and wealth determinants (Inoguchi *et al.*, 2011). The Japan-US Security Treaty is not specific about its objectives and areas of activity. Its adaptive nature has led to it being called the alliance for all four seasons. Throughout the years and decades, the alliance has weathered many wars and many crises with Japan always fulfilling its supporter position. The Great East Japan Earthquake and Tsunami and the Fukushima nuclear disaster presented the US armed forces an opportunity to help the Japanese public. The US forces launched Operation Tomodachi, a sizeable rescue effort, along the coast of the Tohoku region. The impact of the operation was immediate as pro-American sentiments reached 82 per cent (Yomiuri online, 2011), a new high for the post Cold War years.

Japan is solid, steadfast, and meticulous in its support of all areas related to economics and finance in the US-led world system. Japan and the US share a common position on issues impacting the free trade system of the World Trade Organization (WTO), the dollar-centred currency system of the International Monetary Fund (IMF) and associated organisations, and the development system of the World Bank and the Organization for Economic Cooperation and Development (OECD) and associated organisations. Japan's position as supporter of a superpower is not exciting and is frequently eclipsed by the shadow of the US. Yet Japan is unwavering in its support, even when confronted with negative consequences. A prime example is the 1985 Plaza Accord that under the Maekawa Report introduced into the market a massive amount of Japanese yen and caused the Japanese economic bubble to rise and eventually to collapse in 1991. The pro-American sentiments of 2011 that accompanied Operation Tomodachi did not ameliorate feelings of public uncertainty about the bilateral alliance. A Yomiuri poll conducted in late 2011 in both Japan and the US reveals that anxiety dominates public feelings toward Japan-US relations (Table 7.1).

In this survey, Japanese respondents indicated that 35 per cent view Japan-US bilateral relations as positive, compared to 41 per cent who view it as negative; 47 per cent of surveyed Japanese "trust very much" or "trust more or less" the US, compared to 42 per cent who "do not trust very much" or "do not trust a bit" the US. Yet the 12 per cent of respondents who chose not to respond to the question should also be considered.

The survey posed a similar set of questions about Japan-China bilateral relations. The response shows that Japanese are uncertain and anxious about the future of both bilateral relations. Japanese public opinion toward China and the trust levels expressed in China toward Japan indicate a new low since the 1972 normalisation of relations between the two East Asian countries.

In this troubled triangle, the duality between security and economy is apparent. Table 7.2 shows the questions posed to Japanese and American respondents and their responses.

Questions E and F try to assess public perceptions of which country Japanese view as more politically important and more economically important. Of the surveyed respondents, 55 per cent view the US as politically more important than China with the latter registering 32 per cent in this question. In terms of economic strength, the results are reversed. Of those surveyed, 67 per cent of Japanese consider China as economically more important than the US, which received 21 per cent for the same question. The response of American respondents reveals that the duality between economics and security is not as apparent. For those surveyed, China both politically and economically is perceived as more important: 52 per cent *versus* 42 per cent for political significance, and 69 per cent *versus* 24 per cent for economic significance.

Given the structural duality of security and economics, what is the optimal foreign policy line for Japan? The tension between the two areas is a critical problem for Japanese policymakers. Complicating the trilateral relations is the initiative for a Trans-Pacific Partnership that the US favours. Pros and cons for the initiative add to feelings of Japanese public anxiety. In some ways, the duality of the trilateral relations is moderated by the introduction of such a partnership.

Specifically, as economic ties and activities between Japan and China increase and overtake those between Japan and the US, the Trans-Pacific Partnership may provide a counterbalance. In this complex web, the Yomiuri poll and other Internet polls provide some insight into the quickly evolving preferences of Japanese citizens regarding foreign policy in general and the Japan-US security alliance in particular.

Japan suffers from ontological insecurity. However, over the years, this quality has been evolving at a slow, unsteady rate that does not attract attention. The transformation of its ontological insecurity manifests itself on issues related to territory and history, among others. The change is reflected in Japan's steadfast and tough response to new claims over old issues that have been settled. For instance, China regularly challenges Japan's sovereignty claim over the Senkaku Islands by intrusions into the area. The government of South Korea raises the issue of individual compensation for wartime sex slaves. The Japanese response is that these issues were settled years ago. In the Korean case, the diplomatic normalisation of relations signalled by the signing of the 1965 Japan-South Korea Basic Treaty dealt with this bilateral concern. From the perspective of the Tokyo government, Japan is simply abiding by the treaty terms and all the areas settled in the 1965 negotiation.

The roots of Japan's ontological insecurity can be traced to how it developed in the 20th century. Its development path led to the notable achievement of it being the first non-Western country to achieve modernisation, followed by its decision to pursue colonial expansion, and bookmarked by its decision to join powers in World War II (WWII) who were eventually convicted of war crimes. The last fact caused it to be, for a while, not given full membership to the UN. How to view the achievements of Japan from the 1850s to the end of the war? What is to be learned? How did Japan go wrong? The Far Eastern Tribunal's verdict is that military cliques were responsible for leading Japan temporarily down the wrong path and that after the war, Japan resumed the correct path.

Japanese have inherited mix feelings about the war. Indeed, many have difficulty acknowledging that the Pacific War was a complete mistake. Two notable Japanese historians who grappled with this dark period, the late Seizaburo Sato and Takashi Ito, chose to refer to this period, not as the Greater East Asian War or the Pacific War, but as simply "that war" (Sato and Ito, 1995).

For many Japanese, "that war" is really two wars: the first among imperialist powers and the second against Pacific Asians. This separation allows Japanese to also separate their feelings. In the former, Japan admits that it was just as aggressive and exploitative as other imperialist powers; in the latter, Japan harbours feelings of guilt for the great suffering it caused Pacific Asians. Dividing the conflict into two wars creates ambivalent feelings about the topic for many Japanese.

Westernisation and national solidarity form two pillars in the Japanese conception of national identity. Achieving modernisation was the first step in reaching a high level of Westernisation. For many Japanese, the goals (rich nation and strong army) set in Meiji Japan in 1868 were reached. The history and ambitions of a nation are an intricate part of a national identity, including that of Japan. Hence, to view the war and, in doing so, all the development and progress that preceded it, as purposeless is tantamount to severing a part of modern history and with it a part of Japan's national identity. For this reason Japan struggles to characterise "that war" as completely wrong. The tension between the conceptualisation of national identity and the collective memory that emanates from modern history creates distance between the official apologies offered annually and the general public's absence in expressing what many outside observers would consider genuine repentance. The public hesitation is a product of how the Japanese have been unable to process the notion that Japan is unilaterally responsible for the war and of how Japanese sympathy for wartime suffering has not translated into compassion for humans over all. The end result is that Japan's neighbours and other countries remain skeptical of Japan's intent and any progress forward is slow.

Japanese see themselves as different and separate from other countries in Asia. This sense of detachment stems from historical experience. First, Japan's economic success before and after WWII reinforced its sense that the country was superior to other Asian states. As the only non-Western state to enjoy repeated economic success, disdain for other Asian states grew out of Japan's sense of superiority. The ability to grow from the ashes of war to a member of the OECD, a club for industrialised states, further cemented Japan's notion of self. Second, the cultural debt that Japan owes to China does not nurture a sense of closeness, but rather stimulates a desire to keep China at arm's length. The impulse to develop its own system of thought can be traced to the start of the 17th century in Tokugawa Japan.

These feelings, perceptions, and sense of self in relation to Asia are compounded by the political debt to neighbouring Asians that Japan incurred during the last world war. In part because of these historical experiences, Japan chooses to deal with related issues by distancing itself from them. The policy of the Tokyo government is to argue that wartime debts were settled when bilateral and international treaties and agreements were reached. For key critical issues, the Japanese government insists that conclusions cannot be reached until more objective historical research and analysis is completed.

Attitudes of detachment, disdain, and cultural debt produce a robust complex between Japan and the other regional Asian states. For relations with Japan to move forward in the region, the complex demands resolution. During the 20-year recession, Japan embarked on a "return to Asia" and in choosing this path aspects of the complex have improved.

The crux of Japan's ontological insecurity is World War II. Three lenses that capture the larger themes of the war also offer three distinct narratives that impact Japan's ontological understanding: "democracy against fascism", "anticolonialism against colonialism", and "democracy against tyranny of all sorts" (Inoguchi, 2007).

The first lens is the struggle of democracy against fascism in WWII. Many Japanese concur with this assessment, but at the same time they feel that the war from this viewpoint can be characterised, at some level, as a fight among imperialist powers. Japanese appreciate that the war shaped their post-war foreign and domestic

Table 7.3

Profile of 17 Prime Ministers who Coped with Foreign Policy (1989-2012)

Takeshita	Japan-US trade disputes; consumption tax hike; corruption scandal; resistance to US pressure on SDF shouldering global negotiations.
Kaifu	No accomplishment; a trial at improving relations with Russia.
Uno	Sex scandal.
Miyazawa	Bubble collapsed;
Hosokawa	Political reform;
	Pro-alliance position (*vis-à-vis* Russia and multilateral security).
Hata	No accomplishment.
Murayama	Foreign policy alteration reconfirmed; US-Japan alliance reaffirmed; Murayama speech on history issues.
Hashimoto	Presidential election defeat.
Obuchi	Death; tilting toward non-US (silk road diplomacy).
Mori	Mishaps; tilting toward non-US (Russia).
Abe	Yasukuni Shrine fixed; coalition extended to India, Australia.
Fukuda	Re-focus on G8 and global climate; rejecting SDF role in Afghanistan.
Aso	Pro-alliance enlarged.
Hatoyama	Pro-alliance position adjustment attempted (Futenma Air Field relocating and East Asian Community Formation).
Kan	Nuclear disaster; crisis management failure.
Noda	Pro-alliance position reaffirmed.
Abe (2)	Yasukuni Shrinem Senkaku islands, Collective Self-defense, Asia Pivot and Trans-Pacific Partnership.

Source: Author made this table in reference to the followings; *Ukeru Magosaki, Sengoshi No Shotai* [The True Identity of Postwar History] .Tokyo: Somotosya, 2012; Naikaku, Hosokawa (1993). *Kara Noda Shinshusyo Tanjyo Madeno Rekidai Seiken* [Successive Political Power from Hosokawa (1993) to Noda]
http://jp.reuters.com/article/marketsNews/idJPnTK049757320110831

policies. As one of the imperialist powers, Japan emerged from the conflict disarmed, democratised, and allied with the US. The bilateral alliance formalised in the Japan-US Security Treaty has become a cornerstone of stability and prosperity for the region (Inoguchi, 2006).

The second lens of anticolonialism was paramount in preparing the way for the wave of decolonialisation that swept over Asia in the post-war period. Most Japanese agree that WWII spurred forward the liberation of Asia.

The last of the three lenses is democracy against tyranny. This perspective applied to the last world war and can also be employed to depict the troubles of some current states. In the decades following the war, Japan has chosen a peaceful and democratic path. The Japanese concern is that regional struggles against tyranny could draw their country into the conflict and force it to make hard decisions. Committed to its US alliance, Japan is also aware that the spillover of such foreign policy choices could escalate relations with China or North Korea. Just as democracy and peace have led to prosperity in Japan, Tokyo is convinced that the best path for Asia is the one that Japan chose seven decades ago.

There are many layers to how WWII impacted Japan into the 21st century and to how the Japanese understand the war, their role in it, and their place in contemporary regional politics as determined by this war. The problem is that the Japanese social construction of memory, history, and identity does not fit well with the narratives that emerge from the three lenses. The emotional outpouring on 15 August, every year, reflects the Japanese struggle to accept the three narratives.

Was Leadership Change Prompted by Foreign Policy Needs?

Seventeen men, one of them twice, have led Japan as PM in the post-Cold War period (Table 7.3). Change in state leadership is usually prompted by domestic factors with international incidents sometimes confirming domestic problems. The reason is often that the leader is weak and incompetent in handling domestic policy. The high turnover of Japanese PMs in the last 25 years is due to the following factors: prolonged economic recession; electoral system change that included the elimination of medium-sized electoral districts and the introduction of a single-member district system, as well as a proportional representation system; diverging career paths of parliamentarians; and foreign policy considerations.

The post-Cold War years were tumultuous ones for Japanese politics and for Japan-US relations. The main party of Japan, the Liberal Democratic Party (LDP), experienced severe factional infighting and corruption scandals. Japan-US trade frictions were at an all-time high. The rise and fall of the economic bubble further aggravated LDP intra-party relations and Japan-US relations.

What brings about leadership change? Many factors can be attributed to why a certain leader exits a political office. Frequently, an unresolved or hidden foreign policy matter prompts a leader to step down. However, foreign policy is never given as the reason for leadership change, especially if it is a hidden issue. Instead domestic factors are cited. Domestic factors can range from corruption to intra-party politics to administrative reform to the most encompassing factor—economics. The bursting of the economic bubble followed by the long recession and then compounded with a consumption tax hike have provided fodder for many political leadership exits. Leadership change in Japan has also provided opportunities for the government to complete unfinished work. Irrespective of individual PMs and their achievement or lack of achievement over the last 25 years, a set of structural work remains as their legacy. How issue areas are prioritised depends on the strength of the administration, the strength of the PM, and a whole web of demands that are placed on the government. Issue areas include trade disputes, good governance practices of business and government, increasing the domestic market, engagement of JSDF in transborder operations, and location of US military bases. The collapse of the Soviet Union and its absence from international politics has placed a different kind of spotlight on the Japan-US alliance. The rationale for the alliance must be reconsidered. As Japanese PMs re-think the scope and aim of the alliance, domestic and international factors also come into play (Magosaki, 2012; Thalakada, 2012).

Is Japan Most Befitting This World Order?

As authors like Mueller (1989) argue that war is about to disappear or Goldstein (2011) who argue that war is on the decline, Japan's role in UN peacekeeping and peace-building operations is growing. Japan participated in the UN operations in Cambodia. The individual sent to Cambodia did not come from the JSDF, but from the Police Agency. Japanese lawmakers interpreted Article 9 of the Japanese constitution as discouraging JSDF personnel from being dispatched to foreign countries. This interpretation also prevented the lawmakers from passing new legislation that would have permitted JSDF involvement in future UN operations.

Peace and stability are Japan's strength. For the most part, the Asian region has not recently witnessed conflict beyond small-scale disputes. In terms of economic upheaval as experienced in the US and Europe, Japan is a beacon of stability, and therefore strength. This set of conditions reflects directly onto the strength of the Japanese yen and its exchange rate with other major currencies such as the US dollar.

The world is changing. Is Japan prepared to meet the emerging world order? The three core qualities that anchor Japanese foreign policy remain, yet they are undergoing change at a surprising rate. First, ranking number three in GNP after the US and China, Japan shares the concern that the status of the US as a superpower is waning (Hikida, 2012) and that the US faces a similar fate to that of Britain after WWII. Second, Japan is replacing "bilateralism at any costs" with "multilateral regionalism." In tandem with the transition from the hub-and-spoke hierarchical order to the "ad hoc coalition of the temporarily willing" and further to the multilateral regional groupings by the US, Japan is placing the key terms of its foreign policy line from loyalty to trust, from compliance to coordination. Third Japan's ontological insecurity has lessoned and self-confidence has grown. As a result, Japan is self-assured in its foreign policy pronouncements, such as a country's international policy should not be defined merely by nation interests, but by universal beliefs of "sharing the sorrow with those killed in war." A phrase used and made famous by Junichiro Koizumi to explain his Yasukuni Shrine visits.

If war is on the decline and if the effectiveness of UN peacekeeping and peace-building operations is on the rise, then is Japan most befitting the 21st century? That is, is Japan in harmony with the time? This question must be continuously posed. It is not a matter of whether Japan should disarm, but one of whether Japan is prepared. For each phase of history and each level of war, the actors must be ready.

II

The Rise of Abegeopolitics

Abe's Ascent to Power and the Coincidence of Business Cycle and China's Assertiveness

Shinzo Abe's second time as Japan's PM started on 26 December 2012. Two factors worked to his benefit: Abe's ascent coincided with a marked improvement in the Japanese economic outlook after 20 years of recession; and China's reactive assertiveness (International Crisis Group, 2014) became louder after PM Yoshihiko Noda nationalised the Senkaku (Diaoyu) Islands. Abe made sure to accrue all the political points possible from these two factors (Inoguchi, 2013; 2014a). Once in the office of PM, Abe launched Abenomics with much fanfare. His first arrow, released in March 2013, targeted the quantitative easing of money. Deflation was the bull's eye. Whereas China argued that its assertiveness was in response to Noda's island policy, Abe argued that Japan's non-violent assertive stance was in response to China's frequent assertive actions. For instance, on 31 January 2013, China's navy targeted a Japanese Coast Guard vessel with fire-control radar. The combative decision of the mainland greatly benefitted the development of what is currently referred to as Abegeopolitics (Inoguchi, 2014b).

The Purposes of Abegeopolitics

Abe in the first 18 months of office embarked on 49 foreign trips. He loves to travel, but his travel has purpose—four purposes specifically. First, Japan views the US as being in a predominantly isolationist mood, and as such, Abe wants Japan to take the extra initiative of reaching out and following what he calls pro-active pacifist diplomacy. This policy line is one of bilateral and multilateral cooperation with all friendly states and the pursuit of international law, prosperity, and non-violent peace. Second, Abegeopolitics is designed to re-assure those concerned about Abenomics. The logic is that although the theory behind the quantitative easing of money raises concerns about the policy's effectiveness in increasing the consumption price index to two per cent per year while maintaining the Nikkei Stock price index as high as possible, TV and news stories of Abe travelling and meeting foreign leaders provide reassurance. Third, Abegeopolitics target the positive and brisk expansion of Japanese trade, investment, and technology markets. Again, this policy is intended to offer some counterbalance to the increasing vulnerability that accompanies Abenomics and the resulting drop in the yen exchange rate with the US dollar. Given the amount and extent of imports that Japan must purchase from abroad, there is naturally an increasing sense of vulnerability. Fourth, with an ironic twist, Abe resorts to a tactic of the ancient Chinese strategist Sun Zi. He advocated *yuanjiao jingong,* that is, keep distant friends close and attack nearby enemies. In the case of Japan, this means keeping friendly ties with 200 states and managing relations with two neighbouring states that are often critical of Japan—China and Korea. In addition to these four objectives, the origins of Abegeopolitics have deep roots.

The Origins of Abegeopolitics

The seeds that germinated into Abegeopolitics started with Japan's unconditional surrender in 1945 and the ensuing years of allied occupation. The impact of those years and the long-term consequences that the post-war constitution had on Japan's sovereignty and sense of self-agitated Abe (2006) to the point that he wrote a book called *Toward Beautiful Japan*. In this volume, published prior to his first time as PM in 2006, Abe explicitly states his love of country, mourns his fellow citizens' loss of confidence, and grieves over his country's compromised sovereignty. He vows that as PM, his first order of business would be to rebuild national confidence and spirit. The historical legacy of the war weighs most heavily in Abe's mind. He laments over the unnecessary compromises he believes Japan made during the transitional period after the war. And he also laments the negative impact they had on diminishing public respect for the flag and anthem and on public awareness about the war dead. The unnecessary compromises for Abe include: the constitutional outlawing of war as a means of international dispute settlement for Japan; constitutional limitations placed on the JSDF and its "war" capabilities; the long-term placement of US armed forces within Japan and the special status or extraterritorial rights ceded to US forces. Abe's strategy is to step out from the shadow of the US, especially given the US isolationist mood, by expanding opportunities for Japan; in areas of trade, investment, technology, and diplomacy. Abe's strategy is also tempered by China's assertive mood. Constrained by the pacifist constitution, Abe seeks to make Japan more alert, politically astute, and aggressive in its foreign policy stance.

Abegeopolitics in Action

Geopolitics sounds old school, especially when the modern buzzword is globalisation and when discussions at all levels of government and business start with the premise that the "world is shrinking." Yet regional politics and geographic proximity matter in governmental day-to-day decisions and in times of crisis. Japan's foreign policy is constructed around three main cornerstones (Inoguchi, 2014c), and the thrust of Abe's key policies are connected to, and reinforce, these cornerstones: the first, improving defence and deterrence capability has a strong affinity with Abegeopolitics; the second, pursuing discovery and innovation to maximise limited domestic resources shares an affinity with Abenomics; and the third, encouraging and promoting multilateral networks and institutions has an affinity with Abe's rationale for foreign travel.

Defence and Deterrence

Since the 1991 bursting of Japan's economic bubble, national defence spending has flat-lined as government revenue faltered and the region around Japan enjoyed relative stability and peace. A stagnate defence budget has affected Japan's ability to defend itself and deter attacks. Kivimaki (2014) and Goldsmith (2014) have researched the reasons behind East Asia's long peace since 1980. It is usually not recognised as an impressive fact, but the long peace is significant.

East Asia's long peace acts as a backdrop to Japan's defence and deterrence policy. Two key concepts are strongly connected to this policy as it has evolved over time—stability and prosperity. Although high economic growth references the past, and not the present, the goal of Japan's policy has sought to maintain domestic and international stability and prosperity. Japan reaches for its objective by seeking to invigorate its US alliance and propel its high technology advantage. Without the alliance, Japan's defence and deterrence capabilities would be substantially hindered. To enhance the alliance, Japan needs to contribute, and its technological edge allows it to make a valuable contribution that assists US armed forces and their technology. Both alliance and technological edge have progressed simultaneously.

Internal Self-transformation

Political actors have a choice when confronted with change: they can either focus on self-transformation or the transformation of others. Abenomics focuses on the former. The most visible example is the attempt by Abe to cleanse Japan of the deflationary mindset with a quantitative easing of money.

Prolonged domestic stagnation and turbulent relations with China and North and South Korea from 2012 to 2014 prompted Japan toward self-transformation. As China's economy has flourished with double-digit growth over the last three decades and Japan's economy has languished for the last two decades, the regional economic centre of Asia has shifted from Japan to China. Regional economic links have developed along two tracks. Non-Chinese regional states have pursued increased economic ties with other regional players. In contrast, Japan, China and South Korea have focused on increased economic trade and investment at the international level. Of the three states, China's globalisation is the most dramatic. In recent years, particularly since 2012, this economic pattern has been accompanied by increased anti-Japanese rhetoric by both China's new leader Xi Jingping and South Korea's new leader Park Geun-Hye. This development is troubling to the government and people of Japan. Noda's decision in the autumn of 2012 to nationalise the Senkaku Islands generated a scathing response from China. In the last days of 2012, Abe was sworn in as PM, and as the new national leader, he is critical of the anti-Japanese posturing of China and South Korea.

To mark the first anniversary of being sworn into office, Abe visited the Yasukuni Shrine on 26 December 2013. It was an opportunity for Abe to show respect to the war dead, a gesture valued by his right-wing supporters. However, for China, 26 December 2013, marks the 100th anniversary of Mao Zedong's birth (1893-1976). Responses from both Beijing and Seoul were vehement and warned of further deteriorating relations with Japan. At the start of 2013, China's Navy had employed fire-control radars to target Japan's coast guard vessels. Japan chose not to react to this provocation. The Chinese then proceeded to have their air force tail and manoeuvre "unusually close" to a Japanese reconnaissance aircraft (Inoguchi, 2014b). Such actions have created an anti-Chinese and anti-Korean mood among Japanese citizens. Abe has chosen to exploit these public sentiments but cautiously as he understands and values the economic interdependence that binds his country with China and South Korea.

Research and development in science and technology will remain important as the process of self-transformation commences. Abenomics is focused on three goals: (a) to replace the deflationary mindset of the Japanese public with one that promotes consumption and investment through the use of monetary policy; (b) to control and cap huge government budget deficits by excising selected non-priority budget items and focusing resources on priority areas, such as science and technology; and (c) to ensure that Japan's science and technology maintains its advantage through substantial investment by government and corporations in science and technology research and development.

Networks and Multilateralism

Abe's trips abroad are designed to reinforce Japan's position and voice in international institutions and to explore foreign connections, new and old. Japan seeks to build a presence in multilateral institutions for two reasons. First, the familiar institutions created in the 20th century, that is, the UN, the WTO, the IMF, and the World Bank are increasingly viewed as large, lumbering organisations that have lost their relevance. Japan's approach is to re-invigorate these agencies with new groups, for instance, the introduction of the G4 (Japan, Germany, Brazil and India) into the UNSC. Second, Japan realises that emerging economies are actively setting up their own organisations and that these new endeavours are making the older organisations extraneous. The New Infrastructure Investment Bank, an offshoot of the G22, is one example. Japan is cognisant that its foreign policy is US-alliance centred and that in the past the other 190-plus countries were not given sufficient attention in Tokyo's foreign relations agenda. Japan may be deeply involved in globalisation, but it is not exploring the extent of its soft power in technology, economic prowess, and cultural richness. One factor holding Japanese back from employment in multilateral institutions is their low proficiency in English.

Abegeopolitics is a perspicacious platform for the moment. Whether it has the ability to endure and succeed remains an open question.

III

Speculating on Asian Security (2013-2033)

What will the next two decades bring in terms of power competition in Asia? This is a speculative exercise but the actors are definite: Japan, China, and the US. I presume that state strategies will be more critical in this exercise than the strength of a hegemonic order and the possible transition from US supremacy to global governance supported by states, societies, and international organisation who mostly share a common understanding of international norms and rules. This section examines and analyses the difficulties faced by each of the three countries in pursuing their strategic goal. The US goal is "primacy", whereas the Chinese goal is "equality" and the Japanese goal is "peace." Whether these goals can be achieved is uncertain as the means that is supposed to help these states reach their goal is problematic. For the US, the level of investment in R&D (research and development) is at risk; for China, the extractive institutions may do more harm than good; and for Japan, its ability to be decisive in a fractious, fragmented power structure is uncertain. Before considering the future dialectics of Asian security, I turn to the past dialectics of Asian security, starting in 1813, to contrast and compare the key qualities that characterised the past 200 years with those of the next 20 years.

Two Benchmark Years: 1813 and 2033

The year 1813 is an important benchmark for combined Asian wealth or GDP (Maddison, 2003; Maddison and Wu, 2007; Frank, 1998). The Mughal empire ruled India, the Qing empire ruled China, and the Tokugawa Shogunate ruled Japan (Jones, 1981; 1988). It was a time of prosperity for all three dynasties. Yet this year also marks the start of the decline for all three powers (Ferguson, 2011). Western powers were on their doorstep along with the unstoppable tide of globalisation. The combined Asian domestic product dropped dramatically in the coming years.

In contrast, the West was in a period of industrialisation and military expansion. Its ascendance is marred by the devastating wars of World War I and World War II. After the war, the US led the West in quickly climbing GDP. Pax Americana dominated the industrial age of the second half of the 20th century. Industrialisation and globalisation developed in tandem, trickling down to the non-West and allowing for wealth accumulation as well. Asia experienced three waves of wealth accumulation (Aoki, 2011). Japan was in the first wave. Following the destruction of World War II, Japan industrialised during the first three decades following this conflict. Next, China's economic development gained momentum, starting in the 1980s and continuing into the 2000s and beyond. The third wave of industrialisation includes India and other emerging economies. Their time for economic growth came in the 2000s. Current predictions for 2033 peg Asia's combined GDP as representing 50 per cent of world GDP. Hence, 2033 is the second benchmark year following 1813. I use these two benchmark years to contemplate Asia's power relations in 2033.

The Coming Two Decades of Uncertainty

How power relations in Asia unfold over the next 20 years to 2033 is uncertain, but in evaluating the anticipated power competition, the factors that pose the most challenges to meeting the respective goals of Japan, China, and the US (peace, equality, and primacy) are better understood. In this section I concentrate on these three strategic goals and the cost of their pursuit. Cause for concern and uncertainty can be found in many areas, such as the stagnant economies of OECD countries, especially when compared to growing emergent economies. Another source of uncertainty is the contest between China and the US and how it draws in their respective allies and friends. One problem China is struggling to handle is the demographic impact of its one-child policy. As the elderly population increases, the productive demographic is sharply dropping. The pressure comes from the expectation that with growth comes increased social policy entitlement. The situation is aggravated by the uncertainty of institutions. The last three decades of economic growth in China are built on Dengist economics and politics. Today, many believe that Dengist policies have plateaued in usefulness, and in the 2010s more are adding their voice for change. China is proud of its economic progress but with it has come self-assertive tendencies. Gaps in income and status cause tensions in Chinese society. In 2012, there were 100,000 protests with 1000 participants or more. The Chinese leadership, which are also part of the elite and privileged segments of society, are divided on how to best handle these social cleavages and the ensuing social unrest. Xi Jinping is firmly in power, but not before the world witnessed the dramatic fall of Bo Xilai from power.

Uncertainty also looms for the US. Still struggling to recover from the 2008 Lehmann Brother shock, the US economy continues to suffer from high unemployment and low consumer demand. The massive monetary injection by the US government has not brought the US economy out of its current downturn. The political spectrum in Washington also oscillates between those who demand "small government" and those who call for "no entanglement abroad." Political leadership and economic reality impact the US defence policy. With the rise of China, the US government is convinced that it needs to play a more active role in Asian regional security and in limiting the tensions and fallout between regional actors who come into conflict with China. To achieve this policy goal requires a substantial investment of the US budget on defence, but is this possible given the current economic woes of the US? Whether Washington can play a sustained role in balancing the Asia-Pacific depends on its financial ability to fund R&D on weapons. When the US Congress is dominated by small government ideologues, funding for R&D is cut.

The future of Japanese politics also holds uncertainty. In the post-Cold War years, friction and fragmentation have plagued politics in Japan (Inoguchi and Ikenberry, 2013). What was once a tightly structured society, is part a product of high economic growth witnessed in the 1960s, 1970s, and 1980s, turned to a less cohesive societal structure during the long recession. In the political realm, this transition translated into a stronger civil society that challenged the state. Another foible to cast a shadow over Japan's future is the failure of organisations, regardless of size, to design and implement decisions that integrate long- and short-term policies. Indecisiveness is a common affliction. Examples of some of the critical policy areas to be affected include: Should the country rely on nuclear power generation for energy? Should taxes be raised to maintain the social policy package for the elderly population? If so, how much should they be raised? What kind of collaborative projects should be brought forward to sustain the US alliance? Lastly, what should Japan do to ensure that its economy remains viable in a scientifically and technologically advanced world in which demographically large states flourish? Population forecasts for 2050 place Africa's population at

2 billion, India at 1.6 billion, and China at 1.4 billion. In contrast, Japan's population is estimated to be under 100 million people.

Dialectic Moment?

The task is to speculate on the 2033 power configuration of Japan, China, and the US. Informed speculation requires that shared, key factors in the evolution of the three states be considered. In this exercise, the factor is demography, but not because it is a principal determinant, more because other factors will intervene to influence its development, producing unexpected power configurations.

China

Acemoglu and Robinson (2012) refer to China's institutionalised procedures and practices that direct power and wealth to the communist party elites as extractive political and economic institutions. China's dialectic starts with Acemoglu and Robinson's concept. The "class enemy", once reviled and persecuted in China, has lost many of its associated taboos as China pursued economic development. This class is now able to join the Chinese Communist Party (CCP). These political elites acquire power and wealth from the Chinese practice of state ownership of land and state enterprises. The slogan "socialism with Chinese characteristics" specifies that the state owns all land and that SOEs (state-owned enterprises) are leading players. The practical application is that the state can confiscate land whenever it wants. The frequency of the practice is confirmed by the roughly 500 weekly protests against the confiscation of rural and urban land. The SOE is another form of extractive institution that has special access to state financing and is tax exempt. Such advantages allow SOEs to survive difficult times when their private counterparts go bankrupt. The elites benefit through employment with the extractive institutions, which in turn guarantees the survival of the SOEs who are backed by the People's Liberation Army (PLA) and fall under the umbrella of the CCP. During economic downturns, the business and operation of extractive institutions increase. The issue is that sustained economic development is not possible with the existence of extractive institutions. The question then focuses on long-term viability of extractive institutions. Will they exist in 2033? Will the 500 weekly protests lead to something larger? Will they trigger a military response?

United States

R&D investment in weapons is the most significant uncertainty facing the US. In 2012, President Barack Obama announced a 10-year defence budget plan, including budget cuts. How deeply will the budget cuts affect R&D in weapons? Based on the size of defence budget cuts, it is impossible for R&D weapon programmes not to be impacted. The US, as the largest single actor in the expenditure of R&D weapon programmes, accounts for approximately 85 per cent of worldwide expenditures on weapons. Two factors may influence this area of budget cuts. First, the US is a strong proponent in the ever-advancing technology of weapons, and hence, its commitment to a robust R&D weapon programme. That said, since the 1960s, the ratio of public R&D to GDP has dropped by one-half (The Economist, 2012). In recent years, some have argued for low-tech weapons to be fully explored and exploited first (Caverley and Kapstein, 2012). Second is the China factor. For the last two decades, China has pursued a double-digit defence build-up. The US is concerned about the build-up, but it is more worried by China's foreign and defence policy to refuse the US access to international waters and airspace around the South China Sea area and its coastline where military and industrial facilities are concentrated. To achieve its policy goal, the PLA have divided the western Pacific, west of Hawaii, into zone A and zone B. The demarcation of zone A follows the line of Japanese archipelago along to Taiwan and the Philippines; zone B follows along from Guam and Hawaii. For the US to effectively mount a counter campaign against China's maritime policy, R&D investment in weapons is critical. One expensive option is to collaborate in design and production of materials and components with foreign companies who excel in these areas. The F-35 fighter plane is an example, but the costs are astronomical. Of course, the two powers could pursue reconciliation over confrontation. The effect of such a policy choice would mean that the US would have one less reason to embark on huge investments in weaponry R&D.

Japan

Japan's problem with quick decision-making is well known. Henry Kissinger (2001) observed that Japanese are historically slow in reaching any kind of decision. Some would say, Kissinger exaggerates the problem, but that is not to say that the bottlenecks do not exist. The perceived style of Japanese decision-making is to seek consensus from below, but the reality is that each actor asserts his veto, thereby making the decision process labourious. In this environment, politics suffers from fragmentation and a piecemeal approach. Evolving structural features complicate the problem. (a) Technology allows everyone to participate in politics. (b) Traditional mediating organisations, that is, political parties and interest groups, have much less societal influence. (c) Ideas and opinions cross borders much quicker and easier. Keane (2009) identifies this trend as "monitory democracy", noting its arrival means the end of representative democracy. The question of whether other industrial democracies exhibiting similar conditions remains open (The Economist, 2011).

Three Pursuits Concurrently Unfolding?

In assessing and analysing the security dynamics of the Asian region, a lot of 'ifs' need consideration. In the case of the US, if it continues to prioritise primacy, if US economic conditions do not limit its policy priority, if Washington imposes drastic budget cuts, and if it implements a rebalancing strategy to maintain it primacy in the region, dialectics are inevitable. The current US strategy seeks an "air-sea battle (ASB)—an operational concept designed to help the US air force and navy jointly respond to Anti-Access/Area Denial (A2/AD) challenges, enhance deterrence, and ensure freedom of action around the world over the next generation" (Horowitz, 2012). Budget cuts are expected to be extensive and will have a negative ripple effect, including high-tech procurements, next generation robotic R&D, a new long-range bomber, and C4ISR (command, control, communications, computers, intelligence, surveillance, and reconnaissance). All are viewed as “essential to guaranteeing US military power over the long term” (Horowitz, 2012).

If the US is not willing to adjust its primacy policy in the Asia-Pacific region and anticipated budget cuts remain, then what policy choices does the US have? One option is to stand tall. This harkens back to Ronald Reagan’s concept of standing tall and luring China into an arms race that would cause it to overextend itself. US defence budgets would not be hit as hard. A second option is burden sharing with Japan. For instance, the latter could provide access to its airplane wing technology for the production of F-35s. Such an initiative and outward sign of a strong Japan-US alliance would certainly spark hostile feelings from China. A third option is appeasement. The US could simultaneously pursue global primacy and step back from A2/AD. The result would be a less hostile China. The implementation of this last choice is controversial and its effectiveness questionable.

If the main Chinese policy objective is income equality for the domestic arena and equality of sovereign power in the international context, then dialectical movements are unavoidable. Deng’s economic reforms loosened state regulations and associated privileges. The economic benefits of the reform package are visible in higher domestic incomes and growing economic and political power abroad. The harmful outcomes include gaps between urban and rural places and between party elites and grass-root movements. The overall sense in China is that state regulations need to be loosened further. State regulations are at the centre of what Acemoglu and Robinson label extractive institutions (Acemoglu and Robinson, 2012). State regulations have made China’s elites wealthier, but at what cost to the masses.

If Japan does not remedy its contentious and labourious decision-making process, then its roles in the region and in the world are uncertain. If China’s power keeps growing, if 60 per cent of US forces are focused on the Asia-Pacific region, and if the US pursues its A2/AD strategy against China, what is Japan’s policy position? Public opinion on this issue is unclear. An Internet survey, called “Japan and World Trends”, offers some insight. The survey asks its readers to respond to the following question: "When the United States and China are contesting each other in the Asia Pacific, what do you think is your preference for Japan's foreign policy?" The respondent is to choose one of seven possible responses: (a) neutrality with the current defence level intact; (b) neutrality with a conventional defence build-up; (c) neutrality with nuclear armament; (d) alliance with the US while keeping a strategic and mutually beneficial relationship with China; (e) build an East Asian community, excluding the US and the European Union; (f) another scheme; and (g) don't know.

The third policy choice is the one that both the ruling party and the main opposition party support. Of the respondents, 25 per cent selected this option. Over 50 per cent of respondents chose some form of neutrality, that is, one of the first three options. However, those respondents who indicated option 1 have to be disregarded as it is not a viable option. The third policy direction is also not possible without major implications. The fourth choice received 15 per cent of respondent support. The results of this Internet survey produced similar results to other random sampled surveys, such as the Yomiuri survey. The takeaway from these surveys is that the Japanese public is split on policy direction, culminating in delayed action. In 2033, what will Japan's foreign and security policy be? Even if Japan wants peace, the dynamics produced by the US seeking primacy and China seeking equality may force Japan to prepare, at least, for the use of force.

IV

Conclusion

All three powers seek a role in Asia's regional security in 2033. How these power relations unfold is uncertain. It is a speculative exercise in which I have examined the main policy objective of each state player and the means they must use to reach their goal. Whenever a state prioritises one policy, other factors intrude. The policy goal of the US is primacy, and that intruding other factor for it, is the prohibitive cost of weaponry R&D. The policy goal of China is equality within and outside its borders. At home, equality must involve alleviating the pressure placed on the masses and the economic development process by the extractive institutions. Abroad, equality means equal sovereignty. The intruding other factor in China's case is that the modernisation of its military depends on these very extractive institutions. The policy goal of Japan is peace and armed neutrality. The other intruding factor is regional security and the dynamics in power relations between the US and China, as they reach for their policy objective. Hence, Japan may be forced to acquire a more powerful means to defend itself and deter potential adversaries. Uncertainty will be the dominant feature of the next 20 years as power relations among the three countries unfold. A better way to assess power relations in Asia may be to look toward the domestic arena. How each state pursues its policy goal and how it achieves it may shed more light on the way how regional power relations will unfold among the three countries. For all the discussions about globalisation, the outcome will be determined by the battle at home.

Notes

Key issues of this chapter are borrowed from three recent publications of mine;

1) "Japan's Foreign Policy Line after the Cold War" in G. John Ikenberry and Takashi Inoguchi (ed.), *The Troubled Triangle-Economic and Security Concerns for the United States, Japan and China*. 2013.
2) "The Rise of Abegeopolitics", *Global Asia* 10(3), Autumn, 2014.
3) "Speculating on Asia Security, 2013-2033", *European Review of International Studies* 1(1): 46-56 (March 2014).

Table 7.1-7.3 originally appear in: 1) "Japan's Foreign Policy Line after the Cold War". They have been reproduced in this chapter with permission by Palgrave Macmillan.

References

Abe, Shinzo (2006). *Utsukushii Kuni e* (Toward Beautiful Japan). Tokyo: Bungei shunju sha.

Acemoglu, Daron and James Robinson (2012). *Why Nations Fail: The Origins of Power, Prosperity and Poverty*, New York: Crown Publishers.

Aoki, Masahiko (2011). "The Five Phases of Economic Development and Institutional Evolution in China and Japan", Presidential Lecture at the *XVIth World Congress* of the International Economic Association. Beijing. July.

Caverley, Jonathan and Ethan B. Kapstein (2012). "Arms Away: How Washington Squandered its Monopoly on Weapons Sales", *Foreign Affairs* 91:5.

Ferguson, Nial (2011). *Civilization: The West and the Rest*, London: Allen Lane.

Frank, Andre Gunder (1998). *Re-Orient: Global Economy in the Asian Age*, Berkley, CA: University of California Press.

Funabashi, Yoichi (1999). *Alliance Adrift*. New York: Council on Foreign Relations Press.

Goldsmith, Benjamin (2014). "The East Asian Peace as a Second-Order Diffusion Effect", *International Studies Review* 16:2.

Goldstein, Joshua (2011). *Winning War on War: The Decline of Armed Conflict Worldwide*. New York: Dutton.

Gourevitch, Peter and Takashi Inoguchi and Courtney Purrington (eds.) (1995). *United States-Japan Relations and International Institutions After the Cold War*. San Diego, CA: University of California Graduate School of International Relations and Pacific Studies.

Hidaka, Yoshiki (2012). *Teikoku no shuen, superpower de nakunaru domeikoku, America* (The End of the Empire, the Fall of an Ally: How America will Lose its Superpower Status). Tokyo: PHP Institute.

Horowitz, Michael C. (2012). *How Defense Austerity Will Test U.S. Strategy in Asia*. The National Bureau of Asian Research. pp.1-4. Available at *www.nbr.org/publications/element.aspx?id=612* (posted August 2012).

Jones, Eric (1981). *The European Miracle: Environments, Economies and Geopolitics in the History of Europe and Asia*. Cambridge: Canbridge University Press.

———. (1988). *The Growth Recurring*. Oxford: Oxford University Press.

Keane, John (2009). *The Life and Death of Democracy*. New York: Simon & Schuster.

Kissinger, Henry (2001). *Does the United States Need a Foreign Policy? Toward a Diplomacy for the 21st Century*. New York: Simon & Schuster.

Kivimaki, Timo (2014). *The Long Peace of East Asia*. Surrey, England: Ashgate.

Inoguchi, Takashi (1991). *Japan's International Relations*. New York: Continuum International.

———. (1993). *Japan's Foreign Policy in An Era of Global Change*. New York: Continuum.

———. (1995). "Japan's United Nations Peacekeeping and Other Operations", *International Studies* 50: 2 (Spring).

———. (1998). "Japan's Foreign Policy under U.S. Unipolarity: Coping with Uncertainty and Swallowing Some Bitterness", *Asian Journal of Political Science* 6: 2.

———. (2001). *Global Change: A Japanese Perspective*. New York: Palgrave Macmillan

———. (2006). "Japan's Emerging Role as a 'Global Ordinary Power'", *International Relations of the Asia-Pacific* 6: 1.

———. (2007). "How to Assess World War II in World History: One Japanese Perspective", in David Koh Wee Hock (ed.), *Legacies of World War II in South and East Asia*. Singapore: ISEAS.

———. (2008a). "Japan as a Global Ordinary Power: Its Current Phase", *Japanese Studies* 28: 1.

———. (2008b). "Japan: What Power? What Strategies?" *Politique étrangère* 73 (World Policy Conference). October

———. (2009). "Japan Desperately Needs Grand Strategy", *International Herald Tribune, The Asahi Shimbun* 1: 13, January.

———. (2013). "The Dynamic Dynamite of Asia's Leadership Changes", *Global Asia* 8: 1.

———. (2014a). "Japan in 2013: Abenomics and Abegeopolitics", *Asian Survey* 54: 1.

———. (2014b). "Speculating on Asian Security, 1813-2033", *European Review of International Studies* 1: 1.

———. (2014c). "A Call for a New Japanese Foreign Policy: The Dilemmas of a Stakeholder State", *International Affairs* 90: 4.

Inoguchi, Takashi and Daniel I. Okimoto (eds.) (1989). "Vol. 2: The Changing International System", *The Political Economy of Japan.* Stanford: Stanford University Press.

Inoguchi, Takashi and G. John Ikenberry (eds.) (2013). *The Troubled Traingle: Economic and Security Concerns for The United States, Japan, and China.* Political & International Studies Collection 2013, Series: Asia Today. New York: Palgrave Macmillan.

Inoguchi, Takashi, G. John Ikenberry and Yoichiro Sato (2011). *The US-Japan Security Alliance.* New York: Palgrave Macmillan.

Ikenberry, G. John and Takashi Inoguchi (2003) *Reinventing the Alliance.* New York: Palgrave Macmillan.

————. (2007). *The Uses of Institutions: The US, Japan and Governance in East Asia.* New York: Palgrave Macmillan.

International Crisis Group (2014). "Report Reactive Assertiveness", quoted by Yaping Wang, *The Flawed Logic behind Beijing's Senkaku/Diayu Policy*, 16 May.

Kitaoka, Shinichi (2009). *Global Player Toshiteno Nihon* (Japan as a Global Player). Tokyo: NTT.

Kosaka, Masataka (1968). *Saisho Yoshida Shigeru* (Prime Minister Shigeru Yoshida). Tokyo: Chuokoronsha.

Maddison, Angus (2003). *The World Economy: Historical Studies Statistics.* OECD, Development Centre Studies.

Maddison, Angus and Harry X. Wu (2007). *New Estimates of Chinese Growth Performance and Potential 1952-2020.* The Groningen Growth and Development Centre.

Magosaki, Ukeru (2012). *Sengoshi no Shoutai* (True Identity of Postwar History). Tokyo: Sogensha.

Mueller, John (1989). *Retreat from Doomsday: The Obsolescence of Major War.* New York: Basic Books.

Sato, Seizaburo and Takashi Ito (1995). *Ano Senso wa Nandatta noka?* (That War, What was it?). Tokyo: Chuo Koronsya.

Tanaka, Akihiko (2009). *Post-Crisis no Sekai: Shin-takyoku jidai o ugokasu Power genri* (Post-crisis World: Principals Guiding the New Multipolar Era). Tokyo: Nihon Keizai Shimbun.

Thalakada, Nigel R. (2012). *Unipolarity and the Evolution of America's Cold War Alliances.* New York: Palgrave Macmillan.

The Economist (2011). "Turning Japanese", *The Economist*, 30 July.

————. (2012). "Free Exchange/Arrested Development", *The Economist*, 25 August 25. p.61.

Yan, Xuetong (2006). "The Rise of China and Its Power Status", *Chinese Journal of International Politics* 1.

Yomiuri Online (2011). "*Beikoku ni Shitashimi-Saikou no 82%*" (Pro-American Sentiments Recorded 82%—The Highest Ever), *Yomiuri Online*, 3 December. Access at: *http://www.yomiuri.co.jp/feature/20110316–866918/news/20111203-OYT1T00998.htm* (December 18, 2011).

Zarakol, Ayse (2010). "Ontological (In) security and State Denial of Historical Ciemes: Turkey and Japan", *International Relations* 24:1.

Zarakol, Ayse (2011). *After Defeat: How the East Leaned to Live with the West.* Cambridge: Cambridge University Press.

Others:

The Asia-Pacific Roundtable, CSIS, Kuala Lumpur, Malaysia, May 28-30, 2012, and at the *World Peace Forum*, Tsinghua University, Beijing, China, July 7-8, 2012.

The poll conducted in December 2011 jointly by the Yomiuri Shimbun and Gallup Organization: *Yomiuri Online*, December 18, 2011; Access at: *http://www.yomiuri.co.jp/feature/fe6100/koumoku/20111218.htm* (January 10, 2012).

8

ROHAN MUKHERJEE

India's Foreign Policy

I

Historical Context and Evolution

Although one can look far back into India's colonial and pre-colonial history to chalk out the long-term historical context of its foreign policy, a proper account of modern India's foreign policy must begin in 1947, with the birth of the republic. It was at this point, freed from the shackles of British rule and reeling from the bloody aftermath of Partition with Pakistan, that a visionary set of national leaders began to come to terms with the challenges and opportunities of India's position in regional and global affairs. A key question in this regard was: What kind of power will India be? At the outset, the answer that Prime Minister Jawaharlal Nehru—who was largely responsible for India's foreign affairs in the first decade and a half following independence—struck upon was that India would be a force for peace and unity among the nations of the world.

In a speech to the Constituent Assembly of India on 22 January 1947, Nehru articulated this vision:

> We do not want to fight any nation if we can help it. The only possible real objective that we, in common with other nations, can have is the objective of co-operating in building up some kind of world structure, call it 'One World', call it what you like (CAD, 1947).

In the resolution that followed, this philosophy was accompanied by an assertion of India's sovereignty and greatness: the assembly resolved to enact a constitution,

> Whereby shall be maintained the integrity of the territory of the Republic and its sovereign rights on land, sea and air according to

> justice and the law of civilised nations; and this ancient land attain its rightful and honoured place in the world and make its full and willing contribution to the promotion of world peace and the welfare of mankind (CAD, 1947).

A conflict in Kashmir with Pakistan in late 1947 reminded Nehru that the world was not yet ready for his vision of peace through international cooperation. Although Nehru referred the matter to the United Nations Security Council (UNSC), the Western permanent members of the council—particularly the United States (US) and Britain—were deeply unsympathetic to India's claims. Although this experience soured India's idealist approach to the United Nations (UN), Delhi continued to play an important role in upholding the fundamental commitment to international peace and security enshrined in the UN charter. In 1950, India advocated restraint as the US and its allies sought to enter the conflict in Korea under UN auspices against China. India, for its part, supported the resolution for intervention but sent only a field ambulance unit into battle while declining to officially label China the aggressor in the conflict.

Relations with China, however, did not turn out as well as Nehru had hoped when promulgating the famous *Hindi Chini Bhai Bhai* slogan in the early 1950s. Although India and China agreed upon the Five Principles of Peaceful Coexistence (*Panchsheel*) in 1954 and Delhi ceded any control it had over Tibet to Beijing, by 1955 official Chinese maps had emerged showing portions of territory that India considered its own within China's national boundary. Escalating tensions over the India-China border led to a brief and limited war in 1962 that resulted in a resounding defeat for India, followed by China's first nuclear test two years later—events that transformed South Asian geopolitics for India. In 1965, India faced an attack by Pakistan in Kutch, which Prime Minister Lal Bahadur Shastri's government was able to repel with relative ease compared to the experience with China three years ago. Later in the decade, fearing the looming Chinese nuclear threat, India refused to sign the Nuclear Non-Proliferation Treaty (NPT) on grounds that it would create a world of nuclear haves and have-nots, the subtext being that India chose to reserve the option of exiting the latter group.

India's diplomatic isolation on the NPT was, however, nothing compared to the solitude experienced by Prime Minister Indira Gandhi and her advisors in 1971 when they tried to rally global condemnation of Pakistan's genocide in East Pakistan (Bass, 2013). At a time when both the US and China supported Pakistan for strategic reasons, India chose a defense pact with the Soviet Union, thus effectively abandoning the policy of non-alignment with the Cold War's superpower blocs that Nehru had fashioned since the 1950s (although successive Indian governments continued to reiterate at least rhetorical commitment to it). India's reputation as a peace-loving nation took a beating due to Delhi's military intervention in the East Pakistan crisis, as well as India's first nuclear test in 1974, even though the explosion itself was labelled "peaceful" by the government (Perkovich, 1999).

India's relations with China began warming again toward the end of the 1970s, but relations with the US plunged further as India evinced tacit support for the Soviet invasion of Afghanistan and the US amplified its alliance with Pakistan (alive since the 1950s) in order to fight a proxy war in the latter's strategic backyard. The 1980s saw India involve itself in the Sri Lankan civil war, with disastrous consequences for all sides, and for India's image as a regional power. However, this period was also a time of hesitant initial cooperation among South Asian nations, with the advent of the South Asian Association for Regional Cooperation (SAARC) at Bangladesh's behest. Toward the end of the decade, as Soviet power began to decline, India and China initiated a rapprochement with Prime Minister Rajiv Gandhi's visit to Beijing, the first by an Indian Prime Minister since Nehru.

As is well known, the year 1990 was a watershed for India in almost every respect (Mohan, 2003). A balance of payments (BoP) crisis necessitated emergency assistance from the International Monetary Fund (IMF), which in turn required major domestic economic reform. Externally, India had backed the wrong horse in the Cold War, and now had to deal with a global power (the US) and a regional power (China) that were allied with Pakistan. Delhi responded by redoubling its economic efforts and seeking new strategic partnerships, and by conducting a second round of nuclear tests in 1998, which initially invited the ire of the world's major powers, but soon gave way to recognition of India as an important player that could not be simply "hyphenated" with Pakistan in thinking about South Asia (Talbott, 2004). This was evident in the 1999 Kargil War with Pakistan, when China took a relatively neutral stance compared to the past, and the US worked actively to broker a peace through informal channels.

Subsequently, with President Bill Clinton's visit to India in 2000, relations with the US began a period of warmth and peaked with the signing of the landmark US-India Civil Nuclear Agreement of 2008 (during visit of President Bush). Although many in the US criticised the agreement as giving too much away to India, Delhi viewed it as long-awaited validation of its policies as a responsible nuclear power. While this may be true in the nuclear realm, the question on the minds of international observers of contemporary Indian foreign policy is whether India can be an overall responsible global power, be it in handling bilateral relations with traditional rivals such as Pakistan and China, in promoting regional cooperation in South Asia and the Indo-Pacific region more broadly, or in tackling global issues of peace and security as a non-permanent (and perhaps future permanent) member of the UNSC.

Political Context

The political context of India's foreign policy can be viewed on two levels, the international and the domestic. On both levels, India's democratic constitution and political system is of vital importance. However, despite being a democracy, India has often not hewed to certain theoretical expectations that one might have of democratic powers. For example, it is widely noted that for most of the Cold War the world's largest democracy (India) and the world's oldest democracy (the US) were consistently on the opposing sides of most regional and global strategic equations (Kux, 1993). Moreover, India has done precious little to externalise or promote its democratic values beyond its borders. These outcomes are partly due to the fact that India is what one author has labelled an "improbable democracy" (Varshney, 2013)—a poor nation with high ethnic diversity and public institutions that are still struggling to resolve challenges of representation and effectiveness. They are also due to the global configuration of power and interests that prevailed for much of the Cold War, particularly the American alliance with Pakistan 1950s onward, and the role played by Pakistan both as a conduit for the US-China rapprochement in the 1970s and proxy warrior against the Soviets in Afghanistan in the 1980s. Strategic interests aside, it is still worth investigating the question of how India's democratic political system influences its foreign policy.

There are three broad observations that one can make about the domestic politics of India's foreign policy. First, unlike non-democratic regimes, in democracies it is possible for relatively small constituencies of voters or sections of society to have an impact on foreign policy. The demands, or perceived demands, of such groups are amplified through the free press and a vibrant civil society that facilitates organised representation of interests and input into the policymaking process. In India, various groups have impacted foreign policy on a range of issues, either through organised input or the simple perception on the part of politicians and policymakers that these groups' interests matter for individual or party political survival. The often-cited influence of India's 'Islamic identity' (Mohan, 2003: 17) is a case in point. As observed by a scholar in the 1980s, "The Indian National Congress [party]...has a sixty year old history of sensitivity to the preferences of the country's large Muslim minority regarding West Asia" (Wright, 1982: 1655). Indeed, India's policies toward the Middle East (also known as West Asia in India) have been influenced by the perceived sensitivities of India's sizeable Muslim population, despite the fact that no effort has been made to systematically unearth the latter's preferences, and despite the fact that the Middle East is a highly diverse region with sectarian divides that are mirrored within India's Muslim population. Nonetheless, the putative power of the so-called Muslim vote led India to adopt strong pro-Arab and anti-Israeli stances in the UN throughout the Cold War, and it was only in the 1980s that tentative steps were taken to establish a relationship with Israel, under the Janata government of 1977-1980 (Abhyankar, 2007).

The second observation one can make about the domestic politics of India's foreign policy is the role of sub-national identity and regional political power. Due to various historical, political and geographic factors, certain groups in Indian society share strong ethnic affiliations with groups in neighbouring countries or territories. Prominent examples include Kashmiris living under Indian and Pakistani rule respectively, Indian Punjabis and Pakistani Punjabis, Indian Tamils and Sri Lankan Tamils, Indian Bengalis and Bangladeshis (particularly Hindus in Bangladesh), Indians in the border regions of Uttar Pradesh (UP) and Bihar, and Nepalis in the neighbouring Terai region. In some regions, particularly Kashmir and Punjab, these transborder ties have fuelled insurgencies in Indian territory. In other cases, such as Sri Lanka and Bangladesh, ethnic groups in India have exerted great political and moral pressure to sway India's policy toward intervention of some sort. The pull of regional power centres has grown in India over time with the gradual decline of the Congress Party's dominance in electoral politics, as well as the party's own internal cohesion, since the 1960s. India's semi-federal political structure has frequently empowered leaders at the sub-national level who might have their own specific agenda regarding a narrow transborder issue such as water sharing, immigration, or militancy, which then forces the hand of the federal government due to coalition politics in Delhi.

The issue of federalism and foreign policy leads indirectly to the third observation, which is the growing fragmentation of political power at the federal level in Indian politics. Since independence, India's democracy has witnessed considerable deepening in terms of newly empowered groups joining the political process, particularly as the benefits of economic growth reach hitherto neglected regions and sections of society. Consequently, new parties and formations trading in identity politics have emerged and slowly chipped away at the electoral bases of the two national parties, the Congress and the Bharatiya Janata Party (BJP). The 1990s witnessed the advent of highly unstable coalition politics, when India elected six governments in the span of eight years (the normal tenure for a government being five years). The general decline of single-party dominance and the emergence of different national governments allowed the articulation of alternative worldviews within the policymaking establishment, such as the "genuine non-alignment" of the 1977 Janata government, or the "Gujral Doctrine" of the late 1990s, or the "Hindu Rashtra" of the BJP at the turn of the 21st century (Malone and Mukherjee, 2010). Although the various political dispensations at the federal level may have disagreed on specific policy issues, the one thread common to them all in the post-Cold War world has been economic diplomacy, which provided tangible gains that each government could point to in its record, and also helped to grow the Indian economy. India's domestic politics, although often chaotic, has managed to settle on an equilibrium that seems to satisfy at least the basic needs of a large and relatively poor nation.

Institutions and Processes

For almost the entire Cold War period, Indian foreign policy was decided between the Prime Minister's Secretariat (PMS, later renamed the Prime Minister's Office, or PMO) and the Ministry of External Affairs (MEA), often in a situation where the prime minister was also foreign minister (as Nehru was for his entire tenure from 1947 until his death in 1964). During this period, India's foreign policymaking was relatively centralised—most decisions were made at the highest levels and simply implemented by the relevant ministries and agencies. Following the Nehru era, as with most aspects of domestic policymaking and internal Congress party organisation, foreign policymaking was centralised a great deal more under Indira Gandhi's leadership. Since this period, the PMO has remained a powerful independent actor in the foreign policy establishment (Bandhyopadhyaya, 2003). It is not surprising, therefore, that India's diplomatic history is often recounted in terms of the policies of successive prime ministers, even though in many cases a single prime minister was in office for multiple—in some cases, non-consecutive—terms during which the strategic environment changed, often significantly. This method of compartmentalising India's Cold War foreign policy, while it reflects the stature of figures such as Nehru and Indira Gandhi, tends to over-emphasise their authority within the foreign policy establishment, which did not always go unquestioned (Madan, 2014). Even in military affairs, India has maintained a tradition of civilian control through the Ministry of Defence (MoD)—while some have argued that this tradition has cost India key strategic losses, such as the 1962 war with China (Dalvi, 1968), others more recently contend that civilian control is not the Indian military's only or biggest challenge when it comes to successfully fighting wars (Raghavan, 2009).

Since the end of the Cold War, in addition to the PMO and MEA, the key institutions framing Indian foreign policy are the Cabinet (of growing importance in the era of coalition government), the Indian Foreign Service (IFS, who staff Indian diplomatic posts abroad as well as in the MEA, PMO and other ministries), the MoD, the Indian Parliament, and various manifestations of the defence and intelligence establishment (the armed forces, the Defence Research and Development Organization, the nuclear establishment, the Research and Analysis Wing, the Intelligence Bureau, etc.). Parliament is the only body among these that is directly accountable to the people, and it in turn is intended to hold the other institutions of foreign policy accountable through proceedings in the Lok Sabha, or Lower House of the Indian Parliament. Over time, however, with the advent of coalition government and the increasing complexity of domestic issues facing India, Parliament's attention to foreign policy has waned. Concurrently, since 1999 a new and unelected centre of power has emerged in the foreign policy establishment by way of the National Security Council (NSC), headed by the National Security Adviser (NSA) who holds deputy ministerial rank and is in many respects the topmost bureaucrat in charge of advising the Government on India's (GoI) foreign and security policies—decision-making authority still rests with the Cabinet, PMO, MEA, and other ministries depending on the issue at hand.

The institutional set-up of India's foreign policy establishment creates two major impediments in the policymaking process. First and foremost is the issue of capacity, which has in recent times come under scrutiny (Tharoor, 2012). India's foreign service of 600 officers (not counting support staff) is roughly the same size as that of Belgium and Holland, with an average of four officers per embassy abroad (Bajpai, 2013). Furthermore, India's intellectual infrastructure of policymaking—universities, think tanks, media, lateral expertise inducted into the MEA—is inadequate for a country of its size and ambition (Markey, 2009). Arguably, even the quality of IFS recruits is on the decline, with the most successful candidates in the joint civil service examinations opting for the Indian Administrative Service (IAS) and other services. As a consequence of low numbers and poor quality input into the policy process, India's foreign policy bureaucrats—although among the best in the world—are spread all too thinly across the ever-widening spectrum of Indian diplomacy.

The second challenge arising from the institutional set-up for foreign policy pertains to the lack of coordination and effective communication between the different agencies responsible for a particular file. This is particularly challenging in an environment where the technical complexity and breadth of an issue requires various ministries or agencies to be involved, but recommendatory and decision-making powers lie at the highest levels of the MEA or NSC and the Cabinet or PMO respectively. The resulting gulf between politicians (or political appointees) and bureaucrats can create hurdles for policy, particularly in the case of international negotiations where mixed signals carry significant costs (Mukherjee and Malone, 2011: 320-21). Due to the lack of institutionalised communication and coordination across ministries or agencies, coordinated policymaking often relies on personal networks and initiative—sometimes, an international issue, especially if it is not of great strategic relevance but perhaps important for normative reasons (such as the Millennium Development Goals, or the MDGs), may receive greater than usual attention due to personal proclivities of the official involved. The challenge with an individualistic policymaking process is that individuals may frequently come into conflict without any institutionalised means of resolution, leading to unseemly turf battles between high-ranking members of the foreign policy establishment whose bureaucratic politics at home at times impact their behaviour abroad (Iype, 1998).

Ultimately, the size and functioning of India's foreign policy establishment have constrained its external relations in different but equally important ways. While many of the problems India faces are not unique, it remains difficult to fathom why the IFS has not increased its numbers commensurately with India's rise and the growing complexity of international affairs. In 2012, the MEA announced a plan to expand intake and double the number of officers over 10 years, which by any reckoning is an eternity in world politics. Given that a country such as Brazil is already at double the strength of the IFS (Bajpai, 2013), India's plans cannot but seem disconnected from its diplomatic needs.

Impact of Major Wars

A major war can be defined as "a war fought by the most powerful members of the international system, drawing on all of their resources and using every weapon at their command, over a period of years, leading to an outcome with revolutionary geopolitical consequences including the birth and death of regimes, the redrawing of borders and the reordering of the hierarchy of sovereign states" (Mandelbaum, 1998: 20). The relevant conflict for India since 1947 by this definition is the Cold War, which pitted two superpowers against each other and divided the world along mostly ideological lines. India entered the post-Second World War international system with a strong desire for autonomy and independence of action, having cast off almost a century of direct British rule. Faced with a polarised world, Nehru and his compatriots devised a policy known as non-alignment, which sought to create space for India to make foreign policy decisions based on its own interests by judging the merits of each case. In his speech to the Constituent Assembly of India in 1947, Nehru declared: "I know that there are...separate groups and blocks today and because they exist today, there is hostility between them, and there is even talk of war among them...Therefore India, in so far as it has a foreign policy, has declared that it wants to remain independent and free of all these blocks and that it wants to cooperate on equal terms with all countries" (CAD, 1947).

By the 1950s, other countries of the post-colonial developing world had become interested in the concept of non-alignment, and a single country's foreign policy that had been designed to preserve independence of action evolved into an international third bloc of sorts. Countries that sought to travel the middle path between the two superpowers formed what came to be known as the Non-Aligned Movement (NAM), a development that Nehru did not view as favourably as many thought he did (Dixit, 2003). Despite this development, many in the West viewed India's non-aligned credentials with suspicion, particularly given the mild variety of socialism and redistributive politics espoused by many of India's top leaders, including Nehru. The US in particular took a negative of what they perceived to be Indian neutrality on grave matters of moral consequence, matters in which one could not be neutral between what the respective superpowers stood for. Restated more pithily, this amounted to US Secretary of State John Foster Dulles' famous dictum, "Those who are not with us are against us" (Appadorai and Rajan, 1985). India countered by arguing that non-alignment did not amount to neutrality. V.K. Krishna Menon, who was close to Nehru and played a vital role in India's foreign affairs during the latter's tenure as Prime Minister, remarked in the UN that "there can no more be positive neutrality than there can be a vegetarian tiger" (Reddy, 1968: 34). He asserted that India was not neutral between war and peace, between imperialism and freedom, or on questions of ethics.

That India was not neutral on questions of imperialism and war was clear from its opposition to the actions of the British and French during the Suez Canal crisis of 1956. However, it also became clear that year that Indian neutrality tended to drift in a particular direction, when India remained silent upon the Soviet Union's invasion of Hungary, an act that was in many respects at par with that of the Western powers at Suez. Despite these events, the US remained a strong supporter of India's economic development into the 1960s, and President John F. Kennedy was responsive to Nehru's request for military aid during the war with China in 1962. During this period, India benefitted from aid competition between the two superpowers. From Washington, Delhi received assistance for agricultural commodities, general imports, power development, transportation, public health, education and multipurpose projects. From Moscow, Delhi received aid focused on the development of heavy industries, oil exploration and refining (Shah, 1983).

India was able to walk this tightrope reasonably well until the Cold War came close to home, in the 1971 crisis in East Pakistan where the Pakistani army began slaughtering thousands of Bengalis, the majority of whom were Hindu (Bass, 2013). At a time when the Chinese and Soviets were deeply at odds in world politics, and Pakistan was secretly brokering a rapprochement between China and the US, India argued it had no choice but to rely on the Soviets for assistance in pressuring Pakistan to stop the killing and stem the flow of refugees into India, which at the height of the crisis amounted to 10 million individuals. India and Pakistan soon went to war over this crisis, resulting in a resounding victory for the former and territorial dismemberment for the latter—East Pakistan became the independent nation of Bangladesh. As a consequence of this conflict, Delhi moved visibly closer to Moscow and India's relations with the US remained frosty for the next two decades.

More generally, the Cold War impacted India's foreign policy in three ways. The first, as already discussed, was the emergence of non-alignment as the basis for India's relations with the world. Second, India sought for much of the Cold War to keep the superpowers out of its own backyard, the Indian Ocean and the Indian Subcontinent. Although India could not prevent superpower involvement in Pakistan and Afghanistan, and frequently objected to their presence in the Indian Ocean too (e.g., at Diego Garcia), Delhi did enjoy considerable levels of influence in its neighbourhood, particularly in Nepal, Bhutan, Bangladesh and Sri Lanka, various bilateral animosities between India and its neighbours notwithstanding. Finally, India's de facto orientation toward the Soviet Union meant that generations of Indian diplomats were socialised in a world where Moscow and Delhi were much closer than Delhi and Washington. The end of the Cold War required a major reorientation of this worldview, and even today many Indians remain skeptical of warmer ties with the US. A 2006 survey found that although India's elites feel more warmly towards the US government than the Chinese government, they place similar levels of trust in both (Kapur, 2009).

II

Strategic Priorities

Since independence, India has faced numerous bilateral disputes in its region. The most prominent among them has arisen from disagreements and frequent conflict with Pakistan. The last 60 years have witnessed two major wars between the two countries and two major acts of aggression by Pakistan, in addition to numerous small-scale incidents across their borders. During the Cold War, Pakistan received billions of dollars worth of military aid and equipment over the years from its major patrons, much of which was employed in conflicts with India and to sponsor what India termed 'cross-border terrorism' in India-occupied Kashmir. Pakistan's abiding alliance with China since the 1950s, even more than the former's erratic relationship of convenience with the US, causes grave concern for India, especially due to China's transfer of nuclear weapons technology and missile systems to Pakistan.

The Indo-Pakistani rivalry, which had somewhat fallen into a manageable pattern from the mid-1970s to the early 1990s, intensified following India's (and then Pakistan's) nuclear weapon tests of 1998, the Kargil war of 1999, and a 2001 terrorist attack on the Indian parliament, the latter of which led to a tense military standoff. Prime Minister Vajpayee and President Musharraf subsequently initiated a peace process that led to superficially improved relations between 2003 and 2007. The deadly terrorist attacks in Mumbai in November 2008 created fresh challenges in Indo-Pakistani relations. International pressure eventually forced Pakistan to recognise Pakistani links to the attack, and after a long freeze in bilateral high-level contacts, they resumed in 2009 and intensified in 2010.

Increasingly, China is more worrying for India than is Pakistan. While India has experienced significant economic success over the past 20 years, China has consistently outstripped India's growth by 2-3 per cent each year. Consequently, the Chinese economy has expanded to more than two-and-a-half times the size of India's economy in 2012 (World Bank, 2013), which has allowed China to invest significantly in its military sector. The overall trend in Sino-Indian relations remains positive, yet potential flashpoints exist. The border issue remains intractable. The prospect of progress through dialogue was belied for Delhi when Chinese Premier Wen Jiabao on a visit to India in 2010 stated flatly that the border issue "will not be easy to resolve...it requires patience" (Chakravarty, 2010). This statement prompted a recent group of prominent Indian strategists and public intellectuals to urge the Indian government to upgrade its border infrastructure and develop capabilities to deter a Chinese attack (Khilnani *et al.*, 2012). Tibet is another potential source of conflict. China remains extremely sensitive to the Dalai Lama's leadership of the Tibetan government-in-exile in India, along with approximately 100,000 Tibetan refugees. India worries about the Dalai Lama's successor taking potentially more radical stances toward the Chinese (Madhukar, 2011). If this were the case, India could be unwittingly drawn into a standoff between Tibetans in exile and the Chinese government.

While certain redline issues such as Tibet and the border may spark an India-China conflict, trade offers some reason to be hopeful. India-China trade has increased steadily since the end of the Cold War and stands at US $65.8 billion in 2012 (Department of Commerce, 2013), making China India's largest trading partner. Although the structure of bilateral trade advantages China, India largely exports raw materials to and imports capital goods from China, and currently runs a trade deficit with China amounting to US $38.7 billion in 2012 (Department of Commerce, 2013). The growing mutual dependence between the Asian giants is a positive sign, suggesting that the low politics of trade might gradually create the bedrock for more conciliatory high politics (Athwal, 2008: 11-12).

With regard to the wider South Asian region, India has faced a number of challenges with neighbouring countries such as Nepal, Bangladesh and Sri Lanka. Most of India's neighbours are weak states: in the Fund for Peace's 2013 Failed States Index, six of India's neighbours ranked among the 30 most unstable states in the world (FSI, 2013).[1] The weakness of these states magnifies the already complex challenges arising out of the sheer asymmetry of size and influence between India and its neighbours, which by inherently breeds insecurity among the latter. Political factions, insurgent groups and ideological movements in these states have frequently resorted to anti-Indian rhetoric and politics when seeking to challenge or overthrow governments in power. Moreover, the shifting socio-political alignments that sustain these weak regimes make it challenging for Delhi's foreign policy establishment to form lasting relationships or cooperative mechanisms with the political elites of these states. Events in Nepal, as of June 2012, offer an example of this type of situation, where a split in the ruling Unified Communist Party saw a breakaway radical group criticising the party for, among other things, its conciliatory policy toward India (Jha, 2012).

On balance, however, although India's relations with Nepal have fluctuated over time, its relations with Sri Lanka and Bangladesh have improved in recent years. As India's decade of intervention—the 1980s—in Sri Lanka's civil war has receded, and as the civil war itself has come to a close with a decisive victory for the government against the Liberation Tigers of Tamil Eelam (LTTE), India has found it easier to maintain a distance from Sri Lankan affairs except in the face of domestic political pressure from Indian Tamils to protect and promote the interests of Tamils in Sri Lanka. This pressure is exacerbated by the weight of Tamil Nadu's two regional political parties in any coalition government that formed in Delhi. With regard to Bangladesh, relations have improved since the election of Sheikh Hasina as Prime Minister of Bangladesh in 2009 and her historic visits to India in 2010 and 2012, as well as Prime Minister

1. *Failed States Index 2013*, The Fund for Peace, 2013. *http://fsi.fundforpeace.org/rankings-2013-sortable.*

Manmohan Singh's visit to Bangladesh in 2011 during which India and Bangladesh made record progress on border demarcation and trade (though they were unable to move forward a long-standing water-sharing dispute). Improvements in India's relations with its neighbours, while encouraging, will however remain hostage to political winds in the latter countries, more so than in the normal course of states' domestic politics because South Asia's states exhibit considerable weakness (Paul, 2012).

Political Priorities

Democracy remains the cornerstone of India's political system, but it is unclear the extent to which the country seeks to or needs to externalise it domestic values. Although India is the second largest contributor to the UN Democracy Fund, it has taken few bilateral measures to promote democracy directly in other countries. In fact, India has in recent years shied away from taking positions on democratic and human rights issues in other countries, especially if there are strategic gains to be made. A prominent example of this was the change in India's approach to Myanmar, where India gradually shifted away from its pro-human rights and pro-democracy stance and adopted a more neutral attitude toward the military junta, much to the chagrin of Western observers (Varadarajan, 2010). This change was largely driven by the growing strategic relationship between China and Myanmar, which included large-scale infrastructure investments by Beijing.

Strategic considerations do not always drive India's political priorities in the external realm. Sometimes, ideological differences on key issues such as sovereignty and intervention play an important role in shaping in India's approach to fundamental political questions debated in forums such as the UNSC. Nowhere has this been clearer than in UNSC debates over humanitarian intervention and the Responsibility to Protect (R2P). India has frequently found itself in the same camp as China and Russia in arguing for greater restraint by the international community when considering interventions in civil wars or internal conflicts across the world (The New York Times, 2012). This stance does not always make sense from a strategic perspective—India does not have major oil interests in Syria, for example—yet India's so-called hawkishness on sovereignty becomes more explicable when considering a broader historical view. In particular, the puzzle of the *shift* in India's stance of sovereignty only makes sense once one considers the domestic exigencies of maintaining territorial integrity and social cohesion.

The shift is evident when one counts the major instances of sovereignty violation by India since independence. Between 1947 and 1989, India engaged in 19 non-humanitarian military interventions that compromised the sovereignty of other countries (Pearson and Baumann, 1993); a rate of 0.44 interventions per year. These instances include the coercive integration of some of the larger Princely States following India's independence, the forcible liberation of Goa from Portuguese rule, Prime Minister Nehru's Forward Policy deployed during the border conflict with China, India's intervention in the Bangladesh crisis of 1971 (a quasi-humanitarian intervention), and interventions (by invitation) in Sri Lanka and the Maldives in the 1980s. Between 1990 and 2005, the rate was only 0.2 interventions per year, which mostly took the form of relatively minor border incidents with Pakistan and Bangladesh (Kisangani and Pickering, 2008).

Even on the question of humanitarian intervention, India's priorities have shifted over time. India was actively involved in the discussions that shaped the UN Declaration of Human Rights, and adopted many human rights provisions from the UN charter into its own Constitution. Indian leaders at the time also espoused an ideology of 'One World,' or the notion that the international system of nation states was but a milestone in the global journey towards an overarching sovereign that would peaceably regulate relations between all countries (Bhagavan, 2012). India's initial support for the UN grew out of this feeling that international morality could and should often trump domestic sovereignty and authority, particularly when human rights were at stake. India's campaign in the UN against the Apartheid regime in South Africa most clearly reflected and articulated this philosophy.

However, since the end of the Cold War, India has been loath to engage in both humanitarian and non-humanitarian military interventions in other countries. Part of the reason behind this shift lies in Indian fears of a UNSC with a greatly expanded ambit under American leadership. Almost three-fourth of the UN's 67 peacekeeping missions as of 2012 were undertaken after 1990. Since the early 1990s, the organisation has involved itself in numerous conflicts around the world. India's 6th term on the UNSC, in 1991-92, witnessed an explosion of UNSC activity on conflicts in a host of countries including Iran, Iraq, Kuwait, Israel, Lebanon, Cyprus, the former Yugoslavia (and its successor states), Libya, Angola, Somalia, Liberia, South Africa, Mozambique and Cambodia.

In addition to international factors, a major reason behind India's reluctance to both engage in and support unilateral or multilateral sovereignty violations is internal. Specifically, India's own tenuous hold on its border regions and insurgency-ridden districts, coupled with frequent human rights abuses by Indian armed forces in Kashmir and the Northeastern states, makes it difficult for Delhi to endorse the emergence of any new norms that shift the global consensus away from absolute to more contingent ideas of sovereignty, which is precisely what West-driven discussions around R2P have sought to do. Thus India has conducted a steady and unyielding campaign within the UN calling for greater reflection, preparation, and political consensus prior to the launch of humanitarian interventions. India has warned that peacekeepers should not become "agents of regime change" (PMIUN, 2011) or become embroiled in civil wars. Unlike China and Russia, which have been outright spoilers, India has taken the slightly more constructive stance of admitting the importance of intervention while counseling restraint in its implementation.

Thus on two key political issues in international affairs—democracy and sovereignty—India has evinced a move away from externally oriented postures toward a more internally oriented approach that has been described as a "defensive crouch" (Sidhu *et al.*, 2013: 2). Instead of supporting international efforts to spread democracy to other countries, or to arrest internal conflict through armed intervention, India has channelled its efforts into critically engaging with current methods of promoting democracy and stability across the world. Until India's own domestic politics and security environment change, Delhi is unlikely to deviate from this default position of prioritising a narrowly defined national interest, state sovereignty, and strategic autonomy. India's foreign policy in many respects remains non-aligned, although less interventionist than before.

Economic and Social Priorities

Declining interventionism in Indian foreign policy has been accompanied by the rise of economic diplomacy. Economic diplomacy refers to how states—often with the significant involvement of non-state actors—conduct their international economic relations (Bayne and Woolcock, 2007: 3). This practice has two aspects: first, the use of statecraft to promote a nation's economic interests; and second, the use of international economic instruments to further a nation's political or strategic interests. Since economic liberalisation in the early 1990s, India has done reasonably well on the former but lagged on the latter.

The purpose of India's economic diplomacy has been largely to create external relationships that produce higher levels of wealth that can be harnessed for internal development. The shift toward economics in foreign policy was brought about by the BoP crisis that led to economic liberalisation in 1991. A 'mixed' economy run on socialist principles had produced historically low levels of growth, sluggish public enterprises, and few gains in service delivery, particularly for the millions of Indians living in poverty. Liberalisation represented both an external imposition by the IMF and an internal turn away from Nehruvian economic principles that prioritised centralised planning, nationalised industries, and a heavily regulated private sector. Much of this orthodoxy changed with the advent of economic reforms, which also created new links and deepened existing connections between India and the world economy. Reforms unleashed a period of unprecedented economic growth, which in turn made India an important partner and player in international affairs. Economic diplomacy was designed to continue the task of creating mutually beneficial economic relationships between India and other countries.

On the social front, India is an extremely heterogeneous society with multiple cleavages along religious, caste, and linguistic lines. The Constitution of India recognises 22 official languages (not including English), while the Census of India enumerates another 100 major languages spoken in India, in addition to numerous languages with less than 10,000 speakers (Census of India, 2001a). India is also home to many of the major world religions. Hindus make up the majority of the population (80.5%), followed by Muslims (13.4%), Christians (2.3%), Sikhs (1.9%), Buddhists, Jains and others (1.9%) (Census of India, 2001b). At the time of independence, India's leaders sought to accommodate the religiously plural nature of its society. For the Indian Constitution, they chose the principles of dis-establishment of religion in the state and non-separation of religion from public life, resulting in a state that is secular and a society that does not exclude religion from the public sphere (Mahajan, 2008). Along with its other liberal democratic provisions, the Constitution has permitted religious plurality to flourish despite the dominance of a single religion. While contemporary India has been witness to a surge in Hindu nationalism, care must be taken to distinguish political variants of Hinduism (e.g., *Hindutva*) from the religion itself.

Poverty and socio-economic inequality have been major facets of modern India's existence. In 2010, India was home to 394 million individuals living on less than US$ 1.25 a day, which the World Bank (2014a) defines as extreme poverty. Economic inequality—measured by the Gini coefficient—has marginally increased since the 1980s, by about three percentage points (World Bank, 2014a). Inequalities between regions and between social groups threaten to undermine the overall growth trajectory of the Indian economy. The overlapping nature of social and economic inequality in the case of Muslims and Dalits (lower-caste Hindus), for example, has important political implications in the age of economic liberalisation, which has proved somewhat of a social equaliser and pathway to political empowerment (Prasad *et al.*, 2010). Since the late 1980s, the rise of identity-based political parties along caste and regional lines has changed the face of Indian politics and the calculus of political power at the federal level. The number of claimants to the state and its resources are correspondingly higher, politics more divisive, and policymaking more stunted.

India's socio-economic priorities are therefore to sustain high levels of economic growth (already a challenge since the global downturn of 2008), promote economic development in manner that especially benefits disadvantaged regions or social groups, and manage the extreme heterogeneity of its society in a way that does not undermine the state's authority and legitimacy. Since the early 1990s, these priorities have ensured an economic orientation to external affairs with an emphasis on trade and foreign investment. In 2012, international trade accounted for almost 55 per cent of India's GDP (gross domestic product), up from 17 per cent in 1991 (World Bank, 2014b). Foreign direct investment (FDI) remains low, at 1.3 per cent of GDP in 2012 (World Bank, 2014b), suggesting that India has not fully harnessed the potential of global economic integration.

Economic integration is particularly important for fostering higher levels of interdependence with other countries in ways that might mitigate conflict in future. The various tools of economic diplomacy—trade, investment, foreign aid, and cross-border production, to name a few—can be viewed on a scale in terms of their increasing ability to foster interdependence by raising the costs of disruption to all countries in a relationship. Instruments that are more substitutable tend to be less conducive to creating interdependence. In this regard, foreign aid is perhaps the most substitutable economic relationship between two countries, followed by trade. Foreign direct investment creates assets owned by the firms of one country in an another country, but this channel too is less substitutable than cross-border production networks of the kind that have emerged in East and South East Asia. By integrating firms operating in multiple countries into one supply chain, these networks tend to increase the cost of disruption to bilateral relations between these countries (Suri and Kapur, 2013), as has been witnessed in the growing economic embrace between China and Association of Southeast Asian Nations (ASEAN).

By comparison, India has done well in trade but little else. As shown above, its FDI linkages remain weak; and cross-border production networks are almost non-existent in South Asia for a variety of reasons to do with politics, weak infrastructure, and non-complementary markets (Kapur and Iyengar, 2006). Thus although India is well on the path to economic growth, the ability of its economic diplomacy to serve its strategic interests is presently minimal. The election of a strongly pro-business and pro-trade government under Narendra Modi in early 2014 offered some hope that this scenario would change, but India continued to lock horns with the World Trade Organization (WTO), effectively blocking the latter's multilaterally negotiated Bali agreement on trade facilitation which infringed on India's large-scale domestic food subsidy programme (Bellman and Kenny, 2014).

National Security Considerations

A state's threat environment—both internal and external—largely shapes its national security priorities. In this regard, one can think of India's priorities, as many have done before (e.g., Tanham 1992), in terms of concentric geographical circles radiating outward. At the centre of this construct is the Indian state itself, which faces considerable internal threats emanating from its own soil. Chief among these are insurgent and separatist movements, leftist militias (the Naxalites), and domestic terrorism. Insurgencies have threatened the Indian state since independence, particularly in the Northeastern states, Punjab, and Kashmir. Although the insurgency in Punjab subsided after a tumultuous period in the 1980s, the Northeast and Kashmir remain hotspots for all kinds of movements ranging in their demands from greater autonomy to statehood within the Indian republic to outright separation. By one estimate, since independence roughly 116 terrorist, insurgent, and extremist groups have been active in the Northeastern states of Assam, Manipur, Meghalaya, Nagaland, Tripura, Mizoram, and Arunachal Pradesh, and 32 groups have been active in the Indian state of Jammu and Kashmir (SATP, 2014a). In 2007, according to an estimate, there were

30 armed insurgent groups operating in the Northeastern states (Hussain, 2007).

Aside from regional militants, a multi-state leftist insurgency known as the Naxalite movement has engaged in a low-intensity conflict with the Indian state since the 1960s. Originally inspired by and designed along Maoist lines of guerilla warfare against the class enemies of the rural poor, the movement today represents a group of highly armed and well-trained militias whose demands are based on the unemployment and land-related grievances of rural Indians, particularly those of excluded social groups such as indigenous tribes. In 2006, Prime Minister Manomhan Singh declared the movement India's greatest internal security threat (PTI, 2006), a view that he reiterated four years later (PTI, 2010). In 2011, the movement was active in 182 of India's 640 districts, 83 of which were identified by the government as worst hit and in need of urgent programmatic action to promote security and economic development (MHA, 2011).

Terrorism and counter-terrorism related incidents have exacted a high cost in human lives—in the period, 1994-2014, an estimate records 63,363 deaths, where 47 per cent of them are terrorists themselves, 38 per cent civilians, and 15 per cent security forces (SATP, 2014b). In addition to regional movements and the Naxalite movement, India also faces the threat of homegrown terrorism from both Islamic and Hindu groups. Organisations such as the Students Islamic Movement of India and Indian Mujahideen are prominent homegrown Islamic groups engaged in terrorism, whereas organisations such as Abhinav Bharat and others under the umbrella of the Rashtriya Swayamsevak Sangh (RSS) are Hindu groups involved in similar activities.

Moving outward from the core, the second geographical ring includes India's neighbouring countries in South Asia (excluding China). In this region, there are essentially two types of threats: neighbouring countries posing a direct conventional or nuclear military threat to India, and neighbouring countries posing indirect threats to India by supporting or aiding insurgent groups operating within. In the former category lies Pakistan. Having engaged in four wars and numerous smaller conflicts across their border since 1947,

India and Pakistan are locked in an enduring rivalry, one that is exacerbated by the overt nuclear weapons capabilities of both states since 1998. However, while India's nuclear posture of 'no first use' provides it with a useful deterrent, Pakistan's asymmetric nuclear posture since 1998 presents a constant threat to India (Narang, 2009), and in turn allows Islamabad to continue probing Delhi's resolve and capabilities through conventional military tactics (as in Kargil in 1999) and support for terrorist attacks on Indian soil, most notably on the Indian parliament in 2001 and in Mumbai 2008, among numerous other incidents.

In the category of indirect regional threats, the most important challenge India faces is the material support provided by neighbours to insurgent and terrorist groups operating on Indian soil, particularly in Kashmir and the Northeast. In addition to material support, states contiguous with India are able to provide safe havens for the personnel and finances of insurgent groups operating within India. During the Cold War, China under Mao had been an active supporter of separatism in India's northeast (Garver, 2001: 5). In the post-Cold War world, Pakistan remains the main sponsor of cross-border terrorism in India—mostly in Kashmir—while Bangladesh allows insurgent groups operating in India to establish camps in border areas, and Nepal's Maoists aid leftist guerrillas across the border. Some neighbours such as Bhutan and Myanmar have unwittingly provided safe havens to such groups mostly due to their inability to effectively police their borders with India or to decisively expel any unwelcome elements operating in the border regions. In similar fashion, the territories of states neighbouring India are often used by insurgent groups to smuggle weapons into the country—in 2009, the Indian Home Minister hinted that the Naxalites were obtaining arms smuggled through Nepal, Bangladesh, and Myanmar (PTI, 2009).

The third and final concentric circle of India's threat environment spans Asia and contains China. Having suffered a humiliating defeat in 1962, Delhi is keenly aware of the persistent border dispute between the two countries, and the growing power and influence of India's neighbour to the north. Although a robust land border in the form of the Himalayas makes a land-based attack by China costly,

Indian strategists remain concerned about China's expanding naval capabilities and the 'string of pearls'—or military and commercial naval facilities—that China has constructed at strategic points in the Indian Ocean, including Chittagong in Bangladesh, Hambantota in Sri Lanka, and Gwadar in Pakistan. Most importantly, China has a greater and more highly developed and deliverable nuclear arsenal than India. Like India, China maintains a no-first-use policy on its nuclear weapons, although the credibility of that commitment may be questioned in a hypothetical crisis scenario. Thus India's national security concerns operate at three levels—domestic insurgencies and terrorism, a fractious and hostile neighbourhood, and an expanding major power to the north.

III

Emerging Trends

Although prognosticating with regard to international politics is an inherently fraught exercise, it is possible to discern some emerging trends over the last decade that signal potential shifts in India's relations with the world. In the realm of India's strategic priorities, it is clear that Pakistan today is less important than it was 10 years ago, and that China and the US loom much larger in the Indian strategic imagination than before. Particularly in the context of the US pivot to Asia and Japan's growing desire to provide for its own security in partnership with India, Delhi remains concerned on the one hand about provoking China and on the other hand about America's declining ability and willingness to confront China in its own backyard—the East and South China seas—and perhaps eventually the Indian Ocean. Nonetheless, India's own relationship with each major player in these equations has witnessed significant improvements, be it through the compartmentalisation of the border dispute with China, the signing of the India-US civil nuclear agreement, or the relative calm in India-Pakistan relations following the terrorist attacks of 2008. In each case, India has shown a remarkable ability to either set aside differences or bracket them in a way that allows an economic relationship to grow apace. Even in the case of Pakistan, India has pushed for most favoured nation status (MFN)—a status that India had granted Pakistan in 1996—in order to boost bilateral trade, and the Nawaz Sharif government in Pakistan has edged ever closer to reciprocating since coming to power.

In the political realm, however, relations with Pakistan may not improve in the near future with the election in 2014 of a BJP, or Bharatiya Janata Party, government under the leadership of Narendra Modi, a leader controversial for his alleged role in the 2002 Hindu-Muslim riots in Gujarat (where he was Chief Minister), where 790 Muslims and 254 Hindus were killed and scores more of both religions injured (BBC, 2005). Indeed India-Pakistan relations have cooled after an initial period of optimism following Modi's election, when he invited the leaders of South Asian Association for Regional Cooperation (SAARC) countries to his swearing in ceremony and was seen engaging in positive diplomacy with Nawaz Sharif. Within a matter of weeks, Delhi had called off diplomatic talks with Pakistan as the latter's envoy in India sought to meet with Kashmiri separatists. In a similar vein, during a trip to Kargil in August 2014—the first by an Indian prime minister since the 1999 armed conflict in this sector of Kashmir—Modi denounced Pakistan for promoting cross-border terrorism in India (Pandit, 2014).

Modi and his party embody a muscular Indian nationalism under the brand of *Hindutva*, or Hinduness, which espouses cultural uniformity and assimilationist ideas with regard to minorities in India. Although the BJP was in power between 1998 and 2004, it was led in that period by a relative moderate Prime Minister, Atal Bihari Vajpayee. Even under his tenure, many have argued that India pursued a more nationalist foreign policy, particularly with regard to the decision for India's second round of nuclear tests in 1998 after a hiatus of 24 years (Hymans, 2006; Bajpai, 2009). The resurgence of *Hindutva* in Indian politics, symbolised by Modi's election, might portend a major shift in relations with countries that potentially threaten India, particularly in the event of a crisis such as a Pakistan-backed terrorist attack, for example. However, it is equally likely that in the interest of economic prosperity and domestic stability, the BJP government—potentially over two terms from 2014 to 2024—

will engage its neighbours through productive economic diplomacy (Madan, 2014).

In the economic realm, India is gradually augmenting its strategy of using foreign policy to achieve economic goals such as greater trade and investment. In the near future, it will be in a position to use these relationships to achieve over-arching strategic goals in the manner that the US and China do. Foreign aid will be a major component of this strategy, and already India has begun increasing its aid budget considerably. In 2012, the MEA's aid budget touched US$1 billion (GoI, 2013: 106). The Development Partnership Administration (DPA), established in 2013 in the MEA with a five-year budget of US$15 billion, is likely to play a major role in India's economic diplomacy in the future. This is particularly true when one views foreign aid as part of a larger deal or package including trade and investment that India can offer countries in the developing world, especially South Asia and Africa. In this manner, foreign aid can be used to win lucrative contracts for Indian firms abroad, to secure market access, and to obtain a variety of other policy concessions and adjustments to suit India's strategic interests. South Asia, however, will remain poorly integrated until India takes the lead in developing cross-border production networks as mentioned above. Overall, India is likely to go from a country that seeks economic relationships to another that uses its economic relationships to maximise its strategic interests. Although presently this is not the case, it may very well be so 10 or 20 years down the line.

Finally, in the social realm, India's social cohesion is likely to interact with two variables in the near future—the rate of economic growth, and the level of socio-political pluralism. Given the election of an ideologically Hindu nationalist government with pro-market economic policies, it is possible that India will witness the types of social dislocation and ferment associated with rapid economic growth and majoritarian politics. Much will depend on whether the ruling party is able to contain its more extreme factions and supporters, and whether it is able to protect the interests of minorities. In any event, a return to pre-global downturn rates of economic growth is likely to also result in the continued empowerment of previously excluded and disadvantaged groups such as Dalits that might mount credible state-level challenges to the majoritarian consensus in Delhi, thereby bringing some balance into an otherwise lopsided political situation. In terms of external policy, the emergence of a discontented religious minority might create fertile ground for both internal and externally-aided security threats. And in the most extreme of scenarios, internal religious strife might turn outward in the form of provocations toward neighbouring countries, especially Pakistan and Bangladesh. At a more mundane level, India's social evolution might signal a greater willingness to engage with foreigners and develop meaningful partnerships in areas such as health, education, and science and technology research. However, it might equally entail a return to more nativist conceptions of India that seek to exclude foreign influences and actors from the domestic scene.

Overall Assessment

The conduct of foreign policy is in many ways a slow and gradual enterprise requiring great patience on the part of statesmen and analysts alike. It therefore makes little sense to speak of Indian foreign policy in categories as stark as success and failure, which presume some ideal standard of measurement and some temporal cut-off point at which measuring the outcome of a work in progress becomes justifiable. While an indicator for failure in bilateral relations—the outbreak of war—is somewhat readily available (and even this can be debated), there seems to be no equivalent for success. For example, should India measure its own success in comparison to what the US or Pakistan have achieved with China? The costs that the US-China and Pakistan-China relationships carry may be undesirable for Indian policymakers, and therefore measuring Indian policy's success against them produces little insight.

The most reasonable measure of success lies not in comparison with some ideal or with other countries, but with India's own past and its stated foreign policy objectives. In this context, one can ask two simple questions of any policy. First, did India achieve the objectives it set out to achieve through the policy? Second, was India able to maximise its strategic interests—economic, military, or political—through the policy? Looking at India's foreign policies following the Cold War, one can identify three over-arching policies and three specific policies that are the most likely candidates for evaluation.

In terms of over-arching policies, since the Cold War, India has pursued economic diplomacy in its relations with all countries, strategic autonomy in its relations with the great powers, and critical engagement in its relations with international institutions. In the case of economic diplomacy, India has certainly met its objective of widening and deepening its economic relationships with other countries, and this has led to greater prosperity within India and more stable partnerships with a host of diverse countries including the US, China, Japan, Russia, Iran, and Israel. Economic relationships have provided a vital buffer to help mitigate political differences between India and the US, India and China, and India and Iran, to name a few cases.

In the case of strategic autonomy, India has pursued a policy of eschewing alliances with and major commitments to any of the great powers while protecting its decision-making autonomy in forums such as the UNSC and on issues such as China's rise or Iran's nuclear weapons programme. By and large, India has successfully relied on strategic autonomy as a means to protecting its freedom of action; like non-alignment, strategic autonomy has allowed India to decide each case for external action (or inaction) on its own merits, without reference to any over-arching ideological or political commitments. The policy has helped Delhi benefit from the existing competition in Asia between the US and China—the most visible emblem of India's success in this regard was the India-US nuclear deal of 2008, which essentially legitimised India's nuclear programme and gave it access to global supply networks of nuclear supplies and technology—all motivated by Washington's desire to create a credible partner in Asia that might act as a counterweight to China. Beyond this nuclear deal, however, the benefits of strategic autonomy to India in the context of the Sino-American rivalry have been limited (Tellis, 2012). Whether this policy has improved bilateral relations with the great powers is even less certain. The US, for one, has found India a difficult interlocutor precisely due to the latter's dogged adherence to the creed of strategic autonomy (Ganguly, 2012).

In the case of critical engagement with international institutions, India's objective has been to carve out exceptions for itself on issues ranging from trade to climate change and nuclear non-proliferation. It has been largely successful in doing so, just as China has in many of the same forums. Critical engagement has meant strenuous representations in favour of exceptional treatment for India as a developing nation or a conscientious objector to the status quo. In certain regimes, such as the one for humanitarian intervention, India has sought not exceptions for itself (even though it would certainly do so if the occasion demanded it), but an alternative consensus on basic principles. Again, in all its interactions with international institutions, India has largely been able to by and large achieve its pre-determined objectives. However, whether this has maximised India's national interests varies from issue to issue. On trade, it is not entirely clear that torpedoing the Doha round (along with China) helped India's economic interests, although it did aid the government politically at home. Similarly, arguing for common but differentiated responsibility in a manner that has slowed progress in global climate change negotiations is also likely to harm Indian interests and impede the drive for domestic energy efficiency in the long term. On the issue of nuclear non-proliferation, however, India has emerged a clear winner by holding out long enough for the regime to de facto accommodate Indian interests.

A frequently discussed development in India's multilateral policy is Delhi's predilection for rising power groupings such as BRICS (Brazil, Russia, India, China, and South Africa), IBSA (India, Brazil, and South Africa), and the BASIC (Brazil, South Africa, India, and China) coalition of countries at the 2009 Copenhagen climate change summit. This strategy is in some sense typical of a rising power seeking to maximise influence in world politics, somewhere in between the "universalism of the weak" that characterised India's Cold War foreign policy (Mohan, 2010), and the unilateralism of great powers such as the US today. It is, however, a strategy unlikely to produce major gains for India, particularly given the divergent priorities and interests of countries involved in a grouping such as BRICS, for example. Although the BRICS countries—at their meeting in Fortaleza, Brazil, in mid-2014—began the process of establishing an alternative development bank and currency pool that signalled their collective desire for a world less dominated by the West, the structural imbalances of a coalition involving a mammoth China, diminutive South Africa, rising India and Brazil, and declining Russia—not to mention the political and strategic differences between these countries—are sufficient to preclude any major multilateral challenge to American or Western hegemony in the near future (Pant, 2013).

In terms of specific policies, one can consider the extent to which India has been able to constrain China in Asia, contain Pakistan in South Asia, and address security threats at home. In each of these cases, India has fallen short of its objectives. China's power and influence have grown unabated and India has made negligible headway in building economic and security partnerships with countries on the Chinese periphery, particularly in South East Asia, where ASEAN and China have grown closer over time. Japan for its part has made considerable overtures to India for a deeper partnership, but the relationship has not moved significantly beyond high-level statements and dialogues. India has therefore been unable to successfully balance externally against China's rise. On Pakistan and homeland security more generally, India's counter-terrorism and intelligence establishments have suffered major weaknesses and reversals. Even in the realm of conventional war and nuclear deterrence, India has found it difficult to contain Pakistani belligerence and adventurism in Kashmir. Finally, with regard to domestic insurgencies, although the Indian state has made much headway in breaking the back of major insurgent movements such as the United Liberated Front of Asom (ULFA) in the Northeast, the situation in Kashmir remains bleak and the Naxalite movement remains strong and constitutes the most serious threat to the Indian state's security and legitimacy.

India has therefore not progressed in any major respect toward achieving its specific objectives regarding China, Pakistan, and internal security. Nonetheless, India has made major strides in terms of economic growth and (to a great extent) redistribution. It has also made significant diplomatic gains through over-arching policies of economic diplomacy, strategic autonomy, and critical engagement with international institutions. While there is much that remains to be done, the fact that the Indian state remains not just a viable enterprise, but a flourishing venture in its 67th year of independence, is in itself a remarkable feat of domestic and foreign policy given the levels of poverty, institutional weakness and domestic turmoil at which India began its journey in 1947. The future holds many opportunities, and it will remain the duty of Delhi's able policymakers to seize these opportunities and convert them into gains for every last citizen of the largest democracy in the world.

References

Abhyankar, Rajendra M. (2007). "India's West Asia Policy: Search for a Middle Ground", in Atish Sinha and Madhup Mohta (eds.), *Indian Foreign Policy: Challenges and Opportunities*. New Delhi: Foreign Services Institute and Academic Foundation.

Appadorai, A. and Rajan, M.S. (1985). *India's Foreign Policy and Relations*. New Delhi: South Asian Publishers.

Athwal, Amardeep (2008). *China-India Relations: Contemporary Dynamics*. Routledge, Abingdon.

Bajpai, Kanti (2009). "The BJP and the Bomb", in Scott D. Sagan (ed.), *Inside Nuclear South Asia*. Palo Alto: Stanford University Press. pp.25-67.

———. (2013). "Foreign Policy on a Shoestring", *The Times of India*, 13 October.

Bandhyopadhyaya, Jayantanuja (2003). *The Making of India's Foreign Policy*, 3rd ed. New Delhi: Allied Publishers.

Bass, Gary J. (2013). *The Blood Telegram: Nixon, Kissinger, and a Forgotten Genocide*. New York: Alfred A. Knopf.

Bayne, Nicholas and Stephen Woolcock (2007). "What is Economic Diplomacy?" in Bayne and Woolcock (eds.), *The New Economic Diplomacy: Decision-making and Negotiation in International Economic Relations* (2nd edition). Aldershot: Ashgate.

BBC (British Broadcasting Corporation) (2005). "Gujarat Riot Death Toll Revealed", 11 May. *http://news.bbc.co.uk/1/hi/world/south_asia/4536199.stm*

Bellman, Eric and Peter Kenny (2014). "India Blocks WTO Agreement to Ease Trade Rules", *The Wall Street Journal*, 27 July.

Bhagavan, Manu (2012). *The Peacemakers: India and the Quest for One World*. New Delhi: Harper Collins.

Census of India (2001a). "Abstract of Speakers' Strength of Languages and Mother Tongues", Part A and Part B. *http://www.censusindia.gov.in/Census_Data_2001/Census_Data_Online/Language/Statement1.aspx*

———. (2001b). "Distribution of Population by Religion", Table 21. *http://censusindia.gov.in/Census_And_You/religion.aspx*

Chakravarty, Pratap (2010). "India-China Border Tensions Belie Warm Words", *Agence France-Presse*, 25 December.

Constituent Assembly of India (1947). *Proceedings*, Vol. II. Accessed at *http://164.100.47.132/lssnew/constituent/vol2p3.html*

Dalvi, John 1968, *Himalayan Blunder: The Curtain-raiser to the Sino-Indian War of 1962*. Bombay: Thacker.

Department of Commerce (2013). *Export Import Data Bank*. Accessed at *http://commerce.nic.in/eidb/default.asp.*

Dixit, J.N. (2003). *India's Foreign Policy 1947-2003*. New Delhi: Picus Books.

Ganguly, Sumit (2012). "Thing Again: India's Rise", *Foreign Policy*, 5 July.

Garver, John W. (2001). *Protracted Contest: Sino-Indian Rivalry in the Twentieth Century*. Seattle: University of Washington Press.

GoI (Government of India) (2013). *Demand No. 32: Ministry of External Affairs. Notes on Demands for Grants, 2013-14, Union Budget.*

Hussain, Wasbir (2007). "Ethno-nationalism and the Politics of Terror in India's Northeast", *South Asia: Journal of South Asian Studies* 30(1): 93-110.

Hymans, Jacques E. C. (2006). *The Psychology of Nuclear Proliferation: Identity, Emotions, and Foreign Policy*. Cambridge: Cambridge University Press.

Iype, George (1998). "War in MEA Cripples India's Battle for World Support", *Rediff News*, 14 July. Accessed at *http://www.rediff.com/news/1998/jul/14bomb4.htm*

Jha, Prashant (2012). "Maoist Meet Exposes Crisis", *The Hindu*, 21 July.

Kapur, Devesh (2009). "Public Opinion and Indian Foreign Policy", *India Review* 8(3): 286-305.

Kapur, Devesh and Kavita Iyengar (2006). "South Asia: The Limits of Integration in Improving Regional Security", in Ashley J. Tellis and Michael Wills (eds.), *Strategic Asia 2006-07: Trade, Interdependence, and Security*. Seattle and Washington, D.C.: National Bureau of Asian Research.

Khilnani, Sunil, Rajiv Kumar, Pratap Bhanu Mehta, Prakash Menon, Nandan Nilekani, Srinath Raghavan, Shyam Saran and Siddharth Varadarajan (2012). *Non-Alignment 2.0: A Foreign and Strategic Policy for India in the Twenty First Century.* New Delhi: Centre for Policy Research.

Kisangani, Emizet F. and Jeffrey Pickering (2008). "International Military Intervention, 1989-2005", *Inter-University Consortium for Political and Social Research, Data Collection* No 21282. Ann Arbor: University of Michigan.

Kux, Dennis (1993). *India and the United States: Estranged Democracies*. New Delhi: Sage Publications.

Madan, Tanvi (2014). *A Modi Foreign Policy: The Knowns and Unknowns*. Brookings Institution, *http://www.brookings.edu/blogs/up-front/posts/2014/05/16-india-modi-foreign-policy-madan*

Madan, Tanvi (2014). "Officialdom: South Block and Beyond", in David Malone, Srinath Raghavan and C. Raja Mohan (eds.), *The Oxford Handbook of Indian Foreign Policy*. New Delhi: Oxford University Press.

Madhukar, Abhishek (2011). "Exiled Tibetans Elect Political Heir to Dalai Lama", *Reuters*, 27 April.

Mahajan, Gurpreet (2008). "Religion and the Indian Constitution: Questions of Separation and Equality", in Rajeev Bhargava (ed.), *Politics and Ethics of the Indian Constitution*. New Delhi: Oxford University Press.

Malone, David M. and Rohan Mukherjee (2010). "Polity, Security, and Foreign Policy in Contemporary India", in T.V. Paul (ed.), *South Asia's Weak States: Understanding the Regional Insecurity Predicament*. Stanford: Stanford University Press.

Mandelbaum, Michael 1998, "Is Major War Obsolete?" *Survival* 40(4): 20-38.

Markey, Daniel (2009). "Developing India's Foreign Policy "Software"", *Asia Policy* 8: 73-96 (July).

MHA (Ministry of Home Affairs) (2011). "Lok Sabha Starred Question No. 1: Naxal Hit Areas, Answered on 22.11.2011", Government of India, retrieved from SATP (South Asia Terrorism Portal), *http://www.satp.org/satporgtp/countries/india/maoist/documents/papers/DATA_%20 Extent_Naxal_Violence.pdf*

Mohan, C. Raja (2010). "Rising India: Partner in Shaping the Global Commons", *The Washington Quarterly*: 133-48 (July).

Mohan, C. Raja (2003). *Crossing the Rubicon: The Shaping of India's New Foreign Policy*. Viking, New Delhi.

Mukherjee, Rohan and David M. Malone (2011). "From High Ground to High Table: The Evolution of Indian Multilateralism", *Global Governance* 17: 311-29.

Narang, Vipin (2009). "Posturing for Peace? Pakistan's Nuclear Postures and South Asian Stability", *International Security* 34(3): 38-78.

Pandit, M. Saleem (2014). "Modi Slams Pakistan for 'Proxy War' against India, Visits Kargil", *Times of India*, 12 August.

Pant, Harsh V. (2013). "The BRICS Fallacy", *The Washington Quarterly*: 91-105 (Summer).

Paul, T.V. (ed.) (2012). *South Asia's Weak States: Understanding the Regional Insecurity Predicament*. Stanford: Stanford University Press.

Pearson, Frederic S. and Robert A. Baumann (1993). "International Military Intervention, 1946-1988", *Inter-University Consortium for Political and Social Research, Data Collection* No 6035. Ann Arbor: University of Michigan.

Perkovich, George (1999). *India's Nuclear Bomb: The Impact on Global Proliferation*. Berkeley and Los Angeles: University of California Press.

PMIUN (Permanent Mission of India to the United Nations) (2011). *Explanation of Vote on Côte d'Ivoire Resolution by Ambassador Hardeep Singh Puri, Permanent Representative*. Security Council. 30 March.

Prasad, Chandra Bhan, D. Shyam Babu, Devesh Kapur and Lant Pritchett (2010). "Rethinking Inequality: Dalits in Uttar Pradesh in the Market Reform Era", *Economic and Political Weekly* XLV(35): 39-49.

PTI (Press Trust of India) (2006). "Naxalism Biggest Challenge: PM", *Hindustan Times*, 13 April.

———. (2009). "Naxals Get Arms from Abroad: Chidambaram", *The Hindu*, 24 October.

———. (2010)., "Naxalism Biggest Threat to Internal Security: Manmohan", *The Hindu*, 24 May.

Raghavan, Srinath (2009). "Civil-Military Relations in India: The China Crisis and After", *Journal of Strategic Studies* 32(1): 149-75.

Reddy, T. Ramakrishna (1968). *India's Policy in the United Nations*. Cranbury: Associated University Presses.

SATP (South Asia Terrorism Portal) (2014a). "India: Terrorist, Insurgent and Extremist Groups", *http://www.satp.org/satporgtp/countries/india/terroristoutfits/index.html*

———. (2014b). "India Fatalities: 1994-2014", *http://www.satp.org/satporgtp/countries/india/database/indiafatalities.htm*

Shah, M.A. Zafar (1983). *India and the Superpowers*. New Delhi: Vikas Publishing House.

Sidhu, W.P.S., Pratap Bhanu Mehta and Bruce Jones (2013). *Shaping the Emerging World: India and the Multilateral Order*. Washington, D.C.: Brookings Institution Press

Suri, Manik and Devesh Kapur (2013). "Geoeconomics vs. Geopolitics: Implications for Asia", in Inderjit Kaur and Nirvikar Singh (eds.), *Oxford Handbook of the Economics of the Pacific Rim*. London: Oxford University Press.

Talbott, Strobe (2004). *Engaging India: Diplomacy, Democracy, and the Bomb*. Washington, D.C.: The Brookings Institution

Tanham, George K. (1992). *Indian Strategic Thought: An Interpretive Essay*. Santa Monica: RAND.

Tellis, Ashley J. (2012). *Nonalignment Redux: The Perils of Old Wine in New Skins*. Washington, D.C.: Carnegie Endowment

Tharoor, Shashi (2012). *Pax Indica: India and the World of the 21st Century*. New Delhi: Penguin.

The New York Times (2012). "The Enablers", *The New York Times*, 14 February.

Varadarajan, Siddharth (2010)., "Facing up to the Myanmar Challenge", *The Hindu*, July 26.

Varshney, Ashutosh (2013). *Battles Half Won: India's Improbable Democracy*. New Delhi: Viking.

World Bank (2013). *World Development Indicators*. Accessed at *http://databank.worldbank.org/data/views/variableSelection/selectvariables.aspx?source=world-development-indicators*

———. (2014a). *Poverty & Equity: Country Dashboard, India. http://povertydata.worldbank.org/poverty/country/IND*

———. (2014b). *World Development Indicators. http://databank.worldbank.org/data/home.aspx.*

Wright Jr., Theodore P. (1982). "Ethnic Group Pressures in Foreign Policy: Indian Muslims and American Jews", *Economic and Political Weekly* 17(41): 1655-660, 9 October.

9

SARTAJ AZIZ

Strategic Vision of Pakistan's Foreign Policy

Completion of the first year of the new government is an appropriate time to review its foreign policy achievements and also list the goals and challenges that lie ahead. This review is presented under three inter-related sections:

I. The Strategic Vision.

II. The Main Achievements.

III. The Future Challenges.

Strategic Vision

As the Pakistan Muslim League (N) [PML(N)] 2013 election Manifesto emphasised,

> Pakistan today is at war within, while isolated abroad. Its independence and sovereignty stand compromised; its economic weaknesses are forcing us to go begging bowl in hand, while foreign states undertake unilateral strikes on its territory and non-state actors use it as a sanctuary to pursue their own agendas, oblivious to Pakistan's national interests.

Keeping this perspective in view, the first important foreign policy objective is to safeguard Pakistan's security and eliminate the growing culture of extremism, intolerance and violence from the society through concerted political and military strategies and a policy of non-interference in the affairs of other countries. Henceforth, top priority will be accorded to country's own security rather than the agendas and priorities of other countries.

The second important objective is to make economic revival and sustained development, the centrepiece of our foreign policy. A persistent low rate of growth, an average of less than three per cent over the past six years, has not only increased our dependence on others but also widened the gap between expectations and reality. That is why, the Prime Minister has repeatedly emphasised that 'external influence flows from internal strength'. The government therefore has vigorously set out to pursue three major priorities: expanding investment and trade (not aid), resolving the energy crisis, and addressing extremism and terrorism.

The third important priority of a peaceful neighbourhood automatically flows from these two objectives. Prime Minister's slogan of "peace for development" means building a peaceful external environment so that core national objectives of economic development could be robustly advanced.

A fourth pillar of this vision is to turn Pakistan's strategic geographical location from a liability into an asset through trade, transport and energy connectivity with China, Central Asia and West Asia. This in turn could also help to re-balance our geo-strategic and geo-economic priorities.

The government is fully aware of the complex and difficult external environment in which these policy objectives and priorities have to be pursued but if there is clear vision, backed by strong political will, Pakistan can achieve Qauid's dictum of "peace within and peace without" in a relatively short period of time.

Achievements

One year is not a long period to expect all the tangible outcomes of the far-reaching changes introduced since June 2013. Yet, the list of achievements, so far, is impressive:

a. *Reinforcing Strategic Partnership with China*: Our time-tested and all-weather relationship with China has been transformed into a strong strategic partnership, with focus on trade, investment, energy infrastructure and connectivity. Counter-terrorism cooperation continues to strengthen, while Pakistan's support to China's core interests of Tibet and Taiwan remains unwavering. Mutual collaboration in regional forums like Shanghai Cooperation Organisation (SCO), Conference on Interaction and Confidence Building Measures in Asia (CICA) and Heart of Asia has stepped up.

A monumental achievement is the initiation of the China-Pakistan Economic Corridor (CPEC), which is considered to be a "game-changer" in terms of trade, investment, connectivity and regional economic integration. China is poised to offer investments and loans to the tune of $ 35 billion for energy and other infrastructure projects over the next 8-10 years.

b. *Reaching out to Afghanistan*: Our Afghan policy is aimed at building a friendly and good-neighbourly relationship, in which flawed concepts of the past like 'strategic depth' have no place. The key principles enunciated by the Prime Minister include mutual respect for sovereignty and territorial integrity, non-interference and no favourites. The Prime Minister has had four meetings with the Afghan President in the past one year. Our efforts are focused on intensified political dialogue, measures to prevent use of territory against each other, support for Afghan peace and reconciliation process, streamlining transit trade issues, up-scaling bilateral assistance, enhanced border management, refugee return, counter-narcotics, and intensified dialogue at regional and international level. Pakistan's constructive engagement has helped reduce trust deficit. Pakistan's contribution to the process of stabilisation in Afghanistan is being acknowledged regionally and internationally.

We have played a positive role in Afghan elections, by helping with border security and maintaining strong neutrality. Pakistan now looks forward to working closely with the new democratic choice of Afghan people, manifested through a credible electoral process, to build a strong, peaceful and fruitful relationship between the two countries.

c. *Improving ties with India*: It is manifestly clear that South Asia cannot have durable peace and stability unless Pakistan and India make peace. This requires building a qualitatively new environment in which mutual concerns are addressed in a credible way and efforts are made to promote an agenda of peace and development. It is in this perspective that the

Prime Minister has stressed that the main dynamic in South Asia should be cooperation, not confrontation.

Mr Narendra Modi is the choice of the Indian electorate, and we have already started our interaction with the new government. The Prime Minister's early outreach to Mr Modi to congratulate him on Bharatiya Janata Party's (BJP) electoral victory and later participation in the swearing-in ceremony in New Delhi are reflective of his sincere commitment to turning a new page in the relationship. The Prime Minister's initiative has been widely commended at the international level.

The government will continue to seek sustained and result-oriented dialogue, meaningful progress towards resolution of outstanding issues including Kashmir, and enhanced cooperation on economic issues. The two Foreign Secretaries will be meeting shortly to evolve a roadmap for such a dialogue.

d. *Strengthening ties with the United States (US):* The strategic relationship with the United States (US) is being reoriented on the basis of mutual interest and mutual trust. The effort is to transform the substantive content of the relationship, and to change the narrative. The US is a key partner in trade and investment, counter-terrorism, and regional stability. We have endeavoured to build on the positives while working sincerely and meaningfully to address each others' concerns. Pakistan's democratic transition is playing an important role in this context.

Prime Minister's visit to Washington in October last year and his interaction with President Obama as well as senior Administrator officials and key legislators was of far-reaching importance. The Prime Minister placed his central emphasis on enhanced market access, US investments in energy and other projects, defence and security cooperation, counter-terrorism, and people-to-people exchanges.

The Prime Minister's visit was followed by a resumption of the Strategic Dialogue at the Ministerial level, which the

Adviser and Secretary Kerry co-chaired. The work of several Joint Working Groups was reviewed and a new group was created on education. We also agreed to strengthen our dialogue and cooperation on regional issues, particularly working to advance common objectives of peace and stability in post-2014 Afghanistan and sustainable peace and progress in South Asia.

While challenges remain, we are committed to deepening mutual collaboration and making this important relationship truly beneficial for the socio-economic development of the people of Pakistan.

e. *Comprehensively up-grading relations with European Union (EU):* Our intensive engagement with European countries—both bilaterally and in the EU framework—has produced significant results. Trade, investment and cooperation in social sectors are on the upswing, while counter-terrorism cooperation and security ties continue to strengthen. A ministerial level strategic dialogue was held in March 2014 and the next EU-Pakistan Summit is planned before the end of this year.

A major achievement for the government has been the grant of the Generalised Scheme of Preferences+(GSP+) status to Pakistan in December 2013. This would help boost Pakistan's textile exports, generate employment, and contribute to efforts for economic revival. This would also help address the issue of extremism and terrorism by creating economic opportunities and reducing the appeal of radicalism.

f. *Re-invigorating relations with Saudi Arabia, Iran, Turkey and other Islamic countries*: Solidarity with the Islamic World has always been a central tenet of Pakistan's foreign policy. Pakistan has long-standing exemplary relations with the Kingdom of Saudi Arabia. These relations were further strengthened through several high level exchanges in the past year.

Our historic relations with Turkey are also being translated into concrete political and economic partnership. As a result, economic cooperation with Turkey crossed a new threshold in the past 12 months. Many Turkish companies are making important investments in several key sub-sectors.

Iran is an important neighbour. The Prime Minister's visit to Iran in May not only provided an impetus to bilateral relations, but also helped to remove perceptions and to evolve a roadmap to enhance bilateral trade and economic cooperation. The key areas of focus remain border security, forward movement in IP gas pipeline projects, exploring practical ways to increase trade in the face of sanctions, and pursuing balanced relations in the Gulf region.

Pakistan's traditional relations with fraternal countries like the United Arab Emirates (UAE), Qatar and Bahrain are expanding through deeper political dialogue, growing accent on energy cooperation, investment in infrastructure project, export of skilled manpower and increased trade. We have intensified efforts to conclude a Free Trade Agreement with Gulf Cooperation Council (GCC) countries.

g. *Promoting Regional Cooperation:* Pakistan's close engagement with Economic Cooperation Organization (ECO), South Asian Association for Regional Cooperation (SAARC) and Organisation for Islamic Cooperation (OIC) remains crucially important. In the face of changing global and regional context, Pakistan's balanced approach avoiding interference in internal or intra-regional affairs that are not directly of concern, has been widely appreciated.

The revival of the Pakistan economy in the past one year, as clearly highlighted by many positive economic indicators and also decisive steps to attract foreign investment in energy and some other sectors, have significantly expanded prospects for deeper economic cooperation with other countries.

h. *Safeguarding national security, nuclear programme and geo-strategic interest:* Pakistan's nuclear deterrence has served to maintain peace in region. Our diplomats have effectively defended Pakistan's position on strategic issues at multilateral fora. We have also successfully mobilised international support for Pakistan's counter-terrorism efforts.

The military operation launched in North Waziristan in June this year, preceded by the operation in Karachi, will not only re-establish the writ of the State in all parts of Pakistan but also counter the growing culture of violence and intolerance.

i. *Looking after Pakistani diaspora and promoting soft image:* As expected of any democratic government, there has been a strong emphasis on looking after the Pakistani community abroad. In Saudi Arabia, a massive effort was undertaken to protect interests of Pakistanis during Saudization campaign and consular facilities are being improved in many countries.

Overall, there is a visible transformation in the international image of Pakistan, which now finds itself in the mainstream of the global community.

Future Challenges

In terms of security and stability, South Asia stands at a crossroad, with elections having taken place in Bangladesh, India and Afghanistan, the recent announcement of US post-2014 military disengagement in Afghanistan, the process of Iran-US rapprochement underway, and the changing political and security landscape in the Gulf and Middle East region.

Coming years could witness many challenges like turmoil and instability as also opportunities for new avenues of cooperation emerging from political changes and strategic re-alignments. While consolidating the gains made over the past one year in Pakistan's key relationships, as enumerated above, our focus in the coming year would also be on:

- Evolving a joint strategy with the new Afghan government to control extremism and terrorism so that our respective territories are not used for attacks or subversion against each other and expand, economic cooperation between Pakistan and Afghanistan.
- Carrying forward the peace process with the new government in India through focus on economic revival

and expanded people-to-people contacts, while at the same time intensifying the dialogue on all-outstanding issues like Kashmir, Siachin, Sir Creek and Water.

- Launch several new initiatives to expand energy and trade connectivity with Central Asia and West Asia. The proposed Economic Corridor from Gwadar to Kashgar will be further extended to other Central Asian countries, and apart from expanding CASA-1000 electricity import project, additional projects will be undertaken to import gas from Iran, Turkmenistan and Qatar.
- Deepening engagement with the Russian Federation, as Russia and China cooperate, in SCO and other fora, to integrate Eurasia into the world economy without ideological overtones of the Cold War era.
- Building deeper trade and economic linkage with Southeast Asia/Association of Southeast Asian Nations (ASEAN).
- Reviving closer ties with and seeking new avenues of cooperation with Africa and Latin America.
- Serving Pakistani diaspora and mobilising their potential to advance our national interests.

The core elements of our approach would remain: (a) constructive engagement; (b) non-interference; and (c) advancement of trade, investment and economic cooperation. We would continue to maximise our diplomatic space and enhance foreign policy options:

- The barometer would be how to protect our security and promote the agenda of peace and development.
- We would continue to pursue balanced relationships, and eschew involvement in issues where no direct interests are at stake.
- In the internal context, de-radicalisation and building a grand national narrative, would be the additional focus of these efforts.
- Further improving Pakistan's image abroad, which in turn will depend on more effective control of terrorism, movement on human rights, and positive image of a more tolerant society.

10

APARNA PANDE

Neighbours Without Fences

India and Pakistan

Good Fences Make Good Neighbours.

—17th century proverb.

Introduction

Notwithstanding ties of history, culture, ethnicity, and language, Pakistan and India still remain hostile. Neighbours divided by the impact of the British Indian Empire's partition in 1947. The split of a unified subcontinent along religious lines into the states of India and Pakistan have framed the fundamental relations between the two neighbouring states. As such, India inherited the secular Indian nationalist worldview of the Indian National Congress (INC), just as Pakistan continues to pursue the Islamic nationalism of the All India Muslim League (AIML). Subsequently, issues of national identity coupled with disputes over land and resources have bred enormous mistrust, and left a bitter legacy which continues to frame ties between these two neighbours for the last six decades.

To understand India-Pakistan relations, there is a need to comprehensively understand the underlying issues of their relationship. For each state, its national identity framed its foreign policy. Indian leaders, conscious of their multi-religious and multi-cultural population portrayed India as a secular—not a Hindu—state, encouraging minorities to feel that they were part of a 5000-year-old civilisation. India regretted partition as the 'vivisection of Mother India' and saw the creation of Pakistan as the unfortunate result of the 'two nation theory.' In external relations, this translated into emphasising historic linkages with other nations and a tendency to effectively overshadow Pakistan. In light of this, for Pakistanis, India became an existential threat: unreconciled to their nation's birth, which could only be contained through military parity.

In legal terms, India recognises the sovereignty of Pakistan, which resulted from India's partition. India also accepts the independence of Bangladesh, which was born out of the partition of Pakistan. But in South Asia, India's primary goal remains regional integration which it sees as the way forward with its immediate neighbours. Pakistan, on the other hand, has insisted on trying to be an equal to its much larger neighbour whom it accuses of seeking to be a regional hegemon. Pakistan's desire for equivalence with India can be traced to the pre-Partition era, when the Muslim League sought parity with the Congress. In some ways, it is an ideological cornerstone of Pakistan's worldview.

This chapter will provide a historical context to the relations between India and Pakistan dating back to Partition before discussing the evolution of the foreign policies of these two countries. It will examine the role of institutions in each country, their conflicts and wars, as well as their views on the issues of military and economic parity. Further, the influence of the Cold War on both countries' ties with other nations (including the United States [US], China, Afghanistan and the rest of the Muslim world) and the changes ensued with demise of the Cold War will be reviewed before assessing future prospects.

Contesting Identities: Legacy of Partition

The last few decades of British rule in India saw a scramble for power between the two leading communities in the British Raj, namely Hindus and Muslims. The Indian national movement and the demand for parliamentary democracy ultimately led to the rise of both majority and minority consciousness in India. While the INC that emerged in 1885 sought a territorial national identity, organisations like the Hindu Mahasabha (HMS) sought a religious one. Similarly, two strands emerged in Muslim political consciousness, those who believed in territorial nationalism and others who believed in religious nationalism. While many Muslims joined the Congress, others instead joined the AIML set up in 1906.

Right from 1906, the key problem espoused by the Muslim League was numerical inferiority and the solution was safeguards for Muslims, initially both from the British and the Congress. The initial claim for safeguards was later encapsulated in the demand for parity with the Hindus. The ground for demanding parity with the Hindus was based on the belief that Hindus and Muslims were two separate nations living in India and both had equal right to India and its territory. Attempts were made in 1916 and 1928 to try to get the Muslim League and the Congress on one platform, but these failed to bring about any long-term understanding.

The initial Muslim demand for separate electorates gradually evolved into a demand for the independent Muslim state of Pakistan and the Congress leadership's continued intransigence prevented any compromise on the issue. Thus, in 1947, the subcontinent was partitioned into the two independent states of India and Pakistan. Among the lasting legacies of partition was that of mistrust between these two newly-created countries.

Even though India emerged as a new nation in 1947, geography, history and the national struggle against British colonial rule provided the basis for an Indian identity, which emphasised civilisational heritage, and a multi-ethnic, multi-linguistic and multi-cultural identity.

The idea of Pakistan, however, was recent. The name was coined in 1933, the Pakistan resolution passed in 1940 and the country emerged in 1947.[1] The shared civilisational heritage with India meant that Pakistan's founders had two choices, either to accept the

1. In his Presidential address to the AIML in 1930 Sir Muhammad Iqbal, leading poet and thinker and to many Pakistan's 'spiritual founding father', stated: "I would like to see the Punjab, North West Frontier Province, Sind and Baluchistan amalgamated into a single state...... formation of a consolidated North-West Indian Muslim state appears to me to be the final destiny of the Muslims at least of North-West India." Iqbal's scheme caught the imagination of some Indian Muslim students at Cambridge who in 1933 coined the phrase 'PAKSTAN' as an acronym for the states of Punjab, Afghania (the North-West Frontier region), Kashmir, Sindh and Baluchistan. For them 'Pakstan'—later Pakistan—"means the land of the Pak—the spiritually pure and clean. It symbolises the religious beliefs and the ethnical stocks of our people; and it stands for all the territorial constituents of our original Fatherland."

heritage and constantly feel their identity was challenged or to create a new identity, separate from that of India. Therefore, a conscious decision was made by its founding fathers to construct an ideology-based national identity; one based on and derived from Islam.

Most Pakistanis incorrectly believe India has not accepted the creation of Pakistan. Except for the statements at independence and a few stray comments made periodically by Hindu right-wing organisations, most Indian leaders have accepted partition and the existence of Pakistan. In a speech at Aligarh Muslim University in January 1948, India's first Prime Minister Jawaharlal Nehru stated that India had no desire to undo Partition and take over Pakistan:

> It is to India's advantage that Pakistan should be a secure and prosperous State with which we can develop close and friendly relations. If today by any chance I were offered the reunion of India and Pakistan, I would decline it for obvious reasons. I do not want to carry the burden of Pakistan's great problems. I have enough of my own (Nehru, 1958).

Five decades later on his trip to Lahore in 1999, Indian Prime Minister, and leader of the Hindu nationalist Bharatiya Janata Party (BJP), Atal Bihari Vajpayee stressed that India had accepted Pakistan's creation.[2]

Just as many Pakistanis misunderstand Indian intentions towards their state, there are also some Indians who have not forgotten Partition and often voice displeasure that Pakistanis want to repeat it by tearing India apart further. During the years immediately after Partition, Nehru came under tremendous pressure and criticism for his attempts to create a secular country, especially from Hindu nationalist politicians and refugee leaders. In a letter to Deputy Prime Minister and Home Minister Sardar Patel, Nehru deplored the "constant cry for retaliation and of vicarious punishment of the Muslims of India, because the Pakistanis punish Hindus. That argument does not appeal to me in the slightest. I am

---

2. The BJP's ideological roots come from the HMS and the Rashtriya Swayamsevak Sangh (RSS) who espouse the ideology of Hindu nationalism. In yesteryears they also championed the idea of *Akhand Bharat* or undivided India though they have not do so for some time now. However, the BJP has never opined such a policy.

sure this policy of retaliation and vicarious punishment will ruin India as well as Pakistan."[3]

Furthermore, Nehru's close confidant Krishna Menon stated that a view commonly held by radical Indian strategic thinkers is that Pakistan wants to break up India and create a new Muslim state in all of South Asia. "In Pakistan's view the Partition [of India, in 1947] is only the beginning. Her idea is to get a jumping-off ground to take the whole of India" (Cited in Brecher, 1968).

The degree to which any talk about Partition can still awaken emotions in India and Pakistan was publicly visible in August 2009. A former Foreign Minister and BJP leader, Jaswant Singh, released his biography of Jinnah, titled *Jinnah: India, Partition, Independence*. In a lengthy 600 plus pages, Singh blames the Congress leadership, and not the Muslim League, for Partition. Singh also refers to Jinnah as an Indian nationalist. Singh's views are surprising considering the ideological origins of his party. The BJP's ideological mentor organisations are the Hindu chauvinist HMS and the Hindu right-wing militant organisation RSS, who believe Partition led to the 'vivisection of Mother India'. The reactions to Singh's book were sharp, he was initially expelled from his party and the western Indian state of Gujarat even banned the book.[4]

Mainsprings of Indian and Pakistani Foreign Policies

At independence, India benefitted by being the direct successor of the British Raj. On a functional level, India inherited the administration, the capital, the basic institutional architecture, and the majority of assets and resources. In addition to this, British India had been a signatory to the League of Nations as well as the Charter of the United Nations (UN); when 'British India' no longer existed, India took over its seat in all international organisations. Above all, India inherited the name and with it the civilisational heritage.

3. "Nehru to Patel, 20 February 1950, SPC, Vol.10, p.5", Cited in Guha (2007): 241.

4. The ban was later overturned by the Supreme Court of India, and Mr Jaswant Singh too returned to the BJP.

Pakistan, however, had to deal not only with creating a new state and administrative machinery from scratch, but also keeping the disparate provinces together and managing a massive refugee problem. These issues were exacerbated by the fact that India initially withheld assets and funds (later on released under pressure from Mahatma Gandhi, India's founding father), and the balance of trade was skewed against Pakistan as it inherited the primary products producing regions but lost the factories to India.

In such an atmosphere, the two countries fought their first war, over Kashmir. A newly independent state, Pakistan, facing both internal and external problems saw the war as an attempt by India to 'wipe out Pakistan'. The massive military disparities between the two countries only ended up exacerbating Pakistan's feeling of insecurity and desperate need for allies and alliances.

It is in this environment that the founding elites in both countries formulated the key principles of their foreign policy.

The foreign policy of a country is influenced by both its geography and its history. India's geographical size, demography and natural resources along with its civilisational heritage are believed to guarantee India's rightful place in the world arena. Nehru, who was India's first Prime Minister and Foreign Minister for 17 years, laid down basic guidelines for India's foreign policy—a legacy that remained by and large unchanged by his successors. In a speech in March 1949, Nehru (1961) stated:

> Remember that India, not because of any ambition of hers, but because of the force of circumstances, because of geography, because of history and because of so many other things, inevitably has to play a very important part in Asia.

Desirous of building its economic strength, there was an excessive emphasis on economic autarky or self-sufficiency and avoiding reliance on outside powers. Indian leaders believed that India could teach the world more with a non-assertive, non-aggressive soft power approach than by joining military alliances.

In sharp contrast, Pakistan's founding elite and policymakers, both civilian and military, sought security—from the perceived

Indian threat—through alliances. In the words of Pakistan's first Prime Minister Liaquat Ali Khan, Indian leaders "resented" the Partition and had "mental reservations" about the creation of Pakistan.[5] Hence, Pakistan's leaders believe that even after the creation of Pakistan, its territorial integrity was still under threat and there was a constant need for self-preservation.

The crafting of a national identity and framing of foreign policy had the fear of India in common. The argument that Pakistan was created so that the Indian Muslims could live their lives according to the "Islamic way of life," and no longer be under the majority rule of the Hindus was repeatedly made.[6] Hence, Pakistan's Islamic identity would be an "ideological safeguard," protecting its territorial integrity and preventing any disputes and disruptions from within.[7]

During the 1930s and 1940s, Nehru as Congress spokesman and President, travelled around the world and built relationships in the US, UK, Europe, the Middle East and even in East and Southeast Asia. These relationships formed the bedrock of India's ties with these countries after Independence. Most countries around the world and most colonial states not only knew where India was situated and what its leaders sought, but also supported the Indian national movement.

In contrast, the problems that Pakistan's leaders faced were complicated. In the words of Pakistan's first Foreign Minister, Sir Zafrulla Khan (1951), not only did they have to "introduce our new state to the rest of the world," but there was "a certain amount of confusion abroad as to what this Pakistan was. We tried to explain that the subcontinent hitherto known as India had been divided into the sovereign states of Pakistan, and India. That instead of helping matters merely made the confusion worse. That India had been divided into India and Pakistan sounded absurd." Thus Pakistan's leaders and policymakers had an uphill task in simply ensuring that

5. Speech by Liaquat Ali Khan on his trip to the US in 1950. See, Khan (1950).

6. Ibid.: 10-11.

7. Ibid.: 16.

the rest of the world knew where the new country was located and why it was created.

An analysis of the foreign policy establishments of both countries is now in order before we move on to a study of their policies during and after the Cold War era.

Foreign Policy Establishments

Foreign policymaking is by its very nature somewhat confidential and secretive. Since both India and Pakistan are parliamentary democracies and inheritors of the same British Raj; at least at independence there was a fundamental similarity in their institutions. Changes, however, have occurred over time, not only in the institutional setup but also the role (and power) of various institutions.

Multiple institutions are involved in foreign policymaking in India, including the Ministry of External Affairs (includes the embassies and the Indian Foreign Service), the Prime Minister's Office (PMO), the Cabinet Secretariat and Committees, the National Security Advisor and the National Security Council Secretariat. In addition to this, the Parliamentary Committees as well as the Ministries of Home, Defense, Commerce and Finance are also a part of the Indian foreign policy process. Nehru's legacy paved the path for subsequent Prime Ministers to prioritise foreign policymaking as a key component of their role.

With the legacy of colonial rule looming, for India's leaders the paramount security—and foreign policy—concern was maintaining India's territorial integrity. India's neighbours were hence seen as a key part of its security especially since India shares borders and ethno-linguistic-cultural-religious similarities with them. This has resulted in Ministries like home affairs and defence gaining an increasing say in foreign policy. India's military and intelligence establishments also provide inputs into foreign and security policy. With economic policy being critical to foreign policy, finance and commerce ministries have played a key role. However, civilian supremacy has ensured that their input is limited.

If we turn to Pakistan, the institutional set up has by and large similar contours. The key institutions are: the Ministry of Foreign Affairs (includes embassies and the Foreign Service of Pakistan), the PMO, National Security Council or Defense Committee of Cabinet (the two have been used alternately over the decades), Ministries of Finance, Defense and Interior and Pakistan's Military and Intelligence establishments and agencies (Chief of Army Staff, Chairman Joint Chiefs of Staff Committee and Director General, Inter-Services Intelligence Directorate [ISID]).

In comparison with several other countries, scant literature exists on Pakistan's foreign policymaking process. Retired officers of Pakistan's Foreign Service say the foreign policy debate is somewhat limited, a view endorsed by experts. Years of military rule have led to ascendance of the military and intelligence institutions in Pakistan's foreign policy decision-making.

In the initial decades the army's influence was limited mainly to Pakistan's relations with the West, especially US and the UK, and the various military pacts later joined. During General Zia ul-Haq's rule (1977-1988) in addition to establishing military dominance in domestic politics, the influence of the military and especially Pakistan's intelligence organisation, the ISID in foreign and security policies became entrenched. The real change came after the Soviet invasion of Afghanistan in 1979 and Pakistan's involvement in the anti-Soviet Afghan jihad. Increasingly, since 1979, the Inter-Services Intelligence (ISI) developed a virtual veto power over issues related to external and security policy. As a former Pakistani foreign secretary once remarked, "the space they [ISI] gained as an expedient, later on they claimed as a right."

In India, changes have taken place especially since the 1990s. The end of one-party supremacy—the Indian National Congress—and the rise of coalition governments ensured that domestic politics has an increasing impact on foreign policy. The weakening of national level parties and the corresponding rise of strong regional parties have resulted in situations where state governments play an important role in framing policies with India's neighbours. The growing role of media in shaping public opinion and hence on impacting foreign policy can be seen in both countries in recent decades.

It is in this context that we will now examine the key areas of conflict between India and Pakistan, including the wars they have fought.

Conflicts/Wars (Areas: Water, Border, Refugee, Minorities; 1948, 1965, 1971, 1999)

The roots of the key areas of conflict between India and Pakistan lie in the legacy of partition, whether it is the problems facing minorities, the dispute over Kashmir as well as issues like Siachen, Sir Creek and the water dispute. The two countries have fought four wars in the last six decades, three over Kashmir, and one that resulted in the creation of Bangladesh.

Minorities and the 'Other'

One of the long-term legacies of Partition was the creation of countries, which had substantial religious minorities. Pakistan had a large Hindu minority in 1947 and India had a large Muslim minority. Over time due to riots, internal displacements and the 1971 creation of Bangladesh, Pakistan's Hindu minority has been reduced to less than 2 per cent of its population today. However, in India, the Muslim minority stands at around 14 per cent of its population, which translates into India having almost as many Muslims as Pakistan does.

The physical and psychological impact of Partition, the uprooting of people and the communal riots left a bitter legacy, which shaped both Pakistani and Indian perceptions of each other. The rise of religious revivalist ideologies and organisations in India and Pakistan owes a lot to this defining of the 'other.' Hindu revivalist organisations in India like the RSS and right-wing Hindu nationalist parties like the Jana Sangh, the BJP, and the Shiva Sena have a common 'other': 'Islamic Pakistan'. Similarly for Islamist revivalist organisations in Pakistan like Deobandi[8] parties, Jamaat e Islami[9] and jihadi groups like Lashkar-e-Taiba (LeT), the 'other' is 'Hindu' India or 'Hindustan'.

Over the years, both countries have developed the policy of deeply scrutinising any policy or incident, which affects the minorities, and thus domestic policy ends up influencing foreign policy.

India and Pakistan view any analysis by the other of how they treat their minorities as interference in internal affairs. Both sides, however, continue to be focused on this issue. In February 2010, when the Pakistani Taliban, a terror network operating out of Pakistan's tribal areas, kidnapped and killed Sikhs, India protested about the treatment of minorities in Pakistan. In March 2013, when India hanged Muhammad Afzal Guru for his role in the 2001 terror attack on the Indian parliament, Pakistan's National Assembly passed a resolution condemning his hanging and expressed concern about the situation in Jammu and Kashmir (CNN-IBN, 2010; 2013).

---

8. The Deobandi movement is a reform movement which centres on the Dar ul Ulum madrasa founded at Deoband (northern India) in 1867. The founders of the Deoband madrasa believed that Muslim societies had fallen behind the West because they had been "seduced" by the "amoral and material Western culture." This happened because Muslims had deviated from the true path and original teachings of the Prophet. The way out was to 'purify' Islam and remove any 'un-Islamic' influences which had crept in from Hinduism. This was to be done by training Ulema in Hadith and Quran and sending them out to various towns and villages across the British Raj where they would issue *fatwas* and guide Muslims back to the true teachings of Islam. During the Indian national movement, clerics belonging to the Deoband movement split into two, with some siding with the Congress and others with the Muslim League. After 1947, Deobandi clerics who stayed in India remained traditionalist but those who went to Pakistan, over time, became more revivalist, and the 1970s onwards, developed close ideological and organisational ties with the Wahhabis.

9. The Jamaat e Islami was founded in 1941 by Maulana Abul Ala Maududi. Maududi believed that Islam was not just a religion and faith but a way of life. Maududi's ideal political system was a 'theo-democracy' which meant "limited people's sovereignty under the suzerainty of God." Desirous of establishing this view all over South Asia, Maududi was not an early champion of either the Muslim League or Quaid-e-Azam Jinnah. The goal of Maududi and his followers was the establishment of an Islamic state but they would have preferred more pious leaders as the head of that state. However, once Pakistan was created, Maududi and others with views similar to him believed that this was a great opportunity to create the ideal of perfect Islamic state. In 1947, Jamaat e Islami split into two—Jamaat e Islami Hind which was India-based and remained a traditionalist proselytising organisation, and Jamaat e Islami which was Pakistan-based and over time became a revivalist organisation.

Kashmir: 'Unfinished Business of Partition'

The one issue, which most epitomises how the rest of the world looks at India-Pakistan ties, is that of Kashmir. The divergence of views on Kashmir starts from how the two countries refer to the issue: for Pakistan, Kashmir is the 'unfinished business of Partition,' whereas for India, it is a settled issue that only needs dialogue and discussion.

Jammu and Kashmir, one of the 562 princely states in pre-Partition India and large in size and population had, on the dissolution of the British Raj, the choice of acceding to either Pakistan or India. Kashmir was contiguous to both countries, had a Muslim-majority population and was ruled by a Hindu Maharaja Hari Singh. Maharaja Singh, the ruler of Kashmir, initially refused to join either country. However, when faced with a rebellion in his kingdom, aided by Pakistan, he signed the Instrument of Accession to India. Thus, within a few months of Partition, India and Pakistan faced each other as enemies on the battlefield. India's appeal to the UN in 1948 and the subsequent ceasefire led to the de facto division of Kashmir along an ad hoc boundary, presently referred to as the Line of Control (LoC).

Around the same time, the Cold War exacerbated the India-Pakistan conflict. India believed, especially after the US-Pakistan Mutual Defense agreement of 1959 that the US-dominated UN would always side with Pakistan. Since the 1960s, India has refused to accept either a UN monitored plebiscite or international arbitration, maintaining Kashmir was a bilateral issue between India and Pakistan in which no external power has the right to interfere.[10] That has remained India's stance ever since. Pakistan, however, has tried to portray Kashmir as an international conflict and repeatedly looked to its allies for aid in resolving the Kashmir dispute. In this regard, Pakistan portrays Kashmir as part of the broader 'Hindu-Muslim,' conflict dating back to Partition.

---

10. In 1964, Indian representative at the UN, M.C. Chagla, requested that the UN Secretary-General should not come to India solely to discuss the Kashmir dispute. During the discussions between Indian and Pakistani Foreign Ministers after the 1965 conflict, Indian Foreign Minister Swaran Singh insisted that Kashmir was a bilateral issue. Cited in Burke (1973).

Pakistani leaders and strategic thinkers put forth three broad reasons for Kashmir belonging to Pakistan, ideological, economic and strategic. Ideologically for Pakistan, the basis of India's partition and the creation of Pakistan was the 'two-nation' theory. Since Pakistan comprised the Muslim-majority parts of the British Indian Empire, Kashmir, as a Muslim-majority state, should automatically have gone to Pakistan. Kashmir is also the 'K' in the acronym, Pakistan.

Economically, Pakistani planners have put forth historical arguments for why Kashmir should be part of Pakistan. All the trade and communication routes in Kashmir have historically been through what is present-day Pakistani Punjab. The Indus water issue, which is discussed later in this chapter, also ties in here as these rivers flow through Kashmir and then enter Pakistan. If Kashmir were part of Pakistan, there would be no fear of India cutting off the water supply to starve Pakistan.

Strategically, Pakistan has always feared calculated encirclement from India. The north-western province of Pakistan, Khyber Pakhtunkhwa, formerly North Western Frontier Province (NWFP), borders Kashmir, and if all of Kashmir were to fall into Indian hands, then Pakistan would be completely surrounded by India. The key political party in this province before Partition, a secular Pashtun party, was a close ally of the Congress and its leadership was keen to either join India or be independent. Any moves by India to obtain all of Kashmir were seen as one step in the final aim of taking over both Kashmir and then NWFP and thus undoing Partition. The Pashtunistan issue and the tensions with Afghanistan coupled with Afghanistan's close ties with India further fed into Pakistan's fears. Until 1971, Pakistan already faced encirclement by India in East Pakistan and was fearful of the same in the West. After 1971, the belief that encirclement by India had led to the defeat and loss of the Eastern wing meant there was a need to prevent any such action in the West and Kashmir was all the more crucial.

Kashmir was also a key part of Pakistan's geo-strategic location and importance to global powers like China and the US. The argument ran thus: If Pakistan had Kashmir and thus access to Central Asia, China would want to build close ties with Pakistan. Pakistan's access to the 'soft underbelly of the Soviet Union,' would also make it indispensable to the Americans.

Hence, Pakistan asserts that as a Muslim majority region Kashmir belongs in Pakistan and therefore Indian sovereignty over Kashmir is unacceptable. Pakistan has demanded that plebiscite should be held in Indian-controlled Kashmir in accordance with the UN resolutions to ascertain the will of the people about joining India or Pakistan. Pakistan also believes that India has been violating the human rights of Kashmiri Muslims, which has resulted in the popular and indigenous uprising against Indian occupation since 1989.

India's claim to Kashmir has ideological, historical, economic, strategic and legal dimensions. According to Indian policymakers, Kashmir was a part of every Indian empire right from the ancient times. For India, the existence of a Muslim majority state within the Indian union reflects the secular nature of India's polity, notwithstanding India's overwhelming Hindu majority.[11] There is also a fear that allowing secession of one part of India could open the gates for possible balkanisation of modern India.[12]

Legally speaking, India's position is that Jammu and Kashmir lawfully acceded to India in 1947 when the Maharajah signed the Instrument of Accession. India believes that successive elections in Jammu and Kashmir 1950s onwards, have helped ascertain the will of the people and thus Kashmir is now an integral part of India. It is left to Pakistan to end its 'occupation,' of the Northern Areas and Azad Kashmir and let them join the rest of Indian administered Kashmir.

Over the years, successive Indian governments have been willing to consider acceptance of the LoC as the international boundary between Pakistan and India to resolve the dispute. However, there is also a demand for Pakistan to end all support to Kashmiri terrorist

---

11. There is also a view put forth by many Indian Muslims that the presence of a Muslim-majority state in a Hindu-majority country gives them a sense of security and assurance.

12. For many Indian leaders, especially Indian Muslim leaders, a second partition of India and on the grounds of religion might spell enormous trouble for the Muslim minority, which is already held responsible for the partition by Hindu right-wing groups.

groups and to give up the option of use of force to gain control of the state.

Kashmir's strategic position too is critical for India as it borders Tibet and Nepal on one side and Central Asia on the other. Kashmir, like Nepal and Tibet, was part of India's buffer zone with China and part of its security. The historical land routes for trade from Europe to Asia went through Kashmir and the Indian argument was that Kashmir was India's connection to the future trade and energy routes in Asia. An additional factor was that Nehru's ancestors came from Kashmir and he often admitted these "emotional and personal reasons," played a role in framing his Kashmir policy.[13]

India and Pakistan have fought two full-fledged wars—1947 and 1965—and a border war—1999—directly over Kashmir. The 1965 war was conducted at a time when growing military disparity between the two countries led Pakistan's leaders to believe that they could use Kashmiri disenchantment with Indian rule in their favour.[14] Counting on local Kashmiri support Pakistani leaders like Ayub Khan and Zulfikar Ali Bhutto approved Operation Gibraltar which involved the training and sending across the border, by Pakistan, of guerillas into Indian Kashmir. However, things did not pan out as they had expected. The local Kashmiri populace, even though angry at their government, did not side with the intruders and actually handed over most of them to the police and local authorities. Operation Grand Slam followed with the crossing of Pakistani troops across the ceasefire line and full-scale war between India and Pakistan. The war came to an end with a UN-sanctioned ceasefire and subsequent talks brokered by the Soviet Union.

13. Nehru's speech to the Indian Constituent Assembly, 7 September 1948: "May I take the House into my confidence? In the early stages...I was so exercised over Kashmir that if anything had happened or was likely to have happened in Kashmir, which according to me, might have been disastrous for Kashmir, I would have been heart-broken. I was intensely interested, apart from the larger reasons which the Government have, for emotional and personal reasons; I do not want to hide this: I am interested in Kashmir." See, Nehru (1949).

14. In 1964, a sacred hair of the Holy Prophet was stolen from the Hazratbal mosque near Srinagar. This led to riots and demonstrations not just in Kashmir, but also in East Pakistan and West Bengal.

In 1971, India and Pakistan fought their third war, this time not over Kashmir but East Pakistan. However, Kashmir dominated the deliberations at the post-war conference at Simla. The ceasefire line in Kashmir was now called the LoC and it "shall be respected by both sides without prejudice to the recognized position of either side. Neither side shall seek to alter it unilaterally, irrespective of mutual differences and legal interpretations. Both sides further undertake to refrain from the threat or the use of force in violation of this Line."[15] India and Pakistan, however, have interpreted the key sentences differently.[16]

It is in this context that one will be able to understand the 1999 Kargil conflict in which India and Pakistan fought a border war over Kashmir. Akin to 1965, intruders backed and supported by the Pakistan army entered into Indian-administered Kashmir in an attempt to gain territory and force India to discuss Kashmir. India decided to conduct a border war and also sought international support. International pressure, led by the US, finally resulted in the withdrawal of Pakistani troops.

Fear of the Jugular: Indus Waters Dispute

The Kashmir dispute when it originated had no ties to the water issue, i.e., the Indus Waters dispute. Over the years, however, Pakistani leaders and policymakers have coupled the two by referring to the fear that India might 'grab the jugular,' i.e., cut off the supply of water to Pakistan. This is tied into Pakistan's fear of Indian encirclement.

---

15. Text of Simla Agreement, 1972.

16. India interprets this statement to mean that till the Kashmir dispute is peacefully resolved, neither country will use war or violence as a means to change the status quo. Indian analysts and leaders also insist that in a secret meeting at the Simla conference President Zulfikar Ali Bhutto and Prime Minister Indira Gandhi agreed to resolve the Kashmir issue by legitimising the status quo over a period of time, thereby bringing the dispute to a gradual end. Pakistani leaders disagree with this Indian interpretation. They insist there was no secret pact between the two leaders. Also Pakistani analysts interpret "without prejudice to the recognized position of either side" to mean that the Pakistani view on Kashmir remains intact and that Pakistan has a right to raise the Kashmir issue at international fora. There is also the view that the agreement was forced on Pakistan because it lost the war and therefore a forced pact is not valid. Taken from interviews with former Indian and Pakistani diplomats. Also see, Raza (1997).

The northwestern part of the Indian subcontinent is irrigated by the Indus waters system, which comprises the river Indus and its five tributaries: Jhelum, Chenab, Ravi, Beas and Sutlej. When Punjab was partitioned along the Radcliffe boundary line in 1947, the waterways and canals created by the British were divided between the two countries. Of these three rivers, Indus, Jhelum and Chenab flow through India and then into Pakistan. Pakistan, the lower riparian state in this system, thus became dependent on flow of river water from hostile India.

Through the 1950s, numerous efforts to resolve this water issue failed. However, the two countries agreed to allow international arbitration and referred the matter to the World Bank. A treaty was finally signed in 1960 under the aegis of World Bank President Eugene Black. The Indus Waters Treaty set up a transitional period of 10-13 years after which the three eastern rivers (Ravi, Beas, Sutlej) would fall exclusively to India and the three western rivers (Indus, Jhelum, Chenab) exclusively to Pakistan. A permanent Indus Commission was also set up. In addition to this, the Treaty set up a fund to pay for the creation of canals and waterworks in Pakistan before the end of the slated time period.[17]

India has always abided by the Indus Water Treaty and has never cut off the supply of water to Pakistan even during wars, in 1965, 1971, or 1999. Despite the fact that Pakistan's fear has never been proven historically, Pakistani leaders and analysts still believe that with India controlling Kashmir and the upper reaches of the Indus water system India has Pakistan 'by the jugular.' This, tying in with the concomitant belief that India wants to wipe out Pakistan's existence, has never allowed Pakistani policymakers to fully trust the Indians to keep their part of the Indus bargain.

Since 1960, Pakistan has routinely pointed to instances when it believes India has broken the Indus Waters Treaty by either stopping or slowing down the water supply to Pakistan. The Indus Water Treaty contained provisions which allowed India to establish run-

17. Countries like the US and other international donors provided funding for the construction of these waterworks and canals.

of-the-river power projects with limited reservoir capacity for power generation purposes.

Availing this provision over the decades, India has constructed run-of-the-river power projects on Chenab (Baglihar) and Jhelum (Kishenganga) rivers. Both of these rivers' waters were assigned to Pakistan as part of the Indus agreement. Hence, Pakistan has objected to these projects on grounds that they would give India a strategic leverage in times of tension or war. Fortunately, the Indus Waters Treaty provides an adjudication mechanism to resolve conflicts, which both countries have resorted to in order to resolve their issues.

Siachen and Sir Creek

In addition to the key issue of Kashmir, there are other minor areas of border dispute between India and Pakistan as well that date back to Partition. The issue of Siachen is tied both to the conflict over Kashmir as well as the issue of demarcation of the border. The conflict emerges from the fact that neither the 1949 ceasefire agreement nor the 1972 Simla agreement mentioned whether the Siachen glacier fell in Indian or Pakistani administered territories.

Prior to 1984, neither India nor Pakistan maintained a military presence on the glacier. However, concerns about Pakistan's intentions led the Indian military to launch Operation Meghdoot in April 1984 and since then has maintained control over the glacier. Pakistan launched several counter attacks and the two countries have fought many minor conflicts in trying to hold on to the Siachen glacier.

Over the years, there have been attempts to come to an agreement whereby both countries will withdraw their military presence from the glacier mainly because they lose more soldiers to inclement weather conditions than to actual conflict and also to protect the fragile ecosystem from the presence of troops. However, mistrust of each other's intentions has prevented a resolution.

Sir Creek refers to a strip of water in the Rann of Kutch marshlands. India and Pakistan fought a minor border conflict over the Rann of Kutch in early 1965 before the full-fledged war later that year.

The dispute over Sir Creek originates from how each side has interpreted the maritime boundary line between the regions of Kutch and Sindh. At Partition, Kutch became part of India and Sindh a part of Pakistan. Pakistan lays claim to the entire Sir Creek on the basis of the 1914 resolution signed between the government of Sindh and the ruler of Kutch in which the eastern flank was marked as the boundary, in essence making the creek part of Sindh province Pakistan. India's argument has been that according to the Thalweg Doctrine in International Law, river boundaries between two states are taken as mid-channel.

Although the creek itself has little military value, it has both symbolic and economic value to India and Pakistan. Each country believes territory legitimises identity. Further, the Sir Creek like the rest of the Rann of Kutch is rich in oil and gas below the seabed. Even though this issue should be easy to resolve, unfortunately issues of mistrust between the two establishments have prevented this from happening.

Loss of East Pakistan: 'Cutting off one's limb'

Kashmir is the core dispute between the two countries and reflects the issues of identity and mistrust. The war of 1971, which led to the break-up of Pakistan and the creation of Bangladesh, only increased this mistrust, along with the fear of India trying to wipe out Pakistan by breaking away one of its wings, East Pakistan.

In 1947, Pakistan comprised two wings, East Pakistan (or East Bengal) and West Pakistan (comprising the provinces of Punjab, Sindh, NWFP and Baluchistan). Population-wise and linguistically East Pakistan was the largest province of Pakistan with over half the population who spoke Bengali. The need to bind the various provinces together and the desire to have 'one nation, one religion, one language' (Pakistan, Islam and Urdu) led Pakistan's founders to emphasise a uniformity which was resented by the Bengali majority.

The differences between the two wings of Pakistan were more than just geographical in nature. With power being held by mainly West Pakistanis, elite East Pakistanis felt deprived of a say in Pakistan's domestic politics and foreign policy. Although contributing heavily to

Pakistan's economy, East Pakistanis sensed they were not given their due share in development funds. In 1969-70, West Pakistan's per capita income was 61 per cent higher than Bengali per capita income (Hyder, 1972). This was exacerbated by the fact that East Pakistan's share in the civil and military services was disproportionately less than their population share. In 1947, Bengalis constituted only 1 per cent of Pakistan's army; by the 1960s the number was up to only 7 per cent (Hasan, 2000). In 1966, only 27,648 civil servants were Bengalis out of a total of 114,302 (Burki and Baxter, 1975).

In the 1960s, an East Bengali-led political party, the Awami League, formed by former Prime Minister Huseyn Suhrawardy and later led by Mujibur Rehman, grew in strength and popularity as a party which demanded more autonomy for East Pakistan. The famous 'Six Points,' put forth by the Awami League in 1966 asked for a federation in Pakistan on the basis of the Lahore Resolution of 1940.[18] This meant a parliamentary form of government, a separate paramilitary force for East Pakistan and the federal government only having control over defense and foreign affairs. These demands for autonomy were for West Pakistan's leaders their worst nightmare. Bengali demands for autonomy were seen as proof of attempts by India (acting through East Bengalis) to break up Pakistan.

Speeches by Indian leaders either expressing solidarity with East Pakistanis or threatening Pakistan only increased the paranoia. In the early 1950s, Sardar Patel had stated: "Artificial boundaries cannot separate them (Hindus of East Bengal) from us. If we can express sympathy with the people of South Africa and run to their assistance, it is easier to do so in the case of the people in East Pakistan" (Razvi, 1971).

In 1970, when East Pakistan's Bengalis overwhelmingly voted for the Awami League, a military crackdown ensued. Not only did Indian leaders support East Pakistan during the civil war in Pakistan in 1971, but also the Bangladeshi government in exile was based in

18. The Lahore Resolution stated that the "Northwestern and Eastern zones of India shall be grouped to constitute Independent States in which the constituent units shall be autonomous and sovereign." This was used by the Awami League to ask for more autonomy for East Pakistan. Cited in Sayeed (1968).

the Indian state of West Bengal. Indian Prime Minister Indira Gandhi campaigned around the world seeking support for India's stance and condemnation of Pakistani military action and genocide in East Pakistan. In the resultant war with India, Pakistan lost badly and East Pakistan became Bangladesh.[19]

Let us now turn to the issue of parity.

Parity *versus* Regional Integration

Just as the issue of mistrust has prevented a resolution of conflicts between India and Pakistan, Pakistan's desire for parity with India as well as the fear of Indian hegemony has framed its military and economic policies.[20] India's response has been similar to what it has offered its other South Asian neighbours—regional integration based on a shared civilisational heritage as well as economic (and strategic) benefits. Further, Pakistani desire for equality is seen by India as a sign of Pakistan ignoring the fundamentals of geography. Most Indian leaders and policymakers insist that they accept Pakistan and its creation and are willing to give it sovereign equality but not equal weight.

At regular intervals Indian leaders have often mentioned the idea of a confederation between India and Pakistan based on the civilisational and historical ties between the two countries. Although not necessarily an attempt to undo Partition or wipe out Pakistan, these statements are seen by Pakistanis as doing just that. Understanding this fear Nehru in an interview in March 1957,

---

19. Although desirous of helping East Bengalis in their struggle, India was reluctant to go beyond humanitarian assistance and basic training of the Bengali refugees. The large influx of Bengali refugees into both West Bengal and India's northeastern states leading to economic and social tensions played a key role in changing Prime Minister Indira Gandhi's mind. From memoirs and documents released, what we also realise is that the Indian army was reluctant to start a conflict with Pakistan during the summer and monsoon seasons and wanted to wait till winter. It was December 1971 when the two countries fought. For details please see Guha (2007).

20. General Zia ul Haq said this in an interview to Indian Kuldip Nayar, 29 January 1980: "Pakistani leaders would like 'equality' to be the 'determining factor' in any India-Pakistan relationship." Cited in *President of Pakistan General Zia ul Haq: Interviews to Foreign Media.* Vol III. Islamabad: Directorate of Film and Publications. Ministry of Information and Broadcasting. Government of Pakistan. p.43; In September 2009, Prime Minister Gilani stated that Pakistan desired a relationship on an "equal" basis with India. See, Indian Express (2009).

stated that though a "confederation," between India and Pakistan "independent states with common defense and economic policies" would have been the logical course of development "if we talk about it, our Neighbours are upset because we are so much bigger."[21]

Military Parity

Pakistan's strategic and military planners have always feared an attack from India because of the level and plain terrain along the India-Pakistan border. With people on both sides of the border ethnically and linguistically similar and no mountainous or other barriers separating the two countries, this fear has been all consuming. Thus in 1947 from the view of Pakistan's leaders, the fear of India marching across Punjab and Rajasthan into the heart of Pakistan was a reality they had to guard against. This fear has been kept alive through the years.

India's counterarguments to Pakistan's fears have been that both countries have enough armed forces on their border to ensure their safety. Further, mines and moats on the Pakistani Punjab side provide enough guarantees to Pakistan that Indian tanks will not simply be able to roll into Lahore one day from Amritsar. Furthermore, India has often offered a no-war pact or treaty to Pakistan to guarantee that the latter does not have to fear an Indian attack.

Since mistrust lies at the core of the relationship, offers of no-war pact and guarantees have made no difference. At the heart of Pakistan's fear lies the disparity between armed forces of the two countries.

In 1947, the British Indian army was so divided between India and Pakistan that Pakistan got one-third.[22] During the division of assets between the two countries, Pakistan felt it was deprived of its complete share. Hence, at the core of Pakistan's defence policy

21. *New York Times*. 2 March 1957.

22. Pakistan received 8 infantry regiments, 6 armoured corps units, eight and a half artillery regiments and 34 engineer units. The navy obtained 16 of the 48 vessels including 2 frigates and 2 sloops. The air force was given 2 out of the 10 squadrons. Of the various ordnance factories in British India, Pakistan received none. Please see Siddiqui (1960).

lies the desire at any cost for military parity with India. The result has been Pakistan's high military expenditure, the search for allies like the US, Saudi Arabia, and China who would supply military aid, and the obsessive focus on its eastern frontier with most of its army being trained for war with India.

India's security concerns emanating from China, have resulted in India's military—both conventional and nuclear—build-up being Sino-centric. Further, India's status as a regional power—and belief in being a future great power—have meant that India needs to maintain a certain level of military strength. Even though India's military build-up has not been oriented towards Pakistan, Pakistani fears of perceived Indian hostility have resulted in the perennial search for parity with India. Hence, over the decades both countries have invested a lot of money in defense expenditure, and an arms race has ensued.

No War Pact

Military parity was one way to resolve Pakistan's fear of Indian aggression; a no-war pact might have been another. Indian leaders instead have offered a 'no war' proposal and Pakistani leaders initially countered it by offering a joint defence proposal. The reason was simple: a no-war proposal did not resolve Pakistan's quest for equivalence nor resolve the Kashmir dispute. Rather it prevented Pakistan from resorting to war if it felt that was the only way out.

Joint defence, on the other hand, not only gave a semblance of parity but the mechanism set up might help solve other issues. Pakistani leaders have often asserted that they would be willing to consider a no-war proposal, only if it also included a mechanism or institution to resolve India-Pakistan disputes and if India agreed to abide by any decisions made by this arbitrating mechanism. Since India refused to accept international arbitration in what it considered a bilateral problem, the no-war proposals have never had any future. Also for most Pakistani leaders, resolution of Kashmir dispute is seen as a more powerful way to bring about peace than a no-war pact.

Nuclear Policy: Parity, Not Deterrence

India's views on nuclear weapons changed over the decades. In the initial years under Nehru, India sought civilian nuclear power but not nuclear weapons. India instead sought a global elimination of nuclear weapons and championed this policy for decades. Defeat in the Sino-Indian war of 1962 and the Chinese nuclear test of 1964, however, led to a change in this policy. India, perceiving the threat from its northern neighbour focused not just on developing nuclear power, but also a nuclear weapons programme. In 1974, India conducted its first nuclear tests.

India's tests in 1974 had a profound impact on Pakistan. Until the 1971 breakup of Pakistan, Pakistani leaders believed that their large population gave them some sense of parity with India. The loss of East Pakistan—and the majority of Pakistan's population—coupled with the disastrous military defeat at the hands of India did not result in a realisation that maybe it would be impossible for Pakistan to have a military balance with a much larger neighbour. Instead, the desire for military parity with India became more important so as to prevent any further break up of Pakistan.[23]

Desirous of achieving military parity with India and fast realising by the early 1970s that conventional military parity was difficult, Pakistan's policymakers, both civilian and military, looked to nuclear weapons to provide the solution. Nuclear weapons were seen as the magic wand, which would make Pakistan India's equal, guarantee territorial integrity even without the support of allies and also give Pakistan respectability in the Muslim world as the first Muslim country with nuclear weapons. The primary goal of Pakistan's nuclear weapons programme was to achieve military parity with India, and

23. In an interview with the Americans in January 1972, the head of Pakistan's Army Lt Gen Gul Hasan stated the need for American aid in order to maintain the army "at pre-war size." When asked by the Americans if this would be possible keeping in mind both the reduction in size of the Pakistani territory and elimination of the need to now maintain a force in East Pakistan, Gul Hasan's answer was that "a credible force would still be needed to serve as deterrent against any hostile intentions by India." Department of State, Telegram, Secret, From American Embassy Islamabad, 22 January 1972, Subject: Conversation with Pak Army Commander in Chief Lt Gen Gul Hasan. Cited in Khan (2000).

nuclear weapons were seen as a method of balancing the asymmetric relationship between India and Pakistan.

India refused to sign the Nuclear Non-Proliferation Treaty (NPT), as it believed that the treaty indulged in 'nuclear apartheid', by dividing the world into nuclear haves and nuclear have-nots.[24] Pakistan refused to sign the NPT, unless India signed the treaty first. Similarly when the Comprehensive Test Ban Treaty (CTBT) was being deliberated in Geneva in 1996, three countries—India, Pakistan, and Israel—did not sign the treaty. India refused to sign on grounds similar to the ones shaping its stance towards the NPT claiming it was an unequal and unfair treaty, while Pakistan stated it would sign only if India signed first.

In May 1998, the Hindu-right wing BJP government of India conducted nuclear tests, and this increased pressure on Pakistan to follow suit. The US tried to dissuade Pakistan from testing its nuclear weapons. However, belligerent statements by Indian leaders directed at Pakistan and asking Pakistan to accept the new reality simply increased Pakistan's fears of an existential threat from India and reinforced the desire for parity.

Exploding five devices on 28 May 1998—and an additional one on 30 May—the Pakistani rationale for the blasts was reflected in the centrality of India in their strategic outlook and the desire for parity: "We have done it. We are India's equal" (Anderson, 1998). Content to not test the nuclear weapons as long as India did not do so, Pakistan felt justified in testing if only to ensure the balance. Once again, the only way Pakistan could contain and prevent India's alleged hostile intentions was to have a balance in the military field.

In the nuclear arena too, it is parity not deterrence which Pakistan seeks *vis-à-vis* India. This is evident from the fact that Pakistan has consistently refused to sign the Fissile Material Cut off Treaty (FMCT). The only explanation is that if it signs the treaty then Pakistan will have less fissile material than India, and it would like to

---

24. Statements by Ms Arundhati Ghose, Ambassador/Permanent Representative of India to the UN Offices at Geneva, in the Plenary of the Conference on Disarmament on both 20 June 1996 and 8 August 1996. Accessible at *http://www.indianembassy.org/policy/CTBT/ctbt_cd_june_20_96.htm and http://www.indianembassy.org/policy/CTBT/ctbt_cd_august_8_96.htm*

continue building its fissile material arsenal until it has as much or more than India does.

Pakistan continues to seek parity with India, in nuclear and non-nuclear fields. In August 2009, during a press conference, the Pakistani foreign office spokesman expressed the country's continued "concern over the domination of India in traditional and nuclear arms." However, he further stated that "minimum nuclear deterrence would be maintained in the region for lasting peace in the region" (Online International News Network Pakistan, 2009).

In an attempt to defuse the nuclear tensions since 1998, India has suggested a 'no first use' policy, which Pakistan did not respond favourably to until 2008, when Pakistan's then civilian President Asif Ali Zardari stated that Pakistan too has a "no first use policy" (Gilani, 2008). However, he was immediately overruled by the military and even his own cabinet disagreed with him.[25]

Parity: Economic, not only Military

If we look at countries around the world, in almost every case it is neighbours who are among the top trading partners. For France, it is Germany; for US, it is Mexico and Canada. In the case of India, and Pakistan, however, this has not happened. Further, in an age of regional trading arrangements, like European Union (EU) and Association of Southeast Asian Nations (ASEAN), South Asia's regional organisation, South Asian Association for Regional Cooperation (SAARC) falls far behind.

It is clear that issues of mistrust and parity have prevented regional economic integration. Unlike other regional economic groupings, SAARC has not taken off. Despite the fact that individual economies in South Asia (especially India and Bangladesh) have been growing fast, the inter-regional trade has been miniscule. Although treaties for a South Asian Free Trade Area (SAFTA), and South Asian

25. In March 2009, then Pakistani Prime Minister Gilani stated that any internal instability in Pakistan could prompt an Indian attack on Pakistan. Reflecting the perennial Pakistani desire for parity, Prime Minister Gilani stated: "When seen with the widening force differential between ours and Indian armed forces, it explains to us New Delhi's emboldened posture and its urge to find space for a conventional war." See, The Daily Times (2009).

Preferential Trading Agreement (SAPTA), have been put forth, they have yet to be implemented across the board. Not only has Pakistan often stated that the resolution of Kashmir would help trade ties, but it has sought to focus more on groupings outside the region, than within. The main rationale is that Pakistan would much rather avoid a regional grouping where India is the dominant player. India too for a long time preferred to focus outside the region but in recent years it has sought to bolster SAARC and push regional integration.

Since economic ties are considered the building blocks for regional ties, when we turn to India and Pakistan, we see that even though in 1947 the two countries were critical to each other, things changed soon after. Although the only time there was no official trade between the two countries was the period between 1965-1974, yet by 2001 bilateral trade stood at only $250 million. It is only in recent years that trade has gone up and in 2013 it stood at $ 2.4 billion.[26]

A key part of free trade is the need to remove tariff and non-tariff barriers. According to World Trade Organization (WTO) guidelines, all its member states are required to offer this condition to other member states or what is referred to as offering MFN or Most Favoured Nation status.

India offered Pakistan MFN status in 1996, but it has taken Pakistan almost two decades to agree to offer India the same. This is despite the fact that at regular intervals, reports by relevant government departments as well as the corporate sector have championed such an idea.[27] The reason why Pakistan was reluctant to give India MFN status was political not economic. Pakistan's leaders over the years argued that unless the Kashmir issue was resolved, it made no sense to build economic or cultural ties. India's argument

26. See Murshed and Mamoon (2010); FICCI paper on India-Pakistan Trade, 2014, *http://www.ficci.com/events/21770/Add_docs/India-show-Pakistan-2014.pdf*

27. In 1996, a report of Pakistan's Ministry of Commerce referred to the ease and benefits of trade with India namely: low transportation costs, low prices and cultural similarities leading to similar tastes and preferences. See, Government of Pakistan (1996); In the same year, a study by the Karachi Chamber of Commerce and Industry stated that granting India Most Favoured Nation (MFN.) status as per World Trade Organization (WTO) guidelines was "an economic and geopolitical imperative." See also, Karachi Chamber of Commerce and Industry (KCCI) (1996), cited in Government of Pakistan (1996).

was the reverse, as Indian leaders believed that building economic and cultural ties would help resolve political disputes.

Since 2008, civilian governments in Pakistan have attempted to give India MFN status but it has taken six years for the process to reach some sort of conclusion. What is interesting to note is that on Pakistan's insistence, the two countries will refer to their trade ties not as MFN, but Non-Discriminatory Market Access (NDMA). The specific language used is tied to Pakistani governments' fear that if they are perceived as offering MFN status to India then they will face a backlash from various segments of Pakistani society where the anti-India sentiment is high.

A key factor here again traces to the issue of identity and nationalism. The phrase, Most Favoured Nation, when translated into local languages would make India appear like a close Pakistani ally, instead of the existential threat that it has been portrayed as over the years.

Fear of Indian Hegemony

During the initial years after Partition, both India and Pakistan worked to ensure their territorial integrity and unity. Each state thus ended up perceiving the other as trying to prevent its territorial unity. Being the smaller of the two countries, for Pakistan, any statements emanating from India that critiqued Partition or denied the 'two nation theory', were seen as attempts by hegemonic India to reclaim its territory.

Not only do Pakistanis fear that India plans to undo Partition, but that the end goal of all Indians is to create *Akhand Bharat*, an Undivided India. This was a term used by Hindu revivalist organisations as well as right-wing Hindu nationalist parties. *Akhand Bharat* territorially refers to the entire Indian subcontinent as being one entity.[28] Pakistanis often refer back to the statement made by Hindu right-wing nationalist organisations at Partition about the indivisibility and territorial unity of the Indian subcontinent as proof of Indian imperial designs. In 1947, the HMS had declared: "India is

28. Thus it would include modern day India, Pakistan, Bangladesh, Nepal and even Sri Lanka.

one and indivisible and there will never be peace unless and until the separated parts are brought back into the Indian Union and made integral parts thereof."[29] Although never a mainstream belief in India, these views have caused a lot of fear in Pakistan.

India is thus seen as both hegemonic and imperialist. Hyderabad and Junagadh are cited as Indian imperialist adventures at the time of Partition, and Goa and Sikkim a few years after Independence. India's treaties of friendship with Nepal, Sri Lanka and Bhutan are also seen as evidence of an Indian desire for subservience from neighbours. Furthermore, India's close ties with Afghanistan have been cited as an attempt by India to spread its wings. This only increases the Pakistani desire to break out of this India-dominated region and seek security outside.

India has always projected itself as a peaceful status quo power, with a very large army, which is willing in its national interests to send out its forces. Indian policymakers and leaders argue that Goa was part of India, Sikkim volunteered to join India, Nepal and Bhutan are critical to India's security, and India sent troops into Sri Lanka only when they were requested. India's neighbours, especially Pakistan, do not always see these incidents in the same way as India portrays them.

In 1971, when East Pakistan broke off and Bangladesh was created, the fear of India trying to undo Partition and wipe out Pakistan's existence became a near-reality. If *Akhand Bharat* had been the real aim of Indira Gandhi, then India would have merged East Bengal with West Bengal and not just walked away. Similarly, a weakened West Pakistan would have been easy prey for India's army. The calculated decision not to undo Pakistan was reflected in a letter from Indira Gandhi to President Nixon in December 1971 where Gandhi stated that India does "not want any territory of what was East Pakistan and now constitutes Bangladesh. We do not want any territory of West Pakistan."[30]

---

29. *The Statesman*, 9 June 1947. Delhi.

30. Department of State, Confidential, 17 December 1971, Letter from Indira Gandhi to President Nixon dated 15 December 1971. Cited in Khan (2000).

The theory of *Akhand Bharat* or Undivided India as India's ultimate strategic goal has been disproved by historic reality. Yet this did not keep it from losing its salience in Pakistani strategic thinking. The paradigm was adjusted and adapted. Even after Pakistan obtained nuclear weapons and thus nuclear deterrence, the fear of India trying to break up Pakistan has not dissipated. This is because it is not a fear rooted in realistic analysis, but rather psycho-political in nature.

Cold War and Post-Cold War Differences (Ties with US; Ties with Muslim Countries; China, Afghanistan)

Emerging from colonial rule the leaders of both India, and Pakistan were avid champions of anti-colonialism. The key difference between the focus of India and Pakistan with respect to anti-colonialism was that Pakistan's anti-colonialism had a Pan Islamic dimension to it. The Pan Islamist orientation of Pakistan's foreign policy and close ties with the Muslim Middle East are easy to understand as they flow from its ideological identity and perceived existential threat from 'Hindu' India. Not only did Pan Islamism help bolster Pakistan's national identity, but also provided strength in numbers and resources from the wider Muslim *ummah* (community).

India's policy during the Cold War was framed by its civilisational heritage, colonial legacy and the views of its founding elite, especially Nehru. As one of the first colonies to achieve independence, India championed anti-colonialism and anti-racialism. Even before independence, leaders like Nehru had built ties with leaders in other colonies who were fighting for independence. India provided extensive support to countries in Southeast Asia (especially Indonesia) and Africa. It is in this context that India held the Asian Relations Conference in New Delhi in March 1947, which was attended by leaders from various Asian countries.

Fear of being subjected to external influences led to India seeking to stay out of the Cold War and follow the policy of non-alignment. As early as 7 September 1946, Nehru stated in the Constituent Assembly that: "We propose as far as possible to stay away from the power politics of groups aligned against one another, which have led in the past to world wars and which may again lead to disasters on an even faster scale." In this speech, he said that India sent "greetings" to both the USA and the Soviet Union as well as to her Asian neighbours.[31] By being a part of the non-aligned movement, India thus sought to avoid participation in the Cold War bloc politics. India was aided in this policy because most of the non-aligned countries were former colonies and hence had similar outlooks and challenges.

In contrast, Pakistan's policy during the Cold War was to seek close alliances and ties with countries—like the US—who would provide resources and strength to help stand up to the perceived perennial threat from India.

Ties with the US

The loss of China to Communism and the start of the Cold War led to a global search for allies by American policymakers. India was a natural candidate as ally from the American point of view but independent India, under a left-leaning and non-aligned Nehru, did not respond positively to initial American overtures. Over time, Americans saw India as a difficult country to deal with and impossible to have as an ally. Pakistan, a large Muslim state with more Western-leaning policymakers starting with Liaquat and Ayub, coupled with its geo-strategic location at the crossroads of South Asia, Central Asia, South East Asia and West Asia, was considered favourably.

Pakistan entered into a number of Cold War security arrangements with the US and obtained economic and military assistance: the South East Asia Treaty Organization (SEATO) in 1954, the Central Treaty Organization (CENTO) or the Baghdad Pact in 1955 and a mutual defence treaty with the US in 1959. The latter ensured that Pakistan would get economic and military assistance from US to preserve the 'independence and integrity of Pakistan,' and in return the country provided the US with an air base in Peshawar. Pakistan was a frontline American ally during the anti-Soviet Afghan jihad of the 1980s, and the US has accorded a major non-NATO ally status to Pakistan after the 9/11 attacks in New York.

31. Nehru's speech on 7 September 1946, "Future Taking Shape" taken from Nehru (1961).

During the Cold War years not only did India and the US have 'estranged' relations, but Indian leaders perceived American policy as benefitting Pakistan. They saw the US as acting like an offshore balancer or as hyphenating India-Pakistan together and treating them equally (Rudolph and Rudolph, 2006). From the Pakistani point of view, US policy helped them achieve a sense of parity with India by way of supplying conventional military weapons and providing economic support. From the Indian point of view, US policy hurt the natural order of things, affecting regional security. Indian leaders have always resented the influence of any external power in the South Asian subcontinent, unless that power accepts Indian preponderance (dominance?).[32]

Despite these differences, the US and India never viewed each other as enemies. In each of the agreements signed with Pakistan, including the treaties of CENTO and SEATO, the US emphasised that the support and equipment was only to be used against 'communist aggression.'

At the end of the Cold War, many segments of the American policy community, whether Democrat or Republican, saw the need to build closer ties with India and to 'de-hyphenate,' the relationship between India-US-Pakistan.[33] India's rising economic power, its support for counter-terrorism and the need to include a nuclear-India among the world powers also played a role. Starting from President Clinton's visit in 2000, and especially since 2005, the US started building closer ties with India—including defence and economic—culminating in the 2006 Indo-US Nuclear deal. The deal finally came through in 2008.

The Afghan Factor

This brings in another dimension of India-Pakistan relations, that of ties with Afghanistan. In 1947, Afghanistan was the only country

32. Often referred to by scholars as "Indira's Doctrine" (akin to Monroe doctrine).

33. Nicholas Burns, Under Secretary for Political Affairs, *On-the-Record Briefing on the Status of the U.S.-India Civil Nuclear Cooperation Initiative and the Text of the Bilateral Agreement for Peaceful Nuclear Cooperation* (123 Agreement). Accessible at *http://www.usindiafriendship.net/viewpoints1/burns-07272007.htm*; Also see, Indian Express (2005).

to object to Pakistan's admission to the UN. Constant tensions and conflicts continued due to the support of succeeding Afghan governments for the creation of a state of 'Pashtunistan'[34] and by a refusal to recognise the Durand line as the international border between the two countries.

This led Pakistani leaders and strategists to perceive a 'pincer effect' (Stephens, 1953): the belief that on both the East and West, it was surrounded by hostile nations determined to break it up and wipe out its existence and therefore the only way to prevent this was to fight back. In later years, Afghan support for Baluch irredentism has also been a factor in their relations and Pakistan's fears.

Thus from the point of view of Pakistani policymakers, there was a need to have a 'friendly' (read 'anti-Indian') government in Afghanistan to discourage India-Afghan alliance. Also for the Pakistani military, Afghanistan would provide 'strategic depth' in case India ever attacked Pakistan.

Afghanistan's ties with India played a role in this perception. Since 1947, India had friendly ties with Afghanistan, not just historic ties, but also educational and economic. From the vantage point of Kabul, close ties with a bigger country, India, which could provide economic resources, was a way of balancing Pakistani interference.

Similarly, from the Indian point of view, not only were there historic ties with Afghanistan, but also Afghanistan is India's pathway to Central Asia. Furthermore, from a strategic point of view, it has always been beneficial for New Delhi to have a friendly government in Afghanistan, especially because that would help counter any Pakistani attempts to use Afghan territory against India. Thus India's support for Afghanistan's reconstruction and development since 2002 and its roughly $2 billion aid package to the latter's needs to be viewed in this context.

Pakistan's fears about an Indian-Afghan pincer movement have been as unfounded as its fear of an *Akhand Bharat* trying to undo Pakistan. During the 1965 and 1971 wars between India and

---

34. A homeland for Pashtuns, which would include the Pakistani province of North West Frontier Province (NWFP) and parts of Pakistani Baluchistan.

Pakistan, Afghanistan stated that Pakistan need fear nothing from the Afghan border citing Afghanistan as its neighbour. As recently as October 2011, Afghan President Hamid Karzai stated that Afghanistan would support Pakistan in any war with the US (Morgan, 2011). However, this has not reduced Pakistani suspicion of India-Afghan collaboration against Pakistan.

Pakistan has always viewed its ties with the US in the regional or South Asian context, i.e., its rivalry with India and desire for strategic balance (read: 'parity') with India. Warmer ties between India and the US and de-hyphenation of the India-Pakistan-US relationship has led Pakistan to seek closer ties with China and countries in the Muslim world.

The Muslim World

Right from 1947, Pakistan's ties with the Muslim world, especially the Middle Eastern countries, were an important part of its identity and ideology-based foreign policy. 'Islamic' Pakistan would be able to stand up to 'Hindu' India because it would have the support of the larger Muslim *ummah*. Pakistani diplomats championed the cause of self-determination for fellow Muslims at the UN soon after Pakistan's independence. Pakistani efforts on behalf of Indonesia, Algeria, Tunisia and Eritrea were significant, but it was as a vocal champion of the Palestinian cause that Pakistan tried hard to establish its credentials as a leading Muslim country.

Pakistan was among the key proponents of international cooperation among Muslim states. However, due to the deeper belief in nationalism and strength of anti-colonialism in other recently de-colonised Muslim countries, Pakistan's attempts at Pan Islamism failed during the 1950s. Its efforts bore fruit only by the 1970s.

Pakistan's Middle Eastern focus has to be seen in the context of its strategic insecurity against India and its psychological unease with its own identity. The ties of Islam were expected to ensure that the Muslim countries would always side with Pakistan, not India. Pakistan's leaders did not take into account that 35 million Muslims had stayed behind in India after partition and that in subsequent years their number had increased significantly.

India had been a leader of the non-aligned movement, which Pakistan could not join initially as it was a member of western alliances. Several Muslim countries, notably Egypt, played an important role in non-alignment. Further, India's leaders like Nehru and Maulana Abul Kalam Azad, had built ties with their counterparts in other countries and were able to put forth India's point of view in order to counter Pakistan.

Indian diplomats made it a point to remind Muslim countries of India's own Muslim heritage. India was seen by many Arab leaders as closer to their own anti-colonial worldview than Pakistan, which was seen as a US protégé. Apart from the attraction of close ties with India as the world's largest secular democracy and a potential leader of the third world, India's large Muslim population made it impossible for Muslim countries to decisively choose Pakistan over India. This is why over the years, India has had close ties with almost every Muslim country.

The China Angle

Turning to China, India's ties with its northern neighbour started off in bonhomie, but soon became fraught with tension over the border issue: the legacy of imperial fault lines, both countries differed on where the border line should be drawn. In 1962, the two countries fought a war which India lost. Through the 1970s and 1980s, Sino-India ties were barely existent. It is only from the 1990s that things have improved especially in the economic arena. As of June 2014, China is one of India's top trading partners with their bilateral trade standing at around $ 100 billion (Press Trust of India, 2014). However, China's ties with and its economic and military (including nuclear) aid to Pakistan forms a key part of how India views the Chinese threat.

Pakistan's relations with China started during the 1950s and initially it was primarily an economic relationship. Over a period of time, it has grown into a multifaceted relationship with primarily economic and military (including nuclear) dimensions. Pakistanis and Chinese often describe their countries' ties as "loftier than the Himalayas and deeper than the Indian Ocean." Chinese support both economic and military, over the years has been a great asset to Pakistan.

In some respects, it is a classic realpolitik situation: both countries have their worries about India and so find the other useful. During the Cold War due to China's ideological differences with the Soviet Union and the tensions with the US, Pakistan was China's window to the world in many ways.

China supported Pakistan during both its wars with India during the 1960s and 1970s and continued to provide economic and military support. Starting from the 1970s, Chinese companies have invested in Pakistani infrastructure and obtained raw material from Pakistan. At periodic intervals, China has also provided loans and aid to Pakistan to tide over emergency situations. However, like Pakistan's other allies, China has built good ties with India as well.

Future

Geographically, linguistically, culturally and historically, South Asia is a vital part of the personality and identity of both India and Pakistan. India has always emphasised these bonds with all its neighbours, including Pakistan. Pakistan, however, has attempted to escape its South Asian identity and sought a contrived Middle Eastern identity.

In 1947, there might have been a rationale for Pakistan fearing Indian intentions. Soon after Partition, many Indian leaders did make statements about the inability of Pakistan to survive but India's views have since then changed significantly. Most Indians now recognise the need for stabilising an independent Pakistan and there is wide recognition that partition cannot be undone, except at great cost, which no one is willing to incur.

The core of the issue lies within the two countries, not outside. The Pakistani state's insecurity, its fear of existential threat and its abiding mistrust of its larger neighbour, India have prevented the evolution of a normal relationship with the latter. Similarly, India as the larger country in South Asia, as the country that is more stable and at ease with its identity, would benefit by offering some unilateral gestures of friendship especially in areas like trade and visa policy as that will help build a grounds well of support within Pakistan. Instead of seeking to open ways to build people-to-people ties, economic relations and look at challenges that both countries seek, the two nations seem to be locked in a vicious cycle.

Despite the fact that since 2008 successive Pakistani civilian leaders have sought better ties with India (both the PPP [public-private partnerships]-led government and the current PML [Pakistan Muslim League]-N-led government), military establishment's mistrust of and desire for parity with India have prevented change beyond the surface level. This is because civilian democratic rule is new to Pakistan and even after six years of civilian control, its foreign and security policies continue to be framed by the military-intelligence establishment. The views of this establishment with respect to both Pakistan's neighbours and allies have not changed drastically. Despite the rising internal jihadi menace, India is still perceived as the bigger threat to Pakistan's security.

Similarly, in India, even though every Indian Prime Minister since the time of Nehru has sought to repair ties with Pakistan and resolve issues, this has not happened. While the Indian military–intelligence establishment does not have a say in most areas of foreign and security policy, in the case of Pakistan its sphere of influence has increased especially with respect to issues like Kashmir, Siachen and cross-border terrorism. In fact, during the May 2014 between the new Indian Premier, Narendra Modi, and his Pakistani counterpart, Nawaz Sharif, security issues were a central topic, with India emphasising the importance of Pakistan containing the anti-India terrorism growing within its boundaries.

Both Pakistan and India appear to prefer a conflict management approach to their relationship instead of focusing on conflict resolution. India is unlikely, over the next few years, to change its stance over Jammu and Kashmir. Given that Pakistan considers resolution of that dispute in its favour a core national interest, it is unlikely that Pakistan will fully normalise relations. Although so far there is no sign that Pakistan intends to give up its option of sub-conventional warfare against India, New Delhi might be willing to accommodate Pakistan over greater trade and travel if Islamabad shows signs of shutting down India-centric terrorist groups operating from Pakistan.

India-Pakistan relations over the next 5-10 years will also depend on the state of civil-military relations in Pakistan and on Pakistan's ties with both the US and China. If the military remains ascendant and in control of foreign and national security policies, Pakistan is likely to repeat the pattern of announcing steps for normalisation of ties—such as granting MFN status to India in trade or loosening visa restrictions—without fully implementing them. The Pakistani military continues to prefer emphasising resolution of the Kashmir dispute over opening trade ties or expanding travel between citizens of the two countries.

Expectation of support from the US and China in terms of military hardware, in particular, has been a major factor in Pakistan's willingness to believe that it can maintain parity with India. If the US (and possibly China) deny Pakistani requests for military hardware, Pakistani civilian politicians might be able to make more of an argument to their military for normalisation of relations with India. Expansion of Pakistan's nuclear arsenal, however, might keep the country's hardliners confident in their belief that it can forever compete with India, which they see as a permanent enemy.

References

Anderson, John Ward (1998). "Pakistan Sets off Nuclear Blasts: Today We Have Settled a Score, Premier Says", *Washington Post*, 29 May.

Brecher, Michael (1968). *India and World Politics: Krishna Menon's View of the World.* New York: Oxford University Press. pp.170-71.

Burke, S.M. (1973). *Pakistan's Foreign Policy: An Historical Analysis.* London. Oxford University Press. pp.320, 380.

Burki, Shahid Javed and Craig Baxter (1975). "Socio-Economic Indicators of the Peoples Party Vote in Punjab", in William Howard Wriggins (ed.), *Pakistan in Transition.* Islamabad: Islamabad University Press. pp.161, 167. Cited in Haqqani, Husain (2005). *Pakistan Between Mosque and Military.* Washington, DC. Carnegie Endowment for International Peace. p.61.

CNN-IBN (2010). "Taliban Attack on Sikhs, Pakistan Dismisses India's Concerns", *CNN-IBN.* 20 February.

———. (2013). "Pakistan Passes Resolution on Afzal Guru, India Says Don't Interfere", *CNN-IBN.* 15 March.

Gilani, Iftikhar (2008). "Zardari Proposes Nuclear Free South Asia", *The Daily Times.* 23 November.

Government of Pakistan (1996). Pakistan-India Trade: Transition to the GATT Regime. Islamabad: Ministry of Commerce. September. p.1.

Guha, Ramachandra (2007). *India After Gandhi: The History of the World's Largest Democracy.* New Delhi. Harper Collins. pp.445-65.

Hasan, Mubashir (2000). *The Mirage of Power: An Inquiry Into the Bhutto Years, 1971-1977.* Karachi. Oxford University Press. pp.202-08.

Hyder, Khurshid (1972). "Pakistan Under Bhutto", in *Current History* 63(375): 202 (November).

Indian Express (2005). "US has Dehyphenated Ties with India: Rice", *Indian Express*, 13 May.

———. (2009). "Pakistan wants Relationship with India on 'Equal Footing' Gilani'", *Indian Express.* 6 September.

Karachi Chamber of Commerce and Industry (KCCI) (1996). *Freer Trade With India: Its Raison d'etre and Impact.* Karachi: Research and Development Cell. March. p.1.

Khan, Liaquat Ali (1950). *Pakistan: The Heart of Asia.* Cambridge: Harvard University Press. p.14.

Khan, Muhammad Zafrulla (1951). *Pakistan's Foreign Relations' in Pakistan Horizon.* Karachi: Pakistan Institute of International Affairs. pp.4-5.

Khan, Roedad (ed.) (2000). *The American Papers: Secret and Confidential India, Pakistan, Bangladesh Documents, 1965-1973.* Karachi: Oxford University Press. pp.744, 787.

Morgan, David (2011). "Karzai: Afghans Would Side with Pakistan in War", *CBS News*, 22 October.

Murshed, Syed Mansoob and Dawood Mamoon (2010). "Not Loving Thy Neighbor as Thyself: Trade, Democracy and Military Expenditure Explanations Underlying India-Pakistan Rivalry", *Journal of Peace Research* 47(4): 463-76 (July).

Nehru, Jawaharlal (1949). *Independence and After.* New Delhi: Ministry of Information and Broadcasting. p.95. Cited in Brecher, Michael (1953). *The Struggle for Kashmir.* New York. Oxford University Press. p.44.

Nehru, Jawaharlal (1958). *Jawaharlal Nehru Speeches. Vol 1. September 1946-May 1949.* The Publications Division. Ministry of Information and Broadcasting. Government of India. pp.337-39.

———. (1961). *India's Foreign Policy*. New Delhi: Publications Division, Government of India. pp.1, 22.

Online International News Network Pakistan (2009). "No Accord Exists Between Pakistan and US for Drone Attacks: FO Spokesman", *Online International News Network Pakistan*. 9 August.

Press Trust of India (2014). "India's Trade Deficit with China Mounts to $9 bn in January–April", *Press Trust of India*, 9 June.

Raza, Rafi (1997). *Zulfikar Ali Bhutto and Pakistan, 1967-1977*. Karchi. Oxford University Press. pp.211-12.

Razvi, Mujtaba (1971). *The Frontiers of Pakistan: A Study of Frontier Problems in Pakistan's Foreign Policy*. Karachi. National Publishing House. p.50.

Rudolph, Lloyd I. and Susanne Hoeber Rudolph (2006). "The Making of US Foreign Policy for South Asia: Offshore Balancing in Historical Perspective", *Economic and Political Weekly* 41(8): 703-09 (Feb. 25-Mar. 3).

Sayeed, K.B. (1968). *Pakistan: The Formative Phase 1857-1948*. Karachi: Oxford University Press. p.113.

Siddiqui, Aslam (1960). *Pakistan Seeks Security*. Lahore. Longman & Greens. p.56.

Stephens, Ian (1953). *Horned Moon*. (Unknown binding).

The Daily Times (2009). "'Internal Threat has Weakened Pakistan' Weakness May Prompt Indian Attack: Gilani", in *The Daily Times*, 27 March.

11

NATANA J. DELONG-BAS

Foreign Policy of Saudi Arabia

Introduction

Foreign policymaking in Saudi Arabia today is the product of a complex interplay of multiple identities and roles and pragmatic and value-driven interests and objectives. For Saudi Arabia, foreign policy is not simply a matter of driving a particular programme or idea forward, but must also take into consideration the desired outcome, rendering policymaking an equation in which both inputs and outputs must be carefully considered and constantly evaluated and re-evaluated for potential adjustment. As foreign policymaking is considered to be more of a strategy than a tactic, it must be consistent enough to be clear, and relatively predictable at the same time, that it needs to be sufficiently flexible to adapt to changing contexts, circumstances, and perceived strategic interests.

The three main drivers for Saudi foreign policy today are the objectives of peace, prosperity and stability, suggesting that national security lies at the heart of policymaking. As national security itself must take into consideration a variety of national needs—military, political, financial, economic, social, religious, cultural, and humanitarian—all of which have interplay with the surrounding regional and global contexts, Saudi foreign policy must also reflect consideration of those needs. Within these contexts, Saudi Arabia's national (Saudi), micro-regional (Arabian Gulf), macro-regional (Arab), and Muslim (global) identities all come into play, particularly its roles as:

a. Custodian over the two holiest cities of Islam, Mecca and Medina, and, thus, oversight of the Hajj.[1]
b. The world's largest producer and exporter of oil.
c. A leader in the global struggle against terrorism and extremism, and increasingly in the post-Arab Spring context
d. The most stable, financially powerful, and politically influential of the large Sunni majority countries of the MENA[2] region.

As regional dynamics have become particularly unstable in the context of the aftermath of the US-led invasion of Iraq and overthrow of Saddam Hussein's regime in 2003, the Arab Spring, the bloodshed and conflict in Syria, and the rise of ISIS,[3] Saudi Arabia's role both regionally and globally has become increasingly central as a source of stability and influence.

A Brief History of Saudi Foreign Policy

Early History

Although the Kingdom of Saudi Arabia is a relatively recent arrival to the global political scene, having been formally established in 1932,[4] the Saudi royal dynasty has a longer history of rulership and policymaking dating back to the 18th century. Historically, the Arabian Gulf was not a single political entity with set borders, but a fluid territory with recognised tribal settlements, pastures and migration paths. Failure to respect these 'understood' boundaries resulted in inter-tribal disputes, warfare and the creation of alliances,

1. The pilgrimage to Mecca is required of all Muslims once in a lifetime, provided that they are physically and financially able. Between 2 and 3 million people make the *Hajj* each year, rendering it the largest annual religious gathering in the world. The logistics of *Hajj* management and the structure for issuing visas by country is described in Bianchi (2004).
2. Middle East and North Africa.
3. The Islamic State of Iraq and Syria, also known as the Islamic State of Iraq and the Levant (ISIL), and Da'esh.
4. The first Saudi dynasty was established through the formation of an alliance with the Al al-Shaykh family in 1744, lasting until 1818. The second dynasty recovered power in 1824 and lasted until 1891. The third dynasty recovered power initially in Riyadh in 1902 and formally united the country in 1932.

as described in pre-Saudi chronicles.[5] It was both normal and accepted for migrations to occur over significant distances due to movement of family members or pursuit of scholarship or commercial interests. As a result, many families in what is today Saudi Arabia have long-standing significant commercial and family relations and scholarly connections extending into southern Iraq, Syria, Bahrain, Qatar, and Kuwait, rendering relations with those entities not simply a matter of state-to-state considerations, but also a deeper personal matter.

Formal political boundaries between countries were introduced during the European colonial era in the Arabian Gulf region, largely to indicate European claims over and patronage systems within specific geographic territories. Only the territory of what is today Saudi Arabia was never formally colonised by Europeans, although Great Britain played the dominant role in the Gulf region, providing subsidies to various rulers to create patronage systems and encourage and direct tribal rivalries and a new political order following the collapse of the Ottoman Empire in the aftermath of World War I.[6]

The Pre-Oil Era

During the pre-oil era, foreign policy was largely determined by financial considerations as the Saudi government was not a major player on the international stage, but more of a dependent nation, relying on two major sources of income—Hajj revenues and subsidies. Access to Hajj revenues required assuring the safety of pilgrimage routes and the undertaking of pilgrimage rites as evidence of its seriousness in fulfilling the role of caretaker of the two holy cities. It also meant protection of the cosmopolitan nature of the Hijaz region, as pilgrims representing different Sunni law schools, Shiis, and Sufis alike make the Hajj, placing the Saudi royal family in the delicate position of having to accommodate pilgrims from a variety of Islamic persuasions at the same time that it appeases the demands of its own ultra-conservative religious establishment. It is a delicate balancing

5. The definitive works on this topic are Juhany (2002), which reviews the chronicles and Determann (2014), which provides a broad analysis of historical writing in Saudi Arabia, showing the interplay between political developments and how history is conceived.

6. For a broad overview of Saudi-European relations, see Nonneman (2001).

act that has sometimes proven challenging, particularly during years when some visiting pilgrims have made political declarations in the context of the Hajj, which is supposed to unite all believers as one, regardless of differences in nationality, tribal or ethnic background, or sect. Similarly, subsidies tended to have conditions attached, typically with respect to political and economic relations with other countries, especially Great Britain. Formal political ties have been maintained with Great Britain, although the exploration for oil in the 1930s was entrusted to an American company, SOCAL (Standard Oil of California), opening another door of revenues and tying Saudi Arabia closer to the United States (US).

Foreign policy was considered to be sufficiently important to Saudi Arabia that the first ministerial body founded by King Abdulaziz, in 1930, was the Ministry of Foreign Affairs. He appointed his son, then-Prince and, later, King Faisal (r. 1964-1975), as Minister, a position which he held, with a brief break from 1960-1962, until he was assassinated in 1975. At that point, his son, Saud Al-Faisal, was appointed Minister, a position he has held ever since. From a Saudi perspective, the advantage of having such long-serving Ministers is that it assures continuity in policy, while assuring a known entity for policymakers from other countries, as opposed to the uncertainties introduced by constant elections and changing of governments and alliances. Given Saudi Arabia's foreign policy priorities of stability and security, having that level of stability reflected in the government indicates institutional seriousness about policy objectives.[7]

The Rise of the Oil Era, the Cold War and Saudi Islamic Identity

The conclusion of World War II, the rising global dependence on oil for the spread of the military-industrial complex, and the

7. Although the *Majlis al-Shura* (Shoura Council), founded in its current form in 2000, has a foreign affairs committee, the *Majlis* is limited to being a consultative body that makes recommendations to the Council of Ministers. It does not legislate or direct policy per se. That power remains in the hands of the Foreign Minister, who is subject to the King's approval. Nevertheless, having a mechanism for input to the Foreign Minister is considered evidence of a shift from a supposedly personality-driven policy to one that has more of an institutional base. This has become a particular concern for other countries as the senior members of the Saudi royal family are aging and some are experiencing serious health concerns.

onset of the Cold War between the US and the Soviet Union placed Saudi Arabia in an increasingly strong relationship with the US in the latter half of the 20th century. Throughout the Cold War, the US and Saudi Arabia were largely ideologically united in containing the global spread of Soviet communist influence. Cold War dynamics were played out on the Arab political stage through increasing rivalry between Saudi Arabia and Egypt for regional hegemony. Although Saudi Arabia, under King Saud (r. 1953-1964), initially supported Gamal 'Abd al-Nasser's Free Officers Revolution in 1952, which overthrew the Egyptian monarchy, over time, Nasser's secular Arab nationalist ideology and growing ties to the Soviet Union came to be perceived as a domestic security concern. Then-Crown Prince Faisal's rising influence led to a shift in pursuit of a foreign policy that emphasised a Saudi image focused on Islamic identity and claimed a key global role for Saudi Arabia in world Islamic affairs.

First as Crown Prince and then as King, Faisal established, financed and/or heavily influenced a variety of Islamic institutions with global reach, including the Muslim World League (1962), Organization of the Islamic Conference (1972), World Assembly of Muslim Youth (1972), and International Islamic Relief Organization (1975). These organisations were specifically designed to assert Saudi Arabia's leadership in service of the global *ummah* (community) and thus served as informal instruments of Saudi foreign policy.[8] The assertion of a specifically global *ummah* was intended to serve as a counter-weight to national borders that had been artificially imposed by the Europeans and to encourage the *ummah* not to allow itself to be divided by national politics at the expense of the greater common good. This appeal to the global identity of being Muslim was intended to remind Muslims that their primary identity was based on religion and a shared history rooted in the same, rather than on political constructs or alternative ideologies not rooted in religion, particularly Arab nationalism and Soviet communism. This policy objective was later further institutionalised within the Saudi government with the creation of the Ministry of Islamic Affairs, Endowments, Call and Guidance in

8. Global community of Muslims, united by faith in Islam.

1999 with Shaykh Saleh bin Abdulaziz Al al-Shaykh as Minister. This ministry oversees both domestic and international Islamic affairs and charitable endowments and is responsible for financial support for Muslims globally, particularly with respect to construction of mosques, religious educational institutions, and missionary work, giving Saudi Arabia extensive reach into and influence over religious interpretation in areas where such assistance is accepted.

Saudi Arabia as a Regional Arab Player

Saudi Arabia has also sought to play a major regional role based on its Arab identity, beginning with membership in the Arab League, founded in 1945 to create an Arab regional bloc of economic and social unity. Despite common aspirations centred on better education, health care, social security and jobs, the League didn't host its first official Arab Summit until 13 January 1964. Outside of issuing statements in support of Palestine, it has generally failed to develop any comprehensive strategy for addressing regional concerns or upgrading living standards within member countries.

Frustration with the Arab League's inability to achieve its projected goals led Saudi Arabia to turn to a smaller regional focus—the Arabian Gulf countries—which, despite their wealth and power, have nevertheless been faced with significant socio-economic challenges, including poverty, social inequality, and unemployment, all of which have served to create breeding grounds for extremism. Saudi Arabia was a founding member of the Gulf Cooperation Council (GCC), established on 28 May 1991. By June 1991, the GCC had already enacted an Economic Unity Agreement (EUA) to coordinate economic development plans between the countries to strengthen and expand their collective international economic and geopolitical influence. Over time, a common external tariff of 5 per cent was agreed upon, in addition to a common market and a customs union, all of which were the first of their kind in modern Arab history. Saudi Arabia has, throughout, been a consistent leader within the GCC, seeking to expand cooperation and influence.

Saudi-US Relations

The dawn of the oil era brought Saudi Arabia into a mutually beneficial relationship with the US, typically described as bilateral, that has remained close at multiple levels, including financial, military and strategic, until today.[9] The role of ARAMCO in developing and expanding Saudi Arabia's oil producing, refining and exporting facilities placed the US in the position of privileged partner with Saudi Arabia from the beginning. This relationship expanded into US military assistance and sales to Saudi Arabia in the 1950s and deepened with the collapse of monarchies throughout the Middle East in the 1950s and 1960s. It was during a visit by King Saud to the US in 1957 that the Eisenhower Doctrine was declared, pledging, "assistance, including the dispatch of armed forces, to nations requesting American help 'against overt aggression from any nation controlled by international communism.'"

Initially, the mutual support was based on the need to maintain stability so that the flow of oil, which was critical to the US military-industrial complex and growing demands in Europe, could continue. The spread of the Cold War rendered the relationship more of a strategic alliance intended to contain the spread of Soviet influence as, throughout the 1970s, it spread into Egypt, Libya, Algeria, Ethiopia, Somalia, the Peoples' Democratic Republic of Yemen, and Iraq, as well as Africa, Central America, and, most ominously in the long-term, Afghanistan. The US-Saudi cooperation in this regard continued through the collapse of the Soviet Union and Saudi Arabia has remained cautious with respect to Russia ever since; although business relations have expanded in the 21st century, Russia's support for the al-Assad regime in Syria, which Saudi Arabia has come to vehemently oppose, has presented a political challenge at the same time that both play powerful roles globally as major energy producers and suppliers.

---

9. A complete history of US-Saudi relations, with particular attention to the role of the oil industry, can be found in Bronson (2006). This is not to say that the relationship has been without its challenges, particularly where issues of human and women's rights and religious freedom are concerned. See Lippmann (2012) for details.

Although it is often asserted that Saudi Arabia's relationship with the US was uniformly strong historically until 9/11, there have been times of strained relations, particularly in response to the Israeli invasion and occupation of Egypt in 1956; the Israeli conflict with Egypt and Syria during the June 1967 war; and the October 1973 attempt by Egypt to recover its territories that had been seized by Israel in 1967. In these instances, Saudi Arabia perceived the need for regional stability and Saudi security in the face of a powerful Israeli military threat to Arab nations as a more critical concern than US-Saudi relations. It was in response to the October 1973 Egyptian-Israeli War, for example, that Saudi Arabia, along with other oil-producing countries, engaged in an oil embargo to protest against Western support, particularly by the US, UK, and the Netherlands, for Israel. Initially, at the beginning of the embargo in 1973, Saudi Arabia also claimed a 25 per cent stake in ARAMCO, expanding it to 60 per cent by 1974 and full control by 1980.

The dual embargo and nationalisation of ARAMCO marked major Saudi foreign policy initiatives, powerfully expressing collective Arab and specifically Saudi anger over Western support for Israeli expansionist policies. Yet, as the US economy, in particular, entered into a downward spiral with skyrocketing inflation and slowed economic growth, Saudi Arabia also had to consider the longer-term financial, strategic and political impact of the embargoes. Given the intertwining of the Saudi and US economies, as evidenced by the sheer volume of mutual investments and joint ventures, the reality of the US being the world's largest investor in Saudi Arabia, Saudi Arabia's holding of major US debt instruments, Saudi Arabia's ongoing need for American-manufactured defense equipment and structures, and Saudi Arabia's continued use of the US dollar as the medium of exchange for international financial transactions, Saudi Arabia ultimately concluded that use of this soft weapon was not in its strategic interests in the long run.[10] Consequently, it has not endorsed any further oil embargoes, despite ongoing anger

10. Until today, the overwhelming majority of Saudi bank reserves remain held in US dollars. See Anthony (2011).

and frustration over the failure to achieve a just resolution to the Palestinian-Israeli conflict.

Instead, in response to these challenges and security needs, a number of important joint Saudi-US initiatives were undertaken, beginning in the mid-1970s with the Saudi Arabia-US Joint Commission for Economic Cooperation, which was established to strengthen and expand both the nature and extent of defence cooperation, as well as to re-circulate the hundreds of millions of dollars accrued by Saudi Arabia during the oil embargoes. Yet, even this shared strategic interest has not always resulted in smooth operations, as there have been several instances of US Congressional resistance to arms sales to Saudi Arabia, such as during the late 1970s when there was significant opposition to the sale of F-15 fighter aircraft to Saudi Arabia, despite having sold such weaponry to other countries without similar challenges; and in the 1980s, when the Reagan administration failed to complete the sale of advanced defensive weaponry to Saudi Arabia, costing the US nearly $60 billion in lost revenues and jobs (Anthony, 2013).

Challenges to Saudi Arabia's Islamic Identity and Leadership

In the midst of these economic and political developments, Saudi Arabia has also had to contend with competing interpretations of Islam that challenge its claimed position of leadership of the Muslim world, which has been a major focus of Saudi foreign policy from the outset. The most significant of these challenges began with the 1979 Islamic Revolution in Iran, which deposed a secular ruler in favour of a new state based on Shii identity, religious interpretation, and expansionism, thus posing an existential threat to Saudi Arabia.[11] At the same time, militant strains within the Sunni tradition began to express themselves within Saudi Arabia itself, presenting both a domestic challenge and a regional security concern. Domestic challenges began in 1979 with the seizure of the Grand Mosque in Mecca by millennial militants (for details, see Trofimov, 2007),

11. Whether relatively real or perceived depending on the circumstances, the claim of the Iranian/ Shii threat has been a staple of Saudi foreign policy since the Islamic Revolution.

accompanied by an uprising of the Shii population in the Eastern Province, purportedly encouraged and supported by the new Islamic Republic in Iran.[12] Although these challenges were put down in the short term, continued religious opposition to the Saudi monarchy continued through the rise of the Sahwa movement throughout the 1980s and 1990s,[13] becoming a serious security concern following Saddam Hussein's invasion of Kuwait in 1990-91 and the subsequent Saudi invitation to US troops to defend Saudi national territory. The Saudi government invitation and policy of asserting national security as a priority was upheld by the Council of Senior Ulama, thus enjoying endorsement from the official Saudi religious establishment. However, the Sahwa protested the presence of non-Muslim troops in the homeland of Islam's two holiest cities. Popular opposition to the government stance and support for the Sahwa indicated a shift in popular attitudes from one of obedience to the government to opposing it for placing national security as a higher priority, as opposed to the doctrinal purity and Islamic identity it pledged to uphold. Although the Saudi government was, again, able to forcibly silence the opposition for a time, the underlying issues, particularly the primary place of Islamic identity over national security concerns, did not go away.[14] They resurged most powerfully through the rise of Al-Qaida, supported by the Taliban, in Afghanistan in the second half of the 1990s and the terrorist attacks against the US on 11 September 2001, and within Saudi Arabia beginning in 2003.[15]

In the aftermath of 9/11, Saudi Arabia found itself in the uncomfortable position of being, on the one hand, blamed for the ideology leading to Al-Qaida as a global terrorist organisation and, on the other, as being the most important global partner in the General War on Terrorism spearheaded by the US, beginning with the October 2001 retaliation against Afghanistan, and continuing

12. Details of this relationship and Saudi Shii history can be found in Ibrahim (2006).

13. Details can be found in Lacroix (2011).

14. For a discussion of the Saudi religious interpretation known as Wahhabism, both historical and contemporary, see DeLong-Bas (2008).

15. A full history can be found in Hegghammer (2010).

through the occupation of Afghanistan and invasion and occupation of Iraq in 2003. Saudi Arabia continued its strategic relationship with the US in forming the Saudi Arabia-US Joint Terrorist Financing Task Force, permitting regular, intensive, extensive and effective cooperation that has led to the foiling of numerous terrorist plots. It has also served to expand discussions of joint concerns and assuage fears about potential foreign investors in both economies.

Saudi Arabia as an Independent Actor

Despite close strategic cooperation between the US and Saudi Arabia in addressing terrorism and extremism as global security priorities, the relationship became strained during the events of the Arab Spring, beginning in December 2010, as they viewed the potential opportunities and challenges from different perspectives, based on foreign policy objectives. The US, with a foreign policy of promoting the spread of democracy globally, saw an opportunity for popular sovereignty to come to power.[16] Saudi Arabia, on the other hand, held stability and regional security as primary foreign policy objectives. From a Saudi perspective, the end result of the US policy of supporting democracy has been the destabilisation of societies, the kindling of religious warfare, and the installation of dictatorships that do not respect religious or ethnic minority rights, none of which are in favour of the Saudi priorities of stability and security (Freeman, 2014). These differing approaches have led to more of a "transactional" relationship between Saudi Arabia and the US, in which each situation has to be individually evaluated, rather than allowing a single policy objective to pre-determine the approach, as had been the case, for example, during the 1980s, when containing the Soviet Union was the agreed-upon principle (Gause, 2012).

Thus, although there remain common interests and mutual benefits in the US-Saudi relationship, Saudi Arabia today is taking into greater consideration its own domestic and regional concerns

16. Ironically, initial US support for burgeoning democracy rapidly deteriorated when it became apparent that genuinely popular elections would result in Islamist parties taking power—a reality that Saudi Arabia had warned would happen.

as a priority over its relationship with the US. One indication of US recognition of this reality is the Jeddah Communiqué of 2014, establishing a joint US-Saudi strategy for building a regional coalition to combat ISIS, including an end to terror financing, sealing borders, moving away from violent extremism, and addressing the deepening rift between religious conservatives and the rest of society to assure stability and prosperity. It also specifically includes recognition of Saudi Arabia's commitment to help train the Syrian opposition.

Perhaps the biggest indicator of the shift in Saudi-US relations and in Saudi Arabia's rising claim to global leadership can be found in Saudi Foreign Minister Prince Saud Al-Faisal's refusal to deliver the opening remarks at the UN General Assembly in October 2013, an address he has given for decades, followed by Saudi Arabia's rejection of its hard-fought election to a two-year non-permanent seat on the United Nations Security Council (UNSC) to protest the UNs' ongoing inability to resolve justly the Palestinian-Israeli conflict and end the bloodshed in Syria, and to force recognition of the perceived double standard in the Security Council of holding only certain countries accountable for the violations of international laws and treaties and UN Resolutions, while allowing others, namely Israel, to repeatedly violate them. Saudi analysts see these actions as presaging "concrete policy changes and rectifications in the coming months and years that are going to set the tone for a completely transformed Saudi foreign policy" that will put to use Saudi Arabia's status as the world's energy superpower, economic engine, and last remaining political heavyweight in the Arab world (Obaid, 2013).

Priority Areas for Saudi Foreign Policy

Saudi foreign policy today is driven by a combination of strategic, political, economic, social, and national security priorities, that are best summarised by the objectives of peace, prosperity and stability. These driving objectives reflect Saudi Arabia's consideration of the domestic, regional and international spheres. King Abdullah is working at and with all of these levels to rebuild an image of Saudi Arabia internationally as one of a moderate (*wasatiyya*) interpretation of Islam in dialogue with other faith traditions and guided by humanitarian concerns; a regional hub for advancement in science, medicine, and technology; a reliable and desirable partner for business and financial relations and foreign exchanges; a key player in the global energy market, not just in terms of fossil fuels, but also for renewable energy resources; and a source of regional stability at a time when the region is plagued by bloodshed and chaos.

Domestic Priorities as Drivers of Foreign Policy

Domestically, Saudi policies are based on five long-term priorities, focusing largely on the economy, but recognising the need for international engagement. Those priorities include:

a. Diversification and expansion of the economic base.
b. Reduction of fossil fuel energy consumption while expanding renewable energy resources.
c. Expansion of job opportunities for the burgeoning youth population.[17]
d. Enhancement of cooperation between the public and private sectors,[18] and
e. Increase of investments, both local and foreign (SUSRIS, 2014).[19]

In order to achieve these objectives, Saudi Arabia has long maintained the need for *gradual* domestic reform, having learned a harsh experience with the 1979 uprising in Mecca that was at least partially the result of rapid modernisation and development without accompanying social adjustment. Revolution is not part of Saudi culture; there is a preference instead for consultation and presenting demands to public figures, indicating a certain level of solidarity between the government and the people (SUSRIS, 2011). Inasmuch as Saudi Arabia recognises the multiplicity of voices

---

17. Between 60 and 70 per cent of the Saudi population is under the age of 30, making addressing the needs and aspirations of youth a pillar of domestic stability.
18. The overwhelming majority of the Saudi economy is based on the public sector, both the oil industry and government employment, making expansion of the private sector a critical policy issue.
19. Prince Muqrin was named Deputy Crown Prince in March 2014.

seeking inclusion and expression in the political process, the Saudi government nevertheless takes the position that the state remains the dominant player in Saudi society as the central source of wealth and infrastructure, so that inclusion of these diverse identities in the "unified, singular Saudi identity" must be conducted "through the state apparatus and narrative" (Al-Faisal, 2011). Evidence of Saudi government seriousness includes the institution of the Basic Laws of Governance, the Majlis al-Shura, and the National Dialogues, as well as work toward increasing government transparency, expansion and reform of education, and stronger inclusion of both women and Shiis in the public sphere and in terms of expanded rights for citizens.[20] Saudi Arabia also points to greater media openness, the formation of debate clubs in Saudi universities, continuation of the long-standing practice of public *majlis* discussions between the people and public officials, judicial reforms, encouragement of the development of Saudi nationalism, and the establishment of the Bay'ah Council to assure a smooth succession process as evidence of its institutional support for public inclusion in issues of national importance (Al-Faisal, 2011a).

Domestically, major challenges facing Saudi Arabia include the ongoing threat of terrorism, extremist positions standing in the way of gender equality, the need to reform the judiciary, upgrading of the educational system, and the need for social and economic reforms, including a decreased dependence upon foreign workers (Fatany, 2013). In other words, not only are development and prosperity needed throughout the region, but also at home, particularly with a burgeoning youth population in need of education leading to gainful, meaningful employment—only part of which has been realised by the

20. Rights for non-citizens remain a serious challenge, both with respect to non-Saudi spouses of Saudi nationals, especially when children are born to the union as only those with a Saudi father have been eligible for citizenship and, thus, benefits such as public education and health care, which are open only to citizens, and with respect to foreign workers who are sometimes subject to abuse of various kinds, including having passports confiscated so that they cannot leave the country, not being paid for months or years at a time, or facing physical abuse, as has been the case in several spectacular incidents involving drivers or maids. Although there have also been cases of children, in particular, being abused by a driver or maid, the majority of the cases have involved Saudi nationals abusing foreign workers.

Nitaqat programme, which is intended to "Saudize" the workforce.[21] Greater integration of women in the public sphere, particularly in business, medicine, and the Shoura Council, has also been set as a domestic priority by the King, albeit with oftentimes strong opposition, particularly in religious circles.

Given the omnipresence of social media throughout the MENA region, many analysts expected Saudi Arabia to experience its own Arab Spring, as Saudi youth are often described as "netizens," rather than citizens, given their proclivity for using social media and the internet. Saudi Arabia has the highest Facebook user rate in the GCC with over 6 million users and Facebook being the third most visited website in the Kingdom. Saudi Arabia also has more than 3 million active Twitter users recording 50 million tweets per month and leading the world's growth rate, up 3,000 per cent from 2011 to 2012, as compared to the global rate of 300 per cent. YouTube has also proven immensely popular, with more than 90 million videos being viewed daily and a growth rate of use of 109 per cent in 2013 (SUSRIS, 2013). The impact of such widespread use of social media was the circulation of grievances and criticisms at an unprecedented rate, obligating the government to respond in a way that had never previously happened (Lacey, 2011). Yet, despite strong expressions of discontent, Saudi Arabia did not share in the social upheavals experienced elsewhere.

Part of Saudi Arabia's ability to weather the storms of the Arab Spring was due to its financial strength and the government's willingness to address public concerns. As Saudi youth joined with other regional youth in expressing frustration with high rates of unemployment and public sector corruption, the Saudi state responded by financing projects designed to meet the needs of the

21. Introduced in 2011 to prioritise hiring of Saudi nationals over foreign workers, this programme became very controversial in late 2013 and early 2014 when it was announced that any foreign worker overstaying their visa or without a valid one would be subject to deportation. There has been resistance to the programme because of its cost—Saudi workers demand about three times the salary paid to a foreign worker, rendering the cost prohibitive to some employers—and because of the sheer volume of workers involved. There are about 7 million expatriate workers in Saudi Arabia out of a total population of about 28 million, which is about 25 per cent.

youth population, including expanding housing assistance and loan programmes, offering monthly allowances, and raising salaries. Greater attention was also given to better integrating students from outlying tribal areas into urban schools also, thereby shifting allegiances from local to national leaders and further bolstering a sense of Saudi national identity and pride. All of this was in addition to a government anti-poverty programme launched several years before the Arab Spring with the express goal of reducing poverty levels from 13.3 per cent in 2010 to 2.2 per cent by 2020 (Obaid, 2011).

The Saudi government's willingness to listen to the voices of its youth and produce concrete solutions to address their concerns and problems stood in marked contrast to the responses of other governments faced with similar challenges. Rather than being further disillusioned by an unresponsive government, Saudi youth chose to support a government that listened to and addressed their needs, demonstrating that the social contract of consultation (*shura*) and response remained intact. Some analysts have also noted that the culture of obedience to the government in exchange for comfortable living remains intact among many youth who continue to rely on the culture of influence (*wasta*), rather than merit or productivity, for entitlement (Alterman, 2010).

Strategic Priorities

Strategic priorities for Saudi Arabia include: maintaining the Middle East as a nuclear weapon-free zone at the same time that it asserts the regional right to obtain nuclear power for civilian purposes; [22] using political and financial power to maintain/create regional stability, especially through the auspices of the GCC; and positioning itself as the global voice for respect for and defense of religion, especially Islam, which is a pillar of legitimacy for the Saudi monarchy. All of these priorities have peace, prosperity and security as their central objectives.

---

22. Saudi Arabia has made it clear that it will demand the same rights to develop nuclear capacities for domestic energy production granted to any other Middle East country, including and specifically Iran. See, Al-Faisal (2014).

Saudi Arabia as a Zone Free of Weapons of Mass Destruction

Saudi Arabia's stance on regional nuclear and other mass-destruction-weapons issues historically has been one of the consistent oppositions to their proliferation in the Middle East. Saudi Arabia has requested that the Middle East be guaranteed to be a zone free of weapons of mass destruction by the five permanent members of the UNSC and that military sanctions be implemented against any zone member seen to be developing such weapons (Al-Faisal, 2014a). It is a policy that is both principled and pragmatic with security at its heart—principled in the sense of opposition to the presence of such enormous destructive capability because of its potential harm to both the human and natural environments, and pragmatic from a security perspective in terms of considering the potential for regional destruction, if not annihilation, given the presence of so many rogue regimes in the region, as well as a regional history of political instability. Particularly with sectarian tensions that constantly fluctuate due to the quest for regional hegemony and geopolitical influence, the presence of nuclear weaponry in the Middle East is seen by Saudi Arabia as a recipe that can only lead to disaster. Therefore, Saudi Arabia has consistently opposed the presence of such destructive weapons for all states with no exceptions.

Today, Saudi concerns about the proliferation of nuclear weapons in the Middle East are focused on Iran, which it accuses of pursuing a nuclear programme geared toward the development of weaponry, rather than the peaceful generation and use of energy. Israel is similarly accused of creating disruption, both because it is widely believed to have and be capable of making nuclear weapons, and because it has refused to participate in the P5+1 negotiations designed to keep the Middle East nuclear weapon-free.

At the same time, Saudi Arabia has expressed concern about ongoing US-Iranian negotiations over the Iranian nuclear programme as potentially leading to a political rapprochement between the two countries. This is undesirable from a Saudi perspective because it would further extend Iranian influence and potentially sideline Saudi Arabia as a regional partner for the US (Freeman, 2014). It would also deter an ongoing US presence in the Middle East, which Saudi

Arabia believes is critical to maintaining stability, although the US has been so focused on the weapons themselves that the central issue of regional security is perceived to have been ignored (SUSRIS, 2014a). Although Foreign Minister Saud Al-Faisal has been adamant that the Middle East remain a nuclear-free zone, in a demonstration of *realpolitik*, there have been recent warnings in non-official circles that, if Iran succeeds in building a nuclear weapon, the GCC will have to carefully consider all options, including acquisition of a nuclear deterrent.[23]

Regional Cooperation and Stability

Saudi Arabia was a founding member of the GCC[24] and has encouraged a regional shift toward being more independent and self-reliant in managing its own affairs, particularly in the aftermath of the Arab Spring and as the Saudi-US relationship has shifted on certain issues. On 19 December 2011, King Abdullah proposed taking the GCC to the next level by developing it into a single political, economic and military entity—the Gulf Union—with a "capitol" based in Riyadh, along the lines of the European Union (EU). Under this project, each state would retain its own sovereignty, but all would coordinate their foreign and defense policies, with the possibility of extending coordination to other policy areas. The advantage of the Gulf Union would lie in a more coherent regional focus that takes into consideration the common needs of member states (SUSRIS, 2014a). Its members would include the current GCC states and the possible additions of Jordan and Morocco. The decision-making body would replace the current GCC Secretariat.

One of the initial indicators of progress toward the Gulf Union was the creation of a customs union that came into effect on 1 January 2012. The five-year development plan places Saudi Arabia in a central position to lead regional and international stabilisation,

---

23. Although he does not currently hold an official government position, many analysts look to Prince Turki Al-Faisal, former chief of general intelligence and former Saudi Ambassador to the UK and US, as an astute observer and a strong gauge for the likely future direction of Saudi foreign policy. See, Al-Faisal (2014).

24. The other members of Bahrain, Kuwait, Oman, Qatar, and the United Arab Emirates (UAE).

based on its oil production capacity and thus ability to stabilise global energy markets and provide foreign aid to stabilise fragile Arab and Muslim states (Obaid, 2012).

The next indicator of progress came in September 2013 when Saudi Arabia called for the creation of an Arab League military force of between 75,000 and 100,000 to be positioned along the Jordanian-Syrian border as the most legitimate way to bring an end to the atrocities of al-Assad's security forces. In the past, Egypt would have been expected to participate heavily, but has not been able to step up to the task because of its own domestic preoccupations, leaving Saudi Arabia as the only major regional player left to take on leadership. The symbolism of the move is that it represents a major post-colonial action, showing the capacity of Arab countries to act independently and assure their own security, rather than farming it out elsewhere. Saudi analysts believe this was an important step in the Arab world taking over full management of its own affairs (Obaid and Khashoggi, 2013).

At present, Saudi Arabia is the central player in Gulf Union plans, with strong support from Kuwait and the UAE. Ironically, the main challenge to Gulf Union success has not come from outside, but from within, namely from Qatar. Since the Arab Spring, Saudi Arabia and Qatar have been locked in a struggle for influence in Egypt. Both possess extensive fossil fuel reserves and financial resources, so both have been able to pour enormous financial support into Egypt. Following the overthrow of former President Hosni Mubarak, Qatar backed Mohamed Morsi and the Muslim Brotherhood as the appropriate new leaders of Egypt, largely due to ideological affinity, while Saudi Arabia backed the Egyptian military, ultimately under General Abdel Fattah al-Sisi when the Morsi government was removed from power, as a reflection of its own pragmatic concerns for both Egyptian and regional stability.[25]

Such was the anger against Qatari policy in Egypt that Saudi Arabia spearheaded the Riyadh Agreement, signed in late 2013,

25. It was also perceived to have been a snub to the Muslim Brotherhood, which was held responsible by the Saudi monarchy for the rise of domestic opposition movements in Saudi Arabia, up to and including Al-Qaida of the Arabian Peninsula (AQAP).

outlining 37 actions required from Qatar in order to continue membership in the GCC and re-establish relations with other member countries. Qatar's repeated failure to take these actions led to talk of suspending its membership in the GCC altogether. Saudi Arabia further threatened a closure of its borders and a sea blockade of Qatar to force it to reverse its actions (Karasik, 2014). As a result of this relative regional isolation, Qatar has drawn closer to Iran and Turkey, particularly working with the latter on an alternative plan to the Saudi initiative for resolution of the Israeli-Palestinian conflict, causing further friction between these two states.

To protest the ongoing disagreement within the GCC, in March 2014, Saudi Arabia, the UAE, and Bahrain recalled their ambassadors from Qatar, although Kuwait and Oman did not, raising questions about just how united the GCC really is. At the same time, Saudi Arabia also began working in 2014 to integrate Jordan into the GCC to try to limit regional instability, particularly by helping it deal with the refugee crisis of more than 1 million Syrians seeking asylum in Jordan, and bolstering security, giving the Jordanian state more power to limit the export of militant jihadist fighters (Nerguizian, 2014).

Although many Western analysts look at these developments and question the GCC's capacity to overcome its ideological differences at the level of regional security and, especially, foreign policy,[26] Saudi Arabia remains committed to the cohesion of both the Gulf and the broader Middle East region as an important geopolitical player on the global stage.

A Global Voice for Respect for Religion

One of the pillars of the Saudi monarchy's claims to legitimacy and, therefore, its foreign policy, is its role in defending Islam and the religious freedom of Muslims. In the aftermath of 9/11 and the global rise of Islamophobia, Saudi Arabia has played a prominent

---

26. See "Gulf Cooperation Council: Role in Regional Dynamics", panel at "Framing and Charting the Region's Issues, Interests, Challenges, and Opportunities: Implications for Arab and U.S. Policies", 23rd Arab-US Policymakers Conference and National Council on US-Arab Relations, Washington, DC, 28-29 October 2014, posted by *SUSRIS*, 10 November 2014, particularly the remarks by Dr Abdulaziz Sager for a positive assessment and Ambassador Stephen A. Seche for a negative view.

global role in calling for respect for religious beliefs and sensitivities, including demands for criminalisation of defamation of religion and religious figures and the violations of rights of religious and social minorities in other countries.[27] Saudi Arabia has been particularly concerned by the use of social media as a means of spreading offensive anti-religious, particularly anti-Islamic, propaganda, such as the Danish cartoons of 2005, a 2012 film on the Prophet Muhammad and periodic reports of extremist preachers in the US threatening to burn Qur'ans, which Muslims believe to be sacred revelation. Social media enables such stories to quickly "go viral," being projected into millions of lives, sometimes with deadly results.

Although many in the West perceive these issues to be a matter of freedom of speech, for many Muslims, particularly in Saudi Arabia, they serve as simply yet another example of the hegemonic West engaging in willful and reckless disregard of Muslim sensitivities that is perceived to have been at least tacitly approved by Western governments and is designed to maintain Western dominance in Muslim lands, thereby making it, from a Muslim perspective, an issue of sovereignty and an assertion of cultural superiority, rather than free speech. There are also concerns about a double standard in the West in which racial epithets and Holocaust denials are criminalised, but mocking God and religion is considered "protected speech." From their perspective, therefore, the West is not genuine in its protection of freedom of expression, but selective according to cultural sensitivities, as evidenced most powerfully by the global rise of Islamophobia to the point where it has become mainstream in many Western societies. Saudis particularly perceive a double standard as, for example, the US insists that Saudi textbooks and preachers be revised and reformed to be more 'tolerant' at the same time that US

---

27. Reported in Saudi Press Agency (2014). Some have declared this stance to be hypocritical, given the lack of religious freedom within Saudi Arabia, where public practice or proselytising of any religion other than Islam is prohibited. Historically, Shiis have also been banned from publicly celebrating or expressing certain aspects of their beliefs. Although some restrictions had been lifted in recent years, the events of the Arab Spring and concerns about Iranian influence among Shii populations have resulted in crackdowns on Shii practices due to concerns about politically dissident behaviours and foreign influences. For a discussion of sectarian tensions in the Arabian Gulf, see Wehrey (2013) and Potter (2014).

politicians hold anti-Muslim hearings and have outlawed the Sharia (Islamic law) in some states.[28]

As a global leading voice for Islam and Muslims and as the custodian of the two holy cities, Saudi Arabia believes itself to be obligated to speak out and defend Islam and Muslims globally, including by making certain correct information available, encouraging interfaith dialogue,[29] and assuring that Muslims enjoy freedom of religion wherever they live, making defence of Islam a major strategic priority of Saudi foreign policy.

Political Priorities[30]

Political priorities for Saudi Arabia today are: regional stability and regional leadership—both of which have become particularly critical in the post-Arab Spring context. Although many in the West viewed the events of the Arab Spring as an opportunity for regional movement toward democracy, or at least greater popular political participation, Saudi Arabia viewed the Arab Spring with apprehension, seeing potential for tremendous regional unrest and political instability, the creation of conditions conducive to the further rise of terrorism and extremism, increased tensions between Sunnis and Shiis, as well as extremists and moderates, and demands from domestic populations that were not necessarily realistic when compared to financial realities, massive demographic challenges, and timelines required for reforms to be implemented, jobs to be created, and the economies to be stabilised and expanded.[31] Simply overthrowing old governments did not assure that the underlying problems would be easily fixed.

---

28. For a particularly biting critique, see Al-Fahad (2012).

29. Saudi support for interfaith dialogue was most powerfully expressed through King Abdullah's $50 million endowment to found the King Abdullah Bin Abdulaziz International Center for Interreligious and Intercultural Dialogue in Vienna, Austria, to bring the five major world religions—Christianity, Islam, Hinduism, Buddhism and Judaism—together for serious discussion not only about religious issues and beliefs, but how they can be collectively put into practice to improve the human condition and address real-life problems globally.

30. For a broad overview of political issues in the Gulf in general, see Gause III (2009).

31. See, for example, Cordesman (2013).

Unlike Western countries on the outside seeing a golden moment of opportunity, Saudi policymakers and government officials warned of the political instability to come, as simply electing new governments and having new officials in place should not be equated with problem-solving or a cure to long-standing economic challenges. Indeed, many Saudi officials voiced concerns that such intense short-term focus on popular sovereignty was leaving aside longer-term critical security concerns, particularly the potential for widespread violence, and economic disruptions that almost always follow major social upheavals.[32] Therefore, in response to the new realities created by the Arab Spring, Saudi Arabia has declared a deliberate foreign policy of engaging in diplomacy, advisory missions and financial gifts to assure regional stability (Al-Faisal, 2011a). Although it has been claimed that Saudi foreign policy has always had non-interference in the internal matters of other countries as a basic pillar,[33] Saudi Arabia has clearly intervened in matter of other countries in cases where it perceives its national interests or own security to be threatened. This has proven particularly true in Lebanon, Iraq and Egypt in recent years.

Lebanon

Saudi Arabia has a long-standing diplomatic and business presence in Lebanon, dating to Saudi efforts to help heal the sectarian rifts that erupted in civil war in Lebanon between 1975 and 1990. Central to this conflict were changing demographics and reaction against the confessional system, based on a 1932 census, which assigned political positions by sect, so that a Maronite Christian had to serve as president, a Sunni Muslim as Prime Minister, and a Shi'a Muslim as Speaker of the Parliament. The power distribution

32. It has been observed that, rather than bringing "democracy," "human rights," or "reform," the reality of the Arab Spring has been a negative impact on regional economies (particularly Egypt), central authority (Libya), and has even led to civil war (Syria). HRH Prince Turki Al-Faisal, Chariman King Faisal Center for Research & Islamic Studies, "New Regional Conditions: A Saudi View," Keynote Speech delivered at The College of William and Mary, Williamsburg, VA, 11 March 2014.

33. For a recent statement of this variety from a retired Royal Saudi Navy Commodore, see Al-Mulhim (2014).

tended to control the distribution of financial resources and targeting of development projects, leaving the growing Shii population at the bottom of the chain.

Saudi Arabia played a pivotal role in concluding that conflict through the 1989 Taif Accords,[34] which reconfigured the distribution of power in the legislature, to be more in line with actual population figures, thus increasing Shii representation—an end result that one could argue was not necessarily in keeping with its broader regional policy of containment of the purported "Shii threat."

Nevertheless, Saudi Arabia worked with the new Lebanese government, particularly Prime Minister Rafik Hariri (in power from 1992-1998 and 2000-2004), to assure development and stability. Hariri was a close ally and longtime business partner to Saudi Arabia, which deepened the ties between the countries. Hariri's assassination in 2005 greatly angered Saudi Arabia, particularly given that the perpetrators still have not been brought to justice. Thereafter, Saudi Arabia has repeatedly expressed concern about subsequent governments' failures to both find justice and to curb the growing power and influence of Hizbullah, particularly with respect to its use of southern Lebanon as a launching site for missiles and other threats against Israel, arguing that this threatens regional security—a staple of Saudi foreign policy.

Saudi Arabia has also expressed concern about Iranian influence among the Shii population of Lebanon[35] and the Shii population's ongoing support for al-Assad's regime in Syria, which Saudi Arabia vehemently opposes. To counter Iranian influence and rebuild Lebanon, Saudi Arabia pledged $3 billion to support the Lebanese army in January 2014, particularly seeking to bolster Lebanese security against the expansion of groups such as ISIS and Jabhat al-Nusra.

Saudi Arabia's ongoing interests in Lebanon thus clearly have both political and security dimensions at heart.

---

34. Kuwait and Algeria served as co-mediators.

35. For details on Saudi-Iranian rivalry as pertains to Lebanon from an international relations perspective, see Wehrey *et al.* (2009) and Mabon (2013).

Iraq

Despite close cooperation and coordination with the US on many regional issues, the US-led invasion of Iraq in 2003 created a policy rift between the two countries, as the US claimed a need to address alleged weapons of mass destruction and engage in regime change geared toward the introduction of democracy in Iraq, while Saudi Arabia focused on regional security concerns.[36] Saudi Arabia opposed the invasion from the beginning, arguing that it would weaken the main regional counterbalance to Iran and embolden Iran to expand its quest for regional influence. Saudi Arabia also warned about the instability and insecurity within Iraq that would result, particularly when the US failed to provide a plan for and engage in comprehensive post-invasion reconstruction efforts, in opening the door to the rise of militias. Although Saudi Arabia had initially opposed the invasion, it shifted its policy in the aftermath, always with security in mind, counseling against the US withdrawal from Iraq, arguing that the lack of a US presence would further embolden increasingly powerful militias and leave them freer to build their own constituencies—a circumstance that Saudi Arabia believes significantly contributed to the rise of ISIS.[37]

Saudi Arabia's concerns with respect to the Iraqi government installed during the American occupation focused in part on structural issues and in part on the shift to a Shii identity under Prime Minister Nouri al-Malaki (in power 2006-2014), who Saudi Arabia accused of being under Iranian influence. As always, security concerns were at the heart of Saudi policy. Saudi Arabia pointed, for example, to the undermining of effectiveness of the Iraqi military in the aftermath of the overthrow of Saddam Hussein as the US pushed for a complete sweep of all Baathists from their positions with the de-Baathification Decree, which sought to eradicate Baathist ideology from the government and in the public sphere. The problem was that

---

36. For full details of the new security challenges introduced by the 2003 invasion, see Cordesman and Obaid (2005).

37. Sager (2014). Indeed, the power structure in Iraq has degenerated into such chaos that Saudi Arabia has distanced itself from all factions so as not to be caught in the cross-fire. Al-Faisal (2013).

anyone who had wanted to have any government position at any level under Saddam Hussein had been required to swear allegiance to Baathism, so that being a member of the Baath Party was not so much an indicator of genuine loyalty to the ideology as it was a matter of pragmatism in securing employment.

The actual impact of sweeping full members of the Baath Party out of government jobs, which included universities and hospitals, was the overnight unemployment of between 500,000 and 1 million people, including teachers, doctors, lawyers and professionals, who had no hope of otherwise finding gainful employment. More importantly, it deprived Iraq of their knowledge and expertise at a time of already immense instability and insecurity while the country was attempting to rebuild. Perhaps most critical in Saudi eyes: the head of the Coalition Provisional Authority, L. Paul Bremer, decided to abolish outright the former army, police and security personnel because of their affiliation with the old regime. Not only did this immediately deprive an additional 300,000-400,000 people of their jobs, salaries and pensions, but it also left Iraq without any semblance of an experienced or functional domestic security apparatus, making it dependent on the Coalition forces led by the US for security (Holt and Jawad, 2013). This became even more problematic in light of US domestic pressure to withdraw US troops at the same time that Prime Minister al-Malaki, reconstituted the Iraqi military, but appointed Shii commanders selected for their personal loyalty to him, rather than those with training and qualifications. The impact was grave—when ISIS forces attacked Mosul in June 2014, these forces fled.

Saudi Arabia's ongoing concerns in Iraq are not inherently rooted in sectarianism, despite concerns about Iranian influence. Rather, the issue is that the Iraqi government favoured ideology over effectiveness at the military level, leaving Iraq susceptible to serious incursions by ISIS (Al-Faisal, 2014). Iraqi security, stability and military effectiveness are, therefore, important political priorities for Saudi Arabia, rooted in its objective of regional security.

Egypt

Egypt has proven to be a regional flashpoint, beginning with the peaceful overthrow of the Hosni Mubarak regime during the Arab Spring. Mubarak was a long-time friend and staunch ally of Saudi Arabia,[38] rendering his removal from government a serious challenge for Saudi policy, not only because of the loss of an important ally in favour of an uncertain new regime, but, even more importantly, because of the regional instability that resulted and the potential for the threat of regime change to spread into the Gulf. Egypt's status as a financially weak state, long dependent on subsidies, as well as one of the most populous, rendered attention to Egypt's economy and demands of the bulging youth population central to any future hope for regional stability.[39]

Despite anger over Mubarak's "resignation," Saudi Arabia accepted the new reality of a popularly elected government and provided $4 billion in aid, despite its concerns about Muslim Brotherhood influence and Qatari financial support. When the will of the people was later expressed in protesting the incompetence of Morsi's government and demanding a referendum that resulted in millions asking the armed forces to step in and take over the government, Saudi Arabia was the first world leader to recognise the new government and offer support in the form of an unconditional $5 billion in grants, loans and deposits, which it delivered, in contrast to Europe and the US, which promised, but then threatened to freeze, loans (Al-Faisal, 2014a).

Egypt marks a case of Saudi Arabia using its financial power to uphold its political priorities, providing regional leadership in the attempt to sustain stability by encouraging development as a means of legitimising new governments brought to power by popular acclaim (Obaid and Khashoggi, 2013a).

---

38. In the words of Prince Turki Al-Faisal, "abandoning him or any close ally during a revolutionary uprising was not and will never be a policy option for the Kingdom, which must uphold and defend its values." See Al-Faisal (2014a).

39. For outstanding coverage and analysis of the implications of the Arab Spring, particularly in Egypt and Tunisia, see Cole (2014).

Economic and Social Priorities

Economic and social priorities of Saudi foreign policy include: maintaining its role as the world's premier producer and exporter of energy, both fossil fuels and renewable energy, including solar, wind and nuclear;[40] diversification of the economy by attracting foreign investments and business partners; using its membership in the World Trade Organization (WTO) and leading GCC efforts to create a common market to expand its global financial reach; putting its financial power to use for humanitarian purposes; and creating and projecting an image of a "modern" country that remains faithful to its culture, religion and heritage, yet is on the cutting edge of developments in science, technology and medicine.

Saudi Arabia is one of the main economic engines of the MENA region, representing over 20 per cent of GDP (gross domestic product), over 50 per cent of regional stock market capitalisation, and serving as the world's largest producer and exporter of oil. It also possesses about 25 per cent of the world's known oil reserves, in addition to significant shale oil and gas resources. It is the world's third largest holder of net foreign assets and is home to 5 out of the 10 top regional companies, including the top 2—ARAMCO and SABIC. It has been projected that, by 2050, Saudi will have the 6th highest GDP per capita in world. In addition, Saudi Arabia is the largest US trading partner in the MENA region and the 9th largest in the world (Westphal, 2014).

Saudi Arabia's significant financial resources have permitted it to play an increasingly influential role on the global stage. It is the only MENA country and Arab state to hold membership in the G20. It also won entry into the WTO in 2005, further integrating Saudi Arabia into the global economy, expanding its financial reach globally, and also opening its own economy to further outside investment,

40. The King Abdullah City for Atomic and Renewable Energy is poised to make Saudi Arabia one of the world's largest green energy generators. See, Al-Faisal (2013).

reaching out particularly to China,[41] India,[42] and, more cautiously due to political differences over al-Assad's regime in Syria, Russia[43] as business partners and diffusing US influence in the process.

Yet, Saudi Arabia does not simply interact with other major global financial powers. It has been a major financier for projects in poor Muslim countries through soft loans of between $4 and $5 billion annually, financed by Saudi Arabia's Development Fund. Saudi Arabia is among the top five foreign aid donors in the world, having provided aid for building infrastructure in more than 90 countries and forgiving debts in many others, placing it behind only the US, China, and Japan and on par with leading EU countries. It is further the largest single donor to Egypt, Lebanon, Jordan, Pakistan, Palestine[44] and other Muslim majority countries. Saudi Arabia also gives generously to humanitarian causes, having donated over $100 billion since 1980 to people struck by natural disasters around the world, showing how financial power can be put to use for foreign policy as guided by philanthropy (Reported in Saudi Press Agency, 2014).

In a current example of *riyalpolitik*,[45] Saudi Arabia has further placed its financial power behind the new governments in Egypt and Tunisia to encourage development, which it believes is critical to future stability. It has been the main contributor to GCC stabilisation

---

41. Saudi Arabia's main export to China is oil and petrochemicals. Saudi Arabia is China's largest trading partner in Western Asia. Aluminum of China has partnered with several Saudi companies to build a $3 billion aluminum facility in Saudi Arabia. China Railway Company also won a $1.8 billion contract to build a monorail in Mecca.

42. Saudi Arabia is India's 4th largest trading partner. Saudi Arabia is India's largest supplier of oil and the 6th largest global market for Indian exports.

43. Saudi Arabia mainly exports petrochemicals to Russia and imports from Russia barley, reinforced steel, copper, pipes, drilling equipment and semi-processed metal items.

44. Despite ideological concerns about HAMAS, which has ties to the Muslim Brotherhood, Saudi Arabia remains the world's largest contributor to the Palestinian Authority and has given hundreds of millions of dollars to rebuild and develop Palestine, including schools, roads and security. See, Al-Faisal (2014a).

45. A term coined by F. Gregory Gause III to describe Saudi Arabia's use of financial power to achieve political and policy objectives.

plans in Bahrain and Oman, valued at $10 billion each.[46] Saudi Arabia has also provided over $500 million in humanitarian assistance to Iraq (Westphal, 2014).

Finally, from a soft power perspective, Saudi Arabia also seeks to become the regional hub for achievement in technology, medicine, and science. Saudi Arabia's King Faisal International Prizes in science and medicine[47] have long been recognised as precursors to the Nobel Prizes. Saudi Arabia now seeks to be a stronger participant, rather than just recognising achievement, in the fields of science and technology through its 2009 foundation of the King Abdullah University for Science and Technology (KAUST), which focuses exclusively on graduate education and research and aims to be the "Arab MIT." Seriousness of the endeavour is reflected in its holding the third largest university endowment in the world, second only to Harvard and Yale, and its attraction of top-level scholars and researchers from around the world. It is recognised globally as one of the fastest growing and most productive research centres in the world, placing Saudi Arabia at the heart of global conversations about scientific and technological advancement.

Security Priorities

Security priorities, both national and regional, tend to be the most important guiding objectives in the development of Saudi foreign policy. It is only in the context of regional security that the development necessary for political, economic and social progress and prosperity can take place, ultimately leading to long-term regional

46. Although Oman was only marginally effected by the events of the Arab Spring, much of which was resolved through financial packages to the population, Saudi Arabia has concerns about Oman's longer-term stability because Sultan Qaboos is terminally ill with pancreatic cancer, hence a succession crisis is looming. Saudi Arabia has worked hard to establish significant economic and political relations over the past year to prevent Iranian influence from spreading there. Saudi Arabia also has security concerns with respect to Oman because it is known that supply lines for Al-Qaida run through Oman into Yemen, where Al-Qaida of the Arabian Peninsula is based. See, Obaid (2012) and Karasik (2014).

47. Prizes are also given for service to Islam, Islamic Studies, and Arabic language and literature. The prizes are sponsored by the King Faisal Foundation.

peace.[48] Policy considerations for Saudi Arabia related to security include: Saudi Arabia's role as an ongoing partner in the General War on Terrorism (GWOT); the jihadist threat, both domestic and regional, presented by the civil war in Syria and the rise of ISIS; containment of sectarian and religious rivalries, particularly the sectarian conflict in Bahrain and the threat of a potentially nuclear Iran; resolution of various long-standing conflicts, most importantly in Palestine; and protection of Saudi Arabia's borders, particularly with Yemen.

Saudi Arabia as a Partner in the General War on Terrorism (GWOT)

Since the terrorist attacks of 9/11 that placed Saudi Arabia on the global radar as a "breeding ground" for terrorism and extremism, the country's foreign and domestic policies have made prevention and eradication of terrorism and extremism and the conditions that breed them a top policy priority. It has worked closely with the US, in particular, in a variety of joint ventures designed to combat terrorism and extremism politically, militarily and financially.

Although Saudi Arabia was initially in defensive, responsive mode with respect to homegrown extremism, it has sought to shift to a more aggressive approach of leadership in combating what is increasingly a global problem. Minister of Foreign Affairs, Saud Al-Faisal, has assured the global community that Saudi Arabia "will not hesitate to participate in any international serious effort seeking to mobilise and intensify international action against terrorism wherever it occurs and whatever its motives and reasons or those who stand behind it and without discrimination between their sex, color or doctrine" (Saudi Press Agency, 2014a).

As evidence of its seriousness in combatting the issues on a global level, Saudi Arabia called for the founding of an International Center to Combat Terrorism to be based at the UN in 2005. The declared objectives of this Center were to share global intelligence on the whereabouts of terrorists and to share knowhow and expertise on dealing with terrorists to countries lacking both, by way of providing financial resources to beef up counterterrorism methods

48. This has been stated very clearly by, for example, Al-Faisal (2013).

and operations. Saudi Arabia additionally pledged $100 million to the Center on 13 August 2014, with the immediate goal of combating ISIS, militarily, politically, economically and intellectually.[49]

Saudi Arabia has also engaged a variety of programmes domestically to reform and rehabilitate those arrested for crimes of terrorism[50] and has undertaken a "retraining" campaign for *imams* deemed to be extremist.[51] The Grand Mufti and Council of Senior Ulama continuously issues *fatwas* condemning terrorism, extremism, and attacks on civilian populations, as well as a range of violent actions. Reforms have also been introduced to the religious curriculum in public schools, although opinions vary as to how comprehensively this has been done.[52]

At the same time, Saudi Arabia has also exercised leadership in calling for a more comprehensive approach to fighting terrorism, noting that simply rooting out particular terrorist groups or organisations or picking off particular leaders does not address the root causes that led to their creation. Rather than focusing on the symptoms, the Kingdom has demanded "dignity, security and peace" for all people as the cornerstone for a new order in the Middle East.[53]

In addition, Saudi Arabia has called for a more expansive approach to terrorism, noting the Western tendency to focus on Sunni jihadist groups and while ignoring comprehensive what

49. Despite strong Saudi support for this initiative, the Center has not, thus far, fulfilled its objectives, leading to criticism by Saudi Arabia that failure to implement Center objectives led, in part, to the creation of ISIS and other similar groups. This criticism was raised most recently and bluntly by Al-Faisal (2014).

50. The Munasaha programme, begun in 2008 and run by the Interior Ministry under the auspices of Prince Mohammed bin Naif, enjoys a strong global reputation and claims to have graduated more than 3,000 men. For details of the programme's purpose and structure, see Royal Embassy of Saudi Arabia. Initiatives and Actions to Combat Terrorism, posted at: *http://www.sauidembassy.net/files/PDF/Reports/Counterterrorism.pdf*, accessed November 11, 2014.

51. There is significant debate about how comprehensive some of these measures have been, as ongoing concerns about religious textbooks, in particular, continue to surface periodically. At the same time, concerns have been expressed by international human rights organisations with respect to how "extremism" and "terrorist crimes" are defined, as cases have been reported of young men being imprisoned on "terrorist charges" without any known supportive evidence.

52. See, for example, Doumato and Starrett (2006).

53. Reported in Saudi Press Agency (2014).

Saudi Arabia considers to be "Shia terrorist organisations," a label they apply to Hizbullah in Lebanon, the al-Asad regime in Syria, the Houthis of Yemen, and elements within the Iraqi government, particularly former Prime Minister Malaki and his associates, as well as Iran in general. Acknowledging the reality of multiple ideologies among terrorist organisations is, from a Saudi perspective, critical to recognising the multiple threats they represent to global and regional security.

The Jihadist Threats of Syria and ISIS

The greatest security threat and, thus, foreign policy concern for Saudi Arabia today is the rise and expansion—geographically and financially—of ISIS in the shadow of Syria's ongoing civil war that has claimed more than 200,000 lives and displaced more than 3 million people, both internally and as refugees seeking asylum in surrounding countries. The crisis has been described by Saud Al-Faisal as "this century's biggest humanitarian disaster in terms of savageness and crime-committing" (Saudi Press Agency, 2014) and has exponentially fuelled the spread of terrorism and extremism, not only because such groups have found safe haven in Syria, but also because of the rising sense of anger and despair among victims who have lost all semblance of personal security.

Saudi Arabia has consistently denounced Bashar al-Asad's regime for killing its own people and has accused Iran and Hizbullah of sending militias into Syria to support al-Asad, which Saudi Arabia considers to be an unacceptable infringement upon Syrian sovereignty.[54] The bloodshed and carnage among a Muslim majority population is a serious concern for Saudi Arabia in its leadership role within the Muslim world and as a threat to regional stability. Inasmuch as transnational migration has been a reality throughout the history of Middle East, there is a difference between migration undertaken for educational or employment purposes, in which case those migrating are expected to be self-sufficient, and migration that takes place by refugees seeking asylum, whereby they become

54. See, for example, Al-Faisal (2014).

dependents either upon the new state or charitable organisations that are typically overstretched when migrations of this volume take place. Being host to large portions of refugee populations places both logistical and financial strains upon the host countries, and also introduces the potential for political unrest as tensions may rise between host and refugee populations and refugee populations often bring with them political ideas and objectives that can cause unrest among domestic populations. Thus, Saudi concerns about the Syrian crisis are not limited to broader political concerns about regime change and Iranian influence, but also have a practical dimension with respect to the realities that it creates in the lives of both refugees and host countries.[55]

From the beginning, Saudi Arabia called for support to the moderate opposition to al-Asad's government, in keeping with its own foreign policy goals of containing Iranian influence and preventing Russia from gaining a stronghold there (Obaid and Khashoggi, 2013a). In the early days of non-violent protests, there appeared to be a window of opportunity for peaceful regime change. However, Saudi Arabia blames hesitancy on the part of the West, particularly the US, for loss of that opportunity and the rise of a bloody civil war (Sager, 2014). From a Saudi perspective, the failure of the US, UK, and France to effectively intervene in Syria opened a new chapter in global relations—one of American and European military disengagement in the Middle East, due to lack of political will and economic power to unilaterally engage other militaries (Obiad, 2013). That disengagement is expected to lead to regional realignments of sovereign borders and military alliances, as the region looks within, rather than to the outside (namely, to the US or Europe) for security, which is in keeping with Saudi regional policy goals.

Saudi Arabia has repeatedly warned against leaving al-Asad in power and has further made it clear that he cannot be part of the anticipated political solution for Syria. This marks a very different stance from Saudi Arabia's position on, for example, Bahrain, in

55. The burden of managing the economic, political, and financial chaos resulting from the Syrian conflict falls on the GCC in general and Saudi Arabia in particular. See, Obaid and Khashoggi (2013a).

which a mediated, political solution, pursued as national dialogue, between rulers and the demands of the ruled, was supported with the goal of maintaining the rulers intact, albeit in a reformed fashion. In the case of al-Asad, by contrast, the sheer loss of life and livelihood and the particularly brutal military campaign undertaken against civilians has placed him outside of any claim to being a legitimate ruler. Instead, Saudi Arabia supports the unconditional removal of al-Asad and his supporters in favour of the Syrian Coalition Council, which has been recognised by the Arab League, US and major European countries as the legitimate representative of the Syrian people, which it therefore asserts should be leading efforts toward the creation of a national reconciliation government in order to bring stability to Syria (Al-Faisal, 2014).

For Saudi Arabia, ISIS and Syria are inextricably linked as the Saudis hold the al-Asad regime as largely responsible for the circumstances that permitted the creation of ISIS; while, ironically, ISIS is currently the most prominent opponent to the al-Asad regime (Gause, 2014). Saudi Arabia feels that both need to be eliminated, while also recognising that a military solution alone will not resolve the issues. What is really needed is for the Arab states to work together, not only on military cooperation, but also on changing the surrounding context, namely ending the long-standing conflicts and providing comprehensive justice in Syria, Iraq and Palestine.[56]

ISIS has been described as the greatest existential threat to Arab societies and Muslim populations everywhere as it seeks to overtake the states of the Middle East, conquer their territories, and use their resources to attack the US, Europe, Russia and China in order to take control of the world's energy reserves. As the greatest immediate threat is to the Arab world, some analysts are pressuring these countries to step up to the plate to protect themselves (See, for example, Freeman, 2014).The greatest regional challenge to this happening is the fact that many countries are too focused on seeing each other as the enemy, rather than as part of the solution.

---

56. Op-Ed piece in *The Times* by Prince Mohammed bin Nawaf Al Saud, Ambassador to UK, 25 September 2014.

Whatever their differences, both Saudi Arabia and Iran have a vested interest in removing ISIS from the scene as both are existentially threatened by it.[57] Although Saudi Arabia and Iran have different reasons for combatting ISIS, they nevertheless share the common goal of its eradication. Saudi Arabia has thus chosen to engage in *realpolitik*, recognising the importance of including Iran in the ideological battle against ISIS and thereby showing the Saudi capacity for pragmatism over ideological purity where foreign policy is concerned.

In terms of leading regional military action against ISIS, Saudi Arabia has armed insurgents against the al-Asad regime, along with Qatar and Turkey (Nerguizian, 2014). It also brought together regional states in the signing of the Jeddah Communique on 11 September 2014. Saudi Arabia and some other Sunni majority countries have also participated with the US in air strikes against ISIS, but with limited effect. Some analysts have suggested that Muslims, in general, and Saudi Arabia, in particular, must lead the fight against ISIS because only Muslims have the religious and doctrinal credentials to combat the more pervasive challenge presented by ISIS' deviant ideology (Freeman, 2014). Saudi Arabia has put its religious credentials to work in this regard, using ideological counterarguments to combat ISIS, such as by having Saudi religious authorities declare members of ISIS to be apostates and criminals.[58]

---

57. ISIS has declared the goal of removing both governments from power—the Saudi monarchy because of its purported failure to fully, literally and exclusively implement Sharia, and the Iranian government because it is Shii.

58. This is a fairly standard way for Saudi religious authorities to denounce terrorism and extremism, whether of the Al-Qaida or ISIS variety. As non-state actors engaged in military activities, they are subverting the social order and committing criminal acts because they have no legitimate, recognised political authority to carry out such actions. Declaring someone to be a *murtadd* (apostate) is even worse than being a *kafir* (unbeliever) in Saudi eyes because one can be an undeliberate *kafir*, in the sense of not knowing any better, while a *murtadd*, by very nature, is a deliberate rejection of Islam. The Saudis historically have been cautious with respect to use of the term *murtadd*, so its frequent use with respect to ISIS is a strong indicator of the serious nature of ISIS' deviancy, rendering them subverters of Islam, rather than Muslims. Religiously, these are very serious charges and render members of ISIS subject to the death penalty.

Thus, where Syria and ISIS are concerned, Saudi Arabia has moved at multiple levels to declare, influence, and implement its foreign policy objectives, always keeping security at the centre.

Containment of Sectarian and Religious Rivalries[59]

In the aftermath of the US-led invasion of Iraq in 2003 that brought a Shii-dominated government to power, the loss of Egypt as a major Sunni regional stabiliser due to domestic political issues, and the resulting rise of Iran as a now relatively unchecked regional power (due to the loss of Iraq as a counterweight) with a reportedly expansionist policy, Saudi Arabia has been particularly concerned about the impact of sectarian issues affecting regional stability. Saudi Arabia sees Iranian hands behind the destabilisation of countries with Shii majorities, particularly Iraq and Bahrain, as well as those with Shii minorities, including Kuwait, Lebanon and Yemen, at the same time that it lacks a major, stable regional ally, given the relative instability of Lebanon, Egypt and Iraq.[60] The failure to establish a stable government in Iraq, in particular, is held responsible, in Saudi eyes, for creating a safe haven for the expansion and consolidation of terrorist groups, particularly ISIS, as well as for Iranian expansionist ambitions.

Saudi Arabia typically portrays Iran as a regional threat that seeks to place the Shiite minority (roughly 10-15% of the global Muslim population) in a position of authority, which it bolsters through claims of willingness to stand up to the West. Regardless of whether the Iranian threat is a myth or a reality, Saudi Arabia perceives it to be a sufficient reality to drive policymaking, largely from a security perspective, although an ideological dimension is also present. Nowhere was this clearer than in Bahrain during the Arab Spring uprisings,[61] as Saudi Arabia called for the GCC to engage the Peninsula Shield Forces to step in to protect vital strategic infrastructure,

59. For a full overview of the Saudi-Iranian struggle for regional hegemony since the 2003 US-led invasion of Iraq, see Wehrey *et al.* (2009).

60. Gause (2014). For a fuller discussion, see Gause, III, F. Gregory (2011). *Saudi Arabia in the New Middle East*. New York: Council on Foreign Relations.

61. For a comprehensive study of events in Bahrain, including sectarian dynamics, during the Arab Spring, see, Matthiesen (2013).

including oil refineries, airports, seaports, and other economic installations[62]—"a duty that the kingdom will always fulfill."[63]

From the Saudi perspective, the intervention by the GCC was intended to restore a political environment suitable for dialogue—an environment it accused "Shiite theocratic revolutionary movements"[64] working for Iran of destabilising the region (Obaid, 2013). Saudi support for dialogue between the monarchy and opposition was bolstered by a 10-year economic package of $10 billion offered by the GCC and financed mostly by Saudi Arabia. Saudi Arabia has consistently supported the concept of political reconciliation between the government and the opposition, focusing on internal dialogue within Bahrain (namely, trying to push purported Iranian influence out of the process) and following the recommendations of an independent commission that was established to investigate the clashes of 2011. Saudi Arabia has backed the Crown Prince as the central figure for negotiations as part of its broader support for Gulf monarchies in general and has accused the opposition, namely the Wefaq Party, of refusing to negotiate outside of its own terms and of boycotting the elections that are supposed to be representative of Bahraini popular political will. The opposition's refusal to participate in the elections robs them of the legitimacy the government would like for them to have, creating an obstacle to further national reconciliation, which Saudi Arabia supports as the ultimate goal.

The Challenge of Palestine: Ending the Longest-Standing Regional Conflict

Saudi Arabia has been actively involved in attempts to resolve the Israeli-Palestinian conflict since the 1980s, beginning with the September 1982 and September 1983 King Fahd Peace Plan that later (in 2002) became the Arab Peace Initiative. This Initiative offered

62. This was not the first time a collective regional military force was assembled. During the Iran-Iraq war, the GCC formed the Dar al-Jazeerah (Peninsula Shield) to engage in collective self-defense.

63. Al-Faisal (2014a). Despite accusations by some parties that GCC forces confronted protesters, Saudi Arabia insists that no GCC personnel were involved in any actions against protesters.

64. Op-Ed, in *Al -Monitor*, 17 October 2013, authored by Nawaf Obaid.

Israel complete normalisation of relations in exchange for Israel's withdrawal from the Occupied Territories and a just solution for the Palestinian refugee issue, including establishment of a Palestinian state. Saudi Arabia has continued to push this proposed solution forward, most importantly achieving, in 2007, the backing of all Arab states during the Riyadh Arab League Summit. Saudi Arabia later acquired the backing of the Organization of the Islamic Conference (OIC) for the same, expanding supporters to 57 countries. However, despite clearly broad Arab and Islamic support for this proposal, it has not been accepted and Israeli-Palestinian violence has not only continued, but escalated. Much of this violence might have been avoided, from a Saudi perspective, had the Initiative been followed (See for example, Sager, 2014).

On the one hand, Saudi Arabia's position on the issue has remained constant, demanding a two-state solution, justice for displaced Palestinians, right of return for those forced to leave their homes, and an end to Israeli abuse of Palestinian rights, including human and property rights. Saudi Arabia has repeatedly stated that peace for the Palestinians is the only way to reach a comprehensive peace globally. On the other hand, Saudi Arabia is calling to task other countries, particularly the US, and organisations, specifically the UN, for their double standard in dealing with Israel, which Saudi Arabia believes prevents the achievement of international peace and security and perpetuates and expands injustice, the violation of rights, and the spread of conflicts and wars around the world.[65]

To protest these realities and as an indication of its seriousness in insisting that this central issue be comprehensively and justly addressed, despite having been one of the first 50 countries to sign the charter that created the UN on 26 June 1945, Saudi Foreign Minister Saud Al-Faisal cancelled his annual speech to the UN General Assembly in October 2013, followed by Saudi Arabia's rejection of its election to a 2-year seat on the UNSC, a position that it had lobbied to attain, until such time as the Council is "reformed and enabled, effectively and practically, to carry out its duties and responsibilities

65. Remarks made by Al-Faisal, reported in Saudi Press Agency (2014).

in maintaining international peace and security."[66] Saudi Arabia cited failure to reach a just solution to the Palestinian issue after 65 years, inability to create a WMD-free zone in the Middle East, and failure to stop al-Asad's regime from killing its own people as "irrefutable evidence and proof of the inability of the Security Council to carry out its duties and responsibilities" (Saudi Press Agency, 2013). The Saudi Foreign Ministry further accused the Security Council of engaging in double standards and failing to perform its duty and responsibility to preserve international peace and security.

Central to the Saudi vision of resolution is recognition that a ceasefire in current hostilities is not itself the final objective, but should open the door to a fair, comprehensive and constant peace in the Middle East, directed by the Arab Peace Initiative, including the establishment of a viable, independent Palestinian state with East Jerusalem as its capitol. Current realities of ongoing Israeli incursions into East Jerusalem, including seizure of Palestinian homes, businesses, and land, and the closure of the Al-Aqsa Mosque complex[67] to visitors,[68] are further complicating attempts to provide a just solution, as the creation of "facts on the ground" make right of return even more challenging.

Saudi Arabia has further continually warned that this conflict will continue to fuel terrorism and extremism as long as it exists because of the blatant oppression of the civilian Palestinian population and accompanying denial of both Palestinian identity and statehood. It is these circumstances that continue to fuel terrorist dreams and actions. Military responses alone will never be sufficient to end terrorism and extremism; as long as the circumstances that allow them to incubate and create perceptions of legitimacy because

66. Ibid.

67. This is considered the third holiest site in Islam because it is believed to be the location from which the Prophet Muhammad ascended into Heaven during his mystical Night Journey, making Jerusalem a sacred site for Muslims. The site on which the mosque is located is also home to the Temple Mount, the most sacred site to Jews, rendering sovereignty over the location a sensitive and often contentious issue.

68. These developments occurred in late October 2014 and continued into November 2014. Tensions over control of the site continue to fuel tension and clashes between Israeli security forces and Palestinians, feeding fears of a new Palestinian Intifada.

a struggle against clear injustice and oppression exists, so will terrorism. Thus, from a Saudi perspective, attention needs to be given not just to the military actions of terrorist organisations, but, more critically, to the core issues, contexts, and collective frustrations that led to their creation in the first place.[69]

At the same time, this time around, the resurgence of Palestinian-Israeli violence has not had the same domestic impact in Saudi Arabia that it has had in the past. This is not because the issue has disappeared or is no longer of concern—quite the opposite—but is likely due to the emergence of other regional realities, namely ISIS and the Iranian nuclear programme, that present a more immediate existential threat to Saudi Arabia than Palestine does at the moment (Gause, 2014). At the same time, domestic issues, including the youth bulge, ongoing issues with unemployment, inevitable regime change given the age and health circumstances of the senior royals, and internal tensions over changing parameters of the role of religion in the public sphere and gender issues, also seem to be of higher priority. In other words, the difference at this point is the presence of multiple other variables in the foreign policy equation, the very existence of which render foreign policymaking ever more challenging.

Protection of Saudi Arabia's Borders

The final security issue Saudi Arabia has to address increasingly today is its ability to protect its borders and, thus, its own people, making recognition and enforcement of borders a foreign policy objective. Although ISIS has made a few incursions across the Saudi border, the country's biggest concern lies with Yemen to the south.

Despite unification in 2000, Yemen has a long history of fragmentation and tribal warfare, which has led Saudi Arabia to maintain relations at multiple levels, including tribal figures, regional politicians, and the central government. Political fragmentation combined with a weak central state incapable of controlling vast, mountainous territories outside of the major cities, presented an opportunity during the 1990s and 2000s for terrorist groups,

69. See, for example, Al-Faisal (2014).

including, ultimately, Al-Qaida of the Arabian Peninsula (AQAP) to take root and train (Al-Faisal, 2013). Despite decades of Saudi financial and economic support for the Yemeni people, poverty remains rampant and the borders between Yemen and Saudi Arabia are not sufficiently well-protected to prevent refugees and Al-Qaida terrorists alike from crossing into Saudi Arabia. Added into that already volatile situation were the events of the Arab Spring, which took root in Yemen.

Initially, Saudi Arabia supported President Ali Abdullah Saleh's regime as a matter of promoting regional stability. However, as time went on, the revolution became less about unemployment, the economy and curbing government corruption, and more about the resignation of Saleh. Rising demonstrations, clashes and violence led to concerns about insecurity spilling out of Yemen's borders and the potential for terrorist groups, like Al-Qaida of the Arabian Peninsula, to take advantage of the chaos so as to seek a stronger hold for themselves. Saudi Arabia thus shifted from supporting Saleh to working on a transition plan to remove him from power in exchange for immunity, marking a different approach than had been taken in Bahrain or Egypt. However, Saleh's refusal to step down ultimately resulted in Saudi Arabia pushing him to sign an agreement allowing a unity government to come to power (Obaid, 2013). Much of Saudi Arabia's policy was driven by the need to protect its borders from both refugees and terrorists.

Post-Arab Spring, Saudi Arabia is particularly concerned by the Houthi Shii sect in the north, which it claims is receiving both arms and financing from Iran in opposition to the central government (Al-Faisal, 2014a). To counter Houthi and Iranian influence, Saudi Arabia has strongly encouraged and supported national dialogue as a means of expanding the power of the central government and sharing revenues between different regions, particularly through the Peace and Partnership Agreement concluded on 21 September 2014, which was intended to end violence and in-fighting in favour of resuming development and building. Saudi Arabia has repeatedly accused the Houthis of failing to abide by the agreement, particularly where security issues are concerned (Reported in Saudi Press Agency,

2014). Saudi Arabia recognises a clear need for development in Yemen, but believes it cannot occur without guarantees of security for the country)—a condition that would require the elimination of what Saudi Arabia believes is Iranian influence through the Houthis (SUSRIS, 2014a)—and greater attention to border security.

The Way Forward in a Globalising World

Saudi Arabia clearly faces many foreign policy challenges, as well as opportunities, today. First, the Saudi monarchy finds itself more accountable than in the past to public opinion within Saudi Arabia and also more broadly in the Islamic world with respect to conflicts having an impact on Muslims. If Saudi Arabia continues to claim to be a Muslim leader, there is tremendous accompanying pressure to be responsive, which means having to deliver, rather than just talk about, issues, particularly hot-button topics, such as Palestine and human rights, particularly where expatriate Muslim workers are concerned. There is a global expectation for Saudi action and money to be put behind its words. Failure to do so comes at the price of its perceived legitimacy, pressuring Saudi Arabia to take a more activist stance on the global stage, while also building in support for the same. Responsiveness is also applicable on the global stage as Saudi Arabia has been under increasing pressure to address its record on human rights issues, both in terms of investigating charges of human rights abuses and in terms of protecting the expatriate population from abuse by employers, and women's status, particularly with respect to family law and employment.[70]

Secondly, Saudi Arabia is faced with the challenge of institutionalising its policymaking, particularly as succession issues loom. Although, for a long time, Saudi foreign policy was viewed as the product of a few key players at the top of the royal family (namely, the King and the Foreign Minister), the reality today is one of looking to long-term stability—a central objective of Saudi foreign policy—

70. Human Rights Watch has issued a serious of reports addressing these issues in detail. See, for example, Human Rights Watch (2008) and Human Rights Watch (2013).

which, given the multiple variables and identities involved in foreign policymaking, requires establishing institutions for statecraft.

Third, Saudi Arabia finds itself in a unique moment of opportunity, both regionally and internationally, as the largest and most stable Sunni country in the MENA region at the same time that it finds itself in rivalry with other countries for regional hegemony, most importantly, Iran and Qatar. Although the rivalries are of different types—Sunni *versus* Shii, long-term regional issues *versus* short-term competition over use of financial resources to purchase and project (through the media) influence in other countries and an image of Islamic leadership—the contemporary reality of weak states in Iraq (evidenced by ongoing sectarian rivalries and the foundation of ISIS) and Afghanistan (evidenced by political fragmentation and economic weakness), as well as fragile (Egypt) and failed (Yemen, Syria) states, has opened the door to a variety of players in the quest for power. All represent an immediate security threat to Saudi Arabia, so it is expected that security will remain the main driver of Saudi foreign policy for the future, particularly because some of these groups have called for an end to the Al Saud. Saudi Arabia also faces a credibility gap, as it has strongly and repeatedly denounced ISIS and its atrocities, but has yet to take significant, systematic action to dismantle it, outside of financing to and some arming of rebels and participation in air strikes against ISIS targets. With respect to the more complex challenge of debunking ISIS ideology, the major work has been engaged by Jordan, with only very minimal Saudi participation.[71] A variety of Saudi *shaykhs* and scholars have denounced ISIS and its ideology, but only in terms of condemnation, rather than detailed exegesis.

Finally, Saudi Arabia has offered strong indications of its intent to break with its past pattern of close parallel to US foreign policy, although military and business relations remain strong. Saudi Arabia

---

71. Specifically, the Open Letter to Al-Baghdadi, which was initially signed by 126 Islamic scholars from around the world, only one of whom was Saudi-Seyyed Abdullah Fadaaq, who is a self-described Shafii and Sufi scholar in the Hijaz. He is neither on the Council of Senior Ulama nor on the Permanent Committee of Ifta, so is not representative of the Saudi religious establishment.

is increasingly diversifying its pool of business partners and foreign investments, particularly with China, India, Russia and Europe. It has also made both official and unofficial statements, distancing Saudi policy from US policy, particularly on the issue of Israel/Palestine, suggesting that Saudi Arabia will continue to pursue pragmatic policies in keeping with its projected objectives of security, stability and prosperity in the years to come.

References

Al-Fahad, Abdulaziz (2012). "Globalization and its Discontents", *ForeignPolicy.com.* Middle East Channel blog. 18 September.

Al-Faisal, Turki (2014). "Keynote Address", delivered by HRH Prince at 23rd Arab-US Policymakers Conference *Framing and Charting the Region's Issues, Interests, Challenges, and Opportunities: Implications for Arab and US Policies.* National Council on US-Arab Relations. 28 October. Published by *SUSRIS*, 1 November.

———. (2014a). "New Regional Conditions: A Saudi View", Keynote Speech delivered HRH Prince, Chariman, King Faisal Center for Research & Islamic Studies at The College of William and Mary, Williamsburg, VA. 11 March.

———. (2013). *Saudi Arabia's New Foreign Policy Doctrine in the Aftermath of the Arab Awakening.* Speech delivered at Belfer Center for Science & International Affairs, John F. Kennedy School of Government, Harvard University. 25 April.

———. (2011). *A Saudi National Security Doctrine for the Next Decade.* Remarks given at Royal Air Force Molesworth, UK. 8 June.

———. (2011a). *A Tour D'Horizon of the Saudi Political Seas.* Speech delivered at World Affairs Council of Washington, DC at the National Press Club. 15 November.

Al-Mulhim, Abdulateef (2014). "Defending Our Borders", *Arab News*, 1 October.

Alterman, Jon B. (2010). "The Real Threat in the Persian Gulf", in *Middle East Notes and Comment.* CSIS. 19 June.

Anthony, John Duke (2011). "Saudi Arabian Ambassadors to America in Context: The Diplomatic and Geopolitical Lives of Ambassadors Prince Bandar, Prince Turki, and Adel Al-Jubeir," *SUSRIS*, December 5.

———. (2013). *Saudi Arabia-U.S. Relations Reconsidered.* Address to National Council on US-Arab Relations. 31 October.

Bianchi, Robert R. (2004). *Guests of God: Pilgrimage and Politics in the Islamic World.* New York: Oxford University Press.

Bronson, Rachel (2006). *Thicker Than Oil: America's Uneasy Partnership with Saudi Arabia.* New York: Oxford University Press.

Cole, Juan (2014). *The New Arabs: How the Millennial Generation is Changing the Middle East.* New York: Simon & Schuster.

Cordesman, Anthony H. (2013). "Saudi Arabia and the Arab 'Frontline' States", *SUSRIS.* 4 November.

Cordesman, Anthony H. and Nawaf Obaid (2005). *National Security in Saudi Arabia: Threats, Responses, and Challenges.* Santa Monica, CA: Praeger Security International.

DeLong-Bas, Natana J. (2008). *Wahhabi Islam: From Revival and Reform to Global Jihad*. Revised edition. New York: Oxford University Press.

Determann, Jörg Matthias (2014). *Historiography in Saudi Arabia: Globalizaion and the State in the Middle East*. London: I.B. Tauris.

Doumato, Eleanor and Gregory Starrett (ed.) (2006). *Teaching Islam: Textbooks and Religion in the Middle East*. Boulder, CO: Lynne Rienner Publishers.

Fatany, Samar (2013). *Modernizing Saudi Arabia*. CreateSpace Independent Publishing Platform. p.14.

Freeman, Jr., Ambassador Chas W. (2014). "The Collapse of Order in the Middle East," Remarks to the 23rd Annual Arab-U.S. Policymakers Conference. 28 October. Published in *SUSRIS*, 31 October 31.

Gause III, F. Gregory (2014). "Threats and Neighbors, Choosing Lesser and Greater Evils: A Conversation with F. Gregory Gause, III", *SUSRIS*, 19 August.

———. (2011). *Saudi Arabia in the New Middle East*. New York: Council on Foreign Relations.

———. (2012). "Confronting a 'New Middle East': A Conversation with F. Gregory Gause", *SUSRIS* interview, 4 January.

———. (2009). *The International Relations of the Persian Gulf*. New York: Cambridge University Press.

Hegghammer, Thomas (2010). *Jihad in Saudi Arabia: Violence and Pan-Islamism since 1979*. New York: Cambridge University Press.

Holt, Maria and Haifaa Jawad (2013). *Women, Islam and Resistance in the Arab World*. Boulder, CO & London: Lynne Rienner Publishers. pp.115-16.

Human Rights Watch (2008). "Perpetual Minors: Human Rights Abuses Stemming from Male Guardianship and Sex Segregation in Saudi Arabia", *Human Rights Watch*, 19 April posted at: *http://www.hrw.org/print/reports/2008/04/19/perpetual-minors*

———. (2013). "Challenging the Red Lines: Stories of Rights Activists in Saudi Arabia", *Human Rights Watch*, 18 December posted at: *www.hrw.org/reports/2013/12/18/challenging-red-lines*

Ibrahim, Fouad (2006). *The Shi'is of Saudi Arabia*. London: Saqi.

Juhany, Uwaidah M. Al (2002). *Najd Before the Salafi Reform Movement: Social, Political and Religious Conditions During the Three Centuries Preceding the Rise of the Saudi State*. Reading, UK: Ithaca Press in association with the King Abdul Aziz Foundation for Research and Archives, KSA.

Karasik, Theodore (2014). "Focus KSA: Special—Dr. Theodore Karasik Interview—Region in Crisis", *SUSRIS*, 22 August.

Lacey, Robert (2011). "Another Look Inside the Kingdom: A Conversation with Robert Lacey", *SUSRIS*, 28 October.

Lacroix, Stéphane (2011). *Awakening Islam: The Politics of Religious Dissent in Contemporary Saudi Arabia*. Trans. George Holoch. Cambridge, MA: Harvard University Press.

Lippmann, Thomas W. (2012). *Saudi Arabia on the Edge: The Uncertain Future of an American Ally*. Dulles, VA: Potomac Books.

Mabon, Simon (2013). *Saudi Arabia and Iran: Soft Power Rivalry in the Middle East*. London: I.B. Tauris.

Matthiesen, Toby (2013). *Sectarian Gulf: Bahrain, Saudi Arabia, and the Arab Spring That Wasn't*. Stanford, CA: Stanford University Press.

Nerguizian, Aram (2014). "The Struggle for the Levant: Geopolitical Battles and the Quest for Stability", Posted at *http://csis.org/publication/struggle-levant-geopolitical-battles-and-quest-*

stability on 18 September.

Nonneman, Gerd (2001). "Saudi-European Relations 1902-2001: A Pragmatic Quest for Relative Autonomy", *International Affairs* 77(3): 631-61.

Obaid, Nawaf (2011). "'Conspicuously Quiet' in Saudi Arabia", *The Washington Post*, 9 March.

———. (2012). *Saudi Arabia: The Kingdom in a Post "Arab-Spring" Environment.* Presentation prepared under the auspices of the King Faisal Center for Research & Islamic Studies, Riyadh, Saudi Arabia. February.

———. (2013). "Saudi Arabia Shifts to More Activist Foreign Policy Doctrine", *Al-Monitor.com*, 17 October.

Obaid, Nawaf and Jamal Khashoggi (2013). "Arab D-Day", *New York Times*, 8 September.

———. (2013a). "Syria Tragedy a Turning Point for West", *CNN.com.* 16 September.

Potter, Lawrence G. (ed.) (2014). *Sectarian Politics in the Persian Gulf.* New York: Oxford University Press.

Sager, Abdulaziz (2014). "Price of Not Heeding Kingdom's Advice," *Arab News*, 11 September.

Saudi Press Agency (2014). "Prince Saud Al-Faisal: Kingdom of Saudi Arabia is Keen to Spare No Effort to Achieve the World Community's Collective Objectives under UN Umbrella", *Saudi Press Agency*, 28 September.

———. (2014a). "UN Week: Prince Saud Al Faisal Speech to the Global Counter Terrorism Forum", *Saudi Press Agency*. 23 September.

———. (2013). "Foreign Ministry Makes Statement on Saudi Arabia's Apology for Not Accepting Security Council Membership", *Saudi Press Agency*, 18 October.

SUSRIS (2011). "Perspective of a Shura Council Member: A Conversation with Eng. Usamah al-Kurdi, Part 1—The 'Arab Spring' and Saudi Arabia", *SUSRIS*, 25 April.

———. (2013). "New Details on Social Media in Saudi Arabia", *SUSRIS*, 12 January.

———. (2014). "Deputy Crown Prince Muqrin Outlines Priorities in SPA Interview", *SUSRIS*, April 25.

———. (2014a). "Focus KSA: Arabian Gulf & Regional Challenges Conference", Interview with Mark Katz. SUSRIS. 23 September.

Trofimov, Yaroslav (2007). *The Siege of Mecca: The Forgotten Uprising in Islam's Holiest Shrine and the Birth of Al Qaeda*. New York: Doubleday.

Wehrey, Frederic (2013). *Sectarian Politics in the Gulf: From the Iraq War to the Arab Uprisings*. New York: Columbia University Press.

Wehrey, Frederic Theodore W. Karasik, Alireza Nader, Jeremy Ghez and Lydia Hansell (2009). *Saudi-Iranian Relations Since the Fall of Sadadm: Rivalry, Cooperation, and Implications for U.S. Policy*. Santa Monica, CA: The RAND Corporation.

Westphal, Ambassador Joseph (2014). "Framing and Charting the Region's Issues, Interests, Challenges, and Opportunities: Implications for Arab and U.S. Policies", Luncheon *Keynote Address* to 23rd Arab-US Policymakers Conference and National Council on US-Arab Relations. Washington, DC. 29 October.

12

YOAV TENENBAUM

Israel's Foreign Policy

Foreign Policy Decision-Making Process in Israel

Henry Kissinger is widely quoted as having said that Israel has no foreign policy, only a domestic policy. The irony of Kissinger's remark notwithstanding, it reflects the important role that domestic factors play in shaping of the Israeli foreign policy. To be sure, an understanding of the role played by the internal dimension in shaping foreign policy is particularly called for when dealing with liberal democracies, Israel included. The Realist and Neo-Realist Schools of international relations and their relegation of domestic factors to a secondary role in shaping of the foreign policy would fail to explain the complexities entailed in Israel's foreign policy decision-making process.

Suffice it to witness the constant endeavours by Prime Minister, Benjamin Netanyahu, to strike a delicate balance between the demands of his domestic constituencies and the expectations of the international community in order to be able to appreciate the importance of the domestic dimension while formulating Israeli foreign policy.[1]

Of course, Kissinger may have referred primarily, even though doubtless not exclusively, to the internal political squabbles which are part and parcel of the decision-making process in Israel, foreign policy being no exception. After all, back in the 1970s, Kissinger, as Secretary of State, had to deal with the consequences of intense political rivalries between the then Israeli Prime Minister, Itzhak

1. See, subsequent discussion of Netanyahu's Bar Ilan Speech, in which, for the first time, he expressed his readiness to accept a Palestinian state in the context of final peace agreement with Israel.

Rabin, and his Defence Minister, Shimon Peres, and, to a lesser extent, between each of them and Foreign Minister Igal Alon.

Graham Allison's Governmental Politics Model may partially explain this phenomenon, which, it has to be stressed, has characterised Israeli foreign policy decision-making process, to a greater or lesser extent, since 1948.[2]

Israel's political system, which, on the one hand, reflects the diversity of Israeli society, has produced, on the other hand, a fragmentation of political parties vying for influence. Foreign policy is thus shaped not only on the basis of national interests and strongly held values, but also by domestic political considerations.

Israel's political system itself is influenced by extra-parliamentary forces, such as the Israeli inhabitants in the West Bank (Judea and Samaria) or the Peace Now Movement, particularly in the late 1970s and the 1980s.

Although parliamentary in form, Israeli democracy is vibrant in a manner reminiscent somewhat more of a direct rather than a representative democracy. A humorous anecdotal remark attributed to the late Gold Meir, who held the post of Foreign Minister and subsequently Prime Minister, may serve to stress this point. In a meeting at the White House with then US President Richard Nixon, the latter posed the following rhetorical question: "Mrs. Meir, do you know how difficult it is to be the president of a country of two hundred million people?" Golda Meir retorted: "Mr. President, do you know how difficult it is to be the prime minister of a country of three million prime ministers?"

Domestic politics in Israel is a constraint on foreign policymaking, which compels decision makers to be aware of the inner limits delineated by it. Further, it constitutes an important input into the decision-making process, which may serve either as a break or as an accelerator, depending on the issue concerned and the prevailing circumstances.

For instance, even a dovish government in Israel would most probably refuse to accept any final accord with the Palestinian

---

2. For an analysis of Allison's model, see Allison and Zelikow (1999).

Authority, which would not leave most Israeli inhabitants (rather than most Israeli settlements) within Israeli sovereign territory. On the other hand, even a hawkish prime minister would be aware that accepting a final peace settlement based on the creation of a Palestinian state and the withdrawal of Israeli military forces from most of the West Bank (Judea and Samaria) would elicit the support of most Israeli citizens.

The first and most intense political rivalry which was caused by different foreign policy outlooks saw Israel's first Prime Minister, David Ben-Gurion, and his Foreign Minister, Moshe Sharett, in a constant political struggle, which culminated in Sharett's resignation in 1956. Sharett was more sensitive to international opinion than Ben Gurion. He thought that foreign policy ought to be a central feature of Israeli national security policy, rather than a secondary element in it. The differences between the two was manifested in the exchange between them, whereby Ben Gurion argued that it didn't matter what the Gentiles said, but rather what the Jews did; to which Sharett retorted that what mattered was not so much what the Gentiles said, but rather what they did, implying that Ben Gurion's dictum was only half-true.

The differences between Sharett and Ben Gurion were also manifested in their respective attitude to the United Nations (UN) Organisation (UNO). Sharett never agreed with Ben Gurion's dismissive utterance *UM SHMUM* (A derogatory Hebrew phrase implying that the UN counted for little and merited scant respect by Israel).

Rhetoric apart, to claim that Ben Gurion was unaware of the importance of the diplomatic dimension in Israel's national security strategy would be as simplistic as contending that Sharett was too eager to please his international interlocutors. After all, it was Ben Gurion who supported the UN Partition Plan of 1947, and even the more modest Partition Plan proposed by the Peel Commission in 1937-38.

Further, Ben Gurion was acutely conscious of the importance of having a major power support, Israel, both diplomatically and militarily. On the other hand, Sharett could be very firm when dealing with foreign diplomats as when he warned them, following Israel's move of its Foreign Ministry from Tel Aviv to Jerusalem in 1953, that should they refuse to meet with him in Jerusalem, they would essentially become as effective as tourists with diplomatic immunity (Sharett, 1978). Moreover, Sharett did not believe that peace with the Arab World was possible no matter how forthcoming Israel would be towards it. He thought that peace might be possible perhaps within 10 to 30 years. He urged moderation to elicit the support of Israel's friends in the international system, rather than as a means to achieve peace with the Arabs. He was less optimistic than Ben Gurion on the chances of attaining peace, but thought that Israel could moderate the conflict by avoiding aggressive retaliatory military attacks.[3]

Incidentally, he did not oppose retaliatory military attacks following terrorist attacks on Israeli civilians, but thought these should be measured and undertaken always sensitive to Israel's wider international interests. Indeed, Sharett agreed with Ben Gurion that, in the wake of the Holocaust and in the light of the persecutions that Jews had to endure, Israel could not afford not to retaliate when attacked. The sense of vulnerability felt by Israeli citizens might increase to dangerous levels. There was a domestic psychological dimension which rendered Israeli retaliation necessary. The difference, then, between Ben Gurion and Sharett on this issue was one of tactics and proportions, rather than principle.

In a sense, this conceptual difference between the "hawks" and the "doves" or, as they were known during the 1950s, between the "activists" and "moderates," was to characterise the Israeli national security debate both outside and within government. On the whole, the Foreign Ministry has tended to follow the moderate line whereas the Defence Establishment has been inclined to pursue a more activist policy.

The increasingly limited role played by the Foreign Ministry in the shaping of Israeli foreign policy has been a source of controversy and criticism. Some notable academics have bemoaned the process

3. See, for instance, *Sharett and His Legacy*, "Israel and the Arabs—War and Peace: Some Reflections on the Years 1947-1957 by Moshe Sharett, Extracts from an address at Beit Berl delivered in October 1957", *http://www.sharett.org.il/English/war-and-peace.htm*

of marginalisation of the Foreign Ministry from the decision-making process.[4] In a country in which the military dimension of national security policy takes precedence over the diplomatic and political dimensions, the input of the defence establishment is more pronounced than that of the Foreign Ministry. Further, the Prime Minister's Office (PMO) has centralised, if not altogether monopolised, the shaping of foreign policy with regard to Israel's relations with the US, its principal ally, and the peace process with the Arab World. Indeed, other crucial policy matters such as Iran's nuclear programme are also mainly within the purview of the PMO. Thus, Israeli foreign policy on the major, strategic issues is formulated generally outside the province of the Foreign Ministry.

Although such criticism is warranted to some extent, one should bear in mind that the multifaceted relationship with the US is handled by various institutional organs, with the Foreign Ministry having an important role in its day-to-day management. Thus, although major decisions in this regard are taken at the PMO, other less prominent matters are decided at the diplomatic level. To claim that the Foreign Ministry is excluded from the shaping of policy towards the US would thus be only partially right.

With regard to the peace process with Israel's Arab neighbours, the Foreign Ministry has a less visible role, no doubt, although it can't be said to be totally relegated from the decision-making process. The same would apply to Iran's nuclear programme. One should be careful to distinguish in this context between two simple but crucial questions: Who takes the decisions? How are those decisions taken? On major issues pertaining to Israel's policy towards the US and in the Middle East, generally decisions are taken either by the Prime Minister or with his direct and active participation. However, the input of the Foreign Ministry in the decision-making process could not be dismissed out of hand without reliable information. Considering that sensitive documents are not released to the public for many years after the events, one could not categorically be able to

4. See, for instance, Klieman (2013). For the perspective of an academic who served for many years in the Israeli Foreign Ministry, including as its Director General, see Liel (2014).

affirm that the Foreign Ministry has no input in the decision-making process.

To be sure, the role of the Foreign Ministry in the decision-making process depends also on the Foreign Minister and his or her relationship with the Prime Minister. Thus, for instance, Moshe Dayan was a very influential Foreign Minister, serving under Prime Minister Menachem Begin, at least until the peace agreement with Egypt in March 1979. The Foreign Ministry under his stewardship had an active role in the shaping of Israeli Foreign Policy. The same could be said about Abba Eban between 1966 and 1969, when he served as Foreign Minister under Prime Minister Levy Eshkol. Abba Eban was directly involved in formulating and implementing Israeli foreign policy; the Foreign Ministry under his leadership was active in the diplomacy conducted by Israel both prior to and in the wake of the Six Day War of 1967.

Moshe Sharett, as the first Foreign Minister of Israel, had a central role in establishing the Israeli Foreign Ministry and in enlisting the best and the brightest to work for it. Although, as previously stated, his relationship with the Prime Minister was far from being harmonious he struggled politically to enlist adherents within the government for his moderate line, winning a few battles in Cabinet against Ben Gurion. During those years, Israel had such distinguished and capable diplomats as Abba Eban, who served as Ambassador to Washington and to the UN, and Eliahu Elath, who was accredited as Ambassador in London. A former Oxford academic, Walter Eytan, was the first Director General of the Foreign Ministry. He was the architect of Israel's diplomatic corps. Later on, he would serve for 11 years as Ambassador in Paris. The Foreign Ministry was both visible and active, if not always significantly influential in determining Israel's policy on the major, strategic issues.

To be sure, the relegation of the Foreign Ministry to a secondary role in the national security decision-making process is bemoaned by the Winograd Commission, which was established by the Israeli government in the wake of the Second Lebanon War in 2007. In its recommendations, the Commission calls for the "Full incorporation of the Ministry of Foreign Affairs (2007) in security decisions with political and diplomatic aspects."[5]

Incidentally, as a result of the recommendations submitted by the Winograd Commission, an agreement was signed between the Israeli Defence Force and the Foreign Ministry aimed at providing the latter with raw intelligence material necessary for its intelligence and political analyses (Ravid, 2007a).

Indeed, the Director General of the Foreign Ministry when the Winograd Commission published its findings and recommendations, Aharon Abramovitch, proudly stated that, as a result of the Second Lebanon War and the Winograd Commission, "the ministry is now increasingly involved in the diplomatic-security decision making process." He went on to elaborate:

> The ministry is involved in this process since the stage of the preparations for cabinet discussions, the preparation of position papers, discussions at the National Security Council, and taking an active part in the cabinet meetings. Our contribution has also grown significantly in terms of implementing the decisions.

However, some Foreign Ministry officials reacted in a critical vein to Abramovitch's words, saying that "Ambramovich is priding himself with achievements which never existed. He is being inaccurate and preparing the ground for the next steps" (Nahmias, 2007).

The conclusions of the Winograd Commission following the Second Lebanon War reflected a growing awareness in Israel that shaping national security policy requires a coordinated, coherent effort in which the diplomatic dimension, and the input of the Foreign Ministry, is given a prominent role. Indeed, many years previous to the publication of the Winograd Commission Report, the Agranat Commission, which was set up in the wake of the Yom Kippur War of 1973, urged the Israeli government to strengthen the Research Department of the Israeli Foreign Ministry so as to accord it, among other things, a more pronounced role in the decision-making process on national security matters (Knesset Website, 2008).

5. On the Foreign Ministry's reactions to the findings and recommendations of the Winograd Commission, see Ravid (2007).

Landmarks in Israeli Foreign Policy since 1967

On the 29 November 1947, the General Assembly of the UN endorsed a partition plan entailing the establishment of a Jewish state and an Arab state in what was then Mandatory Palestine. The Arab leaders rejected the plan as they were opposed to the establishment of a Jewish state in any part of Mandatory Palestine. The Jewish leaders, notwithstanding their reservations, decided to accept it. As a result, a series of attacks by Palestinian Arabs against the Jewish population evolved into a major military confrontation between the two sides.

Following the declaration of independence by David Ben Gurion, who was to become the first Prime Minister of Israel, the surrounding Arab states joined the Palestinian Arabs in a war aimed at thwarting the establishment of the State of Israel. The war ended in 1949, with heavy casualties in both sides. One per cent of the Jewish population in Palestine in those years, i.e., around six thousand people, died during the war. The Armistice Lines agreed upon by Israel and its Arab neighbours left the newly established Jewish state in control of a larger portion of territory than originally allotted to it by the UN partition plan, including the western part of Jerusalem, which would remain divided with Jordan until the end of the Six Day War in June 1967.

Notwithstanding the Armistice Agreements signed with Israel, the Arab countries refused to engage in peace negotiations with Israel, let alone recognise it as a sovereign state. To be sure, Jordan's king, Abdullah, did negotiate with Israel, in secret, in order to reach a final peace agreement with it. However, his assassination on 20 April 1951 by a Palestinian Arab in Jerusalem put an end to those negotiations.

Israel's aspiration to be recognised by its Arab neighbours would be dashed for many years to come. The first country to extend official recognition to Israel would be Egypt, but this would be only 30 years after the Armistice Agreements. Israel would attempt thereafter to concentrate on internal economic development and on eliciting external diplomatic and military support aimed at offsetting the all-out boycott imposed by the Arab world against it.

The establishment of the State of Israel was due to a combination of dire need, international support and remarkable organisation. Following centuries of persecution and pogroms, which culminated in the Holocaust, the need for a sovereign Jewish state was deemed to be obvious, not an option to be countenanced. In the wake of the Holocaust, a convergence of Jewish need and international support created a propitious diplomatic environment for the creation of such a state. To be sure, the Zionist cause was based on an uninterrupted historical link between the Jewish people and the Land of Israel. In addition, Zionist leaders argued that their case was also founded on international law. The Balfour Declaration of the 2 November 1917, which committed the British government to see with favour the establishment of a Jewish national home in Palestine, and the San Remo Conference of April 1920, in which the Allies confirmed the pledge contained in the Balfour Declaration, were two important legal foundations upon which their case relied. The UN partition plan of 1947 and the subsequent invitation for Israel to be a full member of the UN sealed the case for a Jewish state.

UN Security Council (UNSC) Resolution 242

UNSC Resolution was adopted in the wake of the Six Day War of June 1967, during which Israel captured the Sinai Peninsula and the Gaza Strip from Egypt, the West Bank (Judea and Samaria) and East Jerusalem from Jordan and the Golan Heights from Syria.[6]

Every peace agreement (including framework agreements for peace, as well as interim accords) between Israel and its Arab neighbours makes direct and explicit reference to Resolution 242 as the legal cornerstone upon which it is based.

The Camp David Accords between Israel and Egypt of September 1978 and the Peace Agreement signed by both countries in March 1979 were founded on Resolution 242; which was also mentioned as the basis for the Oslo Accords between Israel and the Palestinian Liberation Organization (PLO) of September 1993. Resolution 242

6. See full text of UN Security Council Resolution in *http://unispal.un.org/UNISPAL.NSF/0/7D35E1F729DF491C85256EE700686136*

was referred to as the legal basis of the peace agreement, which was signed by Israel and Jordan in October 1994.

Resolution 242 is the only UNSC resolution on the pacific resolution of the Arab-Israeli conflict which has been accepted by both Israel and its Arab neighbours.

Israel, Egypt and Jordan endorsed Resolution 242 already in November 1967. Syria refused to follow suit until 1973. Following the Yom Kippur War of October 1973, the Syrians adopted UNSC Resolution 338, which called on the warring sides to negotiate peace on the basis of UNSC Resolution 242, thus endorsing it as the basis for peace.

Indeed, UNSC Resolution 338 is usually mentioned in official documents, alongside UNSC Resolution 242, as the basis for peace between Israel and its Arab neighbours.[7]

The PLO refused, for many years, to endorse Resolution 242 as it did not make any explicit reference to the Palestinian Arabs as a separate entity.

To be sure, there is a general reference in Resolution 242 to "achieving a just settlement of the refugee problem," which may be interpreted as alluding to Palestinian Arab refugees (as well as to Jewish refugees from Arab countries). However, apart from that, the Palestinian Arabs as a separate factor in the conflict are not specifically mentioned in Resolution 242.

Still, as already mentioned, the Oslo Accords between Israel and the PLO were based on Resolution 242. Thus, the PLO and the Palestinian Authority, which was established in the wake of the Oslo Accords of September 1993, have recognised Resolution 242 as a basis for peace.

UNSC Resolution 242 was not adopted under Chapter VII of the UN charter, which would have been unequivocally binding, having been adopted in the light of a situation deemed to be a "threat to the peace, breaches of the peace and acts of aggression." Resolution 242 was endorsed under Chapter VI of the UN charter, which obtains in

7. See full text of UN Security Council Resolution in *http://avalon.law.yale.edu/20th_century/un338.asp*

cases related to the "pacific resolution of disputes." However, having been adopted by both sides to the conflict, it could be said to be binding, albeit in a consensual, rather than an enforced, manner.[8]

It should be noted that, although UNSC Resolution 242 has been accepted by both sides to the Arab-Israeli conflict, Israel and its Arab neighbours have accorded it a different interpretation.

For instance, Resolution 242 calls on Israeli armed forces to withdraw "from territories occupied in the recent conflict."

The Arab side has consistently argued that Israel was obliged under the terms of Resolution 242 to withdraw completely to the lines prevailing prior to the outbreak of the Six Day War of June 1967. In other words, according to this interpretation, Israel must return to the territorial status quo ante. Israel, on the other hand, has contended that Resolution 242 speaks for itself. Israel is not requested to withdraw from all the territories, but from "territories." The absence of the article 'the' or of the word 'all' preceding the term "territories" is not accidental, but a clear allusion to the fact that the drafters foresaw a withdrawal of Israeli armed forces to an unspecified line that might be different from the one existing prior to the Six Day War. There was certainly no obligation to withdraw fully to the boundaries existing before the War, which, anyway, were Armistice Lines and not final and mutually-agreed borders.

This particular phrase has been a bone of contention between the two sides. A further interpretative dispute between the Israelis and the Arabs and their respective supporters for many a year has been over whether Resolution 242 calls on Israel to withdraw unilaterally or only in the framework of a peace agreement with its Arab neighbours.

Indeed, the Arab side and many a political and legal commentator siding with it have protested that Israel does not implement UN resolutions, alluding in this regard first and foremost to UNSC Resolution 242.

---

8. See both Chapters VI and VII of the UN Charter in "Charter of the United Nations", United Nations Website. *https://www.un.org/en/documents/charter/*

According to their line of reasoning, Israel should have withdrawn completely from the territories it had captured during the Six Day War, in the same manner, for example, that Iraq was requested to withdraw from Kuwait following the invasion of the latter by the first in August 1990. Israel has been treated differently than other countries that violate UN resolutions, so it has been argued.

The counterargument advanced to refute this dwells on the difference between a UNSC Resolution which requests a country to withdraw unilaterally, i.e., Iraq with reference to Kuwait, and one that calls on it to withdraw in the context of a peace agreement, following negotiations between the warring sides, i.e., Israel as regards the territories it captured during the Six Day War.

Also, it has been contended, Israel captured those territories in a war of self-defence against countries calling for its destruction and undertaking aggressive and illegal actions against it. Iraq invaded Kuwait without being under any threat of attack by the latter, let alone being menaced with physical extinction.

There is a legal difference, according to this counterargument, espoused among others by the Cambridge University scholar Sir Elihu Lauterpacht, between unlawful territorial change by an aggressor and lawful territorial change in response to an aggressor.[9] Of course, the Arab side has contended that Israel was the aggressor in the Six Day War, and thus any territorial change in its favour would be *ipso facto* illegal.

Israel has argued that Resolution 242 does not oblige Israel to withdraw completely from all the territories captured during the Six Day War referring to the words of Lord Caradon (Hugh Foot), the British Ambassador to the UN at the time of the drafting of Resolution 242 and one of its drafters, who subsequently said that

9. For a full quote of Sir Elihu Lauterpacht's comment, see Hertz (2005): 105. "... Territorial change cannot properly take place as a result of the 'unlawful' use of force. But to omit the word 'unlawful' is to change the substantive content of the rule and to turn an important safeguard of legal principle into an aggressor's charter. For if force can never be used to effect lawful territory change, then, if territory has once changed hands as a result of the unlawful use of force, the illegitimacy of the position thus established is sterilized by the prohibition upon the use of force to restore the lawful sovereign. This cannot be regarded as reasonable or correct."

the absence of the article "the" or the word "all" was intentional. Indeed, Britain's Foreign Secretary, George Brown, expressed himself in a similar vein.[10]

Further, the then US Ambassador to the UN, Arthur Goldberg, who was involved in the drafting of Resolution 242, stressed that it was drafted the way it was on purpose. According to Ambassador Goldberg, Israel was not requested to withdraw fully to the lines existing prior to the Six Day War.[11]

The fact that a Soviet-led effort at tabling a resolution calling on Israel to withdraw completely to the boundaries existing prior to the Six Day War was rejected by the US and Britain, which instead put forward what was to be known as Resolution 242, proves, according to Israel, the existence of a diplomatic-legal process preceding the adoption of Resolution 242 which validates the interpretation that the drafters did not intend to call on Israel to withdraw fully to the lines prevailing before the Six Day War.

The Arab side has contended that Israel should withdraw completely from the territories captured during the Six Day War, stressing that Resolution 242 emphasises "the inadmissibility of the acquisition of territory by war." The capture of any territory by Israel during the Six Day War could be deemed to be, according to this interpretation, inadmissible, thus foreclosing any legal right for Israel to retain territory beyond the lines existing prior to that War.

Israel has found the aforementioned argument to be questionable, arguing that the clause on "the inadmissibility of the acquisition of territory by war" is a general principle mentioned in the preamble of Resolution 242 and not in its operative clauses, in which Israel is called to withdraw "from territories," thus legally allowing a modification of the pre-existing lines. Prof Ruth Lapidoth, a former Legal Advisor to the Israeli Foreign Ministry, has also argued that there is a difference between the terms "acquisition" and "occupation."

> 'Acquisition' refers to gaining title, ownership, or sovereignty over the land or territory. 'Occupation,' on the other hand, refers to

10. See, Israel Ministry of Foreign Affairs (MFA) (n.d.).

11. Ibid.

provisional presence, or holding of the territory pending negotiations on peace or any other agreed-upon determination as to the status, ownership, or sovereignty of the territory. The Security Council did not, in this preambular provision, denounce 'occupation' as such" (Lapidtoh, 2011).

Israel has argued that it has implemented Resolution 242 by withdrawing from the Sinai Peninsula, in exchange for a peace agreement with Egypt. Indeed, as part of the Oslo Agreement, Israeli forces withdrew from most of the inhabited areas of the West Bank (Judea and Samaria) and the Gaza Strip, returning to some of them only as a result of the terrorist attacks that beset Israel during the so-called Second Intifida, which led to the deaths of more than a thousand Israelis, most of them citizens.

Israeli leaders, both from the left and right of the political spectrum have already conveyed their readiness to withdraw from most of the West Bank (Judea and Samaria) in the context of a final peace agreement with the Palestinian Authority, thus following the precepts of Resolution 242, according to Israel's official position.[12]

Israeli Foreign Policy in the Wake of the Yom Kippur War of 1973

Following the Yom Kippur War of October 1973, Israelis felt relieved at the final outcome of the War, but distraught because of the manner it came about. Israel was caught off-guard. Israeli decision makers were surprised. A phenomenon known as Groupthink had characterised the decision-making process prior to the outbreak of the War. The foremost expert in Groupthink, Irving Janis (1972), defined it as "A mode of thinking that people engage in a cohesive-in-group, when the members' striving for unanimity override their motivation to realistically appraise alternative courses of action."

The first days of the Yom Kippur War were perceived by Israeli decision makers in particularly grim terms. Moshe Dayan, who served then as Defence Minister, was the gloomiest of them all, fearing what

12. For an up-dated, current, Israeli interpretation of the Resolution, See Gold, (2013). Dore Gold was appointed in December 2013 as Foreign Policy Advisor to Israel's Prime Minister, Benjamin Netanyahu. He served as Israeli Ambassador to the UN between 1997 and 1999, during Netanyahu's first term as Prime Minister.

he termed the destruction of "the Third Temple," the reference being to the destruction of the State of Israel.[13]

As the days elapsed, Israel managed to recover from the initial shock and counter-attacked successfully pushing the Syrian army to within 40 kilometres from Damascus and reaching on the west side of the Suez Canal a position of a 100 kilometres from Cairo.

The emergency military equipment Israel got from the US during the War helped to re-supply its dwindling weaponry following the first days of the War. President Richard Nixon gave strict orders to comply with every Israeli request for arms (Byron, 2010).

Indeed, Golda Meir, who served as Israeli Prime Minister then, used to refer to Nixon as the best friend Israel had in the White House since Israel's inception. Golda Meir, with whom the President kept in frequent touch throughout the War, referred for the rest of her life to Richard Nixon as "my president," and said, "For generations to come, all will be told of the miracle of the immense planes from the US bringing in the materiel that meant life to our people."[14]

The US is Israel's most important friend and ally. The support accorded to Israel by the US is based on a combination of pragmatic reasoning and moral tenets. The US regards Israel as a stable and reliable ally in an unstable and sometime hostile region. Further, Israel's parliamentary democracy, surrounded by authoritarian political regimes, has traditionally been highly regarded by the US. Indeed, both countries share common values and embrace a similar political culture, factors that help enhance the bilateral special relationship.

To be sure, Israel enjoys a solid support of a majority of the US population. Public opinion polls conducted in the US have consistently shown that Israel elicits a considerably greater sympathy than the Palestinian Authority and the Arab countries.[15] Such support is reflected in both Houses of Congress, where Israel has enjoyed since the 1950s an overwhelming bi-partisan backing.

---

13. See, for instance, Rabinobich (2013).
14. See, Twersky (1998) quoted in Byron (2010).
15. See, for instance, Bard (2014); Lipka (2014).

In the aftermath of the Yom Kippur War, through the active mediation of the US Secretary of State, Henry Kissinger, Israel signed an interim accord with Syria and a disengagement agreement and subsequently an interim accord with Egypt. Although no Arab state was yet ready to recognise Israel and negotiate peace agreements with it, these accords represented a diplomatic leap beyond the violent reality of October 1973 into a more tranquil regional structure, albeit a rather precarious one.

The Shaping of a new Foreign Policy under Begin and Dayan

Following the election of the centre-right Likud alignment in 1977, which ended an uninterrupted period of 29 years of the Labour Party's domination, there was trepidation throughout the international community. It was feared that any prospect for peace, however tenuous, would be dashed; indeed, that war might be resumed.

Likud's leader, Menachem Begin, was seen as an obdurate, extreme politician, who would alienate the Arab leadership from engaging with Israel in peace negotiations. To be sure, none of the Arab leaders had consented to recognise Israel as a sovereign state or to deal with it directly until then. The prospect of Begin becoming Prime Minister did not seem to modify Arab positions one way or the other, at least not in public.

Indeed, Egyptian President Anwar Sadat used to say, in the wake of the 1977 Israeli elections, that he saw no difference between Begin, Rabin who had served as Israeli Prime Minister between 1974 and 1977, Peres, who had served as Israeli Defence Minister between 1974 and 1977, and was then the Labour Party's leader, and Golda Meir, whom he used to call "The Old Lady," who had served as Israeli Prime Minister between the years 1969 and 1974. As far as Sadat was concerned, Begin was neither worse nor better than the rest.

To be sure, President Sadat was not trying to imply that Begin was not as extreme and obdurate a politician as he was portrayed to be. Rather, his intention was to depict the whole Israeli leadership, whether Labour or Likud, as being equally unacceptable as peace partners.

The same President Sadat used to stress that no peace between Israel and its Arab neighbours would be possible in his own generation.

Notwithstanding the aforementioned, Begin's first concrete act in the realm of foreign policy following his election was to appoint Labour Knesset Member Moshe Dayan as Foreign Minister. A singularly bold and original appointment, Dayan, renown world-wide as a former Defence Minister and Army Chief of Staff, would introduce a pragmatic dimension to Begin's foreign policy. Dayan's appointment led to protestations in the Labour Party and to consternation within Begin's Likud Party. Nevertheless, Begin stood firm and managed to overcome all opposition.

A twofold message could be said to have been conveyed by Dayan's appointment: Begin was fully cognizant of the diplomatic difficulties entailed in his election as Prime Minister and wished to portray internationally as pragmatic an image as possible by appointing Dayan. In addition, Begin wanted to relay a clear message that he was serious about pursuing negotiations with Israel's Arab neighbours and believed that an experienced and pragmatic foreign minister, who would need no introduction in the Middle East and beyond, could serve him well in this regard.

Begin and Dayan set out from the outset to enquire through secret diplomatic channels whether there was even the slightest possibility for an opening leading to peace with any of Israel's Arab neighbours. This led to secret meetings in Morocco between Dayan and Hassan Tuhami, Egypt's Deputy Prime Minister and Sadat's special emissary, a meeting that took place two months prior to President Sadat announcement in November 1977 that he would be ready to speak before the Knesset in Jerusalem.[16]

Thus, Sadat's subsequent visit to Israel between 19 and 21 November 1977, which stunned the international community, was a corollary not only of his own imaginative decision to break the

16. On the secret meeting between Dayan and Tuhami in Morocco, see Israel State Archives (ISA), Prime Minister's Office (PMO) ISA/A/4313/4, "Highlights from Meeting of September 16 1977, 21:00, 17 September 1977". *http://www.archives.gov.il/NR/rdonlyres/7BFFC442-E877-4377-989E-DE3ED63389AA/0/Egypt12.pdf*

psychological barrier, as he himself said, but also of Israel's proactive diplomacy.[17]

Of course, in terms of cause and effect, it would be difficult to prove that Israeli diplomacy was directly responsible for Sadat's decision to visit Israel. However, had it not been for the active diplomatic efforts of Begin and Dayan, Sadat might have been more reluctant to embark on his mission to Israel as the secret talks that had preceded it had made clear to him, among other things, the general outlines of Israel's possible territorial concessions.[18]

Sadat's visit to Israel represented both a diplomatic and a conceptual volte-face by Egypt. From the long-held stance of refusing to hold direct negotiations with Israel, Sadat now consented to deal with Israel's leaders face-to-face, and in Jerusalem. From refusing to recognise Israel in any way or form, Sadat now appeared before the Knesset and in his speech explicitly welcomed Israel as an integral part of the region.

Few are the cases in Modern History in which public diplomacy has played such a dramatic role reflecting a radical change of positions as it did during Sadat's visit to Israel.

One of the reasons leading Sadat in his quest for a direct dialogue with Israel was the joint statement issued by the US and the Soviet Union on the 1 October 1977 on the principles for the re-convening of the Geneva Peace Conference, first convened in the wake of the Yom Kippur War of 1973.[19] Seeing it as an attempt by the US to re-

17. For a summary of Sadat's visit to Israel, see ISA, Prime Minister's Office, "Documents on the Background to Sadat's Visit and the Israeli Government's Reaction—F. Sadat's Visit to Jerusalem," *http://www.archives.gov.il/ArchiveGov/Templates/Articals/Article.aspx?NRMODE=Published&NRNODEGUID=%7bC0784AEB-F7CC-497D-86DD-06AB7E224CED%7d&NRORIGINALURL=%2fArchiveGov_Eng%2fPublications%2fElectronicPirsum%2fSadatVisit%2fSadatVisit%2ehtm&NRCACHEHINT=Guest#6*

18. During the aforementioned secret meeting in Morocco, Tuhami said to Dayan that Sadat considered Begin and Dayan strong leaders with whom he could deal, and that he would be ready to meet Begin, but only after a commitment on the part of the latter that he would be ready to withdraw from all Arab lands occupied by Israel in 1967. ISA, PMO, "Highlights from Meeting..." *http://www.archives.gov.il/NR/rdonlyres/7BFFC442-E877-4377-989E-DE3ED63389AA/0/Egypt12.pdf*

19. See MFA, 51: "Press Conference with President Carter, 29 September 1977". Vols 4-5: 1977-1979. *http://mfa.gov.il/MFA/ForeignPolicy/MFADocuments/Yearbook3/Pages/51%20Press%20conference%20with%20President%20Carter-%2029%20Sept.aspx*

introduce the Soviet Union into the peace process, Sadat, who had endeavoured to distance Egypt from Soviet influence, believed that he should pursue a direct diplomatic path to offset the effects of this joint statement. Israel issued a critical response to the US-Soviet statement thus finding itself in tacit agreement with Egypt.[20] Indeed, in a meeting that took place in the wake of President Sadat's visit to Israel with Prime Minister Begin and Foreign Minister Dayan, the US Ambassador to Israel, Samuel Lewis, was reported to have said: "(in a jocular tone) We have to think of this in historical terms. Perhaps because of the joint communiqué we helped bring Sadat to Jerusalem."[21]

Following Sadat's visit, Begin presented an Israeli peace plan composed of two elements: a general outline of a peace agreement between Israel and Egypt; and a Self-Rule plan for the Palestinian Arab inhabitants of the West Bank (Judea and Samaria) and the Gaza Strip.

According to Begin's peace plan, Israel would be ready to withdraw completely from the Sinai Peninsula, leaving under Israeli control, though not sovereignty, the military airfields that had been constructed by Israel, following the Six Day War and the Israeli civilian settlements in Northern Sinai that had been set up since then as well.[22]

The Self-Rule Plan entailed the establishment of an autonomous entity in the West Bank (Judea and Samaria) and the Gaza Strip, which would last for a period of five years, pending final status negotiations. This represented an ideological change on the part of Begin, who had traditionally supported the claim to extend Israeli sovereignty over those territories, on the basis of Israel's unbreakable

---

20. See MFA, 52: "Israel government reaction to joint US-Soviet statement on the Middle East". 2 October 1977. *http://mfa.gov.il/MFA/ForeignPolicy/MFADocuments/Yearbook3/Pages/52%20Israel%20government%20reaction%20to%20joint%20US-Soviet%20s.aspx*

21. ISA, PMO, ISA/A/4350/3, Top Secret, 23 November, 1977. *http://www.archives.gov.il/NR/rdonlyres/AA5AB7B2-013B-40B7-9434-99B6C60C7C75/0/Egypt34.pdf*

22. See, MFA, 103: "Statement to the Knesset by Prime Minister Begin Presenting Israel's Peace Plan, 28 December 1977". Volumes 4-5: 1977-1979. *http://mfa.gov.il/MFA/ForeignPolicy/MFADocuments/Yearbook3/Pages/103%20Statement%20to%20the%20Knesset%20by%20Prime%20Minister%20Beg.aspx*

historical links to them. In addition, he believed that the strategically vital areas of the West Bank (Judea and Samaria) could not be relinquished under any circumstances.

To be sure, following his election as Prime Minister, and the appointment of Dayan as his Foreign Minister, Begin had decided not to extend unilaterally Israel's sovereignty over the West Bank (Judea and Samaria) and the Gaza Strip pending the outcome of future peace negotiations. Now, in the wake of Sadat's visit, Begin went a considerable step forward, as far as he was concerned, and presented a Self-Rule Plan, which might prevent Israeli sovereignty over those territories at least for five years, if not longer.

Begin's Self-Rule Plan, which was to serve subsequently as the basis of the Full Autonomy Plan agreed to by Egypt and Israel during the Camp David negotiations in September 1978, was an attempt to strike a delicate balance between different interests and long-held values.

By virtue of being an interim solution, the Self-Rule Plan did not deal with the thorny questions of final borders and the ultimate status of the territories concerned. It left those matters to be negotiated subsequently thus affording an opportunity to show Israeli goodwill without deviating radically from previously-held positions. Begin could contend, as he did, that he was offering the Palestinian Arabs something that had not been offered previously, by Jordan and Egypt prior to the Six Day War, or by the British Mandate or the Ottoman Empire, before Israel was set up, without actually renouncing his claim to sovereignty over those territories.

Further, although Israel would thus end its military control of the West Bank (Judea and Samaria) and the Gaza Strip, it would still retain overall security control during the interim period, without being involved in the daily life of the Palestinian Arab inhabitants.

The Self-Rule Plan reflected Dayan's own long-held view that the Israeli-Palestinian-Jordanian settlement would have to be based on a functional rather than a territorial compromise; in other words, that instead of trying to agree upon a final border, the parties concerned would have to work out a solution that would provide the Palestinian inhabitants the fullest degree of autonomy while affording Israel the right to exercise strategic security control and allowing Israeli citizens to visit freely and even live in those areas. He made his views in this regard clear to the new US Administration, even prior to his being appointed foreign minister.[23]

The enthusiasm sparked by Sadat's visit to Israel dissipated somewhat as the talks between Israel and Egypt reached a deadlock. Following a few months of diplomatic impasse during 1978, in which Sadat refused even to talk over the phone with Begin, US President Jimmy Carter decided to invite both leaders to a secluded conference at the presidential retreat of Camp David to try to break the deadlock.

The Camp David Conference, which lasted 13 days, was a remarkable success of personal mediation by Carter and his delegation. What transpired at Camp David remained secret for the duration of the Conference. The Conference itself was not a secret. Its deliberations were. At the end of it, Carter was able to announce that two framework agreements had been reached between Israel and Egypt: one for a bilateral peace agreement and the other for a Full Autonomy Plan for the Palestinian Arabs of the West Bank (Judea and Samaria) and the Gaza Strip as an interim accord pending final status negotiations.[24]

Mistakenly referred to as a peace agreement between Israel and Egypt, the Camp David Accords were a framework agreement, signed on 17 September 1978, which ultimately led to the signing of a peace agreement between the two countries in Washington D.C. on 26 March 1979.

This constituted a major diplomatic breakthrough for Israel. For the first time since its inception, Israel was to have normal diplomatic relations with an Arab state; not just any Arab state, but the most

23. See, for instance, Foreign Relations of the United States [FRUS], 1977-1980, Volume VIII, Arab-Israeli Dispute, January 1977-August 1978, Memorandum of Conversation, Washington, 31 January 1977. *http://static.history.state.gov/frus/frus1977-80v08/pdf/frus1977-80v08.pdf*

24. See United States Embassy in Israel, "The Middle East Peace Process: Camp David Accords, September 17, 1978—The Framework for Peace in the Middle East". *http://usembassy-israel.org.il/publish/peace/campdav.htm*

powerful and influential one. The implications were not only diplomatic, but also strategic. No major war against Israel had been fought without Egypt. Egypt's leadership had been essential in the forging of the various anti-Israel diplomatic coalitions and military alignments. With Egypt out of the anti-Israel diplomatic and military equation, Israel's position became seemingly stronger, the dangers facing it less ominous.

The strategic importance entailed in the peace agreement with Egypt has led every Israeli government since then to adopt a benign attitude towards Egypt even when the latter pursued a reserved, if not hostile, posture towards Israel. Indeed, Egypt seems to have resolved to maintain a cold peace with Israel whereby it refrains from violating the letter of the peace agreement while refusing to go beyond the modalities of a formal diplomatic relationship.

To be sure, Egypt's public opinion, as that of other Arab countries, has been opposed for many a year to any links with Israel. In this respect, it might be possible to understand Egypt's policy towards Israel as an attempt to maintain a delicate balance between Egypt's contractual obligations and the hostile disposition of its population towards Israel. Still, considering the autocratic nature of Egypt's regime, it might be equally possible to argue that the Egyptian leadership did precious little to encourage a change of attitude towards Israel.

Whereas the Camp David Framework Agreements led to a formal peace agreement between Israel and Egypt, which has lasted to the present, it did not lead to implementation of the Full Autonomy Plan for the Palestinian Arabs of the West Bank (Judea and Samaria) and the Gaza Strip.

The negotiations to that end between Israel and Egypt failed to materialise and were actually interrupted shortly thereafter by Egypt, which contended that Israel was not serious about them. To be sure, Dayan resigned as Foreign Minister due to disagreements with Begin over the same issue. He differed with the Prime Minister regarding both the manner and the substance of the negotiations concerning implementation of the Full Autonomy Plan.[25]

It could be argued that Begin was not interested, to begin with, in implementing the Full Autonomy Plan as agreed to at Camp David; that he went along with the negotiations as he was contractually obliged to without actually seriously intending to pursue them to their ultimate end. According to this line of logic, Begin feared that a fully autonomous entity in the West Bank (Judea and Samaria) and Gaza might lead to the establishment of a Palestinian state, which might pose a mortal danger to Israel. Further, he never intended to renounce Israel's right to set up civilian settlements in those territories or Israel's sole security control over them. He might have feared that implementing the Full Autonomy Plan as agreed to at Camp David might curtail considerably Israel's freedom of action. Begin agreed to it as a tactical price to achieve the much more important strategic objective of a peace agreement with Egypt.

On the other hand, it could be argued that Begin did intend to implement the Autonomy Plan, but one that resembled more his original proposal following Sadat's visit to Israel than the more expansive scheme agreed upon at Camp David, at least as interpreted by the Egyptians. According to this scenario, Begin was sincere in his wish to proceed with the negotiations aimed at implementing the Full Autonomy Plan, but a genuine difference of opinion with Egypt over the nature of such autonomous entity led their breakdown.

Whatever the truth, no Israeli government managed to break the diplomatic deadlock regarding the Israeli-Palestinian conflict until the Madrid Peace Conference, held in the wake of the First Gulf War, in October 1991. The corollary of an intensive shuttle diplomacy by US Secretary of State, James Baker, the Conference, co-chaired by US President George H.W. Bush and Soviet President Mikhail Gorbachev, was attended by an Israeli, an Egyptian, a Syrian, a Lebanese and a

25. MFA, 52: "Letter of Resignation of Foreign Minister Dayan and Interview with Him, 21 October 1979; and a letter of 2 October 1979". Volume VI: 1979-1980. *http://mfa.gov.il/MFA/ForeignPolicy/MFADocuments/Yearbook4/Pages/52%20Letter%20of%20resignation%20of%20Foreign%20Minister%20Dayan.aspx*

joint Jordanian-Palestinian delegation. The Israeli delegation was headed by Prime Minister Itzhak Shamir, who had replaced Begin as Likud leader when the latter resigned in 1983. Bilateral talks in Washington between Israel and a joint Jordanian-Palestinian delegation followed the Madrid Peace Conference.[26]

The Oslo Accord—A Volte-Face in Israeli Foreign Policy?

The bilateral negotiations between Israel and the joint Jordanian-Palestinian delegation in Washington continued through the election of the Labour Party headed by Itzhak Rabin in 1992. Returning to the post of Prime Minister, in which he had last served between 1974 and 1977, Rabin was determined to pursue the negotiations in earnest. He had agreed with his arch-rival within the Labour Party, Shimon Peres, that he would appoint him as Foreign Minister, but that the peace process would be handled from the Prime Minister's Office with the Foreign Ministry having a secondary role.

Nevertheless, as time elapsed and the negotiations in Washington were not progressing at a significant pace, informal talks between two Israeli academics, Dr Yair Hirschfeld and Dr Ron Pundak, and one of the key members of the PLO, Ahmad Qurei, better known as Abu Ala, which had been held in the Norwegian capital, since January 1993, were subsequently elevated into a more formal level, under the guidance of Foreign Minister Shimon Peres, with the full, if somewhat reluctant, acquiescence of Prime Minister Rabin. The secret Oslo negotiations were being conducted in parallel to the open negotiations in Washington.[27]

Finally, on 13 September 1993, the Declaration of Principles on Interim Self-Government Arrangements, better known as the Oslo Accord, was signed by Israel and the PLO. It stipulated a

---

26. See Office of the Historian, US State Department, Milestones: 1989-1992, the Madrid Peace Conference, 1991. *http://history.state.gov/milestones/1989-1992/madrid-conference*

27. Listen to the personal recollection in this regard by Dr Yossi Beilin, who served then as Deputy Foreign Minister, and is widely-regarded as the main architect of Israel's diplomacy leading to the Oslo Acccord. *http://www.youtube.com/watch?v=j-vLx8WdOMs* (Hebrew); and in the following English-language interview, *http://www.youtube.com/watch?v=bDOu6oOGGvk* (English)

mutual recognition between the two and the establishment of an autonomous Palestinian Arab entity for an interim period of five years in the Gaza Strip and Jericho, first, to be followed by the other inhabited areas of the West Bank (Judea and Samaria), later. Thereafter, final status negotiations would be held between Israel and the newly established National Palestinian Authority aimed at reaching a mutually-acceptable peace accord that would put an end to the claims by either side.[28]

Thus, the Oslo Accord was not a final peace agreement, but rather an interim accord. Also, Israel did not pledge itself in advance to accept an independent Palestinian state as part of the final agreement to be signed in the wake of the five-year interim period; as the PLO did not commit itself to accept, it would renounce the so-called Right of Return (the reference being to the Arab refugees and the Palestinian claim that they should have a right of return to what is today Israel) or accept any pre-established boundaries. It is in vogue to claim that the Oslo Accord entailed the acceptance by both sides of a two-state solution. That is patently wrong. However groundbreaking it undoubtedly was, the Oslo Accord did not include any reference to the two-state solution—nor, indeed, to any other final-status arrangement—as that would have presumed an advanced agreement by Israel and the PLO as to the outcome of the final status talks, which was clearly not the case.

Nevertheless, the Oslo Accord represented a diplomatic volte-face by both Israel and the PLO as they recognised each other, an almost inconceivable scenario for most Israelis and Palestinian Arabs until then. The impact of the Oslo Accord was enhanced by the secrecy of the negotiations leading to it.

A comparison between two secret diplomatic negotiations would suffice to illustrate the magnitude of the impact that ensued from the Oslo Accord. Public opinion worldwide, and particularly in Israel and Egypt, was stunned when US President, Jimmy Carter, announced that a framework agreement for peace between Israel and Egypt had been signed at Camp David in September 1978, following 13

28. See MFA (1993).

days of intensive negotiations. However, whereas at Camp David, in September 1978, the very fact that negotiations were taking place was public knowledge, very few individuals were actually aware that negotiations were being conducted in Oslo between Israel and the PLO in 1993. Thus, the impact of the news that an agreement had been reached at Oslo was even greater due to the fact that those negotiations were not public knowledge.

Reactions in Israel to the Oslo Accord were, in a sense, as expected, with most of the centre-right vehemently in opposition and the centre-left largely in favour. Opinion polls conducted during that period show that the Oslo Accord enjoyed an increasing support among Israelis from the moment the agreement was announced until it was officially signed, but that it decreased considerably as terrorist attacks against Israelis took place, and also in the light of PLO leader Yasser Arafat's "Jihad" speech in South Africa in May, 1994.[29]

Although diplomatically bold, it would seem that the move finally undertaken by Rabin was intended to be conceptually more modest. Rather than reach a final accord with the PLO entailing not only mutual recognition but also the establishment of some form of a Palestinian state, Rabin appeared to have preferred to follow the Camp David path by agreeing to an interim solution involving the creation of an autonomous Palestinian entity. Rabin might have realised that selling domestically an agreement with the PLO would be no easy task for him and his government. Endeavouring to convince Israeli public opinion to accept a final accord with the PLO would have been, so he seemed to have thought, a considerably more difficult challenge to overcome. On the face of it, the main tenets of the Oslo Agreement were quite similar to the Full Autonomy Plan agreed to at Camp David in September 1978 by Israel and Egypt. Rabin's decision could thus be seen abroad as bold while he could argue at home that his diplomatic move, although groundbreaking in many respects, was less radical than it appeared to be.

---

29. See Leon (1995); for Israeli official reactions to Arafat's "Jihad" speech in South Africa see, Haberman (1994; 1994a).

Thus, the Oslo Accord was perceived by the international community as a major breakthrough in Israeli foreign policy; domestically, it would seem that Rabin wished to sell it as a logical implementation of the autonomy plan that Begin himself had agreed to at Camp David. If a right-wing leader as Begin could consent to such a plan, why couldn't he do likewise? Why would the opposition to it be so fierce?

Rabin knew that the mutual recognition with the PLO would be a bitter pill to swallow for many an Israeli (including himself!). Maybe that's why he wanted to avoid reaching an agreement that would have gone beyond the main parameters of what his right-wing predecessors had formally agreed to.

To be sure, Yossi Beilin, who served then as Deputy Foreign Minister and who was one of the main architects of the Oslo Accord, revealed subsequently that he had tried to persuade Rabin to go for a final agreement with the PLO at Oslo. Rabin, according to Beilin, retorted that going for a final agreement might be detrimental for should it fail, there might not be an alternative to fall back to, whereas an interim agreement that failed would have less adverse consequences.[30]

On the other hand, Peres attempted to sell the Oslo Accord domestically by describing it as a more radical modification in Israel's foreign policy than Rabin seemed to wish. He went so far as to compare it with De Gaulle's volte-face decision to leave Algeria and agree to its full independence.

Peres even claimed in the wake of the Oslo Accord that the study of history was becoming irrelevant as history was nothing more than a story of wars in the new era of peace and reconciliation. Indeed, he went on to argue that within five years (he said so in 1994), the Israeli Defence Force would not have to defend the country but rather the peace.[31] In an overly-optimistic mood, following the Oslo Accord, Peres even said that "It is no wonder that war, as a matter of

30. Yossi Beilin, conversation with the author, 11 February 2014. Tel Aviv, Israel.

31. See, for instance, Peres being interviewed for a children's programme on Israeli television in 1994, in which he depicted his highly optimistic vision of a post-Oslo Middle East (Hebrew). *http://www.youtube.com/watch?v=foQMLDmyKcM*

conducting human affairs, is in its death throes and that the time has come to bury it."[32]

The Israeli government was conveying a sense of elation, which could be understood as the Oslo Accord brought in its wake a significant wave of diplomatic support for Israel. All of a sudden, there was a widely-held expectation by many Israelis that the Oslo Accord would become the diplomatic key to the whole Arab world and to restoring Israel's international image. The peace agreement signed by Jordan and Israel on 26 October 1994, only reinforced that view. Once the PLO had recognised Israel and Yasser Arafat was meeting with Israel's leaders, there seemed to be no obstacle to other Arab leaders meeting with Israelis and engaging in talks with them. This was the major benefit accruing to Israel's diplomacy in the wake of the Oslo Accord.

Although diplomatically a major success, politically the Oslo Accord turned out to be a more complex phenomenon for Israel's decision makers. Faced by terrorist attacks and what was perceived to be as double-talk by Yasser Arafat on the peace process, Israeli public opinion became less certain of the benefits accruing from the agreement with the PLO. To be sure, Israel's centre-right opposition parties failed sometimes to rise to the challenge, engaging on occasion in what was perceived to be inflammatory rhetoric, which did not always help in conveying an articulate opposition credo to the Oslo Peace Process.

The murder of Prime Minister Rabin by Igal Amir, an extreme right-winger, on 4 November 1995, changed the whole rhetoric of political discussion in Israel, with Labour and the Left accusing the Likud and the right-wing parties of having fomented a toxic political atmosphere leading to the assassination. A paradoxical process ensued: opinion polls conducted following Rabin's assassination indicated clearly that the Labour Party would win a general election by a large margin. However, when elections were held in a few

---

32. Quoted in Gerber and Isaac (1996). He is also quoted as having written that "We are in transition from a world of identifiable enemies to one of unidentifiable problems."

months time, on 29 May 1996, the centre-right opposition leader, Benjamin Netanyahu, won against all odds, although by a small margin. Certainly, a spate of terrorist attacks on Israeli civilians that had taken place in the months preceding those elections reduced the support enjoyed by Labour and its new leader, Shimon Peres. However, as a result of Rabin's assassination, and the sharp—and on occasion inaccurate and unfair—attacks on Netanyahu, a modification of the latter's mode of conduct into a more restrained and measured one rendered him more electable than would have appeared only a few months previously.

Israeli diplomacy from the signing of the Oslo Accord in 1993, through the signing of the Oslo II Accord on 28 September 1995, and until the election of Netanyahu as Prime Minister in 1996, was singularly dynamic. Israeli foreign policy enjoyed a long honeymoon. International support for Israel was widespread. This came to a halt, to some extent, following Netanyahu's election. To be sure, there was no dramatic drop in the diplomatic support enjoyed by Israel, 1996 onwards. Indeed, the Israeli government, headed by Netanyahu, signed two further interim accords with the Palestinian Authority, the Hebron Agreement on 17 January 1997 and the Wye River Memorandum on 23 October 1998. However, having opposed the Oslo Accord from the very beginning, Netanyahu's subsequent endorsement of it on the eve of his election in 1996 was regarded by many with skepticism.

Whether he was sincere in implementing the Oslo Peace Process or not, Netanyahu had to face a mounting challenge from his right-wing coalition partners as well as from some members of his own Likud Party, who were weary of his seeming moderation and were opposed to the two agreements he signed with the Palestinian Authority.

When the so-called Second Intifida broke out in September 2000, Israeli public opinion turned more sharply against the Oslo Agreement. Indeed, even Labour Party doves such as Shlomo Ben-Ami, who had also served as Foreign Minister, expressed their criticism of the Oslo Peace Process.[33] In the midst of terrorist attacks on Israeli civilians almost on a daily basis, and the rupture of the negotiating process, the Israeli public tended increasingly to identify the term "Oslo" with violence and insecurity.

The Oslo Peace Process failed in producing a stable interim accord that would lead to a final agreement. However, as far as Israeli foreign policy was concerned, it could be said to have represented a diplomatic and a political landmark. As a result of the Oslo Accord of 1993, the PLO became the sole interlocutor to settle the Israeli-Palestinian conflict, whereas previously Israel had seen Jordan and the representatives of the Palestinian Arabs in the West Bank (Judea and Samaria) and the Gaza Strip as its negotiating partners. Also, domestically, the idea of a peace settlement based on the creation of an independent Palestinian state gradually gained considerable support among Israelis. In a country in which the internal political dimension plays an important role in shaping foreign policy, this change in public opinion is worth noting.

33. See, for instance, Bar-On (2000).

"Many Israeli observers have noted the inherent foolishness of claims by Prime Minister Ehud Barak and Acting Foreign Minister Shlomo Ben-Ami that 'there is no longer a "partner" for the peace process.'

"Numerous Israelis with leftist views have also expressed "disappointment" with Arafat following the Palestinian uprising at the end of September 2000." *http://www.pij.org/details.php?id=251*

See also, "The Day Peace Died", Interview with Shlomo Ben-Ami, *Haaretz Weekend Edition* 14 September, 2001.

"We had a number of working assumptions, but I think the most important of them was the basic assumption that has been shared by the Americans, the Europeans and the Israeli center-left for years: that Oslo created a rational order in the Middle East based on give-and-take, which in the future would lead to an acceptable compromise; that in 1993 a quasi-state of the Palestinians was established, in terms of orderly international relations. *In retrospect, this turned out to be a mistaken assumption, It turned out that for [Palestinian leader Yasser] Arafat it was a huge camouflage net behind which he fomented, and continues to foment, political pressure and terrorism in different dosages in order to undermine the very idea of two states for two nations*" (my emphasis). *http://www.weizmann.ac.il/home/comartin/israel/ben-ami.html*

Benjamin Netanyahu's Bar Ilan Speech

Benjamin Netanyahu was elected at the head of the Likud Party to form a government in 2009. This would be his second term as Prime Minister, after having served in the same post between 1996 and 1999.

Netanyahu could have formed a coalition government with parties to the right of the Likud and with ultra-orthodox parties, which stress more domestic issues than foreign policy matters. Nevertheless, his wish was to form a large coalition, if possible with the former ruling Kadima Party. Having failed to reach an agreement with Kadima's leader, former Foreign Minister, Tzipi Livni, on the terms for such a government, Netanyahu turned to the Labour Party's leader, Ehud Barak, who had defeated him back in 1999, in order to establish a coalition government that would rely less on individual votes from the right and be more amenable to international public opinion.

With Barak holding the second-most important post as Defence Minister, Netanyahu tried to tread carefully between his domestic constituency and his international interlocutors.

Netanyahu made it clear from the outset that he would be ready to resume peace negotiations with the Palestinian Authority. His official stance against the establishment of an independent Palestinian state was seen as a stumbling bloc both by the US and the Palestinian Authority, which had previously negotiated with various Israeli governments that had endorsed that idea. To be sure, Netanyahu was prepared to accept a fully autonomous entity in the West Bank (Judea and Samaria) and the Gaza Strip, but feared that an independent Palestinian state would constitute an unacceptable danger to Israel's security.

Facing stiff resistance by US President Barak Obama, who also demanded that Israel freeze completely all settlement activity beyond the 1967 lines as a pre-condition to the negotiations with the Palestinian Authority, Netanyahu announced that he would be making an important statement on the peace process; which he did, following a series of consultations, on 14 June 2009. Netanyahu delivered a speech at the University of Bar Ilan, near Tel Aviv, which could be deemed to have been an important conceptual and political landmark for Netanyahu and his Likud Party.

Israeli Prime Minister Benjamin Netanyahu's much awaited speech on the peace process reflected his endeavour to strike a delicate equilibrium between the political and diplomatic dimensions.[34] It attempted to strike a balance between his domestic audience's expectations and the international community's demands; between the ideological precepts embraced by many of his political allies and the pragmatic need to adapt to a new US administration bent on exerting considerable pressure in order to advance its own agenda in the region.

Netanyahu's rhetoric during the speech was rather different than some of his predecessors'. It was positive in the objectives that were delineated, although cautious in the path that was depicted to arrive at them.

The intellectual basis of his arguments was distinctively unapologetic. He came out against the widespread paradigm that the Palestinian-Israeli conflict was caused by the capture of the West Bank (Judea and Samaria) and the Gaza Strip by Israel during the Six Day War of 1967. Indeed, he stressed the difference between cause and effect. The latter was the effect of a conflict that began even before the State of Israel was established. Furthermore, he reminded his audience that the Palestinian Arabs could have had a state of their own had they endorsed the UN Partition Plan of 1947, which the then Jewish leadership accepted.

Moreover, on the issue of Palestinian Arab refugees, while stressing the humanitarian need to solve their plight, he referred to the hundred of thousands of Jewish refugees from Arab countries that were integrated by a poor and war-torn Israel, without much outside help.

In addition, Netanyahu prefaced his readiness to accept a demilitarised Palestinian state by arguing that the territories of the West Bank (Judea and Samaria) are the cradle of Jewish civilisation. Some previous Israeli leaders tended to convey the impression

---

34. For the full text of Netanyahu's Bar Ilan University's Speech on 14 June 2009, see MFA (2009).

that those territories were a demographic burden to Israel. The Palestinians were expected to relieve Israel of this burden. Netanyahu seems to have altered the basis of discussion in this regard too. Whatever the burden entailed in any possible Israeli control of the West Bank, Israel had to accept reluctantly the fact that it may have to foreswear its own aspirations regarding those territories and endorse Palestinian sovereignty, albeit with certain conditions.

As for the nature of any future Palestinian state, Netanyahu was less innovative in content than seems to be the case. He spoke of a demilitarised state, having no right to sign any military pacts, especially with Israel's enemies, accepting limitations on the sovereignty applied to its airspace and enjoying no full control of its own border crossings, from which offensive weapons could be smuggled.

These terms were then taken for granted by the other major parties in Israel. Both the main opposition party, Kadima, and the Labour Party, which formed part of Netanyahu's coalition, accepted the idea of a Palestinian state in the West Bank and Gaza as part of a peace agreement only on condition that such a state be demilitarised and its sovereignty limited in areas where Israel's vital security interests would be at stake.

What distinguished Netanyahu's stance on this issue from previous Israeli leaders was the fact that he mentioned, clearly and explicitly, the caveats for the establishment of such a Palestinian state. To be sure, Netanyahu was also politically motivated to do so. Indeed, this was part of the same balance he was trying to strike between the fears of his domestic public and the exigencies of his international interlocutors. To help his political allies, indeed his own Likud party, digest the idea of a Palestinian state, he had to stress the security limitations upon which such a state would be founded so as to alleviate the ideological and strategic pain entailed in it for them.

Thus, Netanyahu had to emphasise the conditions upon which such a Palestinian state would be set up, not only as a true reflection of his own beliefs, but also in order to help moderate any adverse reaction within his own domestic audience.

Of course, the fact that Netanyahu mentioned, publicly and openly, his readiness to accept the establishment of a Palestinian state under certain conditions, rather than a Palestinian autonomous entity, constituted in itself a major ideological and political change. To be sure, the first Likud leader to have endorsed the idea of a Palestinian state in the context of a peace agreement was actually Ariel Sharon, whose hawkish image had been more pronounced than Netanyahu's. However, as he faced growing resistance within the Likud, particularly following his plan entailing the unilateral withdrawal of Israeli armed forces and civilian settlements from the Gaza Strip and the northern part of the West Bank (Samaria) in 2005, Sharon resigned from the Likud and formed a new party, Kadima.[35]

Many people were expecting a vague speech by Netanyahu, with precious little new in terms of contents. His speech, though, was innovative. It said something new, and said so in a manner that opened doors in Washington and Europe without closing doors in Jerusalem. Netanyahu's Bar Ilan speech thus became a political term and diplomatic catchphrase, denoting a change of rhetoric and official stance on the part of Israel's Prime Minister on a central foreign policy issue. It would facilitate Netanyahu's future international dealings as it removed a contentious diplomatic obstacle from Israel's foreign policy agenda.

The skeptics were not sure that beyond the new rhetoric, a new policy really emerged. So far, since then, Netanyahu has been consistent in his rhetoric. Indeed, he has been stressing time and again that he is ready to accept a Palestinian state and that the Palestinian leadership should equally accept to recognise, at the end of the negotiating process, that Israel is a Jewish state, the state of the Jewish people.[36] This has led to a diplomatic impasse as Mahmoud Abbas (Abbu Mazen) has consistently refused to do so, and has even received support for his refusal from the Arab League.[37] Thus, although the President of the Palestinian Authority is ready to

35. For an assessment of the Kadima Party, formed by Ariel Sharon, see Pipes (2005).

36. See, for instance, Ravid (2014).

37. See, for instance, Daraghmeh (2014). See also, *Dunya News* (2014).

accept the two-state solution, he is adamantly opposed to recognise Israel as a Jewish state.

What kind of a Palestinian state is Israel ready to countenance in the context of a final peace agreement?

A Demilitarised and Neutral Palestinian State: Some Precedents

Netanyahu said he would be ready to accept a Palestinian state, as part of a peace agreement, as long as such was demilitarised and was forbidden from signing any pacts, particularly with Israel's enemies.

Following Netanyahu's Bar-Ilan Speech, in which he first mentioned the idea, the Palestinian leadership reacted vehemently against it. Other Arab observers, as well as some European foreign ministers, expressed reservations at the conditions attached by Netanyahu to the establishment of a Palestinian state. Indeed, many have protested that the Palestinian state Netanyahu envisages does not conform to the widely-accepted notion of sovereignty in the international system.

To begin with, it should be stressed that none of the major political parties in Israel would countenance the creation of a Palestinian state that would not be demilitarised and would not be barred from signing military pacts with other countries, particularly enemies of Israel.[38]

There is one country that is totally demilitarised, indeed that has no army since 1948, and yet it would be difficult to claim that its sovereignty has been impaired on that account: Costa Rica. The most stable democracy in Latin America, Costa Rica is no less independent and sovereign for having no army of its own.

Indeed, Oscar Arias, former president of Costa Rica and Nobel Peace Prize Winner argued himself that a future Palestinian state should be demilitarised. Based on the experience of his own country, Arias said that: "A small, poor state like Palestine doesn't need an army." He added, however, that courage was needed for such a

---

38. For a brief, historical analysis of this issue from both Israeli and Palestinian perspectives respectively, since the signing of the Oslo Accord in 1993 until 2009, see The Reut Institute (2009).

decision to be adopted by the Palestinian leadership (Slomovich, 2009).

To be sure, Costa Rica has no army due to an internal decision, rather than to an external imposition. In the case of a Palestinian state, as envisaged by Netanyahu, its demilitarisation would be an external condition to which the Palestinian leadership would have to consent to. Nevertheless, the fact that a country has no army, as the Costa Rican example clearly shows, does not render it particularly any less sovereign or independent.

As for the stipulation that such a Palestinian state should not be allowed to sign any pacts, particularly with Israel's enemies, one can think of a historical example in which a condition of neutrality was asked by external forces and willingly accepted by the country itself: Austria.

According to the agreement signed by the four Allied powers and the Austrians in 1955, Austria was permitted to regain its independence, albeit with one serious caveat. It was strictly prohibited from annexing itself to Germany (Anschluss). No one then or at present would contend that Austria has its sovereignty curtailed in any significant way because of that. Further, Austria's neutrality, which prevents it from being part of any pact or alliance, is not seen either by Austrians or by foreigners as a stain on its sovereignty. Certainly, Austria has an army of its own; but then Costa Rica, which does not, follows a policy of neutrality as well since 1949.

The conditions advanced by Netanyahu for the establishment of a Palestinian state have some notable precedents in current history. Obviously, the precedents mentioned above are not tailor-made. However, Israeli decision makers would argue that these precedents demonstrate that a state can be demilitarised and neutral, and yet be sovereign and proud.

Indeed, even the President of the Palestinian Authority, Mahmoud Abbas, also known as Abbu Mazen, has gone on record as having agreed in principle to the establishment of a demilitarised Palestinian state, wherein foreign forces, such as North-Atlantic Treaty Organization (NATO) troops, might be stationed to safeguard the peace between the two states (Jerusalem Post, 2014).

Israel's Dilemma

Israel has a dilemma. On the one hand, it must display power to deter its actual and potential enemies, but on the other hand it should convey an image of vulnerability to elicit international support. No matter how one looks at it, there is no easy answer to untangle this dilemma.

When Israel was vulnerable, international backing was forthcoming. In the 1950s and 1960s, Israel enjoyed worldwide support. Israel's very existence was seen to be at stake. Surrounded by a seemingly powerful alliance of Arab states bent on its destruction, tiny Israel was popular (See, for instance, Gilboa (2006)).

To be sure, this widespread sympathy did not always translate into concrete diplomatic moves to the benefit of Israel's foreign policy. Still, public opinion, in general, tended to side with Israel, particularly in the so-called western world.

Even under a right-wing Likud government, led by the seemingly obdurate Itzhak Shamir, Israel experienced a singular honeymoon with world public opinion during the First Gulf War in the winter of 1991 as its populated areas were being targeted by Iraq's Scud missiles. Certainly, Israel's case was enhanced by Shamir's decision not to retaliate, which helped to convey an image of victimhood, and by the fact that a wide international coalition was fighting Iraq, thus putting Israel, *ipso facto*, on its side (Gilboa, 2006).

An argument has been advanced, more often than not, that whenever Israel pursues an active and generous peace policy, a considerable shift for the better in world public opinion consequently ensues. Contemporary history vindicates this argument, in most cases, but one should be careful to distinguish between a passing, short-term phenomenon and a more consistent, longer-term process.

Israel's unilateral withdrawal from the Gaza Strip in 2005 elicited worldwide applause; but its effect was short-lived. Gaza is usually referred to, outside of Israel, as being, in one way or another, under Israeli occupation notwithstanding the fact that no Israeli is present there. Any measure Israel has taken to defend itself from the Hamas-controlled territory of Gaza has been accompanied by worldwide criticism, albeit with some balancing words of understanding for the difficulties encountered by Israeli civilians. The international benefits of the unilateral withdrawal have long since been forgotten, even though Israel continues to enjoy understanding for the plight of its citizens whenever they are attacked from the Gaza Strip.[39]

The Oslo Accord between Israel and the PLO in September 1993, and the second interim agreement that followed it a year later, is a different case. The diplomatic benefits that accrued for Israel as a result were many and noteworthy. Israel enjoyed a period of a few years of widespread international sympathy.

However, once the Palestinians were perceived once again as being the victims of Israeli occupation, during the so-called Second Intifida, world public opinion shifted, once again, in a considerable manner away from Israel. Incidentally, this happened under a Labour-led government, headed by Prime Minister Ehud Barak, which had pursued a dovish peace policy, not only during the failed Camp David Summit Meeting in July 2000, but also subsequently in the course of the Taba Summit negotiations in January 2001.[40]

Israeli Prime Minister Ehud Olmert's far-reaching proposals to the Palestinian Authority, indeed his dovish public rhetoric directed at the Palestinians, helped Israel in getting diplomatic support from many a country, particularly from the US.[41]

It should be borne in mind, however, that the US was being led then by a staunchly pro-Israel administration. President George W. Bush, who did not conceal his personal sympathies for Israel, pursued a policy which was widely perceived by Israelis as being singularly friendly to their state. Indeed, Condoleezza Rice, who served as Secretary of State during President Bush's second term, wrote subsequently that she was utterly surprised by how far-reaching were the Israeli Prime Minister's peace proposals (IPT News, 2011). In other words, in terms of cause and effect, Olmert's peace plan did not lead to the US administration adopting a favourable attitude towards Israel. That attitude had prevailed prior to Olmert's proposals of

---

39. See, for instance, Holehouse (2014) and Finley (2014).

40. For an Israeli version of events, see MFA (2000; 2000a).

41. On Ehud Olmert's peace plan, see Isacharoff (2013).

2008, which, according to Rice's post-factum evidence, had actually surprised her considerably.

To be sure, Olmert and many prominent members of his party Kadima (that had been founded by his predecessor, Ariel Sharon) have stressed the benefits of a dovish peace policy by reminding their audience that European leaders came to Israel and appeared with Olmert as a show of support in a press conference during Operation Cast Lead in Gaza in the winter of 2008-09.

Without belittling the importance of that press conference, one has to bear in mind that the presence of the European leaders side by side with Olmert might have been not only a sign of support, but also a manifestation of fear. They might have wanted to control as much as to embrace Olmert. After all, European leaders were not only sensitive to Israel's predicament, but also fearful of its consequences. They sympathised with the aggrieved Samson, but might have wished to hold him tight to prevent him from demolishing the premises.

As it has been proven, a dovish peace policy can be helpful to enhance Israel's image and secure diplomatic backing, even if it has little chance of producing peace. The benefits of such a policy, though, may be short-lived. The seemingly weak and oppressed side—the Palestinians—can always reverse the positive image portrayed by the peace policy of the more powerful side—Israel. Public diplomacy has its limitations when the other side is perceived as considerably weaker, as Israel has learned on many an occasion.

Thus, the image of Israel as a vulnerable state has been demonstrated to have a greater chance of eliciting long-term international support than any peace policy that is not accepted by the other side. The situation is rather different when Israel is engaged in a mutually-acceptable peace process, so long as it lasts and the sides concerned are not engaged in an adversarial relationship. The moment the peace process faces obstacles or is actually derailed, Israel's diplomatic stance tends to elicit less support in the international arena.

An image of vulnerability on the part of Israel reflects the truth as it is perceived by the Israeli population. Translating that truth into a diplomatic strategy has not always been an easy task for Israel.

It was certainly easier for Israeli diplomacy to portray an image of vulnerability, prior to the Six Day War or subsequently whenever it faced attacks on its civilian population, so long as it did not resort to military retaliation, particularly if deemed 'disproportionate.'

The dilemma still remains for Israeli decision makers: how does Israel achieve widespread international support by reflecting its vulnerability without running the risk of seeming weak?

Israel's Vulnerability

Israeli foreign policy could be said to have veered since Israel's inception between two different objectives: aspiring Israel to be accepted as a normal sovereign entity, which forms an integral part of international society, and wishing the same international society to regard it as exceptionally vulnerable, facing singular threats.

Faced by constant threats of extinction, Israel has stressed that it is the only country in the world, the very legitimacy of which is being violently challenged.[42]

For almost 30 years, the entire Arab world refused to recognise Israel and launched an all-out diplomatic campaign aimed at delegitimising it. Israel's very existence was questioned, its borders constantly challenged. Only President Sadat's volte-face in November 1977 altered this reality. It would take 15 years between Israel's first peace agreement with an Arab state (Egypt) and its second peace agreement (Jordan), and 15 years between the Camp David Framework Accords and the interim Oslo Accord between Israel and the PLO.

Nevertheless, although Israel does not face at present a unified Arab world bent on its destruction, the challenges posed to its security and legitimacy are still considerably menacing.

In the south, the Islamic Hamas movement controls the Gaza Strip. In the north, Lebanon is under the de facto control of the Hezbollah. Both the Hamas and the Hezbollah call for destruction of the State of Israel. Both are armed with weapons that could

42. For an academic reference to Israel being the only country whose existence is being questioned and challenged, see Gilboa (n.d.).

potentially wreak havoc on Israeli civilian centres. The Hezbollah, which is armed like few countries in the region, presents a particularly serious challenge to Israel.

In the east, Iran constitutes a strategic menace to Israel, enhanced by its nuclear policy. Its leadership is perceived by Israelis as being obsessed with the very existence of Israel; almost every means has been traditionally valid in their pursuit of a policy of delegitimising Israel, including the denial of the Holocaust as a historical fact.[43]

Syria, which is currently absorbed in internal strife, is a further threat to Israel as its leadership has traditionally adopted the most extreme positions on the Arab-Israeli conflict and supported the most radical Palestinian groups bent on Israel's destruction and derailing of the peace process. Although the civil war has had positive side-effects for Israel, as its enemies are immersed in ever-growing violent clashes, the chaos that might ensue could spell particular trouble for Israel and pro-Western forces in the region that would have to deal with a fragmented, unstable Syria.

There is no region in Israel, no citizen in the country, no matter how far to the south or to the north he or she lives, that is immune from the weaponry of its enemies.[44]

The power to inflict harm on Israelis is enhanced by the apparent lack of any compunction by some of those willing to do so to aim

43. For the latest statement by Iran's spiritual leader in this regard, and Israel's reaction to it, see Keinon (2014). For previous statements by Iran's leaders questioning or denying the Holocaust, see, for instance, BBC News (2005).

To be sure, Iran's Foreign Minister called the Holocaust a 'horrifying tragedy' in an interview with a German television station, for which he was criticised in Iran. See, Jerusalem Post (2014a).

Beyond any genuine disagreement that may exist within the Iranian leadership on this issue, one has to bear in mind that the statement by the Iranian Foreign Minister was intended for a foreign audience. Israel has always been sensitive to statements issued by its neighbours destined for foreign audiences as distinct from those advanced in their own language for a domestic audience.

44. See the comment by Head of Military Intelligence, Aviv Kochavi, to the effect that about 200,000 missiles are aimed at Israel at any time. Harel (2012).

More recently, Kochavi said that 170,000 rockets and missiles are aimed at Israeli cities: "for the first time in many decades, the enemy has the ability to drop considerable amounts of munitions on the cities of Israel" the Head of Military Intelligence said. He went on to add that those weapons represented a huge intelligence challenge for Israel. Ginsburg (2014).

their lethal weapons on civilians. Israeli civilians have been killed in thousands primarily as a result of intended and targeted attacks against them. It is not just the narrowness of its geography that places Israel's civilian population in danger, but also the menacing objectives of its enemies and their lack of moral restraint on many occasions.

The perception that prevails among Israelis is that they are particularly vulnerable, a perception which is translated into a national security policy that is aimed at achieving the following objectives: militarily, to produce a sense of deterrence among Israel's enemies, and to have the most sophisticated means to defend Israeli civilians and to retaliate should deterrence fail; diplomatically, to create propitious international conditions to avert an attack or to legitimise an Israeli response to it in case of failure; politically, to create a sense of national unity in the face of danger, which goes beyond any divergence of opinions that exist within Israeli society.

Diplomatically, Israel also faces an automatic hostile majority comprising Muslim and non-aligned countries, in most international forums, which leave it precious little room for manoeuver. To be sure, US consistent support in the Security Council of the UN has protected Israel from many an attempt to censure and apply punitive sanctions against it. Indeed, the backing that Israel enjoys in the US has become a singular asset for Israeli diplomacy.

Certainly, the message that Israeli foreign policy has to convey is not simple. Israel has one of the most powerful armies in the world. Its intelligence services are among the most sophisticated, having achieved remarkable results both in the region and beyond it. Further, Israel is believed to possess nuclear military capacity, although it has never confirmed that.

Owing in part to the deterrence achieved by Israel's security forces, and the firm attitude displayed by Israeli diplomacy on the core issues, Egypt, Jordan and the mainstream of the PLO have resolved to negotiate with Israel and reach either peace agreements (in the case of Egypt and Jordan) or interim accords (in the case of the PLO).

Yet, Israel is still vulnerable, very much so. A tiny country with no defensible borders, beset by terrorist attacks, faced by short and long range missiles aimed at its civilians, Israel is paradoxically both very powerful and very vulnerable. Without its singular power, Israel would not exist. Without its singular sense of vulnerability, Israel would not need to be that powerful.

Thus, Israeli foreign policy has to convey both a message of deterrence and a sense of vulnerability; it has to convince its international interlocutors that it aspires to achieve peace based on painful concessions without impairing its perceived deterrence; it has to be diplomatically flexible without appearing to be weak, as adverse consequences of the latter might be considerably more significant than positive effects of the first.

There can be little doubt that a peace agreement signed between Israel and the Palestinian Authority would go a long way towards enhancing Israel's international image. The question is whether such a peace accord would improve considerably Israel's international standing in the long run. The positive effects of previous peace agreements and interim accords did not prove to be sustainable. Of course, one could contend that the diplomatic impact of a final peace agreement between Israel and its Palestinian Arab neighbours would be more profound and long-lasting than any peace accord signed with any Arab country.

In any event, beyond the diplomatic effects of such a final agreement between Israel and the Palestinian Authority, some crucial questions would still remain. After all, those wishing to destroy Israel would not be deterred by any agreement signed by Israel and the Palestinian Authority. Their aim is not to get a different accord with Israel. Their ultimate objective—and they say so clearly and explicitly —is the destruction of the State of Israel. How would the Hamas, which controls the Gaza Strip, react? Indeed, how would Hezbollah in Lebanon and its patron Iran react? There are groups affiliated with Al-Qaeda, mostly based in Gaza. How will such an agreement alter their ideology? How will it deter them from launching attacks against Israel?

These are open questions with which Israeli foreign policy has to deal while shaping a peace policy towards the Palestinian Authority. The consequence of such a peace policy, however successful its results, might be incomplete as long as there is an active desire still lingering to destroy Israel.

To be sure, an Israeli-Palestinian final accord might facilitate the forging of closer regional links between Israel and some of the Suni-led countries in the Middle East, which do not perceive Israel as being their primary threat, but rather Iran and its allies. The existing tacit mutual interest shared by Israel and those countries could be rendered into an open and formal relationship, once the Palestinian leadership signs a peace agreement with Israel. Even progress in the Israeli-Palestinian peace process, short of a formal agreement, might help in this regard.[45]

However, even in the light of the above optimistic scenario, Israel would still remain the target of countries and armed groups the aim of which will be to seek its destruction in the long run, and thwart any regional peace attained and imperil any sense of security entertained by Israelis in the short run. Thus, in Israel's case, opportunity comes accompanied by risk. In a sense, in shaping policy, Israel's policymakers are ever aware that any nuance entailing a diplomatic opportunity might be fraught with danger (The Oslo Accord, for instance), as any menace implying significant risk might constitute a springboard for a diplomatic opportunity (The Yom Kippur War, for example).

The implicit core message of Israeli foreign policy can be summarised as follows: Israel is not a powerful country that feels vulnerable. Israel is a vulnerable country that is powerful to prevent its demise. Israel's power is also aimed at persuading its foes that pursuing violence is futile. Following the cold peace with Egypt and lack of full normalisation with Jordan, as well as the perceived failure of the Oslo Accord, the aspiration entertained by Israelis has changed. Prior to the peace agreement with Egypt, Israelis depicted peace as a scenario entailing full normalisation; their aim now is more modest.

---

45. See, for instance, Spiegel-Feld (n.d.).

As an Israeli political source puts it, "Security is my first aim; peace can follow suit."[46]

The Israeli-Palestinian Conflict: At the Core of Regional Problems?

The notion that a stable Middle East is dependent predominantly on a tiny country like Israel and on its conflict with the Palestinian Arabs being resolved was never particularly convincing to Israeli decision makers. The fact that the international community tends to stress the centrality of that conflict, at the expense of other regional and internal conflicts in the Middle East, has only further confounded Israelis. The belief that, a resolution of the Israeli-Palestinian conflict *per se* would lead to a much more stable and peaceful Middle East, has generally not been shared by those involved in the shaping of Israeli foreign policy.[47]

To be sure, there are those in Israel—mostly political doves on the left and left-of-center wing of the Israeli political system—who believe that a resolution of the Israeli-Palestinian conflict would go a long way to solving the Arab-Israeli conflict. According to that point of view, the Israeli-Palestinian conflict is the most important conflict besetting Israel, the resolution of which would radically alter Israel's position in the Middle East and beyond it. However, even they would not necessarily subscribe to the notion that resolving the Israeli-Palestinian conflict would have a dramatic positive effect on the various, complex problems besetting the Middle East.

In a sense, it could be argued that Israeli foreign policymakers have seen the conflict with Arab countries—and presently with Iran—as a strategic military challenge for Israel, and the conflict with the Palestinian Arabs—certainly since the 1970s—as a strategic diplomatic challenge, entailing much human suffering for Israeli civilians, but constituting only a tactical menace to its security.

However, it would be difficult to contend that Israeli decision makers, whether from the right or from the left, have ascribed a

46. Conversation with the author, 12 October 2012, Jerusalem.

47. See, for instance, MFA (2014).

markedly potential positive regional influence to a resolution of the Israeli-Palestinian conflict, beyond the expected positive effects on Israel's relations with the Arab world and its general diplomatic standing in the international community.

The so-called Arab Spring has rendered Israel's skeptical attitude in this regard even more coherent than ever before. It behooves to look at it in terms of cause and effect, inferring logically what would have happened had Israel and the Palestinian Authority reached a final agreement. Suffice it to imagine what would have happened had a peace agreement between Israel and the Palestinian Authority been reached prior to emergence of the so-called Arab Spring.

Following such an accord, what would have happened in Syria? Would the cruel civil war now taking place in that country not have occurred? Would the Asad regime have behaved any differently towards those opposing his rule? Would they have conducted themselves any differently towards his regime? Would the Iran-backed-Hezbollah not have intervened directly in that civil war?

What about Egypt? Would Hosni Mubarak not have been deposed? Would Muhamad Morsi not have been elected? Would the violent confrontation between the Army and the Muslim Brotherhood have been averted?

Would an agreement between Israel and the Palestinian Authority have created a different reality in the Sinai Peninsula, where Jihadist groups are challenging Egypt's sovereignty and Israel's security?

Would the Iranian regime not have pursued its nuclear programme? Would it have discontinued its support for Hezbollah? Would it have altered its attitude towards Israel and the Sunni countries as a result of that accord?

Would Al-Qaeda and any of its affiliated terrorist organisations in the Middle East and beyond have altered either their ideology or their actions on account of such an agreement?

What would have been different, what wouldn't have happened that actually did, in this region and beyond, had the scenario aforementioned become a reality?

This is not merely an exercise in counterfactual history, but rather a logical attempt to ascertain accuracy of the oft-repeated argument that Israel and its dispute with the Palestinian Arabs are at the core of the Middle East problems.

Israeli public opinion reflects the official position of most—though hardly all—Israeli politicians at present, who would be ready to accept a Palestinian State in exchange for a peace agreement and an end of the conflict with the Palestinian Arabs.[48]

However, beyond that, in terms of cause and effect, it would be safe to assume that no Israeli decision maker or political representative in the Knesset from any of the major parties would contend that any of the major events taking place in the region wouldn't have happened had the conflict been resolved.

As far as Israel is concerned, in order to contend persuasively that the conflict between Israel and the Palestinian Arabs is at the core of the regional problems, it ought to be possible to demonstrate that its resolution would have prevented at least any of the major events that have taken place in the area or would have created a considerably different regional reality than the one prevailing at present. This is not merely a conceptual credo by those who shape Israeli Foreign Policy, but reflection of a deeply-held assumption that peace with the Palestinian Arabs might transform Israel's place in the region, but not the region's multifaceted and serious problems.

48. See, for instance, Haaretz (2012). For Polls conducted during 2013 on this question, see Jewish Virtual Library (2013).

References

Allison, Graham and Philip Zelikow (1999). *Essence of Decision: Explaining the Cuban Missile Crisis.* Second Edition. Longman.

Bar-On, Mordechai (2000). "The Impasse and the Alternative", *Palestine-Israel Journal* 7(3 & 4).

Bard, Mitchell (2014). "American Public Opinion Toward Israel", *Jewish Virtual Library.* Updated March. *http://www.jewishvirtuallibrary.org/jsource/US-Israel/American_attitudes_toward_Israel.html*

BBC News (2005). "Iranian Leader Denies Holocaust", *BBC News*, 14 December. *http://news.bbc.co.uk/2/hi/middle_east/4527142.stm*

Byron, Jim (2010). "How Richard Nixon Saved Israel", *The New Nixon*. Richard Nixon Foundation. *http://blog.nixonfoundation.org/2010/10/how-richard-nixon-saved-israel/*

Daraghmeh, Mohammed (2014). "Mahmoud Abbas Says He Won't Accept Israel as a Jewish State", *The Boston Globe*, 8 March. *http://www.bostonglobe.com/news/world/2014/03/08/abbas-recognition-israel-jewish-state/x04iawYOn8Iw7iJO2HvOAL/story.html*

Dunya News (2014). "Arab Summit Refuses to Recognise Israel as 'Jewish State' (AFP)", *Dunya News*, 26 March. *http://dunyanews.tv/index.php/en/World/216689-Arab-summit-refuses-to-recognise-Israel-as-Jewish*

Finley, J.C. (2014). "US & UN Condemn Gaza Rocket Attacks on Israel", *UPI*, 12 March. *http://www.upi.com/Top_News/World-News/2014/03/12/US-UN-condemn-Gaza-rocket-attacks-on-Israel/8791394656512/*

Gerber, Roger A. and Rael Jean Isaac (1996). "Shimon Says: Introduction and Compilation", *The Middle East Quarterly* III(3), June.

Gilboa, Eytan (2006). "Public Diplomacy: The Missing Component of Israel's Foreign Policy," *Israel Affairs* 12(4): 715, October. *http://uscpublicdiplomacy.org/pdfs/gilboa_israel_publicdiplomacy_Oct06.pdf*

———. (n.d.). *Public Diplomacy and Israel's Foreign Policy.* pp.721-22. *http://uscpublicdiplomacy.org/pdfs/gilboa_israel_publicdiplomacy_Oct06.pdf*

Ginsburg, Mitch (2014). "170,000 Rockets are Aimed at Israel's Cities, Says IDF Intelligence Chief", *The Times of Israel*, 29 January. *http://www.timesofisrael.com/170000-rockets-are-aimed-at-israels-cities-says-idf-intel-head/*

Gold, Dore (2013). *The Assault on Resolution 242.* Jerusalem Center for Public Affairs. 11 November. *http://jcpa.org/article/the-assault-on-resolution-242/*

Haberman, Clyde (1994). "Rabin Says Arafat's 'Jihad' Remark Set Back Peace Effort", *New York Times*, 20 May. *http://www.nytimes.com/1994/05/20/world/rabin-says-arafat-s-jihad-remark-set-back-peace-effort.html*

Haaretz (2012). "Poll: Most Rightist Israelis Would Support Palestinian State, Dividing Jerusalem", *Haaretz*, 31 December. *http://www.haaretz.com/news/national/poll-most-rightist-israelis-would-support-palestinian-state-dividing-jerusalem.premium-1.490926*

Harel, Amos (2012). "Some 200,000 Missiles Aimed Consistently at Israel, Top IDF Officer Says", *Haaretz*, 2 February. *http://www.haaretz.com/news/diplomacy-defense/some-200-000-missiles-aimed-consistently-at-israel-top-idf-officer-says-1.410584*

Hertz, Eli E. (2005). *Reply.* New York. p.105.

Holehouse, Mathew (2014). "David Cameron Condemns 'Barbaric' Missile Attack on Israel", *Daily Telegraph*, 12 March. *http://www.telegraph.co.uk/news/worldnews/middleeast/israel/10693432/*

David-Cameron-condemns-barbaric-missile-attack-on-Israel.html

IPT News (2011). "Rice: Abbas Rejected Olmert Peace Plan", *IPT News*, 1 November.*http://www.investigativeproject.org/3373/rice-abbas-rejected-olmert-peace-plan*

Isacharoff, Avi (2013). "Revealed: Olmert's 2008 Peace Offer to the Palestinians", *Jerusalem Post*, 24 May. *http://www.jpost.com/Diplomacy-and-Politics/Details-of-Olmerts-peace-offer-to-Palestinians-exposed-314261*

Isreal Ministry of Foreign Affairs (MFA) (1993). *Declarations of Principles on Interim Self-Government Arrangements*. 13 September. *http://www.mfa.gov.il/mfa/foreignpolicy/peace/guide/pages/declaration%20of%20principles.aspx*

———. (2000). "The Middle East Peace Summit at Camp David–July 2000", 11 July. *http://mfa.gov.il/MFA/AboutIsrael/History/Pages/The%20Middle%20East%20Peace%20Summit%20at%20Camp%20David-%20July%202.aspx*

———. (2000a) "Israel-Palestinian Negotiations, December 2000-January 2001", 24 December. *http://www.mfa.gov.il/mfa/foreignpolicy/peace/guide/pages/israel-palestinian%20negotiations%20-%20dec%202000-jan%20200.aspx*

———. (2007). "Winograd Commission Submits Interim Report", Par. 16, Clause b. 30 April. *http://www.mfa.gov.il/mfa/pressroom/2007/pages/winograd%20inquiry%20commission%20submits%20interim%20report%2030-apr-2007.aspx*

———. (2009). *Address by PM Netanyahu at Bar Ilan University*. 14 June. *http://mfa.gov.il/MFA/PressRoom/2009/Pages/Address_PM_Netanyahu_Bar-Ilan_University_14-Jun-2009.aspx*

———. (n.d.). "Statements Clarifying the Meaning of UN Security Council Resolution 242", *http://www.mfa.gov.il/mfa/foreignpolicy/peace/guide/pages/statements%20clarifying%20the%20meaning%20of%20un%20security%20c.aspx*

———. (2014). *PM Netanyahu Meets World Leaders in Davos*. 24 January. *http://mfa.gov.il/MFA/PressRoom/2014/Pages/PM-Netanyahu-meets-world-leaders-in-Davos-24-Jan-2014.aspx*

Janis, Irving (1972). *Victims of Groupthink: A Psychological Study of Foreign-Policy Decisions and Fiascoes*. Boston: Houghton Mifflin. p.9. Knesset Website (2008). "Agranat Commission", *Knesset Website*. *https://www.knesset.gov.il/lexicon/eng/agranat_eng.htm*

Jerusalem Post (2014). "Abbas Suggests NATO Troops be Stationed in Future Palestinian State", *Jerusalem Post*. 3 Frbruary. *http://www.jpost.com/Diplomacy-and-Politics/Abbas-suggest-NATO-troops-be-stationed-in-future-Palestinian-state-340164*

———. (2014a). "Iranian Foreign Minister Under Fire for Condemning Holocaust", *Jerusalem Post*, 24 February. *http://www.jpost.com/Middle-East/Iranian-foreign-minister-under-fire-for-condemning-holocaust-342396*

Jewish Virtual Library (2013). *Israeli Public Opinion Polls Regarding Peace with the Palestinians*. Updated November. *http://www.jewishvirtuallibrary.org/jsource/Society_&_Culture/ispopal.html*

Keinon, Herb (2014). "After Iran's Leader Questions Holocaust, Lieberman Hits Back at 'Hitlerian' Khamenai", *Jerusalem Post*, 23 March. *http://www.jpost.com/Iranian-Threat/News/After-Irans-leader-questions-Holocaust-Liberman-slams-Hitlerian-Khamenei-346203*

Klieman, Aharon (2013). "The Sorry State of Israeli Statecraft", *Israel Journal of Foreign Affairs* VII(2): 9-18. *http://israelcfr.com/documents/7-2/7-2-2-AharonKlieman.pdf*

Lapidtoh, Ruth (2011). "The Misleading Interpretation of Security Council Resolution 242 {1967}", *Jewish Political Studies Review*. Jerusalem Center for Public Affairs, (JCPA). *http://jcpa.org/wp-*

content/uploads/2012/08/JPSR-23-3-4-Lapidoth.pdf

Leon, Dan (1995). "Israeli Public Opinion Polls on the Peace Process", *'Palestine-Israel Journal* 2(1), *http://www.pij.org/details.php?id=676*

Liel, Alon (2014). "The Generals Have Won: The Grim Shape of Israeli Diplomacy", *i24News*, 18 March. *http://www.i24news.tv/en/opinion/140318-israel-is-suffering-from-a-diplomatic-lobotomy*

Lipka, Michael (2014). *Strong Support for Israel Cuts Across Religious Lines.* Pew Research Center, 27 February. *http://www.pewresearch.org/fact-tank/2014/02/27/strong-support-for-israel-in-u-s-cuts-across-religious-lines/*

Maoz, Jason (2009). "Thirty Six Years Ago Today, Richard Nixon Saved Israel—But Got No Credit", *Commentary*, 6 October. *http://www.commentarymagazine.com/2009/10/06/web-exclusive-thirty-six-years-ago-today-richard-nixon-saved-israel%E2%80%94but-got-no-credit/*

Nahmias, Roee (2007). "Lebanon War Upgraded Foreign Ministry's Status", *YnetNews.com*, 24 October. *http://www.ynetnews.com/articles/0,7340,L-3463366,00.html*

Pipes, Daniel (2005). "Assessing Kadima", *Middle East Forum*, 28 November (updated 24 January 2013). *http://www.danielpipes.org/blog/2005/11/assessing-kadima*

Rabinobich, Abraham (2013). "Moshe Dayan's Yom Kippur War", *The Jerusalem Post*, June 10. *http://www.jpost.com/Opinion/Op-Ed-Contributors/Moshe-Dayans-Yom-Kippur-War-328029*

Ravid, Barak (2007). "Foreign Ministry Lauded for Diplomatic Role in War", *Haaretz*, 2 May. *http://www.haaretz.com/print-edition/news/foreign-ministry-lauded-for-diplomatic-role-in-war-1.219540*

————. (2007a). "Foreign Ministry to Start Receiving Raw Intelligence Reports, Thanks to Winograd", *Haaretz*, 5 November. *http://www.haaretz.com/print-edition/news/foreign-ministry-to-start-receiving-raw-intelligence-reports-thanks-to-winograd-1.232518*

————. (2014). "Netanyahu: Israel Prepared to Make Peace, But Abbas Must Recognize Jewish State", *Haaretz*, 4 March. *http://www.haaretz.com/news/diplomacy-defense/1.577867*

Sharett, Moshe (1978). *Ioman Ishi* [Sharett's Diaries]. Volume II. 11 February 1954: 348; 28 February 1954: 380; 8 April 1954: 444-45. Tel Aviv: Sifriat Maariv.

Slomovich, Natanel (2009). "Costa Rican President: Palestinians Don't Need an Army", *Ynet News*, 28 November. *http://www.ynetnews.com/articles/0,7340,L-3811953,00.html*

Spiegel-Feld, Danielle (n.d.). *Time to Take the Saudi Plan Seriously.* Israel Policy Forum, *http://www.israelpolicyforum.org/commentary/time-take-saudi-plan-seriously*

The Reut Institute (2009). *Demilitarized Palestinian State.* The Reut Institute. 23 July. *http://reut-institute.org/Publication.aspx?PublicationId=3679*

Twersky, David (1998). "Remembering Nixon, The 'Anti-Semitic' Prez who saved Israel during the Yom Kippur War", *Jewish World Review*, 14 October. *http://www.jewishworldreview.com/0798/twersky1.asp*

13

LEILA BIJOS

The Brazilian Contemporary Foreign Policy

Challenges in the 21st Century

Introduction

Brazil's foreign policy has a history of continuity and renewal, and certain national characteristics have generated permanent interests. For instance, Brazil is a country of continental proportions and contains two huge hydrographic basins, the Amazon and the River Plate; it has 10 neighbouring countries, some with densely populated borders giving rise to major commercial activity and trade relationships; and the country's population of around 200 million is ethnically and socially diverse, originating from different parts of the world, which has created special links with Germany, Italy, Japan, Lebanon, Poland, Portugal and Ukraine, to name some of the most notable.

Latin Americans have many ethnic origins, including indigenous peoples, early settlers who came predominantly from the Iberian Peninsula, entrepreneurs (especially from the United Kingdom [UK] in the 19th century), Africans who came as slaves, and more recent immigrants from southern Europe, particularly Italians in Argentina and southern Brazil. All these people brought along different social mores and traditions that included particular gender relationships, but the dominant culture was established by the colonisers and reinforced by the Roman Catholic Church.

The end of the Cold War and the effects of globalisation induced the Government of Brazil (GoB) to discuss its physical and functional identity, and its role in the new international reality, how to leave its isolation and look forward to a more relevant role in the international community.

In this context, Brazil's foreign policy is a by-product of the country's unique position as a regional power in Latin America, a leader among developing countries, and an emerging world power. Brazilian foreign policy is based on the principles of multilateralism, peaceful settlement of disputes, and non-intervention in the affairs of other countries. Brazil engages in multilateral diplomacy through the Organization of American States and the United Nations (UN), and has increased ties with other developing countries in Africa and Asia, especially during the two terms of President Luiz Inacio Lula da Silva. Brazil's coming of age in world politics has made it necessary for its diplomatic agenda to broaden and become more complex, and this has created a challenge to coordinate domestic and foreign policy agendas, and systematically keep track of the positions defended by Brazil abroad.

Due to its significant contributions of uniformed personnel to UN Peacekeeping Operations, Brazil has been offered leadership roles therein and is currently providing the Force Commander to the UN Stabilisation Mission in Haiti (MINUSTAH), and to the UN Mission in the Democratic Republic of the Congo (MONUSCO).

Instead of pursuing unilateral prerogatives, Brazilian foreign policy has tended to emphasise regional integration, first through the Southern Cone Common Market (MERCOSUL) and now through the Union of South American Nations (USAN).

Brazil is also committed to cooperation with other Portuguese-speaking nations through joint-collaborations with the rest of the lusophone world, in several domains which include military cooperation, financial aid, and cultural exchange. This is done in the framework of the Community of Portuguese Language Countries (CPLP), for instance. President Lula da Silva visited Africa several times, including state visits to Angola, Mozambique and São Tomé and Príncipe. Brazil is also strongly committed to the development and restoration of peace in Timor L'Este.

Brazil's political, business, and military ventures are complemented by its trade policy. In Brazil, the Ministry of Foreign Relations continues to dominate trade policy, causing the country's commercial interests to be, at times, subsumed by a larger foreign policy goal: enhancing Brazil's influence in Latin America and the world. For example, while concluding meaningful trade agreements with developed countries (such as the United States [US] and the European Union [EU]) would probably be beneficial to Brazil's long-term economic interests, the GoB has instead made its leadership role within MERCOSUL a priority as well as expanded trade ties with countries in Africa, Asia and the Middle East.

Asia presents itself as one of the most promising diplomatic targets in the 21st century. It is one of the most dynamic regions of the world, with cultural richness, ethnic diversity, religions and sociopolitical institutions. Brazil and Asia have a solid and consistent profile. In addition, Brazil has many citizens of Asian extraction. The union and cooperation between Brazil and Asia, specifically in the context of the Association of Southeast Asian Nations (ASEAN), will consolidate partnerships as emerging economies, globalisation, consolidation of new economic blocs and regional integration with Latin Amerian countries. Globalised capitalism is intended to facilitate Western relationships, a bond that links Brazil to Western developed countries in the context of markets opening, cooperation in science and technology, and transfers of expertise in production and productivity, among others.

Brazil's soft power diplomacy involves institutional strategies such as the formation of diplomatic coalitions to constrain the power of the established Great Powers. In recent years, it has given high priority to establishing political dialogue with other strategic actors such as China, India, Russia, and South Africa through participation in international groupings such as Brazil, South Africa, India, and China (BASIC), the India, Brazil, South Africa dialogue forum (IBSA) and the Association of five major emerging economies, Brazil, Russia, India, China, and South Africa (BRICS). The BRICS states have been amongst the most powerful drivers of incremental change in world diplomacy and they benefit most from the connected global power shifts.

Brazil is aware of its importance in the world as a global player and is investing in cultural diplomacy. Cultural relations are actions inserted in the practical reality of every internationalist, diplomat or political scientist. These relations have expanded, and the specialist has the opportunity to contemplate an extensive range of themes that show the need for adjustment, organisation and interaction with the world, by means of a constant demand for economic and cultural exchange. Brazil saw the need to adapt to the new international reality and seek a more relevant role in the international scenario through the use of soft power relationships.

Brazil's development throughout the last two decades, along with its increasing involvement in great international themes, are supported by a foreign policy that aims at an increasing inclusion in the international commuity. Consequently, the number of international partners grows exponentially every day, showing the need to consolidate old partnerships, as well as to attract new ones, particularly with Asian countries, which have a remarkable cultural richness. As an example, India, Iran, Japan, the Philippines, and Taiwan are countries immersed in thousands of years of history, diversity and religious syncretism.

Culture can play an important role in overcoming obstacles, promoting cooperation and reducing mutual distrusts. Countries such as France, Germany, Japan, Spain, the US, and the UK, among others, have already recognised the value of using culture as a facilitator for their international inclusion. In order to achieve and consolidate these goals, the objectives of international inclusion of a country must be addressed based on some theoretical tools that may help with the proposed task: language teaching, cooking lessons, geopolitics, and the most important, getting in touch with citizens.

In this sense, the role of cultural diplomacy is highlighted, which provides innumerable inputs in a society that is changing from a purely political conception to a predominantly economic society. Culture creates bonds that were once non-existent between different peoples; it does not depend on origins, geographical localities or the economy. It possesses a universal character because its reach is unlimited. The culture of a country represents its identity, one that distinguishes it from other nations. Culture, as a diplomatic tool of foreign policy, facilitates international inclusion of the state, which will lead to the delimitation of diplomatic relationships, as happened globally during President Lula's government. Lula included Brazilian cuisine in official dinners, like *caipirinha*, cheese bread and milk fudge. Soft drinks as *Guaraná* (an Amazonian fruit) have been exported all around the world, *rapadura* to China and *caipirinha Garota de Ipanema* to France, Germany, and Italy.

Although the present course of Brazilian foreign policy started in the second half of President Fernando Henrique Cardoso's government, there were no qualitative changes at that time. The former president had not possessed the will or political basis to implement modifications that could go far beyond timid critical rhetoric. Lula's inauguration in 2003 transformed this situation and, at the beginning of his administration, Brazilian foreign policy showed development and leadership that surpassed many expectations. To fulfill his strategy, Lula's government's international relations were characterised by three dimensions: economic diplomacy, a political dimension, and a social agenda. The first dimension is a realist one, the second aimed at offering resistance and assertiveness, whereas the third is a propositive one.

President Lula showed himself as a labourer and as an example of a common man who rose as a union leader, founded the Labour Party and became President of the Republic for two terms (2003-2010), with more than 52 million votes from the Brazilian citizens.

Lula's main goals were to transform Brazil into an honest and equitable country, without famine, beginning with a food security programme: "Zero Hunger", "First Job Employment", and "Family Fellowship" (Silva *et al.*, 2003). His objectives included: to set as a priority of Brazilian foreign policy to reaffirm an economic and political space aiming at South American unification. It started with the rejection of the Free Trade Area of the Americas (FTAA), identified as a regional annexation project of the North American governments, which originated in the launching of the South American Community of Nations (CASA) in December 2004.

President Lula emphasised that Brazil needed to state what it stands for, doing justice to the struggle for survival in which its children are engaged; internationally, affirming its sovereign and creative presence in the world. Brazilian foreign policy should reflect the desire for change expressed by ordinary people (Brazilian Ministry of External Relations, 2008: 17).

Brazilian diplomatic policies obtained more emphasis on different approaches in the current government of Dilma Rousseff; both from the point of view of doctrinal innovation of Lula's policy and as a result of changed circumstances and the emergence of new opportunities.

The Cabinet of Brazil is composed of the Ministers of State, and senior advisors to the executive branch of the federal government Cabinet officers are appointed and may be dismissed by the President. There are currently 24 Ministries of State and 14 other cabinet-level offices.

Ministers assist the President in the exercise of executive power. Each minister is responsible for the general administration of a government portfolio, and heads a corresponding government ministry. Ministers prepare regulations, monitor and evaluate federal programmes, and formulate and implement policies for the sectors they represent. They are also responsible for establishing strategies, policies and priorities for the use of public resources. The most important minister is the Chief of Staff, while other high profile ministers include Finance, Justice, External Relations and Defence.

The current cabinet features a record number of women ministers (10, making up 26% of the cabinet), signalling President Dilma Rousseff's wish to appoint women to key sectors of her government. The cabinet consists of 25 Ministers, and the Vice-President, Michel Temer (PMDB), Chief of Staff Aloísio Mercadante (former Minister of Education), Central Bank head Alexandre Tombini, Inspector General of the Union Jorge Hage, Institutional Security Cabinet Army General José Elito Carvalho Siqueira, the Public Defender General, the Attorney General of the Union Luís Inácio Lucena Martins, and nine Secretariats in several areas. Women have been invited to be part of the Cabinet, especially Minister of Culture Marta Suplicy, Minister of Environment Izabella Teixeira, Minister of Planning, Budget and Management Miriam Belchior, Minister of Social Development and Hunger Alleviation Tereza Campello, Secretariat of Institutional Relations Ideli Salvatti, Secretariat for Social Communication Helena

Chagas, Special Secretariat for Human Rights Maria do Rosario, Special Secretariat for Promotion of Racial Equality Luiza Barrios, and Special Secretariat for Women's Rights Eleonora Menicucci.

Foreign policy and international relations determine the relationship of a country with the world. In this context, the Ministers of Finance, Justice, External Relations and Defence are high profile specialists. Their decisions may affect Brazil's domestic policy, attracting or discouraging new investors in the country. The Ministers may use their power to defend, whenever necessary, Brazilian national interests and the values of the nation.

The Central Bank of Brazil on presenting the results of the Census of Foreign Capital in the country (2010-11) highlighted FDI (foreign direct investments) and showed that the Netherlands were the major investor country in Brazil under the FDI-equity capital modality, with a stock of US$163.3 billion, or 27.8 per cent of the total, encompassing 838 enterprises. Dutch investments were concentrated on manufacturing, US$92.5 billion, and financial activities, US$29.1 billion. As immediate investors, the US represented US$108.1 billion, or 18.4 per cent of total stocks, encompassing the majority of direct investment enterprises—2,910. US investments were predominantly made in financial activities and extractive and manufacturing industries, with investments valued at US$30.1 billion, US$30 billion and US$23.2 billion, respectively. Spain was the third largest investor in 2010, with US$72 billion, 12.3 per cent of the total, encompassing 1,088 enterprises, highlighting investments in manufacturing, financial activities and extractive industry, totalling to US$20.3 billion, US$18.8 billion and US$10.8 billion, respectively. In 2011, these countries continued as major investors, with FDI-equity capital stocks totalling US$160.9 billion, US$103.2 billion and US$82.3 billion, respectively. Spanish FDI growth in the information and communications sector rose from US$10 billion to US$22.7 billion.

Brazilian foreign policy is firmly oriented towards the search for peace, for negotiated solutions to international conflicts and on principles of multilateralism, aiming at the construction of a peaceful and harmonious world order. In this context, Brazil is participating in new groupings, including the G20, BRICS, the

IBSA, the Pacific Alliance, the Arab South America Summit (ASPA), BRASIL-CARICOM, the Cooperation Forum Latin America East Asia (FOCALAL), and the Community of Portuguese Language Speaking Countries (CPLP), among others.

In addition to reducing trade barriers, these groups have begun several other projects for regional integration, including visa-free travel, a common stock exchange, and joint embassies in several countries.

Emphasis is put on the Latin American Integrated Market (MILA), which currently integrates the stock markets of Colombia, Chile, and Peru, and is seen as a foundation for the economic integration of Pacific Alliance members. In November 2010, these three stock markets began their integration, and soon became a unified market, considered the largest in Latin America by a number of issuers, in fact, the second by market capitalisation and the third by turnover. In 2014, the Mexican Stock Exchange was incorporated into MILA and it has acquired a total of 3.79 million shares of the Lima Stock Exchange (BVL), equivalent to 6.7 per cent of the shares of Series A of that market.

Notwithstanding its development, Brazil has a significant amount of its population living with an income that is not enough to cover basic necessities. The main continuous determinant of poverty in Brazil may be, in the words of Draibe (2002: 2):

> That the Governments under strong international pressure, had radically decided for one side of the balance—to make only fiscal and economic adjustment. In doing that, they took important steps in the direction of destruction of the old Welfare State. Concerning Latin America, it was in fact still an embryonic Welfare State, born in only a few countries of the region.

Nevertheless, Draibe shows that the "dismantling" of the State, which has been anxiously awaited by some citizens, is not happening, especially in its social programmes. What is happening is:

> A movement of gradual inflexion of the past social protection, seen mainly on the institutional policies and programmes level, through the introduction or reinforcement of at least three main characteristics: decentralization, new parameters for movement of

> resources and the redefinition of public-private relations in finance and in provision of goods and social services. The new social policies establishment, developing from this parameter, is still characterized by expansion and a multiplicity of participatory mechanisms and, in the great majority of the programmes, by reinforcement of the government regulatory power (Draibe, 2002: 2-3).

Facing a national policy of economic adjustment, it became even more necessary to establish a counterpoint for poverty elimination and one of its faces is the popular microcredits for excluded populations.

Presently, President Dilma Rousseff, who took office in January 2011, is consolidating the social programmes launched during the eight presidential terms of Luis Inácio Lula da Silva, which combined an array of cash transfer programmes, sharply expanding his version of the model, called the Family Grant. The Family Grant aims at breaking the cycle of poverty in Brazil, giving the poor small cash payments in exchange for keeping their children in school and taking them for regular medical check-ups. Each month, poor families receive about US$24. The target is to reach at least 11.4 million families—more than a quarter of Brazil's population. The programme was launched with the support of the World Bank and the Inter-American Development Bank, whch provided US$3 billion in loans for the programme. Its total cost over the President's four-year term will be close to US$7 billion. Its annual cost—about a third of one per cent of Brazil's GDP (gross domestic product)—will be more than offset by savings during President Lula da Silva's administration.

Summary of the Political Context of Brazilian Foreign Policy

As Brazil moves into the 21st century, the racial and ethnic mix of its population has grown more complex. Focusing on the economic arena (salary and status), we may say that after centuries of domination, most African-Brazilian citizens continue to live below the poverty line. Thus, Brazilians consider the issue of poverty to be determined by race and the absence of economic and social participation in society. Poverty remains in the majority of Brazilian provinces. During the past two decades, the Brazilian people have made significant progress in the battle to forge a true racial and ethnic melting pot, but they are still far from declaring victory.

By analysing the fundamental problems of the most impoverished members of society in Brazil, especially people of African origin, their rights and individual contributions to collective decisions and the conditions that make them able to improve their chances of survival and insertion into the capitalist system, we may refer to their displacement, as most of the indigenous people and those of black African descent have been taken from their native lands by oligopolistic groups.

Likewise, once living in urban areas, they become affected by criminality and by the globalisation process, leading to displacement from traditional rites, festivals and customs that are important tools for the transfer of knowledge and native cultures.

In this context, one questions: how should countries face the unbalanced aspects of globalisation in its different aspects? (DIAS, 2002) The openness of global financial markets, for example, contrasts drastically with the closed nature. The start of the 21st century is witnessing global interactions on a scale and intensity unparalleled in history—within and between business, governments and people. As global interaction and integration grow, issues of global governance are becoming more and more critical. Problems, whether economic, social or environmental, increasingly spill over into neighbouring, and even distant lands. Policy decisions by governments have international implications, and truly global problems are emerging. While globalisation offers great potential to improve human livelihood around the world, there is a concern that the process is getting out of control (UNU, 2001).

Social Policies in Latin America

Although Brazil is considered to be the fifth largest nation in the world and is the largest country in South America, it shows high inequality levels. Economically, Brazil also achieved the sixth position in ranking of the countries with the most significant GDP in the world, but the number of people excluded is astonishing (World Bank Report, 2011). The country passed only 5 per cent of other countries in its inequality ranking. Based on the Monthly Employment Research (Pesquisa Mensal de Emprego—PME), published by the Brazilian Geography and Statistics Institute (IBGE, 2010), it would take at least 20 more years for Brazil to achieve a comparable level to that of other countries with the same development pattern (IPEA, 2010). The Brazilian economy has shown a significant growth rate during the past four years, due, mainly, to the proper execution of national monetary policy, aiming to ensure stability in the internal market and reduce the effects of economic risks that can cause negative impacts on the economy.

The labour market remains a key element in the process of upward social mobility. In this context, the unemployment rate reached 5.3 per cent in October 2012 and approximately 1.7 million jobs were created that year (*Brazilian Economic Outlook*, Ministry of Finance, 2012). Thus, it is expected that increasing formalisation and expansion of policies to guarantee basic income, access to public services and inclusion of the poor in the formal economy, continue to advance the socio-economic inclusion of the poorest.

The expectation is that the Brazilian economy will be even stronger with the expansion of the middle class, or 'C' class. According to the Brazilian Institute of Applied Economic Research (IPEA), the "C" class will increase by 15 million people by 2014, reaching 59 per cent of the population. This means an enormous consumption potential, which is fundamental to stimulate an increase in productive capacity in Brazil.

Emphasis is put on the increase in cash transfers in recent years, especially of minimum wage and *Bolsa Família Program*, which has substantially and comprehensively reduced poverty levels in the country. In 2009, the year of the economic crisis, poverty continued its downward trend for the aforementioned reasons and had little impact on the job market (Neri, 2010).

It is also notable that there was an increase in the buying power of monthly wages, contituting real gains for the population. The stronger growth of the economy, coupled with cash transfer programmes and inflation control, ensured a significant income increase. 'Lower income' encompasses the population below the average poverty line, which was 41.1 per cent of the northern population, 51.3 per cent of the northeastern, 17.6 per cent of the southeastern, 17.3 of the southern, and 18.2 from the mid-western (Ministry of Finance, 2010).

The 9.5 per cent increase in minimum wage has allowed improvements in the purchasing power of the population over the last year. These improvements include a smoother rise in the essential products' 12-month period rate, like food & beverages, and a reduction in the cost of a staple food basket. For example, one minimum wage used to buy only 1.38 staple food basket in June 2008. From then on, the power of the minimum wage to purchase a staple food basket has increased by 29 per cent (Dieese and LCA, 2010).

Nonetheless, Brazil is expected to grow just 2.1 per cent in 2013, according to Nomura Securities. That would make 2013 the third consecutive year of sub-3 per cent growth, a significantly slower rate than the emerging-market peers such as China and India.

Complicating matters, inflation at around 6 per cent has also been higher than targeted. President Rousseff's challengers are expected to make slow growth and persistently high inflation a key part of their campaigns against her. Her popularity briefly dropped in June when an increase in bus fares triggered nationwide protests by Brazilians angered by rising costs and poor public services (Fick and Kiernan, 2013).

According to the latest census, undertaken in 2010, the population of Brazil was 190,732,694, although this number has grown significantly since then. Therefore, because of rapid increases, the results of the census are already out of date. The Instituto Brasileiro de Geografia e Estatística (IBGE), which runs the Brazilian census and compiles the latest population data, completed its latest estimate in July 2013, and reported that it believed Brazil had a population of 200,674,130 in 2013. This is the first time Brazil's population has topped 200 million, and it continues rising faster than previous estimates as its ever-growing middle class live longer than their parents (*World Population Review*, UNFPA, 2013).

This new scenario presents more women looking for job opportunities, as well as participation in discussions concerning racial inequalities and discrimination in the work place. International Labour Organization (ILO) data show 73.3 per cent of white men in the labour market in comparison to 73.4 per cent black men; 53.0 per cent of white women compared to 52.7 per cent of black women, totalling 62.7 per cent workers at the national level. Index rates present 30.2 per cent as total inclusion of women in the labour market in Brazil in a period of 10 years (1995-2005) (PNAD/IBGE, 2005).

From 2005 to 2013, due to the strong recovery of emerging economies around the world, the Brazilian market has been converted to a stable and attractive investment environment. Consequently, the Brazilian economically-active population grew at an accelerated pace, which, in turn, made it possible to achieve an income increase and the inclusion of even larger groups in the so-called middle class. It is expected (in 2014) that Brazil will have the fifth smallest unemployment rate among developed and emerging economies.

This controversial analysis of growth and real benefits for the population highlights that although Brazil has recently achieved the rank of the 16th world economy in terms of size of its GDP, it is still far from the most developed countries, when compared to the more important indices such as GDP, competitiveness, Human Development Index (HDI) (UNDP, 2012), capacity in doing business (Report "Doing Business"), and there still exists great social, regional, urban and rural inequality.

Between 1980 and 2012, Brazil's HDI rose by 1.2 per cent annually from 0.522 to 0.730 today, which gives the country a rank of 85 out of 187 countries with comparable data. The HDI of Latin America and the Caribbean as a region increased from 0.574 in 1980 to 0.741 today, placing Brazil below the regional average. HDI trends tell an important story both at the national and regional level and highlight the large gaps in well-being, opportunities and life expectancy that continue to divide our interconnected world (*International Human Development Indicators*, UNDP, 2012).

The negative aspects of shortfalls in development relate to water supply, and access to sanitation and garbage collection, which are basic services important for maintaining good living conditions. Presently, safe water is available in 93.2 per cent of urban households, but negative rates show that 31.4 per cent of households in the northern region do not have safe water, although the statistical data from the National Household Sample Survey (PNAD) (2010) says that water supply increased 1.5 per cent points (the data do not specify whether it is safe water or if it is only a basic supply).

Sanitation services are found in 70.6 per cent of the total households in the country (PNAD, 2010), but in the northern region a precarious inequality situation shows 12.6 per cent. In the northern region, 10.5 per cent count on sanitation services, northeast 34.5 per cent, centre-west 37.2 per cent, southeast 84 per cent and southern 60.6 per cent (Brazilian Institute of Geography Statistics [IBGE], 2010).

Demographic analysis demonstrates a decrease in the percentage of young and an increase in the elderly in the total population. In 2005, the percentage of children from 0-9 years old was 17.1 per cent, whereas in 2006 this number had decreased to 16.5 per cent. The population over 40 years old in 2005 was 31.5 per cent and there was an increase to 32.3 per cent in 2006. The same trends are shown in all regions, but percentages are higher in the south and in the southeast (PNAD, 2010). The reality shows that the population of both men and women is getting older, due to a decrease in fertility rates (which had been 2.1 births per woman and diminished to 2.0 births in 2010); on the other hand, there has been an increase in life expectancy for the Brazilian population (overall).

Migration occurs in adults during the reproductive age, 37.9 per cent of those 18-39 years old, and 33.7 per cent of those 40-59 years old. People migrate from the rural areas to urban centres. In this context, women are nearly always the poorest of the poor.

Nonetheless, expectancy of life at birth, from 2006-2010, presented an increase of 3.5 years, with women's life expectancy improving more than that of men (72.3-75.8 years for women and 65.1-68.7 for men). Governmental policies have been implemented to improve Brazil's progress in reaching human development goals in the rural sector, and to prevent the spread of large-scale slums in the cities, as well as to address other structural problems such as water pollution, shortage of educational facilities, deterioration of public health and lawlessness. When women are considered the poorest of the poor, they disproportionately lack access to land and water, to education and to other social services. Too often, women are excluded from decision-making, not only in governmental processes at the national, regional and local levels, but also within their own families.

On analysing the GNI (gross national income) per capita in PPP (purchasing power parity), emphasis is put on aggregate income of an economy generated by its production and its ownership of the factors of production, less the incomes paid for the use of factors of production owned by the rest of the world, converted to international dollars using PPP rates, divided by midyear population. As an example, the northeastern region has presented real GDP growth, which ranged from 13.8 per cent in 2003 to 14.1 per cent in 2004. In addition, its participation in the GDP per capita from 1985 to 2004 was 64.0 per cent. It has little by little been advancing through 2013, despite the absence of major government infrastructure.

Geographical factors, such as sparse and irregular rainfall, recurrent drought, poor soils, and historically unfavourable economic and social factors, contributed significantly to development. Over half of the local population living below poverty levels, and persistent anachronistic political models, makes the northeastern region of Brazil, especially the semi-arid region of Brazil, at the highest risk for human security, due to lack of nutritious food, resulting in an increase in nutritional deficiencies.

Statistical data show that 10.6 per cent of Brazil is located in a semi-arid region, and 12.7 per cent in the 'hunger polygon'. This area encompasses eight states in the western portion of Brazil's northeastern region (not including the state of Maranhão). The region also has 85 municipalities in the North of Minas Gerais, affected by irregular rainfall and drought seasons. It is within these areas that the greatest risks of food shortages and nutritional insecurity occur and, figuratively speaking, they comprise 'the cartography of hunger'.

The deline in the infant mortality rate in that region was the most significant result registered in the country, 37.2 per cent in 2008 and 33.9 per cent in 2010 (MS, SVS, SIM),[1] which seems to indicate the beneficial effect of implementation of sanitation policies and investment in infrastructure and the health and education sectors in most of the country's urban centres.

Concerning education, the gross rates of attendance at school in 2010 showed a significant increase in some age groups. For children from 0 to 3 years old, the percentage doubled from 7.4 per cent in 1996 to 15.5 per cent in 2006. In the age group from 4 to 6 years old, the rates changed from 53.8 per cent to 76.0 per cent in the same period, representing a growth of 40 per cent. The 2010 results confirm that access to school for children from 7 to 14 years old is practically universal, without any distinction related to gender or race (Table 13.1).

However, the situation is worse for students from 15-17 years old—the age that corresponds to secondary education. Evidence shows that while access to school was increasing from 69.5 per cent to 82.2 per cent between 2006 and 2010, the net frequency rate of attendance for that age group in 2010 did not reach more than 47.1 per cent.

Conditions for women are also very important for equality of opportunities, as an outcome of inequality may be attributed to differences in 'circumstances', including family background, and partly due to 'personal efforts'.

Brazil on the Brink of Becoming a Developed Country

A realistic picture of Brazil still shows deep inequalities, but it also shows that they are being competently addressed, with prospects for achieving prosperity and a durable growth cycle in the near future.

Brazil's industrial economy is strong and diversified; at the same time the country is a major agricultural, beef and mining producer. Brazilian international trade is well balanced, with four large

1. MS: Ministério da Saúde (Ministry of Health), SVS: Secretaria de Vigilância em Saúde (Secretariat for Health Surveillance), SIM: Sistema de Informações sobre Mortalidade (Mortality Information System).

Table 13.1

Commitment to Education

Educational System				
Compulsory	*Primary*	*Secondary*	*Higher Education*	*Source*
12 years	9 years	3 years	4 to 5 years	4

Public Expenditure on Education (US$ million)

		Fundamental Education					
Years	*Children Education*	*from 1st to 4th grade*	*from 5th to 8th grade*	*Secondary Education*	*Higher Education (University)*	*Total*[iii]	*Source*
2007	0.3	1.2	1.0	0.5	0.9	4.0	3
2008	0.3	1.2	1.1	0.6	0.8	4.0	3
2009	0.3	1.1	1.2	0.7	0.9	4.2	3
2010	0.6	1.0	1.2	0.6	0.8	4.2	3
2011	0.7	0.3	1.1	0.5	0.8	4.2	3
2012	0.9	0.3	0.4	0.7	1.9	4.2	3

Illiteracy rate 2006 (%)

Illiteracy rate of the population from 15 years old or more compared to Latin America and the Caribbean			*Students that have concluded Fundamental Education – Female (Brazil)*			*Source*
Total	*Men*	*Women*	*1 858 615*			2
9.5	8.8	10.3	Latin America and the Caribbean (%)			1
			Total	Men	Women	
			11.1	11.3	11.0	2

Functional illiteracy (15 years old or more)[iv]

Total	*Men*	*Women*	*Rural*	*Urban*	
23.5%	24.1 %	23.0%	45.8	19.3	1 and 4

Enrolment[v]

Children' education				*Primary School*		*Secondary school*		
Nursery School		*Pre-school*		33,282,663		8,906,820		3
1,427,942		5,588,153		*Men*	*Women*	*Men*	*Women*	
Men	*Women*	*Men*	*Women*	17,086,427	16,196,236	4,091,657	4,815,163	3
742,740	685,576	2,864,454	2,723,699					

Population with higher education (12 years and over) %

	2012		2012		
	Men	*Women*	*Men*	*Women*	
Brazil	43.7	56.3	42.5	57.5	1
North	41.7	58.3	40.0	60.0	1
Northeast	39.6	60.4	39.7	60.3	1
Southeast	45.2	54.8	44.4	55.6	1
South	43.1	56.9	41.1	58.9	1
Centre-east	43.2	56.8	42.4	57.6	1

Female ratio of higher education (2012)						
Education	*Humanities and Arts*	*Social Sciences*	*Natural Sciences and Computing*	*Engineering, Production and Construction*	*Agriculture and Veterinarian*	*Source*
62.9%	81.7%	54.6%	42.6%	30.8%	42.1%	3
	Health and Social Welfare			*Services*		3
	72.3%			70.6%		3

Gross primary enrolment (% of school-age population)				
Men	146	*Literacy (% of population age 15+)*	*Youth literacy rate (% aged 15-24)*	*Source*
Women	135	89	96.8	1 and 5

Notes: Does not include inactive and pensioners.

a. For 2000 municipality, data are estimations. For 2011 and 2012, state and municipality data are also estimations. b. The results are based on data sent to OECD/WEI. c. Based on direct expenses. d. Ministry of Education. e. *Human Development Report* (2010/2012). f. According to that published at INEP website (*http://www.inep.gov.br/estatisticas/gastoseducacao/PIB_nivel_ensino.htm*). Values are calculated based on mathematical approximation methodology of two decimals digits. g. Functional Illiteracy refers to the inability of an individual to use reading, writing, and computational skills efficiently in everyday life situations. Illiteracy is the inability to read or write simple sentences in any language. h. It is important to notice that parents in rural areas do not enroll children in schooling systems, first because they need their help in agriculture; so most of them go to school for the first time when they are 10 years old and stay for some 6-7 years just to get basic literacy and insert themselves in the labour force. When they are 17 years old or more, they feel more mature and know they need an official certificate to get a better job, thus most of them stay longer at school. Nonetheless, young men leave school in search of work, while women stay in school longer and finish the educational cycle. As well, it's important to highlight that the data is shown by the total population, including also those who did not declare scholar attendance.

Sources: 1. IBGE/PNAD, 2012. 2. *Latin America and the Caribbean Yearbook 2010.* Santiago de Chile: CEPAL, 2012; *Latin America and the Caribbean Yearbook 2010.* Santiago de Chile: 2012. Available in: *http://www.eclac.cl/publicaciones/*. 3. IInstituto Nacional de Estudos e Pesquisas Educacionais Anísio Teixeira–INEP (National Institute of Educational Studies and Research Anisio Teixeira)–Ministry of Education, Census on Higher Education. *http://portal.inep.gov.br/web/censo-da-educacao-superior.* 4. Institute for Applied Economic Research–IPEA-Diretoria de Estudos e Políticas Sociais (DISOC) (Directorate Studies in Social Policies) *http://www.ipea.gov.br/portal/index.php?option=com_content&view=article&id=151.* 5. National Institute of Geography and Statistics –IBGE (2010). *Public Expenditure on Education. 2010: Population Census. http://www.ibge.gov.br*

poles of origin and destination in terms of foreign relations (the European Union, accounting for around 28% of Brazil's international trade, the US for around 20%, Latin America another 20% and the Pacific Rim also 20%). The Brazilian economy reveals a high level of complementarities in relation to the different economies that have developed and are developing. Brazil is highly competitive in the sectors of agriculture, cattle and industrial products, despite, for that very reason, facing protectionist barriers in some developed markets.

Twenty-nine years after the election of civilian President Tancredo Neves (15 January 1985), who accepted the challenge of being a candidate for the President of the Republic after 23 years of military rule, Brazilian democracy is firmly established, its institutions are strong, and they resist political crises with hardly a dent.

Brazil is flush with natural resources: the world's largest biodiversity and its largest fresh water reserves (a strategic factor in this century). The country is close to self-sufficiency in oil and has outstanding renewable energy sources, particularly sugar cane.

These and other basic characteristics of Brazil signal clear priorities for Brazilian foreign policy: strengthening of the World Trade Organization (WTO), full participation in all the mechanisms for promoting sustainable development, human rights and the non-proliferation of weapons of mass destruction; the consolidation and broadening of MERCOSUL, one of the bases of Brazil's new international identity; the strengthening of some of the country's traditional partnerships, such as the one that unites it with Argentina in a strategic alliance, or the launching of new partnerships, such as that being forged with BRICS; and full and active participation in discussions on hemispheric integration and in new areas of international trade.

It is in order to move these priorities forward that Brazil is engaged in intense diplomatic activity in the various circles within which it moves: MERCOSUL, South America, the Southern Hemisphere and the world. This packed diplomatic agenda has directly involved the President of Brazil, Dilma Rousseff, in the exercise of presidential diplomacy, which has achieved prominence both inside and outside the country. That diplomacy clearly reflects some of Brazil's priorities and reveals a nation that is committed to searching out and strengthening partnerships within the developed and developing world, whilst exercising a discreet yet affirmative protagonism in its own region and in relation to issues of particular interest to Brazilian society, such as environmental protection and sustainable development.

Through the major courses followed and by specific achievements of the diplomacy of the Fernando Henrique Cardoso government, it is possible to find many points of innovation that meet the necessities and challenges of Brazil and also to identify the origins of Brazilian foreign policy, which have endowed Brazilian diplomacy with the character of a fundamental instrument of national sovereignty and development.

The following topics refer to the analysis of the Brazilian educational scenario.

Brazilian Educational Reality

Education and knowledge are essential to the economic development and welfare of the society, and quantitative and qualitative schooling indicators and scientific production have shown an evolution in recent decades in Brazil. Nonetheless, the social and economic indicators present low performance when one considers their impact on the living conditions of the population as a whole.

There is a specific bottleneck showing that knowledge as well as education can be the most efficient promoter of economic and social development. On examining results, especially concerning the dimension of knowledge, we can visualise the HDI projections up to the year 2022, which show that progress is related to education. Nonetheless, if the tendencies shown in the country in the last decades continue, the probable scenario will be low quality basic education, related to the density of social inequalities.

It is important to highlight Brazil's performance in the past two decades, which diverged completely from the period 1955-1980. At that time, there was an unprecedented transforming desire to modernise the material basis of the national economy, conducted through a social convergence between main political forces of the nation.

The modernisation of society, with the spread of a broad urban workforce and an advanced middle class employed in public service and in both large private foreign corporations and Brazilian enterprises, advanced a qualified social structure and provided the population with very good living conditions. It revealed the singular progress of productive forces, due to economic cycles (sugar cane, gold, coffee and industrialisation), which inserted themselves in several political regimes over time (empire, republic, dictatorship and democracy), but neglected to attach it to a distribution system that could reduce social inequalities.

Social and economic inequality is visible when one examines the available data: of 40 million Brazilian households, 10 million are considered unhealthy and 2 million do not have electricity. Around 21 million people have no access to clean drinking water. Apart from these elementary necessities, which show a deprivation of basic human rights, like the right to life, only 8.2 per cent of the population of Brazil had access to computers in 2002. Therefore, there was no widespread access to information. Summing up this negative scenario, it is important to emphasise that school conditions provide an oppressive structural inequality pattern.

To reverse the data, Brazilian society has to express itself in the process of modernisation to correct the mistakes. It is necessary to have a clean, active, planned and able country to envisage a future of improved living conditions in Brazil.

In 2001, the GoB announced affirmative action programmes to increase the number of non-white students at Brazilian universities, considered as anathema to Brazilians' long-established impression of their country as a democracy. Although significant race-based policy initiatives had been taken in a few municipalities, these were the first policies implemented on a large scale and at the federal level. Implementation of affirmative action was seen as a top-down policy, although it was brought on by pressure from the black movement and Brazil's international commitments, particularly at the UN Conference Against Racism in 2001. According to Telles (2013), "since then, affirmative action has progressively expanded to many public universities, and federal law now requires it at all federal universities." Consequently, affirmative action has engendered much discussion about race and racism, including lively debate about affirmative action, whereas public discussion of race and racism was rare prior to 2001. The discussions spread out at the university councils, especially in the most competitive public universities, increasing their popularity.

It is important to highlight that public universities are completely free of charge in Brazil, and tend to be superior to private universities, but the students who are enrolled in public universities come disproportionately from the private secondary schools that Brazil's privileged classes attend. Paradoxically, most Brazilians attend the poorly resourced public schools, and those who graduate and go on to college predominately go to private universities, which account for 70 per cent of higher education students in Brazil (Paixao and Carvano, 2008). Many middle class or upper middle class families do not enroll their children in public secondary schools, as it is an indicator of low socio-economic status in Brazil.

This situation has given birth to quota systems, which have become the default affirmative action programme, especially because they fit well with the Brazilian system of university admissions, which tend to be based entirely on entrance examinations. Quota-based programmes guarantee a certain percentage of university admission slots to students on the basis of race and/or class. As some universities do not feel comfortable accepting coloured or disadvantaged students, a few universities like the State University of Campinas and Federal University of Minas Gerais have begun to use point systems, which give additional 'points' to the applications of those from disadvantaged backgrounds. Notwithstanding, the point system does not provide a guarantee of access to university education for a number of beneficiaries. Although affirmative action has not eliminated racism, it is moving forward in its goal of inserting non-white people in Brazil's federal and state universities (Telles and Paixão, 2013).

Policies in 2016 will require that all federal higher educational institutions implement quotas on the basis of attendance at public high school; family income; or being indigenous, black or brown. As a Quota Law was approved in 2012 by the National Congress, the GoB expects that the number of quota students in higher education will increase by roughly three times (Paixao and Carvano, 2008).

Brazilian reality includes many people who are suffering, impoverished and discriminated against in society. To involve indigenous, black, or brown people in Brazilian society, it is necessary to have a development agenda, so that poverty can be reduced.

In fact, during this period the average income of the poorest (10.4%) headcount rate at $ 2.00 a day PPP. The poverty gap is the mean shortfall from the poverty line (counting the non-poor as having zero shortfall), expressed as a percentage of the poverty line. This measure reflects the depth of poverty as well as its incidence, and it reached 5.4 per cent in Brazil.

In this context, as measured by the Gini coefficient, which is the most commonly used indicator of income inequality, income concentration in the country presents a data of 5.5 per cent by 2012.

In the period as a whole, the average income growth of the poorest 20 per cent was some 20 percentage points higher than that of the richest 20 per cent. Therefore, while the perception of the poorest in Brazil was that they were living in a country with a high rate of economic growth, for the richest 20 per cent, the country was going through a period of economic stagnation.

As for the inequality generated by the labour market, the first fundamental aspect to be noticed is wage discrimination based on race and gender. As in nearly all countries in the world, the wages of Brazilian women are much lower than those of men. This differential has remained stable, with a slight rising trend between 2001 and 2004, and therefore, has not contributed to the fall in income inequality. Wage differentials by race are also high in Brazil, although much lower than gender differentials, and despite the falls recorded in the past decade, their quantitative importance in explaining the recent fall in income inequality is close to none (IBGE, 2010).

In addition to race and gender discrimination, the labour market can also be a generator of inequalities if it is segmented. As regards spatial segmentation, possible reductions in high wage differentials between the Units of the Federation (UFs) could be a potential source to explain the fall in income inequality. However, over the past decade, labour markets in the different UFs have not become more integrated and, therefore, this aspect has not contributed to reducing the degree of income inequality (Souza, 2012).

The monthly income rate per capita is the basic data information usually used to analyse the socio-economic conditions of the population, showing in 2010, that in 39 per cent of the households in the northeastern region, the families received only half of the minimum wage. The same condition was identified in 32.5 per cent for the northern region households. South and southeast regions present lower percentages at 12.5 per cent and 13.6 per cent respectively, meaning that families have higher income wages (IBGE, 2007). In this context, the Brazilian Family Expenditure Survey was conducted by the Brazilian Institute of Geography and Statistics to show the population life conditions based on their household budget and corresponding expenditure.

Afro-Brazilians and women represent 42 per cent and 44.5 per cent, respectively, of the Brazilian Economically Active Population (EAP). Summed up, they correspond to 55 million persons or 68 per cent of EAP in Brazil, that is, a vast majority: 36 million blacks of both sexes and almost 19 million white women. Nevertheless, special attention is given to 14 million black women who represent 18 per cent of the Brazilian EAP, who are submitted to a double, or sometimes triple stigma of discrimination (gender and race, also linked to social discrimination (ILO, 2006). Life expectancy for white women is 71 years-old, and 40.7 per cent of Afro-Brazilian black women die before reaching 50 years old (SEADE, 2005). In terms of quality of life, white men rank 41°, white women 69°, and Afro-Brazilian men 114°, showing the lowest quality of life rate (GDI or Gender Development Index).

It is not possible to face social exclusion with simple solutions or with short term planning, because it is a complex phenomenon with many interrelated elements that mutually reinforce each other. Violence, criminality, social protests, the absence of access to financial services and health systems and education are some limitations that can condemn the excluded to live in poverty and miserable conditions (BID, 2008).

Governmental authorities and research institutions are worried about declining growth indices in the world, combined with other elements. Investments have been made to improve the average years of education of the population, especially children and youth from vulnerable families who were previously excluded from the educational system, and who are now able to attend secondary school. The consequent increase in student heterogeneity has heightened the challenges of retaining children in school until graduation as well as providing high quality education. Despite the magnitude of the changes, few attempts have been made to compute and explain the patterns of enrolment, graduation, and dropout rates in Latin America over the past two decades.

Increasing educational achievement around the world is one of the key aims of the Millennium Development Goals (MDGs). Cash transfer programmes, both conditional and unconditional (Baird *et al.*, 2013), are a popular social protection tool in developing countries that aim, among other things, to improve educational outcomes. The debate over whether these programmes should include conditions has been at the forefront of recent global policy discussions. This systematic review aims to complement the existing evidence on effectiveness of these programmes in improving schooling outcomes and help inform the debate surrounding the design of cash transfer programmes.

Monthly Wage of Employed and Active Population Per Gender

The participation of women in the labour market is registered in four categories, which correspond to about 70.0 per cent of the female workforce—general services 30.7 per cent, agricultural work 15.0 per cent, administrative jobs 11.8 per cent, and commerce 11.8 per cent. The highest participation of women in the workforce occurs in the centre-east region, with 36 per cent; in the northeast region, 26.6 per cent were identified as involved in agricultural jobs; the southeast region had the most significant percentage of women in the administrative sector; and commerce absorbed 15.5 per cent in the northern region (IBGE, 2010).

Table 13.2

Monthly Wage of Employed and Active Population Per Gender and Monthly Income Brazil, 2010[2]

Monthly Income and Household Situation	*10 Years Old and Above (in 1000 People)*			*Monthly Income of 10 Years Old and Above (R$) (1)*		
	Total	*Men*	*Women*	*Total*	*Men*	*Women*
Total	156,284	75,326	80,957	587	764	423
Less than 1/2 minimum wage	12,958	3,992	8,965	89	100	84
More than 1/2 to 1 minimum wage	27,107	12,555	14,552	316	313	320
More than 1 to 2 minimum wages	32,075	17,758	14,316	522	528	513
More than 2 to 3 minimum wages	12,046	7,608	4,438	879	880	878
More than 3 to 5 minimum wages	9,036	5,702	3,334	1,360	1,358	1,365
More than 5 to 10 minimum wages	7,269	4,652	2,617	2,415	2,419	2,409
More than 10 to 20 minimum wages	2,557	1 742	814	4,899	4,923	4,847
More than 20 minimum wages	970	751	219	11,761	11,818	11,567
Urban	131,091	62,152	68,938	647	847	467
Rural	25,193	13,174	12,019	277	374	173

Note: Not included in the population without income declaration.

Source: IBGE, National Household Survey (PNAD) 2010.

2. The statistical data concerning Monthly Wage of Employed and Active Population per Gender, emphasises women of 10 years old and over, who are actively working. (Some families allow girls who are 10 years old to work as baby sitters or maids to help parents with income.)

According to Brazilian legislation, work is legally authorised from 18 years old onward; however, children can develop apprentice work during the school year as interns at private enterprises or even in the public service, receiving scholarships as well as expense allowances or even they can do some labour activity as a form of participation in a social programme, as, for example, the conditionality of the Bolsa Família Programme.

Nevertheless, in the past six years, there has been an increase in the number of working children from 10 years old on, which indicates that they are inserted in the informal sector of the economy in urban areas, as rural workers, as well as workers in agricultural small family businesses. In light of this, they have been studied and considered in surveys and research data as compounds of labour force and participants in the family income.

Considering the combination of gender/ethnicity, the situation of Afro-Brazilian women is much worse than others, in all fields. Women's average pay still remains at 50 per cent of that of men, while black women earn 50 per cent of white women's average wages (ILO, 2010). According to the International Labour Organization (ILO), if the present development rates continue, in a period of 475 years women will reach equal levels with men (ILO, 2010). Families often consider women as important only to do household tasks; consequently, girls and women are not motivated to attend formal classes.

Educationally, for the same stereotypical reasons, women's fields of study tend to be in the humanities or health and medical services. Black and poor students dropout of school at an early age, as families need them in the labour force in the agricultural areas and the income they can generate to protect families from famine. Adults from 25 to 39 years old present high illiteracy rates; ranging from 21.6 per cent to 37.1 per cent in the northern region. In the northeast, 22.6 per cent of adults who are 25-39 years old are not able to learn due to poverty, difficult access to school, difficulties in learning as educational methods are old-fashioned, curricula and teaching materials are not adequately suited to regional patterns, teachers lack the necessary skills for the profession, absence of infrastructure and facilities, and the monthly wage corresponds to US$ 30.

Focusing on health, statistical data show that there are 13 million people suffering from hypertension, 4.5 million with diabetes and there is no financial budget to cover treatment for these conditions in public institutions. In addition, 50 per cent of the Brazilian women do not have access to adequate neonatal treatment.

The Brazilian Ministry of Health considers that this chaotic health situation indicates that diseases such as tuberculosis and syphilis can return to large urban centres such as Rio de Janeiro and the triple frontier (Argentina, Uruguay, and Paraguay), if financial resources are not approved in the annual governmental budget to improve the situation. This is evidenced by an increase in HIV/AIDS cases and a high mortality rate in children, especially indigenous and migrant ones.

Social and public policies should be aimed at improvement of the educational level of health councillors, that of administrative staff, and offering them in-service training courses, at federal, state and municipal levels. In this context, elementary school teachers should be trained to deal with pregnancy at their institutions, which show a high level of pregnant teenagers in the country. It is of fundamental importance to train and sensitise students to HIV/AIDS, sexually transmitted diseases, abortion causes, as well as to listen to the women and inform them of the necessity of family planning.

It is important to integrate actions to support youth and education that addresses sexuality with clear and easy-to-understand information, concerning methods to avoid pregnancy, such as oral contraceptive pills, the contraceptive patch (Evra), injection, spermicides, condoms, intrauterine devices or diaphragms (IUDs), standard family planning, such as natural birth control methods, and others. Reports on the actions of the Ministry of Health between 2006 and 2012 indicate that, during this period, reproductive health was made a priority. A broader agenda has been established in the first term of President Dilma Rousseff's government. One basic point means guaranteeing access to family planning, and providing education on methods of contraception. As to reduction of maternal mortality, one of the strategies is the creation of prevention committees in all Brazilian municipalities with more than 50,000 inhabitants.

Particular attention should be paid to the serious problem of maternal mortality, requiring action to provide full health care for women, taking into account the challenges posed by HIV/AIDS, and infectious and parasitic diseases that continue to represent public health problems, such as malaria, tuberculosis and leprosy. Up to 2003, about 310,000 cases of AIDS had been diagnosed in Brazil. The southeast and southern regions presented the largest concentration of cases in the period between 1980 and 2003—84 per cent. The southeast, however, despite the high incidence rate, is the only region that shows a consistent declining trend in HIV/AIDS since 1998. Comparing recently figures with those of 2012, the national rate fell by 31.5 per cent—from 18.7 to 12.8 people infected by

HIV per 100,000 inhabitants—and the rate in the southeast region, 41 per cent—29 per 100,000 to 17.1 per 100,000. There was an increasing trend in the number of cases in some states of the north and northeast regions, related to alterations in the socio-economic patterns of the disease, which began to strike harder in poorer segments of the population (IPEA/IBGE, 2011).

Due to a high rate of AIDS mortality, the Brazilian Government implemented antiretroviral therapies that are easily available in the market, thus launching in 2004 a programme for universal and free access to antiretroviral drugs, which has been established throughout the country. Another indicator to analyse the fight against HIV is the rate of condom use (12.9%) in relation to other contraceptive methods, used by women aged 15-49 years.

In 1981, the first case of AIDS was reported in Brazil. A prompt governmental response to the epidemic was required. The Brazilian STD/AIDS programme was expanded and strengthened on all fronts: prevention, treatment, research, human rights and social organisation, as well as access to antiretroviral (ARV) therapy and treatment, offering eight generic versions of drug therapies at low-cost. More recently, the biggest challenge is to achieve a significant drop in new cases. In 2004, the Brazilian government spent US$ 260 million in ARV medicine, almost 80 per cent was used to acquire eight kinds of imported medicines. In 2005, about 170,000 people were undergoing ARV treatment. For 2008, the estimate is that 215,000 people will be undergoing treatment, costing some US$525 million in imported medicines (Brasil Ministério da Saúde, 2006).

In the Brazilian areas where reliable statistics exist, the gender differences become obvious as do the policy responses to fight HIV/AIDS; but the great majority of newly infected are now young women. The governmental response to tackling the disease needs to be built around that fact. The daily lives of women in the Brazilian municipalities should be a catalyst in developing and sharing best practices on how to improve social and public policies, develop new partnerships, and expand and develop knowledge networks in the near future.

Recent Advances and Challenges in Higher Education in Brazil

On focusing our attention on the State, and the requests of the population, we become aware of society's interest in social welfare, in broad involvement in the formal sector of the economy, and the Brazilian reform project as part of a wider social development policy that attaches priority to actions in the field of education. Brazil, like other Latin American countries, is committed to promoting educational reforms that will make it possible for the nation to overcome significant disadvantages *vis-à-vis* its rates of schooling and the level of knowledge of developed countries.

The governmental model that was adopted in Latin American universities, in the last hundred years, unfortunately presented lower levels of financing in comparison to developed countries, due to modest terms of governance. For decades, the higher educational institutions were oriented to assembly gathering, structure and decisions, which made decision-making in the institutions difficult.

Contemporary pressure has led to new exigencies of internationalisation of education, an axiological construction of processes that are opened with the emergence and consolidation of experiences of social convergence in confrontation with neo-liberal policies. This pressure shows a qualitative growth in polity struggles envisaging human dignity. It is important to re-evaluate educational policies, aiming at humanising curricula, to avoid the austerity of the past, which was intended to achieve high professional training, but was absolutely inefficient.

On undertaking an international exchange, a Brazilian student will see upon his arrival in the destination country that higher education institutions abroad are much more advanced than in his country, also offering liberal arts, a choice of disciplines, which can aggregate value to human life, dignity, liberty, and equality. Values are highlighted for life in society and inner growth. It is necessary to rescue the knowledge produced throughout history, to generate a new knowledge for the present challenges to humanity; as well as to design spaces for discussing the problems of society.

Academic mobility has been at the core of discussions since the 1980s, the challenge of implementing internationalisation of higher education in each institution, as well as organising the exchange of graduate students.

The historical evolution of higher education in Brazil should be considered, since formal Brazilian institutions were only officially authorised in the 20th century. Brazil's experience was different from the historical context of Spanish-speaking America. Brazil also took a long time to open its universities, which underwent a long period of military government during the 1960s and 1970s, when military officers intervened in the institutions, sometimes suppressing courses, firing professors, sending professors and students to prison, and exiling some of Brazil's most brilliant minds.

Educational reforms were initiated during the 1980s and 1990s, upon the opening of private higher educational institutions, in an expansionist view, which caused a decline in educational standards throughout the country. The internationalisation of higher education implies academic mobility, a syllabus restructure, quality schooling, and teaching of foreign languages.

Education and knowledge are essential for the economy and for the well-being of society. Quantitative and qualitative schooling indicators, as well as scientific production, show an impressive evolution in recent decades in Brazil. Nonetheless, the economic and social indicators present a meagre performance when one considers improvement in the living conditions of the population.

It is clear that Brazil needs a network of qualified universities, specialised in undertaking research focused on economic development. It is necessary to increase productivity in research, create a culture of innovation, based on improvement in international scientific collaboration, with research papers co-authored by professors from different countries, as well as motivating students to become authors.

The search for quality in education shows that the great majority of countries have understood that competition among universities is not only local, national, or regional, it is global. The same kind of globalisation that swept the world in terms of business and the dissemination of culture, has already arrived in the world of higher education.

In particular, we know of no effort to estimate the social returns on investment in school quality, permitting a comparison of the returns to improving rather than expanding the school system. Specialists outline a method for estimating the rate of return of quality and find that it exceeds substantially the social return to quantity. Examples can be given of the universities of Bologna, Oxford, and Paris, which became notable for their excellence, since the Middle Ages and started attracting foreign students. At that time, rich families used to support their children so that they could travel abroad, and opt for internship opportunities in colleges outside their home countries.

Presently, educational statistical data show that there are more than 3 million students away from their countries of origin, which represents an increase of 75 per cent in only the past decade. Future projects evaluate that by 2025, there will be around 8 million foreign students in China, Europe, the Republic of Korea, the US, and in Arab countries, like Saudi Arabia. King Abdullah of Saudi Arabia invested US$10 million to build the King Abdullah University for Science and Technology (KAUST), to reduce inequality in the field of education and promote the broadening of schooling in his country.

Historically, education has been considered as the fundamental element to transform a country in a competitive economy in the hegemonic world. The harmonisation of social, environmental and economic goals through strategic planning and daily management of the economy and society must envisage an equilibrium among different sustainable factors (social, cultural, ecological, environmental, territorial, economic and political); also taking into account efficiencies (allocation, innovation, Keynesian, social and eco-efficiency), as fundamental elements for the country's involvement as a prominent international actor.

Security and "Local Connections" to Terrorism

In the late 1960s, there was a recurrence of terrorism in Latin America. This was not nationalist separatist in character, but drew its inspiration from the extreme left. They emerged in Uruguay, a country that for many years had been the most progressive in Latin America, and even in the 1960s was among the more liberal. The Tupamaros, who stood for radical political and social change, attracted some of the energetic, best and most idealistic from the younger generation, and they were engaged in bank robberies and kidnappings but not in indiscriminate murder.

Initially their illegal activities and acts of serious crime were very successful, proving that a civilian legitimate government could be easily shaken up and disrupted. The Tupamaros initially attracted a great deal of attention in the international media, but in the final analysis the only result of their illegal operations was the destruction of freedom in a country that almost alone in Latin America had an unknown democratic tradition, however imperfect.

The campaign of the Tupamaros caused the rise of a military dictatorship and destroyed the valuable democratic system, and, at the same time, brought about the destruction of their own movement. By the 1970s, the remaining Tupamaros were in exile bemoaning the evil doings of an oppressive regime that they themselves had created. The gravediggers of liberal Uruguay, as Regis Delray later wrote, had also dug their own graves. Facing defeat, the Tupamaros had no other option. They tried their hand at establishing a united front of the left together with non-terrorist parties. But, unfortunately, they fared badly in popular elections due to their bad track record.

Terrorism in Argentina commenced a few years after the outbreak in Uruguay, on a far more massive scale. Both the terrorist operations there and the subsequent backlash were more indiscriminate and bloody. In contrast to their Uruguayan comrades, Argentinean terrorists consisted of two groups—the "Montoneros", and the smaller, but better-equipped and organised, GRP (more doctrinally leftist in character, consisting mainly of students)—became prominent. The Montoneros, who had the left wing as a base of recruitment, began their terror campaign with the killing of ex-President Arambure in May 1970. Initially, a considerable number of foreigners (or locals representing foreign economic interests) were among the victims. Gradually, the attacks turned against the army, the police, politicians and moderate leaders. There were also many victims of bomb attacks whose lives were sacrificed apparently for no reason.

In the period 1975-76, terrorism in Argentina reached its height. There were 646 political murders in 1976 alone. Also, military installations in some provincial cities were attacked. Argentina is perhaps the only recorded example of urban guerrilla activity—that is, where terrorists came close to establishing liberated zones in urban areas. But the terrorists overreached precisely because they engaged in large-scale operations that made it easier for the army to combat them. Once the army received a free hand to retaliate, it showed no mercy. About 4,000 members of the Montoneros and the GRP were detained, and thousands more were arrested. Some died in combat. Thus, a very heavy price was paid for the ill-conceived terrorist campaign. True, within a decade, military rule in Argentina, as in Uruguay, gave way to a civilian government that gradually became more democratic; but the experience of these countries showed that even weak and ineffective governments were capable of defending themselves when terrorists had no hope of gaining the support of significant sectors of the population. For any terrorist organisation to be successful, the support of the masses is essential.

Latin America deserves mention in this article because of the strategy of its so-called urban guerrillas, despite the fact that guerrilla activities in Brazil were short-lived. Abraham Guillen, a refugee from Spain, advocated guerrilla cells consisting of no more than five or six members who would be constantly on the move. But in his writings Guillen also suggested stronger political action, and clandestine existence and constant mobility was not possible in combination with open political propaganda. There were also the writings of Brazilian Carlos Marighella, who had been a member of the Communist Party, but left it because it had been too tame for his taste; he was probably more widely read among his European admirers than in his "native country". His "mini-manual" was translated in many languages, but his advocacy of a scorched earth policy, sabotage of transport and oil pipelines, and destruction of food supplies, was quite unrealistic. Marighella assumed that the masses would blame the authorities for these disasters, but the masses were less naïve than he thought. Even among the extremists, not many accepted his strategy.

These violent political theories can be categorised into an approach called the strategy of provocation, an approach that had failed everywhere else. The strategy was based on the assumption that violence would produce repression, which would generate more revolutionary violence, which in turn would provoke yet more draconian measures by the government, which would shatter its "Liberal Façade". Eventually society would be totally polarised, and in the confrontation between the left and the right, the extreme left was bound to win.

As Latin American extremists later admitted, the strategy overestimated the strength of their movement and underestimated the forces of repression. If the terrorists succeeded in frightening the police, usually weak and ill-equipped and untrained for war, this led them to face the army, which was not hampered by state regulations and laws and could use repressive measures, including torture, as they saw fit. The Brazilian "urban guerrilla" campaign lasted three years, but it never reached the intensity seen in Uruguay and Argentina. It finally ended with Marighella being shot in a police ambush in São-Paulo in November 1969, and the other guerrilla commanders eliminated in similar circumstances.

The police in Latin American countries used tough methods against extremists, but it is also true that their adversaries had not shown an excess of humanity in their operations: agricultural workers were killed because they had stumbled on an arms cache or hideouts; drivers were murdered because the guerrillas needed their cars; and sailors were cut down after a getaway at gunpoint.

Most of the Latin American countries witnessed urban terror, and it would be tedious to survey all of them. Venezuela was one of the first to confront urban terrorism, and in some respects the country seemed predestined for it, since two-third of the population lived in urban centres and a substantial part of the powerful Communist Party supported the guerrilas. Terrorism in Venezuela failed not because of massive police repression—the measures taken by the Democrat Betancourt were half-hearted—but because the rebels caused more irritation and hardship for the general public than for the government, disrupted daily life, and brought about a public groundswell of revulsion against themselves.

In Colombia, violent revolution was also not very successful at that time. This country had one of the most violent political traditions in Latin America. The rebel movement M-19 appeared on the scene not when repression was most violent, but, on the contrary, when a democratically-elected Government had taken over and when economic development was strong. In later years, there was to be a resurgence of terrorism in Colombia, but this had more to do with the appearance of drug cartels and their growing power than with revolutionary zeal.

Transnational Links and "Local Connections" of Terrorism in Latin America

According to the April 2007 *Country Report on Terrorism* by the US State Department, only four Latin American groups were defined as terrorist organisations: (a) Fuerzas Armadas Revolucionarias de Colombia (FARC). (b) Ejército de Liberación Nacional (ELN, or National Liberation Army). (c) Autodefensa Unida de Colombia (AUC, or United Self-Defence [forces] of Colombia). (d) Sendero Luminoso (Shining Path). The first three organisations operate in Colombia, whereas Sendero Luminoso is Peruvian. Of the four organisations, only the AUC is rightist. The 2006 *Country Reports on Terrorism* mentioned that no Islamist group of terrorist cells operated in Latin America. The Latin American region, therefore, has not been seen as a hotspot in the US-led "War on Terror".

In the 1970s and 1980s, Latin America was considered to be one of the two regions, along with the Middle East, where anti-US terrorist attacks were the most frequent. In the 1970s and early 1980s, terrorism was sometimes employed as a tactic by rebel groups in Argentina, Chile and Uruguay. There were attempts by the Argentine Montoneros to establish links with Palestinian organisations operating in Lebanon. By the end of the 1980s and during the 1990s, yet another shift occurred in the perception and manifestation of terrorist threats in Latin America, with the growing focus on the link of drug trafficking to terrorism. The concept of "narco-guerrilla" appeared in the late 1980s and became "narco-terrorism" following the attack by terrorists associated with Al Qaeda on the World Trade Center (WTC) in New York on of 11 September 2001.

Guerrilla warfare and State repression is what has usually characterised the Latin American context of political violence. When compared to Middle Eastern, mainly Palestinian, organisations and even to Western European rebel groups (such as the Irish Republican Army [IRA] or the Basque ETA) and, for instance, to the Liberation Tigers of Tamil Eelam (LTTE) in Sri Lanka, Latin American armed groups, including groups that have used terrorist means, with some rare exceptions, developed only regional links, at most. The popular figure of Ernesto Che Guevara or the moral leadership of Fidel Castro for the Latin American left has always been more a source of inspiration than a vehicle of the internationalisation of revolutionary struggle. One of the reasons why internationalisation of terrorism has historically not been successful in Latin America (for instance, in contrast to the Middle East) is that the prime motive of that pattern has been ideological without a material interest to support it. In other words, Latin American armed groups that resorted to terrorism had no real incentives to expand their struggle beyond their local (national) context.

Terrorism in Latin America was not an exclusively leftist phenomenon. It faded away even before it did so in other regions in the early 1980s. The main reason was the military defeat of these groups in their own countries and the lack of the popular support they hoped to build up for their struggle. With the return of democratic governments in the 1980s, most of Latin American leftist armed organisations went through the transformation process experienced by all the Latin American left. In particular, they abandoned the idea of revolution and declared support for progressive change to embrace democracy.

Terrorist Bombings in Argentina

During the years 1992-1994, two bombings devastated the Argentinean Jewish Community and marked the arrival of Middle

Eastern terrorism to South America for the first time. On 17 March 1992, a car bomb was exploded near the site of the Embassy of Israel in Buenos Aires. The bomb explosion killed 29 and injured over 250 people. Among the victims were Israeli diplomats, children, clergy and passersby. The Islamic Jihad claimed responsibility for the explosion soon after it happened.

On 18 July 1994, a second bombing took place at the Jewish community centre in Buenos Aires. Eighty-seven people were killed and over 100 people injured. These were the two most significant terrorist attacks in Latin America.

The Main Danger Zones

It is observed that ethnic conflicts are not the only sources of terrorism; religious and social tensions also lead to terrorist activities within a national community. In some Latin American countries, the grievances of the native American population, such as in Peru and Mexico have provided the impetus for political violence. Tribalism in Africa has provoked widespread violence in recent years, and in the future this could affect South Africa, where ethnic differences coincide with social tensions. North Africa seems to be a main danger zone, where religious fanaticism is greater and where a higher level of education combines with unemployment, especially among the younger generation.

However, terrorism experts express serious concerns about the potential for expansion of Islamist terrorism in Latin America, due to new waves of immigrants from the Middle East and South East Asia into the region, including the Caribbean countries and free trade zones of Iquique (Chile) and Colon (Panama).

Predictions of population growth are risky because of a number of variables. All over the world, hundreds of millions of people have left the countryside in search of a better and comfortable life in the big cities. Thirteen cities in Asia, two in Africa, Cairo and Lagos, and four in Latin America, Mexico City, São Paulo, Rio de Janeiro, and Buenos Aires, have 10 million or more inhabitants, and some cities will soon have close to 20 million residents.

Forty years ago, the situation was quite different. Some of the mega-cities did not even have half a million inhabitants, like Lagos and Dacca. This trend might slow in the future. But, the consequences are irreversible. Rural poverty has been transferred to the big cities and urban poverty has become the most significant and politically explosive problem in the world. Guerrilla warfare has dwindled, but urban terrorism is on the rise. In Bombay, Calcutta, Karachi and Lagos, nearly 50 per cent of the population live in very poor conditions. The situation in Rio de Janeiro and Mexico City is similar. These cities are inhabited by what was once known in Britain and France as the "dangerous class".

Mega-cities Getting Out of Control

Rapid urbanisation and the emergence of slums have brought about many unfortunate consequences; insufficient social services, growing crime rates, including organised crime and terrorism. In some countries, the mega-cities have become unmanageable; Bombay, Cairo, Calcutta, Dacca and Karachi are classic examples. The mega-cities of Asia, Africa and Latin America are becoming the 21st century's breeding ground for terrorism and other forms of political violence.

In the future, there might be "no-go-zones"—where police and soldiers may not dare to trespass even in daytime—springing up in the big cities. In these areas, terrorist gangs might be able to organise and train, and keep their arms caches without fear of detection or seizure. To a certain extent, this has already taken place. It is far easier to mobilise people in the big cities for violent action than in the countryside. As control is lost in the mega-cities, even intervention by the army is challenged by well-armed gangs, for example, in Rio de Janeiro. The security authorities in the mega-cities of Latin America will have to be very vigilant about the activities in *favelas* (slums) to prevent a resurgence of terrorism.

Drugs and Terrorism in Latin America

Colombia has experienced violence that has dominated much of its history in the 20th century. Its two major armed guerrilla forces, the *Fuerzas Armadas Revolutionarias de Colombia* (FARC), originally an offshoot of the Colombian Communist party, and the National Liberation Army (ELN), have been active for decades with many ups and downs in their history. In the 1990s as the central government was weak and under international pressure to do more against the drug cartels, the fortunes of the FARC improved and whole regions in the south of the country passed out of control of the central government. For many years, they had received substantial financial support from the drug cartels that sought to function outside the power of the Government.

The income of the drug cartels declined somewhat as some positive initiatives of the government were successful against the coca growers. Also the drug cartels had no particular interest in replacing a weak central government by a stronger one headed by the guerrillas, so the financial help given to the latter was reduced. To replenish their finances, the FARC engaged in a massive campaign of kidnappings involving hundreds of people, most of them not even very rich. The terrorist situation in Colombia was further complicated by the existence of a good deal of criminal banditry that also engaged in similar activities, not to mention the activities of counter-insurgency gangs. The bandits did not bomb oil pipelines as the FARC did, but they too kidnapped civilians and took money from the drug cartels.

The issue, finally, is not whether the concept of "narco-terrorism" is a valid one. The drug cartels are not guerrillas and terrorists and *vice versa*; there is no giant conspiracy linking every act of guerrilla warfare with the drug trade. But the heavy involvement of guerrillas and terrorists in the drug trade has decisively contributed to the survival and indeed, the strengthening of some Latin American guerrilla movements, and it has equally decisively affected their character. A new species of terrorist has come into being, different in character, outlook, motivation and potential from guerrilla and terrorist groups of the past.

Many of those who doubt the extent of guerrilla and terrorist groups' involvement in the drug business tactically assume that they are revolutionary in inspiration and pure in motivation. They ignore the fact that terrorists other than left wingers have been involved in the narcotics business, which is worldwide and covers many countries. Until President Noriega's fall, the centre of the drug trade was Panama. Noriega, too, had his defenders, but it can hardly be argued that he was a pillar of Marxism-Leninism. The various "contras" have been equally involved in smuggling drugs and protecting growers. In actual fact, political ideology has not been a matter of paramount importance concerning the involvement of guerrillas and terrorists in the drug business, whether it is plied in the Far East (including the "Golden Triangle"), in Afghanistan, in Lebanon and Syria, or in other parts of the world.

With regard to Latin America, the population pressure and the mega-cities getting out of control is a matter of serious concern for the continent. The population density in Rio de Janeiro, São Paulo and Mexico City could become breeding grounds for terrorism in the future. Properly coordinated intelligence controlling organised crime, criminal gangs and drug dealers is a top priority for the region. If the situation gets out of control, terrorism could rise and become a challenge for governance and national security. The public would then lose confidence in the rulers.

In Brazil, there is no serious threat of terrorism to the society and for governance. The economy is booming and Brazil is an economic giant. Also, Brazil is an emerging world power. With a population of 200 million, there is 'peace' in the society. Due to the country's healthy economic policies, Brazilians have hope for the future. Therefore, there are no possibilities of an upsurge in terrorism in Brazil in the near future. But the intelligence agencies will have to be vigilant due to the "global trends" of terrorism. In general, in Latin America, terrorism is not going to be a serious challenge for governance as 'terrorism' has been curbed at the right time by utilising 'state power'. Due to poor international links, terrorist organisations have been of 'national character' only, in Latin America. But future international links among the existing organisations will have to be monitored very carefully in order to keep the region free of terrorism.

Also, it is extremely important that "narco-terrorism" is fought to the end to eradicate terrorism in Latin America. Wilkinson and Stewart (1989) have argued that "terrorism" is a label placed on individuals or groups of individuals to cloud factual issues surrounding social reform in Latin America; that hidden agendas, from East-West involvement, focusing on national security concerns, political-economic motivations and media exploitation, tend to distort the sovereign interests of people. Indeed, associated names like "terrorist", "Communist-supported revolutionaries" and "Marxist guerrillas" are labels that tend only to heighten ideological sentiment and play to emotion rather than intellect. In Latin America, these labels often represent those striving for social justice from the liberation perspective. But the author of this article is of the view that 'terrorism' cannot by justified for this purpose, because it hampers national security, governance, economic development and public life in any state, including Latin America.

Civil Society and Citizen Participation: Addressing Public Issues in Brazil

Although Brazil does not face any serious threat of terrorism to the society and for its governance, it suffered the reactions of civil society in 2013. While security issues seemingly dominate government action, more and more nation states are coming under pressure from their own citizens. Some political analysts have diagnosed a crisis of representative democracy and argued for a stronger role of civil society. Citizen action, citizen initiatives, and protest movements have gained in importance, especially with the 'Arab Spring'. Citizen participation has become a key issue for governments, with a plethora of different meanings attached to it (Arndt, 1987). Furthermore, the question of what civil society can bring to the table in attempting to attack the global challenges of the 21st century, with demands for political democratisation, economic recovery, social democratisation and educational reformulation has become a point of particular attention. While some governments and the corporate sector would like to see civil society primarily in the role of service providers, citizens are increasingly aware of the political mandate of civil society (Hall and Midglet, 2008).

The reactions of organised civil society in Brazil should be noted since the inauguration of the soccer stadiums in 2013, also known as the Brazilian Spring, initiated by the Free Fare Movement, a local entity that advocates free public transportation. The demonstrations were initially organised to protest increases in bus, train, and metro ticket prices in some Brazilian cities, but grew to include other issues, such as corruption in government, creating a crisis of representative democracy (Rawls, 1971). Since then, social relations have been tense in Brazil and civil society has become a customs inspector over state actions. Effective changes in the juridical order (Annoni, 2002) were a request from civil society, as well as in the rules of Congress, including the effective use of the Federal budget, calling for a really participative budget, transparency in all accounts, and benefits to every segment of the population. The movement started in May 2013, when President Dilma Rousseff kicked the first symbolic ball on the newly-laid pitch of the brand new Mane Garrincha Stadium in the Brazilian capital. At a cost of 1.2 billion reais ($590.1 million), the colonnaded stadium was the most expensive of the 12 that Brazil was building for the 2014 32-nation World Cup, and a prime candidate to become a white elephant in a city with no major soccer club. Relations between the State and society in the mobilisation process for the conquest or implementation of rights became tense, with the support of the NGOs (non-governmental organisations). NGOs derive an important part of their legitimacy from the claim that they are able to have an open dialogue with governmental institutions. This ability, it is argued, contributes to aid effectiveness and efficiency in human rights demands (Arendt, 1997; Aston and Goodman, 2013; Axt and Schwartz, 2006). Donnelly (2013) predicts an assertive exercise, activating the obligations of the duty-bearer and through the contractual right defends the rights of NGOs as legitimate political entities. The Universal Declaration of Human Rights, for example, presents itself as a "standard achievement for all peoples and all nations", and the governments protect human rights, and legitimate the citizens' demands for security. Joel Feinberg calls for rights in a "manifesto sense" (Feinberg, 1980: 153). Human rights do imply a manifesto for political change, including liberty, democracy, law (justice) (Dworkin, 2011), which implies education, employment, shelter and health.

Relevance is put on the military regime in the 1960s, when people could not participate freely in the political process and there was limited freedom of expression or belief. For 23 years, the people of Brazil were oppressed by military authorities who used political persecution, torture, disappearances, and massacre even at the universities to grab professors from the classrooms and students who were sent to prisons (Alvarez et *al.*, 2000); Huggins, 2006; Haritos-Fatouros, 2002; Garland, 2001), murdered, and declared disappeared. Only in 1988, Brazil faced the return to democracy, and the electoral process was restored, with a new Constitution, which was ratified on 5 October 1988, by the 1988 Constituent Assembly. As of March 2012, it has been amended 70 times and has 250 articles.

The idea of "human capabilities" has become increasingly popular in recent discussions of human rights (Donnelly, 2013; Sen, 2003), as it motivates the citizens to get together, develop or realise their wishes. Their capabilities increased as they started to interact with each other, advocating their cause through particular kinds of mechanisms, structured in terms of networks on social media (Facebook, LinkedIn, Twitter, e-mails messages, blogs and links). Historically, citizens used to march through the avenues with guns, tools and stones in their hands, feeling their vulnerability and weakness to convince the government of their particular demands. The government, seen as an opponent to requests, used the coercive powers of the state to frighten them, emphasising the control of the state, abusing and violating their rights.

The recent civil society movements in Brazil have changed the scenario of the 2014 elections and presented new candidates, new political parties and many criticisms concerning democracy and contemporary politics. To examine the variables for the next decades, it is necessary to conceptualise the institutional rules, partnership decision-making, a project-design for the country and the region. The role of NGOs and NGDOs (non-governmental development organisations) is brought to the scene to show the right to popular participation, civil liberties such as the freedom of speech, press, and assembly, the empowerment of citizens in their participation in politics and how they exercise control over the State.

Environmental protection of the Amazon

President Dilma Rousseff is finishing her three-year mandate and will soon start her election campaign for 2014. She is running against time to initiate more programmes to show to her electorate that she can compensate for the delays and mismanagement that fuel criticism from her opponents. One of her opposition's main criticisms of her is the need to protect the Amazon and exercise sovereignty while also eradicating poverty, improving the standard of living and, especially, achieving sustainable development. This includes an open dialogue since 1978 with the eight countries that have sovereignty over the Amazon Basin.

After 36 years of operation, during which the Amazonian Cooperation Treaty Organization (ACTO) was administered by rotating Pro Tempore Secretariats attached to the countries' respective Foreign Ministries and Governments of the Treaty: Bolivia, Brazil, Colombia, Ecuador, Guyana, Peru, Venezuela, Countries in the Amazon Domain, and Suriname. The signatory members decided to accept the Brazilian government's kind offer to make Brasilia the headquarters for this new organisation. The main objective of the Treaty was to play a major role in the region, in the South American continent and, indeed, in the global arena. All countries were worried about the survival of the human species on the planet and the advanced stage of destruction of the Amazon Rain Forest.

The main issues included the Amazon's potential, its vast wealth, the richness of the soil, the quality of the air, the number of species in the Amazon, its biological diversity, and also the indigenous population. In addition, the Treaty called for fostering the promotion of regional integration, and a wide scope of projects in science and technology to protect fresh water, the biodiversity it nurtures, the extraordinary potential it offers, as well as the cultural diversity of its people. The technical, scientific and cultural cooperation includes political and economic policies to fight poverty, the success of health, education, gender, culture and sanitation policies, and all issues to consolidate sustainable and sustained development to protect the future of humankind.

With regard to President Dilma Rousseff's political will, it is based on the endeavour to achieve more equitable living conditions for the region's inhabitants. President Dilma Rousseff has the responsibility of keeping the growth of influence, presence and prestige that Brazil had gained during the two terms of government of President Lula; and maintaining its strong economic development and sustainable path, continuing the five catalysts to Brazil's growth in the 21st century: the ending of cycles of domestic and foreign indebtedness; the modernisation of industrial plants, with particular focus on mechanical and electrical engineering; expanded access to credit by both industry and Brazilian families; the emergence of a new middle class to become strong consumers; and finally, recognition within Brazil of the value of innovation and technical creativity.

System of Power and Society (2004–2014)

Discussions about systems of government have historically followed two main positions: that of the ideal model and that of the historical example. An ideal model shaped according to fixed values considered to be all-important is the oldest form of analysing the question and was found in Greek thought from Herodotus, followed by the speculations of Plato and Aristotle (Jaguaribe, 2009: 35). Both Plato and Aristotle seek the ideal characteristics the state should enjoy in order to ensure justice among the *Polis* and a virtuous harmony in the souls of men. Aristotle emphasises the ideal characteristics of the state, and as Plato points out, the conditions necessary to ensure social balance in the relationships between rich and poor, patricians and plebeians, and the virtuous conduct of everyone.

In speaking about Brazil, the typical controversy between Presidential power and Parliamentary power has been almost exclusively conducted according to the above-mentioned two viewpoints.

In this context, since Independence, Brazilian society has gone through three main periods of unequal length beginning on the 19th century and going up to the first decades of the 20th Century, when Brazil was an agrarian society controlled by a rural patrician class and a trading bourgeoisie, ruled by a democracy of notables. The government used to say that it was governing in the name of the people but without the latter having a voice, and mainly not in their interests, by a landowning-trading oligarchy among whom and in favour of whose interests, the parliamentary system of the Empire and the presidential system of the Old Republic operated. The government was called Old Republic from 1889-1930, and it ended with a military coup as noted by Jaguaribe (2009: 37).

The military coup was called the 1930 Revolution, followed by the short periods of the 1934 Constitution, the 1946 Constitution, which allowed the establishment of a middle-class democracy that combined, under the protection of the bourgeoisie and the political weight of the middle class, the interests of the former with many of the aspirations of the latter. Brazil lived a period of transition in which the old agrarian society became industrialised and urbanised. As a consequence of this period of industrialisation, the demands of the masses grew during the governments of Getulio Vargas and João Goulart in 1954 and 1964, respectively. The traditional family values and conservative ethics resulted in *coups* of a preventive nature. The Brazilian conservative and traditional family was worried that the dissemination of Communism in the country would lead to atheism. The result was a military government, which lasted 20 years from 1964 to 1985.

To modernise Brazil, it was necessary to achieve compatibility between an essential institutional stability and work for the acceleration of socio-economic development in which a modern industrial society could achieve higher living standards, access to education, technological modernisation and participation in a democratic process.

Transitional processes aiming at achieving compatibility between stability and change, on one hand, and economic and social development on the other, were not easy. Presidents like Vargas and Goulart, who wanted changes, were overthrown by *coup d'état*, consequently damaging stability and respectability of the Brazilian institutions. The military government from 1964 onward tried to guarantee institutional stability through repressive methods, showing its authority and curbing participation of the masses.

The military government proved to be equally inadequate to the process of social change. Abusive and repressive methods, imprisonments and deportations mobilised the population to demand a return to democracy.

Causes for the breakdown of authoritarianism, such as splits in the military, led to the success of the demand for democratic elections in Brazil. Democratisation finally occurred in 1974; and according to specialists such as Jaguaribe (2009: 41), it coincided with the 'Third Wave' of democracy. Three strong Presidents were Castello Branco, Costa e Silva (March 1964–December 1968), and General Ernesto Geisel (1974-1979). Branco tried to govern in a more democratic way, but had to accept Silva as his successor. Under Costa's reign, the military regime implemented and strengthened its diplomatic relations with the US as it was beneficial to Brazil's development during that period. Hard-line President Costa e Silva died unexpectedly in October 1969, and was succeeded by General Garrastazú Médici, who governed until 1974. He was extremely unpopular and had as his main objective to turn Brazil into a great authoritarian power, controlling the country against a widespread movement of revolutionary or "guerrilleros" who started terrorist attacks and rampant kidnapping of diplomats, including the US Ambassador to Brazil. Torture, corruption and denial of political rights were commonplace, which resulted in the nomination of General Ernesto Geisel (1974-1979), who announced the politics of regime transformation of the dictatorship, replacing in the first instance several military commanders, appointing trusted liberal officers and beginning Brazil's political opening, known as the return to democratic rule. President João Figueiredo's term of office marked the last few years of military regime and the election of the first civilian president in 1985. The election of Tancredo Neves marked the re-democratisation of the country, followed by the adoption of a new

Constitution in 1988. Unfortunately, Tancredo Neves died before assuming office and his Vice-President, José Sarney, became the first President after the dictatorial regime. Incidents occurred later on, such as the impeachment of President Collor de Mello in 1989, showing the evidence of creeping democratisation, which emphasised the eradication of authoritarian features and the necessity of cooperation with the opposition to avoid disruption of the system.

Institutional stability grew with a President elected by an absolute majority through universal suffrage and a secret ballot, who is responsible for the stability of institutions and acts as a moderator of the functions of the State and has supreme command of the armed forces. On the other hand, there is a Vice-President, appointed by the Party, who works together with the President, and relies on maintaining the confidence of the House of Deputies. The Vice-President is co-ordinator of the programme of government and interacts with the leaders in the Congress and with all legal political parties. He works, assisting the Chief of State, within a system that attends to the needs of the people in conditions of reasonable stability for the government.

The process of political representation in a modern democracy like Brazil shows two important correlations that appear between the level of development of the society's economic and cultural development, and the quality of the political class it generates, especially concerning the institutional arrangements and processes for choosing the Foreign Minister, who must be a distinguished career diplomat, with extensive experience abroad. His candidacy will then be submitted to the Congress for consideration and he will assume power upon the President's official appointment and public approval. The complexity of international issues requires a level of expertise that parliamentarians do not have. All foreign negotiations are linked to the Executive and the Legislative branches of government. However, there is distance between the decision-making process and foreign policy, and a widespread view that the legislative branch is indifferent or apathetic towards foreign policy.

Brazilian foreign policy was defined in the second half of Fernando Henrique Cardoso's government (1995-2003), and further developed under the leadership of President Luiz Inácio Lula da Silva. Lula was the first leader of the Workers' Party (PT), founded in 1980 as a labour-based movement of opposition to the military dictatorship regime to gain the elections for President (2003-2010).

Under Lula, the PT strengthened its base, overtly committed the Party to socialism, and specifically to agrarian reform, participatory democracy, redistribution of wealth, independence from the "North American hegemonic power", and to regional solidarity within Latin America.

Relations with the Congress were tightened by the PT representatives, who worked hard to have all international agreements and rules approved, including the programme Bolsa Familia (Family Stipend), a programme of cash transfers to the poor, and *Minha Casa Minha Vida* (Houses for the poor). The issues had to be included in the Agenda of the Plenary of the Chamber of Deputies (Lower House of the Congress), through permanent committees, such as international acts, which have to be fully processed and transformed into legislative decrees. In addition, there are provisional measures that sometimes "lock" the agenda of the House, since they have priority. In other words, there is an agenda external to international acts, specific to the Brazilian presidential system, that affects the speed with which such matters make their way through Congress. Proposed legislative decrees are submitted by the Executive, which are always under pressure. What seems relevant in this process is to investigate how relevant in the agenda the different national interests are, what the relevant factors are, why this process occurs and, lastly, how this question is processed at the international level (Kubalkova, 2001).

The process of foreign policy-making is not easy as it has to accommodate domestic interests and international issues, related to international negotiation processes, agreements, and international activities. Parties, unions and other political players able to influence the decision-making process are fundamental actors. The relationship between the Executive and the Legislative branches of government, with regard to external relations, is regulated by the Constitution. Given the constitutional attributes that the Executive and the Legislative branches have in foreign policy matters, it is correct to state that Congress plays a legitimising role in relation to the political decisions of the Executive concerning the international arena. Summarising, the Congress is the locus of the political parties and, hence, a legitimately constituted channel of representation for societal interests.

In this context, foreign policy and international relations determine the relationship of the country with the world. In this context, the Ministers of Finance, Justice, External Relations and Defence are high profile specialists. Their decisions may affect Brazil's domestic and foreign policy, attracting or discouraging new investors to the country. The Ministers may use their power defending, whenever necessary, the Brazilian national interests and values.

Conclusions

As final conclusions, Brazil's Foreign Policy should be analysed in several contexts. It is necessary to envisage the plurality of actors and the domestic interests and preferences that form the country's agenda.

The main focus of our analysis was the Brazilian role as an important player in the international scenario, assuming regional leadership, with influence over changes in the system that enlists cooperation for development. While Brazil reaches higher standards in social areas, it tries to create mechanisms to enlarge its partnerships around the world, through technical cooperation, science and technology and educational good practices, which include the institutionalisation of teaching and use of foreign languages, joint research, the exchange of students, professors and researchers, double diploma programmes, wide utilisation of teleconferences, distance learning systems, and the university campus, to open a wide variety of possibilities, in public and private institutions. The President should take into account that the Executive entails many more agencies than the Presidency and the Prime Minister's office alone. It should be taken into consideration that foreign issues have been increasingly spread over other public policies and, as a consequence, they have been equally present at several other executive agencies. Nevertheless, the President should keep in her mind that the Brazilian presidential system functions as a coalition, and it has to listen to the people's demands. The President needs to create a basis of support among the political parties and to form her cabinet from this coalition. Brazilian foreign policy is thus entangled in the political bargain that characterises the coalition government. If President Dilma Rousseff hopes to win the 2014 elections, she must accept more members of other parties in her ministerial cabinet. In addition, it is necessary to listen to the popular demands for improvements in education, health, housing, security and transparency.

Democracy cannot be imposed; it is borne through dialogue. During the last 10 years, Presidents Luiz Inácio Lula da Silva and Dilma Rousseff have sought to redefine Brazil's place in the world. Brazil has to take control of its development as an independent nation and reduce its dependence on economic vulnerabilities imposed from outside, without succumbing to the temptations of isolationism. In this context, Brazil should formulate a strategy in its relations with great emerging countries like China, India, Russia and South Africa. These alliances play a fundamental role in forming a new international economic and trade geography. At the same time, the standard of excellence of foreign relations has to be maintained with great partners from the developed world: the US, the European Union and Japan. Brazil needs to develop diverse partnerships and more balanced relations with all the regions of the world. Brazilian foreign policy has to focus on long-term objectives to guarantee the well-being of its people, with economic and social development for all, and for the establishment of a world of peace and solidarity.

References

Annoni, Danielle (2002). *Direitos Hhumanos & Acesso à Justiça no Direito Internacional.* 1 ed. Curitiba: Juruá.

Arendt, Hannah (1997). *As Origens do Totalitarismo* (trad. Roberto Raposo). Sao Paulo: Companhia das Letras.

Arndt, Heinz Wolfgang (1987). *Economic Development: The History of an Idea.* Chicago and London: The University of Chicago Press Ltd.

Ashton, and Goodman (2013). "Law Cases at the Court", *The Law Times* 155. Michigan University.

Axt, Heinz Jurgen and Oiliver Schwartz (2006). *Conflict: A Literature Review.* University of Duisburg Essen, Department of Social Sciences.

Baird, Sarah, H.G. Francisco Ferreira, Berk Özler and Michael Woolcock (2013). *Relative Effectiveness of Conditional and Unconditional Cash Transfers for Schooling Outcomes in Developing Countries: A Systematic Review.* Oslo, Norway: The Campbell Library.

Banco Central do Brasil (2011). *Census of Foreign Capital in the Country: 2010 and 2011 Results.* Brasília: Editora do Banco Central do Brasil.

Barros, Ricardo Paes et al. (2007). *A Queda Recente da Desigualdade de Renda no Brasil.* Texto para Discussão N° 1258. Rio de Janeiro: Instituto de Pesquisa Econômica e Aplica (IPEA).

Bijos, Leila (2004). *Women and Development: The Regional Microfinance Programme for Women in the Urban Informal Sector: 1980-2002—A Case Study: Brazil–Bolivia.* Doctoral Dissertation. Brasilia: University of Brasília.

————. (2006). "Gender, Power, Financial Access, and Development in Latin América: Comparing Brazilian and Bolivian Cases", *Law and Business Review of the Americas* 12(3), Summer. Texas, US: Southern Methodist University (SMU) Dedman School of Law.

Brahy, Nicholas and Tobin, Brendan (2005). "Protecting and Strengthening Traditional Knowledge Innovation System", *Work in Progress* 17(2): 19-21 (Summer). United Nations University.

Brasil Ministério da Saúde (2006). *HIV/AIDS, Hepatites e Outras.* Secretaria de Atenção à Saúde, Departamento de Atenção Básica. p.il. Cadernos de Atenção Básica n. 18. Série A. Normas e Manuais Técnicos. *http://bvsms.saude.gov.br/bvs/publicacoes/abcad18.pdf*

Brazilian Ministry of External Relations (2008). *Brazilian Foreign Policy Handbook.* Bureau of Diplomatic Planning. Brasilia: Alexandre de Gusmão Foundation.

Bruschini, Cristina, Maria Rosa Lombardi and Sandra Unbehaum (2006).*"Trabalho, Renda E Políticas Sociais: Avanços e Desafios"*, in *O Progresso das Mulheres No Brasil.* BRASÍLIA: UNIFEM, Ford Foundation, CEPIA.

Centerpoint (2007). *Newsletter.* Washington, D.C.: Woodrow Wilson International Centre for Scholars. May.

Donnelly, Jack (2013). *Universal Human Rights in Theory and Practice.* Cornell University Press, USA.

Dworkin, Ronald (2011). *Justice for Hedgehogs.* Harvard University Press.

Feinberg, Joel (1980). *The Nature and Value of Rights.* Princeton University Press, USA.

Fick, Jeff and Jack Kiernan (2013). "Brazil's Economy Posts Worst Quarterly Performance in Two Years", *The World Street Journal (Global),* 3 December. Access: *http://online.wsj.com/news/articles/SB10001424052702304355104579235794103297608* (15 December 2013).

Fontenelle-Mourão, Tânia (2006). *Mulheres no Topo da Carreira: Flexibilidade e Persistência.* Brasília: Secretaria Especial de Políticas para as Mulheres.

Haritas-Fatouros, Mika (2006). *The Psychological Origins of Institutionalized Torture.* London: Routledge.

Huggins (2006). *People v. Huggins*. The Lego Case. Supreme Court of California.

Garland, David (2001). *The Culture of Control: Crime and Social in Contemporary Society*. Oxford University Press, New York.

IBGE (2007). *Síntese de Indicadores Sociais: Uma Análise das Condições de Vida da População Brasileira*. Rio de Janeiro: Instituto Brasileiro de Geografia e Estatística (IBGE).

ILO (2006). *Gênero, Raça, Pobreza e Emprego: O Programa GRPE no Brasil*. Brasília: International Labour Office.

———. (2007). *Guide for Locating Vulnerably Spots to the Sexual Exploitation of Children and Juvenile Alongside of the Brazilian Highways Mapping*. International Labour Office.

IPEA/IBGE (2004). *Brazilian Monitoring Report on the Millennium Development Goals*.

Hall, Anthony and James Midgley (2008). *Social Policy for Development*. London: SAGE Publications.

Kúbalková, Vendulka (ed.) (2001). *Foreign Policy in a Constructed World*. New York: M E. Sharpe. See also: Diniz, Simone and Claudio Oliveira Ribeiro (2008). "The Role of the Brazilian Congress in Foreign Policy", *Brazilian Political Science Review* 2(2): 10-38. Sao Paulo

Ministry of Finance (2010). *Brazilian Economic Outlook*. 3rd Edition. January. p.37. *http://www.fazenda.gov.br/divulgacao/publicacoes/economia-brasileira-em-perspectiva/brazilian_economy_outlook_eng_ed3_jan2010.pdf*

Ministry of Finance (2012). *Brazilian Economic Outlook*. 17th Edition. December. Access: *http://www.fazenda.gov.br/divulgacao/publicacoes/economia-brasileira-em-perspectiva/brazilian_economy_outlook_eng_ed17*

Neri, Marcelo (2014). *Inequality in Brazil: Measurement, Trends, Impacts and Policies*. Strategic Affairs (SAE/PR) and EPGE/FGV. Institute for Applied Economic Research (IPEA) and National Institute of Geography and Statistics (IBGE). Paper presented at WIDER/Helsinki. September. Brazil is a Small World, p.4. *http://www1.wider.unu.edu/inequalityconf/sites/default/files/IGA/Neri.pdf*

Ogata, Sadako (2006). *Infrastructure Development and Human Security*, Keynote address at the Annual Bank Conference on Development Economics. Tokyo. May 30.

Piovesan, Flavia (2006). "*Direitos Civis e Políticos: A Conquista da Cidadania Feminina*", in *O Progresso das Mulheres no Brasil*. Brasília: UNIFEM, Ford Foundation, Cepia–Cidadania, Estudo, Pesquisa, Informação e Ação.

PNAD (2010). *The National Household Sample Survey*. *http://ibge.gov.br/english/estatistica/populacao/trabalhoerendimento/pnad2011/default.shtm*

PNAD/IBGE (2005). *Pesquisa Nacional por Amostra de Domicilios. Sintese dos Indicadores*. Ministério do Planejamento, Orçamento e Gestão Instituto Brasileiro de Geografi a e Estatística—IBGE, Diretoria de Pesquisas Coordenação de Trabalho e Rendimento, Rio de Janeiro. *http://www.ibge.gov.br/home/estatistica/populacao/condicaodevida/indicadoresminimos/suppme/default_educacao.shtm*

PNAD/IBGE (2012). *Pesquisa Nacional por Amostra de Domicilios. Sintese dos Indicadores*. Ministério do Planejamento, Orçamento e Gestão Instituto Brasileiro de Geografi a e Estatística—IBGE, Diretoria de Pesquisas Coordenação de Trabalho e Rendimento, Sintese dos Indicadores. *http://www.ibge.gov.br/home/estatistica/populacao/condicaodevida/indicadoresminimos/suppme/*

Posthuma, Anne Caroline (1999). "*Transformações do Emprego no Brasil na Década de 90*", in *OIT/MTE, Abertura e ajuste do mercado de trabalho no Brasil: Politicas Para Conciliar os Desafios de Emprego e Competitividade* 13(34).

Rawls, John (1971). *A Theory of Justice*. USA: Harvard University Press.

SEADE (Fundacao Sistema Estadual de Analise de Dados) (2005). *Life Conditions*. Sao Paulo Government. *http://www.seade.gov.br/*

Sen, Amartya (2003). *Rationality and Freedom*. Cambridge, Massachusetts: The Belknap Press of Harvard University.

Secretaria Especial De Políticas Para As Mulheres (n.d.). *Memória 2003-2006*. Brasília, D.F.: Presidência da República.

Souza, Pedro H.G. Ferreira de (2012). "Poverty, Inequality and Social Polices in Brazil, 1995-2009", *Working Paper* number 87. Institute for Applied Economic Research (IPEA). February. *http://www.ipc-undp.org/pub/IPCWorkingPaper87.pdf*

Telles, Edward and Marcelo Paixão (2013). "Affirmative Action in Brazil", *Lasa Forum Spring* XLIV(2): 10-11. *http://lasa.international.pitt.edu/forum/files/vol44-issue2/Debates4.pdf*

UNDP (2012). *Human Development Report 2012—Sustaining Human Progress: Reducing Vulnerabilities and Building Resilience.* Note: tables use data available to the HDRO as of 15 November 2013. All indices and indicators, along with technical notes on the calculation of composite indices, and additional source information are available online at: *http://hdr.undp.org/en/data. http://hdr.undp.org/sites/all/themes/hdr_theme/country-notes/BRA.pdf*

UNFPA (2004). *State of the World Population—The Cairo Consensus at Ten: Population, Reproductive Health and the Global Effort to End Poverty*. New York.

———. (2005). *A Promessa de Igualdade: Equidade em Matéria de Gênero, Saúde Reprodutiva e Objetivos do Desenvolvimento do Milênio*. Brasília.

———. (2013). *World Population Review, 2013. http://worldpopulationreview.com/countries/brazil-population/; http://www.unfpa.org/swop; http://www.unfpa.org/transparency-portal/unfpa-brazil*

UNIFEM (2006). *O Progresso das Mulheres no Brasil*. Brasília: UNIFEM, Ford Foundation, Cepia.

United Nations General Assembly (2006). *The United Nations Global Counter-Terrorism Strategy*. 6 September. 60th session, Agenda items 46 and 120.

Wilkinson, Paul and Alasdair M. Stewart (ed.) (1989). *Contemporary Research on Terrorism*. Aberdeen: Aberdeen University Press.

World Bank (2011). *World Bank Report*. Washington, D.C.

Internet Access

Draibe, Sônia M. (2002). "*Brasil: a Proteção Social Após Vinte anos de Experimentação Reformista*", Paper Presented at Taller Inter-Regional *Protección Social en una Era insegura: Un Intercambio Sur-Sur sobre Políticas Sociales Alternativas en Respuesta a la Globalización*. Santiago, Chile (May 14-16). Available at *http://www.comciencia.br/reportagens/ppublicas/pp10.htm*

Alvarez, Sonia E., Evelina Dagnino and Arturo Escobar (*organizadores*) (2000). *Cultura e Política nos Movimentos Sociais Latino-Americanos: novas leituras*. Ed. UFMG, Belo Horizonte (Humanitas).

Alvarez, Sonia E. (1990). *Engendering Democracy in Brazil: Women's Movements in Transition Politics*. Princeton, New Jersey: Princeton University Press.

Arendt, Hannah (1994). *Sobre a Violência* (trad. André Duarte). 2ª edição. Rio de Janeiro: Relume Dumará.

———. (1987). *Economic Development: The History of An Idea*. Chicago and London: The University of Chicago Press, Ltd.

———. (2005). "*A Crise na Educação*", in *Entre o Passado e o Futuro* (tradução Mauro W. Barbosa de Almeida). São Paulo: Perspectiva. pp.221-47 (Coleção Debates).

Banco Interamericano de Desarrollo Informe (2008). *Los de Afuera? Patrones Cambiantes de Exclusión en América Latina y el Caribe.* Washington, D.C.: Progreso Económico y Social en América Latina. Co-published by David Rockefeller Centre for Latin American Studies, Cambridge: Harvard University.

Bandeira, César (2007). *A Violência na Contemporaneidade.* 1ª ed. Fortaleza: Sindicato dos Bancários do Ceará.

Barker, S.L. and D.M.F. Castro (2002). *Gravidez na Adolescência: Dando Sentido ao Acontecimento. Conselho Federal de Psicologia: Adolescência e Psicologia: Concepções, Práticas e Reflexões Críticas.* São Paulo: Conselho Federal de Psicologia. pp.78-84

Bezerra, Angélica Gonçalves (2006). *Quem Cria a Criminalidade é o Criminoso?* (Trabalho de conclusão de curso (Serviço Social)). Londrina: Universidade Estadual de Londrina.

Biasoli, Paola *et al.* (2005). *"Adolescência e Violência: Habilidade, Competências e Estratégias Resilientes Para Promoção da Paz"*, in Tânia Mara Campos Almeida and Liana Fortunato Costa, *Violência no Cotidiano: Do Risco à Proteção.* Brasília: Ed. Universa.

Bijos, Leila (2003). *"Violência: O Cotidiano da Mulher", Revista Dialogos* 3(1): 50-57. Brasília: Universidade Católica de Brasília.

———. (2005). *Mulher e Desenvolvimento: O Programa de Microcrédito Regional Para as Mulheres no Setor Informal Urbano: 1980-2002—Um Estudo de Caso: Brasil-Bolívia* (tese de Doutorado). Universidade de Brasília.

———. (2009). *Discriminação Étnica-Racial: "Nikkeis" Brasileiros no Japão.* Brasília: Editora Universa.

Bijos, Leila and Verônica Arruda (2012). *"A Diplomacia Cultural como Instrumento de Política Externa Brasileira"*, in *Relações Internacionais, Gestão do Conhecimento e Estratégias de Desenvolvimento: debates interdisciplinares na primeira década do novo milênio* (org. Nilzo Ivo Ladwig & Rogério Santos da Costa). Palhoça: Ed. Unisul. pp.165-84.

Birman. Joel. O Mal-Estar na Modernidade e a Psicanálise: a Psicanálise à Prova do Social. *PHYSIS: Revista Saúde Coletiva,* Rio de Janeiro, 15 (Suplemento): 203-224, 2005.

Blodgett, Steven Alvah (1999). *The Evolving Relationship Between the United Nations and the International Non-Governmental Organizations: An Assessment of the Need for Institutional Reform.* p.4, *apud*: Ricardo Neiva Tavares (1999). *As Organizações Não-Governamentais nas Nações Unidas,* Brasília: Instituto Rio Branco.

Bronfenbrenner, U. (1993). "The Ecology of Cognitive Development: Research Models and Fugitive Findings", in: R. Wozniak and D. Fischer (eds.), *Development in Context, Acting and Thinking in Specific Environments.* Hillsdale, New Jersey: Erbaum. pp.3-44.

Caliman, Geraldo (2006). *Paradigmas Da Exclusão Social.* Brasília: Editora Universa. UNESCO.

Carnoy, Martin (2002). *Mundialização e Reforma Na Educação: O Que os Planejadores Devem Saber* (Trad. Guilherme João De Freitas Teixeira). Brasília: UNESCO.

Casassus, Juan (2002). *A Escola e a Desigualdade* (Trad. Lia Zatz). Brasília: Editora Plano.

Castro, A.L.S. (2002). *Os Adolescentes em Conflito Com a Lei. Conselho Federal De Psicologia: Adolescência E Psicologia: Concepções, Práticas E Reflexões Críticas.* Conselho Federal De Psicologia, São Paulo. pp.122-29.

Costa, Valeriano M. Ferreira, Álvaro De Vita and Eliana Marcondes Pralon (1998). *Reforma Das Políticas Sociais Num Contexto De Descentralização: O Papel Dos Programas Municipais De Garantia De Renda Mínima No Combate À Pobreza, Cadernos Do Centro De Estudos De Cultura Contemporânea.* Nº 65. São Paulo: Cedec.

Degnbol-Martinussen, John and Paul Egberg-Pedersen (2004). *Aid: Understanding International Development Cooperation.* New York: Zed Books.

Dias, Marco Antonio (2002). *Educação Superior: Bem Público Ou Serviço Comercial Regulamentado Pela Omc?* Cumbre Iberoamericana De Rectores De Universidades Estatales, Porto Alegre. 26 April.

Dieese (Departamento Intersindical de Estatistica e Estudos Economicos) and LCA (Solucoes Estrategicas em Economia) (2010). *http://www.dieese.org.br/balancodosreajustes/2010/estPesq55balReajustes1sem2010.pdf*

Estatuto Da Criança E Do Adolescente (1990). *Estatuto Da Criança E Do Adolescente.* Conselho Municipal Dos Direitos Da Criança E Do Adolescente. Lei N° 8060 De 13 De Julho De.

Faleiros, Vicente (2010). *Estado E Sociedade: Parcerias E Práticas Contra A Violência Sexual*, Brasília: Universa.

Foucault, Michel (1979). *Microfísica do Poder*, 23ª Edição. Rio De Janeiro: Edições Graal.

Freud, Sigmund (1971 [1929]). *Malaise Dans La Civilisation.* Paris: Presse Universitaires De France..

Friedman, M. and R. Friedman (1980). *Free to Choose: A Personal Statement.* New York: Avon.

Furtado, Celso (2008). "*A Difícil Leitura Da Realidade: Prefácio*", in Ignacy Sachs, *Desenvolvimento: Includente, Sustentável, Sustentado.* Rio De Janeiro: Garamond. p.7.

Garmezy, N. Masten A. (1994). "Chronic Adversities", in M. Rutter, E. Taylor and L. Herson (eds.), *Child and Adolescent Psychiatric.* Oxford: Blackwell Scientific Publication. pp.191-207.

Hall, Anthony and James Midgley (2008). *Social Policy for Development.* London: Sage Publications.

IBGE (2010). *Censo Demográfico* de 2010. Access: *www.ibge.gov.br/Home/Estatistica/.../Censo2010/*

ILO (2010). *World of Work Report 2010: From One Crisis to the Next?* Geneva, Switzerland: The International Institute for Labour Studies (IILS), International Labour Office. *http://www.ilo.org/public/portugue/region/eurpro/lisbon/pdf/worldwork_2010.pdf*

IPEA (Institute for Applied Economic Research) and IBGE (National Institute of Geography and Statistics) (2011). *Censo Demografico 2010: Resultados Preliminares.* Rio de Janeiro. *http://www.ibge.gov.br/home/estatistica/populacao/contagem2010/contagem.pdf*

Jaguaribe, Helio (2009). *Brazil, the World and Man Today: Various Studies.* Brasília: Fundação Alexandre De Gusmão.

Kalifa, D. (1995). *L'encre et le Sang: Écrits de Crimes et Societé a la Belle Époque.* Paris: Arthème Fayad.

Kelly, L. and F.J. Manly (2004). *Multivariate Statistical Methods.* London: Crc Press Llc. 3rd Edition.

Kuznets, S. (1955). "Economic Growth and Income Inequality", *American Economic Review* 45(1): 1-29.

Landim Assumpção, Leilah (1993). *A Invenção Das Ongs: Do Serviço Invisível a Profissão Sem Nome (Tese De Doutoramento Apresentada Ao Programa De Pós-Graduação Em Antropologia Social Do Museu Nacional E Da Universidade Federal Do Rio De Janeiro).* Rio De Janeiro: Universidade Federal Do Rio De Janeiro.

Laus, Sonia Pereira (2003). "*Alguns Desafios Postos Pelo Processo de Internacionalização da Educação Superior no Brasil*", in *Internationalization of Higher Education in Latin America.* Financiado Pela Divisão De Educação Superior E Ciência E Tecnologia Do Banco Mundial E Pelo Programa De Gestão Institucional Da Educação Superior (Imhe) Da Ocde.

Lopes, Carlos (2005). *Cooperação E Desenvolvimento Humano: A Agenda Emergente Para O Novo Milênio.* São Paulo: Unesp.

Mazza, Williame (2001). "*Parente. O Alcance da Imunidade Tributária dos Impostos Sobre o Patrimônio, Renda e Serviços das Entidades de Educação e de Assistência Social do Terceiro Setor*", in *Terceiro Setor E Tributação.*Vol. 4. (Coord. José Eduardo Sabo Paes). Rio De Janeiro: Forense. pp.3-47.

Marx, K. and F. Engels (1976). *Manifesto Del Partito Comunista. Serie Le Idee*: 18. Roma: Editori Riuniti.

Mauger, Gérard (2009). *La Sociologie de la Délinquance Juvénile*. Paris : Éditions La Découverte.

Menezes-Filho, L. (2001). *A Evolução da Educação no Brasil e Seu Impacto no Mercado de Trabalho.* Instituto Futuro Brasil, São Paulo: Departamento De Economia.

Merle, Marcel (1999). *"Un Imbroglio Juridique: Le 'Statut' des Oing, Entre le Droit International et les Droits Nationaux"*, *in* Transnational Associations (1995). p.267; *Apud*: Ricardo Neiva Tavares (1999). *As Organizações Não-Governamentais Nas Nações Unidas*. Brasília: Instituto Rio Branco. p.21.

Meynaud, Jean (1999). *Les Groupes de Pression Internationaux*. p.182; *Apud*: *Apud*: Ricardo Neiva Tavares (1999). *As Organizações Não-Governamentais Nas Nações Unidas*. Brasília: Instituto Rio Branco.

Miliband, Ralph (1972). *O Estado na Sociedade Capitalista*. Rio De Janeiro: Zahar Editores.

Mingoti, S.A. (2005). *Análise de Dados Através de Métodos de Estatística Multivariada: Uma Abordagem Aplicada*. Belo Horizonte: Editora Ufmg.

Miranda, Jorge (1990). *Textos Históricos Do Direito Constitucional*. 2ª Edição. Lisboa: Casa Da Moeda.

Mirza, Christian A. (2006). *Movimientos Sociales y Sistemas Políticos en América Latina: La Construcción de Nuevas Democracias*. Buenos Aires: CLACSO; *apud:* Julia Sant'anna (2007). *"Novos movimentos sociais e os movimentos de esquerda na América Latina"*, *Democracia Viva* 35: 4-8, Junho. Rio de Janeiro: IBASE.

Moraes, Alexandre de. *Direitos Humanos Fundamentais*, 6ª Edição, São Paulo: Editora Atlas S.A., 2005.

Oliveira, Henrique Altemani de. *Política Externa Brasileira*, São Paulo: Saraiva, 2005

Paes, José Eduardo Sabo. *Fundações, Associações e Entidades de Interesse Social: aspectos jurídicos, administrativos, contábeis, trabalhistas e tributários*, 8ª edição, Rio de Janeiro: Forense, 2013.

Paixão, Marcelo and Luiz M. Carvano (2008). *Relatório anual das desigualdades raciais no Brasil, 2007-08*. Rio de Janeiro: Garamond.

Piovesan, Flávia (2008). *Declaração Universal dos Direitos Humanos: desafios e perspectivas* 17(2), Set/Out/Nov. Revista de Política Externa, São Paulo: Editora Paz e Terra.

Pochmann, Márcio (2009). *Qual desenvolvimento? Oportunidades e dificuldades do Brasil contemporâneo*, 1ª edição. São Paulo: Publisher Brasil.

Pochmann, Márcio *et alii*. (2004). *Atlas da exclusão social*. São Paulo: Cortez.

Porto, Maria Stela Grossi (2000). *"A Violência Entre ä Inclusão e a Exclusão Social"*, *Tempo Social* 12(1): 187-200, Maio De.

Puente, Carlos Alfonso Iglesias (2010). *A Cooperação Técnica Horizontal Brasileira Como Instrumento Da Política Exterior*. Brasília: Funag

Ribeiro, Darcy (1975). *A Universidade Necessária*. Rio De Janeiro: Paz E Terra.

Rummert, Sonia Maria (2005). *Projeto Escola De Fábrica: Atendendo A "Pobres e Desvalidos da Sorte" Do Século XXI. Perspectiva: Revista Do Centro De Ciências Da Educação Da Universidade Federal De Santa Catarina. Florianópolis* 23(2), Junho/Dezembro.

Sachs, Ignacy (2008). *Desenvolvimento: Includente, Sustentável, Sustentado*. Rio De Janeiro: Garamond.

Sawaia, Bader (2001). *As Artimanhas da Exclusão: Análise Psicossocial e Ética da Desigualdade Social*. Petrópolis: Vozes.

Sen, Amartya (1990). *On Ethics and Economics*. Basil: Blackwell, Oxford.

Silva, Luiz Inácio Lula Da and Celso Amorim (2003). *Guimarães, Samuel Pinheiro. A Política Externa do Brasil.* Brasília: Ipir/Funag. p.31.

Síveres, Luiz (2006). *Universidade: Torre Ou Sino?* Brasília: Editora Universa.

Smith, David Horton (1979). *The Diversity of Transnational Associations and NGOs: Variations According to Structural-Functional Types.* Transnational Associations. pp.245-49.

Soares, Barbara and Mulheres Musumeci (1999). *Invisíveis: Violência Conjugal e as Novas Políticas de Segurança.* Rio De Janeiro: Civilização Brasileira.

Spaece-Net (2004). *Evolução Do Programa De Modernização E Melhoria Da Educação Básica.* Secretaria Da Educação Do Estado Do Ceará.

Sposati, Aldaísa De Oliveira (1998). *Exclusão Social Abaixo da Linha Do Equado.* Puc/Sp, Maio De: Apresentado no Seminário Sobre Exclusão Social.

Sposati, Aldaísa De Oliveira (2004). *A Menina Loas: Um Processo De Construção Da Assistência Social.* São Paulo, Cortez.

Steiner, João S. (2006). *"Conhecimento: Gargalos Para Um Brasil No Futuro", Revista de Estudos Avançados* 20(56): 231-48, Jan./Abr. São Paulo: Instituto De Estudos Avançados.

Stiglitz, Joseph E. (2007). *Globalização: Como Dar Certo (Tradução Pedro Maia Soares).* São Paulo: Companhia Das Letras.

Tavares, Ricardo Neiva (1999). *As Organizações Não-Governamentais Nas Nações Unidas.* Brasília: Instituto Rio Branco.

Tedesco, Juan Carlos (1998). *O Novo Pacto Educativo.* São Paulo: Ática.

Telles, Edward and Paixão, Marcelo (2013). "Affirmative Action in Brazil", *Lasa Forum* XLIV(2), Spring.

Telles, Edward (2004). *Race in Another America: The Significance of Skin Color in Brazil.* Princeton, Nj: Princeton University Press.

The San Diego Union-Tribune, 3 January 2004, p.A18.

Weber, Max (2012). *A Ética Protestante e o Espírito do Capitalismo.* São Paulo: Editora Cia. das Letras.

Acesso à Internet

Ação Educativa. Debate sobre relação entre educação e desigualdade abre IX Seminário de EJA, 2006. Acesso em 01/05/2012, às 18:08 e disponível endereço:http://www.acaoeducativa.org.br/base.

Bava, S.C. and V. Paulics (n.d.). *V. Experiências inovadoras em uma nova governança democrática.* Access: *http://www.direitoacidade.org.br/artigo_interno* (01 May).

United Nations University (2001). A New Concept for Education and Higher Education. Tokyo. *http://www.unu.edu*

14

TSELISO THIPANYANE

Foreign Policy of Major States: South Africa

Introduction

Whilst the racist policies under the Apartheid system influenced South Africa's foreign policy and informed its hostile and aggressive relations with many African states that led to its isolation by the international community, the country today is an important member of the international community and plays a significant role in international affairs. The country's post-Apartheid founding values, 'human dignity, the achievement of equality and the advancement of human rights and freedoms,' amongst other values, now define its national interests and inform its foreign policy.

This chapter reviews South Africa's foreign policy in the context of how this policy informs and affects the country's international relations and the impact this has had on it's national interests and objectives. Part one of this review provides a historical context and evolution of South Africa's foreign policy. Part two looks into the political context that informs the country's foreign policy, while part three entails an analysis of key institutions and processes that inform and develop South Africa's foreign policy. Part four assesses the impact of conflicts (regional and international) and the Cold War on the country's foreign policy. Part five provides an overall assessment of South Africa's foreign policy performance, including its successes and failures, especially in relation to emerging strategic, political, economic and social trends and concludes with recommendations on how best the country can respond to contemporary and future challenges in relation to its foreign policy.

I

Historical Context and Evolution of South Africa's Foreign Policy

South Africa was established in 1910 as a self-governing entity under the British colonial empire. It was a merger of four British colonies; the Cape of Good Hope, Natal, the Orange River Colony and the Transvaal—the latter two were Afrikaner Republics wrested by the British, whilst the Cape Colony had been annexed from the Dutch in 1806 (Wilson and Thompson, 1975).

The country obtained full parliamentary sovereignty from Britain with the passing of the 1931 Statute of Westminster[1] and became a republic in March 1961.[2] However, South Africa's entrance in international relations and the world of foreign policy began in 1948 with the institutionalisation of racism under the notorious Apartheid system—a system the international community and the United Nations (UN) later declared a crime against humanity.[3]

Whilst racism was already institutionalised in South Africa when the Union was formed in 1910, the advent of the Apartheid system in the country in 1948 deepened and increased its magnitude and impact. This was followed by flurry of legislation intended to give effect to the racist policies of the government. These measures include: The Population Registration Act 30 of 1950 (classified South Africans in different racial categories); the Group Areas Act 41 of 1950 (restricted different racial groups to different residential and business areas); the Prohibition of Mixed Marriages Age Act 55 of 1949; the Immorality Amendment Act 1950 (criminalised sexual relations across racial categories); the Suppression of Communism

1. The Status of the Union Act 69 of 1934 declared the Union as a sovereign independent state.
2. This followed a whites-only referendum held on 5 October 1960. The country only obtained judicial independence in 1950 when it stopped sending appeals to the Privy Council in Britain. See, South African History Online: *http://www.sahistory.org.za/topic/becoming-republic-and-withdrawal-commonwealth-1961* (accessed 10 May 2014).
3. The International Convention on the Suppression and Punishment of the Crime of Apartheid, which entered into force on 18 July 1976, proclaimed that the inhuman act of policies and practices of the Apartheid system violated the principles of international law and purposes and principles of the Charter of the UN in particular, and constituted a serious threat to international peace and security (Article 1).

Act 44 1950; the Reservation of Separate Amenities Act 49 of 1953 (separate public amenities such as parks, libraries, beaches, sports facilities etc., for different racial groups); and the Bantu Education Act 1953 (separate and inferior education for African learners). The Apartheid system with its laws, policies and institutions brought extreme socio-economic and political hardships, pain and suffering to many South Africans and African people in particular. Resistance to the Apartheid system was met with harsh, cruel and deadly response by the Apartheid regime.

Due to Cold War politics and the support the Apartheid regime received from several Western countries like the United States of America (USA) and the United Kingdom (UK), there was minimal international opposition to the Apartheid system at its initial stages. However, the Sharpeville massacre of 21 March 1960, where over 69 peaceful and unarmed protesters were shot and killed by the Apartheid regime was the turning point in relation to opposition to the Apartheid system by the international community. The massacre and related events triggered massive international campaigns against the regime.

The UN Security Council (UNSC) resolution 134 (1960) adopted on 30 March 1960, was a direct response to the Sharpeville massacre through which the UN 'deplored' the racist policies and practices of the Apartheid regime and called upon the regime to 'abandon its policies of Apartheid and racial discrimination.'[4] The Apartheid regime, however, ignored and resisted calls to abandon its racist policies and practices, and went on to hold a whites—only referendum in October 1960, withdrew from the Commonwealth in March 1961, and declared itself a republic on 31 May 1961.

The disregard of international demands on the Apartheid regime to end its racist policies and practices led to more concerted international and domestic pressure against the regime. At the international level, the International Labour Organization (ILO) adopted a resolution on 29 June 1961 that effectively suspended South Africa's membership in the organisation. At the domestic level,

4. France and Britain abstained from Resolution 134 that was adopted by nine votes.

the African National Congress (ANC) established in 1912 to fight for the political rights of black South Africans, formed an armed wing (*Umkhonto weSizwe*—MK) in December 1961 in order to wage an armed struggle against the Apartheid.

These measures, however, did not bring about any significant changes initially, and the Apartheid regime responded with more brutality against its opponents in general and black South Africans in particular. Imprisonment, torture, banishment and death became the order of the day for opponents of the Apartheid regime (Truth and Reconciliation Commission, 1998). Neighbouring states like Lesotho, Botswana and Mozambique, that offered support to opponents of the Apartheid regime also felt the wrath of the regime and had their territorial integrity and economic and political systems undermined in many ways. The invasion of Angola between 1980 and 1985, military strikes in Lesotho (1982), Mozambique (1981 and 1983), Swaziland, Botswana and Swaziland, support of the civil war in Mozambique, and support of a military coup in Lesotho in January 1986, are examples of these activities—manifestation of the foreign policy of the Apartheid regime and its aggressive behaviour towards its neighbours (Truth and Reconciliation Commission, 1998).

South Africa's racist policies and its hostile foreign policy and actions ultimately forced the UN to adopt even harsher measures against the regime. In this regard, the UN General Assembly through resolution 1761 (1962) requested UN member states to take several punitive measures against the country, individually or collectively. These measures included cutting diplomatic ties with the regime, boycotting its goods, imposing arms boycotts against it, denying port access to its registered vessels and landing and passage rights for aircrafts registered under its laws.[5] The UNSC, through resolution 181 (1963), imposed an international arms embargo against the regime and called on the Apartheid regime to abandon its racist

5. The General Assembly in its resolution also expressed concerns about the conduct of some UN Member States, that provided support to the Apartheid regime in the pursuit of its racist policies and established the Special Committee on Policies of Apartheid, later remained the Special Committee against Apartheid.

policies.[6] Other measures adopted by the UN included cultural, educational, scientific and sporting boycotts against the regime, and the suspension of the country's participation in meetings of the UN General Assembly[7] and other organisations and conferences of the UN.[8] These measures turned the Apartheid regime into a pariah state, and after many years and much suffering by the oppressed people of South Africa and neighbouring states, helped to end the Apartheid system.

Foreign policy under the Apartheid regime was characterised by defiance and contravention of international norms and standards provided by the Charter of the UN and the Universal Declaration of Human Rights that inform healthy and peaceful relations amongst nations of the world. This policy, according to the African National Congress (ANC), was 'an extension of the [regime's] oppressive and violent nature' (ANC, 1992). In describing the impact of the policies of the Apartheid regime, the 'Declaration on the Destructive Consequences in South Africa' adopted by the UN General Assembly in December 1989 stated:

> Affirming that apartheid, characterized as a crime against the conscience and dignity of mankind, is responsible for the death of countless numbers of people in South Africa, has sought to dehumanize entire peoples and has imposed a brutal war on the region of southern Africa, which has resulted in untold loss of life, destruction of property and massive displacement of innocent men, women and children and which is a scourge and a affront to humanity that must be fought and eradicated in its totality.

The anti-Apartheid struggle, in contrast to the Apartheid regime and its aggressive foreign policy, was informed by a commitment to the principles of the Charter of the UN and the Universal Declaration

---

6. France and Britain abstained from the Security Council resolution adopted on 7 August 1963.

7. Adopted on 12 November 1974.

8. As per resolution 3324 (1974) of the General Assembly on 18 July 1976, the International Convention on the Suppression and Punishment of the Crime of Apartheid entered into force. This Convention declared Apartheid as a crime against humanity and that its policies and practices violated principles of international law and constituted a 'serious threat to international peace and security.'

of Human Rights. The Freedom Charter, adopted on 26 June 1955 by the oppressed people of South Africa and those opposed to Apartheid, espoused these principles and also outlined a vision for a new South Africa fundamentally and radically different from the Apartheid regime.

In relation to foreign policy, the Freedom Charter provided for a post-Apartheid South Africa that will 'respect the rights and sovereignty of all nations,' 'maintain world peace,' and pursue the settlement of international disputes by negotiations and not war. This was a response to the aggression of Apartheid South Africa towards the majority of its citizens and its neighbours and to the politics and consequences of the Cold War that saw Apartheid South Africa being supported by Western countries for a long time whilst the ANC, received much of its military support from the Soviet Union then.

II

Political Context of South Africa's Foreign Policy

The inauguration of Nelson Mandela on 10 May 1994, as South Africa's first democratically elected president is a historic moment in the struggle against racism and the struggle for freedom and human rights in South Africa. It also marked a turning point in South Africa's foreign policy under Apartheid—an end of hostile relations with the international community and the beginning of normal and peaceful relations. Nelson Mandela outlined these changes in his inaugural speech when he said:[9]

> We, the people of South Africa, feel fulfilled that humanity has taken us back into its bosom, that we, who were outlaws not so long ago, have today been give the rare privilege to be host to the nations of the world on our own soil.
>
> We have triumphed in the effort to implant hope in the breasts of the millions of our people. We enter into a covenant that we shall build

9. Nelson Mandela's inaugural speech-Pretoria, 10 May 1994. Available at *http://www.anc.org.za/show.php?id=3132* (accessed on 10 May 2014).

> the society in which all South Africans, both black and white, will be able to walk tall, without any fear in their hearts, assured of their inalienable right to human dignity—a rainbow nation at peace with itself and the world.
>
> Never, never and never again shall it be that this beautiful land will against experience the oppression of one by another and suffer the indignity of being the skunk of the world.

Mandela's position on South Africa's relations with the international community and its neighbours was a reflection of the principles of the 1955 Freedom Charter, which inspired the struggle against Apartheid and set out a vision of a post-Apartheid society many South Africans fought and laid down their lives for: a South Africa at peace with its neighbours.[10]

The Freedom Charter constitutes the foundation upon which South Africa's new constitution and the post-Apartheid foreign policy are based. It is also the foundation of the constitution of the ANC,[11] the ruling party in South Africa since 1994, and has informed and continues to inform policies of the ANC and that of the government of South Africa.[12] The Freedom Charter also informed the 'Ready to Govern: ANC Policy Guidelines for a Democratic South Africa' that the ANC adopted in 1992 for the negotiations leading to South Africa's first democratic elections in 1994. The intended foreign policy of a democratic South Africa, shaped by the country's internal policies and the needs and interests of its people, was, according to the ANC's Policy Guidelines, going to help the new South Africa contribute to "the democratization of international political and

---

10. The ANC has always had an international perspective from its inception. Its struggle against Apartheid also took a significant internationalist approach. See Charles Nqakula (High Commissioner of the Republic of South Africa to Mozambique). 'The Foreign Policy of South Africa from 1994 to 2012: Input by Charles Nqakula—High Commissioners of the Republic of South Africa, Mozambique, Maputo, 6 March 2013. Available at *www.dirco.gov.za/maputo/speeches2011/remarks_by_charles_nqakula* (accessed on 14 May 2014).
11. The ANC adopted the Freedom Charter in April 1956 as part of its policy framework.
12. The ANC's Constitution, as amended and adopted at the 53rd National Conference in Mangaung, South Africa, in December 2012, describes the Freedom Charter as the "essential philosophy of the ANC", See, *http://www.anc.org.za/show.php?id=10177* (accessed 18 May 2014).

economic relations", promote "peaceful co-existence and cooperation on a democratic basis with its neighbours in the region and further afield", and "actively promote the objectives of democracy, peace, stability, development, and mutually—beneficial relations among the people of Africa as a whole" (ANC, 1992).[13]

The advancement of human rights which featured prominently in the Freedom Charter also influenced the ANC's Policy Guidelines on the role of human rights in the country's new foreign policy—human rights were at the heart of the anti-Apartheid struggle. In this regard, the ANC's Policy Guidelines refers to human rights as 'beacons' that will guide policy advances in the post-Apartheid South Africa. Nelson Mandela reiterated this position in December 1993 when he indicated that: "South Africa's future foreign relations will be based on our belief that human rights should be the core concern of international relations" and that human rights "will be the light that guides our foreign affairs." He outlined the following as pillars upon which the foreign policy of post-Apartheid South Africa will rest upon (Mandela, 1993): [14]

- That issues of human rights are central to international relations and an understanding that they extend beyond the political, embracing the economic, social and environmental;
- That just and lasting solutions to the problems of humankind can only come through the promotion of democracy worldwide;
- That consideration of justice and respect for international law should guide the relations between nations;
- That peace is the goal for which all nations should strive, and where this breakdowns, internationally agreed and non-violent mechanisms, including effective arms-control regimes, must be employed;
- That the concerns and interests of the continent of Africa should be reflected in our foreign policy choices;

---

13. ANC, "Ready to Govern. ANC Policy Guidelines for a Democratic South Africa", *http://www.anc.org.za/show.php?id=227* (accessed on 28 May 2014).
14. Available at *http://www.sahistory.org.za/article/insights-mandela039s-reign* (accessed on 28 May 2014).

- That economic development depends on growing regional and international economic cooperation in an interdependent world.

The ANC's positions on foreign policy and international relations, including Mandela's 1993 reflections in this regard, were consolidated in its foreign policy document: *ANC: Foreign Policy Perspective in a Democratic South Africa* (ANC, 1994), which informed foreign policy and international relations under the post-Apartheid government and continues to do so. The transformation of Apartheid-based foreign policy and related international relations into that of a free, democratic and non-racial country were at the heart of these developments.[15]

The ANC's foreign policy positions as informed and grounded in the Freedom Charter have remained unchanged after two decades in power as the ruling party in South Africa's post-Apartheid government. The South African government's 2011 white paper on foreign policy still envisages a country that is a 'good international citizen' committed to play a 'leading role in conflict prevention, peacekeeping, peace-building and post-conflict reconstruction,' and the promotion of democracy in Africa by working with the African Union 'to discourage unconstitutional changes in governments' (Department of International Relations and Cooperation, 2011).[16] Human rights, the aspirations of a society living in 'human dignity, equality and freedom', are values that continue to inform South African's foreign policy and international relations according to the white paper, values rooted in South Africa's long liberation struggle against Apartheid.

In 2012, the ANC's National Policy Conference reaffirmed the centrality of the values of the Freedom Charter in South Africa's international's objectives—friendship and peace. The ANC's National Policy Conference also affirmed that its international relations policy, as the governing party, is directly informed by the country's domestic

15. Available at *http://www.anc.org.za/show.php?id=230*

16. Available at *http://www.safpi.org/sites/default/files/publications/white_paper_on_sa_foreign_policy-building_a_better_world_20110513.pdf* (accessed on 28 May 2014).

policy and that it remains 'committed to [its] founding values of a struggle for a humane, just, equitable, democratic, and free world, particularly Africa' (ANC, 2012).[17] The 'building of a better Africa and better world', 'continental and international solidarity' and 'transformation of global governance', the UNSC in particular, were seen as key pillars of South Africa's foreign policy by the National Policy Conference.

Since the end of the Apartheid system of government in 1994, South Africa's foreign policy has been influenced and shaped by policies of the ANC[18] as informed by the Freedom Charter. The ANC regularly expands and revises the organisation's foreign policy and international relations positions at its National Policy Conferences, and the ANC-led government is required and expected to express these positions in the country's foreign policy.[19]

III

Key Institutions and Processes that Inform and Shapes South Africa's Foreign Policy

The authority to develop and implement national policy for South Africa, including foreign policy, vests in the President of the country and is exercised by him or her with the support of Cabinet.[20] The President is particularly assisted in this regard by the minister in charge of the Department of International Relations and Cooperation

17. Available at *http://www.anc.org.za/docs/pol/2012/policy_conferencev.pdf* (accessed on 29 May 2014).

18. South Africa's foreign policy, however, has to be within the context and parameters of the supreme law of the land—the 1996 Constitution of the Republic of South Africa. Section 2 of the Constitution provides that any South African law or conduct that is inconstant with its provisions is invalid.

19. In terms of Rule 25 of the ANC's Constitution, it is an act of misconduct for any ANC official in government to fail, refuse or neglect to comply with policies and resolutions of the party. Such misconduct could lead to the suspension or expulsion of the concerned member. See African National Congress Constitution at *http://www.anc.org.za/show.php?id=10177* (accessed 28 May 2014).

20. As per section 85 of the Constitution of the Republic of South Africa, 1996. Section 85(2) (b) of the Constitution provides: 'The President exercises the executive authority, together with the other members of the Cabinet by developing and implementing national policy.'

(DIRCO), whose strategic objectives include advising government on foreign policy, coordinating South Africa's international relations and promoting the country's foreign policy objectives.[21] This authority of the President includes 'negotiating and signing' international agreements and international human rights treaties that bind the country and informs and shapes its foreign policy and international relations.[22]

At Cabinet level, the International Cooperation, Trade and Security (ICTS) cluster, comprising Cabinet ministers from Defense, International Relations and Cooperation, Finance, Trade and Industry, Rural Development and Land Reform and Environmental Affairs departments, is responsible for the formulation of government's foreign policy and foreign policy positions. The cluster also monitors implementation of the country's foreign policy.[23] The DIRCO, formerly the Department of Foreign Affairs (DFA), is responsible for the coordination of implementation of South Africa's foreign policy (DIRCO, 2013).[24]

The Parliament of South Africa, through the National Assembly, also plays a major role in the country's foreign policy and international relations. Whilst the negotiating and signing of international agreements falls within the mandate of the executive branch of the executive branch of government, such agreements must meet with the approval of Parliament before they could bind the country and also need an enactment of Parliament before they could be part of the country's domestic law.[25] The President, Cabinet and the Minister

---

21. See, *http://www.dirco.gov.za/department/index.html* (accessed on 30 May 2014).
22. These agreements, however, should not be in conflict with the country's Constitution, see section 231 of the Constitution of the Republic of South Africa, 1996.
23. See, *http://gov-zas.websiteinprogress.co.za/about-government/international-cooperation-trade-and-security-cluster* and *http://gov-zas.websiteinprogress.co.za/about-government/structure-and-functions-south-african-government#gov_cluster* (accessed 30 May 2014).
24. See Measures and Guidelines for the Enhanced Coordination of South Africa's International Engagements, 2013. Available at *http://www.dfa.gov.za/docs/2013/measures_guidelines_book.pdf* (accessed on 30 May 2014).
25. Section 231 of the Constitution of the Republic of South Africa. Self-executing international agreements only need Parliamentary approval and should not be in conflict with provisions of the Constitution or an act of national legislation.

of International Relations and Cooperation Affairs in particular, are also accountable to the National Assembly of South Africa's Parliament for the content and implementation of the country's foreign policy, and could, individually and collectively, be sanctioned for conduct inconsistent with provisions of the country's constitution and relevant laws.[26]

The Portfolio Committee on International Relations and Co-operation is the main committee of the National Assembly responsible for oversight of South Africa's foreign policy and its implementation, and in particular, the activities of the Minister of International Relations and Co-operation and the Department of International Relations and Co-operation in this regard. The Committee also oversees the budget of the Department of International Relations and Co-operation and considers relevant draft laws pertaining to foreign policy and international relations, international treaties and international agreements and their implementation. The Committee also has powers to summon any person, official and institution to appear before it in the fulfillment of its oversight responsibilities.[27]

Constitutional bodies established to support South Africa's constitutional democracy, such as the South African Human Rights Commission (SAHRC) and the Commission for Gender Equality and the Commission for the Protection and Promotion of the Rights of Cultural, Religious and Linguistic Communities, play an important role in the country's foreign policy and international relations. The SAHRC can, for example, comment and report to the National Assembly on how the country discharges its international human rights treaty obligations and make recommendations in this regard. The SAHRC also has observer status in the UN Human Rights Council and the African Commission on Human and Peoples' Rights, and occasionally reports on the country's human rights record in relation to international human rights treaties in these bodies.

26. Section 55(2) of the Constitution provides that the National Assembly 'must provide for mechanisms—to ensure that all executive organs of state in the national sphere of government are accountable to it; and maintain oversight of the exercise of national executive authority.'

27. See *http://www.parliament.gov.za/live/content.php?Item_ID=215&CommitteeID=14 and http://www.parliament.gov.za/live/content.php?Item_ID=35* (accessed on 1 June 2014).

The South African judiciary, led by the Constitutional Court, also plays an important role in the country's foreign policy and international relations. The Constitutional Court has the authority to determine the constitutionality of any law or conduct of the executive (government) and legislative (Parliament) branches of government[28] and has made pronouncements on South Africa's foreign policy and international relations.[29]

In one of its earliest decisions, the South African Constitutional Court in *S v Makwanyane and Another* made it clear that all government's conduct must be steeped in human rights and said in this regard:[30]

> The rights to life and dignity are the most important of all human rights, and the source of all other personal rights in Chapter Three. By committing ourselves to a society founded on the recognition of human rights we are required to value these two rights above all others. And this must be demonstrated by the State in everything that it does.

In *Mohamed and Another v President of the Republic of South Africa and Others*,[31] South African government immigration officers had arrested, interrogated and handed Khalfan Mohammed to the US Federal Bureau (FBI) for removal to the US in violation of South Africa's Alien's Control Act (Act 96 of 1991). Mohammed was a suspect in the bombing of US embassies in Kenya and Tanzania in August 1998 that killed over 223 people.[32] The Constitutional Court, in re-emphasising that all government's actions and decisions,

---

28. Section 167 (4) of the Constitution provides that the Constitutional Court may 'decide on the constitutionality of any parliamentary bill' and may 'decide that Parliament or the President has failed to fulfill a constitutional obligation.'

29. In Glenister v President of the Republic of South Africa and Others, [2011] ZACC 6; 2011 (3) SA 347(CC); 2011 (7) BCLR 651 (CC) 917 March 2011)., paras 191-3, the Court said at paragraph 205: "We add that any obligation binding upon the Republic under international law must not conflict with express provisions of the Constitution, including those in the Bill of Rights."

30. (CCT3/94) [1995] ZACC 3; 1995(3) SA 391 (June 1995), at paragraph 144.

31. (CCT 17/01) [2001] ZACC 18; 2001 (3) SA 893 (CC); 2001 (7) BCLR 685 (CC) (28 May 2001).

32. He was convicted and sentenced to life in the US. See, *http://www.huffingtonpost.com/2011/10/05/judge-terrorist-can-sue-o_n_996286.html* (accessed on 7 June 2014).

including those pertaining to foreign policy and international relations, are bound by the country's constitution and its Bill of Rights, and that the government may not be party to any violation of human rights, said:[33]

> For the South African government to co-operate with a foreign government to secure the removal of a fugitive from South Africa to a country of which the fugitive is not a national and with which he has no connection other than that he is to be put on trial for his life there, is contrary to the underlying values of our Constitution. It is inconsistent with the government's obligation to protect the right to life of everyone in South Africa, and ignores the commitment implicit in the Constitution that South Africa will not be party to the imposition of cruel, inhuman or degrading punishment.

The South African Constitution also requires the judiciary and any other domestic forum or tribunal to consider international law when interpreting any provision of the country's Bill of Rights.[34] The judiciary is also required by section 233 of the Constitution to prefer interpretation of any legislation that is consistent with international law over interpretation to the contrary. In this regard, the Constitutional Court in *Glenister v President of the Republic of South Africa and Others*, said:[35]

> There is, thus, no escape from the manifest constitutional injunction to integrate, in a way the Constitution permits, international law obligations into our domestic law. We do so willingly and in compliance with our constitutional duty.

South Africa's international treaty obligations also have an impact on its foreign policy. As an example, the 1992 Treaty establishing the South African Development Community (SADC) which South Africa ratified in 1994 provides for human rights, democracy and the rule of law as some of the principles that SADC member states must

33. At paragraph 58.

34. See section 39(1) of the Constitution of the Republic of South Africa, 1996.

35. [2011] ZACC 6; 2011 (3) SA 347(CC); 2011 (7) BCLR 651 (CC) (17 March 2011), paragraph 202.

abide by.[36] The SADC Treaty also provides for the establishment of the Tribunal with the responsibility of interpreting provisions of the Treaty and other instruments of the SADC; decisions of the Tribunal are final and binding. The member states of SADC are obliged to give the Treaty the force of national law.[37] The South African judiciary also plays an important role in ensuring that South Africa's foreign policy and international relations are in compliance with the country's constitution and laws, and that the country adheres to international agreements and treaties it has entered into and approved by Parliament.[38]

IV

Impact of Conflicts (Regional and International), the Cold War and Other National Security Concerns on South Africa's Foreign Policy

Conflicts and national security concerns have shaped and continue to influence foreign polices of many countries and their implementation. South Africa is no different in this regard, given its aggressive conduct towards its neighbours under the Apartheid system, role in the Cold War and its new role in peace-building attests.

Whilst foreign policy in Apartheid South Africa was characteristic by aggression and destabilisation of its neighbours; a vision of a prosperous African continent that is peaceful, democratic, non-racial, non-sexist and united, informs international relations in post-Apartheid South Africa. This vision is also reflected in section 198

36. See Articles 5 and 21 of the SADC Treaty: *http://www.sadc.int/files/9113/5292/9434/SADC_Treaty.pdf* (accessed on 12 June 2014).

37. See Articles 4, 5, 6, 9 and 16 of the SADC 1992 Treaty.

38. See Government of the Republic of Zimbabwe v Fick and Others (CCT 101/12) [2013] ZACC 22; 2013(5) SA 325 (CC); 2013(10) BCLR 1103 (CC) (27 June 2013). In enforcing South Africa's compliance with its international treaty obligations, the Constitutional Court, at paragraph 71 said: "When the farmers' rights to property, their human rights in general and the right of access to courts in particular were violated, Zimbabwe was, in terms of article 6(6) of the Amended Treaty, obliged to cooperate with the Tribunal in the adjudication of the dispute. After the Tribunal had delivered its judgment, Zimbabwe was duty-bound to assist in the execution of that judgment and so is South Africa."

of South Africa's Constitution pertaining to principles governing the country's national security:

> [T]he resolve of South Africans, as individuals and as a nation, to live as equals, to live in peace and harmony, to be free from fear and want and to seek as better life.

This new vision has influenced much of the post-South Africa's foreign policy and the country's response to conflicts and national security concerns in the region and worldwide, and as indicated above, is informed by provisions of the Freedom Charter.

The white paper on foreign policy, Building a Better World: The Diplomacy of Ubuntu (Department of International Relations and Co-operation, 2011), provides for values that informs South Africa's foreign policy response to regional and international conflicts and the national security concerns. These values include 'creating a better South Africa' and a 'good international citizen,' the 'pursuit of a better Africa,' and 'regional and continental integration', and are regarded as essential for South Africa's prosperity and security. The white paper also indicates that South Africa will play a leading role in 'conflict prevention, peacekeeping, peace-building and post-conflict reconstruction,' and will work with the African Union to 'discourage unconstitutional changes of government' that have contributed to many conflicts in Africa.

The position of the Department of International Relations and Co-operation on South Africa's national security concerns as reflected in the white paper was endorsed by the national policy conference of the ANC held in 2012, which reconfirmed the commitment of the ANC and government to 'work towards peace in the continent and in the world' (ANC, 2012). The policy conference also supported resolutions prohibiting the presence of foreign militaries in Africa, such as the US and its African Command (AFRICOM), and acknowledged that South Africa's role in 'peace keeping, post-conflict reconstruction and development' cannot be separated from the country's national interests.

In keeping with these policy positions, South Africa has adopted numerous instruments and agreements pertaining to regional and global conflicts and broader national security concerns. These instruments and agreements once adopted, form part of South Africa's foreign policy and inform its international relations.

At the international level, South Africa ratified the Rome Statute of the International Criminal Court adopted to deal with serious crimes arising out of conflicts that threaten international peace and security; the crime of genocide, crimes against humanity, war crimes and the crime of aggression.[39] The country has also domesticated the Rome Statute into national law through enactment of the Implementation of the Rome Statute of the International Criminal Court Act 27 of 2002—a serious and important commitment to respond to atrocities of regional and international conflicts and a departure from Apartheid policies of aggression towards neighbouring states and their destabilisation.[40]

The country has also signed and ratified the Convention on the Prohibition of the Development, Production, Stockpiling and Use of Chemical Weapons and their Destruction (Chemical Weapons Convention).[41] This was in response to the chemical and biological weapons manufactured, acquired and used by the Apartheid regime against black South Africans and its opponents, and the assistance it received in manufacturing these weapons from countries such as the US and Israel (Truth and Reconciliation Commission, 1998: 517). This was followed by ratification of the Convention on the Prohibition of the Use, Stockpiling, Production and Transfer of Anti-Personnel Mines and on their Destruction (Mine-Ban Convention)[42] in pursuit of the country's post-Apartheid foreign policy and international relations perspective.

39. Adopted in Rome on 17 July 1998. South Africa signed the treaty on 17 July 1998 and ratified it on 17 November 2000.

40. The legislation came into effect on 16 August 2002. See, *http://www.justice.gov.za/legislation/acts/2002-027.pdf* (accessed on 12 June 2014).

41. The Convention was adopted on 13 January 1993 and came into effect on 29 April 1997. South Africa adopted the Convention on 13 September 1995.

42. South Africa ratified the Convention on 26 June 1998 and it came into effect on 1 March 1999. Over 300,000 mines were destroyed in line with the requirements of the Convention.

At the regional level, and in response to the challenge of conflicts in Africa, South Africa played a key role in the formation of the African Union (AU) and the adoption of its constitution, the Constitutive Act of the Africa Union, on 11 July 2000. The promotion of 'peace, security, and stability' and the 'establishment of a common defense policy for the African continent,' are some of the important objectives and principles of the Constitutive Act.[43]

The African Union has adopted several instruments and agreements to address conflicts and security concerns in Africa in line with the objectives and principles of the Constitutive Act. These instruments, which South Africa is party to, include the OAU Convention on the prevention and Combating of Terrorism,[44] the Protocol to the OAU Convention on the Prevention and Combating of Terrorism,[45] the Protocol Relating to the Establishment of the Peace and Security Council,[46] and the African Union and Non-Aggression and Common Defense Pact.[47] There is also the African Nuclear-

43. See Articles 3 and 4 of the Constitutive Act of the African Union.

44. Adopted on 1 July 1999 and came into operation on 6 December 2002. South Africa signed the convention on 14 July 1999 and ratified it on 7 November 2002.

45. Adopted on 8 July 2004 in Addis Ababa but not yet into operation on 26 February 2014. South Africa ratified the treaty on 25 March 2007. According to this Protocol, African state have undertaken to fight terrorist activities, not allow their territories to be used for terrorist activities—some the measures in this regard include: prevent 'the entry and training of terrorists in their territories', 'identify, detect and freeze or seize any funds or assets associated with terrorism,' 'take appropriate actions against perpetrators of mercenary activities' and use the Protocol as a legal basis for extradition purposes where no such agreements exist between States—see Articles 3 and 8.

46. Adopted on 9 July 2002 (Durban, South Africa) and came into force on 26 December 2003. South Africa ratified the Protocol on 15 May 2003. According to the Preamble of the Protocol, 'no single internal factor has contributed more to socio-economic decline on the Continent and the suffering of the civilian population than the scourge of conflicts within and between our States.' According to the Protocol, the Peace and Security Council is 'a standing decision-making organ for the prevention, management and resolution of conflicts'.

47. Adopted on 31 January 2005 (Abuja) and came into force on 18 December 2009. South Africa has not ratified the instrument but signed it on 24 January 2006. This provides for mutual assistance amongst African states in response to aggression and the establishment of an African Standby Force pending the establishment of an African Army at the 'final stage of the political and economic integration of the Continent.'

Weapon-Free Zone Treaty (Pelindaba Treaty),[48] which 'prohibits the development, stockpiling, testing of nuclear explosive devices and dumping of radioactive waste' in Africa. South Africa, the only African country with nuclear weapons that it dismantled towards the end of the Apartheid regime and end of the Cold War, played a major role in the adoption of this treaty, which it ratified on 13 March 1998 (De Klerk, 1993; De Villiers *et al.*, 1993).

The Southern African Development Community (SADC) established to promote peace and security and economic growth amongst other objectives, which South Africa joined after much aggression and destabilisation of its member states, has adopted several treaties and agreements pertaining to conflicts and security concerns in the region.[49] South Africa has played a central role in the activities of SADC and continues to do so.

In 14 August 2001, the SADC adopted the Protocol on Politics, Defense and Security Cooperation, which provides for the development of common foreign policy positions and regional co-operation on matters relating to security and defence, the 'development of a collective security capacity,' and the conclusion of a 'Mutual Defense Pact in order to respond to external military threats to the region.' The Protocol also provides for the establishment of the Organ on Politics, Defense and Security responsible for the coordination of policies and activities pertaining to politics, defense and security in the region.[50] The Mutual Defense Pact was signed in 2003 and makes provision for an 'immediate collection action' by SADC member states in response to an armed attack against a fellow member state. Partly in response to the destabilising activities of Apartheid South Africa in the region in the past and the role of

48. Adopted on 11 April 1996 under the auspices of the Organization of Africa Unity (OAU), but and came into force on 15 July 2001 after establishment of the African Union.

49. See Articles 5 and 21 of the SADC Treaty: *http://www.sadc.int/files/9113/5292/9434/SADC_Treaty.pdf* (accessed on 12 June 2014).

50. Signed on 14 August 2001 and entered into force on 2 March 2004: *http://www.sadc.int/files/3613/5292/8367/Protocol_on_Politics_Defence_and_Security20001.pdf* (accessed on 13 June 2014.

Rwanda and Uganda in the conflict in the Democratic Republic of Congo (DRC), Article 8 of this Pact provides:[51]

> States Parties undertake not to nurture, harbor or support any person, group of persons or institutions whose aim is to destabilize the political, military, territorial and economic or social security of a State Party.

These developments show a clear determination by post-Apartheid South Africa to move away from previous policies of aggression and destabilisation of the Apartheid regime that were also associated with politics of the Cold War. They reflect a new South Africa committed to live in peace with its neighbours.

V

Way Forward in a Globalising World: Overall Assessment of South Africa's Foreign Policy Performance and Recommendations

There is no doubt that the post-Apartheid South Africa, led by aspirant leaders like Nelson Mandela, has clearly turned the tide in terms of its foreign policy positions under the Apartheid system. The country has moved away from policy positions informed by racism, hostility and aggression to neighbouring states and disregard of international norms and standards, to policy positions grounded and informed by the advancement of human rights at national and international levels and the promotion of democracy, peace, stability and development in Africa in particular.

The challenge and concern, however, is the progress post-Apartheid South Africa has made and will continue to make in translating its new and progressive foreign policy positions into meaningful and concrete actions that will in turn ensure that the country plays a leading and positive role in international affairs. The other concern is the extent to which narrow and short-term political and economic interests will blunt or adversely affect and undermine

51. See, *http://www.sadc.int/files/2913/5333/8281/SADC_Mutual_Defence_Pact2003.pdf* (accessed on 12 June 2014). The Member States of the SADC also signed the Memorandum of Understanding on Establishment of SADC Standby Brigade in 2007 to respond to collective security concerns in the region.

the country's commitment to a foreign policy and international relations that characterise a good international citizen. It is in this context that the performance of post-Apartheid South Africa's foreign policy is assessed.

Advancement of Human Rights

Positive Developments

Following its readmission in the UN on 23 June 1994,[52] South Africa has played a significant role in the promotion and protection of universal rights and in advancing the work of the UN. In his first address to the 49th Session of the UN General Assembly on 3 October 1994 as South Africa's first democratically elected president, Nelson Mandela said:[53]

> Democratic South Africa rejoins the world community of nations determined to play its role in helping to strengthen the United Nations and to contribute what it can to the furtherance of its purpose.

On the role the new South Africa was to play in advancing human rights at a global level and in making the world a better place, Nelson Mandela in the same address went on to say:

> The millions across our globe who stand expectant at the gates of hope look to [the UN] to bring them peace, to bring them life, to bring them a life worth living. We pray that the new South Africa which [the UN] helped to bring into being and which you have so warmly welcomed among the community of nations will, in its own and in the wider interest, make its own contribution, however small, to the realization of those hopes.

Since 1994, the country has adopted several key human rights instruments such as the International Covenant on Civil and

---

52. See UN General Resolution 48/258 of 23 June 1994 at *http://www.un.org/documents/ga/res/48/a48r258.htm.*

53. Address by President Nelson Mandela to the 49th session of the UN General Assembly on 3 October 1994, at *http://db.nelsonmandela.org/speeches/pub_view.asp?pg=item&ItemID=NMS204&txtstr=human%20rights*

Political Rights, the Convention on the Elimination of All Forms of Discrimination against Women, and the International Convention on the Elimination of All Forms of Racism,[54] and has and continues to discharge many of its obligations under these instruments. The country has also participated actively in UN bodies such as the Human Rights Council[55] and its Universal Periodic Review (UPR) mechanism, and has hosted key UN human rights conferences such as the World Conference against Racism (2001) and the World Conference on Sustainable Development (2002). Several South Africans have served and continue to serve in key UN bodies such as the Office of the High Commissioner for Human Rights, UN Women and various UN Treaty Bodies.

At the regional level, South Africa joined the Organization of Africa Unity (OAU) in May 1994 and has played a leading role in human rights related activities of the organisation. In his first address at the OAU meeting of Heads of State and Government in Tunis on 13 June 1994, Nelson Mandela as president of South Africa, outlined the vision that would inform South Africa's role in the OAU:[56]

> We have entered this eminent African organization and rejoined the African community of nations inspired by the desire to join hands with all the countries of our continent as equal partners...It will never happen again that our country will seek to dominate another through force of arms, economic might or subversion...The objectives we will pursue [are] the creation of a South Africa that would be a good neighbour and an equal partner with all the countries of our continent, one which would use its abilities and potentialities to help advance the common struggle to secure Africa's rightful place within the world economic and political system...If freedom was the crown which the fighter of liberation sought to place on the head of mother Africa, let the upliftment, the happiness, prosperity and comfort of her children be the jewel of the crown.

---

54. For a list of international human rights instruments that South Africa is party to, see, *http://www1.umn.edu/humanrts/research/ratification-southafrica.html*

55. In 2001, South Africa tabled a resolution on gay rights at the UN Human Rights Council: A/HRC/17/L.9/l9/Rev.1. This was despite a strong opposition to this issue by most African states.

56. Statement by President Nelson Mandela at the OAU Meeting of Heads of State and Government, 13 June 1994, Tunis, at *http://www.anc.org.za/show.php?id=4888*

South Africa ratified key human rights instruments of the OAU, the African Charter on Human and Peoples' Rights and the African Charter on the Rights and Welfare of the Child, and played a significant role in the establishment of the African Court on Human and Peoples' Rights.[57] The country also played a major role in the establishment of the African Union (AU),[58] a more human rights oriented body than the OAU that it replaced. The promotion and protection of 'human and peoples' rights in accordance with the African Charter on Human and Peoples' Rights and other relevant human rights instruments' is one of the objectives of the AU according to its Constitutive Act and also one of the principles governing the Union's functions. Several South Africans have also served in various human rights bodies of the OAU/AU, particularly the African Commission on Human and People's Rights and the African Court on Human and Peoples' Rights, and continue to do so.

In Southern Africa, the South African Development Community (SADC), of which South Africa is a key member since 1994, adopted several instruments to promote and protect human rights. Among these is the 2008 Protocol on Gender and Development, which provides for the empowerment of women, gender equality in the public and private sectors, and the elimination of gender based discrimination,[59] and the 2003 Charter of the Fundamental Social Rights in SADC providing for labour rights and the 'recognition of human rights in international and regional human rights instruments.'[60]

Promotion of Democracy, Peace, Stability and Development

Soon after the end of Apartheid, the new South African government expressed its intentions to promote democracy, peace and stability at regional and international levels. In the country's

57. The Court began its operations in November 2006.

58. The African Union was launched in Durban, South Africa on 9 July 2002. The country also hosts one of the organs of the AU, the Pan-African Parliament—a body established to ensure full participation of African peoples in issues affecting the continent.

59. Adopted on 17 August 2008 in Johannesburg, South Africa. The Protocol has not come into force.

60. See, *http://www.sadc.int/files/6613/5292/8383/Charter_of_the_Fundamental_Social_Rights_in_SADC2003.pdf*

first official address to the UNSC in May 1994, the then Deputy-Vice President of South Africa, Thabo Mbeki, in his address said: [61]

> We have become a democracy and a country that can be counted on to subscribe and adhere to the pursuit of the important goals of international peace and security.....The victory that has been won in South Africa belongs as much to the people of our country as to this Organization and the peoples of the world. As we proceed to confront the enormous challenges of consolidating this victory, we shall continue to count on your support. Precisely because we are conscious of what the world has done for us, we too are determined to contribute what we can to the making of a better world for all.

Other than the many international and regional instruments South Africa is party to at the UN level and in Africa, the country has played a vital role in peace building and post-conflict reconstruction in several countries and continues to do so. It helped in the mediation conflicts in Burundi and Sudan, played a leading role in the peace talks in the Democratic Republic of Congo (DRC), and has deployed many of its security personnel in UN and AU peace-keeping missions in the Darfur region of the Sudan and the DRC, and makes regular financial contributions as well. As an example of this commitment and contribution, in 2000, South Africa was rated 91 in the world by the UN Department of Peacekeeping Operations (DPKO) in terms of the country's support and contribution in peacekeeping operations, this improved to 14 in 2013.[62]

In support for democracy and the democratisation process in Africa in particular, South Africa played an important role in getting the AU to reject unconstitutional changes of governments and the

---

61. Statement by Thabo Mbeki, First Deputy Vice-President of South Africa at the 3379th meeting of the United Nations Security Council, S/P.3379 of 25 May 1994, at, *http://www.dfa.gov.za/docs/speeches/1994/mbek0525.htm*

62. See, *http://www.un.org/en/peacekeeping/resources/statistics/contributors.shtml* (accessed on 22 June 2014). South Africa was part of the Intervention Brigade of the UN Organization Stabilization Mission in the DRC (MONUSCO) mandated by the UNSC through Resolution 2098 to use force to neutralise and disarm the M23 rebels in eastern DRC. See also, Mmanaledi Mataboge (2013) "SA revels in M23's defeat following its CAR debacle", *Mail* and *Guardian*, 8 November 2013, at, *http://mg.co.za/article/2013-11-07-sa-revels-in-m23s-defeat-following-its-car-debacle* (accessed on 22 June 2014).

suspension from the AU and its activities of governments that come into power through unconstitutional changes. In 2007, AU adoption of the African Charter on Democracy, Elections and Governance[63] consolidated this position and further provided amongst others, political pluralism, role and rights of opposition parties and the participation of citizens in democratic process and governance of public affairs as principles states have to adhere to.[64] The country, through the auspices of the SADC in particular, has also played a significant role in the restoration of democracy in the countries such as Lesotho, the Democratic Republic of Congo and Madagascar.[65]

After destruction and destabilisation of the economies of the neighbouring states during the Apartheid era, estimated to exceed US$ 60 billion between 1980 and 1988,[66] the new South Africa has played a central role in addressing the destructive effects of its policies and in helping to promote economic development in Southern African states and in the rest of the African continent. During opening of the Lesotho Highlands Water Project in January 1998, one of the biggest engineering projects in Africa, Nelson Mandela said:[67]

> The interdependence of the countries of our region is such that none can prosper in isolation, or enjoy freedom and security on its own. Economic growth, human rights, security and stability are all conditions of the success of our joint endeavors to bring development and prosperity through co-operation. Failure in any one of these conditions affects the others, and affects us all.

---

63. Adopted on 30 January 2007 and entered into force on 15 February 2012. South Africa ratified the Charter on 24 December 2010.

64. See Article 3 of the African Charter on Democracy, Elections and Governance.

65. On 30 January 2014, SADC heads of state and government lifted the suspension on Madagascar after facilitating the democratic elections, following the 2009 coup; see, *http://www.sadc.int/files/1413/9109/9609/Communique_of_the_SADC_Extraordinary_Summit_-_January_2014.pdf* (accessed on 23 June 2014).

66. See, International Labor Organization (1990). Special Report of the Director-General on the application of the Declaration concerning action against Apartheid in South Africa and Namibia. Geneva: ILO.

67. See, *http://db.nelsonmandela.org/speeches/pub_view.asp?pg=item&ItemID=NMS549&txtstr=human%20rights* (accessed on 23 June 2014).

As one of the biggest and most advanced economy in Africa, South Africa has done a lot since the end of Apartheid to develop Africa's economy in terms of infrastructure development and the promotion of regional integration. In 2000, South Africa helped to establish the Southern African Free Trade Area and Africa Free Trade zone in 2008[68] and played a key role in transforming the Southern African Customs Union (SACU) that undermined economic growth of neighbouring states during the Apartheid into an organisation that now plays a key role in enhancing economic development, diversification, industrialisation, the integration of the economies of its member states (Botswana, Lesotho, Namibia, South Africa and Swaziland) and the development of common economic policies and strategies amongst its member states.[69]

The country has also played a crucial role in the formation of Africa's strategy to respond to challenges of poverty and development in the continent and its marginalisation in global affairs—the New Partnership for Africa's Development (NEPAD)[70] and its voluntary peer review mechanism, the African Peer Review Mechanism (APRM).[71] South Africa's membership in the Brazil, Russia, India, China and South Africa (BRICS)[72] trade alliance is intended to help

68. See, *http://www.osisa.org/economic-justice/south-africa-and-regional-economic-integration* (accessed on 23 June 2014).

69. See Article 2 (objectives) of the Southern African Customs Union Agreement of 2002 which replaced the Apartheid based agreement of 1969. Available at, *http://www.sacu.int/main.php?include=docs/legislation/2002-agreement/part1.html*

70. NEPAD was adopted by the OAU in 2001 and ratified by the AU in 2002, see, http://www.nepad.org/ (accessed on 23 June 2014). The Africa Union Summit in 2010 endorsed the integration of NEPAD in AU's programs and activities and the UN Secretary- General has also established the Office of the Special Adviser on Africa (OSAA) in May 2003 (A/RES/57/7 of November 4, 2002) to promote support for NEPAD in the UN system, see, *http://www.un.org/africa/osaa/nepad.html* (accessed on 23 June 2014) and the UN General Assembly resolution on international support for NEPAD, A/RES/67/294 of 15 August 2013.

71. The objectives of the APRM are to promote political stability and attain high economic growth and sustainable development in the continent through a voluntary peer review of performance of African states that have signed up to the mechanism in terms of policies, standards and practices pertaining to political, democratic, economic and corporate governance and socio-economic development. See, *http://aprm-au.org/about-aprm.*

72. South Africa joined the economic and political association of Brazil, Russia, India and China in December 2010 to form BRICS.

develop the country's economy and promote economic integration in Africa (Department of Government Communication and Information System, 2013).

Concerns and Challenges

While South Africa has certainly made significant and impressive progress in its foreign policy and in its international relations, there are concerns and challenges in the country's performance as far as the advancement of human rights and democracy at the international and regional levels are concerned, and in ways adopted to balance human rights considerations with economic and geopolitical interests.

Human Rights

International and regional human rights instruments

While the country has done well in the ratification of regional and international human rights instruments, the failure to ratify other key human rights instruments, delays in the ratification of key instruments and the failure to discharge some of its treaty obligations, especially reporting obligations, is a concern.

At the international level, South Africa has not yet ratified the International Covenant on Economic and Social Rights despite signing the treaty on 3 October 1994[73] and several undertakings to ratify it. The same applies to the Optional Protocol to the Convention against Torture and other Cruel, Inhumane and Degrading Treatment and Punishment which the country signed on 20 September 2006. The country is yet to sign the International Convention on the Protection of the Rights of All Migrant Workers and Members of their Families. The country has not done very well in discharging its treaty reporting obligations and has, in some cases, taken more than 10 years to submit its treaty reports—one glaring case in this regard being the International Covenant on Civil and Political Rights

73. This was as at 23 June 2014, see, *https://treaties.un.org/Pages/ViewDetails.aspx?src=TREATY&mtdsg_no=IV-9-b&chapter=4&lang=en.*

(ICCPR) where the country's treaty report has been overdue since 2000.[74]

At the regional level, where it is one of the most influential members, the country has not granted access to its citizens and NGOs (non-governmental organisations) to take matters to the African Court on Human and Peoples' Rights, despite ratifying the Protocol to the African Charter on Human and Peoples' Rights on the Establishment of the Court on 7 July 2002.[75] The country also takes long to ratify important regional instruments and generally does so 2-3 years after their adoption.[76] The country's record in relation to the African Charter on Human and Peoples' Rights is not very good either and it owes four treaty reports since the submission of its last report in May 2005.[77]

South Africa's response to international and regional human rights instruments since the end of Apartheid era sends confusing and worrying messages about the direction of the country's foreign policy. Unlike other areas of international relations that have to balance various interests, meeting treaty reporting obligations and ratifying already signed human rights treaties should be a straight forward matter that only requires political will and capacity—South

---

74. For a detailed report on the country's performance on international human rights treaties, see the report compiled by the Office of the High Commissioner for Human Rights for South Africa's second round review under the UN Human Rights Council Periodic Review, A/HRC/W 6.6/13/ZAF/2, available at, *http://www.bing.com/search?q=South%20African%20Treaty%20Reporting&pc=cosp&ptag=A79FEF560EC514B869EF&form=CONBDF&conlogo=CT3210127.* See also, *http://tbinternet.ohchr.org/_layouts/TreatyBodyExternal/Countries.aspx*

75. Article 34(6) of the Protocol requires individual State Parties to make declarations allowing their citizens and NGOs to bring matters pertaining to human rights violations to the Court. See also the address of the Vice-President of the Court in May 2014, *http://www.achpr.org/sessions/55th/speeches/opening-statement-court/.*

76. See, *http://www.au.int/en/treaties.*

77. See report of the African Commission on this at, *http://www.bing.com/search?q=South%20African%20Treaty%20Reporting&pc=cosp&ptag=A79FEF560EC514B869EF&form=CONBDF&conlogo=CT3210127* (accessed on 24 June 2014). In 2011, the country had also not submitted its treaty reports to the African Committee on the Rights and Welfare of the Child responsible for the Africa Charter on the Rights and Welfare of the Child which South Africa ratified in January, 2000, but has since submitted some of the outstanding reports. See *http://www.pmg.org.za/report/20111116-department-women-children-and-persons-disabilities-sadc-gender-protoc* and *http://www.pmg.org.za/report/20130313-department-women-children-and-people-disabilities-2nd-3rd-4th-united-*

Africa could not and should not be facing serious capacity challenges in this regard.

General Position on Human Rights Issues at Regional and International Levels

As far as international relations are concerned, political and economic interests appear to be gaining an upper hand over the country's commitment and support for human rights values and principles that underpin its foreign policy. Examples of this phenomenon are seen in the voting patterns of the country in UNSC where it served as a non-permanent member for two terms in 2007/08 and 2011/12, the country's subtle support or tolerance for authoritarian regimes in the AU, and its quiet diplomacy approach in relation to the human rights record of some of its powerful political and economic allies such as China and Russia (Thipanyane, 2011).

In the UNSC, probably due to Cold War politics and alliances and post-Cold War political and economic interests, South Africa voted with Russia and China on several issues that appeared contrary to its own positions on human rights values and principles—this includes not voting against countries such as Zimbabwe, Myanmar and Syria (Bowland, 2012). The country abstained from voting in a UN General Assembly resolution deemed to be critical of Russia's role in the crisis in Ukraine.[78] South Africa has also been associated with resolutions of the AU against the International Criminal Court in support of African leaders, such as President Bashir of Sudan who has been indicted by the Court for crimes against humanity.[79] South Africa's support of the decision by the SADC leadership to suspend the Tribunal, following its findings against the conduct of the government of Zimbabwe in the nationalisation of mainly white-owned farmlands, is another worrying development and an example of where political

---

78. Resolution A/Res/68/262 of 27 March 2014. See also, *http://www.un.org/News/Press/docs/2014/ga11493.doc.htm*

79. See decisions of the African Union in this regard at, *http://summits.au.int/en/sites/default/files/Ext%20Assembly%20AU%20Dec%20&%20Decl%20_E.pdf*

considerations trump human rights issues despite the position of human rights in South Africa foreign policy (Makonese, 2013).[80]

This emerging and worrying trend of South Africa's conduct in international forums, where political and economic interests seem to gain an upper-hand over human rights values raises questions about the government's commitment to values and principles that inform and shape the country's foreign policy so eloquently and forcefully pronounced by Nelson Mandela and Thabo Mbeki, the country's first two presidents in free South Africa. It also makes many wonder whether or not the country is slowly moving away from these values and principles enshrined in its impressive constitution and Bill of Rights.[81]

Promotion of Democracy, Peace, Stability and Development

Democracy

Despite the country's impressive record in the promotion of democracy, peace, stability and development, particularly in Southern Africa and the African continent, there are several concerns and challenges that put a blot on its performance.

South Africa's response to challenges of democracy in Swaziland, where citizens are denied full political rights and freedoms including an effective ban of political parties in violation of treaty provisions of SADC, the AU, and the UN, is a clear example of this phenomenon (Dlamini, 2013). It is difficult to understand why South Africa, and for that matter the SADC leadership, have allowed the untenable political situation in Swaziland to continue for so long with little or no visible action taken against the country (Thipanyane, 2011). Swaziland is heavily dependent on South Africa for its economic

80. See, *http://www.sadc.int/about-sadc/sadc-institutions/tribun/*, *http://www.saflii.org/cgi-bin/disp.pl?file=za/journals/DEREBUS/2013/13.html&query=DEREBUS%202013%2013%20or%202013%20DEREBUS%2013* and *http://www.au.int/en/sites/default/files/Assembly%20AU%20Dec%20490-516%20%28XXII%29%20_E.pdf.*

81. See, Kasambala (2014). "Dispatches: Can South Africa Live Up to its Human Rights Promises?" *Human Rights Watch*, 9 June 2014. Available at, *http://www.hrw.org/news/2014/06/09/dispatches-can-south-africa-live-its-human-rights-promises* (accessed on 24 June 2014).

survival and South Africa could easily exert necessary pressure in this regard.[82]

South Africa's involvement in the Central African Republic is another example. The country sent over 200 soldiers to protect an unpopular president, General Bozize, who came into power through a coup in March 2003. He was overthrown in March 2013 and forced to flee the country.[83] South Africa lost 13 of its soldiers and the country has since been caught up in extensive conflicts between the Christian majority and the Moslem minority that has resulted in the death of thousands of people. This intervention brings into question the real motives and agenda behind the South Africa's military intervention and the foreign policy interest it was pursuing.[84] This intervention is in contrast with the country's role in the DRC where it played a major role in the defeat of the M23 rebels.[85]

Economic Development

Despite South Africa's efforts to promote economic development in the SADC region and in the continent as a whole through the introduction of the New Program for Africa's Development (NEPAD) and other measures, Africa's economic growth and development is still inadequate to address the challenges of poverty and underdevelopment. Intra-trade amongst African states is still at low levels around 5 per cent of total African trade, and Africa's contribution to the world's trade and economy is also low at 3 per cent. Much of the sub-Saharan Africa will not meet the targets set

---

82. The US on the other hand threatened to suspend Swaziland from the African Growth and Opportunity Act (AGOA) that provides some free trade benefits for African countries due to the country's dismal human rights record, see, *http://agoa.info/news/article/5416-swaziland-s-ict-minister-us-using-agoa-to-bully-country.html*. Swaziland was suspended from AGOA on 26 June 2014, see, *http://www.fin24.com/Economy/Swaziland-loses-US-trade-pact-privileges-20140627* (accessed on 27 June 2014).

83. See, *http://www.bbc.com/news/world-africa-21923624*

84. See, 'Central African Republic: Is this what our soldiers died for (13 South African soldiers killed in CAR)'. *http://mg.co.za/article/2013-03-28-00-central-african-republic-is-this-what-our-soldiers-died-for*

85. For South Africa's role in the UN Intervention Brigade in the DRC, see, *http://www.defenceweb.co.za/index.php?option=com_content&view=article&id=31683:un-intervention-brigade-supports-drc-forces-in-latest-clashes--sa-soldier-wounded&catid=56:diplomacy-a-peace&Itemid=111*

under the Millennium Development Goals (MDGs) for 2015 to address poverty and under-development (OECD and United Nations Office of the Special Adviser on Africa, 2011). A significant number of African states are also yet to sign the APRM of NEPAD.

There are concerns as to whether South Africa's membership in the BRICS alliance would benefit the African continent and whether the country will stand up to the conduct of its alliance partners like China that negatively affects Africa's interests.[86] The increasing role of China and its need for Africa's natural resources to fuel its booming economy is also raising concerns in some quarter that the former might be its new coloniser with equally devastating effects on Africa's economy and development as the Europeans did (Gumede, 2012: 248-53).

Recommendations

Increasing interactions between states today have heightened the importance and significance of relations between them. States that manage these relations well will succeed and benefit the most from them in terms of addressing the challenges of poverty and underdevelopment and other national priorities and interests. Foreign policy informs these relations and determines to a large extent, what a country would gain from its relations with others and how.

For South Africa to meet its foreign policy objectives of a peaceful and prosperous Africa and a better world, it will have to address many of the challenges highlighted in this chapter, especially those pertaining to human rights, democracy, development and security.

Human Rights

While post-Apartheid South Africa has done well in relation to the advancement of human rights, the country has to discharge its international and regional human rights treaty obligations in a much better way and should ratify outstanding instruments. As a leading economic powerhouse in Africa, South Africa should lead by example

86. See Besada *et al.* (2013).

and encourage other African countries to discharge their human rights treaty obligations too.

Notwithstanding the country's political and economic interests necessary to address the massive challenges of poverty and unemployment and the need for high economic growth rate, the country has to be more vocal in supporting the respect for human rights at regional and international levels—respect for human rights is crucial for sustainable development, the fight against poverty and the attainment of peace. The South African Parliament and civil society organisations also need to play a bigger role to ensure that the government does discharge its regional and international human rights treaty obligations accordingly, and that the country becomes more vocal and effective champion of human rights and democracy in the Africa and in the world.[87]

Democracy, Peace, Security and Development

While the country's record in the support of peace-keeping activities of the UN and the AU has improved over the years, it could still do a bit more in relation to the size of its economy and influence. However, it is also important that the country puts more effort in the prevention of conflicts in Africa and around the world. It can do so by being more active and vocal in championing human rights and democracy issues in Africa in particular, and in helping to address the underlying causes of conflicts and insecurity. It could also use its influence to ensure that the AU and its relevant bodies are more effective in responding to issues of democracy, peace and security, including emerging threats posed by climate change, terrorism and cyber threats.

A lot more effort is required in relation to economic development and the fight against poverty and inequalities in Africa and the world in general. South Africa has to work harder to promote regional integration and in enhancing trade amongst African countries. The country's support for NEPAD and the APRM should continue and more African countries should be encouraged to sign up to this

87. For a detailed discussion on the role of the South African Parliament, see, Chenwi (2011).

mechanism. South Africa's involvement in the BRICS should be of benefit to Africa's interests, and concerns that countries like China will not do much to promote regional integration in Africa should be addressed.

Conclusion

Relations that any state shares with other states have a major bearing on its success or failure, including the well-being of its people in terms of security and economic growth. These relations are also important for regional and global peace, security and prosperity. Failure to manage these relations can lead to numerous challenges, including conflicts, wars, and change of governments.

The 2011 White Paper on Foreign Policy of the country's Department of International Relations and Cooperation states:

> South Africa's vision for 2025 is to be a successful and influential member of the international community, supported by a globally competitive economy on a sustained growth path that has made significant inroads in addressing unemployment, inequality and poverty in South Africa, and contribute to the development of our region and continent. In a rapidly evolving global environment, South Africa will frequently be faced with key strategic decision points. Its response will determine its success in the future.

For post-Apartheid South Africa to make a significant contribution in the making of a better world, especially in the promotion of democracy, peace and stability and development in Africa, the country has to address the challenges and concerns raised in this chapter in relation to its foreign policy and international relations. This would require the country to remain committed to human rights, values and principles that inform its foreign policy and international relations.

References

African National Congress (2012). *Recommendations from the 4th National Policy Conference*. Available at *http://www.anc.org.za/docs/pol/2012/policy_conferencev.pdf*.

Besada, Hany, Evren Tok and Kristen Winters (2013). "South Africa in the BRICS: Opportunities, Challenges and Prospects", *Africa Insight* 42(4). Available at *http://www.nsi-ins.ca/wp-content/uploads/2013/10/2013-South-Africa-in-the-BRICS.pdf*

Bowland, Cayley (2012). "Coming into Our Own: An Analysis of South Africa's Voting Patterns and the Achievement of its Foreign Policy Goals in the United Nations Security Council", *South African Institute of International Affairs*.

Cawthra, Gavin (2010). *The Role of SADC in Managing Political Crisis and Conflict: The Cases of Madagascar and Zimbabwe*. Maputo: Friedrich-Ebert-Stiftung Mozambique. Available at *http://library.fes.de/pdf-files/bueros/mosambik/07874.pdf*

Chenwi, Lilian (2011). ""Using International Human Rights Law to Promote Constitutional Rights: The (Potential) Role of the South African Parliament", *Law, Democracy and Development* 15. Available at *http://www.saflii.org/za/journals/LDD/2011/9.pdf*.

De Klerk, F.W. (2013). "South Africa, The Nation that Gave Up its Nukes", *Los Angeles Times*. 22 December.

Department of Government Communication and Information System (2013). *South Africa Yearbook 2012/2013*. Pretoria: Department of Government Communication and Information System. Available at *http://www.gcis.gov.za/sites/www.gcis.gov.za/files/docs/resourcecentre/yearbook/2012/14%20International%20Relations.pdf*

Department of International Relations and Co-operation (2011). *Building a Better World: The Diplomacy of Ubuntu. White Paper on South Africa's Foreign Policy*. Pretoria, Department of International Relations and Cooperation.

De Villiers, J.W., Roger Jardine and Mitchell Reiss (1993). "Why South Africa Gave Up the Bomb", *Foreign Affairs* 72 November/December.

Dlamini, Lomcebo (2013). *Swaziland Democracy and Political Participation: A Review by AfriMap and the Open Society Initiative for Southern Africa*. Johannesburg: Open Society Foundations. The report can be accessed at: *http://www.afrimap.org/english/images/report/AfriMAP%20SWZ%20Democracy%20%20PP%20main%20text%20Web%20FINAL.pdf*

Gumede, William (2012). *Restless Nation: Making Sense of Trouble Times*. Cape Town, Tafelberg.

Makonese, Makanatse (2013). 'The SADC Tribunal Conundrum-lawyers Look to the African Court for Direction", *DEREBUS 13*.

Mandela, Nelson (1993). "South Africa's Future Foreign Policy", *Foreign Affairs*, November/December.

Organization for Economic Cooperation and Development (OECD) and United Nations Office of the Special Adviser on Africa (2011). *Economic Diversification in Africa: A Review of Selected Countries*. Available at: *http://www.un.org/africa/osaa/reports/economic_diversification_africa_2011Jan.pdf*

Thipanyane, Tseliso (2011). "South Africa's Foreign Policy under the Zuma Government: A Human Rights-based Policy or a Pragmatic Approach Based on Political and Economic Considerations?'", *Africa Institute of South Africa Policy Brief Briefing* No 64.

Truth and Reconciliation Commission (1998). *Volume Two: Truth and Reconciliation Commission of South Africa Report*. Pretoria: Truth and Reconciliation Commission.

Wilson, Monica and Leonard Thompson (eds) (1975). *The Oxford History of South Africa. Vol. II. South Africa 1870-1966*. Oxford: Oxford University Press.

Annexure

Economic and Social Profile of Major Powers

Countries	*Population (millions)*	*GDP Per Capita (US Dollars)*	*Military Spending (US Dollars - Billions)*	*Armed Forces (number)*	*Social Expenditure as per cent of GDP (%)*	*Deficit as per cent of GDP (%)*	*Human Development Index*	*Unemployed (%)*	*Population in Poverty (%)*
US	316.13	53,143	640.22	1,492,200	20.0	96 (-7.5)	0.914	5.7	14.5%
UK	64.09	39,337	57.89	169,150	23.8	103.2 (-5.8)	0.892	6.2	
Germany	80.62	45,085	48.79	186,450	26.2	88.5 (0.1)	0.911	5.4	
France	66.03	41,421	61.22	325,600	33.0	103.8	0.884	9.9	
Russia	143.49	14,612	87.84	1,364,000		9.4 (2.7)	0.778	5.5	11.0
China	1,357.38	6,807	188.46	2,993,000			0.719	4.5	18.6
Japan	127.34	38,492	48.60	259,800	22.3	196.5 (-8.0)	0.890	3.8	
India	1,252.14	1,499	47.40	2,728,700		49.7 (-3.8)	0.586	3.4	60.6
Brazil	200.36	11,208	31.46	713,480		(-2,0)	0.744	6.9	6.8
South Africa	52.98	6,618	4.11	62,100		(-4.6)	0.658	25.0	26.2
Saudi Arabia	28.83	25,852	66.99	249,000			0.836	5.6	
Israel	8.06	36,151	16.03	184,500	15.8	80.0 (-5.4)	0.888	6.9	0.7
Pakistan	182.14	1,299	7.64	947,800		(-8.0)	0.537	5.1	50.7

Sources: *http://data.worldbank.org/indicator* for Population, GDP per capita; 2012-13

http://www.sipri.org/ Stockholm International Peace Research Institute for military spending; 2013

http://data.worldbank.org/indicator/MS.MIL.TOTL.P1 for Armed Forces; 2012

http://www.ilo.org/dyn/sesame/ifpses.socialdbexp for Social security services; 2013, other than Japan which is 2010

http://stats.oecd.org/Index.aspx?datasetcode=SOCX_AGG for Social security services as percentage of GDP

http://data.worldbank.org/indicator/GC.DOD.TOTL.GD.ZS for government deficit as per cent of GDP; 2012-13

http://hdr.undp.org/en/data for Human Development Index; 2013

http://www.principalglobalindicators.org/Pages/Default.aspx and http://data.worldbank.org/indicator/SL.UEM.TOTL.ZS for unemployment, as per cent of total labour force; 2013-14

http://data.worldbank.org/indicator/SI.POV.2DAY for population living on less than 2/day at 2005 prices, as percentage of total population; 2012

Selected Bibliography

Albright, Madeline (2006). *The Mighty and Almighty*. New York: Harper Perennial.

Baker III, James A. and Lee H. Hamilton (2006). *Co-Chairs, the Iraq Study Group Report*. Fifth Vintage.

Banerjee, Ajit M. (1958). *The Organization of Government of India*. Bombay: Asia Publishing House.

———. (1996). *Reinventing Governance: Issues and Options*. New Delhi: Tata-McGraw Hill Publishing Co. Ltd.

Banerjee, Ajit M. and Murari R. Sharma (2007). *Reinventing the United Nations*. New Delhi: Prentice-Hall.

Bremer III , Ambassador L. Paul (with Malcolm McConnell) (2005). *My Year in Iraq: The Struggle to Build a Future of Hope*. New York: Simon & Schuster. pp.36-37.

Bush, George and Brent Scowcroft (1998). *World Transformed*. Alfred A. Knoff.

C-Span (2014). *US-Russia Relations Discussion*. Aspen Institute, Washington D.C. 5 May. Access at: *http://www.c-span.org/video/?322887-1/discussion-usrussia-relations*.

Cooney, James A. (1998). *Foreign Policy: The US and the World*. Walker Publishing Co.

Dror, Yehezkel (1997). *Ventures in Policy Sciences*. New York: Elsevier.

Felbab-Brown, Vanda, Ronald Neumann and David Sedney (2014). "Small Steps Will Save Our Gains in Afghanistan", *Wall Street Journal*, 10 October.

Garekhan, C. (2014). "Islamic State", *Indian Express,* 31 October.

Haas, Richard N. (2013). *Foreign Policy Begins at Home*. Basic Books.

Haqqani, Husain (2014). "Pakistan Military", *Hindu Newspaper,* 6 September.

Hinshaw, Drew and Patrick McGrosenty (2014). "The Reform of Africa's Strong Men", *Wall Street Journal*, 6-7 December.

Huntington, Samuel P. (1996). *The Clash of Civilization and the Remaking of World Order*. New York,: Simon and Schuster.

Ignatius, David (2014). "Islamic State in Iraq and Syria", *Washington Post*, 4 September.

Kissinger, Henry (1994). *Diplomacy*. New York: Simon and Schuster Paperbacks.

———. (2014). *World Order*. New York: Penguin Press.

Kober, Stanley (2013). "CATO", *Huntington Post*, 7 December.

Nye Jr., Joseph C. (2002). *The Paradox of American Power.* Oxford University.

Palmer, Glen and Clifton Morgan (2012). *Theory of Foreign Policy.* Princeton, New Jersey: Princeton University Press.

Robinson, Eugene (2014). "Our Challenge with Fundamentalist Islam", *Washington Post*, 4 September.

Schaem, Douglas E. and Malik Kaylan (2014). *Russia and China Axis*. New York: Encounter Books.

Sharma, Murari R. and Ajit M. Banerjee (2009). *The United Nations International Civil Service*. New Delhi: Academic Foundation.

Sharma, Sudesh K. (1978). *Dynamics of Development*. Delhi: Concept Publishing Company.

Shambaugh, David (2013). *China Goes Global: The Partial Power*. Oxford University Press.

Sinha, Uttam Kumar, Tasneem Meenai, K. Santhanam and C. Uday Bhaskar (eds.) (2005). *UN: Multilateralism and International Security*. New Delhi: Shipra Pubications.

Hook, Steven W. and John Spanier (2015). *American Foreign Policy Since World War II*. 20th Edition. Washington, DC: CQ Press, a Division of SAGE Publications, Inc.

Zakaria, Fareed (2014). "Arab World", *Washington Post*, 4 September.

Websites:

http://countrystudies.us/israel/106.htm

http://en.wikipedia.org/wiki/India%E2%80%93Pakistan_relations

http://en.wikipedia.org/wiki/Foreign_policy_of_the_United_States

http://en.wikipedia.org/wiki/Foreign_relations_of_China

http://en.wikipedia.org/wiki/Foreign_relations_of_France

http://en.wikipedia.org/wiki/Foreign_relations_of_German

http://en.wikipedia.org/wiki/Foreign_relations_of_Saudi_Arabia

http://en.wikipedia.org/wiki/Foreign_relations_of_the_United_Kingdom

http://www.britannica.com/topic/foreign-policy

http://www.foreignaffairs.com/articles/49408/nelson-mandela/south-africas-future- foreign-policy

www.boundless.com

Index

V

W